Journal
1935–1944

MIHAIL SEBASTIAN

Journal

1935–1944

Translated from the Romanian by Patrick Camiller

With an Introduction and Notes by Radu Ioanid

IVAN R. DEE

CHICAGO 2000

Published in Association with the United States Holocaust Memorial Museum

Library of Congress Cataloging-in-Publication Data:
    Sebastian, Mihail, 1907–1945.
    [Jurnal. English]
    Journal, 1935–1944 / Mihail Sebastian ; translated from the Romanian by Patrick Camiller; with introduction and notes by Radu Ioanid.
        p.   cm.
    Includes bibliographical references and index.
    ISBN 1-56663-326-5 (alk. paper)
    1. Sebastian, Mihail, 1907–1945—Diaries.   2. Jews—Romania—Diaries.
3. Holocaust, Jewish (1939–1945)—Romania—Personal narratives.
4. Romania—Biography.   5. Romania—Politics and government—1914–1944.
I. Ioanid, Radu.   II. Title.
DS135.R73 S38713 2000
940.53'18'092—dc21   00-031535

CONTENTS

INTRODUCTION
by Radu Ioanid

"Forgive me, but I don't believe you," said Woland. "That cannot be. Manuscripts don't burn."
—Mikhail Bulgakov, *The Master and Margarita*

On 29 May 1945, as he rushed to cross a street in downtown Bucharest, thirty-eight-year-old Mihail Sebastian, a press officer at the Romanian Ministry of Foreign Affairs, was hit and killed by a truck. As it happened, Sebastian was late to an appointment at Dalles Hall where he was to teach a class about Honoré de Balzac.

The deceased had been born Iosif Hechter, in 1907, in Brăila on the Danube. At the time of his death he was well known in Bucharest literary and political circles as a writer of fiction and of literary criticism, and as the author of several successful plays. His sudden demise left his mother and brothers in a state of shock, while members of Bucharest high society shook their heads in disbelief. As time passed, a few former girlfriends thought fondly of him every now and then; here and there a literary critic mentioned his name; a theatre director occasionally staged one of his plays.

Eventually Sebastian's name came to be associated chiefly with his plays, less so with his novels. A far lesser-known contribution to Sebastian's legacy, however, was the diary he had written during the period 1935–1944, and which remained among his possessions when he died. In 1961, as Sebastian's brother Benu emigrated from Romania to Israel, he shipped the diary out of the country via the diplomatic pouch of the Israeli embassy. Benu was right to be cautious; many manuscripts before (and since) had been confiscated by the Securitate, the Romanian secret police, only to disappear for many years if not forever.

Sebastian's extraordinary diary was published for the first time in full in 1996 in Romanian, followed by a French edition in 1998. The diary was nothing short of a time bomb, its publication generating an explosive debate about the nature of Romanian anti-Semitism in general and about Romania's role in the Holocaust in particular. Vasile Popovici, a literary critic, wrote upon reading the diary, ". . . You cannot possibly remain the same. The Jewish problem becomes your problem. A huge sense of shame spreads over a whole period of national culture and history, and its shadow covers you, too."

Sebastian's diary spans a period that saw the rise of three successive anti-Semitic dictatorships in Romania, each more devastating for the country's 759,000 Jews than its predecessor. This triad began with the regime of King Carol II (February 1938–September 1940), which was followed by the rule of Ion Antonescu in alliance with the fascist Iron Guard (September 1940–January 1941), and ended with Ion Antonescu as Conducător (Leader), ruling alone after having violently suppressed his erstwhile Iron Guard allies (1941–1944).

Sebastian's diary is not the sole or even the first literary account of the Nazification of European society to emerge from the postwar years. Victor Klemperer's diary, published under the title *I Will Bear Witness: A Diary of the Nazi Years, 1933–1945*, also recounts the brutal and merciless way in which he was rejected by his native society simply because he was born Jewish. Also like Sebastian, Klemperer recorded and noted the systematic shrinking of the physical and intellectual freedom allowed to him as a consequence of Nazism. Still, while Klemperer wrote as a Jew in the heart of the Nazi Reich in Berlin, he was protected by his wife's "Aryan" status and his own conversion. Sebastian wrote under Romanian fascism (which was characteristically different from German Nazism) and enjoyed no protection from the onslaught, having no "Aryan" relatives and refusing to convert. It is worth noting that this seems to have been a matter of principle for Sebastian. Although he felt few religious ties to Judaism, he scorned the reaction of his fellow Jews who saw baptism as the only possible solution to escape deportation: "Go over to Catholicism! Convert as quickly as you can! The Pope will defend you! He's the only one who can still save you. . . . Even if it were not so grotesque, even if it were not so stupid and pointless, I would still need no arguments. Somewhere on an island with sun and shade, in the midst of peace, security and happiness, I would in the end be indifferent to whether I was or was not Jewish. But here and now, I cannot be anything else. Nor do I think I want to be." At the height of the anti-Jewish persecution in September 1941, Sebastian went to the synagogue because he wanted to be with his fellow Jews: "Rosh Hashanah. I spent the morning at the Temple. I heard Şafran [chief rabbi of Romania] who was nearing the end of his address. Stupid, pretentious, essayistic, journalistic, shallow and unserious. But people were crying—and I myself had tears in my eyes."

It is not only in terms of their "Jewishness" that Klemperer and Sebastian are distinct (and thus too the perspective they brought to their diaries). Perhaps more important was their differing surroundings and the very nature of the fascist movements they endured. If Klemperer survived because of the legalistic technicalities of Nazi definitions of "Jewry," Sebastian survived due to the particularly opportunistic nature of the Romanian fascist regime. For like almost half of Romanian Jewry, Sebastian remained alive until 1944 only because in the eleventh hour the Romanian authorities changed their tactics, and even their position, on the so-called "Jewish problem." When Marshal Antonescu, and others whose voices counted at the time, realized that Romania, which was allied with Nazi Germany, might not be on the winning side in the war, he and his minions ceased deporting and killing Romanian Jews. Thus Romanian Jewry, which had been targeted for extermination between the years 1941 and 1942, abruptly became a bargaining chip, a means by which the Romanian authorities could hope to buy the goodwill of the Allies and soften the postwar repercussions of defeat. Sebastian's diary is, among its many other attributes, a compelling chronicle of the years during which the collective fate of Romanian Jews hung by a thread.

In the nineteenth and early twentieth centuries, Bucharest, where Sebastian lived and died, was affectionately referred to as "little Paris." Filled with charm and personality, Bucharest was also a modern city, electric lighting having been introduced in 1899, one year after the French architect Albert Galleron built the impressive Ateneu Roman concert hall. Beautiful boulevards such as the Calea Victoriei were lined with private palaces and sumptuous hotels, among them the famous Athenée Palace. On the same street a New York–style skyscraper owned by ITT faced the popular restaurant Capşa. Electric streetcars provided public transportation throughout the city, and elegant automobiles carried their owners to meetings for business or pleasure. Bucharest was cosmopolitan, and its upper classes traveled to Paris and Vienna, dressing in the fashions of the West. An aristocracy in decline and a rising bourgeoisie competed with each other for wealth and prestige, and the symbols of their fortunes and status were very much on display. Modern villas dotted the northern part of the city, near the beautiful Herăstrău Park. Bucharest had many other wonderful green spaces too, among them Cişmigiu Park, copied from New York's Central Park, and Parcul Libertaţii, designed by the French architect Eduard Redont. Winters were quite cold and summers too hot in Bucharest, but resorts in the Carpathian Mountains and on the Black Sea were only a few hours' ride by train or car. Like any other capital city, Bucharest had its share of museums, art galleries, universities, newspapers, public and private schools, and, of course, intellectuals.

Ever a city of contrasts, however, Bucharest's high society mingled in the streets with their less fortunate neighbors from the middle class, with barefoot peasants from Oltenia who delivered milk and cheese, and with Bulgarian gardeners who sold fresh vegetables. Quite unlike the city precincts of elegant villas and hotels, Bucharest's suburbs contained ugly industrial enterprises and neighborhoods where the lower middle class and poor lived in cheap houses, often situated on unpaved streets. Here and there Eastern markets and a certain way of dealing reminded foreign visitors that "little Paris" was in fact closer to the Levant than many Romanians wished to acknowledge.

An image of this colorful and now vanished world is captured in the pages of Sebastian's diary. It is not simply a Holocaust memoir but the journal of a life in transit. He wrote about his daily life in Bucharest, his love affairs, his vacations, and the musical performances—especially symphonies—that he adored. Sebastian was so much in love with music, especially with Beethoven and Bach, that it sometimes became more important to him than his admittedly active romantic life. He was twenty-eight years old when he began the diary, already famous following the publication of his book *De două mii de ani* (For Two Thousand Years) and for the viciously anti-Semitic foreword to the book that had been written by his mentor, Nae Ionescu. Sebastian was an assimilated Romanian Jewish intellectual who struggled to write seriously and to find an existential sense to his life. His accounts of his relationships with his mother and two brothers are personal and intimate, as are his descriptions of his intense and not always happy love life. An avid reader, he especially loved Proust, Gide, Balzac, and Shakespeare.

In addition to its personal side, Sebastian's diary also chronicles the social and political life of the Romanian capital between 1935 and 1944. Sebastian socialized with rich and famous liberal aristocrats, with genuine democrats and reptilian opportunists, with Zionist Jews and Communist Jews, and with actors, novelists, and literary critics. He wrote his novels and plays in Bucharest but also in the not far distant Bucegi Mountains. He took vacations on the Black Sea and sometimes traveled abroad, especially to France.

Sebastian had a strange destiny. He belonged to a group of gifted young intellectuals close to the newspaper *Cuvântul*, who started out as nonconformist and relatively liberal. When *Cuvântul* was transformed into the official newspaper of the Iron Guard, many of Sebastian's friends drifted with their common mentor, Nae Ionescu, toward Romanian fascism. While many of Sebastian's references to his friends and colleagues from this group seem benign at first, the diary ends up capturing Romanian democracy—and many of Sebastian's former friends—in a free fall toward fascism. As Sebastian noted during the early war years, his life was becoming increasingly narrow. Many of his "friends" deserted him, and escalating anti-Semitic legislation made him a pariah.

Romanian politics between the two world wars were slightly more democratic than those of Bulgaria, Hungary, or Poland. The government was an outright model of democracy compared to the fascist and Communist dictatorships that were to follow it. Still, policy between the wars generally was controlled by the will of the monarch. When the king grew displeased with his prime minister, the crown nominated a replacement from the ranks of the opposition. That more malleable nominee, now beholden to the king, was given the task of organizing elections, an arrangement that not surprisingly almost always resulted in the nominee's political party gaining a comfortable majority in parliament. In practical terms, Romania after World War I was a fledgling democracy, inevitably at risk of being tempted by Europe's rising totalitarianism.

Anti-Semitism, which always had been a predominant characteristic of modern Romania, further affected this shaky democracy. Throughout the nineteenth century, Romanian politicians and intelligentsia were heavily anti-Semitic; even the considerable constitutional and political changes brought about by World War I (i.e., the adoption of a modern constitution and of nominal suffrage) did not alter this basic feature. Despite decades of pressure from the Western powers, Romania refused to grant legal equality to its Jews until 1923, and then grudgingly. After 1929, against the backdrop of recurrent economic crises, the so-called "Jewish question" took on an increasingly mass character, such that anti-Semitic activities were not solely the work of radical organizations. Both mainstream *and* fascist parties exploited anti-Semitic agitation. Intellectuals too entered the debate; those oriented toward the fascist Iron Guard were naturally in the forefront of anti-Semitic campaigns against Romanian Jews. In addition to radical solutions to the "Jewish problem," they advocated replacing democracy with a Nazi-like regime possessed of a distinctly Romanian flavor. For all the changes wrought throughout the course of modern Romania, anti-Semitism has been a consistent and dominant element, and remains widespread in intellectual circles to this day.

The tragedy of the Romanian intelligentsia in the period between the world wars was that rather than trying to improve an imperfect political system, they chose to throw it overboard, instead linking themselves with totalitarian personalities and systems. The political scientist George Voicu aptly described Romania's late-1930s abandonment of the Western political model: "The dictatorships that followed (royal, Iron Guard–military, military, and Communist) were not significantly opposed [by the Romanian intellectuals] because sociologically the ground had been prepared: somehow a political culture permissive if not in sync with these solutions appeared." It is exactly this civic desertion, this "Nazification" of Romanian society, that Sebastian witnessed and documented. Captured in this diary, it constitutes one of its most important aspects.

The *maître à penser* of the Iron Guard intellectual generation was Nae Ionescu (no relation to the playwright Eugen Ionescu). The "grey eminence" and one of the principal ideologists of the Iron Guard, Nae Ionescu taught philosophy at the University of Bucharest and later was paid for his pro-Nazi activities by I. G. Farben. He was described by his contemporaries as inconsistent, unscrupulous, opportunistic, and cynical. In the late 1920s, Nae Ionescu, who had already become an influential intellectual but was not yet an Iron Guard ideologist, "discovered" and published the works of Mihail Sebastian. Sebastian never forgot this support and for this reason repeatedly sought a rationale to excuse and explain his early mentor.

One of Sebastian's fundamental choices was to consider himself a Romanian rather than a Jew, a natural decision for one whose spirit and intellectual production belonged to Romanian culture. He soon discovered with surprise and pain that this was an illusion: both his intellectual benefactor and his friends ultimately rejected him only because he was Jewish.

The first big disappointment came from Nae Ionescu. Asked in 1934 by Mihail Sebastian to write a preface to his book *De douǎ mii de ani*, Ionescu wrote a savagely anti-Semitic piece. He explained to Sebastian and his readers that a Jew could not belong to any national community. As he put it, "...Belonging to a particular community is not an individual choice....Someone can be in the service of a community, can serve it in an eminent way, can even give his life for this collectivity; but this does not bring him closer to it. Germany carried on the war due to the activity of two Jews, Haber and Rathenau. Through this, however, Haber and Rathenau did not become Germans. They served, but from outside, from outside the walls of the German spiritual community. Is this unfair? The question has no sense: it is a fact." Nae Ionescu warned Sebastian not even to think of himself as Romanian: "It is an assimilationist illusion, it is the illusion of so many Jews who sincerely believe that they are Romanian. . . . Remember that you are Jewish! . . . Are you Iosif Hechter, a human being from Brăila on the Danube? No, you are a Jew from Brăila on the Danube." Sebastian nevertheless chose to publish Ionescu's anti-Semitic preface, but he responded in a later book with anger and sadness.

Sebastian understood that Nae Ionescu was an opportunist even when it came to his Iron Guard credo, yet the Jewish writer continued to have mixed feelings for the fascist philosopher—"fondness, irritation, doubts, repugnance." When in May 1938 Nae Ionescu was arrested and interned in a concentration camp precisely for his activities as a leader of the Iron Guard, Sebastian was distressed and worried. He continued to try to explain Ionescu's political actions as a "miscalculation," due to "half farce, half ambition." In March 1940, when Nae Ionescu died, Sebastian sobbed uncontrollably, viewing his death as a defeat and an injustice.

Nae Ionescu and his followers hoped that the Iron Guard ideology, with its odd mixture of anti-capitalism, anti-Semitism, and anti-communism, would constitute the solution to Romania's problems. Nae Ionescu, as the political scientist Marta Petreu put it, ". . . prepared and influenced part of the young intellectuals towards the Christian-Orthodox legionary ideology. It is certain that Nae Ionescu's influence . . . had an impact on the most cultivated segment of the young pro-legionary intelligentsia. . . . In the articles of the young legionary intellectuals one finds all the ingredients of this doctrine: attacks against the democratic state and against liberalism, the assertion of heavy nationalism, the rejection of the Western world, the idea of the legionary dictatorship, the ongoing national revolution (following the model of the ongoing fascist revolution), the exaltation of the Orthodox Christianity, etc. The more obscure and mystical an idea of the legionary doctrine, the more successful it was with the pro-legionary young intelligentsia." Sebastian's diary provides a sort of x-ray of this barbarization of the Romanian intelligentsia during these dictatorships. By 1937 Sebastian no longer preserved many illusions about his friends who had become members of the

Iron Guard. Still, he continued to socialize with them, acknowledging in his diary how painful the situation was becoming.

Anti-Semitism was a prevailing theme in the writings of these young intellectuals. They blamed the Jews for everything they perceived to be wrong in Romanian society: liberalism, poverty, syphilis, alcoholism, communism, prostitution, procurement, abortion, homosexuality, socialism, feminism. Before the appearance of the first Romanian anti-Semitic government, Sebastian witnessed the increase in anti-Semitism not only among the Romanian intelligentsia but on the streets of Bucharest itself. In June 1936 he vividly described this phenomenon, advocating Jewish self-defense as a response. When the anti-Semitic Goga-Cuza government was installed at the very end of 1937, Sebastian saw immediately where the country was heading, noting that official speeches as reported in the press for the first time contained the terms "yid" and "Judah's domination." He correctly anticipated the review of citizenship for Jews and rightly predicted that he would lose his job because he was a Jew.

One of Sebastian's closest friends, Mircea Eliade, became rabidly anti-Semitic under the influence of the Iron Guard. A well-known journalist and novelist in Romania between the wars, after World War II Eliade made an exceptional career for himself at the University of Chicago as a historian of religions. Unlike other famous representatives of his generation, however, Eliade never acknowledged his past as an Iron Guard ideologist and is not known ever to have expressed regret for his involvement with this fascist organization.

In the Romanian press Eliade published stridently anti-Semitic attacks. "Is it possible," he asked, "that the Romanian nation will end in the most miserable disintegration in history, eaten by poverty and syphilis, invaded by Jews and torn by aliens, demoralized, betrayed and sold for a few million lei?" This outburst from December 1937 was characteristic. About two months earlier, Eliade had plunged into a long xenophobic exhortation, reproaching the authorities for their *tolerance* toward the Jews, writing, "We didn't lift a finger while we watched the Jewish element strengthening in the Transylvanian towns. . . . Since the war the Jews have invaded the villages of Maramureş and Bukovina and have obtained an absolute majority in all Bessarabian cities. . . . I very well know that the Jews will shout that I am an anti-Semite and the democrats that I am a hooligan or a fascist. . . . I am not a bit annoyed when I hear the Jews shouting: 'anti-Semitism,' 'fascism,' 'Hitlerism.' "

In typical Iron Guard fashion, Mircea Eliade called for violence against the adversaries of his movement. In 1936 he erupted during a conversation with Sebastian, advocating the execution of the pro-Western Romanian foreign minister Nicolae Titulescu: "He should be . . . riddled with bullets. Strung up by the tongue."

If in 1936 Sebastian was still trying to "do everything possible to keep" Eliade as a friend, by March 1937 he seemed to acknowledge that such a friendship was becoming impossible: "We don't see each other for days at a time—and when we do, we no longer have anything to say." During the same years Sebastian described himself as "horrified" that Eliade had participated in the Iron Guard electoral campaign. At the same time, when in August 1938 Eliade was arrested for his Iron Guard activities, Sebastian worried and explained Eliade's behavior as "childish nonsense." Friends in high positions soon appointed Eliade to positions abroad, where he remained out of harm's way.

When Eliade was appointed to diplomatic posts (first in London and then in Lisbon), Sebastian wrote bitterly about his friend who, as he saw it, had betrayed him and who never visited him during the war. ". . . Successes, even when resulting from moral infamy, remain successes," Sebastian wrote. Eliade's opportunism is perhaps best revealed by the fact that he served in three conflicting governments, one right after another, beginning with the dictatorship of King Carol II, who executed C. Z. Codreanu (the leader of the Iron Guard and Eliade's idol) and whose regime eventually put Eliade into a camp. Eliade also served General Antonescu's governments, with and without the Iron Guard.

Another strong supporter of the Iron Guard among Sebastian's friends was E. M. Cioran, a brilliant writer and philosopher who in his Parisian exile after the war would openly regret his "pact with the devil." Earlier, with fascism ascending, he had written, "There are few people, even in Germany, who have a greater admiration for Hitler than I do." Despite this, Sebastian described him in January 1941 as "interesting . . . , remarkably intelligent, unprejudiced, and with . . . cynicism and idleness combined in an amusing manner."

Dinu (Constantin) Noica, a thinker who after the war created a non-Communist school of thought that was tolerated by the Ceausescu regime, joined the Iron Guard in December 1938; he too was a friend of Sebastian. In autumn 1940 he found himself in power with his fellow Legionaries. Noica then admonished Romania to discover anti-Semitism before it was too late, and he spread the ultra-nationalistic hate doctrine of a murderous regime that he claimed he would never disavow.

Like Sebastian's other friends, the theatre director Haig Acterian became an active member of the Iron Guard, participating in the January 1941 anti-Antonescu rebellion that, in its anti-Semitic excesses, could be said to be Romania's equivalent of Germany's *Kristallnacht*. In 1936 Sebastian was amazed by Acterian's adoration of Corneliu Codreanu, the Iron Guard leader, reminding himself that "in 1932, Haig was a Communist." As Sebastian's diary unfolds, the reader senses his vanishing hope that what was happening to his friends was nothing more than an accident, that they would again become "normal" people.

If Eliade, Cioran, Noica, and Acterian had the minimal decency to refrain from openly displaying their anti-Semitism in front of Sebastian, the same cannot be said of Acterian's wife, Marietta Sadova, who was described by Sebastian in 1936 as a future "Leni Riefenstahl in a state run by Zelea Codreanu." "Choking with anti-Semitism," she shouted in Sebastian's presence, "The yids are to blame . . . they take the bread from our mouths; they exploit and smother us. They should get out of here. This is our country, not theirs. Romania for the Romanians!"

Sebastian was exasperated and puzzled by the fascist fanaticism of his friends, but he persisted in his efforts to offer a rational explanation for their "barbarous mistake." In 1937 he still believed there was "more blindness than humbug in their camp, and perhaps more good faith than imposture." In 1939, when King Carol II violently suppressed the Iron Guard following the assassination of his prime minister, Armand Călinescu, executing hundreds of members of the Iron Guard in reprisal, Sebastian was pained by this repression and continued to feel sorry for his ex-friends.

In 1945 the famous playwright Eugen Ionescu, who was a close and unwavering friend of Sebastian's, wrote of the Iron Guard generation, "We were morally rotten and miserable. . . . In terms of me, 1 cannot reproach myself for being a fascist. But the others can be reproached for this. Mihail Sebastian kept a lucid mind and an authentic humanity. Cioran is here in exile. He admits that he was wrong during his youth. It is difficult for me to pardon him. Mircea Eliade arrives these days: in his eyes everything is lost since 'communism won.' He is truly guilty. And he and Cioran and Vulcanescu, and this imbecile Noica and many others are the victims of the odious defunct Nae Ionescu. . . . Because of him all became fascists. . . . He created a stupid and horrendous reactionary Romania."

Sebastian's close friend the well-known novelist Camil Petrescu was not a member of the Iron Guard, but he reflected perhaps better than anyone else the Nazification and opportunism displayed by much of the Romanian intelligentsia. Sebastian was fond of Petrescu and called him "one of the finest minds in Romania . . . one of the most sensitive creatures in Romania." Like Marietta Sadova, Petrescu did not bother to hide his anti-Semitism from Sebastian. Unlike Sadova, however, he was not filled with hate; he was a smiling and casual anti-Semite. Petrescu told Sebastian that because of the Jews' nationalism and communism (which Petruscu considered "Jewish imperialism"), they were the real source of anti-Semitism. Later, during the war, Petrescu bought into the Antonescu regime's official anti-Semitic propaganda clichés, holding the Jews responsible for Romania's military misfortunes and therefore blaming them for their own tragic fate. According to Petrescu, the Jews, especially the Americans, were also guilty for the continuation of the war because they were making compromise impossible.

Of course not all of Sebastian's friends were sensitive or insensitive anti-Semites. Antoine Bibescu helped Sebastian during his military service and refused to allow anyone to utter anti-Semitic allusions in Sebastian's presence. During the summer of 1941, when massive anti-Semitic measures were being implemented in Romania, Madeleine Andronescu, another friend of Sebastian's, told him how ashamed she was for the humiliation being forced on the Jews. A good friend of Sebastian, the diplomat and politician Constantin Vişoianu (later one of the leaders of Romanian post–World War II emigration to the United States), whom Sebastian did not think of as a sentimentalist, said something similar to Sebastian after witnessing a group of Jews in the street: "Whenever I see a Jew, I feel an urge to go up and greet him and to say: 'Please believe me, sir, I have nothing to do with all of this.'" Alexandru Rosetti, Sebastian's benefactor, advised, indeed almost ordered Sebastian to leave Romania for Palestine via Bulgaria and Turkey in 1941, during the height of the deportations of Jews from Bessarabia and Bukovina to Transnistria. Titu Devechi, another good friend, warned him about the massive dimensions of the carnage against the Jews in Bessarabia and Bukovina. In January 1942, in Rosetti's home, Sebastian heard another prominent Romanian intellectual, Andrei Oţetea, speak with "emotion, stupefaction and occasional fury" about the Iaşi pogrom in which twelve thousand Jews were killed and which Oţetea called "the most bestial day in human history."

Sebastian described with fascinating accuracy the Romanian Holocaust as it unfolded around him. In Bucharest he experienced serious discrimination but he was never deported to a concentration camp. Unlike the Jews from Bessarabia, Bukovina, and Transnistria, who were deported and massacred in great numbers, Sebastian's torture took the form of forced labor, confiscations of property, restrictions on his ability to work and earn a living, heavy fines, and tiny food rations. Still, since he was not ghettoized, Sebastian remained in a position to witness the persecution of his less fortunate fellow Jews from Romania's periphery, and to see how Romanian society reacted to the Holocaust.

He filled his diary with rich details (later confirmed by archival documents) of the conditions under which the deportations of Jews from Bessarabia and Bukovina to Transnistria took place during the summer and fall of 1941. At the peak of the deportations, Sebastian knew full well how the Jews were being sent over the Dniester: "The roads in Bessarabia and Bukovina are filled with corpses of Jews driven from their homes towards Ukraine. Old and sick people, children, women—all quite indiscriminately pushed onto the roads and driven toward Mogilev. . . . Already . . . the number of Jews murdered since June is in excess of 100,000." The diary describes in like detail how the Jews from Gura Humorului and Dorohoi were deported in just a few hours.

Sebastian lived through all these events in a "dazed stupor," with "no room for feelings, gestures or words." Like a photographer, he recorded the "nervous animation," "the pale faces," the "mute despair that has become a kind of Jewish greeting," the "small groups of pale, famished, ragged Jews, carrying wretched bundles or sacks." Well informed through his high-ranking Romanian friends, Sebastian even knew how American authorities saw Romania's role in the war against the Soviet Union, as they did Romanian responsibility in the Holocaust.

Sebastian quickly grasped the essence of the state anti-Semitism of the Antonescu regime. In August 1941 he observed, "Everyone is a cog in the huge anti-Semitic factory that is the Romanian state." In October that year: "Organized anti-Semitism is going through one of its darkest phases. Everything is too calculated for effect, too obviously stage-managed, not to have a political significance." Earlier he had described the chaotic way in which these "organized" Romanian anti-Semitic acts were carried out.

On 23 August 1944, Antonescu's regime was overthrown by King Michael and an alliance of several political parties. Sebastian now felt a huge sense of relief, knowing that his life was no longer in danger. But, like many Jews, he was torn between the joy of seeing the liberating Red Army and the plunder that the same army brought with it. One week after the liberation, Sebastian wrote about his elation but also about his "bewilderment, fear, doubt" concerning the liberators who raped, robbed, and looted. At the same time he was already disgusted with the opportunism of the "new ally" (Romania) of the anti-Axis coalition. "In the end," he wrote, "the Russians are within their rights. The locals are disgusting—Jews and Romanians alike." One week after liberation, Sebastian strongly criticized the newly ascendant Communist ideology and refused to work for the Communist newspaper *Romania Liberă* and its "editorial committee terrorized by conformity."

The considerable debate generated by Sebastian's diary after its first Romanian edition in 1996 showed once again that anti-Semitism remains a fundamental element of Romanian culture—called by George Voicu a "culture of idols and taboos." The idols are essentially the same extreme right intellectuals with whom Sebastian socialized. The taboos prohibit any serious critical examination of these idols. A few days before his death in 1997, Petru Cretia, a distinguished Romanian intellectual, wrote, "I have seen irrefutable [evidence of the] fury aroused by Sebastian's *Journal* and of the feeling that lofty national values are besmirched by such calm, sad, and forgiving revelations on the part of a fair-minded (often angelic) witness." Under these circumstances, it remains difficult if not impossible to engage in a serious discussion about any challenge to Romania's self-image and self-definition as a nation of eternal victims, never perpetrators.

Much of the Romanian intelligentsia keeps alive a mainstream cultural anti-Semitism that is perhaps more subtle but no less dangerous. Since the Holocaust it has become more difficult for some of these intellectuals to be at once openly pro-Western and anti-Semitic. And they often depend on recognition and funding provided by the West. Nevertheless their anti-Semitic message remains obvious. Thus while mainstream Romanian anti-Semitic intellectuals do not deny the Holocaust, they barely acknowledge it, and do so only in order to compare it with the crimes of communism. Many pay lip service to Jewish suffering caused by the Holocaust, only to charge immediately that these same Jewish victims were guilty of bringing communism to Eastern Europe and becoming the new perpetrators. Some also allege that a powerful Jewish lobby maintains a monopoly on suffering and thus denies the victims of the Gulag their right to memorials and commemorations. In a March 1998 article, Nicolae Manolescu suggested that Jews sought to monopolize the process of "unmasking the crime against humanity." He also said that "indirect evidence supporting my suspicion is the trial in France against Garaudy, who did not say that there was no Holocaust, but only that a terrible lobby was organized around it. Well the loss of the monopoly over this specific issue seems to make some people nervous. It is not correct and it is immoral," he wrote, "to cover the mouths of the millions of victims of communism fearing that not enough people will remain to mourn the victims of Nazism."

The novelist Norman Manea, a survivor from Transnistria whose article in the *New Republic* in April 1998, "The Incompatibilities," triggered the debate over Sebastian's diary, and Michael Shafir, a political scientist who analyzed this debate, have elicited vitriolic attacks in Romania. Dumitru Tsepenag, a Romanian dissident under communism, has observed that the authors of these types of attacks are responsible for the likelihood that Romania will continue to carry the "infamous tag of an anti-Semitic country." George Voicu has noted that many Romanian intellectuals refuse to acknowledge that "the cultural anti-Semitism of the Romanians is in fact an issue of the Romanian culture, not a 'Jewish issue'; not at all a secondary issue but an essential one. Those whose duty is to research it, to assess it, to solve it, are primarily the Romanian intellectuals. . . . As long as Romanian intellectuals see this issue as a secondary, irrelevant, embarrassing, entertainment-value topic, or even more disturbingly, as an anti-national or false issue that when tackled amounts to a sacrilege, as long as Romanian culture remains under the pressure of idolatrous complexes pulling it back to an obsolete era, Romania will be condemned to a peripheral, exotic status, pervious only in the tiniest degree to the values of European and universal culture." As Sebastian himself put it in his diary in August 1944, a week after the overthrow of the Antonescu regime and a few months before his death, "Romania will regain its senses when the problem of responsibility is posed in earnest. Otherwise, it would all be too cheap."

Principal Figures Mentioned in the Book

HAIG ACTERIAN, theatre producer, active Iron Guard member, husband of Marietta Sadova.

FELIX ADERCA, Jewish novelist and friend of Sebastian's.

SICĂ ALEXANDRESCU, theatre producer.

MADELEINE ANDRONESCU, friend of Sebastian's.

ION ANTONESCU, general, fascist dictator of Romania, 1940–1944.

MIHAI ANTONESCU, minister of justice, later minister of foreign affairs and deputy prime minister in the Antonescu government.

CONSTANTIN ARGETOIANU, politician, prime minister September–November 1939.

ALEXANDRU AVERESCU, general, prime minister March 1926–June 1927.

BABA, nickname of Sebastian's grandmother.

CAMIL BALTAZAR, novelist.

JULES BASDEVANT, French diplomat.

RADU BELIGAN, actor.

JOSÉ BEREȘTEANU, manager of the Comoedia theatre.

ANTOINE BIBESCU, prince, close friend of Sebastian's.

ARISTIDE BLANK, banker.

DORINA BLANK, daughter of Aristide Blank, friend of Sebastian's.

AGNIA BOGOSLAV, actress.

GEO BOGZA, writer and journalist.

GEORGE BRĂTIANU, leader of the right-wing faction of the Liberal party.

TONY BULANDRA, actor.

LENI CALER, actress and friend of Sebastian's.

NICOLAE CARANDINO, journalist.

CAROL II, King of Romania 1927–1940.

DEMETRU CEACĂRU, Jewish journalist.

RADU CIOCULESCU, literary critic and brother of Şerban Cioculescu.

ŞERBAN CIOCULESCU, literary critic and brother of Radu Cioculescu.

ALEXANDRU CIORĂNESCU, literary historian.

GINA COCEA, wife of the novelist N. D. Cocea (also Gina Manolescu-Strunga, also Gina Ionescu).

TANTZI COCEA, actress.

CORNELIU ZELEA CODREANU, leader of the Iron Guard.

PETRU COMARNESCU, art critic, friend of Sebastian's.

IOAN COMŞA, friend and law colleague of Sebastian's.

N. M. CONDIESCU, general, novelist, president of the Romanian Writers' Association.

LENA CONSTANTE, artist, friend of Sebastian's.

NICUŞOR CONSTANTINESCU, theatre director, playwright.

NICHIFOR CRAINIC, extreme right journalist, author of a xenophobic and racist National Christian fundamentalist theory.

NICOLAE CREVEDIA, extreme right anti-Semitic journalist.

JENI CRUŢESCU, friend of Sebastian's.

A. C. CUZA, one of the main "theorists" of Romanian anti-Semitism, leader with Octavian Goga of the heavily anti-Semitic Goga-Cuza government.

GH. CUZA, son of A. C. Cuza, member of the Goga-Cuza government.

ARMAND CĂLINESCU, prime minister 1937–1939, coordinator of the repression against the Iron Guard.

GEORGE CĂLINESCU, literary critic.

TITU DEVECHI, journalist and close friend of Sebastian's.

VICTOR EFTIMIU, playwright.

SANDU ELIAD, theatre producer.

MIRCEA ELIADE, novelist, historian of religions, ardent supporter of the Iron Guard, friend of Sebastian's.

MIHAI EMINESCU, nineteenth-century poet considered the creator of the modern Romanian language, a strong anti-Semite.

GEORGE ENESCU, famous Romanian composer.

ŞTEFAN ENESCU, Sebastian's friend (pen name Ştefan Mincu).

WILHELM FILDERMAN, leader of the Romanian Jewish Community.

BEATE FREDANOV, actress.

SCARLAT FRODA, theatre director and literary commentator.

GRIGORE GAFENCU, politician and diplomat.

MARIA GHIOLU, friend of Sebastian's and wife of Stavri Ghiolu.

ION GIGURTU, foreign minister, prime minister July–September 1940.

GENERAL HENRI CONSTANTIN GIURESCU, historian.

OCTAVIAN GOGA, prime minister December 1937–February 1938, leader with A. C. Cuza of the Goga-Cuza government.

MIRON GRINDEA, journalist.

CORIN GROSSU, writer.

SOLOMON (CHARLES) GRÜBER, lawyer and personal secretary to Wilhelm Filderman.

CAROL GRÜNBERG, friend of Sebastian's.

EMIL GULIAN, poet and Sebastian's friend.

RADU DEMETRESCU GYR, poet and fanatical follower of the Iron Guard.

BOGDAN PETRICEICU HAŞDEU, nineteenth-century writer, strongly anti-Semitic.

POLDY (PIERRE) HECHTER, Sebastian's elder brother, lived in France during the war.

RICHARD (RICCI) HILLARD, journalist, friend of Sebastian's.

EUGEN IONESCU, playwright, Sebastian's friend.

GHIŢĂ IONESCU, political scientist, friend of Sebastian's.

NAE IONESCU, Iron Guard main ideologist, professor of philosophy at the University of Bucharest, early mentor of Sebastian.

JACQUES LASSAIGNE, French art critic.

IONEL LAZARONEANU, lawyer with literary inclinations.

RADU LECCA, commissar for Jewish affairs in the Antonescu government.

ANGELA LEREANU, secretary at Saşa Roman's office.

VASILE V. LONGHIN, judge from Brăila.

EUGEN LOVINESCU, literary critic.

NINA MAREŞ, wife of Mircea Eliade.

VASILE MARIN, Iron Guard ideologist.

ISTRATE MICESCU, lawyer, minister of justice in the Goga-Cuza government.

ION I. MOŢA, leader of the Iron Guard.

FRANKLIN GUNTHER MOTT, head of the U.S. diplomatic mission in Bucharest.

TEODOR MUŞATESCU, playwright.

GHEORGHE NENIŞOR, diplomat and Sebastian's friend.

MARYSE NENIŞOR, wife of Gheorghe Nenişor and Sebastian's friend.

CONSTANTIN D. NICOLESCU, general, former minister of national defense.

IACOB NIEMIROWER, chief rabbi of the Federation of Romanian Jewish Communities until 1939.

CONSTANTIN (DINU) NOICA, journalist, philosopher, strong supporter of the Iron Guard.

VICTOR OCNEANU, publisher.

OCTAV ONICESCU, mathematician.

GEORGE OPRESCU, art critic.

ANDREI OŢETEA, historian.

PETRE PANDREA, left-wing journalist.

LUCREȚIU PĂTRĂȘCANU (wartime name ANDREI), Communist leader.

PERPESSICIUS (DIMITRIE S. PANAITESCU), literary critic.

CAMIL PETRESCU, novelist, friend of Sebastian's.

CONSTANTIN PETROVICESCU, general, pro–Iron Guard minister of the interior.

NORA PIACENTINI, actress.

DIONISIE PIPPIDI, historian.

MIHAI POLIHRONIADE, Iron Guard journalist and theorist.

STELIAN POPESCU, lawyer and politician, director and owner of the newspaper *Universul.*

LILLY POPOVICI, actress and Sebastian's friend.

DRAGOȘ PROTOPOPESCU, right-wing journalist.

GHEORGHE RACOVEANU, Iron Guard journalist.

MIHAI RALEA, minister of labor March 1938–July 1940.

MARIETTA RAREȘ, actress.

LIVIU REBREANU, novelist, director of the National Theatre under the Antonescu administration.

ZOE RICCI, actress.

ALEXANDRU RIOȘANU, head of Siguranța (the secret police) September 1940–June 1941.

NICULAE ROȘU, Iron Guard journalist and ideologist.

SAȘA (SACHA) ROMAN, lawyer, in whose office Sebastian worked as a clerk.

ALEXANDRU ROSETTI, director of the Royal Foundations, Sebastian's close friend and benefactor.

MARIETTA SADOVA, actress, fanatical supporter of the Iron Guard, wife of Haig Acterian.

MIHAIL SADOVEANU, writer.

ION SĂN-GIORGIU, extreme right journalist and playwright.

"BENU" ANDREI SEBASTIAN, the writer's younger brother.

CELLA SENI, the writer CELLA SERGHI, wife of Alfio Seni.

W. SIEGFRIED, stage designer.

SOARE Z. SOARE, theatre producer.

ȚOȚA SOIU, actress, wife of Ion Iancovescu.

THEODOR SOLACOLU, translator and poet.

ZAHARIA STANCU, journalist.

MIHAI STELESCU, Iron Guard leader.

LEOPOLD (POLDY) STERN, lawyer and writer, friend of Sebastian's.

VLADIMIR STREINU, literary critic.

D. I. SUCHIANU, movie critic and journalist.

ALEXANDRU ŞAFRAN, wartime chief rabbi of the Jewish Communities in Romania.

PAMFIL ŞEICARU, journalist, owner of the *Curentul* newspaper.

MIRCEA ŞEPTILICI, actor.

GHEORGHE TĂTĂRESCU, politician, prime minister January 1934–December 1937, November 1939–July 1940.

AL. CRISTIAN TELL, Iron Guard journalist.

IONEL TEODOREANU, writer and poet.

PĂSTOREL TEODOREANU, poet and writer.

TUDOR TEODORESCU-BRANIŞTE, journalist and writer.

CICERONE THEODORESCU, poet.

DEM. THEODORESCU, writer and journalist.

ALICE THEODORIAN, friend of Sebastian's.

VASILE TIMUŞ, theatre manager.

NICOLAE TITULESCU, minister of foreign affairs October 1932–January 1935.

VIOREL TRIFA, president of the students' organization of the Iron Guard.

SANDU TUDOR, journalist at *Credinţa*.

PETRE ŢUŢEA, philosopher, ardent follower of the Iron Guard.

AL. VAIDA-VOEVOD, a leader of the National Peasant party, leader of the anti-Semitic Vlad Ţepeş League.

CONSTANTIN VIŞOIANU, diplomat and politician, close friend of Sebastian's.

TUDOR VIANU, literary critic.

VICTOR P. VOJEN, extreme right pro-Nazi journalist.

PAUL ZARIFOPOL, novelist, literary critic.

HERBERT ("BELU") ZILBER, Communist publicist and friend of Sebastian's.

A. L. ZISSU, leader of the Zionist movement in Romania.

EUGEN ZWIEDENEK, under Ion Antonescu head of the government agency in charge of the Aryanization of Jewish properties.

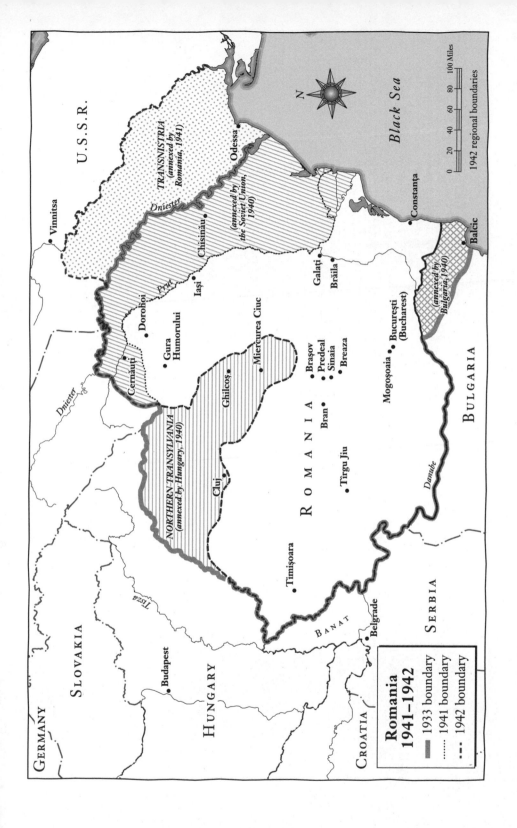

Romania 1941–1942

GERMANY · SLOVAKIA · HUNGARY · CROATIA · SERBIA · BULGARIA · U.S.S.R.

ROMANIA

TRANSNISTRIA (annexed by Romania, 1941)

(annexed by the Soviet Union, 1940)

NORTHERN TRANSYLVANIA (annexed by Hungary, 1940)

(annexed by Bulgaria, 1940)

BANAT

Black Sea

Vinnitsa
Odessa
Chişinău
Iaşi
Dorohoi
Gura Humorului
Cernăuţi
Ghilcoş
Miercurea Ciuc
Cluj
Timişoara
Budapest
Belgrade
Tîrgu Jiu
Bran
Braşov
Predeal
Sinaia
Breaza
Mogoşoaia
Bucureşti (Bucharest)
Galaţi
Brăila
Constanţa
Balcic

Dniester
Prut
Danube
Tisza

N
100 Miles
80
60
40
20
0

1942 regional boundaries

1933 boundary
1941 boundary
1942 boundary

Journal
1935–1944

1935

[Tuesday], 12 February 1935

10 p.m.

The radio is tuned to Prague. I have been listening to a concerto by J. S. Bach in G for trumpet, oboe, harpsichord, and orchestra. After the intermission, there will be a concerto of his in G minor for piano and orchestra.

I am immersed in Bach. Yesterday evening, while writing a long letter to Poldy,[1] I listened to the *Fourth Brandenburg Concerto* from Lyons—for the first time with extremely clear reception—and then to a Mozart concerto for piano and orchestra.

I went to see an eye specialist. He recommended glasses and I have started to wear them. It changes me quite a lot and makes me look ugly.

It was funny when I told him my name. He said that his family has much discussed my *De două mii de ani* [For Two Thousand Years], which he has not read himself. He has heard a lot of people cursing me. I realize that my trial has really been lost. *Cum am devenit huligan* [How I Became a Hooligan] is not reaching the circles where I am cursed even by "hearsay."[2]

On Sunday at Tîrgovişte, where I had gone for a lecture, Samy Herşcovici told me a story that indicates how the "affair" is seen by the public.

The bookseller who was selling tickets for the lecture offered one to a professor at the teachers' training college: "Sebastian? Aha! That yid who got himself baptized."

1. Poldy (Pierre) Hechter: Sebastian's elder brother, a doctor. He lived in France.
2. When Sebastian's publisher invited Nae Ionescu to write an introduction to *For Two Thousand Years*, Ionescu contributed a viciously anti-Semitic piece.

Yesterday evening, Nae[3] was due to speak at the [Royal] Foundation about "National Solidarity." His lecture was banned by the government.[4] The students were herded together on the pavement near the palace, where they booed, shouted, and sang. Then they were driven farther, into Piața Ateneului, where Nae, bareheaded and wearing his coat with a wolfskin collar, made a speech while perched on their shoulders.

"Nae was a fine sight," related Nina.[5]

There were scuffles, fistfights, firecrackers going off. Even some shots were said to have been fired in the air.

Not a word in today's papers.

How disgusting is the issue of *Credința* devoted to Nae. Petru Manoliu, Sandu Tudor, and Zaharia Stancu—about Nae Ionescu![6] I've lived to see this too.

[Monday], 18 February

Yesterday evening, two of Handel's organ concertos, in B-flat major and G minor, from Stuttgart. Very Mozart–Haydn. Could I tell him apart from those other two?

For a week now, beginnings of revolution at the Bar. A few meetings campaigning for a "numerus clausus."[7] On Saturday, the day before yesterday, Istrate Micescu spoke and went right over to the Movement.[8] It is exactly a week since my interview with him appeared. I am obviously losing my touch.

What people! Made of whey, yogurt, and water. M[icescu] told me the other day: "If you want to know who is my master in politics, it is Alain." He spoke then about freedom, about individual resistance to the state, about the stupid idea of a "collective" and how it is exploited by dictatorships. And now look at him, an anti-Semite gone over to the "national revolution."

---

3. Nae Ionescu: chief Iron Guard ideologist and professor of philosophy at the University of Bucharest, early mentor of Sebastian.

4. Following the assassination in 1933 of Prime Minister I. G. Duca by members of the Iron Guard, Nae Ionescu was placed under police surveillance and the publication of his newspaper *Cuvântul* was suspended.

5. Nina Mareș: first wife of Mircea Eliade.

6. Petru Manoliu, Sandu Tudor, and Zaharia Stancu were editors at *Credința*, which a year earlier had harshly criticized Nae Ionescu and the Criterion association.

7. Members of the anti-Semitic League of the National Christian Defense (LANC) and of the Iron Guard were campaigning for the disbarment of Jewish attorneys.

8. Istrate Micescu: lawyer, minister of justice in the anti-Semitic government of Goga-Cuza (1937–1938). The movement to which Sebastian refers is the Iron Guard.

Nae has had a hand in this too. Micescu admitted to Froda[9] that he had had a visit from Nae, who had urged him to take the leadership of what was happening at the Bar. Look at how the professor is going to make a new Romania! What a cruel, ridiculous, terrible affair, in which everyone, including Nae, makes his little contribution.

But spring has come. Yesterday I went with Benu[1] to Băneasa. A March wind was blowing, it was sunny, and I felt young. Not for a long time have I felt such a keen desire to be happy.

[Sunday], 17 March

Midnight

I have come tired from the station (got up at 6 a.m. to go to Brăila, now I am back). But I don't want to leave this note until tomorrow, having vowed in the train to write it.

I traveled with Nae Ionescu. He was going to give a lecture in Galaţi (about "Signs and Symbols"). Nothing interesting in the morning: we read the papers, talked politics, and had a pleasant time chatting with a girl who had struck up a conversation with us. I got off in Brăila and we agreed to meet again in the evening on the return journey.

In the evening we did indeed find ourselves in the same compartment. Professor Vechiu, leader of Argetoianu's[2] supporters in Brăila, was also there with us. All three of us had dinner in the restaurant car. Nae put on a great political act.

It is he who got Vaida's movement off the ground.[3] (Ten days ago he assured me of exactly the opposite.) He and the Iron Guard will support him, but without taking part themselves. He recognizes that the "numerus valachius" is really a platform for agitation, not at all a political program. He accepts the fact that it cannot be implemented. "Things like that could happen only as a consequence of something else, if there were a change in the general framework."

His plan is very simple. Keep Tătărescu[4] in power for the time being— for another three months, say, until Vaida's movement acquires solid foun-

9. Scarlat Froda: theatre director and literary critic.
1. "Benu": Andrei Sebastian, the writer's younger brother. He changed his surname after his brother did. He eventually emigrated from Romania with Sebastian's diary.
2. Constantin Argetoianu: politician, prime minister September–November 1939.
3. Al. Vaida-Voevod: a leader of the National Peasant party. After splitting from his party, he founded the anti-Semitic Vlad Tepeş League, which had as its slogan "numerus valachicus," a kind of numerus clausus.
4. Gheorghe Tătărescu: leader of the Liberal party, prime minister January 1934–December 1937, November 1939–July 1940.

dations and cadres. Then a Vaida government, produced by sixty Iron Guard deputies and some ten to twenty-five from other parties, so that "the Guard will be His Majesty's Opposition." Logically, when this Vaida government falls, the succession will fall to the Guardists.

I do not know what chances this plan has. Rather few, I would think, and in my view he is a fantasy-monger. Quite logical, of course.

What made me feel a little sad for Nae was the tone in which he said everything. Scheming, artful, *"enfant terrible."* What he said to Averescu,[5] how he duped George Brătianu,[6] how he got even with Vaida in Braşov . . .

"I really landed them in the shit."

I certainly prefer him in the lecture hall.

As we traveled back in the compartment, a feeling of vague unease turned into one of pain. What a poseur that man can be! There were two colonels in the compartment. He started chatting and managed to get them both "at sixes and sevens." I could see victory on his lips, a sense of triumph at having flummoxed them. He said some bewildering things—of the kind he uses to startle people by turning the discussion from a local matter to a problem of world history. The talk was of a possible war between France and Germany.

"Rubbish! The whole crux is in Singapore. That's where Europe is playing its cards. And it can play without Germany. That's all there is to it."

In Singapore? Maybe. But anyway, before the problem can be properly discussed, Nae's bolt from the blue put an end to it. The colonels exchanged looks of admiration and astonishment, suddenly alight from the revelation of the truth. Nae could feel this and basked in the warm glow.

In one hour he retold everything I know about him: how he lived through the revolution in Munich, how he gave speeches to the revolutionary ministers, how the revolution finally put an end to the Dachau money factory, how Colonel Epp did this and did that, etc., etc. Things I heard from him years ago, riveted to the wall in his office at *Cuvântul.*

Then he moved on to more recent matters. To Beck in Warsaw[7] he had said that it was necessary to move closer to Germany. To Karl Radek[8]

---

5. Alexandru Averescu: marshal, prime minister March 1926–June 1927.
6. George Brătianu: leader of the right-wing faction of the Liberal party.
7. Jozef Beck: Polish minister of foreign affairs.
8. Karl Radek: member of the executive committee of the Communist International (1920–1924), executed during the Stalinist purges.

he had explained that Stalin's successor would be Genghis Khan. In Berlin he had told a general this, shown a minister that . . .

"And do you know Hitler personally?"

(One of the colonels threw in this question when Nae was in full flow. I well knew that he had never met Hitler. He said so categorically a year ago, and again last summer. But he was at risk of disappointing the colonel, who was so full of admiration.)

"Yes, I've seen him. There's a great politician for you. You see, Trotsky, who is enormously intelligent, and Stalin, who is a fool, . . . (The change of tack was probably out of prudence, but he kept up the lie—a lie of pure bluster—because he could not bear to let slip any of the glory he had promised himself. What a child he is! Five minutes later, Vechiu asked him in turn, "Have you seen Hitler?" And he again replied "Yes," rapidly moving on to something else, either because he felt awkward or because he was bored with having to dream up too many things to say.)

He looked as he must have fifteen years ago holding forth at the Capşa.[9] How young he is, dear old Nae Ionescu!

Saturday, 30 March

Nae's class yesterday was suffocating. Iron Guardism pure and simple— no nuances, no complications, no excuses. "A state of combat is what we call politics. One party contains in its very being an obligation to wipe out all the others. The final conclusion is that 'internal politics' is an absurdity. There can only be a conquest or seizure of power and a merging of the party with the whole collective. From that moment all that exists is household management, since all possibility of reaction has been eliminated. A collective that contains within itself the idea of war is called a nation. A nation is defined by the friend-foe equation." And so on and so forth . . .

I should have liked to tell him how monstrously he contradicted himself, but he was in too much of a hurry and left straight after the lecture.

His whole heresy stems from a wild and terrifying abstraction: the collective. It is colder, more insubstantial, more artificial than the abstraction of the "individual." He forgets that he is speaking of human beings; that they have passions and—whatever one may say—an instinct for freedom, an awareness of their own individual existence.

Even more depressing is the fact that all those theories stem from vulgar political calculation. I am convinced that if he spoke like that yes-

9. Fashionable restaurant in Bucharest.

terday—with so many political allusions and so painfully Hitler-like—it was because an Iron Guardist dressed in national costume was sitting in the front row of the audience. I could feel that he was speaking for him.

I have been listening a lot to Bach recently. Last Sunday the *St. Matthew Passion* at the Ateneu. I think I am really very fond of his music. In any case, I can now easily tell a piece by Bach from any other.

Over the past three weeks I have picked up many of his works on various radio stations. One evening, from Warsaw, there was the *Double Violin Concerto in D Minor,* the *Concerto in D Minor for Three Pianos,* and another concerto, also in D minor, for piano and orchestra. Stuttgart had the *Fifth Brandenburg Concerto,* two cantatas, and a trio sonata for harpsichord, violin, and viola da gamba. (The same evening, from Warsaw, there was a Debussy sonata for flute, cello, and harp. Magnificent.) Later, two preludes and a fugue for organ, from Bucharest. Last Monday the *Second Brandenburg Concerto,* an aria, and a cantata from Budapest, and on Tuesday—again from Prague—the *Third Brandenburg Concerto* and another one in E major. One evening Berlin had a few organ pieces—I no longer remember which ones—and a suite for unaccompanied cello, heartrendingly calm and solemn.

And then, very many things I can no longer recall. (Bach two to three times a week from Stuttgart, after one in the morning. And one evening a delightful *Kleine nachtmusik* by Mozart, also from there.)

Finally, longer ago, Vienna had a memorable performance of the double violin concerto. A Handel sonata, Ysaÿe's *Variations on an Old Theme,* and a sonata by Philipp Emanuel Bach.

A cold rainy spring—I do not mean sad . . .

Sunday, 7 April

Elections at the S.S.R.[1] How wretched! I cannot forgive myself that for one moment I had the naiveté to think the game was serious.

As soon as you give up being alone, everything is lost.

Thursday, 11 April

This evening I listened to a Bruno Walter concert from Prague.

The overture to Gluck's *Iphigènie en Aulide,* a Mozart violin concerto in G major (the first time I have heard it, I think), and Beethoven's *Ninth Symphony.* The Mozart seemed more delicate and melodic than ever.

1. Societatea Scriitorilor Români: the Romanian Writers' Society.

The universities are closed. So tomorrow I no longer have Nae's course.

I saw some appalling things in the street. Wild animals.[2]

Sunday, 14 April

Yesterday Leni[3] came at one o'clock to pick me up at the newspaper. It was a beautiful day, like the middle of June. She was superb. Tailor-made suit, shoes, handbag, a little ribbon around her neck, the brim of her blue hat. With me she has a kind of timidity that makes her look solemn.

She said she had heard of a lover I am supposed to have had for a long time in Brăila.

"That's the reason I haven't called you any more. It's how I explain why you are so reserved. I haven't wanted to disturb you."

I protested and said there was no truth in it.

"So then?"

"So then"—I said to myself: be sensible, kid. "So then, it's just my natural reserve."

"Caution, in other words."

"If you like. But I think it's more a question of self-knowledge. It would be expecting too much of things I don't deserve."

"You don't know what you do and do not deserve. And in particular, you don't know what someone else may be thinking about you."

We went for a walk in Cişmigiu, and I was proud of how beautiful she was. It could be love.

Thursday, 18 [April]

2:30 a.m.

An eventful day. Visited Leni. We are in love; we said it to each other. She is young and beautiful, has an admirably simple way of speaking— and I find it so inexplicable that she is coming closer to me.

But it is not prudent, and I don't know how I'll ever get out of this. How many things have gone wrong because of my ill luck! I had so much going for me to be happy. I had enormous ability, with no complications and no drama. And all that broke down horribly at the age of seventeen and a half. I am disgusted by it sometimes, or more often saddened. Why, Lord, why?

2. Sebastian refers here to the anti-Semitic riots organized by student members of LANC, the Iron Guard, and the Vlad Tepeş League.

3. Leni Caler: actress and friend of Sebastian's.

I would so much like to be happy, and I would have asked so little.

The evening at the Nenişors'[4] and then at Zissu.[5] (I danced.) When I hooted for fun on the way home, she said: "You've so much of the child inside you, yet you're so tired of life."

For someone who has known me for only ten days, that was surprisingly accurate. Yes, it's true. It's terrible how calmly I accept the idea of death.

Sunday, 21 [April]

Went for a walk with Leni and a friend of hers, Jeni Cruţescu, on the Şosea. The first spring morning, after so many rainy ones. It was warm; a lot of green, a lot of yellow. We had vermouths and snacks at the Flora. Leni was delightfully dressed. People turned their heads at us, and I was again proud to be walking beside her.

But in the afternoon I felt a terrible need to see her again. That is not good at all, though I'm beginning to be seriously in love with her. How will I get out of that?

Tuesday, 23 [April]

I met her at a football match (Venus–Juventus), but she arrived late from a theatre rehearsal for the next premiere.

I cannot explain the interest she has in me. She is so beautiful—I am so badly dressed, so awkward. I realize how simple this love could be, how restful.

Wednesday, 22 May

Lunch at Aristide Blank's[6] with Leni, Froda, Mrs. Blank, a guy I've never met before, and two young women—a rather ugly Viennese brunette and a South American blonde who spoke French with a delightful Anglo-Saxon accent.

Coffee and cognac on a terrace, in a kind of courtyard made restful by the colors and the wind blowing through it. Blank is a poseur. Leni

---

4. Gheorghe Nenişor: theatre critic, Sebastian's friend and husband of Maryse Nenişor.
5. A night club in Bucharest.
6. Aristide Blank: a wealthy banker involved in the arts, a well-known member of the Romanian social elite.

was surprisingly ill at ease, but with adorably simple gestures. She is extremely shy, to my amazement. She claims that I intimidate her.

(Yesterday, at the football match at the O.N.E.F. [Stadium], she was uneasy, silent, "melancholic" for a lot of the time, but immediately became talkative, expansive, almost boisterous when Ronea, from the Regina Maria Theatre, joined our group—a man with whom she has certainly slept in the past. Her sudden *"mise à l'aise"*[7] infuriated me. But it is certainly not her fault. I am always the one to blame: I am probably too complicated and basically incomprehensible for her, whereas she has been so straightforward with me from the beginning.)

I did not mean to write about this, however, but about the South American blonde. We exchanged a few words, enough for me to draw a cinema sketch of her. She said:

"I'm South American. Where do I live? Pretty well everywhere. Look, I've just come from Vienna and plan to stay a couple of weeks. Then I'll go back to Vienna and meet up with my husband, who is on a business trip in Africa at the moment. No, I don't live in Germany. I have a house in Hamburg, though I haven't been there for three years. But I'll be going on the Rhine for a while this summer. We have a villa there. Then maybe to North Africa, where we also have a little house."

So, I said, you live on the whole planet.

"No," she smiled with sincere modesty. "No."

Strange people. And we can vegetate for a whole lifetime in Sfinţii Apostoli, Popa Tatu, or Radu-Vodă![8]

[Monday], 10 June

I must see Poldy! The trip that I initially thought to be out of the question must become possible. Things need to be cleared up—so that at least I know where I stand. How funny it would be if there were only a medical matter involved!

But no, I don't have too many illusions. But I do want to know.

Like a fool, I allowed myself to get caught up in a story that I knew from the beginning would lead nowhere. Here I am smitten, jealous of every man with whom she ever slept, preoccupied at every moment with what she is or might be doing, happy when she is smiling, miserable when she is too jolly, trembling when I hear her voice on the telephone. I am rediscovering that ebb and flow of emotions that I have not expe-

7. Relaxation.
8. Streets in Bucharest.

rienced for a long while, since Jeni's time, in the most feverish moments of my love—mornings when everything is simple and unimportant, when it seems neither here nor there whether I see her or not; evenings heavy with melancholy, with a desire to see her that is physically located in the heart.

All this takes a form that is comically sentimental, schoolboyish, adolescent. It sickens me to think that she is meanwhile occupied with a load of trivia that amuse or excite her, in her little life of pleasures, walks, and frivolities. It is altogether likely that she is sleeping around—and I am stupid enough to talk to her gravely and with a ridiculous lack of skill about various overcomplicated "problems."

She, who expected just another man, seems weary of my hesitations, of my excessive complications. And I suffer like a child because of all these meaningless trifles.

She is a "good girl." Will I one day be able to receive her in my bachelor flat, fuck her, drink a glass of wine and smoke a cigarette with her, put a record on the gramophone, and listen with indifference—or at best with amusement—as she talks about her past lovers? If I can, everything will be perfect. That too is a kind of happiness, and I would certainly be happy. But what if I can't? Another failure and it's all over.

Anyway, things are very bad as they stand. It is sickeningly trite that today I bought her a copy of Barbellion's[9] *Journal*—for her about whom Berariu said to me two months ago: "Go chat her up—you can't go wrong—she'll screw with anyone."

And he was probably right.

I'm seeing her tomorrow. She leaves on Sunday.

I broke with Jeni appallingly. The poor girl!

[Tuesday], 11 June

She was supposed to call me and she didn't. Everything can end at that, in the simplest way. Any move on my part would be more than ridiculous, worse than imprudent.

I ought to understand—and do understand perfectly—that it would be out of all proportion to note here every sordid little thing that has happened to me in this "love story." Enough!

Four hours later
More stupid than any lovesick fool, for I have absolutely no excuse.

---

9. Barbellion: pen name of the British writer Bruce Frederick Cummings. His *Journal of a Disappointed Man* was fashionable reading at the time.

I went to see her after all (after phoning twice: the first time she was asleep, the second time on her way out shopping). I told her—and I did it quite well, with perfect gestures, frown, and voice—that I am in love with her. Then I left, because someone was due to call on her at a quarter past eight.

"I got the times mixed up," she said candidly.

What an ass I am!

[Thursday,] 13 June

Chance has it that I am just now rereading a volume of Proust—the second one of *Albertine disparue.*

So many things should make me skeptical about my amatory "sufferings." I am well aware that they will not last, that I shall forget them, that they are all derisory, and that one day they will mean so little as not even to appear ridiculous. Yet such words of wisdom, such calculations that I know to be objectively correct, do not lessen in the slightest today's depression, the absurd need to see her, the physical pain of constantly thinking about her, of seeing again certain moments that now present a mystery I should like to clear up.

I wonder, for example, what happened that day when we went to lunch at Blank's. He took her aside, put his hand around her waist, and talked with her about something or other. Later, in the afternoon, I tried to reach her by telephone. Once she was asleep, the second time she was out. Something tells me that he met her that afternoon, and that when he took her aside he arranged a rendezvous.

And the following evening—on Monday, I think, as we were leaving the Piccadilly where I had met her by chance (she was with J[eni] C[ruțescu], I went with her toward the telephone and she stopped to call someone—whom?

What stupid, childish worries, especially as I know how little point there is in that old old game, so familiar and always the same.

But knowledge is not a cure, just as precise knowledge of the stages of typhoid fever does not spare you from suffering them.

Monday, 17 June

The reading of *Albertine* has given me back a strong inclination for Proust. Maybe I shall also read a volume from *Le temps retrouvé,* the second volume of *Du côté de chez Swann* (especially *Un amour de Swann,* to which

I am drawn by the events in my own life of the past three weeks), and finally some pages from *À l'ombre des jeunes filles* . . .

Meanwhile I enjoyed reading *Marcel Proust* by Robert de Billy; it was not all that interesting, but it did have some letters and photographs that I had not seen before. I am sorry I cannot keep the book—it belongs to Nenişor—but I shall jot down a couple of things here. *"Cette façon de projeter la lumière sur un fait divers, des hauteurs dissemblables, et avec des puissances dissemblables, chandelle ou phare, jusqu'à ce qu'y apparaissent en profondeur toutes les valeurs psychologiques qu'il est susceptible de manifester, est caractéristique de la méthode proustienne"* (page 12).

"Cette poursuite du volume à travers la diversité des formes . . ." (page 13).

"N'est-il pas plus simple d'attribuer à l'étude de la valeur aristocratique, plutôt qu'au snobisme, le goût qu'il avait pour la société des familles dont les racines plongent dans le passé et que les années ont amenées vivantes jusqu'à nous avec d'étranges modifications de leur contexture spirituelle?" (page 86).[1]

A quotation from Proust's preface to his translation of Ruskin's *Sesame and Lilies* perfectly defines his own art of writing: *"J'ai cru pouvoir noter jusqu'à sept thèmes dans la première phrase. En réalité, Ruskin y range l'une à côté de l'autre, mêle, fait manoeuvrer et resplendir ensemble toutes les principales idées—ou images—qui ont apparu avec quelque désordre au long de sa conférence. C'est son procédé. Il passe d'une idée à l'autre sans aucun ordre apparent. Mais, en réalité, la fantaisie qui le mène suit ses affinités profondes qui lui imposent, malgré lui, une logique supérieure. Si bien qu'il se trouve avoir obéi à une sorte de plan secret qui, dévoilé à la fin, impose rétrospectivement à l'ensemble une sorte d'ordre et le fait apercevoir, magnifiquement étagé jusqu'à cette apothéose finale."*[2]

---

1. "This way of casting light upon a trivial event—from different heights and with different powers, candle or headlamp, until all the psychological values it is capable of displaying appear in depth—is characteristic of the Proustian method."

"This pursuit of volume through diversity of form . . ."

"Is it not simpler to attribute to his study of aristocratic values, rather than to snobbism, his penchant for the company of families whose roots go deep into the past and which the years have carried alive down to our own times with strange modifications of their spiritual texture?"

2. "I thought I could detect as many as seven themes in the first sentence. For there Ruskin places alongside one another, mingling them and making them move and shine together, all the main ideas (or images) which appear in some disorder throughout his lecture. It is his mode of procedure. He passes from one idea to another without any apparent order. But in reality, his guiding imagination follows its own deep affinities, which impose a higher logic in spite of himself. Indeed, it turns out that he has obeyed a kind of secret plan which, when revealed at the end, retrospectively imposes a kind of order on the whole and makes it be seen rising magnificently in stages up to the final apotheosis."

I saw Nae on Friday. A completely nonpolitical discussion. He spoke about his last lecture at the faculty, which I missed but which seems to have been exceptional. A revolution in logic, a complete revision of the discipline. Something epochal. . . . The logic of collectives becomes to formal logic what Einstein's physics is to Newton! He went on talking for more than an hour, going over his whole lecture again with that smile of amusement and easily feigned nonchalance, which suits him so well.

It was a beautiful afternoon, and I was glad that at least toward the end he moved away from politics and Iron Guardism.

He is undoubtedly the most interesting and the most complex person I have ever known. In spite of everything that has happened in the past and will happen in the future, he is capable of opening my eyes about his moral values but not of disappointing me about his intelligence.

Leni left this morning. Now it is five in the afternoon—I think the ship left at two, so she is on the high seas.

I saw her on Saturday afternoon, for no more than three-quarters of an hour. But she tried to make up for the irritation of the last few days, and succeeded with a host of fond little gestures, hand-squeezing, and attentive looks. She made a point of using the familiar *tu*, obviously to let me know that our love is beyond all doubt.

Now that she is gone, my fever has suddenly abated—though not yet completely. I hope I can bear these two months of absence with sufficient calm. I also hope that I won't forget her but recover my previous peace of mind, when it was a pleasure to know her, to see and talk with her, without complications and without any difficulty in putting her out of my mind once I had put down the telephone or said goodbye. Anyway, I am a lot clearer about her, and I don't think I shall have to change much in my image of her as a likable, slightly frivolous blonde, more curious than sensual, who happily maintains her personal egoism and feeds on the adoration of quite different people, both men and women, asking them to please her without any sentimentality and giving them in return an uncomplicated smile. An adorable little monster, in relation to whom all my thoughts up to now have been absurdly out of proportion.

I think about her with pleasure, distracted by her memory and hoping that time will relieve me of its more painful edges.

Saturday, 20 July

Too hot for me to write. For sometime now I should have liked to note here at least a long conversation with Nae and then—in another order of things—a very complex dream of which I was quite aware during the night because I repeated it several times on waking up, but of which now, after a few days have passed, I can remember only a few vague remnants.

A desolate moon, with absolutely nothing there. Three days in Constanţa, which could have been restful, did me no good at all. I returned feeling ill, with a temperature of 41 degrees [106 F.]. I am still not back to normal. I have no wish for anything. Ashes and glue—that's all.

Unfortunately I am fully cured of love's passions and torments.

Sunday, 21 July

I shall try to write down a dream just now, as I wake from sleep. . . . I am reading an article by Crevedia[3]—in *Porunca Vremii*,[4] I think—which praises Dinu Brătianu[5] to the skies.

. . . I am at Dinu Brătianu's house. I am holding a jug of water or something like that (I don't think it was a jug of water). Feeling embarrassed, I put it down on the table. He gives me his hand and, when I tell him who I am, he says that he knows me and is extremely friendly.

. . . I am in an adjoining room where there are a lot of people—a meeting, perhaps. Dinu Brătianu says that he had his picture taken earlier in the day. I tell him I have seen a good photograph of him in the window of Julieta. He is surprised: it is years since he has had his picture taken. But I tell him that I did see it.

"That window," I say, "is a fragment of topicality—topicality that lasts a few hours or less, but is nevertheless alive. Whenever you do something that causes a stir—a speech or a letter to Mr. Tătărescu—your photo appears in the window."

What I say seems to have a lot of verve, because everyone laughs and I myself am happy with the effect I have. Meanwhile, however, the bow tie I am wearing has somehow climbed onto my chin and now my mouth, so that I am no longer able to speak. Feeling embarrassed, I apologize to Dinu Brătianu and go into an adjoining room, where a friend—a kind of chauffeur or secretary of mine—arranges my bow tie.

When I return, I find the room is silent. Everyone is listening to a report on student movements. The tone is very anti-Semitic. I feel awkward.

At that point a wedding party for which we seem to have been wait-

3. Nicolae Crevedia: especially anti-Semitic LANC journalist.
4. Rabidly anti-Semitic newspaper.
5. Leader of the Liberal party.

ing all this time returns from church. Puia Rebreanu enters wearing a lamé bridal dress. At that same moment Dinu Brătianu (who has stepped out of the dream) is no longer sitting on his chair; Liviu Rebreanu[6] is there instead. I make a sign that we should stand up, but Rebreanu makes a sign for the lecture to continue. Then the wedding guests rush in. Camil Petrescu[7] holds out his hand to embrace me, but I have two big sweets in my mouth and am unable to reciprocate. He embraces Ionel Jianu[8] and then Paul Moscovici. Meanwhile I have removed the sweets from my mouth and also embraced someone. I think it is Paul Moscovici.

The procession keeps moving, but now it seems to be a baptism rather than a wedding—or both at the same time. Auntie Caroline enters with a baby in her arms and passes alongside me. She is followed by Uncle Avram. Apparently Baba and Frida have died that very day. They have been to the cemetery with the baby and all the wedding guests. They want to name the child after the old ones. At the cemetery a lot of funny things happened with an old woman from the family whom no one recognized; she wept loudly for some distant relatives who died dozens of years ago.

That was roughly it. I think there were some more confused things toward the end. But I have lost quite a bit of the beginning of the dream. Further on, almost everything is there.

Friday, 30 August

Only a last-minute oversight before leaving (it will be four weeks tonight) made me forget this notebook at home. Had I had it with me in Ghilcoș, there would have been so many things to write. I probably would have recorded in it the stages of my detoxification—because a detoxification is what it has been. My natural aptitude for happiness is great indeed. I confirmed this in Ghilcoș, where, after the first days of lazing in the sun, I was cured of the whole business: my confused state following the unhappiness of July, the painful remnants of the affair with Leni (which, fortunately, I now think is well and truly over), and my apathy burdened with so much renunciation. I could observe a total return to health, both moral and physical. One indication of this is the ease with which I now fall asleep, without all those complex mental constructions that I used to enter night after night—before my departure for Ghilcoș—in order to find my way into slumber.

6. Novelist, director of the National Theatre under the Antonescu regime.
7. Novelist, friend of Sebastian's.
8. Ionel Jianu: Jewish art critic.

I was decidedly happy there. Everything seemed right—easy and harmonious. How lucky I was to be reading Charles Morgan's *Fontaine*, so appropriate to my own mood during this blessed August. If I had taken this notebook with me, I think I would have filled whole pages on such themes.

How welcome and diverting was the episode with Margo, and how well concluded. It is a pity that I could not record its various stages—from the time she arrived at the hotel in the provocative company of that Herr Direktor Hellmann from Oradea, to the evening after he had left when I went to bed with her. Everything was so nice that I feel obliged to answer her letter, even though the story is over and done with.

Let us draw a balance sheet. I have come back refreshed, or "re-created." I am proud of myself when I look in the mirror: so young, so visibly healthy (perhaps too visibly). This afternoon I shall go to the photographer's—so that that at least will remain, if nothing else can.

Pensiunea Wagner—a wonderful establishment!

Saturday, 31 August

Had a long conversation yesterday evening with Mircea,[9] Nina, Marietta,[1] and Haig.[2] I was very happy to see them again, and everything seemed in keeping with my optimistic frame of mind.

On the other hand, my walk in town this morning disheartened me. It is still very hot: summer is not yet over. People are pale from the heat, tired, prickly, reluctant to work. I went to pay Montaureanu for my journals[3] and felt depressed by everyone's long yellow faces. And when I went to see Ocneanu,[4] to tell him that I would soon be delivering the manuscript, I found him completely listless.

How long will I manage to keep my present optimism among such bored, indifferent, dead-tired people?

On Monday I go to the office; this evening to the journal.

9. Mircea Eliade: novelist, historian of religions, ardent supporter of the Iron Guard, friend of Sebastian's.
1. Marietta Sadova: actress, fanatical supporter of the Iron Guard, wife of Haig Acterian.
2. Haig Acterian: theatre producer, active Iron Guard member, husband of Marietta Sadova.
3. Virgil Montaureanu: publisher.
4. Victor Ocneanu: publisher.

Saturday, 7 September

Lunch at Capșa with Comarnescu and Soreanu,[5] who suggested that I do a weekly French bulletin for *Excelsior*.[6] Maybe I'll accept, but it would be a little sad to find myself on Soreanu's payroll! Another opportunity to reflect, with resignation and no ill will, on my ineptitude in practical matters and the happy adroitness of others. I shall never get beyond a more or less bearable level of poverty: I shall never have a career, never have money. . . . And, speaking quite frankly, without any reason to deceive myself, I think that I am indifferent to money. All I want from life is a little peace and quiet, a woman, some books, and a clean house.

Comarnescu told me something which, if I were feeling less skeptical at the moment, would strike me as quite monstrous. He has made peace overtures to *Credinţa!*[7] He has had lunch with Stancu! I should say that he is unspeakable. But I shall content myself with observing once more how naive I am. I fell out with the *Credinţa* people over that business; I refused to shake hands with Sandu Tudor. —All that to end up now with such a capitulation. When will I stop getting carried away in my relations with other people? To be disinterested and neutral, never indignant or approbatory: that is the best of attitudes. I am old enough to have learned that at least.

Yesterday evening at the Continental, Sandu Tudor was at a table with Devechi and Onicescu.[8] Two years ago he asked me to put in a word so that Nae Ionescu would bring him onto the journal. Nae laughed, but I think Devechi would have found something like that really bizarre. A cretinous journalist—that is how S.T. would have seemed to him.

But what counts is not whether people are stupid or clever, good or bad, honest or crooked. The only real factor is power—and that can be obtained through money, blackmail, social position, or whatever. Then every other criterion ceases to apply. But it was a pleasure for me to go over to their table and speak to Devechi and Onicescu without noticing Sandu Tudor. I too have my little acts of revenge; others obviously don't care much for them, but they give me satisfaction.

5. Petru Comarnescu: art critic, friend of Sebastian's. Henri Soreanu: journalist.
6. *Excelsior:* economics weekly, published in Romanian and French.
7. Comarnescu had been attacked by *Credinţa*.
8. Titu Devechi: journalist and close friend of Sebastian's. Octav Onicescu: mathematician, friend of Nae Ionescu.

I must admit that, if I went into the Continental yesterday for no particular reason, it was only in the hope (perhaps not openly avowed) that
I would meet Leni there.

And I did meet her. . . . She was there with her sister Olga, Froda,
and Solacolu.[9] She is beautiful. I was pleased to see her, and she seemed
glad too—but I am well aware that her suddenly flashing smile is only
a tic, not an expression, and that it would have been just as nice, just as
enveloping, for anyone else who had approached her table.

Otherwise nothing has changed. She has the same things to do in
town that she had in the summer—the same troubles with her dress-
maker and hairdresser, the same shopping, the same haste and indifference, the same air of frivolity, the same visible lack of sensitivity.

Nothing has changed, but now it will certainly be much easier for
me to break things off. I think I have succeeded in eliminating all the
painful aspects of this love, though some of its roots have remained.
Watch out, kid!

I saw Lilly one evening: we went to a cinema and then to the Corso
(where absolutely all the stares directed at us had a kind of shocked and
aggressive surprise). I was glad to see her again, and I fondly imagine
that one day I will attain the same point of calm and dispassionate sympathy with Leni. I think Leni is less interesting outside a context of love.
But in terms of love, let her make herself at home!

[Wednesday,] 18 September

I have seen a lot of people this week, but I was too lazy to write a page
in my journal for each. Too tiring. I write here only when it gives me
pleasure—though I know that the real pleasure is in rereading, and that
I should therefore be a more diligent "journalist."

The evening before last, I had something more than a surprise with
the painter Siegfried.[1] I felt bored at the thought of our meeting, having stupidly arranged it in a careless moment because I wanted to be
friendly.

When we met, he was with "Jojo" Orleanu—and at first I tried to
keep him with us. "An evening with two homosexuals," I said to myself.
"It'll be entertaining; I'll be able to observe all kinds of gestures and
play-acting."

9. Th. Solacolu: translator and poet.
1. W. Siegfried: stage designer.

How hastily I judge things! Orleanu left soon afterward and Siegfried proved to be an excellent conversation partner, an intelligent, sensitive, and modest young man. He talked about Paris, and he had an exact manner of speech filled with details that evoked the city much better than nostalgic outpourings usually do.

He spoke about his painting and his studies with André Lhote, explained the technique of etching—all very modest and simple, but clear and precise, with a host of accurate observations. He was quite simply instructive.

I do not know how exceptional a person he is. But everything he said to me was tasteful and measured. He is working on the scenery for a play by Géraldy at the Bulandra, and he spoke finely about his future projects. A pleasant evening.

Yesterday evening I repeated the experience with another stranger, a student of Nae's called Mircea Niculescu. Not so interesting, of course, but undoubtedly clever—and, most important of all, a new face, someone from outside my usual circle, another world, other stories, other books.

We spoke "politics"—which was not terribly exciting—but he said useful and heartening things about the chances that Hitlerism might collapse. He is a radical, and that is such a rare species among Romanians.

Finally a day with women.

First a visit to Dorina Blank,[2] who had suddenly and insistently invited me round on such a childish pretext (she wanted me to read and explain a novel she did not understand) that it was obvious she was after something else. She has taken a fancy to me, and she does not try at all to disguise this incipient *béguin*. Marietta Rareş[3] was also there, and Ţoţa Soiu[4] later turned up unexpectedly, but she did not feel inhibited in front of them. "Oh, Dorina, I don't understand you at all," said Marietta, a little embarrassed.

Naturally I shall see her again. (An amusing detail: she, Dorina, was the one who, on the eve of my departure for Ghilcoş this summer, never stopped pestering me on the telephone. For a whim, it has lasted rather a long time. Another, equally amusing, detail. Dorina insisted that Carol Grünberg[5] invite both me and her round to a lunch. The lunch was last Sunday, but Carol did not invite me, even though we had been together on Saturday evening at the premiere at the National. Jealous?)

2. Daughter of Aristide Blank.
3. Actress.
4. Actress, wife of the actor Ion Iancovescu.
5. Friend of Sebastian's.

Finally, on leaving Dorina's, a visit to Leni. The first since our parting in June.

I am content with myself. Apart from a few little gestures of irritation, I did not make a wrong step. She complained that she didn't recognize me, that I had grown cold, etc. (without pressing the point, however, because she is basically indifferent), and I objected with as much good faith as I could affect. Anyway, it was enough for her.

She is still the same. She would like me to love her—not me in particular, but tens of thousands of men, including me. She spent nearly twenty minutes on the phone with a guy who had called to speak with her sister, Olga, but who meanwhile enjoyed "teasing" her a little.

Then she apologized to me, but I tersely said there was no need.

"Don't apologize, Leni dear. I'm happy that you thought me a good enough friend to do something you would certainly never have done with a stranger."

She took the point, but I should not be so naive as to think that she regretted anything. Her capacity to forget is formidable.

No real catastrophe, then. It is still possible to end everything, without suffering. I still have moments of stupid melancholy, when I find any number of excuses for her and make all kinds of plans. I really must stop doing this.

It would be wise not to call her for a fortnight or so. At the moment that doesn't seem too difficult. What if I were to try it out? But I don't know how to make that kind of pledge, nor do I have the courage to do so.

I end the day now, at ten o'clock, by listening to a musical broadcast from Munich. A Bach fantasia and a Schumann symphony. This is a fine epilogue to a few trifles of which, if I were serious, I should perhaps feel a little ashamed.

Saturday, 26 October

The radio is tuned to Juan-les-Pins, which is coming over loud and clear this evening. I have listened to a fragment from Ravel's *Ma mère l'Oye* and to Debussy's *Ménestrels*. Now there are some romances.

If I were to record here everything I have listened to recently, it would come to a very long list. At first I thought it a wild idea of Gheorghe's[6] that I should write music reviews for *L'Indépendence Roumaine*. I

---

6. Gheorghe Nenişor was in charge of arts criticism for *L'Indépendence Roumaine*, a French-language daily.

accepted for the money, with strict guarantees of anonymity. But I am used to it now, after my third contribution, and my weekly concert evening gives me great pleasure.

I have heard a lot of beautiful pieces: a wonderful piano concerto (the third) by Prokofiev, *Rhapsodie Espagnole* by Ravel, a suite for string orchestra by Corelli-Pineli, Beethoven's *Third Symphony* (conducted by Molinari), Tchaikovsky's *Violin Concerto*, Jacques Ibert's *Escales*, Respighi's *Fountains and Pines of Rome*.

I don't know why it is so long since I have written here. Disgust at dwelling so much on myself. . . . But this evening I am pleased that I stayed home and read a book (*Esquisse d'un traité du roman*, by Léon Bopp); I shall correct the proofs of *Orașul cu salcîmi*.[7] I have allowed myself too many wasted nights recently.

Tonight, after the opening of the opera season, we went to Zissu. Maryse was wearing a delightful white dress (like a film actress), Gheorghe in evening dress, Marietta Sadova too, and myself in a tuxedo. Few people, excellent atmosphere, whisky, cocktails, cigarettes. We danced a lot. Maryse was movingly delicate and sensitive, saying many things that disarmed me with their sincerity and forthrightness. "You don't know how much I love you." And I am stupid enough to be flattered by that.

Yesterday morning, at Alcalay,[8] a guy suddenly came up to me with outstretched hand, smiling heartily and eager to talk.

"Are you angry with me?"

"Angry?" I held out my hand without knowing who he was. Ocneanu then introduced us.

"Mr. Niculae Roșu."[9]

I was taken aback by the thoughtlessness of it all. "I don't bear grudges," he said to me several times.

I greatly enjoyed using a formal style of address with him all the time.

"You see, my dear sir, I am not angry. But one thing I must say: your bad faith is monumental."

He grew pale and spluttered something. Ocneanu wrung his hands and tried to make peace between us—but I kept calm, continuing to speak with exaggerated politeness. It was the only way I could hide my repulsion.

The man was a walking platitude. He spoke to me about the Jews—about how they are intelligent and cultured, how they are this, that, and

7. *The Town with Acacias*, a novel by Sebastian published in 1935.
8. A publishing house in Bucharest.
9. Iron Guard journalist and ideologist.

the other. He holds Jews in high regard. He holds me in high regard. He reads what I write, always has. My culture, my style, my talent, etc., etc.

I let him talk, feeling a wonderful satisfaction as he sank beneath the weight of all those platitudes, retractions, and courtesies. It all became clear to me in the end. The poor man is publishing a book and—as he put it without mincing his words—he would not like it to be reviewed in the manner of Pandrea.[1]

"I'll send you the book," he said as we parted.

What a man! I don't remember ever meeting such an abject character. But let's calm down! I can see I'm becoming pathetic.

I have given up following the stages of my love affair (?) with Leni. So many contradictions, so many resumptions, so many blunders, so many discarded projects. I saw her yesterday—and I was quite simply happy at the fact. But it will pass, it will pass.

Monday, 28 October

1:00 a.m.

A Piatigorsky concerto. Frescobaldi, *Toccata*. Boccherini, *Sonata in A Major*. Bach, *Suite in C Major* (unaccompanied cello; I think I heard it once from Leipzig last winter). Weber-Piatigorsky, *Sonatina in A*. Schubert, *Arpeggione sonata*. Scriabin, *Poems*. Glazunov, *Spanish Serenade*. Ravel, *Habanera*. De Falla, *Dance of Terror*.

Thursday, 31 October

Bach: *Passacaglia in C Minor.*
  Mozart: *Piano Concerto in C Major.* Soloist Wilhelm Kempff.
  Brahms, *Symphony No. 1.*

Yesterday evening from Vienna, Beethoven's fourth and fifth symphonies. Weingartner.

The evening before last, from Juan-les-Pins, fragments from Ravel's *Ma mère l'oye* and Haydn's *Farewell Symphony*.

A long lunch today at the Institut Français.

---

1. Petre Pandrea: left-wing journalist.

Sunday, 3 November

Kempff and the Philharmonic on Sunday at the Ateneu—three Beethoven piano concertos, in C minor (op. 37), in G (op. 58), and in E-flat (op. 73).

Some moments of overwhelming emotion, greater than any I have ever had before in music. And a kind of nervous tension, a kind of continual vibration, had me in its grip all day.

It was nice to have Lilly[2] beside me. Farther away, in a box, Jeni.

Monday, 4 [November]

A wonderful evening on the radio. From Zurich a concertino for cello and harpsichord. A sonata by a classical composer whose name I do not fully recall (Andrea something?), the Handel-Goldschlager *Variations* (for unaccompanied harpsichord), *Adagio* by Tartini, *Rondo* by Boccherini.

From Warsaw a trio for piano, oboe, bassoon by Poulenc, remarkable for its humor and inventiveness (*presto, andante, rondo*).

Later, also from Warsaw, a sonata for orchestra by Corelli, Beethoven's *Piano Concerto in C Major* (very Mozartian—which still leaves one before I know all five), and lastly, Prokofiev's *Classical Symphony*.

An amusing visit to Dorina Blank, who offered herself with no talking in circles. A moving letter from Șuluțiu.[3] I'd never have guessed he was such a persistent "admirer."

Friday, 8 [November]

Yesterday evening at the Philharmonic. Mozart: *Symphony in E-flat* (horribly played), Haydn: *Cello Concerto in D Major* (Cassado), Tchaikovsky: *Variations on a Rococco Theme for Cello and Orchestra*, Stravinsky: *The Firebird*.

Evening
What could I still hold against Leni after our talk today? She was nice, kind, and affectionate, without being falsely smart in any way. Little coquetry, a few impulsive outbursts, and above all no hypocrisy of any kind. She will come to my place if I ask her. She could scarcely say that it is hard to receive me at her place because of Froda, but she hinted at it pretty clearly. (Anyway, there was no need, because he phoned while I

2. Lilly Popovici: actress and friend of Sebastian's.
3. Octav Șuluțiu: writer.

was there and the maid sort of stammered on the phone that "the lady is reading"—a lie that embarrassed Leni.)

We walked in the street for half an hour or so, and I said a lot of foolish things. She, on the other hand, said something wonderful, which I shall try to recall. "It's true I'm capricious, flirtatious, and frivolous. But I have never done anything merely out of coquetry, caprice, or frivolity." I regret that I can't remember her exact words. She found a much more suitable expression.

So here I am at a peak of "happiness." Satisfied?

Friday, 15 [November]

I have just returned from Galați, where I spoke yesterday evening at the Liberty circle.

I don't think it is immodest that I enjoy being able to hold the attention of a hall full of people for an hour—while speaking of things that are alien or indifferent to them. During the lecture I had great fun with a host of things that I came up with as I was carried along by the rhythm of speaking.

Wednesday, 27 [November]

How many things I should have noted down! But I don't think I have ever been quite so swallowed up in things (things I don't even carry through to the end: instead I bustle about making them more complicated and putting them off . . .).

I should say a word or two, and even more, about Nae's inaugural lecture. This year he is giving a course on "political logic." His introduction was a little testament of the Iron Guard faith. He flattered the students with an electioneer's persistence, praising "the political generations" as being in the right against "the bookish generations," whose great sin, in his eyes, is that they are bookish. Politics means action, life, reality, contact with existence. Books are abstract. So you are right to do what you are doing; the truth is with you, rah, rah, rah!

At the end (Ghiţa[4] was there, overwhelming in his silence, as well as Mircea and Vasile Băncilă[5]) I reminded him of his article from May 1928, "What Young People Think," in which he asserted in discussion with

---

4. Gheorghe Racoveanu, Iron Guard journalist.
5. Iron Guard follower of Nae Ionescu.

Petrovici[6] that the orientation of the younger generation should be sought not in the street—where the agitators and window-breakers are—but in libraries and the representative values they contain.

"Yes, that's how it was then," he replied imperturbably. "Now it's completely different. Then it was the hour of the intellect—now it is the hour of politics."

Poor Nae! How rapid is his descent. . . .

To stay with politics, I should also record the short sharp discussion I had with Mircea after the theatre on Monday evening, at the Continental. It was not the first. And I have noticed that he is sliding ever more clearly to the right. When we are alone together we understand each other reasonably well. In public, however, his right-wing position becomes extreme and categorical. He said one simply shocking thing to me, with a kind of direct aggressiveness: "All great creators are on the right." Just like that.

But I shan't allow such discussions to cast the slightest shadow over my affection for him. In the future I shall try to avoid "political arguments" with him.

I should also note the trial of *Credința*, at which my pleading went down well.[7] I could sense this not only from the court's attention, but also from the congratulations of the people sitting on my bench and the irritation of those on the opponents'. I sensed it from the silence and from the nervous flow that suddenly raised the proceedings above the previous level of jokes and skirmishes.

Of course, everyone who spoke in defence of *Credința* was at pains to inform the court that I was a yid. Medrea[8] promised to beat me up. I told Maryse,[9] only half joking, that I am waiting for the day when Vulcănescu, Gabriel, Titel, and Tell[1] make their peace with Sandu Tudor, Stancu, and Medrea, and discover that the Jews are alone responsible for the quarrel—especially myself, who has aroused discord among the Christian fraternity. It sounds like a joke, but it's plausible enough.

---

6. Ion Petrovici: philosopher, minister of education in the Goga-Curza government December 1937–February 1938, minister of culture in the Antonescu government December 1941–August 1944.

7. A trial for slander involving members of the former Criterion association.

8. Corneliu Medrea: sculptor.

9. Maryse Nenișor: wife of Gheorghe Nenișor.

1. The philosopher Mircea Vulcănescu, the ballet dancer Gabriel Negri, Petru (Titei) Comarnescu, and Al. Cristian Tell, an Iron Guard journalist, had all been involved in the conflict with the editors of *Credința*.

Otherwise nothing. I become more dull-witted every day and seem no longer to expect any salvation.

Tuesday, 17 December

2:30 a.m.

I am dead tired. Tomorrow morning I have to be writing at my desk by eight at the latest, but I must record here and now the startling admission that Maryse made to me. I shall try to write it down exactly as she said it.

"You don't know how much I've suffered because of you. I wanted to sleep with you, come what may. You obsessed me. One week was complete torture—even physically, you know. Do you remember when I came to collect you from the *Rampa*[2] and we left together in the car? That day I was determined to speak openly with you, because I saw that otherwise you didn't or wouldn't understand. I had made up my mind to take charge of all the most awkward details: to find a room for us to meet, to take you there, to make all the preparations. . . . But it was the day you had a toothache! If you hadn't been in pain, I would certainly have been yours. I wouldn't have hesitated to tell you—and you wouldn't have been able to refuse. No man ever refuses.

"In the early days—after the first evening we were at Zissu, do you remember?—I decided to go to your place one day, to undress, lie down, and wait for you. You'd have found me there and had no choice. But meanwhile you gave me a copy of *Femei*, and I saw that even then I'd only have been repeating an episode from the past. I felt disgusted with myself and called it off, especially as you'd have thought I was copying your heroine.

"Then at the Corso, when we had lunch together, I had come to say everything and to ask everything of you, but you asked me to let you continue writing an article of yours. I never had any reservations, but you refused to understand. . . .

"I'm telling you this now because I think it has passed. It's no longer topical. I wanted it too much then for it to give me any pleasure now. I tell you, I was crazy. With Gheorghe, and with Gheorghe's mother, I spoke of nothing but you. How much I could suffer!

"What? Do you think I wouldn't have been unfaithful to Gheorghe? Do you think I'm not unfaithful to him? Well, I am, with one man or another—not very often, but when I fancy someone, what am I supposed

2. Theatre magazine.

to do? I think I'd be stupid to refuse that. I love him, but I don't think that has anything to do with it. Just once, in Constanţa, when I spent three days alone with a guy who was after me and whom I fancied a lot myself, I did resist—I don't know whether it was from stubbornness or stupidity. Anyway, I haven't gotten over it even today."

[Monday,] 30 December

Sceaux

I am in Paris and still do not quite realize it. I think I shall only recover my reason in ten days' time, after I have left.

There seems indeed to be something unreal in this return that cancels five years of my life, as if they had never existed. On Saturday evening I had dinner at Fanny Bonnard's in Yerres. I found her the same as ever, and it seemed completely absurd to think that there are five years between us. A curious feeling of old age.

One morning I went for a walk in the area around rue de la Clef. Nothing at all has changed—not even myself, for I am not bringing back after these five years anything more than I already knew and experienced in 1930 as a young man of twenty-two to twenty-three. I walked up rue Soufflot, saw again the Sainte Geneviève Library, continued along rue Clovis, rue Mouffetard, rue Monge, rue de la Clef, and rue Lacépède, and went into the Jardin des Plantes where I lingered for a while beneath the great cedar. I am honestly unable to convince myself that the time has gone by.

But I don't intend to write in this notebook, which I have brought along for no purpose.

Maybe I shall sum it all up in Bucharest.

And now, having failed to do it at the right time, I no longer feel like summarizing here the recent stages of my love affair with Leni. We love each other—we said as much and parted in complete harmony, with an embrace. I wonder what will become of me in Bucharest. I have a talent for making my unhappy life as complicated as possible.

1936

Bucharest. Thursday, 6 February 1936

As I left Leni's yesterday evening, I felt that if I committed suicide that very night I would do it contentedly, almost with good humor.

I shall never be able to explain to her how much she means, or could mean, to me. Nor am I myself sure whether I love her with a *grand amour* or with the last of my vital resistance.

Thursday, 20 February

Why does it trouble me to think that she is leaving Bucharest tomorrow? Or why does it make me so happy to have sent her two lilac branches without any message?

She may not even realize who sent them; she may not even look at them—and that would be all the better.

Sunday, 1 March

A wonderful day and an overwhelmingly beautiful evening. A blue sky "rustling profusely" with stars, as I said to Emil Gulian last summer on a night such as this.

But it was not like this. . . . I feel that spring has broken out. I can feel it in many things, but above all in my pressing need to be happy.

And I have to do an article for *Fundații*,[1] just now when all I really want is to love a woman, whoever it may be—Leni, Maryse, Jeni, or none of them, a stranger, no matter who.

I came home alone and—why, I don't know—our Doggy disturbed me for the first time. There was something human in the way he jumped at me, in his lively yet melancholic outburst. Without being literary—I

---

1. The journal of the Royal Foundations.

would even feel ashamed to be asked about this—I felt that he wants to talk to me and suffers for not being able to.

Maybe I'll go to Breaza for a few days.

Monday, 2 [March]

I do not want to write about any of the details of my quarrel with *Vremea*. Some are comical, others upsetting.

I am told that Mircea was "disgusted" when he read my *Rampa* article in the presence of Donescu. He could find no excuse for me and agreed on every point with my "opponent."

I don't want to believe it, nor do I want to ask any more questions. But if even that is possible! . . .

Thursday, 5 [March]

I visited Devechi, whom I had not seen since Christmas.

We left together, and since his car was being repaired I persuaded him to get on a No. 31 bus with me.

Inside the bus, which had too many people on board, he looked dejected and ill at ease. . . . I felt the need to apologize.

"After all," I said, "for you it's an experience of a lifetime to get on a bus."

Yesterday there was a letter from Leni. Loving, cheerful, without any psychological complications. A lovely girl!

Evening at the Nenişors, with Maryse staging a hysterical scene. Crying, laughing and, when I left, forbidding me to say good night. This spring is making all of us a little dizzy.

Tuesday, at the Dalles Hall, Nae's lecture on Calvin. Fine, sober, without any posturing—and with only a few highly vague political allusions. A Nae from the good old times.

Saturday, 14 [March]

Lunch at the Corso with Camil, who had rung for us to revise his *Teze şi antiteze* [Theses and Antitheses] together. Before publishing it, he has a host of doubts and misgivings.

An amusing introduction, in which he declared his admiration for me.

In Romanian literature, he said, there are only three books whose sentiments add up to something profound: *De două mii de ani, Patul lui Procust,* and *Ultima noapte.*[2]

I resolutely freed myself from the eulogy.

"No, Camil, let's drop that. We can talk about *Patul lui Procust,* but leave my books out of it."

That shallow and unchanging tactic of ever-ready admiration I cannot but find somewhat endearing.

But I remain firm in my old affection for him. His little "quirks" always amuse me, never make me indignant. And he is certainly a remarkable fellow. I have been rereading some of his articles from 1922 and 1924. Their precision, tone, and style simply take your breath away.

I didn't go to Nae's class yesterday. It has started to bore me. The last few lectures have been repeats of last year's, rather irritating because of their facile politics.

Last Sunday at the Nenișors, Tudor Vianu took Nae apart for a quarter of hour with extreme violence (though not of vocabulary). In his view, Nae is not at all original: he is a representative of Spengler and some other present-day Germans, and uses them at opportune moments without indicating his sources.

Maybe. I don't know. But there is something demonic in Nae—and I can't believe that that man can be reduced to nothing by academic criticism.

I am vegetating, just vegetating.

Thursday, 19 [March]

Yesterday evening I dined at Lilly's with the whole of our group. Camil, in conversation with Mircea and myself, said in one of those displays of courageous sincerity which suit him so well—as if he had to do violence to his modesty by making it bow to the facts:

"After all, old chap, let's admit that there are only three novelists: yourself, Mircea, and I."

Ineffable Camil. If someone else had been there with us—who shall we say, Sergiu Dan?—he would surely have said that "after all, old chap, there are only four novelists."

---

2. The last two are novels by Camil Petrescu: *Patul lui Procust* (The Procustean Bed) and *Ultima noapte de dragoste, prima noapte de război* (Last Night of Love, First Night of War).

I saw Leni at the theatre, where she had a matinee.

"I've decided not to flirt with you any more," she said.

I objected. She doesn't understand anything and—quite rightly—expects this overlong game to come to an end. But for me there can be only one ending.

Pascal Alexandru's suicide has been haunting me ever since I heard of it. I remember that they used to call him "girlie" at school. It is true that his whole being had something feminine, pallid, delicate. I think that all the way through school—and that means especially in the upper grades—I didn't exchange so much as three words with him. He was anti-Semitic, like all of them. But then I had a kind of sympathy for the tenderness that I felt to be within him, and for the melancholy that made him end up beneath the wheels of a train.

Marioara Ventura, whom I met last week at a lunch at the French Institute, said to me:

"I've been reading you and found you interesting. But I didn't know you were twenty-five years old."

"Twenty-six, madam," I corrected her.

Unfortunately, despite an appearance that is still sometimes youthful, I am growing older all the time.

Friday, 20 [March]

I went to the theatre, because Leni—who had not seen her company's new production—rang and asked me to go with her.

She arrived five minutes after the curtain, and during each interval slipped away to make a phone call.

I would be a complete blockhead if I imagined she does not have a thousand lovers. But I have no doubt that, had I helped her to love me, she would have loved me in her way. I must admit that, given how confusing and cryptic is the game I have been playing, she has always shown an astonishing tact and assurance. I have only to recall how deplorably Lilly behaved in similar situations.

I should not be angry about this evening. It justifies me in lying low for ten days—which is a perfect step toward breaking up—though after the performance we went out to a tavern with Jenica Cruțescu, where Leni told us a lot of distressing things about her setup with Froda. I have the feeling she would gladly be out of it—and I shudder to think how happy something like that would make me.

But there is no point, and I should get used to drawing a line under my life's calculations.

I shall try to write the play about which I have been thinking for some time.[3] I saw the first act (even lines of dialogue) with amazing precision while I was at this evening's performance at the Regina Maria. With my memories of the Wagner villa plus some themes taken over from *Renée, Marthe, Odette*,[4] I could develop something really quite refined. I shall give it a try—and if I weren't tired, if I didn't have so many things to do tomorrow, I think I'd start on the first act right now, even though it is past one in the morning.

Nae's class yesterday was hard to take. Leftovers from last year's course, leftovers of articles, leftovers of chitchat—plus a few crude jokes to arouse the sympathy of an audience that was becoming inattentive. How is it possible?

Half an hour later
I didn't go to sleep after that. I wanted to put on paper a few thoughts I have had about the play, so that I don't forget them. In fact, I woke up writing the scenario for the whole play. I am quite simply delighted with it. The idea seems excellent to me, and whereas half an hour ago I could see only the first act, now I have all three in outline. Perhaps it is a passing exultation, but right now I feel I have come up with something really first class. Let's hope it works out.

Saturday, 21 [March]

It was hard getting to sleep last night. I was in a state of excitement such as I have not known for a long time. (Maybe the last time was in Paris in September 1930, when I was writing the "*Buţă*" chapter[5] that evening in the hotel on the Rue de Rennes. Or maybe that Sunday morning in Brăila in the spring of 1934, when I was writing the Dronţu-Marjorie episode.[6]

Last night I saw the premiere, the theatre, the performance—I was giving out the tickets. (A box for Roman,[7] a box for Nae. I was won-

---

3. Eventually *Jocul de-a vacanţa* (The Game of Holidaymaking).
4. Chapter of Sebastian's novel *Femei* [Women].
5. Chapter of Sebastian's novel *The Town with Acacias*.
6. Characters from Sebastian's novel *For Two Thousand Years*.
7. Saşa (Sacha) Roman: lawyer, in whose office Sebastian worked as a clerk.

dering whether to give Jeni tickets for the premiere, and how, what kind of tickets, etc., etc. Good Lord, how childish I can be!)

If I had had a phone, I might have called Leni there and then—though it was three in the morning—to tell her about it and ask her advice.

This morning I woke up in a more reasonable frame of mind. I do think the outline for the play is good. Today I found a mass of fresh details for Act Two. The main thing now is to work out the scenario in as much detail as possible. Then we shall see. But I have confidence in myself—which doesn't happen too often.

I can see Iancovescu being very good in the man's role. Leni ought to act the woman. In fact she is Leni, everything I expected of her, everything she could be, everything she in a sense is.

If worse comes to worst, and only if she turns it down, the only one to whom I could give the part would be Marietta.[8] She would give it less intensity but perhaps more poetry and an edge of melancholy.

Again, let's hope it works out. I'd be happy if I could draw out all the reserves of emotion, poetry, and grace concealed in my theme.

Monday, 23 [March]

I am not feeling deflated, but the initial fever has passed. On Saturday, and even yesterday, I felt it was something I could finish in a couple of weeks. I think I was mistaken. I may need as much as a few months. I'd be happy to have it ready by September so that I can have it performed then.

I have started writing. Yesterday I sketched out the stage setting, and today I even composed the first scene. I am happy with it. True, it is rather short. I shall probably find it difficult to group several characters and to make them move together on stage at the same time.

I don't know what will come of it, but I have to give it a try. It interests me especially from the point of view of literary technique. I realize that I have come up with a theatrical subject, which would not lend itself to a novel, short story, or anything else. Before now I didn't know what it meant to see a story theatrically. The process of gestation is completely different from that of a novel.

The lure of life behind the scenes, of the auditorium, the publicity posters—all this I find dizzying. There's a bit of the play-actor in me.

8. Marietta Sadova.

And then there is the emotion of writing for Leni! The idea that she will live things thought up by me, speak words written by me! How many times I shall have my revenge on her!

Sunday, 29 [March]

On Friday evening I heard the *St. John Passion* at the Ateneu,[9] and this morning the *Matthew Passion*. I found in it a lot that had remained in my memory since last year, but I also discovered many new things. I felt overwhelmed. I really had the physical sense of being beneath a canopy of sounds. It was a feeling of monumentality, which for perhaps the first time made the term "sonorous architecture" seem more than an empty expression. And how many sweet passages, how many graceful moments!

At the exit, Nae—who had also been to both concerts (what a pensive lion's head he had during the performance!)—called out to me from his new car, a million-lei[1] Mercedes-Benz, and invited me to eat at his place. I had lunch with him and his son, Răzvan, and we went on talking for a couple of hours.

I don't feel like it now, but I ought to write down everything he said in answer to my questions about his course. His logical armor has a thousand chinks. And it is too easy to shrug your shoulders when the questioning becomes more focused and requires you to say yes or no.

"You don't understand," he told me. "My theory of collectives is an escape from solitude, a tragic attempt to break out of loneliness."

Yes, I do understand. But then let him stop speaking of the absolute rights of the collective and insist on the absolute importance of the individual.

I also wonder whether this sense of tragedy is not a little suspect, since it comes down to various theories in justification of the metaphysical value of the term "Captain" and its superiority to the terms "Duce" or "Führer."

Doesn't Nae Ionescu have a sense of humor? How can he take jokes like that seriously?

Saturday, 11 April

Yesterday evening, nearly six hours of music. I started at a quarter to nine with the *St. John Passion* from Budapest—but it was hard listening

---

9. The main concert hall in Bucharest.

1. For comparison, at the time five thousand lei was the monthly income of a middle-class businessman; a luxurious three-bedroom apartment rented for eight thousand lei per year.

to it, because my radio suddenly went crazy. Then I continued at 11:30 with Radio Stuttgart, listening to a Handel overture (the *Theodora*), a Locatelli symphony, Bach's *First Brandenburg Concerto* and his *Double Violin Concerto in D Minor*, a Hebbel song with music by Schumann for choir and orchestra (very beautiful!), and the first part of Schubert's *Third Symphony*. Next, at one o'clock also from Stuttgart, and continuing until 2:30, the *St. Matthew Passion*. I didn't hear it through to the end because I switched it off after "*Barabam!*" Ever greater joy listening to it, with ever more nuances.

Today I am off to Sinaia with Carol[2] and Camil—hoping to stop at Breaza on the way back and remain there until Low Sunday. I should like to be able to work. If I returned with Act One at least! See how modest I am?

Sinaia, [Sunday], 12 [April]

I have been here since yesterday evening. The car journey was nice. Patches of mauve, green, and grey. Restful.

Everything snobbish in me—a liking for comfort and a little posturing—was flattered by the hotel's almost sumptuous decor. But depressing society: whores (Lulu Nicolau, Eugenia Zaharia), journalists (Horia, Ring), gigolos (Polizu), old hags, club gamblers. Yesterday I lost two hundred lei at roulette as soon as I entered the casino. I promise to give it a wide berth—out of disgust more than prudence.

Will I be able to write? I don't know. Maybe at Breaza, where I shall stop from tomorrow evening onward.

Yesterday in Bucharest I saw something that shook me, because I should never have been able to imagine all its thorny complexities. I had stopped with Camil on the Şosea, where work was under way for the Month of Bucharest festivities. Some trees were being transplanted there, and at that very moment they were trying to plant a pine that had been brought from somewhere or other. Two things struck me. The first was the huge piece of earth that had been torn up together with the tree. Not torn up, strictly speaking. A cylinder had been dug around it, a kind of bowl measuring, say, two cubic meters, which encircled it like a barrel. This bowl had to fit into a dug-out area of the same size as itself. But what surprised me even more were the people exerting themselves to hoist the tree. I counted more than fifty of them. What a will to live—indiffer-

2. Carol Grünberg.

ent, powerful, wordless, motionless—there was in that tree, which appeared huge among the people bustling around it.

Tuesday, 14 April

I'd have been happy with my birthday yesterday if it hadn't ended so badly at the casino. I had to stay there until 2:30 in the morning because Carol was losing too much and I couldn't leave him.

Otherwise a nice day. I managed to regain my vision of the play (I mean, I could see it again) and to get myself back into the action. I also started to write the last scene of the first act—Valeriu and Leni. I fear that I've lost touch with it again. I'll try to write it in Breaza; I leave for there at one o'clock.

Later (walking in the park at eight on a splendid evening, beneath a translucent blue sky and stars with a youthful twinkle), I saw quite clearly the shape of a long piece on Jules Renard to be written after I finish his *Journal*. The chapter titles: Jules Renard "anecdotier," J.R. average Frenchman, J.R. *en famille* with parents, children, wife, J.R. the radical, etc.

In another connection, I have decided—once and for all, I think—on the material for the first volume of "The Romanian Novel." There will be six chapters: Rebreanu, Sadoveanu, H. P. Bengescu, Camil, Cezar Petrescu, Ionel Teodoreanu. I have some doubts about Aderca: I think I'll keep him for the second volume, but I won't make a final decision until I reread him. I can see quite well the preface to the first volume, where I shall explain the plan of the whole series and justify the absence of prewar literature. I want to write the book over the summer so that it comes out by Christmas.

But my present concern is still with the play. There is no doubt that I shall write it. The experiment has to be made. More than that, I don't know—either how it will turn out, or what its fate will be.

A conversation this morning in the park between two children aged ten to eleven, in the first classes of secondary school. One in the uniform of the military school, the other with socks, short trousers, jacket, and tie, dressed in the French style as if, with his fair hair and complexion, he was a little boy in the Jardin Luxembourg.

The Soldier: Do you wear the swastika at school?

The Other: What's that?

S: That sign, you know . . .

O: No, I don't.

S: We wear it.

They moved off and then, after a few minutes, returned. The conversation continued. I heard the fair-haired boy explaining to the soldier:

"Religion is separate from the state. The state and religion have nothing in common—it's been like that for a few hundred years. You know, they don't even teach religion in school."

His exact words. Otherwise it would not even interest me to note it here. A society of policemen, like Romanian society, cannot create anything other than whole generations of policemen—that is, people with the mind of a policeman, when they cannot actually be one by trade. I'd like to know what family that fair-haired boy comes from, who doesn't know what a swastika is. I'd like to meet that boy's father and shake his hand.

It reminds me of what Corneliu Moldovanu said a couple of weeks ago when, after some premiere or other, some Gypsy kids were waiting outside with a special edition about the sentence passed on Constantinescu-Iaşi.[3]

"They were right to do it. But it's too little."

And he is a writer!

A lot to record from the hotel, especially concerning Eugenia Zaharia, a whore of quite boundless vulgarity. Entertaining, though, for her vocabulary, her rather violent beauty, and the sincerity (no! let's not spoil a fine word), the complete insensitivity with which she plys her trade. Carol fucked her on the first evening. I think that if five men were with her in the bar, she'd be capable of going "upstairs" with each of them in turn.

She told me that Lucien Fabre wrote *Bassesse de Venise* mainly to take revenge on her, at a time when they had quarreled and she had gone alone to Venice. The funny thing is that it may be true. And it occurs to me that my situation with Leni may not be so different.

"And you're a Ladima,"[4] Camil said to me the day before yesterday at table. Does he know something . . . ?

3. Petre Constantinescu-Iaşi: a university professor who was condemned for pro-Communist activities.
4. A character from Camil Petrescu's novel *Patul lui Procust*.

Thursday, 16 [April]

As I read it, Renard's *Journal* becomes increasingly dear to me. How fond I am of that man, and how absurd his death seems to me—though twenty-four years have passed since then.

That is the only kind of eternity that matters: to be more alive than a living person, and for the memory of you to be just as real as a physical presence.

Reading today his entry of 24 July 1903, I said to myself that I should write a book about Jules Renard in which I explain—through him—my love of France. Renard's radicalism has peasant roots. That reassures me about the fate of French democracy. It will never die.

Since I arrived here I have continued the major scene between Leni and Valeriu which I began in Sinaia. I'm at page 12. I feel it is working. But can I be sure?

To some extent, what gives me the courage to write for the theatre are Renard's notes about his own plays.

I should not like to leave Breaza before finishing at least this scene.

I think that the man's role will be extremely difficult. Only Iancovescu could play it without making it *"raisonneur,"*[5] pretentious and boring. As I write, I like it more, but it also worries me more. After I finish the play—whether I put it on or not—I shall write a general recommendation for each actor on how his role should be performed.

Friday, 17 [April]

Breaza has never been so beautiful before. It is a profusion of colors. Never in my life have I seen so many trees in blossom. I think they are apple trees. Some are so white they look a bit like a picture postcard.

A little while ago—9 a.m.—I stood for a few minutes at the end of the walk with walnut trees, looking up the Prahova Valley toward the mountains. It makes you giddy. The white of the snow on Bucegi, then the white of the apple trees in blossom, then a thousand shades of green—from the dark green of a solitary pine to the yellow, immature, moist, insecure green of the young leaves. In the middle of the landscape—right in the middle, as if placed there by some hidden laws of composition—a house with a dark, burnt roof illuminates by contrast the lively colors around it. Nor should I forget the patches of mauve, the patches of blue,

5. Argumentative.

the grey shadows, the water sparkling in the sun. (I went back after lunch. I was disappointed. There was no water. The Prahova has almost dried up.)

It honestly seemed unreal to me. And after moving away some twenty meters, I returned to make sure that it all really existed and was still in its place.

In the evening, though I tried to write until after midnight, it no longer worked. But now I am rereading everything I have written so far, and it seems good to me. Maybe I did well to start with the main scene. It sets the play's atmosphere. It will be easier for me to write the preliminary scenes.

Sunday, 19 [April], Bucharest

I left Breaza feeling very content, even though I hadn't finished the Leni–Valeriu scene. Two pages were still to be done. I wrote them today, and without flattering myself I think I have done a good job. There are some moments in the scene that I find delightful—exactly what I had envisaged by way of atmosphere and tone. And more important still, the general rhythm of the scene (which is after all a long one) moves forward well.

I counted up the units of dialogue (childishness: but in the same way I counted the lines on the page in my first printed book). There are 149. Isn't that too many? Isn't it too long?

I have confidence in my play. I'd be surprised if I messed it up—though I still have so much to do.

If I now had a whole month free, I'd return to Breaza and be able, I think, to stay in this week's excellent frame of mind. On Friday I wrote ten pages there—an exceptional output for me, who write slowly and with difficulty. I shall try to clear a week for myself in early May.

This morning at the Ateneu a concert with Lola Bobescu (Lalo's *Symphonie Espagnole*). A girl of fifteen to sixteen, whose gestures are still those of a child, with a delightful blend of bravura and timidity. She plays splendidly, but while playing she smiles here and there to someone in the audience—probably a relative or a friend, just as Mlle. Lambert's pupils used to do at exam time in Brăila. Movingly youthful, sincere, and delicate. A girl from one of Francis James's works.

In one of the front rows, Anton Holban applauded with a kind of lewd gusto. He is a delightful boy, with the air of an old maid. "You caught me red-handed with emotion," he said to me.

I have been reading *Album des vers anciens*. Splendid. Very Mallarmé in places, but splendid. How could I have neglected him until now?

Camil—to whom I show some verses by Valéry on the way to Sinaia—said to me: "Yes, it's beautiful. But not more beautiful than my poetry."

Tuesday, 21 [April]

While the play continues to preoccupy me (though I haven't written any more), I am thinking of a short novel that would clear up my chapter with Leni. What happened yesterday evening at the theatre (and out of disgust I prefer to say nothing of it here) has rekindled in me the need to write about it. Two hundred pages, I had in mind. This stupid story will have served some purpose, after all. But for now the play comes first!

Sunday, 26 [April]

I have finished Renard's *Journal*.

Today I made a decision with which I am happy—even if it perhaps causes a little regret deep inside me. I am giving the role to Marietta.

Nothing can be done with Leni. Her indifference is careless, thoughtless, offensive to the point of being impolite or unfriendly. I think that anyone else would at least have feigned some interest. She couldn't even make that effort. My visit to her dressing room on Saturday disgusted me; it was much more depressing than my visit on Monday.

I am glad I spoke to Marietta. It was necessary to take the play away from Leni. I had to make a clear commitment to Marietta so that there could be no turning back.

And then, practically speaking, it is the best solution. Leni is play-acting with Timică and Țăranu—and she does it at the Alhambra. She is actually giving up theatre and going right over to operetta. She takes her distance from Tessa and becomes Miss Speed again. My play, and especially the role she should be playing, are at the opposite extreme.... And she wants too much to make money. She is too eager to "score" a great success with the public to risk experimenting with an original play, especially one of mine.

By contrast, Marietta is happy to play a major role, and the question of money doesn't enter into it (or anyway, only secondarily). Today I read her everything I have written and explained what the scenario will look like. She was excited. I felt that every line was "getting through."

I felt that she understood, identified, saw it before her. And her warmth, her enthusiasm, her generosity! Moreover, since she is so keen to act the part, she will do all she can on stage (and she can do so much when she wants).

If (as rumor has it) Iancovescu moves to the Regina Maria, what an excellent cast I shall have with him, Marietta, and Maximilian. As to the production, in those parts where Haig's touch is too heavy, I shall try myself to bring the text back to life.

I came away feeling over the moon. The reading made everything I had written seem fresher and opened up paths that had no longer been leading anywhere. Back in the street, I saw some new things for the third act (Bogoiu, the tie, "you are compromising me," "I'll see you outside," etc.). As a matter of fact, he is the only one who worries me, because he is poor. I wouldn't want the rhythm to falter suddenly after Act Two, which promises to keep rolling so well.

I shall try to leave on Saturday or Sunday. I have found new reasons to write—and isn't it strange that I find them on the very day when I decide to give up Leni?

Sunday, 3 [May]

General meeting at the Writers' Association. How can they take seriously such ridiculous farces? How can they think for a second that it bothers me whether Kirițescu is elected or not, whether Toneghin is voted in or not?[6]

During the hour I spent there I got worked up, I formed a group, I propagandized—and only when I left did I realize what a pathetic game I had been playing.

What do I have in common with that whole business, with all that plotting and politicking? What an awful dump of a place, a dump filled with literary types. Horrible, really horrible!

More generally, I am in a period of feeling poisoned by literature. I am sick and tired of it. Why didn't I become an ordinary professional— lawyer, civil servant—a plain dealer? Why wasn't I destined to have a house of my own, a life of my own, a love of my own—without complications or anything "interesting," without regrets?

Not even the Viennese show yesterday afternoon (Molnar's *Grosse*

---

6. Menny Toneghin: editor and writer.

liebe) managed to buck me up completely. Still, I had three enchanting hours and a few minutes of high emotion. Lilly Darvaş is a great actress.

But the whole day has left behind a taste of pointlessness. I keep remembering my whole wasted life.

Friday, 8 [May]

An "artists'" lunch yesterday at Lilly's. Myself, Marietta, Elvira Godeanu, Haig, "Kiki,"[7] and someone called Brătăşanu from Ploieşti.

Two things happened, each as unpleasant as the other:

1) It was Lilly who wrote the stupid letter against Nora Peyov in *La Zid*. She told me so herself with more than a touch of pride, begging me not to tell anyone else because—of course—absolutely no one knows or has guessed it.

I shudder to think that although both of them are acting in the same play, and although they see each other, kiss, and visit each other, Lilly can still come up with this kind of plot. I wouldn't have thought her capable of such vulgarity.

2) The second incident concerns Marietta, my good old Marietta Sadova. . . . The talk had turned to the attack on Hefter,[8] who was beaten by a student a few days ago right there in the street. Someone asked what had happened, but Marietta answered in an offhand way: "It's nothing. He'll get over it."

Shall I write how I nevertheless came to read the play to Leni? Not now—I don't feel like writing. Another time.

Thursday, 14 [May]

Tonight from Stuttgart, a sinfonia concertante by Mozart and then—a big surprise!—the *Kleine nachtmusik*.

I was glad to hear it again, because it is so closely bound up with my play. Unfortunately, my radio is on its last legs. I could pick up enough passages, though, and this has brought me back to the play after a few days in which I dropped it. I really ought to go away for at least three days, to pick up the thread that has been momentarily lost. I am reading Oswald Spengler's *Années décisives*: I don't know why it is only now that I do it, because it has been on my bookshelf for ages. A surprise to

---

7. An acquaintance of Sebastian's from Brăila.
8. Alfred Hefter: journalist from Iaşi.

find whole sentences, formulations, ideas, and paradoxes from Nae's course. The whole of last year's course (domestic and foreign policy, peace, war, the definition of the nation), all his "bold strokes" (Singapore, France in its death throes, Russia as an Asiatic power, Britain in liquidation): it is all there in Spengler, with an astounding similarity of vocabulary. And I haven't yet finished it. . . .

The day before yesterday I was in Braşov, at the trial of some Iron Guard students. Nae made a statement (which I read in the papers) that religion does not forbid all murder, and that students therefore naturally feel solidarity with Duca's killers. I don't think I shall attend his course any more—not to "punish" him, but because, quite frankly, Nae Ionescu is beginning not to interest me any longer. The way he sees things is too simple.

Sunday, 17 [May]

I left Breaza a month ago today. Since then my play has been marking time. Isn't it a pity to let it get bogged down like this? Will I ever regain that happy rhythm I found during those five days in Breaza?

I absolutely must go away. Maybe it is a mere prejudice, but it is too deeply rooted by now: I cannot write here. I tried again this evening, but it's no good. The silliest thing about it is that the whole of Act One—each sentence—is clear in my head. But it still doesn't work.

I have looked at my diary and I think that, with a little will, I could leave Wednesday evening and stay until Monday morning. That would be four days of work. I shouldn't let them slip. But I have no money, Mama needs to go away, and on Saturday I have the court case with Aderca's sister. Nevertheless . . .

Tuesday, 26 [May]

Mama left on Friday. She has been in Paris since the day before yesterday.

Nae finished his course on Friday afternoon. I was there. A sober lecture (with just a moment of play-acting, and even that wasn't too exaggerated). A very fine lecture, taut, clever, and with a whole series of happy formulations.

If I had written about it here on Friday, perhaps I'd have summarized it in its entirety. But I didn't feel like anything over the next few days.

On the way out of the hall, Nae said to me: "I gave that lecture for you. For two years you have been giving me funny looks. Well, what do you say now?"

For the moment I said nothing. The lecture really was remarkable— and its solution to the problem of the individual and the collective was certainly interesting (though I can feel the sophistry without being able to put my finger on it). None of that, however, prevents Nae from being an Iron Guardist. At least if he were genuinely that—honestly and without ulterior motives.

I should also have liked to write about the concerts of the Berlin Philharmonic, but I cannot write now. (Bach's *Third Brandenburg Concerto*, a Haydn symphony in D, Beethoven's *Seventh*, Weber's *Oberon* overture, Schumann's *Fourth Symphony*, Brahms's *First*, and the overture to the *Meistersinger*.)

I still see Leni from time to time—less and less often, and with less and less emotion. It was all a stupidly childish business on my part.

I have written two more scenes or so for Act One. I have simplified a situation in which I had badly lost my way. Nearly all the characters were in the scene—I should have left Leni and Bogoiu alone—and I didn't know how to get the others out. The solution came to me unexpectedly, and easily enough. The soundest method is always to sit resolutely at your desk and to wait. . . .

I look at my diary and tell myself that I could still leave next Thursday (5 June) for Breaza, and remain there until Wednesday morning (10 June). That would be five full days of work. But if I manage to finish Act One before then—by filching an evening or afternoon here and there—Breaza could be kept for the second act. What cannot be done in five completely free days! I'll keep my fingers crossed.

A moving letter from Blecher. He wants me to visit him at Roman.[9] I wrote back promising that I would, and I shall certainly do it.

Wednesday, 27 [May], morning

I happen to have been rereading some chapters from *De două mii de ani* (my old habit of taking a book at random from a shelf and leafing through it for an hour). There were a number of things I had completely for-

9. M. Blecher, the writer, was crippled by illness.

gotten. I had a real surprise. Apart from a few passages that are too markedly Jewish, the rest strikes me as exceptional. I didn't know. I wasn't expecting it.

I should be very happy to have that book published again some day, without Nae's preface and without any explanation on my part.

There is no doubt that, of everything I have written, that is the book that will live on.

Yesterday from Rome, a delightful piano sonata in C by Mozart. Later, from Budapest, a violin sonata in E major by Handel.

Sunday, 31 [May]

Yesterday evening, a long visit to Leni's. It is a long time since I have had such a calm and restful conversation with her. . . .

I should have taken her in my arms, kissed her, and said: Come to me tomorrow, Leni. She would have accepted without hesitation. The whole time I was there she made numerous little gestures of affection, of invitation, which I let drop or deliberately refused to understand.

I am more empty than sad—and I live because I once came into existence.

The last three days have been poisoned for me by serious trouble at the office [sic!]. I am not cut out to be an attorney—and if I were honest, I'd have to give it up altogether. But I don't have the courage to break anything off, not even that.

Nor do I even know whether I shall be able to leave Bucharest on Thursday, though I have such a need to—not so much for the play as for myself.

Friday, 5 June

Bogoiu is in danger of becoming too subtle. That cannot be allowed to happen. He must retain a basic optimism, somewhat jovial and emphatic. His note of melancholy must appear, from time to time, out of a rather uncouth robustness and simplicity.

"I am walking with a compass in my pocket and searching for north. If I think about it, that seems to be the only thing I have ever really looked for in my life: the north." Such lines—though I like them in themselves—cannot be Bogoiu's. I shall definitely get rid of them and revive the tone of dullish heartiness that Bogoiu ought to have.

Perhaps to some extent he is a poet, but without realizing it.

As you see, I haven't left Bucharest. Will I be able to tomorrow? I don't know. The Pleniceanu affair is a terrible burden.[1]

Marietta told the Bulandras[2] about the play, and it seems that both of them—especially Mme. Bulandra—are thrilled at the thought of acting in something of mine. But I won't agree to give the part to Toni at any price (even at the risk of its not being performed at all). It would spoil everything.

The ideal interpretation would be Iancovescu, Leni, and Timică. If necessary, Iancovescu could be replaced by Vraca,[3] and Leni—if absolutely necessary—by Marietta. Any other cast would completely foul up my experiment with the theatre.

Monday, 8 June. Breaza

I have finished the first act. I arrived in Breaza at four in the afternoon. By evening I had written three pages. Yesterday, seventeen pages. (I think that is a literary record for me. I don't remember ever having written so much in one day.) Now finally, this morning, the last three pages of the scene with the mechanic—at last linking up with the final scene, which has been written for so long.

Decidedly, Breaza is proving more favorable to my play than anywhere else. It is true that, when I arrived the day before yesterday, I had already sketched everything in my head: scene by scene, almost line by line. But it is also true that in the same situation in Bucharest, I would have managed to write no more than fifteen pages in fifty days—whereas here, in less than two days, I have written twenty-three.

I think that Act Two would go well if I had ten free days at Breaza, working at the same rhythm. I see it very clearly, in great detail. . . . The serious difficulties and resistance will begin again only in the third act; it is the most unclear one at present—or rather, the only unclear one. But it too may become clearer as I write the second act.

I am content. I feel that I have made things simpler and am laying the first act aside with a workman's satisfaction. I am not yet aware of its defects. There must be something: maybe a certain lack of unity in the tone. Most of all, I wonder whether the final scene—of which I am so fond—really blends with the first part of the act. And I don't know

1. A trial involving the wife of Sever Pleniceanu.
2. Toni and Lucia Sturza Bulandra: actors.
3. George Vraca: actor.

whether it is too long. I also ask myself whether Leni's constant presence in the scene is not tiring both for her and for the audience, and whether, for her to stand out in the major scene with Valeriu, she should not be taken offstage earlier for a few minutes, so that her voice (when she returns) carries that touch of surprise that I think is necessary for theatrical dialogue.

I return this afternoon to Bucharest. If the Pleniceanu affair works out in court, I shall have another good stretch for literature and abandon chambers as soon as possible for this Breaza that is so well disposed toward me.

Bucharest, 11 June, Thursday

I am thinking of a book called "Behind the Scenes" that I could bring out in a year or two. I would put into it everything I have written in connection with literary creation, with working techniques, the writer's life, the experience of publishing a book, etc., etc.

The idea came to me in Breaza when, having finished the first act of the play, I was amusing myself by rereading everything in this journal that refers to the play—from the evening I began to write it up to the present. What I noticed was that it is not without interest as a veritable "record of work in progress."

The volume might comprise: 1) The journal of *Oraşul cu salcîmi*—as it was once printed in *Azi*—and any additions since the novel appeared; 2) The journal of the play; 3) The series of articles published in *Rampa* under the title "Voluptatea de a fi scriitor" [The Delight of Being a Writer]—as written and, if possible, reworked, or, if not, completely rewritten; 4) My various polemics with Călinescu, Al. O. Teodoranu, Stancu, and Pandrea. (What a pity I tore up my reply to Lovinescu for *Vremea*.[4] It would have fitted in so well here. I wouldn't be able to write it again.) Also the article with Mircea Dem. Rădulescu and whoever else; 5) My critics confronted and commented upon—especially Roşu's article, to which I would add the note of 26 October from this notebook; 6) Various literary events and anecdotes that I have seen or experienced: for example, my passing through Sburătorul, the "duel" with General Văitoianu, the incident with Lovinescu (the dinner jacket).

I think it could be an entertaining dossier, and the title strikes me as a happy choice.

4. Eugen Lovinescu: literary critic.

The evening before last, I read the first act at Mircea's. Apart from Nina and himself, Marietta and Haig, Maryse and Gheorghe were also there. I think they listened with pleasure and did not grow tired of it. (I realize that my hero annoys Mircea, and I know why. He thinks he is conceited, self-satisfied. But Mircea is mistaken, and I shall try to explain to him why.) I cannot know what they honestly think of the act. Of course, they told me they liked it. But anyway, the reading helped me: I saw the act complete and really had the impression that it holds up well.

I am still working out the details of the third act. I think I'll use Jef here more than I originally intended. And I won't create a love affair between him and Mrs. Vintilă—that would be too easy.

I have been rereading my note from last year, 11 June 1935. How stupid I was, and how miserable.

Am I less miserable today? No. But I am less stupid. I haven't seen Leni for some ten days, *et je me porte très bien, cher monsieur.*[5] I am not really even dying to see her, and I wait rather lazily for the days to pass. One day I shall phone her—one sunny day. I have decided to act as if she is out of town, and the method is successful.

A distressed letter from Poldy. Why, oh why? We, on the Hechter side, are a family with a taste for lamentation. It's true that life has done quite a lot to help me keep this up. But I ought to impose more self-control, more determination to be contented (as far as this is still possible for me).

Friday, 12 June

I am rereading *Les faux-monnayeurs*[6] after ten years or so. How hastily I judged it! And how summary was my article of 1927 in *Cuvântul*! But I'll wait until I have finished the book before revising my overall judgment of it. I shall try to develop what I think in an article for *Revista Fundaţiilor.*

For the moment let me just note one astonishing thing: the great, powerful similarity between Mircea's *Huliganii* and *Les faux-monnayeurs*. Has no one noticed it before? Has not he himself noticed it? I shall ask him, but also after I have finished reading the book.

5. And I'm really fine, sir.
6. Novel by André Gide.

Monday, 15 June

On Saturday and Sunday I went to two football matches at O.N.E.F., together with Camil and his . . . Dragoş Protopopescu.[7]

It was rather embarrassing, especially as on the way out I had to get into Dragoş's car and even sit next to him in front.

I felt like asking him: "Are you an Iron Guardist, or aren't you? If you are, be one entirely." (Without a doubt, I prefer the clear, implacable attitude of someone like Moţa.[8])

But he would be entitled to say in reply: "Are you a Jew, or aren't you? If you are, don't hold your hand out to me again, and don't take mine when I hold it out to you."

There should be—and it's not the first time I say this to myself—there should be more intransigence, more rigidity even, in my life. I am too "supple"—and I utter this word with a touch of scorn for everything in me that is too accommodating.

Dragoş P., who still thinks I am close to Nae, told me a funny thing (in fact, it is only to record it that I am writing this note).

"What's with Nae?" he asked me, because we were just then driving down Şoseaua Jianu behind the professor's home. "He's having a hard time of it. He's burnt his fingers with the Germans. They've been scheming against him. I heard from a very good source that Sân-Giorgiu[9] took to Berlin a letter of Nae's to Blank and showed it to a number of ministers there. Indeed, he seems to have been instructed by the King to do that; the King, who has the original of the letter, gave it to . . . Sân-Giorgiu to show to the Germans. Şeicaru[1] was also involved in the machinations, and he too has a photocopy of the document."

I listened to all this with a curiosity that I tried to hide as best I could. I listened with a bored ear, so as not to put Dragoş on his guard.

"I don't know . . . I don't think . . ."

"Oh yes, I assure you: it's very serious. But I want to have a word with Nae. He should be warned."

Wednesday, 17 [June]

Two days (yesterday and today) stupidly wasted, because of the Pleniceanu business.

7. Right-wing journalist sympathetic to the Iron Guard.
8. Ion I. Moţa: a leader of the Iron Guard.
9. Ion Sân-Giorgiu: extreme right-wing journalist and playwright.
1. Pamfil Şeicaru: journalist, owner of the *Curentul* newspaper.

I went without eating at court yesterday until five o'clock, dizzy with hunger, nervous tension, and impatience. I pleaded well—and lost. I am a good speaker, but I shall never be a good attorney. The Bar amuses me: the adversary, the judges, the rising, questioning, slightly rhetorical phrases that I manage to come up with. And, silly as it seems, I like listening to myself. Just as I am bad at chitchat (my pathetic figure at a society gathering or a social visit!), I am good at public speaking.

But it is of no use to me. I could be a lecturer, not an attorney.

The whole of today wasted at Mrs. Pleniceanu's waiting for the bailiff. And meanwhile so many things I love, or could love, are awaiting me. At least if one of them were . . .

I shall try to leave for Breaza on Friday.

Monday, 22 [June]

Hot, bored, endless troubles in court (still in connection with the Pleniceanu affair), no appetite for anything, except perhaps sun and love.

"Sun and love"—a perfect summary of my ideal of happiness. Yesterday at Snagov I saw the very image of such a life.

I was invited to eat at the home of Maryse's mother, with her and Gheorghe. She has a magnificent villa. It's like a little triangular toy, with dark brown walls and a red roof. White rooms, large and simple furniture, blue armchairs, many flowers, canvas chairs, a chaise longue, a small landing stage with two boats, a lawn, a sunshade, fishing tackle, quietness, water, forest . . . It was like a dream.

I went into the upstairs bedroom for a couple of minutes—and I dreamed I was installed there as master of the house, together with Leni on a holiday that had just started and would never finish. Am I so lazy? I don't know. I am tired, rather, and I have a longing to be happy, what with everything inside me that has had to remain for so long idle, broken, disconsolate.

We went out fishing in the boat and stopped for a while at Snagov Monastery, so moving in its beauty. At the entrance to the nave there was a fresco with a remarkable group of women on the right; a shape so utterly surprising there. The first woman, her thigh draped in long material, had a voluptuous gesture of the leg that I would not have expected to find on the wall of a Romanian monastery. On the other side of the wall, in the church proper, an old scene (*Descent from the Cross?*) looks from the altar toward the exit, curious in the childish awkwardness of its perspectival errors. It reminded me of a painting by Zurbarán in the

Louvre. (Not *The Burial of Saint Bonaventura*?) In a group, an old man raises his hand to his beard—a gesture enchanting in its secular expressiveness.

How many things to record last week! But I keep feeling disgusted with myself, and this journal still seems nothing more than a delusion.

The reception at the Blanks on Thursday evening caused me a drunken night. Perhaps my first joyful bout of drunkenness. And Maryse's presence stimulated rather than discouraged me.

At two o'clock, as we were watching a cabaret show put on by the hostess, I said to Leni, who was "consenting" beside me:

"I'm really drunk. I remember only very few things from my past life."

"For example?" she asked.

"For example, that I love you"—and her hand squeezed mine in a new lovers' pact.

My two-week absence was, I can see, a good strategic device. I think she would be unwilling to lose me. And once again, if I wanted it, if I were capable of wanting it, everything would be extremely simple.

But I saw her again the next day at her place (kind, affectionate, loving, offering herself sincerely enough) and yesterday at the match. This once more gave her the assurance of being "strong"—proof that allowed her to become again inattentive, neglectful, and coquettish.

Right, sir, we'll resume the strategy of silence. It's the only game that still offers the possibility of success in this story.

I had a good time at the Blanks on Thursday evening. Horia Bogdan not only praised me to the skies about my advocacy on Wednesday, but made a terrible fuss about it to Mircea, Nina, Marietta, and everyone. (Leni told me several times to invite her along one day when I'm pleading in court.)

Even more amusing was the fact that Horia Bogdan told his wife all about my advocacy that very evening on their way home from the hearing. If I can believe him—that is, if they weren't just nice words on his part—there seems to have been some discussion about me in chambers.

Well, what if there was?

I didn't make it to Breaza, and I no longer think I shall have time to go. It pains me to note that the play is being left for the holiday months. But will I be free to leave Bucharest? And will I have enough money?

Only a period of getting away from it all, like that August in Ghilcoş, could pick me up again. I'll wait and hope, as much as I am still capable of hope.

Wednesday, 24 [June]

Uproar and anti-Semitic assaults in court. (And two days before, I had been saying to myself that I should give up writing and do nothing but advocacy.)

We may be heading for an organized pogrom. The evening before last, Marcel Abramovici (Auntie Rachel's one from Braşov) was knocked down in the street by twenty or so students, who then dragged him unconscious into the cellar of their hostel and only "released" him a couple of hours later, with a deep head wound, his clothing torn and bloodied.

Yesterday Sicu Davidovici was thrown into the stairwell of the Commercial Court. Marcu Leibovici was also beaten up: there's someone who continues to follow his destiny—I think he was the one most often roughed up at university.

Yesterday evening there was a street-fighting atmosphere on Strada Gabroveni (I had been to see Carol Grünberg). The Jewish shopkeepers had lowered their shutters and were waiting for their attackers, determined to resist them. I think that's the only thing to do. If we're going to kick the bucket, we might as well do it with a club in our hands. It's no less tragic, but at least not so ridiculous.

This morning Leni asked me on the phone not to go to court any longer; she said that she had worried about me the whole of yesterday. She seemed honestly concerned about my fate, and—why not say it?—that made me feel good.

I am reading Stendhal's *Journal* and would like to be somewhere far away, very far away, without papers and news, but with a few classics—and a woman. Perhaps with Leni. Or someone less agitated, a more languid presence. . . .

I have been meaning for a long time—but have kept forgetting—to note here something I heard a week ago from Marietta. Apparently Paul Zarifopol[2] died in a woman's arms, and that woman—believe it or not—was none other than Lisette Georgescu. I would never have imagined any-

2. Novelist, literary critic.

thing like that. I am more inclined to assume that the people I know are virtuous. Probably because of my lack of personal experience.

Thursday, 25 [June]

Camil Petrescu, whom I met this morning at the Capşa, was angry at my suggestion that the trial of the Craiova anti-fascists was out of control.

"Those people shouldn't even have a trial; they should be sent straight off to prison for ten years, or twenty years. Don't give them the chance to make Communist propaganda in court, with witnesses and lawyers."

When we left the Capşa we went a few steps down the street and he repeated what he thought of the latest anti-Semitic attacks.

"It's regrettable, old man. But all Jews have a responsibility for it."

"How's that, Camil?"

"Because there are too many of them."

"But aren't there even more Hungarians?"

"Maybe, but at least they're all in one place, in the same region." (I didn't understand the argument, but I didn't want to insist. What was the point of repeating the long conversation I had with him in January 1934? I am clear about him—and all he can do is depress me, never surprise me.)

He went on to say:

"My dear man, the Jews provoke things: they have a dubious attitude and get mixed up in things that don't concern them. They are too nationalistic."

"You should make up your mind, Camil. Are they nationalists or are they Communists?"

"Wow, you're really something, you know? Here we are alone and you can still ask questions like that. *What else is communism but the imperialism of the Jews?*"

That is Camil Petrescu speaking. Camil Petrescu is one of the finest minds in Romania. Camil Petrescu is one of the most sensitive creatures in Romania. How could Romania ever go through a revolution?

I had lunch at Mircea's. While waiting for him and Nina to come back from town, I read some twenty pages at random of *Le côté des Guermantes*. It was an episode I had completely forgotten (in fact, I have the impression that I've forgotten it all): a lunch that Marcel had with Saint-Loup and Rachel "*quand du Seigneur.*"

Rachel bears a surprising resemblance to Leni. I felt that I was reading the story of my own love.

Wednesday, 1 July

I spent Sunday and Monday in Brăila, where my old class was celebrating the tenth anniversary of the baccalaureate. After fourteen months away, I found Brăila lacking in surprises—unchanged, admirably silent, and uncomplicated. It was a strange feeling to stay at the hotel there. My room—"Hotel Francez"—overlooked Strada Polonă. St. Peter's Church was directly opposite my window, at the end of the street.

At the school I felt more than I would have expected. I sat on the bench—the last bench in the 8th form—and found myself beset with memories. On my right, Ficu's empty place.

Goraş called out the register and we answered in turn—"Present." Now and again we heard "Absent" and a few times "Dead." Four are no longer alive.

Then something amazing happened: Goraş's speech. It deserves to be written down in its entirety, word for word. But I don't think I could do it. Still, I shall try to reconstitute it.

"Gentlemen, there are always misunderstandings (some of them very painful) between form master and class, between teachers and pupils, but I should like you to believe that the traces and regrets they leave in the teacher's heart are no fewer than those they leave in the pupils'. I, for example, have carried a memory for ten years that has caused me a lot of suffering and from which I am glad I can free myself today by telling you about it.

"It concerns one of the most brilliant boys in your year. I am thinking of Hechter. He was in 7-A and had won a prize in Romanian language. At the end-of-year prizegiving—even today I cannot think how it happened—I forgot to call for him to come up. It was hot, I was tired and burdened with worries—so perhaps such a mistake was understandable. All I can say is that it was not deliberate. Once the ceremony was over, I remembered and went to look for Hechter. He said something that annoyed me, and I made a very sharp retort. I immediately regretted it. I realized at once that I was doing the wrong thing. But it was too late. I want to tell him today, in front of you all, how much I suffered for the injustice I did him on that occasion. I assure him that it didn't take me all these years to remember it. It is not the brilliant career he has since made for himself, not those fine literary achievements of his, which make me speak as I now do. I have felt the pain right from the first moment. I should have liked to apologize to him before now. It was not possible. I was not able to do it. I tried once, but I realized it was very difficult. I am doing it today, and I tell you I am glad I can in the presence of his classmates. If possible, he will forgive and under-stand."

I was overwhelmed. It brought tears to my eyes, and I was trembling all over. I replied in a barely audible voice, saying a lot of things badly.

"Headmaster, I have never met anyone before who was capable of doing what you have just done."

That was the truth. The gesture struck me as quite extraordinary, hu-manly speaking. Goraş is an even more complex person than I thought.

At the "banquet" that evening (we all dined at the Monument), I sat next to him all the time and we chatted quite comfortably. I'll send him my books and perhaps write to him.

The next day, on Monday, a long walk by the Danube, as far as the Cropina canal beyond Reni. A fish lunch was awaiting us there, as in a dream. The huge cast-iron kettle in which the fish soup was simmering, the spitted carp around the live coals; it was a sight straight out of Sadoveanu or Hogaş. I had my clothes off all day, bathed in the Danube, went rowing, ate an enormous amount, drank . . .

The return journey was magnificent. Mounted on the ship's cabin, I had the whole Danube in front of me (a Danube wider than at Brăila, with a more orderly forest of willows, almost as in a well-kept park). It was bright sunlight when we left at six, and we caught the last flickers of twilight as we got off at Reni. After an hour in which the little town was alarmed by our invasion (delightful public gardens filled with girls, children, and young lovers!), I resumed my place on the cabin roof as we traveled "in the moonlight"[3] to Galaţi. From there to Brăila, where we arrived at one in the morning. I was rather drowsy.

A fine day, which took me out of Bucharest and allowed me to breathe. It made me aware again that the earth is bigger than the three square kilometers on which I live, fret, and talk.

Visited Leni yesterday—very loving, very warm, not in the least coquet-tish. She told me some interesting things about Jeni Cruţescu's love for her.

"She loves me like a man. There hasn't been anything physical be-tween us—if there had been, I'd have told you—but I'm not sure there won't be some day. She suffers a lot because of me, and I admit that I'm to blame; if she behaves with me like a man in love, I behave with her like a flighty woman.

3. In English in the original.

"Lots of people tell me that I'll cause her nothing but unhappiness, that it will all end in tragedy. We have talked about that ourselves, and once we even decided to part—but it wasn't possible. After a week, she came back feeling miserable."

It's strange that I don't feel at all jealous of Jeni. I listened calmly to Leni as she spoke, and I think it amused me more than it intrigued me. My love for her has never been more natural, more secure. But why, and for how long?

Wednesday, 22 July

My appointment to the *Fundație* came when I was no longer expecting it. For a few days I could not believe it; I thought that everything would turn sour at the last moment. But this morning I got 39,500 lei outstanding. Fantastic! And from now on I'll get 6,000 lei a month (5,935, to be precise).

So that's my holiday taken care of. I'll be able to work and, let's hope, finish the play.

This morning, when I left the *Fundație* and was walking down Calea Victoriei, I suddenly had the happy idea of entering the Columbia store to ask whether the *Kleine nachtmusik* that I ordered last May had arrived for me. It was there. I paid for it, and I am happy that that was my first purchase. Maybe it's a good sign. And the records are magnificent.

Otherwise I do not have the curiosity to write. Nor is there a lot to say.

Had a long, confused dream last night, in which Leni passed through several times.

On Sunday *Lohengrin* from Bayreuth, which I heard in equatorial heat. The voices were admirably clear, the chorus and orchestra blurred.

"But tell me softly at dusk—am I happy?"

Ghilcoș, 2 August. Sunday

I have been here since Friday morning. Back again in the Wagner Villa. Some changes, different people—as always, I am awkward among unfamiliar people with whom I am forced to speak. But the landscape is the same, the air healthy, the firs close by. Yesterday I went to the Bicaz Gorges. At night, by the lake beneath the full moon. Mornings in the sun, on a chaise longue. I am regaining without difficulty that calm sense of happiness that I had last year.

I want to start writing tomorrow. I have no excuse not to, but nor do I feel any great enthusiasm. I have just reread the first act, this afternoon, and it seemed to me long and convoluted. The criticisms that Camil made when I read it to him still pursue me.

Anyway, tomorrow I shall be doing my duty—with resignation if not with relish. That will come too, after I have written the first few pages. *"Le plus difficile,"* says Renard, *"c'est de prendre la plume, de la tremper dans l'encre et de la tenir ferme au-dessus du papier."*[4]

Monday, 3 [August]

I have written little, but written nevertheless. The main thing was to start on the "scheduled" day. It is true that, from the whole day (in which I sat for some five hours with writing paper in front of me), I shall select no more than four pages or so. I have written the first two scenes of Act Two. But I got stuck in the third scene, with Leni and Bogoiu, and I don't think I should press it too hard. I shan't touch it all evening. I'll leave it until tomorrow morning.

I finished the first scene (Bogoiu and the Major) by sacrificing the discovery of the diary—an incident which some time ago, when I was composing the scenario (or scenography, as Stendhal used to say), struck me as particularly funny. But now I have the impression that it is both facile in its effect and very difficult to write. Till tomorrow, then.

A cool evening, but of a perfect purity. The moon right in front of my balcony, in a fir tree. And throughout the valley, a translucent stony blue.

Tuesday, 4 [August]

The mystery of the phone call in Act One will remain unresolved. I'll never know with whom Leni was speaking, or what she said. I don't want to pry open her secrets. Let her keep them.

Evening

I have finished the Leni–Bogoiu scene. I have started the fourth scene (Ştefan–Mme. Vintilă) and got halfway through it. I'd have finished it for sure if the young married couple on the balcony next to mine had not happened to fancy reading aloud all afternoon. They are reading a French

---

4. The most difficult thing is to pick up your pen, dip it into ink, and hold it firmly above the paper.

book in turns: now she, now he. Then they comment on and explain it, passage by passage. Exasperating! An intellectual honeymoon: the most detestable kind.

Without this misfortune it would have been a productive day. Even so, I am happy with it. Eight pages written. And a lot of things made clearer.

I have allowed myself a short break tomorrow morning in order to go up Ghilcoș. But I shall try to make up for it tomorrow afternoon. Let's hope.

Friday, 7 [August]

I didn't "make up for it" Wednesday afternoon, as I had promised myself. The whole day was sacrificed because of the outing on Ghilcoș, where I got lost for nearly two hours (on the way back). But the view was marvelous.

Yesterday it rained from morning till night. A rainy day, but also a day of work. Ten pages. I finished the scene with Ștefan and Mme. Vintilă. Began the Leni–Jef scene, which came to an abrupt halt, however. Impossible to take it any further for the moment. I have abandoned it— and moved on to the scene straight after it, where those two strangers come into the *pensiune*. I can feel that it will work. At the moment (lunch hour) I am at Scene IX-a, page 27. Today I wasted the whole morning on correspondence. But I shall work this afternoon. I have to.

A letter from Jeni, who is at Sovata. Funny how she dates it: "Sovata, on the 3rd of August." That "on" is an old tic of mine, from 1925–1926. She has kept it, doubtless without realizing. That too is a kind of loyalty.

A man can never know what remnants from previous love affairs are in a woman's gestures, habits, vocabulary, and idiosyncrasies.

Sunday, 9 [August]

The fourth rainy day. It's starting to get on my nerves. I surprise myself feeling nostalgia for the city. I'd like there to be a film, a concert. . . . And yet, the thing I look forward to most is the sun.

I think I have been working quite well. Yesterday evening I finished the scenes with the two strangers. There are things that amuse me. But I wonder whether I have not exaggerated here and there, whether I have not pushed too hard, whether I have not resorted to facile effects. I don't know: we shall see. I'm at page 40. Let's see what comes of today.

Yesterday I thought of Ionel Teodoreanu[5] as I walked down the road. I don't know why. I'd have liked to see him. This morning, who do I find in the *pensiune* trying to rent a room from Fräulein Wagner? Ionel Teodoreanu, with his wife. A real joy to see him. They'll be staying in the *pensiune* from tomorrow evening. He's writing a novel. I hope we won't disturb each other.

Monday, 10 [August]

The fifth rainy day. We're in the middle of November. No sign anywhere that it will get better. I have a feeling that it's all over, that I'll never see a clear sky again here in Ghilcoş.

I'm on the final scene—the one about which I wrote in March (that night when I made a first outline of the play) that it was the "major scene, and hard to write."

I approach it with trepidation. How will it work out? If I finish it today or tomorrow, I'll leave myself a free day before moving on to the third act.

Is it possible that I shall return to Bucharest with the whole play written?

I'm not very keen on the pages I wrote yesterday. But I don't want to get held up on them now. I'll have a go at revising them at the end. Right now they seem exaggerated to me. The transition is too abrupt, the effects too calculated.

Evening
I was right. It's hard going. I am at my desk[6]

Tuesday, 11 [August]

Yesterday evening I had just started to write some lines in this notebook when Ionel Teodoreanu knocked on my door. I asked him in and we sat chatting for a couple of hours. When he left, I no longer knew what I had wanted to say in that sentence, and I abandoned it as it was, especially as we had to go to eat.

In brief, I meant to say that the scene at which I had stopped was bothering me. It is the first real stumbling block since I have been at Ghilcoş. And I don't feel like skipping over it to the third act. I want to finish Act Two so that I can put it aside as work completed. Yesterday I

5. Writer and poet.
6. Sentence incomplete.

sat for some six hours with the paper in front of me—and I came away with just a couple of pages (not even two full pages) that can be kept.

I'll give it a try today. To be frank, if the sun were shining, I'd give myself a few hours off and go up Ghilcoş or Ţohard—that might clear my head. But the weather is still bad: the same November sky, a wind that is cold but not strong enough to chase away the clouds.

Teodoreanu is the same fascinating conversationalist I knew in Galaţi. I listen to him with the most intense pleasure—even though he speaks to me only about himself, about literature, and about the novel he is writing. He read me a few passages, and some of them struck me as first class—especially a brief episode with two protagonists, Hans Müller and Mircea Ştefănescu.

"I'm in an anti-lyrical phase," he said. "It's a novel that I'm writing in spite of myself: I think you'll like it."

As for the rest, he is an enchanting companion. His sons, who are staying on my right and are sort of balcony mates, have been given orders to be quiet. Mrs. Teodoreanu makes an exceptional black coffee, and I receive a ration of two cups a day.

His novel is called *Noah's Ark*. It takes place at Borsec, in Frau Blecher's *pensiune*, also known as "the Blecher Fleet."

Since we had been talking about Cezar Petrescu—who, almost without realizing it, used in his books ideas from various conversations or literary confessions—I hastened to say as a precaution:

"You know, there is also a *pensiune* in what I am writing at present, a Pensiune Weber run by a Fräulein Weber up in the mountains, which one of the characters compares to a boat. . . ."

We both laughed at the coincidence, but it was not a bad thing for me to have mentioned it.

"Anyway," he said, "I don't think we shall bump into each other. We're probably moving along different tracks."

"Especially as what I'm writing is . . . a play."

He didn't seem surprised, and he explained why.

"My eldest son, Ştefănucă, told me at lunch today . . ."

(Knocking at the door. I open it: Mrs. Teodoreanu. She has brought my morning coffee. We speak only with our eyes for fear of starting a new conversation. He continues:)

". . . surprised: 'Papa, you know that Mr. Sebastian talks to himself when he writes.' I didn't believe it, but now I understand. . . ."

I explain to him that I do feel the need to speak each line before writing it down.

Friday, 14 [August]

No progress. I'm at a standstill—the last scene of Act Two is putting up stupid resistance.

Act Three, to which I have been trying to draw closer, lacks any shape. For so many days, not a single new idea.

And the sun never returns. I'm beginning to think that is why things are going so badly for me. Yesterday I didn't even try to work. And yet I can't be content with idling about. I keep having pangs of conscience—and each passing hour seems a reproof.

Saturday, 15 [August]

Well, in the end I did finish Act Two yesterday. I think it will need some major additions. I must have a scene with Leni and Ştefan, preceding and preparing the final scene. And I should also dwell a little more on Mme. Vintilă. Maybe the Leni–Jef scene can stay as it is. But I'll have to add something to Leni's "speech" in which she persuades the two intruders to leave.

All these additions seem necessary not only for the internal economy of the act, but also to achieve the right dimensions. Clearly it should be shorter than the first act, but the disproportion seems to me too great. To have seventy-nine pages for the first and only forty-nine for the second: that's a difference not only of thirty pages but, when it's acted, of half an hour.

The sun is back. This morning, two hours naked on a chaise longue on the terrace. I'm convinced that I shall recover my holiday form, which has always been excellent when I've had enough sun.

Yesterday evening a very pleasant stroll with Teodoreanu toward Floarea Reginei.

I'm almost afraid to raise the curtain on the third act. I know so little about what will happen in it.

Thursday, 20 [August]

It seems funny to write it, but when something slightly unfamiliar happens to you, you always have a sense of absurdity and implausibility—so monotonous and well managed is the life we lead.

Well, I have been the victim of an act of banditry. For five minutes or so I was in the movielike situation of having a gun pointed threateningly at me: "Hands up!"

To be honest, he didn't say "hands up." I was with Gulian[7] and his wife, up on Great Țohard. We had reached the summit and were admiring the landscape (which is exceptionally broad and rich in views). I was sauntering along when I heard a voice in front shout out:

"Don't move!"

I didn't realize what was happening; I thought it was Emil's voice or some hiker fooling around. Then, after two or three seconds, the penny dropped. A tall guy was standing in front of us, with a forester's coat, a Mephisthophelean beard, a spiky moustache (both beard and moustache certainly false, though quite well stuck on), and a hunting rifle (double-barreled, I think) pointed at us. "Don't move!"

He made a loading action, no doubt to impress us. There was no need. We were sufficiently impressed.

"Take your clothes off!"

We took our clothes off. We didn't feel like arguing. By happy forethought we were wearing bathing suits underneath. We left our clothes in a heap and moved off a few meters. Still following us with his gun, he ordered us to lie at full length in the grass. As I was staring at him, he asked me a couple of times:

"What are you gaping at, eh?"

Then some terrible words:

"Don't look round, you bunch of motherfuckers!"

He had a rasping voice, with a Hungarian accent. I heard him searching through the pockets—and wondered what else could happen to me. I saw again the events with Terente in 1925.[8] For a moment I wondered whether he might take one of us and try to extort some money. But I was calm enough to joke to Emil:

"Well, it's an experience, after all."

Hortansa Gulian, who has a smattering of Hungarian, told the man to take what he wanted and leave. (Obviously she did this without turning her head and looking at him—which had been forbidden.)

"*Olgos*," he replied in Hungarian. "Shut up!" Then I heard him munching something: he was eating some chocolate and rusks he had found in a handkerchief. Finally I heard:

"Okay, now come and get dressed!"

When I turned my head, he had vanished.

The balance sheet: he had taken my watch (which I greatly regret—

7. Emil Gulian: poet and Sebastian's friend.
8. Referring to a rash of attacks, thefts, and kidnappings in that year in the area near the Danube.

clearly I am unlucky with clocks and watches), my tracksuit top, and roughly eighty lei that I had had in my pocket. Emil lost a silver cigarette case and about five hundred lei. It's funny he left us the other things: beret, sunglasses, trousers.

Then we went back, half frightened, half amused. Our entry into Ghilcoş was priceless: the conversation with the gendarmes, the people looking at us, some wanting details, or smiling with a touch of disbelief, or beginning to feel worried. We are famous. Maybe they'll write about it in the paper.

When I think about it now, my bandit was probably a dilettante. And if we didn't feel too good in his company, he was also a little scared by the operation—afraid to approach us even for a moment. Hortansa was wearing earrings worth tens of thousands of lei, and each of them—of course—a wedding ring. We saved them. I think that if I had had a little cunning, and above all a little presence of mind, I could have saved my watch while I was taking off my trousers.

I also wonder whether his gun was loaded, and whether—had we rushed him with our walking sticks—we might not have put him to flight, or caught him—what a victory!—and taken him down with us to the police. But the gun might have been loaded after all, and it was not worth trying a glorious experiment to save the little we had to be stolen. Only if he had come close to us would I probably have done something.

Now the gendarmes are looking for him in the surrounding area. I'd quite enjoy having a chat with him.

I have begun Act Three after a lot of fumbling. I'm still not completely clear about it. I'm advancing slowly, illuminating short distances as I cross them but not knowing where I will go next. There are days when I write nothing, and others from which I select no more than three or four of the written pieces of dialogue. But I no longer have the distressing feeling of a few days ago—about which I spoke to both Marietta and Mircea—that I won't be able to write any more at all and shall be left with a never-finished play.

It is moving with great difficulty—but it is moving.

Saturday, 22 [August]

I think it has become clearer. It was very hard, but now I sense that I have really achieved clarity once and for all.

Yesterday and today—though not very productive in terms of the number of pages (one and a half yesterday, four and a half today)—have sharpened the contours of Act Three. It has turned out quite different from what I planned, but I'm glad I have recovered a serious tone after the scenes with Bogoiu and the Major, which took it off in a direction that was too crudely comic. It won't be a comic act. I have, for example, given up the scene with the fish caught by the Major—a scene I enjoyed so much in my first outlines. In fact, the Major and Mme. Vintilă no longer appear at all in this act. I didn't pack them off; they went of their own accord, through the inner logic of things.

The play is closing in around Leni, Ștefan, Bogoiu, and Jef. All three love her—each in his way—and when Leni leaves she will abandon all three. I am rediscovering a very old memory from a film I saw in childhood: *The Three Sentimentalists*. It is an emotion regained.

I am surprised at the psychological meanings that Bogoiu and Jef have acquired during the months that I've been writing the play. Originally intended as quite episodic characters with a mostly comic function, they have become linchpins of the whole psychological action.

So far I have written the first three scenes of Act Three, leaving unfinished (at 7:30 p.m.) the scene with Bogoiu and Leni. A summary outline has been done for the whole act.

The only danger is that the elimination of the Major and Mme. Vintilă will leave the act too short. But I am determined not to let this influence me for the moment. I am writing the play as it compels itself to be written. Later, when it is performed, I shall make the strictly necessary amplifications—if any are indeed necessary. I have the impression that, especially given the length of the first act, the play could be divided into two parts, with a single interval after Act One. Acts Two and Three would then be performed almost straight through, with a single five-minute break between them.

I am thinking of various titles ("Holidays" is too flat): "A Sunny Day," "The Game of Holidaymaking," "Playing at Happiness."

I think I have regained the joy of writing. For a moment (which lasted some ten days), it deserted me. If I remain in the mood for work, I shall stay in Ghilcoș until I finish—that is, if necessary, even after the first of September.

Tuesday, 25 [August]

I am halfway through the eighth scene, the high point of Act Three in which Leni and Ștefan have it out. From now on, the rest will be perfectly straightforward. I realize that if I work harder and make a more concentrated effort, I could finish everything in a single day.

But, on the one hand, the rain is back, and since yesterday morning we have again been in mid-November. I miss the sun so much... I'd grown used to working on the balcony—especially between five and seven in the afternoon, when Mount Ghilcoş right in front of me passed through the most delightful glow of twilight. And the presence of Teodoreanu, also bent over a desk on his balcony, was friendly and reassuring. . . .

On the other hand, I am still being bothered by the investigation into what happened on Ţohard. They have summoned me a few times to the police station to show me various suspects. In the end they settled on a guy who, so to speak, offers the highest guarantee of being guilty. I can't swear he is the one, but I do know that his stare frightens me. Now they have summoned me to the preliminary hearing in Miercurea-Ciuc. Obviously, I won't go. But all these parleys, all these trips to the police station, all these statements I have to make (always with the fear of getting an innocent person into trouble) irritate me and, by interrupting the flow, prevent me from working.

All the same, I can now consider the play virtually complete. Two days more, or five or six, and it'll be over. But I should like to finish it here, so that I don't have to leave a single line until Bucharest.

Thursday, 27 [August]

No, I won't finish it either today, tomorrow, or Sunday. I don't know when I'll finish. Although the eighth scene is now over—the one with Leni and Ştefan, which seemed the hardest in this act—not all the difficulties have passed. The very next scene, for example, between Ştefan and Jef, is putting up considerable resistance. I struggled with it the whole of yesterday afternoon, and again the whole of this morning, without coming away with more than five or six snatches of dialogue. Strange how resistances appear when you are least expecting them.

But I haven't got myself worked up about it. I am waiting. The finale is shaping up splendidly, with a wealth of nuances that I didn't suspect ten days ago, when the whole third act seemed lifeless. But will I be able to bring out all these nuances? If I don't extract a moment of great delicacy and refined emotion from the penultimate scene (Leni, Ştefan, Bogoiu, Jef), the only explanation will be that I don't have an ounce of talent.

As for the title, I think I'll stick with *Joucul de-a vacanţa* [The Game of Holidaymaking].

Saturday, 29 August, 4 a.m.

I have finished. To whom shall I wire, as in my first year: "Passed exam. Am happy"?

But have I passed the exam? I'll find out later.

Balcic. Sunday, 6 September

I have been here since yesterday. My accommodation (the Paruşeff Villa), a poor Bulgarian's home, is little more than a hovel. Very clean, though, and literally at the water's edge. The waves break three meters from me. A yard, some chaises longues, and the sea stretched far out before me. I think I am at the midpoint of the bay.

The ceaseless sound of the waves has a rhythmic evenness that lulls me to sleep. My slumber was deep, even, and long, as never happened in Ghilcoş. Yet the roar of the waves never stopped, and my window was wide open all night.

This morning, my first dip in the sea. Rediscovered the great pleasure of swimming. And I swim so badly.

A circle of actors and painters, long lazy conversations, an idle, trouble-free, couldn't-care-less atmosphere that is truly relaxing. Iancovescu, Țoța, Marietta Rareş, Lucian Grigorescu, Paul Miracovici, Baraschi, Mützner. Today we all had lunch together at Judge . . . (I've forgotten his name), and in the afternoon, with the sea in front of me, I listened to Bach (the *Third Brandenburg*), Mozart (a violin concerto), Vivaldi, and Beethoven.

Evening is drawing in, I am alone in the house, and the waves still keep breaking alongside me. . . .

I won't write here about what happened when I passed through Bucharest. Four quite tiring days. I didn't see Leni, and perhaps I won't see her any more. She asked me to visit her on Wednesday—and I didn't find her at home. I'm fed up with it all. I don't want to begin again the ordeal of telephone calls, waiting, suspecting, scheming. It is all such old hat, and so pointless. In a way, that incident will make it easier to find a solution for the play. I'll give the part to Marietta—regretfully, but without hesitating. She'll make of it what she can. I'd like her to act it with Iancovescu at least—but I fear that even that won't be possible and that I'll have to accept Toni in the end. In that case I'll be heading for certain disaster.

On Wednesday evening I read the second and third acts to Marietta,

Haig, the Nenişors, Mircea, and Nina, and by chance the Pencius. A dubious outcome: the first impression was rather depressing. But then I
pulled myself together. There are a mass of criticisms that I should like
to record here. But my ink has run out, and besides, it is too nice outside. Maybe tomorrow.

Monday, 7 [September]

Act Two might work in its present form. Maybe not even the scene with
Leni and Jef needs anything more to be done to it. But the final scene
absolutely must be reworked. In fact, that was what I felt right at the
start, when I first wrote it.

The scene immediately after the two intruders leave is also quite inadequate. The idea is excellent (one of the best things I came up with
in the whole play), but the goods are not delivered. I realized this myself, but it was Haig, in particular, who drew it to my attention.

The whole episode with the two stowaways works very well. They
were all ears and laughed a lot.

That's all I find at the moment to say about Act Two. The picture
is much more complicated for Act Three.

Friday, 11 [September]

I leave this afternoon. I haven't written anything, or read anything. I lay
in the sun—that was just about all. A few happy days. Being lazy is my
highest pleasure. That is why I haven't noted anything here. It doesn't
interest me.

The sea is calm—a mirror.

Bucharest. Tuesday, 15 [September]

I saw Leni and told her I had decided to give the play to Iancovescu and
Marietta. Only if that doesn't work out will I be able to offer it to her
again. She took the news with self-restraint, but the emotion was visible. Maybe not "emotion." Surprise, annoyance, regret—and, very far
off, an urge to burst into tears. Such is the stupid logic of the game we
are playing with each other. So long as she knew that the part was hers,
that I was writing and preserving it for her, she was thoughtless to the
point of indifference. Now that she has lost it, or is threatened with losing it, the part becomes necessary for her and she suffers at no longer
having it.

Nor am I any different. I am rediscovering that "sporadic boorishness" of which Swann spoke. All it takes is a little uneasiness—some doubt, self-questioning, and the idea that I am indifferent to her—and I suffer at not seeing her and think of her day and night. But when it happens (as it did this morning) that I find her dejected, yielding, and ready to love me, then I suddenly regain my distance and stop loving her. This morning I felt she was ugly. Quite simply, I didn't like her—for the first time since I began to love her. But I know it's not true, and that even if it were, it wouldn't be important. The truth is that this morning I and not she was running the show—which forced her to love me, and me not to love her. It is a childishly simple psychological mechanism, which always functions in the same way.

Besides, this doesn't prevent her from being, as before, coquettish and duplicitous—innocent amid a whole structure of lies. I felt bad listening to her explain last Wednesday's incident. My recent rereading of Swann has once again shown me how much our comedy resembles all the comedies of love. Leni too is any old Odette, and even more am I any old Swann.

Saturday, 19 [September]

Long intricate dreams tonight, not much of which I can remember.

I am living in a kind of old house with a lot of other people—a boardinghouse?—in some place or other that is certainly not Bucharest. I am courting a girl and bring her into my room. Someone who seems to be her brother or lover, and who has been watching us from the balcony, enters the room and surprises us. A rather confused drama ensues. The girl and the boy both die, either murdered or by their own hand. I am responsible. I too will have either to be killed or to kill myself. But a woman intervenes, and in a long monologue (which seems to take place at the graveside of those two or at some monument) she tells how it was she who killed them—so that I am saved . . . and wake up.

The second dream was even more confused. I am in a large room with a huge number of people. As far as I can make out, it is a memorial meeting. A little later, things become clearer: it is the anniversary of the magazine *Nouvelles littéraires*. People are holding up large placards with writing on them, all over the vast ballroomlike hall.

A woman is giving a speech. She is interrupted by a man, who shouts out:

"Enough! You've talked too much about the Hebrews. I'm surprised you don't bring Niemirower here too."[9]

9. Iacob Niemirower: chief rabbi of the Federation of Romanian Jewish Communities until 1939.

At that moment an elderly bearded Jew who may actually be Niemirower protests. He takes out a book and starts to read a Jewish prayer. The heckler also takes out a book, from which he reads a Romanian prayer. In reality, nothing can be heard because of the surrounding racket, but one can see the two men reading with great fervor at the back of the hall, on a tall monumental staircase as in a pompous scene from an illustrated magazine.

Some heavy scuffles break out. I, together with a girl or a boy who has been sitting beside me, slip away from the crowd and quickly go home—to the house in my first dream. For a moment I anxiously wonder whether I shall find the door open. It is open. I prepare to run into my room, but I don't have time—because I wake up.

Evidently both dreams were much more complicated, but I cannot remember any more.

Tuesday, 22 [September]

The evening before last, on Sunday, I was at Maryse's to give a reading for Iancovescu. Marietta and Haig were also there, as well as the Nenişors, Ţoţa, and Ghiţă Ionescu.[1]

A good reading, which people found quite easy to follow. Iancovescu was boisterous in his enthusiasm:

"It's the most fantastic thing I've heard for the last forty years. It's a great moment in Romanian theatre. You don't realize what you've done. It's an honor for me to act in it. You don't realize the paths you are opening. What technique! What dialogue! What a wonder!"

I listened with amusement, quite calmly. I am getting to know him. Everything for him is fantastic, unique, epoch-making. Everything: his vineyard in Balcic, his dog, the sunset at Surtuchioi (which was indeed marvelous—I regret not having written in Balcic about that walk). I know how much Iancovescu's superlatives need to be toned down in order to gain a precise idea of what he wants to say. So I don't let myself be taken in by his excesses of enthusiasm. I know my play better than he does. But he really does seem to have liked it a lot, and an honest commitment can be read beneath his downpour of admiration. It is a point won.

His remarks about the third act are quite accurate; he certainly has a keen eye. The scene in which Leni and Ştefan have it out with each other is too explanatory in style. Crudely explanatory. He suggests a simple solution: cut everything up to the scene with Jef and Ştefan (which

1. Political scientist.

he liked a lot, I'm glad to say), write the planned scene with Bogoiu and the Major's fish, drop the first Leni–Ştefan scene, and then link it all up. A five-minute operation.

I don't see things that simply, however. The last act needs to be gone over more thoroughly.

All the readings I have done up to now (Sunday's was the third, not counting the earlier readings of Act One) have been enormously useful to me. They have fixed in my mind the things that work and those that don't work. It seems to me that an audience of five hundred will react no differently from the audience of ten I have dared face up to now.

In Act Two I shall modify the Bogoiu–Leni scene (in the way that Camil and Gulian indicated, with an exciting identity of views). The proof that this change is necessary is that, after the first act, Iancovescu said to me that Bogoiu is a character from the family of Fulda's Fool—which is quite wrong. Anyway, the change is simple and easy to make, more a problem of transcription than of actual transformation.

Act Two will remain almost untouched. The first scene splendidly indicates the change of atmosphere. Again my audience listened with great pleasure to the entrance of the two stowaways. (I shall only change something that Bogoiu says to the police—which doesn't work at all.) Iancovescu gave me here a simple but excellent suggestion.

I think I shall write the third act again, apart from the last four scenes. I'd need three to four days for that, and would go off to work in somewhere like Sinaia, or maybe Braşov or Sibiu. We'll see. I'm not in any hurry at the moment, though Iancovescu assures me that he'll be performing it by Christmas—and has offered to sign a contract straightaway to that effect. But there will be major difficulties. I have a feeling that he won't accept Marietta; that he would prefer Ţoţa. In that case I won't let him have the play. However much I need Iancovescu—and now, especially, I feel he is irreplaceable—I can't let him put on my play with Ţoţa, or with Ţăranu as Bogoiu and—just imagine—Mircea as Jef. I'd sooner wait a year.

Frankly speaking, a year's wait is the solution that would suit me best, because my ideal cast (Leni–Iancovescu–Timică) might be possible by then, and because I am now pretty fed up with the way the whole thing has been dragging on. I am longing to do something else: to read, to write a novel, to put behind me a joke which, I now realize, demands more of my time than it is worth. I feel disgusted when I see the proportions taken by something which has no right to be more than a trifle. Am I so unserious that I imagine this frolic in three acts has a right to preoccupy me, when each year in Paris, Vienna, and London thirty people write thirty comedies that are at least as enjoyable? No, it is time to be serious again.

But 1) I have no money; 2) I don't know if there will be a war or revolution by this time next year; 3) I don't know whether by next year a Jewish writer will still be able to put on a play, even at a private theatre. These are three reasons that spur me on.

I don't know what I shall do.

Friday, 25 [September]

Yesterday evening Mircea flared up in the middle of a fairly calm conversation about foreign policy and Titulescu,[2] suddenly raising his voice with that terrible violence that sometimes surprises me:

"Titulescu? He should be executed. Put in front of a machine-gun firing squad. Riddled with bullets. Strung up by the tongue."

"Why, Mircea?" I asked in surprise.

"Because he's committed treason, high treason. He's concluded a secret treaty with the Russians so that they can occupy Bukovina and Maramureş in the event of war."

"How do you know that?"

"General Condiescu told me."

"And is that enough? Don't you think it's a biased source? Don't you think it's based on fantasy?"

He stared at me with stupefaction, unable to grasp that anyone could doubt such a "truth." Then I heard him whisper to Nina:

"I wish I hadn't told him that."

He'd have liked to add: "because he's too blind to understand it."

The whole incident depressed me. As I write it down, I notice that I no longer have the nervous tension that I felt yesterday, the sense of irreparable discord.

He's a man of the right, with everything that implies. In Abyssinia he was on the side of Italy. In Spain on the side of Franco. Here he is for Codreanu. He just makes an effort—how awkwardly?—to cover this up, at least when he is with me. But sometimes he can't stop himself, and then he starts shouting as he did yesterday.

He, Mircea Eliade, has a blind faith in what *Universul* writes. His informant is Stelian Popescu[3]—and he has a blind faith in him. The most

---

2. Nicolae Titulescu: pro-Western minister of foreign affairs, target of an intense Iron Guard press campaign.
3. Lawyer and politician, director and owner of the newspaper *Universul*.

absurd and trivially tendentious news items find in him a gullible listener. And he has a naive way of getting worked up and raising his voice,
to spout—without so much as a smile—some baloney he has heard in
town at the editorial offices of *Vremea* or *Cuvântul*. Titulescu has sold us
to the Russians. Titulescu has given the Spanish Communists "twenty-
five airplanes ordered in France." If I shrug my shoulders in disbelief,
he looks sorrowfully at me and gently shakes his head, as at someone
completely lost to the truth.

I should like to eliminate any political reference from our discussions.
But is that possible? Street life impinges on us whether we like it or not,
and in the most trivial reflection I can feel the breach widening between
us.

Will I lose Mircea for no more reason than that? Can I forget everything about him that is exceptional, his generosity, his vital strength, his
humanity, his affectionate disposition, all that is youthful, childlike, and
sincere in him? I don't know. I feel awkward silences between us, which
only half shroud the explanations we avoid, because we each probably
feel them. And I keep having more and more disillusions, not least because he is able to work comfortably with the anti-Semitic *Vremea*, as if
there were nothing untoward about it.

Nevertheless I shall do everything possible to keep him.

Wednesday, 30 [September]

Was at Roman on Sunday and Monday. I left overwhelmed, exhausted,
feeling that I wouldn't be able to come back to life. Everything seemed
pointless and absurd. It was humiliating to think that it could be such a
problem for me to ring Leni or to take a call from her. The idea of
putting on my play struck me as trifling.

Now it has all passed. In a way, I have forgotten. This afternoon I
shall go to the law courts, this evening I shall go to the theatre, right
now I am writing in this notebook—and meanwhile Blecher's life at
Roman continues as I have seen it. Will I ever again have the nerve to
complain about anything? Will I ever again be so brazen as to have
caprices, bad moods, or feelings of irritation? He is living in the intimate company of death. It is not a vague, abstract death in the long
term, but his own death, precise, definite, known in detail like an ob-
ject.

What gives him the courage to live? What keeps him going? He is
not even in despair. I swear I don't understand. How many times have
I been on the verge of tears when I looked at him. At night I could hear

him groaning and crying out in his room—and I felt there was someone else in the house apart from us, a someone who was death, fate, or whatever. I came away feeling shattered, bewildered.

If things had a penalty attached to them, I would not go on with my life as I have lived it up to now. I wouldn't be able to. But I forget—and return to the unconscious existence of someone in reasonably good health.

Wednesday, 7 October

I am beginning to miss Leni again. I held out for a couple of weeks, but each day I feel that I am giving way to my longing to see her. I hover around the telephone, fall asleep thinking of her, dream about her, wake up thinking of her. I know it's stupid—I have only to read through this journal to see how stupid it is.

I met her Monday night around half past one, as she was getting out of a car with Froda outside their house. I didn't even see her properly. I spoke indifferently enough; I didn't feel in the grip of emotion. Later, after we had parted, all the memories and expectations opened up again.

I have to be rational and firm. But will I be?

I don't know what the Iancovescu solution will do for the play. It is not at all serious. And this whole business has tired me. I'm a little weary of my manuscript. When I think of it, it seems conceited, cheap, frivolous, irritatingly hearty, compromisingly facile.

In the last few days I have reread some pages of *De două mii de ani*. Will I ever again write anything that serious?

There's a Milstein concert this evening. Maybe I'll come away feeling clearer in the head, more in control of myself.

11 October. Sunday

Celebrations in honor of Stelian Popescu at the Roman Arena. Perpessicius[4] said to me yesterday evening: "A day of mourning." And he added: "It's the most shameful day in Romania since the war."

Maybe I shouldn't be downcast. Maybe, on the contrary, I should be glad that the whole Romanian right, the whole of "nationalism," is re-

4. Literary critic.

grouping around Stelian Popescu. It defines it as something disreputable, and in a sense is even consoling (from a very lofty vantage point).

Nae Ionescu sent him a congratulatory telegram yesterday, on behalf of *Cuvântul*. Should I feel depressed? Not really. I ought to go and tell him: "Now, professor, there's no longer any doubt that your politics are wrong. Only a terrible mistake could put you side by side with Stelian Popescu."

I wonder whether Nae Ionescu at least does not feel rotten deep down inside.

The Romanian Writers' Association also sent a message of support. Neither Tudor Vianu nor Mircea signed it. But Mircea, in his naive way, thought that he was thereby showing solidarity with Nae—which earned him a serious rebuke when Nae found out. For a moment I considered resigning from the Writers' Association, on the grounds that I can't associate myself with celebrations in honor of a paper that insults Arghezi.[5] But if Arghezi himself does not resign . . .

Sad, sad times. What a wave of triviality in which everyone is drowning—out of hypocrisy, cowardice, and self-interest!

Will the day come when it is possible to speak openly about these dark days? I'm sure it will, absolutely sure. I should like still to be here when it does.

Radu Cioculescu[6] told me yesterday evening that he has broken off relations with a family of friends, because the wife—a schoolteacher—signed a manifesto for *Universul*.

This reminded me that he, Radu Cioculescu, also refused to accept tickets for and attend the concerts of the Berlin orchestra this summer, because he couldn't agree to any contact with a Hitlerite institution.

A strange man. Probably the only radical Romanian there is.

Dined yesterday evening at the Continental, with Perpessicius, Șerban Cioculescu,[7] Vladimir Streinu, Pompiliu Constantinescu, and Octav Șuluțiu. Together we constituted an association of literary critics. Perhaps we shall bring out a magazine. I'm not really sure what will come of it.

I'm so remote from all that.

---

5. Tudor Arghezi: major Romanian poet.
6. Literary critic, translator of Proust, and brother of Șerban Cioculescu.
7. Literary critic, brother of Radu Cioculescu.

Wednesday, 14 [October]

Yesterday evening, at the Foundation, Davidescu[8] explained to Perpessicius and Cicerone Theodorescu that Jews don't know Romanian. One of his arguments was to quote the metaphor of a "crammed goose" from a book of mine.

Cicerone told me this little story, and when Davidescu approached me a little later to wish me good evening, I said to him:

"I'm sorry, Mr. Davidescu, but you know I never wrote anything like that—at least I don't remember it."

The discussion then continued quite amusingly for half an hour or so. I am too lazy to reproduce it in full. I get the impression that Davidescu suffers from a case of syphilis with anti-Semitic symptoms. He has a disturbing look in his eyes.

Back home later in the evening, I realized that I had been mistaken about the "goose." So today I am sending the following note to Davidescu:

"Dear Mr. Davidescu, After I left you yesterday evening, I went home and searched for some two hours through my books to be sure whether I had or had not ever used that compromising image which you recalled with such fierce criticism. I hasten to inform you that you were right. The comparison in question can indeed be found in a book of mine. I had forgotten. You will easily find it in *Femei*, second edition, page 27, line 17.

"As a colleague, I am pleased to do you the favor of communicating the exact sentence. Here it is: 'She breathed with difficulty and rolled her eyes a few times, as crammed geese are wont to do.'

"May I also draw to your attention the fact that this is the method by which an excellent foie gras may be obtained.

"I should have no rest if I did not hasten to correct my regrettably poor memory. I am delighted that, in so doing, I am able to restore one of the fundamental arguments in your political and critical system.

"I remain as always your admiring . . ."

Nae Ionescu's telegram appeared in *Universul*—printed between others from Trandafirescu-Nămăești[9] and Muche.[1] that is no mere coincidence. It is a punishment.

8. Nicolae Davidescu: journalist and poet.
9. Journalist at *Universul*.
1. Ion Muche: anti-Semitic journalist at *Porunca Vremii*.

Dem. Theodorescu,[2] whom I met on Monday evening at the National, said to me:

"Yes, Sunday was the most wretched day in the political life of Romania. But you don't know, Mr. Sebastian, what a profound disgust has come over me; you would have to be more familiar with Stelian Popescu."

"All right. But then why did you also sign the congratulatory telegram?"

"What can I do? That's life!"

Friday, 16 [October]

I am at a dangerous point with regard to my play: I am beginning to like the third act. After violently disliking it for quite a while, after thinking at readings (once at Marietta's, another time at Maryse's) that it would be a certain disaster, after blindly agreeing to every suggested alteration—from Gulian or Haig or Iancovescu—now I am beginning to like it!

I would prefer to change only a few details. I'd simplify a few scenes and eliminate some dialogue—but leave intact the scenario, the unfolding of the plot, the general tone of the act. Only the first and the last scene should be revised more thoroughly: the first, to introduce Bogoiu and to justify the absence of the Major and Madame Vintilă; the last, because it is really too hurried, as I knew from the first moment. Otherwise I am inclined to leave the third act as it is—even if in that case Iancovescu refuses to go on with it.

I prefer to make a mistake myself than to have others make one. As I have written it—and not they—I think I have more chance of seeing the truth. I should also mention my inability to redo my own manuscripts. Didn't it happen like that with *Orașul cu salcîmi*?

In today's *Credința*, Manoliu denounces me for working at the Foundation and naturally calls for my dismissal. The only thing that surprises me is that the attack has come so late.

A musical evening. From Radio Bucharest, on discs, Bach's *Double Violin Concerto in D Minor*. Later, from Warsaw, a symphony in G minor by Mozart, and Beethoven's *Violin Concerto*. I thought József Szigeti was exceptional on the violin. And my radio sounded clearer and warmer than ever before! Now I am waiting for a Beethoven cello sonata from Vienna, which should start any minute now. Then to bed.

2. Writer and journalist.

Sunday, 18 [October]

Twenty-nine years old. I feel neither happy nor sad—conscious that I still have some things to do, for which I have to go on living. Otherwise nothing. But I made a serious effort to greet this day with some solemnity, as a lucky day. I have such a need to create for myself little superstitions that augur well. I drank champagne at Mircea's. Everything was fairly awkward.

It was a very nice morning—a marvelous day in a glorious October. That too I put down to my birthday. I also took the Enescu[3] concert at the Ateneu as a good sign. I am most willing to be convinced that I am not a complete and utter goner.

This afternoon, a bungled visit to Leni backstage.

Then a visit to Nae (also half bungled).

Finally the cinema and a group dinner—ending in a painful political argument with Mircea.

But more about all this tomorrow.

I am starting a new year of life—but am I destined really to take on anything else?

Tuesday, 20 [October]

The first two acts came back from the typist this evening. I read them for typing errors, and this has tired me. Everything seems lacking in fun, though it's true that I'm not in the best of "humors."

Thursday, 22 [October]

Yesterday evening I took the first two acts, typed, to Iancovescu. He told me today that he had read the first.

"I'm convinced," he said, "that you are in love with Marietta. A role like that can be written only for a woman you love very much. It's the nicest possible female role—the nicest but also the hardest. Not even Ventura could act it. When I told Țoța that I thought you were crazy about Marietta, he told me that he didn't think so, but that you might be in love with Leni."

This evening I ate at Mircea's, and he told me some amusing details about yesterday's party at Polihroniade's house.[4] Zelea Codreanu,[5] whom

3. George Enescu: well-known Romanian composer.
4. Mihai Polihroniade: Iron Guard journalist and theorist.
5. Corneliu Zelea Codreanu, the principal leader of the Iron Guard.

everyone calls "Captain," was also there. Marietta Sadova had come with Codreanu's book and she asked him to sign it.

"What is your name?" he asked.

"Marietta Sadova," she replied, sure of herself. And since he didn't seem any the wiser, she added:

". . . from the National Theatre."

"Mrs. or Miss?" he asked further, just as we do at the Day of the Book.

I think it was a bit of a blow for poor little Marietta—though (still according to Mircea) it didn't stop her from looking at the "Captain" and listening to him all the time with an ecstatic smile. It is the same ecstatic smile with which she looks at Aristide Blank. Can I say that Marietta is a hypocrite? No. But she's a strange mixture of harsh practicality and openhanded sincerity.

Another detail, as moving and as ridiculous. Haig brought along his whole oeuvre (poems, essays) for the "Captain" and wrote a special dedication for him.

After Codreanu left, Marietta and Haig said in one voice that they had lived through a magnificent day. "Colossal" was their exact term, I think.

In 1932 Haig was a Communist.

A snippet from Sunday's conversation with Nae:

"Look, I'm finished—a broken-down failure of a man. My life divides into two: before 5 July 1933, and since 5 July 1933. Until that day I was a strong person. Since then I've been nothing."

What happened on 5 July 1933? I think it was the day he broke up with Maruca Cantacuzino.[6]

At last we have got ourselves a house. May the gods keep smiling on me!

Sunday, 25 [October]

There is something of Mme. Verdurin in Marietta—not a lot, and not with the same comic violence, but it is there. This morning at the concert she said to me after Enescu had played the Brahms concerto:

"Aren't you feeling a little ill? It has made me ill."

And she had a happy look on her face; she was suffering—almost swooning—from happiness.

6. A Romanian princess.

She is very dear to me, but one day I'd like to capture her studied social tactics in a character in a novel. For example, what subtle intentions could be deciphered from her behavior at this evening's reception at the Blanks, when she obliged me to read the play again!

Tuesday, 27 [October]

Again at Roman, Blecher spoke to me of a woman from Bucharest who knows and "admires" my books. Two years ago, when *De două mii de ani* was published, she wrote to him that she had discovered an author "more intelligent than Gide." Last year, at a concert, she sat next to me and wanted to speak to me, but in the end did not dare. Her name is Maria Ghiolu—the wife of an engineer.[7] They seem to be remarkably wealthy.

The day before yesterday, Blecher sent a letter asking me to phone Mrs. Ghiolu—but he also recommended a whole number of precautions. I should ring on Tuesday or Wednesday, not any other day, at eleven in the morning and not any other time.

I rang her just now. A weak, timid voice, whispering more than speaking, as if afraid that someone in the next room would hear. She gave me an appointment for Thursday at six, in the lobby of the Athénée Palace.[8] That's another "mystery" in this story. We'll see.

I leave at one for Galaţi, where I'm due to speak on Léon Blum as a literary figure.

Yesterday evening at the Dalles Hall, a first-rate chamber concert with the orchestra from Berlin. A lot of Mozart—among other things, the first and the last movement of the *Kleine nachtmusik*. But I was especially moved by a "sinfonia concertante" for violin and viola, its melancholy supremely Mozartian.

But in recent weeks the musical side of things has been much richer than that. I don't have the patience to note it all down.

Thursday, 5 November

For the last ten days, since we began moving into our new home at Strada Antim 45, I have been leading a disorganized life—much more disorganized than before. I do absolutely nothing, yet I feel overwhelmed by things to do. I am worn out, and wait as if for some well-earned hol-

7. Friend of Sebastian's and wife of Stavri Ghiolu.
8. Famous hotel in downtown Bucharest.

iday after months of effort. Everything happening to me takes place some-where outside, as if it did not concern me. I feel as if I am dirty and dusty from a long journey, impatient to reach somewhere where I can brush or change my clothes, take a bath, become a different man. But I am not going anywhere, not expecting anything; nothing is awaiting me.

I look closely at myself (not too closely, though, out of prudence, cowardice, or fear that I may have to bear all the consequences) and tell myself that I am falling apart. In this state of disintegration I have the (semiconscious) stupidity to get involved with people who, not knowing me, "press forward" with a good faith that ought to make me feel ashamed. For example, why did I take that caper with Cella Seni as far as I did?[9] She's a nice girl, who put a lot of herself into this "incipient love"—and now I drop her with the most stupid indifference. Am I really so irre-sponsible in my actions with other people?

I am ashamed—I swear that I am ashamed.

And I am so lacking in energy, good sense, and manliness that I feel everything is going badly—not because I'm a wreck, but because . . . I don't yet have a telephone. Yes, however funny it seems, I wait for them to reconnect me, with the feeling that that will sort out everything.

What will stop me sinking? I don't know. Is there still anything, can anything still happen to pull me out of this?

Friday, 6 [November]

Had lunch at Mircea's yesterday. A discussion of foreign policy—as calm as could be. I tried to speak dispassionately, as if it were a matter of pre-cise facts, not of opinions, impressions, and attitudes.

I especially remember one thing that Mircea said. These were his exact words:

"I prefer a little Romania, with some of its provinces lost but with its bourgeoisie and elite saved, rather than a proletarian Greater Roma-nia."

He was calm. He didn't seem to realize the enormity of what he was saying.

Iancovescu has finally announced the next premiere. It will be a trans-lation—*Nine Thousand* somethings—with Maria Mohor, produced by Popa. Not a word about my play. No phone call, no explanation, no apology.

---

9. The writer Cella Serghi, wife of Alfio Seni.

So the Iancovescu–Marietta solution has fallen through, without any assistance from me. Although it was a solution on which I was never all that keen, the truth is that I did nothing at all to sabotage it. At one point, indeed, I let myself be drawn right into it and did everything possible for things to work out. I hope Marietta won't have reason to blame me now—even if the play is performed by Leni. But will it be performed?

I saw Leni the evening before last, when I went out with her and Froda. It was the third time I had met her since the summer. She is lovely and obnoxious, just as I have always known her. I danced with her at the bar—and then suffered like a fool because Lăzăroneanu[1] (with whom I bet she has slept, is sleeping, or will sleep) came over to our table. I simply cannot start those senseless torments all over again. In the end I was quite all right for those twenty days in which I didn't see her or speak to her on the phone. So now I should begin another twenty days or so of silence.

"In principle" we agreed that I should read her the play, but she has to ring me to fix a time for the reading—and she certainly won't do that. So things will again be left at that for I don't know how long.

One evening I went to the Gambrinus[2] with Camil. I think it was Monday, after the Münzer concert. We spoke about Romanian literature. I recall without smiling his statement:

"Dear Sebastian, there is only one writer today who is capable of producing a great novel—and I am he."

I find it impossible to explain his candor: he is such an intelligent man, and yet so profoundly naive.

Wednesday, 11 [November]

My bad memory for music is extraordinary. Just now (11 p.m.) I was listening to Beethoven's fourth symphony and, apart from a few phrases in the scherzo, I no longer remember anything, even though I have surely heard the symphony several times in my life. The last three weeks or so have been a real musical feast. Enescu, Münzer, and Hubermann concerts. How many things I've heard! The violin concertos by Brahms, Beethoven, and Bach; Beethoven's *Romance in F Major*, Chausson's *Poème*, Beethoven's *Third Symphony* and *Coriolan Overture*, a Brahms symphony (I don't remember which one), Mozart's *Jupiter Symphony*.

---

1. Ionel Lăzăroneanu: lawyer with literary inclinations.
2. Pub in downtown Bucharest, famous for its beer.

The *Kreuzer Sonata*, an Enescu sonata, a Franck sonata (*"surtout jouée par Enesco"*), a Brahms sonata (once with Enescu, a second time with Hubermann), the *Spring Sonata* with Münzer at the piano, two Scarlatti sonatas, Beethoven's fifteen *Eroica Variations*, and a large amount of Chopin.

Now, though very tired, I am waiting for a tremendous program from Stuttgart, due to begin in five minutes: Bach (*Concerto for Flute, Violin, and Harpsichord in A Minor*), Haydn (*Piano Sonata in B Minor*), Schubert (*Rondo in A Major for Violin and String Quartet*), Mozart (*Concertone in C for Two Violins and Orchestra*).

Saturday, 14 [November]

It has been perhaps one of the last magnificent days of autumn. I went to a soccer match at the O.N.E.F. (Venus against CFR), not for the match but for the scenery, which I guessed in advance would be gleaming. I wasn't wrong. A weary, powdered, tender light—and far off a bright, steamy, silvery mist from which the city detached itself in an unreal way, as in a painted canvas or a mounted photograph. And how many colors! I didn't know there were so many red houses in Bucharest. From the stadium they look as if they are made of toy bricks. And the leafless trees jut out of the mist as from a damp exhalation of their own. Everything was very delicately drawn, but with an explosive wealth of color. The red grounds, the multicolored billboards, the still-green grass, the football shirts mingling black, white, and blue, the huge crowd: it was all quite dizzying. At the beginning of the second half, the referee blew his whistle for a minute's silence in memory, I think, of a foreign player who died recently. Suddenly there was a massive silence—a silence of some twenty thousand people. The noise of the city could just be heard in the distance.

"She's sleeping with someone called Berlescu, a kid of around twenty," Camil said at table today, with a studied disinterest that didn't conceal his premeditation and, perhaps, satisfaction. I'd like this incident to help me forget everything once and for all.

Monday, 16 [November]

Had a long telephone conversation this morning with Mrs. Ghiolu; it lasted more than half an hour. She said some things full of childish admiration, which gave me quite a lot of pleasure. She has recently read *Cum am devenit huligan* and was "won over" by it.

"What you write frightens me a little, as if you must have the strength to dominate other people. I think you exert an influence over them from which there is no escape. And you are such a self-possessed man! *Vous êtes probablement d'une sécheresse de coeur*...[3] I'd so much like to be your friend. I have always dreamed of friendship with a man, but a pure, *loyal* friendship. Do you think that's possible? I keep thinking of you, and I've spoken of it with my husband and my friends. Do you have time for us to be friends? Do you want us to be friends?"

She spoke to me in the same (or almost the same) way that Leni did two years ago. Maryse too spoke to me like that. So did Dorina (a few levels down). And when each has got to know me, a disappointed indifference has been the result. The only one who keeps at it is Maryse, though she too is flagging.

On Saturday evening, Enescu played a sonata by Veracini (enchanting: I heard it last year with Thibaud, but I'd completely forgotten it), a sonata in A minor by Bach (absolutely wonderfully played), and a sonata by Mozart. The evening before, Hubermann played the Franck sonata. I'm tired of so much music, but it's been my only consolation recently.

Saturday, 21 [November]

"Wendy and Julie" are two young Englishwomen who were dancing and singing at Maxim's until a few days ago, when the owner terminated their contract and left them lost and penniless in a Bucharest where they don't know a soul. The British consul sent them to Roman—and Roman has passed them on to me. I hope that I'll eventually get quite high compensation for them—something like 25,000 lei—with the help of Comarnescu and Sadoveanu[4] at the Theatre Board.

The whole story has been quite fun. I've met a whole series of fancy men, pimps, and artistic "agents" swarming around "Wendy and Julie"; I've been behind the scenes in the bar, read an employment contract, learned how the establishment is run. It's quite alluring. Wendy, whose real name is Flora Moss, was born in 1911. She has a fiancé in Copenhagen, a policeman by the name of Gunard. I saw a photo of him yesterday evening when I went up to her room. In civilian clothes he looks like a famous sportsman, especially with the long pipe dangling from his teeth. In Danish police uniform he is even more impressive. "For my dear Wendy, for always, Gunard" he wrote on the edge of the picture.

Wendy is slim, with smaller breasts than I have ever seen before, nat-

---

3. You probably have a coldness of heart...
4. Ion Marin Sadoveanu: writer.

urally reddish hair, and a snub nose. She has a childlike gaiety that I find enchanting. Yesterday evening I had promised to stay with her. Of course I didn't stay—and I left her feeling sad, like a child who has been promised an outing to the cinema and then sent to bed.

Julie (Wendy calls her "Miss Julie," which I think she picked up at the bar) is rather plainer, but also very English. Her fiancé, Reginald, lives in London and works as a salesman in a china shop.

Both speak French correctly but with an irresistible accent. As soon as they have the money, they want to go to Sofia to take up a contract. I regret that I can't spend more time talking with them. But it's not possible—Wendy is in love with me. She explained in all seriousness the difference between a *camarade* (stress on the first syllable, pronounced like a Romaniană) and an *ami*. "*Avec un camarade on ne couche pas. Avec un ami on couche.*"[5]

Went to quite a homely little tea party yesterday at Mrs. Ghiolu's. Her house seemed gorgeous, but I didn't look at it all that closely. Entertaining company. On my right, a daughter of Stelian Popescu's (Mrs. Popescu-Necșești), who said that she knows me from the Criterion and that she had asked Mrs. Ghiolu to invite me sometime just with her. Opposite, a youthful Princess Cantacuzino. As I was leaving, I heard that she is very left-wing, being the daughter of Labaiyre, the governor of the Banque de France.

As to Mrs. Ghiolu, I thought her less interesting than at our first meeting at the Athénée Palace, when I was really struck by her. (For I am so plebeian and naive that the event seemed to me really extraordinary.)

She is a "Jeni" type of woman: dark, plumpish, with shaved eyebrows that irritate me. I think that greater repose in her appearance would suit her better, that she is made to be serious, attentive, and submissive. She doesn't have that restless, aggressive quivering that is a feature of slim blondes.

But is it not remarkable that this rich society woman, with a young, handsome, athletic, and wealthy husband, can have a passion for Blecher? And is her timid admiration for someone like me not moving and child-like?

Things will work out with Cella Seni because of my sovereign laziness.

"You are too vile for me not to end up loving you," she said to me the evening before last, as we were on our way back from the Philharmonic concert. That's almost a definition of love. Is it not for the same

5. You don't sleep with a comrade; you do with a friend.

reason—because she is so "vile"—that I love Leni and love her so help-lessly?

It's been a week of which I feel ashamed. Whole days wasted, dizzy nights. I have done nothing and let myself be taken to any occasion that got me out on the town.

Tomorrow I leave for the baptism of Silvia's child in Brăila, but then I am determined to force myself to do a week of serious work. I'd like to write a book, and for that maybe I should go somewhere over Christmas. But I have so many vague plans for Christmas! From time to time I feel a piercing call which I do not yet want to accept, not yet—and I would like so much never to be forced to accept it. It is something for which I pray to God with the last remnant of my hopes.

Monday, 23 [November]

Yesterday evening from Stuttgart, Bach's *Second Brandenburg Concerto* and Mozart's *Piano Concerto in D Minor* (with Edwin Fischer).

Brăila has never before seemed so sad, provincial, godforsaken. The street-car stopped for nearly fifteen minutes on the corner of Strada Unirea, waiting to "cross." Then, on Strada Galați, it didn't move at all because of repairs to the line—and we had to get off and change. In the town center the clock was stopped at 5:20, though it was 10:30 in the morning, and a little farther the clock on the Greek church showed 11:20. A November cold, few people, old houses—not one new person, not one new building, empty shops.

I went with Petrică to the port, and this prevented me from being emotional. But it was still a pleasure to see again the ships, the willows, the heavy chains, the cables. Everything in the town seemed detached from a long time ago, from a previous life.

Thursday, 26 [November]

Yesterday evening Rosetti[6] showed me a letter from General Zwiedenek,[7] written on behalf of the Queen to the Foundation. In it he asked about the conditions under which a novel of hers might be published in translation.

6. Alexandru Rosetti: director of the Royal Foundations, Sebastian's close friend and benefactor.
7. Eugen Zwiedenek: general, head of the military staff of Queen Maria, and under Ion Antonescu head of the government agency in charge of the Aryanization of Jewish properties.

"Until now Her Majesty's works have been printed by Editura Adevărul, which has also made an offer for the present novel.

"Considering, however, that the Romanian national sentiments of that publishing house are not assured, Her Majesty Queen Maria has instructed me to approach your good self."

Literally!

Prodan[8] called Marietta and Lilly to his office in the last few days to rebuke them for verbally obstructing the work of the National Theatre. Among other things he said:

"So what do you want—that I should resign and pack my bags? That Mr. Mihail Sebastian should be appointed in my place? Well, that's not going to happen. It can't happen, because he's a Jew."

Impossible to explain that sudden outburst. But I can't say it doesn't amuse me.

A tooth extraction has kept me indoors since yesterday evening. I can see that I've lost the taste for reading and writing, and my staying at home—which would once have delighted me—now gets on my nerves.

I'm in a grey mood, neither expectant nor despondent, without either longings or loves.

At the Brailowsky recital on Monday evening, I was introduced to Cella Delavrancea, who happened to have the seat next to mine.

"I imagined you to be different. More lively and dark. I was looking at you just now and you seemed like a schoolboy. And you ought to have had a dark complexion. Your writing is so self-assured, so firm. . . ."

I smiled wearily. How many times have I been told the same things?

Tuesday, 1 December

When I bumped into Camil Baltazar[9] at Alcalay on Saturday evening, he said to me:

"If you don't write a study of my work in the *Revista Fundațiilor* in the next three months, I'll never speak to you again."

Just like that.

Domnișoara Christina has been out for three days or so. Mircea is disgusted. He thinks that the bookshops are persecuting him, that the publishers are scheming against him, that Ocneanu is making fun of him,

8. Paul Prodan: director of the Romanian National Theatre.
9. Novelist.

that Mişu at Cartea Românească is full of perfidy. Ciornei didn't put his book in the window. Alcalay did, but it's not visible. Cartea Românească is sabotaging it.

Does it just seem so, or have I really never had such worries? I don't say it with pride, but I have never asked anyone to write an article, never engaged in literary politics, cultivated anyone's favor, or tried to evade anyone's hostility. Maybe it all has to do with my old tendency to laziness, but to some extent it is also because I am aware that my destiny as a writer—if I have one—will be decided a long way from all these little "games."

Whether from pride or from laziness, my indifference is the same—at least in the literary field.

Friday, 11 December

I have just come back from the Philharmonic, where I heard Franck's *Piano Concerto in G Major* and his *Symphonic Variations*, with Arthur Rubinstein. Schumann's *Fourth Symphony* (which I heard this evening with a pleasure it has never given me before) and Richard Strauss's *Till Eulenspiegel*. Altogether a fine evening of music.

Yesterday, at the Ateneu, Bach's *Christmas Oratorio*.

On Monday evening, Casals: Beethoven's *Variations on a Theme by Handel*, the Boccherini concerto, a Bach suite, and three chorales.

Apart from these, more Enescu: the third Brahms sonata, a Schumann sonata, one by Mozart, and one by Bach.

Nothing is happening to me except for music.

A lot of incidents—but nothing significant. I'm not desperate: I am numb and try not to feel anything. The days pass—that's all.

Saturday, 12 [December]

Will I write the book I have been thinking about for some time, without really knowing what might come of it and where it might lead me?

"For some time": to be precise, since the 18th of October, my birthday! When I left Mircea's that day, to buy a couple of bottles of champagne, I suddenly had the picture of a road accident into which I should have liked to be drawn.[1] I could see the first chapter with a wealth of detail so pressing that I thought that, when I got home, I would be un-

---

1. The first reference to what would become Sebastian's novel *Accidentul*.

able to do anything other than write, as if under the command of an imperious voice. Let's call that inspiration.

I did try to write—I don't remember whether it was that evening or a few days later—but it didn't work out.

Nevertheless, since then I have kept thinking of the possibility of such a book. There are a few little things, a few little ideas, that have started to come together around that first image—and to stick to it.

For example, my walk with Cella Seni—the evening she stole an apple on Strada Acadamiei (which made me feel younger as a reflex)—made me feel again like writing a short story. Disheartened as I am, it may be that I shall find some joy in that. It will be a short novel or a long short story, a *récit*. Maybe I'll start on it over the Christmas holidays. But I'd need to get out of Bucharest—and I wonder whether I'll find enough money for that.

Wednesday, 16 [December]

Yesterday evening at the Vişoianus,[2] Marietta called for a legal ban on all foreign films.

"Let them speak Romanian!" she said with a certain violence. I thought she was joking. I pointed out how barbarous are films with a sound track in a language other than the one in which they were filmed.

Marietta grew pale and raised her voice, though it was a kind of "head voice," somewhat dulled by choking as she seemed about to burst into tears.

"This scandal should be stopped once and for all. We are in Romania, and they should speak Romanian."

It seemed tiresome to enter into such a discussion, so I merely said with an irony that she failed to grasp:

"Marietta, my dear, you are in the most disturbing phase of nationalism."

I don't know whether she understood my allusion to her adventure last Friday, when she recited some verse at an Iron Guard festival ("under the spiritual patronage of the legionaries fighting Marxism in Spain") held to raise funds for their "Green House."[3] Nor do I know whether, if she did understand my allusion, she would have been bothered by it. The poor girl feels that she can't hope for anything better under the

2. Constantin Vişoianu: diplomat and politician, close friend of Sebastian's, after World War II one of the leaders of the Romanian emigration to the United States.
3. Iron Guard headquarters.

present regime. Maybe there would be room for a Leni Riefenstahl in a state run by Zelea Codreanu. Anyway, Marietta has put herself forward.

Literature. Anişoara Odeanu has sent me her novel: "A book that ought to have at least ten epigraphs from *De două mii de ani*." In fact, her manuscript contained not ten but two epigraphs. But Camil insisted that she get rid of them. "It's not good for there to be too many epigraphs," he said. Indeed, one is enough—especially as it is from *Ultima noapte*.[4] . . . What a delightful man Camil is!

Saturday, 19 [December]

Two branches of lilies . . . from Cella.

I think it's a year today—that is, precisely fifty-two weeks—since I sent two branches of lilies to someone else—to her.

Sunday, 20 [December]

Projects: 1) Leave for Breaza on the 2nd of January, stay there until the 20th, and start writing a novel for publication in March or April; 2) Immediately start the necessary reading for the first volume of "The Romanian Novel," start drafting it in February–March for publication on the Day of the Book; 3) Discuss with Ocneanu the publication of a volume of chronicles and essays, perhaps to come out in February or at Easter.

This morning at the Philharmonic, Wilhelm Kempff: Mozart, Beethoven (*Concerto in E-flat*). Thursday evening the Brahms concerto. This evening at nine I'll try to pick up Breslau: the *Christmas Oratorio*.

Wednesday, 30 [December]

Came back yesterday evening from Roman, where I had been for the second time to see Blecher.

Maybe it's because I'm getting used to it, but he seemed better than last time. If I lived close by him, I'd probably end up thinking that his tragedy was normal. There are no tragedies lived on a daily basis. I know a little about that from my own life. After twenty-four hours you start getting used to it—that is, accepting it.

4. Camil Petrescu's novel *Ultima noapte de dragoste, prima noapte de război* (Last Night of Love, First Night of War).

As for Blecher, he is much more downcast. He spoke to me of his death, which he thinks is close at hand.

"I tell myself that Jules Renard died in 1911," he said. "At a distance, death becomes so inconsequential. I just have to imagine that I too died a long time ago, in 1911. I'm not scared of death. Then I'll rest and sleep. Ah, how well I'll stretch out, how well I'll sleep! Listen, I've begun to write a novel. But I don't feel that I absolutely must complete it. If I die first, I don't think I'll even regret not having finished it. What a minor thing literature is for me, and how little of my time it takes up! Recently I've thought of taking my own life. But it's difficult: I don't have the means. The simplest would be to hang myself—but I'd still have to bang a nail into the wall, and then Olimpia would come and I wouldn't be able to take it any further. I asked her to buy me some caustic soda on some pretext or other—but my parents didn't allow her to. How stupid I was not to buy a revolver when I could still walk and buy myself one."

The next day—that is, yesterday morning—he apologized to me for what he had said.

"Please forgive me. I don't know what came over me. I don't like to complain. I have a horror of sentimentality."

What move and gladden me most are his undepleted reserves of innocence, humor, and exuberance. With what goodwill and application did he play a number of tangos and foxtrots for me on his accordion! Was he striving to find a joy lost beyond recovery?

He told me of various games last summer, when Geo Bogza[5] came to visit him. They played boats, for example, Blecher giving the signal for departure while Bogza hauled his bed along. They slapped a notice up on the wall: "It is forbidden to climb up to the mast and spit into the machine room."

He showed me a photograph album (Solange, Ernest, Creața, scenes from Berk, from Leysin, from Tekirghiol[6]). I had to stop myself from crying at a picture of him as a splendid young man of seventeen. "*J'étais beau gosse, hein?*"[7]

I left at four o'clock. But why did I not have the courage to embrace him, to say more things, to make a brotherly gesture—something to show that he isn't alone, that he isn't absolutely and irredeemably alone?

Alone is what he is, though.

5. Writer and journalist.
6. Lake near the Black Sea.
7. I was a handsome kid, no?

This morning Mrs. Ghiolu burst out crying on the phone as I told her about Blecher. I still don't really know what there was between them. I think she is ruled by her memory of him: it haunts and frightens her at the same time that it is a source of consolation. For his part, he loved her and still does love her, and he suffers because of her absence. But he is too proud to say anything.

"One day I ran off to Bucharest even though I was ill with a temperature of 40 degrees [104 F.], using all kinds of ruses just in order to see her. And she hasn't made it to Roman once in two years. Would married life be a worse illness than mine?"

While I was on the phone today conveying Blecher's greetings to Ocneanu, Petru Manoliu simply took the receiver out of my hand and said to me:

"A happy new year, Mr. Mihail Sebastian!"

I didn't have the presence of mind to hang up. That kid's mad—or is he just a character?

Dined on Sunday evening at the Cina with Soare Z. Soare.[8] How many illuminating, amusing, and spontaneous things he told me about Leni! I listened and was secretly surprised at my forbearance. I think I can honestly say that it diverted me more than it saddened me.

She makes eighty thousand lei a month at Sică's[9]—for which she sleeps with him, on Froda's advice and with his complicity. Soare and Mușatescu[1] have nicknamed Sică: Alexandrescu-Farado, because each day he buys her a flower from the Farado shop.

She has slept with someone called Walter from Via [?]. She has slept with Izu Brănișteanu—and sleeps with him whenever *Rampa* needs some publicity. She slept with Elly Roman in Vienna while Froda discreetly walked up and down the street outside the hotel. She used to have orgies with Froda and Blank. Then with Froda and Wieder.

In general, Froda has acted docilely through all her love affairs—and has encouraged or even incited them when some profit was to be had. He has been less patient when her caprices have not involved money. He threw Coco Danielescu out of the theatre (the actor who committed suicide a year ago) because he had also slept with Leni.

So who hasn't the dear girl slept with?

I never realized before how much she resembles Odette and Rachel.

8. Theatre producer.
9. Sică Alexandrescu, theatre producer.
1. Teodor Mușatescu, playwright.

But I think I am ceasing to resemble Swann. In June 1935 I'd have screamed with pain if someone had told me all this. In those days I screamed for much less. But now I don't think I'm doing too badly—in this respect, at least.

I keep delaying a note here about the various things that have happened recently between Cella[2] and Camil. They seem to me sensational for an understanding of him. I won't note them down this evening, either. Tomorrow or another time—especially as in the meantime there may be fresh details, priceless incidents.

2. Cella Serghi.

1937

Saturday, 2 January 1937

For the first time I am writing the figures for the new year: 1937. I spent New Year's Eve without emotion, without despair and, it would seem, without any hopes.

I drank a lot, but with no real gusto. The party at Mircea's was quite drab. We used to pass from one year to the next with greater ceremony. Is this another sign of aging?

On Thursday evening—the last day of the year—I visited Nae for the first time in a long while. There was nothing symbolic in this, though.

I wonder whether Nae is not losing control of himself completely. Is it an attack of megalomania, a case of pride accentuated by defeats, or quite simply a phase of acute mysticism? On such occasions in the past I used to find him quite colorful. Now he's beginning to worry me. For the whole of the hour I spent there, he spoke of nothing but foreign policy.

"So, do you like the way the Serbs have been plotting against us?" Those were his opening words. "When I shouted for three years that we should come to a direct understanding with the Bulgarians, no one wanted to listen. Now we have the Serbs reaching an agreement with them— and we're left high and dry. I told the King so many times, but he wouldn't take the point. If we had a revolutionary court, he would be put straight up against a wall. How many wasted opportunities! A year ago the Germans made some extraordinary suggestions to me that we should do a deal with the Bulgarians; we'd have been off to Adrianopole and making an empire for ourselves.[1] Two years ago I brought the King the Polish crown on a plate, but he wouldn't listen. Now we'll be forced to give ourselves to the Germans for nothing. I used to talk to them one way, and now they talk to us quite differently. We'll fall into their hands for nothing."

1. Adrianopole: the old name for the Turkish town of Edirne, near Turkey's frontier with Greece.

"But what about France?" I asked timidly.

"France will also go along with Germany. I told the Germans: you guys have got to do a deal with the French—otherwise it won't work. And then Schacht went to Paris.[2] Look, I'll tell you something that will really amaze you. But be careful: nothing must leave these four walls. I negotiated for the French with the Germans; I had a mandate to do so. And do you know who gave it to me? Léon Blum. Only things are not going so well now with Léon Blum. But when a Daladier government is formed, it'll all be settled straightaway. Look, I've got a letter here from Daladier. When he becomes prime minister, I'll be off to Paris."

Friday, 8 January. Sinaia

I've been here at Roman's villa since Monday evening. It's a splendid house. At first it struck me as both sumptuous and severe, but I'm beginning to make friends with it. I think I could spend a whole lifetime here. But I'll leave on Sunday—and go back to a Bucharest where I feel so disoriented. . . .

I came with the idea of writing, but it hasn't been going too well. The day before yesterday, in some four hours of work, I barely managed to write three pages or so—and even those were full of corrections. Since then, nothing. My writing difficulties really trouble me, and I so much envy Mircea's prolificness. My pen encounters so many obstacles, so many misgivings, so many hesitations. That's not how a novel is written. Besides, I have to agree that novels are not my line. I can write delicate things marked by reflection, revery, and soliloquy—but I don't find it easy to keep darting between characters and let them get on with their lives.

I thought a lot about this yesterday on a walk in the mountains. I have a certain lack of spontaneity, which no other quality can ever overcome. What I write is a little schematic, linear, and abstract, even when it is graceful and suffused with emotion (for I am so sentimental). So I can create stories of two hundred pages, with the tone of a private diary, but not a novel. I also think I could write very well for the theatre; it has a number of standard routines that help me along, because I am so lacking in imagination. Also, the distances are shorter in the theatre. . . . If I were not a Jew and my plays could be performed, I would most likely

2. Hjalmar Schacht: economics minister in Nazi Germany 1934–1937.

have become a "dramatist" and nothing else. As it is, though, the experience of my first play is quite enough.

As to the book I have started to write, I do not yet have a clear picture of it. All I have at the beginning is a vague, highly vague, overview and a clear plan for the first chapter. Further than that, I see nothing and know nothing. I am hoping that things will become clearer as I write. But I find it so hard to get moving! And I have so many other work obligations! Who knows how long I will be held up by this trifle of a book, which I thought might come out this spring! My slow work rhythm has always spoiled the best-laid of my literary projects. Still, I shall try to get down to work in Bucharest (no more going out, hardworking afternoons, sensible evenings), and from time to time I'll take a short working holiday and spend it in Breaza or Sinaia.

Saturday, 9 [January]

My first day's skiing. I'd never have thought it would be so easy. I felt a kind of childish vanity installed on the skis, in a perfect regulation outfit that I had improvised on the day I left Bucharest—but I didn't think I would ever manage anything with my equipment, which looks rather like in the movies.

The day before yesterday in Predeal, where we had stopped for a few minutes at the Manolovici villa, I rather bashfully asked to be given detailed guidance (there were so many people there who had been skiing for years). Someone asked if I was going to learn or not: "Are you scared?"

And I answered quite frankly, without beating about the bush: "Yes."

"Well, you'll never learn then," he answered, cutting short the discussion.

I did learn, though, by a kind of hit and miss. Feeling sure that I'd fall after a few meters, I stormily (yes, I like to say stormily) covered the beautiful slope of the Stîna Regală—and, funnily enough, I did so without falling down. Then I performed a lot of other bewildering "exploits." We were descending for much of the way back, on skis—falling quite often, it is true, but in the end moving quite skillfully for the first day.

Wendy, who was my instructor, said:

"Bravo. You've got talent."

And I wasn't ashamed to feel flattered by this good mark, handed down with objectivity from the teacher's desk.

What a happy morning! Life still has some things to say to me.

Friday, 15 [January]. Bucharest

Since I got back on Sunday evening, there has been nothing in my personal life.

The book has remained where it was; I'll try to start work again this evening.

I don't see anyone. Nothing happens to me.

Moța and Vasile Marin have died in Spain.[3] It's hard for me to talk about that with Mircea. I sense that he's in mourning. As far as I'm concerned, I feel sad when I think about what has happened. There's more blindness than humbug in their camp, and perhaps more good faith than imposture. But then, how is it possible that they don't realize their terrible mistake, their barbarous mistake? What aberration explains it?

I haven't seen Marietta for a fortnight—nor am I in such a hurry to see her now. She's been having an attack of anti-Semitism, which I haven't witnessed myself but which Gheorghe told me about in detail: "The yids are to blame," shouted Marietta. "They take the bread from our mouths; they exploit and smother us. They should get out of here. This is our country, not theirs. Romania for the Romanians!"

One day I'll calmly try to explain to her why a woman who can think like that is completely and utterly unsuited for the role in my play.

Monday, 18 [January]

Holban was cremated yesterday.[4] It's impossible to grasp that he has actually died, that I'll never meet him again in the street or see him in a concert hall.

Also yesterday, a letter came from Blecher—a kind of "testamentary letter" giving me various instructions for his manuscripts after his death. He thinks it must now be very close. I wrote back with difficulty.

On Saturday night I stayed with Camil until two at the Splendid Parc; we talked about Leni and "our past sufferings."

On Sunday morning there was a woman's voice on the telephone:

"I should like to thank you for *Inimi cicatrizate*,[5] which I have read on your recommendation."

She wouldn't say who she was.

"That's all. I just wanted to thank you." And she hung up.

---

3. Leaders of the Iron Guard who fought on Franco's side in the Spanish civil war. Their death was used by the Iron Guard as a major propaganda device.
4. Anton Holban: novelist.
5. *Scarred Hearts*, a novel by M. Blecher.

Sinaia. Saturday, 30 [January]

Back in Sinaia. I arrived this morning: Dinu Noica was waiting for me
at the station. (His extraordinary delicacy, his smooth gestures, his measured speech: what an admirable type of man. Compared with him, I feel
hasty, vulgar, and insensitive. . . .)

I am renting a room opposite the park, modest but clean and pleasant. I want to stay until Wednesday—and above all I want to write. That's
why I've come. But will I be able to? Will it work?

Sunday, 31 [January]

The snow is beautiful as it gently falls. Ideal weather for skiing. But I
won't allow myself a Sunday's skiing unless I earn it by working enough.

Yesterday I wrote all afternoon, and I also wrote this morning. It goes
very slowly. Every sentence takes an enormously long time. I don't know
whether I'm too lazy or too punctilious. I'd like to be able to wander a
bit, to give myself some space and be carried along by the flow of things,
so that I'm not always looking back at what I've done and carefully cal-
culating every step forward. If I go on at this rate, I'll need a year to
finish the book. Besides, I shouldn't forget that these four days away have
been altogether exceptional. Nor should I forget that I'm still on the familiar ground of the first chapter, to which I have given a lot of detailed
thought. What will I do later, when I move on to the parts of the novel
that are still unclear?

I don't know. I would so much like it to come out for the Day of
the Book, at the end of April, but I can't believe it will. I can see myself still working at it this summer—and being forced to postpone other
projects yet again. . . .

But don't let's moan and groan too much. I'm pleased to have this
short break away from Bucharest. I'm alone—and as happy as I am still
able to be.

Monday, [1 February]

I don't know if I deserved this morning's skiing. Anyway, I allowed it to
myself, and I don't feel any remorse. . . .

I was up on the Opler: the skiing area is much smaller and the slope
much gentler than on the sheepwalk. I no longer had a giddy feeling.
Everything seemed less fantastical than at the beginning. But I'm still
enough of a child to be happy with so little.

As for work, I wrote more than six pages yesterday—in exactly seven and a half hours. It's not a record, of course: it's a smooth and normal output. I'll certainly write all afternoon today as well. But as I spend more time at my desk, I realize that it's going to be a long haul. I must stop setting deadlines and schedules for myself in advance. The only sensible plan is to work at a steady pace, without thinking about when I'll finish. Anyway, I don't think there is any chance of having it ready this spring.

Tuesday, 2 February

This morning I got carried away with the review for *Reporter* (I fear I was too harsh with Dem. Theodorescu) and the article for *Independenţa*.[6] But I worked all afternoon until eight, and then from 9:30 till midnight, when I am writing these lines. Even so, the day's yield is derisory: just three pages. Not even three.

I'm really furious with myself. It's not admissible to write so slowly; not admissible to sit for hours to describe a single gesture. Will I never acquire greater ease, greater fluency? At my present rate, God knows when I'll finish a book of two hundred pages, of which I don't think I've written twenty up to now.

Friday, 5 [February]

I came back from Sinaia on Wednesday evening. Am I content with the amount I worked? Yes, in a sense. The twenty pages I've written up to now are certainly not a lot—but they're enough to make me feel that "the ice is broken." Now I know that if I work systematically for forty days or so ("free days," as they say in court, because I'm not counting the inevitable breaks), I'll be able to finish this little story. I'm beginning to see it more clearly. I'm also beginning to take an interest in what happens. And some unexpected little things are indeed "happening" by themselves, through the course of events. Maybe it will finally result in a little book of which I don't need to feel embarrassed.

One possible title is *The Accident*. It's not too evocative, but I've never been good at choosing titles.

---

6. *L'Indépendence Roumaine*, for which Sebastian wrote music reviews under the pen name Flaminius.

Yesterday evening there was a Kreutzberg dance festival. I can't fully assess the value of it, because there must be a whole technique that may in the end successfully replace inspiration, emotion, and natural talent.

But the guy seemed extraordinary. I thought it a happy personal coincidence that the program included the *romance* from the *Kleine nachtmusik*. He danced it with the utmost grace. I thought of my play—and in Kreutzberg's movements I saw what I would have liked to achieve in the way of rhythm and style.

There are curious aptitudes in Kreutzberg: now a mime, now a gymnast, now a true clown. There were moments when he reminded me perfectly of Grock. But in *Till Eulenspiegel* he was a figure out of Breugel.

Nae Ionescu was in a box. We chatted during the interval. Last week he was in Warsaw and Lvov, where he gave a couple of lectures for students. He spoke to them about the new Romania, basing himself—so he said—on the sacrifice made by Ion Moţa in going to Spain "not to fight but to die."

There was also a Parisian journalist in his box—Odette Arnaud, who has come to Romania to write an investigative piece. I arranged to meet her tomorrow morning, because she wants an interview or something like that.

Nae spoke to her about his house, which he called "the finest in Bucharest." He told us of the Florentine furniture he has bought for it, and two fountains he has had brought from somewhere or other. . . . There was something tactless and ostentatious in all this praise. I know how much childishness there is in it, but I think there is also a little boorishness. I felt it especially in the company of that Parisian, so modest and gracious without trying to be. . . .

Friday, 12 [February]

The day before yesterday I went out to a café with Radu Olteanu[7] and Benu. Radu thinks quite seriously that the possibility of an Iron Guard coup in the next few days cannot be dismissed. He thinks it quite possible that the Guard, being mobilized in Bucharest for the funeral of Moţa and Marin, well armed, stirred by fasting, pomp, and parades, will take power into its hands. The Bucharest Garrison—whose young officers at least have become "legionarized"—would not put up any resistance.

7. Lawyer.

I don't take Radu's fears too seriously. But I do register them. They are a symptom, if nothing else.

Nae did not give a lecture, no doubt as a sign of mourning. Tomorrow Mircea won't be lecturing either.

Sinaia. Sunday, 14 [February]

Again in Sinaia. I arrived this morning, but I don't think I'll stay later than Tuesday. Besides, my literary ambitions are very modest: I want to complete the first chapter. Even now it is still not finished, because I haven't written a line since my last *séjour* in Sinaia.

Apart from that, I want to do a little skiing—and to forget Bucharest.

Tuesday, 16 [February]

I've already returned to Bucharest this morning, in Roman's car. Yesterday was taken up with skiing. Three hours in the morning with Mr. Roman and Miss Lereanu,[8] four in the afternoon with Thea.

(I won't write anything about Thea. It was the simplest kind of loving. But I have an intolerably serious way of behaving with women.)

The skiing exercises in the afternoon were very exacting. I fell a number of times. On the way back I fell so badly—there were several meters of ice—that I tore my trousers at the knees and came away with a minor wound, just as in the first chapter of the novel.

As for the novel, I am ashamed to write about it. I have done absolutely nothing.

Bucharest. Monday, 22 [February]

I left Sinaia feeling embarrassed toward Dinu and Wendy.[9] I thought that on Sunday—and again on Monday—the evening was too adolescent, too frivolous. As I stretched out on the sofa with Thea, kissing and embracing her, I had the stupid look of an eighteen-year-old boy off to the cinema to paw his little flirt—or who, even worse, hides himself away with her in a friendly and discreet house.

Dinu and Wendy were our hosts, but I put them in the awkward sit-

8. Angela Lereanu: secretary at Roman's office.
9. Constantin Noica and his wife. Noica was a journalist and a philosopher who became a strong supporter of the Iron Guard and later, under the Communist regime, the founder of an opposing school of thought.

uation of somehow patronizing a "louche" relationship with the wife of a friend of theirs. Everything was unclear: half joke, half excited pleasure. That's a little demeaning for thirty-year-olds.

I considered it was all my fault, and I was a little ashamed of myself. On the other hand, I could understand Thea very well, alone as she was for four weeks in Sinaia after a quarrel with a vulgar and indifferent husband. Why shouldn't she accept friendship or perhaps courtship (or perhaps even an adventure) from a man about whom—for literary or other reasons—she had already begun to feel a certain curiosity? We said good-bye on Monday night in front of her house, with a kiss I had neither requested nor expected and for which there was no longer the pretext of a continuing joke, since we were there alone. Probably for her, my passing through Sinaia was the start of a possible love affair. That would explain why, the day before yesterday at eight o'clock, she rang me from Sinaia to wish me a good morning—a call that gave me so much pleasure. . . .

I thought that was the end of the matter—nor did I consider it important enough to record at length in my journal—but then came yesterday evening's conversation with Dinu. I ate just with him at the Splendid Parc and listened to a confession that was in many ways a revelation. I certainly won't be able to capture all his hesitations, nuances, and details: I'll just give a quick summary of what he said.

So then:

On Saturday 13 February, Dinu—who for some time has been discreetly wooing Thea—sets off for her villa but resolves on the way not to go inside. Two factors make him decide not to pursue his advances: 1) a determination in principle not to be unfaithful to Wendy, even though theirs is a free marriage; 2) the fact that the funeral of Moța and Marin is taking place then in Bucharest, and that this is too grave an event for him to allow himself such frivolity on the same day. But Thea is at the window of her house and sees him passing by; she calls out—and he enters. Once inside, he forgets the two moral impediments and tries to kiss her. Thea refuses him. He leaves feeling depressed—not so much at the rejection as at his own sense of weakness. It is a blot on his honor that he has attempted such a light-minded adventure on the very day of the funeral (in which, he tells me, he participated with emotion).

Sunday 14 February. Wendy is in Predeal. Thea is alone. Dinu has decided to go to her house that afternoon and to renew (perhaps with greater success) the attempt he failed to carry off the day before. But at twelve o'clock someone knocks on the door and puts in a quite unexpected appearance: it is I! For him, I am a welcome rather than an untimely visitor. He immediately glimpses the solution to the moral debate inside himself. He'll do everything possible to throw Thea into my arms, and in any case will try to kindle the possibility of feelings between Thea and myself. In this way he will become a free man again, denied an adventure that he renounced in the most explicit manner. During the meal he tells me of the moral problems of living together with Wendy—but I don't understand a lot of it. After an hour Thea, called from the restaurant where she had been eating, comes in and embraces me. The rest we know.

Bill Witzling has died. He's being buried today in Brăila. He was tall and handsome and always struck me as hale and hearty—a man who made you happy that he existed. More than once I felt unworthy in comparison with him. The poor guy.

After Nae's lecture on Friday (a recapitulation concerning space), Posescu told him in the staff room about some recent theories that seemed to confirm what he had been saying in the lecture. I didn't listen very closely to their conversation and wasn't quite sure of the nature of the problem—but all of a sudden Nae cheerfully turned to me and said:

"You see, Mr. Sebastian, that's why Hitler is right."

Yesterday at Carol's, who'd broken his leg a few days before and had it in plaster. An anti-Semitic conversation with Camil, more anti-Semitic than ever.

Tuesday, 23 [February]

This morning at eight, a woman's voice on the phone.

"I am Thea's sister. Thea asked me to let you know that she has returned to Bucharest."

Thursday, 25 [February]

Yesterday evening, there was a little party at our place. Mircea, Nina, Marietta, Haig, Maryse, Gheorghe, Lilly, Dinu.

I wonder if this won't be the last time I ask them round. The situation is becoming more and more painful. I don't feel I can stand the duplicity that our friendship has required since they went over to the Iron Guard. Mircea's recent articles in *Vremea* have been more and more "Legionary." I avoided reading some of them. The latest one I read only this morning—though it came out on Friday and everyone has been talking to me about it.

Is friendship possible with people who have in common a whole series of alien ideas and feelings—so alien that I have only to walk in the door and they suddenly fall silent in shame and embarrassment?

I haven't been to Mircea's for ten days or so, nor to Marietta's for over a month. Maybe we'll spare ourselves a stormy farewell and let things break up by themselves over time. . . . I'll have to read again the last chapter of *Cum am devenit huligan.*

In the last issue of *Cuget clar* [Clear Thinking], Iorga translates with approval a short article of mine for *Independenţa* (the one with Petre Bellu)—doubtless without realizing that it was I who wrote it, because it was signed "Flaminius." So there I am, translated by Niculae Iorga. Quite a tricky situation.

In the same issue, in the very next item, a regular correspondent lays into Sergiu Dan, Camil Baltazar, and Mihail Sebastian as "those corruptors of the mind."

Monday, 1 March

Yesterday and the day before, with Mrs. Ghiolu at Roman. Blecher is ever closer to death. I don't know how much longer it will last. Now he's suffering from a fresh abscess, which needs to be lanced or left to burst by itself. The whole thing is terrible—but, like last time, I saw that it was becoming bearable, *à force d'obéissance.* Bearable for others, I mean—not for him, who wears a constant grimace from the pain.

As to Mrs. Ghiolu, I don't quite know what to think about her. The fact that she went to Roman is somehow proof that she is less frivolous than I imagined.

Friday evening from Stuttgart, a work by Beethoven, of which I had been unaware: the *Choral Fantasia* (Op. 80). The first part was quite similar to one of his piano concertos, while the appearance of the choruses at the end had a surprise effect. Altogether very beautiful.

Tuesday, 2 [March]

A long political discussion with Mircea at his home. Impossible to summarize. He was lyrical, nebulous, full of exclamations, interjections, and rude remarks. . . . I'll take from all that just his (frank) declaration that he is passionate about the Iron Guard, that he has high hopes for it and expects it to be victorious. Ioan Vodă the Cruel, Mihai Viteazu, Stefan the Great,[1] Bălcescu,[2] Eminescu,[3] Hajdeu[4]—all these are supposed to have been Iron Guardists in their day. Mircea refers to them as all of a piece!

At the same time I can't deny that it was entertaining. In his opinion, the students who carved up Traian Bratu[5] last night in Iaşi were not Iron Guardists but either . . . Communists or National Peasant supporters. Literally. As regards Gogu Rădulescu (Mr. Gogu, as Mircea ironically calls him),[6] the liberal student who was beaten with wet ropes at the Iron Guard headquarters, that was all well and good. It's what should be done to traitors. He, Mircea Eliade, would not have been content with that; he'd have pulled his eyes out as well. All who are not Iron Guardists, all who engage in any other kind of politics, are national traitors and deserve the same fate.

One day I may reread these lines and feel unable to believe that they summarize [Mircea's words]. So it is well if I say again that I have done no more than record his very words—so that they aren't somehow forgotten. Perhaps one day things will have calmed down enough for me to read this page to Mircea and to see him blush with shame.

Nor should I forget his explanation for joining the Guard with such passion:

"I have always believed in the primacy of the spirit."

He's neither a charlatan nor a madman. He's just naive. But there are such catastrophic forms of naiveté!

I'm off tomorrow morning to Brăila, where things look tragic with Babie and Auntie Caroline.

Sunday, 7 [March]

When I returned from Brăila on Wednesday evening, I found a note on the table: "Miss Leni Caler rang and asked you to 'phone her as soon as you're back in Bucharest." Of course, I didn't 'phone her. But on Thursday evening I met her at the opening night at the Regina Maria.

"I thought you were a polite person, Mr. Sebastian."

1. Medieval rulers of Moldavia and Valachia.
2. Nicolae Bălcescu: historian, leader of the 1848 revolution.
3. Mihai Eminescu: nineteenth-century poet, considered the creator of the modern Romanian language, a profound anti-Semite.
4. Bogdan Petriceicu Hajdeu: nineteenth-century writer, anti-Semitic.
5. President of the Iaşi University who was stabbed by a group of Iron Guard students.
6. Gogu Rădulescu was in fact a Communist sympathizer.

"I am, Miss Leni Caler, but I've been very busy today and haven't had a spare moment."

She certainly understood—it was hardly difficult—how much indifference there was beneath my jocular politeness.

In a few words she said what she wanted to ask me. Would I like to read the play this Saturday evening for herself, Froda, and Sică Alexandrescu? I agreed on two conditions: 1) absolute discretion, and 2) the right on my part to cancel the reading if I was not free.

I was glad to be the one with the reservations.

So, yesterday evening I read the play at last—with less emotion than I think I would have done it last summer or autumn. Maybe without any emotion at all. I didn't stress any of the lines that had some hidden meaning for her. I did not look at her, smile in secret understanding, or spark tender emotion within her. Not once did I accept her as my partner in a reading that contained so many partnerships of feeling.

I read the play as it might be read before a readers' panel. If possible, they want to put it on stage this spring, in April. I don't know if that is an acceptable arrangement. How many evening performances would it ensure for me? Thirty at the most. You're never going to have a big success at the end of a season. It would be preferable to leave the play until autumn, to have it open in November and take in Christmas, with time for a tour at the end of winter. That is undoubtedly the best solution. If the opening is postponed till November, I'll agree wholeheartedly that they should take on the play—for an advance of, say, thirty thousand lei.

We argued over the casting. They proposed Lungeanu, and this is exactly how I replied:

"Under no circumstances Lungeanu. Even if it meant the play was not performed for ninety-nine years, I still wouldn't give him the part."

In the end we agreed on Vraca. I think that would give me a really excellent cast: Leni, Vraca, and Timică. For Jef there is a recent young discovery: Mircea Axente. He would seem to be perfect for the role.

I was amused by their reaction to the reading. With each new reading I find how difficult it is to be enlightened about your own mistakes or qualities. Everyone sees them differently. Iancovescu thought Act Two was the best; they thought it the worst. In Act Three, Iancovescu asked me to delete the argument between Corina and Ștefan, on the grounds that it rang "false." Now Froda wants me to delete the "dream scene." What struck Iancovescu as magnificent seems to Froda melodramatic. I listened to them with a smile. They all talk with the same conviction, the same expert assurance—only they say things that flatly contradict each other. To whom should I listen? In the end I think I'll listen only to myself.

Anyway, I no longer take the fate of my play very seriously. It's too old now for me to get excited about it. I look at things from a money angle. I'd be thrilled to get quite a large sum so that I can 1) pay Mama's creditors and finally end that nightmare, 2) have a quiet holiday to finish my novel, 3) get up to date with the rent, 4) restock my wardrobe a little, 5) buy myself some furniture.

Maybe I'm naive to expect so much. But I think I'm being honest with myself when I say that I have no other ambitions ("of an artistic nature"). *Je sais bien à quoi m'en tenir.*[7]

But this play's a real headache. Not one simple, clear-cut situation. I was at Leni's yesterday evening, and we talked in great detail about the possibility of its being performed in their theatre. But at lunchtime today I'm called up by . . . Madame Bulandra. I had to arrange a reading for her too, this Friday afternoon. Good Lord, what will come of all this now?

To see Leni again was not as dangerous as I once imagined it would be. Now that I know where I stand with her, I think I'm cured of any sentimentality. When she was there between Froda and Sică, I looked at her without emotion, with a little irony and a certain indifference. There are no big differences between her and Eugenia Zaharia. And could I ever love Eugenia Zaharia?

There has been only one change in Leni's apartment: a fish tank has appeared on a shelf. I enjoyed watching the little fishes swim through the water, and I couldn't help thinking how symbolic was that fish tank in the Leni–Froda household.

Today's issue of *Memento* spreads a vile rumor that the fish tank is a present from Sică. Even if that's not true, it is a plausible detail—and anyway rather delightful.

No, I'm no longer risking my "heart" at all in that stage galley. Maybe I'll board it as a playwright, but not as just another lovesick individual.

The trial of the arsonists began yesterday,[8] so I'll be tied down for two weeks at the Court of Justice. I'm in a completely absurd state of nervous tension there. Why didn't I turn out to be more thick-skinned in life?

7. I know very well what I should stick to.
8. Involving arson to extract insurance payments.

This morning I met Marie Ghiolu as arranged at a private viewing at the Mozart. I'd just been to the Imre Ungar concert, where I'd heard a prelude and fugue by Bach, a Mozart sonata, and Beethoven's *Appassionata*.

Mrs. Ghiolu was especially beautiful and shone with elegance. She was wearing a hat and a magnificent ermine collar. I felt very dull in my wretched overcoat.

Monday, 8 [March]

This morning I was at the Comoedia Theatre, where a shorthand-typist was waiting so that I could dictate Act Three.

In the manager's office there was a fish tank like the one at Leni's. These people are certainly keen on symbols.

Tuesday, 9 [March]

The first real day of spring. The first day with a light coat.

That too is a joy: to leave off a heavy old overcoat and go out in a light grey one in which you think you look elegant—or anyway in which you feel so much younger!

In the morning, a brief visit to Thea at the magnificent house of her sister, a Mrs. Nadler, in the Filipescu Park. Thea was nice and affectionate, even a touch indiscreet.

All afternoon at the Court of Justice, where the arson trial is still going on. What am I doing there? I'm the only "counsel" there who doesn't pick up any money, and probably the only one who feels he is so utterly wasting his time. At the age of thirty I still don't dare say about myself that I am a counsel without putting it in quotation marks.

Sunday, 14 [March]

A spring Sunday, unbearable in its beauty. I started the morning well at a Cortot recital (Franck, Ravel, Debussy, Bach), but then continued stupidly by playing rummy all day at Carol's. Am I not thickheaded?

I feel alone as I wait for joys that will never come. I think of twenty-year-old boys going today with their sweethearts to Robinson or Nogent-sur-Marne, from where they'll return weary to a springtime Paris so youthful and sensual.

Never more than on a day like today do I feel how pointless my whole life has been.

And I'm too disgusted with everything to write a page of my journal.

There was only one thing to do today—to be with Thea (who was out of town somewhere) and to make love without too many explanations.

Friday, 19 [March]

Was in Brăila on Tuesday for Baba's funeral.[9] She died on Monday, after wandering a whole day in the direction of Baldovineşti, where the gendarmes found her collapsed from fatigue in the middle of the night on the railway. She was ninety-two years old. If she hadn't got lost, I think she might have lived many a year longer.

I heard the news without emotion, and it was also without emotion that I attended the funeral. But a whole world has gone with her—and our whole childhood has lost one of its main heroic figures. Poor Baba: what a long life she had! It's not surprising she lost her memory.

Last Friday, a reading at the Bulandras. I regret not having jotted down my impressions there and then. Now they seem too old and uninteresting. They liked my play but had some reservations. I'm tired of all these points that keep coming up—whether with Iancovescu or Froda or Bulandra.

I'll leave it on hold again for the time being. No new moves, no insistence, just a studied indifference: that's the only attitude to take.

The weather is splendid—but the arson trial is still going on. It doesn't prey on my mind so much, but it still means I am wasting three or four hours a day. When it's over, I'll make a quick getaway to Breaza or Sinaia.

There has been a lot of music recently. The F minor concerto with Cortot and the E minor with Ignaz Friedmann—both by Chopin. Then, again with Cortot, all the preludes, a nocturne ("our" nocturne, from Brăila, in E-flat), a scherzo, a fantasia, the B minor sonata, three waltzes—a whole Chopin recital.

Debussy's *Children's Corner*, a sonatina by Ravel, the *Prelude, Choral and Fugue* by Franck.

Yesterday evening at the Philharmonic, Brahms's *Violin Concerto* (with

9. Sebastian's grandmother.

which I am becoming familiar) played by Thibaud, one of Handel's *Concerti grossi*, and Beethoven's seventh symphony.

A host of other things in recent weeks, which I neglected to note down.

Sunday, 21 [March]

This morning at the Ateneu, a Thibaud concert with the Philharmonic: Mozart's *D Major Violin Concerto* (with a fleetingly melancholic adagio), the Chausson *Poème*, the Beethoven concerto.

I took Leni with me. She was elegant enough for me to find her pleasing—but forgotten enough for me not to get carried away. In short, she was not all that important to me.

Lunch at Maryse's—then to the trot racing at Floreasca. A spring day—a day of idleness.

Thursday, 25 [March]

Blecher has been in Bucharest since yesterday morning, in Room 15 at the Saint-Vincent de Paul Hospital. He came because of the abscess, which still has not drained even though they performed two butcherlike punctures at Roman.

He told me about the train journey, and it made me shudder. They left home well after dark, with the moon already up, passed through deserted streets, encountered Iron Guardists who were amazed to see the moving stretcher, waited in the stationmaster's office, boarded the train through the window, and arrived in Bucharest in the morning, where the porters refused to take him off through the window.

What terrible suffering! Everything becomes absurdly pointless in the face of such pain.

He thought he was about to die. At one point he decided to commit suicide. He tore up all his papers and manuscripts: eighty pages of a new novel and seventy pages of a journal.

I hardly felt like criticizing him for it.

After that, I am ashamed to talk here about Leni. She has again become "engaging," but this time I'll firmly resist. She's a nice tart, but I mustn't forget that she's a tart before being nice.

Mircea was at the Jooss ballet on Wednesday. He told Comarnescu that he found it disgusting because of its "Jewish spirit." He thought the show was Semitic.

That's all he found to say.

Our friendship is rapidly breaking up. We don't see each other for days at a time—and when we do, we no longer have anything to say.

Sunday, 28 [March]

Last Friday evening, the *Matthäus-Passion* from Leipzig. I'd been afraid that spring would pass without my hearing it. Nothing could have consoled me for that. Not only is it a great musical joy; it has become a superstition that seems to bode well for me. I enjoyed it immensely, but I listened with less gravity than before. I'm beginning to be familiar with it. There are passages that I await, anticipate, and then follow as they are played. It no longer holds any surprises, and I no longer listen with the old diffidence. Everything seems to me more intimate, less ceremonious, less austere, more Mozartian than before. Once again, I was happy to discover the tenor aria in Part One: *Ich will bei meinem Jesu wachen,*[1] and so many other things.

Made a long speech yesterday at the Court of Justice—more than an hour and a half. I had a lot of difficulties to resolve, in attitude, tone, and so on. I had to prosecute the case, yet at the same time I didn't want to push too hard. In that respect at least I think I succeeded. I felt that others were listening to me, and for an hour and a half their attention never seemed to waver. But maybe I am wrong. Paul Moscovici, who heard part of the speech, told me this morning that he hadn't been satisfied with it. He said that the "ironic amenity" of my speech had not been the right tone for that court. Probably he is right. He also said that the judges had not listened very closely. That's more serious, if it's true.

Still, I'm glad that he gave me his opinion. It makes me watch myself more closely and stops me from feeling too pleased with my "talents"—though I don't think I've ever got carried away with too much self-admiration.

Yesterday I was at the Military Court, where some Iron Guardists are on trial for kidnapping and torturing the liberal student Aurelian Rădulescu in the Guard's headquarters. Nae Ionescu made a witness statement. I copy from the newspaper what he had to say: "Professor Nae Ionescu, replying to a question from Counsel Vasiliu-Cluj, set forth a theory of constituted organisms, whose particular sensibility means that

---

1. I would keep watch by my Jesus.

they have a right to respond to an action whose consequences affect that organization.

"[. . .] in reply the witness pointed to the fact that, in Western student centers, at Oxford and Cambridge, corrective beatings are commonly applied in student associations.

"[. . .] in reply the witness tried to justify beatings from an educational point of view, saying that he himself had often received one and that it had proved beneficial."

On Thursday evening, a Hermann Scherchen concert at the Philharmonic: Beethoven's *Symphony No. 1*, Mozart's *Serenata notturna* (a delightful piece, but how much I prefer the *Kleine nachtmusik!*), and Mahler's fifth symphony—a splendid, unexpectedly beautiful work, despite my fear that it would be pretentious, grandiloquent, and absurd.

Sunday, 4 April

Exhausting days in court, not so much because of the physical effort as because of the nervous tension.

Bogza's arrest has really shaken me.[2] It seemed to me an act of madness, which would pass as soon as things were explained. I was sure that he'd be released after a night with the police. Chasing newspaper editors, making phone calls, driving around by car—it all depressed me. Again I felt how deplorable was my alarmist temperament.

A conversation with the examining judge (Cornel Stănescu from Office No. VII, a smug flunky type affecting moral outrage) left me groping for words. I tried to convince him and read some of Bogza's less scandalous poems—but none of it had any effect. The man was slavishly obeying orders, or else he just has the cruelty of an imbecile. Maybe I made a fool of myself talking to him so heatedly. In any case, he was laughing away.

The next day the arrest warrant was upheld. I realize that I spoke with too much obvious feeling. An attorney should not appear so involved in a case. But will I ever be able to do anything—anything at all—without some passion?

Besides, I don't need to blame myself. It was a lost cause anyway: if the warrant was upheld, it could only have been because someone else ordered it. For the other counsels, V. V. Stanciu and especially I. Gr. Perieţeanu, showed much greater detachment in presenting the case—

2. Geo Bogza had been charged with disseminating pornography because of the content of one of his books.

and we still lost. To lose in such a trial (where legal justice, not to mention the other kind, cries out to heaven) is enough to make you forever disgusted with the Bar. Personally, though, I didn't need anything else to make me feel disgusted.

It was not so much the confirmation of arrest as the judges' attitude that aroused my indignation. All the time Puiu Istrati had a mockingly skeptical smile on his face, looking as absent as someone propping up a bar in a café. I felt that, whatever was said, the verdict had been fixed in advance—fixed by his position on the bench, his lack of sensitivity, his force of habit, his indifference. What power in the world can jolt the shriveled conscience of a judge with the mind of a bureaucrat? And to think that Bogza's liberty is in the hands of such people! They are the state, the constitutional authorities, justice, morality, truth. . . .

Poor Bogza! He is certainly not aware of anything that is happening—he who is so naive, so childlike, so harebrained!

I used to think that there could be no disagreement on such questions among people of the same background as mine; that, once a threshold of sensitivity was reached, certain things were accepted as a matter of course. Well, how astounded I was at lunch today to realize that Mircea Eliade sides with Puiu Istrati rather than Bogza!

First of all (Mircea says), Bogza is not a writer. He's not even a member of the Writers' Association—and he's more of a journalist than a writer. Second, his poetry is pornographic and pathological.

"Why should I be up in arms over Bogza's arrest?" he shouted. "They've arrested him? So what? He'll spend a month in jail and that'll be the end of it. What's really serious is that those youngsters are being martyred with ten years' imprisonment. . . ."

"Which youngsters, Mircea?"

"The nationalist youngsters. Yes, they're being made martyrs of. And for what? Because they beat Gogu Rădulescu's arse a couple of dozen times? In Oxford and Cambridge, where students have the sensibility of a constituted organism . . ."

I couldn't take the rest: not only because it seemed stupid to hear him repeating Nae word for word, but because I was scared at the way his mind was succumbing to platitude.

I stopped him.

"Mircea, old man, I think we should change the subject. It's Sunday. I haven't seen you for four weeks. Let's talk about something else—otherwise I feel we won't reach the end of our lunch. That would be a pity."

And we did change the subject.

But is friendship possible under such circumstances?

This morning at the Ateneu there was a Bustabo concert, an American girl of sixteen in a white dress with a big behind—the Lola Bobescu type. Tartini's *Concerto in D Minor*, Beethoven's C minor sonata, Lalo's *Symphonie Espagnole*, Szymanowski's *Nocturne and Tarantella*.

Yesterday evening, from Lyons P.T.T., a Mozart bassoon concerto.

On Friday evening, a Fenerman recital: Locatelli sonata, Beethoven sonata, Fauré's *Après un rêve*, Albéniz's *Tango*, a Frescobaldi sonata.

Thursday evening, Bruckner's *Seventh Symphony*, conducted by Perlea.

This last week, of course, I haven't given attention to anything literary. But I did have the idea of a little essay that I may write sometime in the future: "On the Mediocrity of the Theatre."

A play by Denys Amiel (*Ma liberté*) and various thoughts about my own play have made me see once again how impoverished, how conventional, how schematic, how facile and mediocre the theatre is as a genre—at least the "psychological" drama in three acts.

Bucharest. Monday, 18 October 1937

On my way home today, my heart beat fast at the thought—doubtless absurd, but which I may never shake off—that I may find a package from Paris with the missing manuscripts.[3]

I cannot stamp out the childish wish that this bad dream will end. I cannot convince myself that I really have lost the red folder forever, with its 111 pages. Everything is still so vivid, so present within me. . . . I can't let it go. I can't believe it. Yesterday I opened the drawers that I had locked on my departure, and it occurred to me that in one of them I would come across the red folder and the yellow notebook. Maybe it really wouldn't have surprised me to find them there. And now, as I write, I feel that I have them somewhere in my room, among the books on the shelves or the papers on my table—and that I need only look to have them in my hand.

Each time I think of that accursed moment when I first noticed the suitcase was missing, I have the same feeling of gloom, the same refusal

---

3. In Paris a month earlier, Sebastian had lost the draft manuscript of his novel *Accidentul*.

to believe it. It seems absurd, ridiculous, farcical—and I well understand why I laughed that night in the face of disaster. I'd laugh again now.

I compare my present situation with that of two months ago, and I can only rue the collapse. I have lost so much—I who had so little to lose.

A bungled trip, a lost novel, a play withdrawn from rehearsal, probably for good. I was facing an autumn of riches, a winter of hard work. I was looking forward with curiosity to so much that seemed certain to happen—and now I no longer look forward to anything. I'm left with Roman's office, the articles for *Independenţa*, a revulsion against being awake and conscious, a terrible desire to drink, sleep, and forget. I feel at the end of my tether. No one in the world can do anything for me. I have so few deep reasons to live that a happening such as this (which for someone else, in a different situation, would be painful but not disastrous) becomes a reason to think of death.

And today is my thirtieth birthday.

Wednesday, 20 [October]

On Saturday evening I went out with Leni and Froda, first to the Carul cu Bere then to the Melody. I drank a lot, on purpose. (I'd like to drink all the time, so as to forget . . .)

At the Melody, while the three of us talked about this and that, I was "feeling up" Leni beneath the table; she not only "let it be done" but discreetly helped me along. I spent the whole evening with my hand between her thighs. I watched her, but nothing gave her away. She was talkative, cheerful, attentive, pleasant, and self-assured. And her husband was sitting next to her. And she looked him in the eyes. And that is the woman I loved like a dog for two years.

I too finally know Leni the *petite putain charmante*,[4] the one everyone but I has known—of course.

In all likelihood my play will not be performed. There are anti-Semitic pressures that the theatre has no reason to resist. The national conscience does not allow a play by Mihail Sebastian to appear on stage in Bucharest. Well, that's all right: there are enough plays by Fodor László, Pius Fekete, or Franz Molnár.

Sân-Giorgiu literally said to Camil: "I have five thousand lancers at

4. Charming little slut.

my command, and I'll never accept for one moment the staging of Sebastian's play. I've informed Sică of my decision."

For the moment I'm not fully aware of the factors that led to the removal of my play from the repertoire. I don't think that Sân-Giorgiu's
threats are sufficient explanation, nor are Iorga's articles in the press.
There must be a whole set of machinations. But I don't have the patience or the tenacity to clarify matters. I'll let them take their divinely
appointed course. I give up.

On Sunday evening I went to the Comoedia to see the Caragiale play.

Conabie, much less eager to please than he was this summer, addressed me in the second-person singular.[5] Axente, the typist, asked me
with false concern:

"But isn't your play still due to be performed?"

No, it isn't. If it had been, Conabie wouldn't have spoken to me in
that familiar way, and Axente wouldn't have been so offhand. Pathetic
trifles at which I laugh, but I can't help noticing them.

Zaharia Stancu offered me (through Camil, because we don't speak
to each other) an engagement at *Lumea românească*. I turned it down, of
course. But how sad when something like that becomes possible or plausible, in any event not absurd: that I should be in the employ of Zaharia
Stancu!

Camil told me of a conversation he had with Toma Vlădescu. Then
he started probing:

"But what's all this with you and Toma Vlădescu?"

I had to remind him that in 1931, when I was on good terms with
T.V., he (Camil) got me involved in his dispute with V.—without asking
or consulting me.

I don't have any regrets, of course. But isn't it rich that today I am
still "at daggers drawn" with Toma Vlădescu, whereas Camil has lunch
with him and asks me in an angelic voice: "What's all this . . ."?

What childish aspects I must still have if I retain such trifles and even
record them here?

Saturday, 23 [October]

Nevertheless, I can't just sit around forevermore lamenting what happened and what has become of me. There is something stupid in it all,

5. In this case expressing a slight sense of social superiority rather than personal
warmth.

but I have to swallow it and move on. My inclination to do nothing is too strong, and I could encourage it further with another shrug of the shoulders.

So let's draw a circle round the disaster and see what can be done from now on. In the first place, I have to accept that the manuscript is lost for good and stop expecting that it will turn up. (Yesterday evening at the Foundation, as I opened the door, I caught sight of a package on Cioculescu's desk and felt an absurd shudder of hope that it was my papers, my books.)

Is it possible for me to rewrite the manuscript? I sometimes think so when I consider its broad outlines, for I remember the succession of events in it with sufficient clarity. The difficulties begin as soon as I think about the details: I'll never be able to reconstruct those. I wasted whole hours for one word, one shade of meaning, one description of a gesture. I certainly won't recover anything if I try to remember sentence by sentence. On the other hand, if I write at all freely—without remaining faithful to the first version—I'll always suffer from the thought that it is well below my previous standard, and I won't be able to achieve anything this time.

Also, if I was so pleased with the five chapters I wrote before, it was because I saw them growing and was myself surprised at each new element. Isn't it too depressing to write something that no longer holds any secrets for you?

Anyway, I'll try nevertheless. I'm determined not to go out in the evening any more, not to waste any more nights. This year I'll stop being a "first-nighter." And were it not for the three thousand lei from *Independența*, I'd give up going to concerts.

I'd like to do work that is a little more dull and mechanical. I think I'd feel good in the army.

Monday, 25 [October]

On my way home tonight I felt an irresistible need to remember my novel. Thinking that I could reconstitute there and then at least the fifth chapter, I sat at my desk and wrote until three o'clock. Some passages I can recall quite easily, others have disappeared without a trace. There are gaps that I find quite disconcerting. I can see the missing pages well enough, I know where each bit, each sentence fitted on the page (top, bottom, middle), and I seem to have retained the rhythm of the sentences: I hear them, I have the measure of them, I can feel them breathing. And yet I am unable to write them down. With every sentence that

I recall only in a mutilated form, I feel all that I am sacrificing, all that I have lost.

What am I to do? It seems out of the question to work through it methodically from beginning to end. For the time being, I'll try to save what can still be saved: that is, the passages still present in my mind, the ones I can still find alive and unspoiled. Then I'll see if anything can be done with all the sheets that have the value of a mere outline.

I won't promise myself anything. It's an attempt, not a hope as well.

Thursday, 28 [October]

I have just finished rewriting Chapter Five. It had thirty-two pages in the lost version; now it has only twenty-four. As I haven't left out any of the action, the eight-page difference can be explained only by my sacrificing details that I could not and will not be able to recall.

I feel as if I've pulled some half-burnt sheets of paper from a fire. It is shaming and embarrassing to read them again. Everything seems dry, inexpressive, and hurried. I'll put these twenty-four pages aside. They'll serve as a rough outline if I one day decide—and have the time—to go on writing this ill-starred book.

Tomorrow I'll try with the same haste, the same resignation, the same lack of illusions, the same indifference, to reconstitute the rest of the chapters—in the order in which they come.

I've forbidden myself to make any plans or promises until I've completed this first task.

Sunday, 31 [October]

Yesterday evening at the Ateneu, while Enescu was preparing to play again *La fontaine d'arétuse* (which he played admirably and had been asked by the audience to repeat), Mrs. Ciomac leaned across to me and asked:

"Would you be capable of repeating something you had put all your soul into the first time?"

I was on the point of saying a categorical "No!" when I remembered that for several days I had been trying without success to do precisely that—dear, oh dear!

Monday, 1 November

Sometimes I think it is working nevertheless—that the book will be saved in the end. Some passages I have recalled almost intact; others I am writing again, perhaps no worse than the first time. In general, the pages I manage to rewrite without great loss are the neutral ones that I did not like in the old version either. (Oh dear, how resigned I am! I'm beginning to speak of an old version!)

But my despair comes back whenever I approach something that I achieved with great difficulty, and which was so much to my liking before. Anne's entrance into the bar, the atmosphere of the bar, the decor, the moments of waiting—no, I'll never relive them with the emotion, the surprise, the melancholy that I felt the first time up there on Mount Schuller.[6] Some sentences took me whole hours before. Now I feel they are lost, drowned. And again I feel like giving it all up and forgetting about it.

Monday, 8 [November]

I've finished it all. Of the eighty-six pages I had to reconstitute (because twenty-five made up the fragment published in *R.F.R.* and were therefore saved intact), I have lost twenty-eight for good.

The material loss is considerable for a short novel (which is what my book is meant to be), and quite dreadful if I consider not only the number of pages but also their content. The reconstituted pages are insipid, with neither color nor tone. I have not recovered anything of what seemed to me intense, at times passionate, in the lost manuscript. Some passages in it moved me in a childlike way whenever I read them. Now I feel cold and indifferent.

As it is not a novel built around situations, I have lost the very things that were its *raison d'être*: the detailed psychological observations, the precise images and expressions, the appropriate shades of meaning.

The old version seemed to me so good that, whatever else I wrote, the book could no longer be compromised. Now, if the reconstituted chapters are to be tolerable or even excusable, what follows will have to be very good, so good as to make up for and dominate the first part. But is that possible? Will I be capable of it?

No, there's no point in trying to console myself. The loss is irreversible—and perhaps it would have been more manly, more honest, not to try to pick things up from the beginning but simply to abandon it once and for all.

6. The local German name for Mount Postăvaru.

It is very difficult to explain all the intrigues and machinations surrounding my play. *Je ne sais pas me défendre*[7]—that's for sure—and I don't even claim to be trying. But at least I should take what has happened as a lesson in life—though my life no longer has anything to do with any kind of lesson.

In any case, "anti-Semitic pressures" on Sică are not sufficient explanation. I must add: 1) the very active intervention of Froda, who is more scared than anyone in this matter; 2) the fact that Leni is not especially keen to act in my play, and at the end of the day would be happier to take on something like *Absenţe nemotivate* [Unmotivated Absences]; 3) lastly, the fact that no one in the theatre really believes in my play, which strikes them as "interesting" but not a potential winner. With so many motives, was it even necessary to add Sân-Giorgiu's fist and Crevedia's voice?

Thursday, 11 [November]

Yesterday evening, Radio Geneva had Ravel's *Piano Concerto for the Left Hand*, which I have been wanting to get to know for such a long time. Admirable, as soon as I began listening.

Quite a lot of Mozart recently (two exclusively Mozartian concerts with the Salzburg orchestra). This evening I'll hear the *Requiem* at the Philharmonic, also for the first time.

Otherwise nothing new; no expectations, nothing.

Sunday, 14 [November]

This morning in front of the Ateneu (on my way out of the Enescu symphonic concert), Nae Ionescu and Puiu Dumitrescu[8] were discussing the governmental crisis.[9] Who'll be next? they asked each other, shrugging their shoulders, like me or you or him. . . .

Whereas five years ago . . .

Monday, 15 [November]

Mircea has entered the electoral lists. That too is a sign.

7. I don't know how to defend myself.
8. Puiu Dumitrescu: powerful personal secretary to King Carol II.
9. A forthcoming election was to decide the fate of Prime Minister Tătărescu, who was supported by the king but had run afoul of public opinion.

Sunday, 21 [November]

Sunday, alone . . . I'd have like to spend the evening with someone, anyone. Cella and Thea did not answer the telephone. Mircea and Marietta are at the Viforeanus[1] (another contact lost, the Viforeanus). Maryse and Gheorghe in Sinaia.

Only Leni rang me this evening—but why should I keep picking up a story that leads nowhere? (Camil—to complete the list—was at a wedding; Carol in Vienna.)

I went alone to the cinema and then walked in the streets. On Calea Victoriei near Djaburov, someone called out behind me:

"Mr. Comarnescu, Mr. Comarnescu." It was a wretched semijournalist, Emil Flămându, whom I had met a few times cooling his heels in the Foundation's waiting room. He spoke in a drunken mumble:

"Mr. Comarnescu, did you do me that favor? You know, at the general's, I asked you . . . Do you have an answer?"

I explained that he had made a mistake. I was not Comarnescu but Sebastian, and he had never said anything to me about a "favor." He couldn't apologize enough—and went his way.

I can easily see myself as a kind of Emil Flămându later in life. When I wrote *Deschiderea stagiunii* three years ago,[2] I had a quite precise feeling that T. T. Soru (also a kind of Flămându) was myself. And since then I have come down a lot; I have put up less resistance.

I could drink all the time, so as to forget—and I have so much to forget. On Wednesday evening I almost forced Leni and Froda to come with me for a drink after the theatre, and I did indeed end up terribly drunk—one of the worst times in my life. I was like an animal, no longer thinking about anything, and I was happy.

And yet, I'll delay the ending as much as possible.

Friday, 3 December

What Harry Brauner told me yesterday about Marietta challenges everything I knew about her. She got thirty thousand lei from the National Theatre and twenty thousand from the promoters—and she kept it all, without giving anything to Lucia Demetrius. At the same time she sent the text of their play to Germany, signing it only with her own name, on the pretext that it would not be accepted because Lucia Demetrius is "Jewish" (!).

---

1. Mariana and Petru Viforeanu: members of the Criterion literary group.
2. *The Opening of the Season*, Sebastian's sketch about theatrical life.

Isn't it incredible? (On this occasion, I learned that Lucia D.'s mother actually is Jewish. What good methods of investigation our Marietta has! And what timely use she can make of them!)

Sunday, 5 [December]

So it's decided: *Jocul de-a vacanţa* will not be put on stage. I've known it ever since my return to Bucharest—but I still had some vague hopes. Now it's all settled. Instead they're putting on a play by Muşatescu. I received the news (which was not news but only a confirmation) with a feeling of bitterness. But there's been enough time from last night till this morning to give the incident its correct proportions. Obviously it's not at all pleasant. I'm too superstitious not to be troubled when something of mine is a failure; it's as if a hand of cards were to go badly wrong. Since I left for Geneva, I've been having an unlucky streak. When will it end?

The only serious aspect of it all is the money. I haven't got any, and I don't know where to look. I'm beginning to feel poverty as a humiliation. The play could have brought me in a hundred thousand lei—which would not have solved everything, but it would have given me a few months of peace.

I'm waiting for Christmas to go and work somewhere in the mountains. Maybe I could write my novel in twenty days. By January or February I'd like to be handling the production: galleys, final proofs, dedication—in short, to feel that I'm doing something, that something is happening in my life.

This morning I met Antoine Bibescu[3] at the Enescu concert, and this afternoon I went for a stroll on the Şosea with Titu Devechi. I hadn't seen either of them for years. Yet I had nothing to say to them, nor they anything to me. It was as if time had stood still. But goodness knows, that is not at all the case.

The concert was very nice: violin concertos by Bach, Mozart, and Brahms. But there was only one moment of emotion: the last phrases of the andante in the Bach concerto.

3. Prince Antoine Bibescu: close friend of Sebastian's.

Tuesday, 7 [December]

Yesterday (Saint Nicholas), Nina's birthday. I rang in the morning to congratulate her.

"The lady is at the general's," said the maidservant, "and the professor is lunching at his parents'."

Later I went there for dinner and discovered that Mircea had actually been away from Bucharest electioneering for a couple of days and had returned only that evening. The maid's lie at lunchtime horrified me: a family-organized lie in which they did not mind involving the servant. It seemed even sadder than the knowledge that Mircea had been on the campaign trail, wandering from village to village with Polihroniade. Haig Acterian and Penciu were part of the same team. They took turns speaking, and it seemed that Haig spoke with grand, slightly theatrical gestures. I don't know if Mircea made any speeches. It all seems so utterly grotesque. I can't understand how they are not aware of the terrible farce. Marietta, who arrived later, came into the house singing the Iron Guard anthem: *Ştefan Vodă* . . . They're beginning not to feel embarrassed in my presence.

I am seeing a lot of Leni. It is a time when we are able to see eye to eye—and I am not serious enough to refuse. No doubt I'll pay for this light-minded behavior, as I paid on other occasions in the past.

Camil said to me this morning on Calea Victoriei:

"No Reinhardt, no Stanislavsky, not a single stage manager has discovered what I have discovered in the theatre. I am the greatest stage manager there is, because I have deep knowledge of the text as well as an exceptional philosophical culture and an unusual nervous sensibility. These actors are fools: they can't even see how immensely fortunate they are to be working with me."

I was quite disarmed. All I could do was smile—a little surprised but unprotesting.

Lunch with Antoine Bibescu at the Athénée Palace. To be a prince, to possess a huge fortune, to frequent the most prestigious circles in Europe, to be on close terms with all the great French writers, to be performed with some success in Paris, London, and New York—this is not enough to cure you of Bucharest's little vanities. Here is Antoine Bibescu burning to have one of his plays put on by Sică Alexandrescu.

Friday, 10 [December]

Yesterday evening, a Casals–Enescu concert at the Philharmonic. (Schumann's *Cello Concerto*, Brahms's *Double Concerto for Violin, Cello, and Orchestra*.) Very sincere, very pure emotion. In general, I find it so hard to be completely present during a concert! A host of thoughts and images pass through me, some of them quite stupid and meaningless, and when I catch myself wandering off, I scold myself like a schoolchild and return to the concert with a kind of determination to be more assiduous and attentive and to understand more of what I hear.

Antoine Bibescu asked me on Sunday morning whether I had a natural inclination for music. I replied that I didn't: that I had come to music out of curiosity, to enter a domain unknown to me. I think I started to love it through application and effort; only very rarely do I have moments of true abandon. Besides, I'm not sure that what is called "abandon" is the best way of listening to music. I do not trust the muddled, slightly capricious reverie in which I reel about during a concert. On the contrary, I try to listen to each phrase with an analytic or grammatical mind. I try to listen to a piece of music as I would read a book.

Casals brings tears to my eyes. I cannot even bring myself to applaud. I am ashamed to show my "approval." What a magnificent lesson in art, and perhaps in life too! No fuss at all, no dazzle, no verve: everything simple, austere, uncommunicative, as in a great solitude.

Friday, 17 [December]

In yesterday's *Buna Vestire* (year I, no. 244, dated Friday, 17 December 1937): "Why I Believe in the Victory of the Legionary Movement," by Mircea Eliade.

"Can the Romanian people end its days ... wasted by poverty and syphilis, invaded by Jews and torn apart by foreigners ... ?

" ... the Legionary revolution has the people's salvation as its supreme goal ... as the Captain has said.

" ... I believe in liberty, in personality, and in love. That is why I believe in the victory of the Legionary movement."

Evening

Looking at her a short while ago as she spoke in the dressing room, I closely observed each of her features and gestures. She is ugly: a narrow brow, Jewish nose, large mouth, a wart on her thick lower lip. She is thin, her breasts are small and worn out, her arms are too slender, her skin without luster. I also know her hurried way of talking, her artless intonation, her bursts of laughter (which suddenly illuminate her, it is true). I know everything, and none of it pleases me.

She is a woman with neither height nor beauty, no more desirable than last year's Wendy (my young client from the Zig-Zag—"Wendy and Julie"), at best "amusing" or completely insignificant. And yet I love her.

"I love her." Let's not exaggerate. I too am a kind of flotsam carried along by events, by the fear of being alone, by the slothfulness of living. Sometimes I see in her a smile, an incipient emotion, a look that waits and asks . . . and then I don't have the heart to refuse her.

My pathetic visits to the theatre. The doorman, the dresser, the stage-hands, Iancovescu, Roman—what can they think of this poor wretch who, for no apparent reason, comes every other evening to the dressing room to smoke a cigarette?

Sunday, 19 [December]

In normal circumstances, what has happened to me in the last three to four years would have been, I won't say gratifying, but in no way catastrophic. Grave, to be sure, but for that very reason useful.

To have lost a position (*Cuvântul*[4]), a man to whom I felt responsible (Nae Ionescu), a number of friends (Ghiţă Racoveanu, Haig, Marietta, Lilly, Nina, and the closest friend of all, Mircea), to have lost absolutely everything: this may, at thirty years of age, turn out to be not a disaster but a maturing experience.

Should I not feel grateful to life for creating a void around me, for withdrawing all the habits and conveniences I had accumulated over time, for putting me back at square one, not with the thoughtlessness I had at twenty but with the lucidity of my thirty years?

Should I not tell myself that I am ending (totally and forever) a certain period and beginning a new one that will lead me toward different people, perhaps another love, or perhaps another solitude?

Yes, I certainly should. But something is missing for it to be like that—the one thing, in fact, from which there is no escape in my destiny. For all the rest can be built up anew.

Tuesday, 21 [December]

Stupefying results in yesterday's elections to the Chamber. A great success for the Iron Guard: they're talking of thirty to thirty-five deputies.

---

4. The newspaper where Sebastian had worked.

In any case, hundreds of thousands of votes, whole districts swung over to them. It is Germany's "September 1930" all over again.

Yet it was a bright sunny morning, and in the streets, out in the open air, there was a kind of *allégresse* in which I allowed myself to be heedlessly caught up.

Lunch at the Capşa—long, fine, copious—with Blank, Ionel Gherea, Mrs. Theodorian.[5] It was perhaps a sign of irresponsibility, because our fate may be decided this very day. I realize that we no longer have anything to win, anything to defend, anything to hope for. All is virtually lost. There will come prisons, dire poverty, maybe escape, maybe exile, maybe worse.

Yet I am sufficiently unserious to look at events with a kind of amused curiosity, as if I were watching an exciting football match. For there is no question that it is exciting. Right now (ten o'clock) the government has only 37 to 38 percent on paper, and it does not look as if the figures can be falsified at this late stage. If some miracle of arithmetic does not occur this very night, we'll see a Romanian government fall for the first time in elections. Unless the whole regime collapses by tomorrow morning—which is also a possibility.

But to what extent, I ask, can all this change one letter, one comma even, in a destiny that is not mine but all of ours?

Wednesday, 22 [December]

Yesterday's agitation ended with an hour of calm: alone at home, listening to music with only my desk lamp on, the rest of the room in semi-darkness. From Geneva, a Bach organ chorale; from Breslau, a fugue and toccata by Bach for orchestra, and finally Max Reger's *Variations on a Theme by Mozart*, which I heard for the first time last week at the Philharmonic. Everything was quite beautiful and, above all, soothing.

Braşov, Sunday 26 [December]

At last an hour to myself. I've been here since the evening before last, in a villa together with Carol, Grindea,[6] Iova, the Blanks—too many for me to take.

I hoped to find a room somewhere in Poiana or Timiş, but I wasn't lucky and I didn't know how to look. It's impossible for me to work here

---

5. Alice Theodorian: friend of Sebastian's.
6. Miron Grindea: journalist.

with all these people around. I'm not even trying. But with what pleasure, what painful pleasure, I would write! A short while ago, as I walked down the boulevard, I felt the whole novel alive inside me, like an open wound.

So many things that have happened to me recently in Bucharest, so many stupid turns in my never-ending story with Leni, would find in the book a revenge, a solution, an answer.

Again the lost chapters come into my mind. Impossible to forget, impossible to regain them.

The only moments of relaxation are when I am skiing. Yesterday at Poiana, today at Timiş, I was happy as long as I kept skiing. Thick snow, dazzling scenery, the pleasure of flying on skis and leaping over an undulation of the ground, and finally the triumph of stopping almost correctly (or anyway without falling) at the end of the course. . . .

Tuesday, 28 [December]

I leave for Bucharest this evening, in three hours' time. It seems that a Goga government has been, or is about to be, formed. (Someone spoke from Poiana with Miron Grindea, who talked of an absurd list of ministers: Goga[7] as head of government and the War Ministry, Gh. Cuza,[8] Muncă, General Antonescu somewhere or other. A typical government of panic!) I don't know what will happen. We are waiting. But it seems more serious to wait in Bucharest. I can't be so irresponsible as to ski while the whole of our lives from now on is being decided.

But nor can I be so ungrateful as to deny so soon the joys of skiing.

Yesterday and today I performed real feats of bravery in Poiana. Not only did I ski down from Poiana to Prund without falling too often, but in Poiana, especially today on the "exercise field," I solved all kinds of problems that have initiated me into the tricks of the trade. I can now "slalom" reasonably well without sticks. I also tried a slope at the base of the Schuller, which is certainly the fastest slope I have "attacked" until now, and I completed the whole course without incident, executing a perfect turn to the left and a quick regulation stop. On the other hand, I fell badly on the road back—very near the end, which made it even more comical, and anyway at a point near Solomon where there was no longer any difficulty. I am all in (it's not easy to descend, braking all the time, for three-quarters of an hour), but I am proud of myself.

7. Octavian Goga, prime minister December 1937–February 1938, leader with A. C. Cuza of the heavily anti-Semitic Goga-Cuza government.
8. Gh. Cuza, son of A. C. Cuza and a member of the Goga-Cuza government.

I said today, after I had done my first successful "slalom" exercise, that literature will never give me the same joy. And I wasn't lying.

Nevertheless—to be quite honest—all these initiations into skiing also interest me from the point of view of the novel. I have more and more material for the scenes at Gunther's cabin on the Schuller.

I reread the manuscript the evening before last. I suffer line by line when I see how pockmarked my poor manuscript has become—but on the whole the reading has not discouraged me. I'll have to rewrite more carefully everything I have redone so far, but it can certainly be used, even in the deplorable state in which it is today. Everything may perhaps go well from now on, though not, of course, without difficulty.

I'd love to finish writing this book. The poor thing has had too much bad luck for me not to be fond of it. This is probably the kind of tender feeling one keeps for unhappy children.

Wednesday, 29 [December], Bucharest

The Goga government has been installed—and, contrary to what I thought before arriving in Bucharest, it is not a temporary maneuver but a stable formula. It will hold fresh elections, it will govern the country, and it will carry out the Cuzist program to which each minister referred in his speech. For the first time in an official speech one could hear the vocabulary of *Porunca Vremii*: "yid," "the Jews," Judah's domination, and so on.

The first measures of state anti-Semitism are expected for tomorrow or the day after: a citizenship review, probably elimination from the Bar and in any case from the press.

Will I lose my position at the Foundation? It's quite possible—especially if, as today's papers suggest, the Foundations are brought under the Ministry of Propaganda, with Hodoș at its head. But even without that, it is hard to believe that a Cuzist regime will tolerate a Jew in a "cultural position"—even one as lowly as mine.

I don't know what the atmosphere is like in town. Consternation, bewilderment, alarm, or fear? The papers are lifeless, inexpressive, without any note of protest. I think it is only now that we will start learning what censorship means.

In these conditions, is it not a childish stupidity to be writing literature?

I still haven't been into town. My fall yesterday was more serious than I thought at first. My left thigh is swollen and bruised. I walk, or rather hobble, with difficulty, and treat myself with lead acetate. At one moment I was afraid I'd broken something. That's all I need.

Late at night, when I got back from Braşov, I listened to a Mozart piano concerto from Stuttgart—one I don't think I've ever heard before.

This evening from Paris, a sonata in B-flat by Mozart. And finally, as I write this note (eleven o'clock), something that sounds like Mozart—probably a symphony—also from a French station.

A lot of Mozart, really a lot. Perhaps it's the only thing that can console me for everything that's happened.

(It wasn't a symphony but the *Flute Concerto in G Major*—by Mozart, though, so at least I got that right.)

Thursday, 30 [December]

Dimineaţa, Adevărul, and *Lupta* have been banned for the time being.

Petre Pandrea, the county prefect, somewhere in Moldavia.

Victor Eftimiu[9] has resigned from the Peasant party and joined the Gogists.[1] Apparently he'll be given the Theatre Directorate.

Camil Petrescu 'phoned me and commented on Eftimiu's conversion:

"You know, if he's really appointed to the theatre, I'll join the Iron Guard the next day and won't even say 'hello' to you again."

"All I ask, Camil old boy, is that you ring and tell me in advance, so that I don't say 'hello' to you. That'll make things easier for you."

Train passes are being withdrawn from journalists. Jews have been forbidden the occupation of journalist.

"At the end of the day," says Camil, "you have to admit there have been too many abuses."

"I admit it—how couldn't I? I admit everything."

All day at home reading Charles Morgan's *Sparkenbroke.* A book so remote from the present day! It seems a million miles away!

9. Playwright.
1. Members of the Goga-Cuza National Christian party.

1938

Sunday, 2 January 1938

Still at home because of my leg, which has not yet healed. It is worrying me.

They have revoked my permit. Our names in every paper, as if we were a bunch of delinquents.[1]

New Year's Eve at Leni's. Observed a host of things about her—but what's the point of noting them down?

Finishing with her is a serious business. At thirty I'm no longer allowed to behave so childishly.

I ought to write the article for *Revista Fundaţiilor*. But will it be published? I don't think I can possibly stay on at the Foundation. What will this new year bring me, having started on such a gloomy note?

Not a single phone call from anyone. Mircea, Nina, Marietta, Haig, Lilly, Camil—they're all dead. And I understand them so well!

Monday, 3 [January]

I had a moment of terror during the night. I woke up with the clock striking three in the next room: I think I had a fever, and my left leg was hurting; it felt more swollen than before. I checked the swelling with my hand, and I was suddenly frightened at the thought that it was "like a bag of pus."

An abscess, I said to myself, and everything seemed clear and inevitable. I saw again the whole first chapter of *Inimi cicatrizate*. "Cold abscess," "hot abscess," "fistula," "fistular abscess," "at death's door"—all of Blecher's vocabulary. At last I understood how a fistula digs in, how

1. Immediately after taking power, the Goga-Cuza government initiated a series of anti-Semitic measures, including the revocation of Romanian citizenship for Jews and the elimination of Jewish lawyers from the bar association. Sebastian here refers to the withdrawal of his train pass, which he had received as a journalist.

it makes room for itself, how it can sink through flesh "right into the buttock," as Blecher put it, and how I was never able to understand. . . .

Everything seemed clear. I wondered where I would find the money for the initial cost of my treatment: puncture, sanatorium, dressings. And I wondered who might give me a revolver to end it more quickly. Mircea, perhaps. But would he understand? Would he consent to do it, he who thinks of suicide as the ultimate sin?

These thoughts went on all night and all morning, and I took them with me into Dr. Cuper's waiting room, into his surgery, until the moment when he finally explained that it was a local subcutaneous hemorrhage, a burst blood vessel, some clotted blood, circulation problems over quite a wide area—but nothing serious. The pain will persist for six or seven days, and the bruising for three weeks or so. Rest and treatment with x-rays. I actually had the first session there with Dr. Ghimuş.

Maybe the whole incident came at the right time to remind me that there are, or can be, worse misfortunes than an anti-Semitic regime.

I already knew it perfectly well—only I had forgotten.

Tuesday, 4 [January]

In Charles Morgan's *Sparkenbroke* there is an observation about a Jewish character: "*Mais dans ses yeux noirs luisait une ardente imagination, refroidie par cette tristesse ironique qu'ont des civilisés parmi les barbares, et qui est particulière à sa race.*"[2]

Wednesday, 5 [January]

I've finished with her. . . . But if the act itself was quite easy, done without harsh words and with almost a smile, I shouldn't imagine that it will stay so simple.

Now come the hours of absurd disquiet, the choking need to see her, the obsession with the telephone that never rings, the temptation to pick up the receiver and call her, the hope of meeting her "by chance" in the street, the slight alarm on passing the theatre, the urge to look up to her window when I walk down her street (to see whether the lights are on and, if so, who is visiting her, or, if not, where she might be at that hour, etc. etc. etc.).

2. "But in his black eyes was an ardor of imagination, cooled by that ironic sadness of the civilized among the barbarians which is peculiar to his race." Charles Morgan, *Sparkenbroke* (London and New York: Macmillan, 1936), p. 244.

But all this—which I know so well—will have to be borne with resignation. I shall have to hold out until I regain that composure, that restful oblivion, which I have achieved a few times before but carelessly thrown away. For you must admit, old boy, you are too old and you have too many sorrows in life to remain caught up in this sad, banal, and trifling affair.

I won't allow any excuses. It'll be difficult, of course—the proof is that I'm telling you now, just an hour after the "farewell call," when the anesthetizing effect has not yet worn off. It doesn't hurt, but it soon will. No doubt at all about that!

Friday, 7 [January]

I have avoided writing about my visit to Nae the day before yesterday. I came away with mixed feelings: fondness, irritation, doubts, repugnance.

There, in the fading evening light, he sat in his huge office at that long black table, with his head of hair now turning grey, his eye sockets seemingly deeper than before, his eyebrows also beginning to pale, and his face severe and glum. Indeed, he had just said something to me that could have come straight out of Charles Morgan's novel: "Nothing is more vacuous, more threadbare, than irony—for life is too serious to be ironical with it." For a moment I suddenly had the feeling that I had Sparkenbroke in person before me. I couldn't help telling him this, with a certain show of emotion.

But later I found again my old Nae Ionescu: garrulous, quick-witted, childlike, now and then crafty.

"I was just telling them in Berlin . . . I was talking to one of their ministers, and I explained in detail the characteristics of the Hitler regime. The man listened in silence, then stood up and said: 'Professor, I'll go this very day to the Führer and tell him I have spoken with the only man who has understood the National Socialist revolution.'"

Later Nae told me a host of "secrets" about the government, about the temporary ban on *Adevărul*, about various ministers, about the external situation (all "just between the two of us," of course), and finally about perspectives for the future.

Goga's anti-Semitic measures disgust him. He thinks they are a hollow mockery, issued in a barbarous spirit of raillery.

"How on earth can they say that a whole group of Romanian citizens are engaged in the white slave trade? That's a calumny, and any Romanian citizen has a right to prosecute the minister for spreading it around. How can you drive a million people to suicide and social degradation without endangering the very foundations of the Romanian state?"

I tried to reassure him that the slow, or even the impetuous, killing of Jews would not have quite such grave implications of that kind, and that anyway the Iron Guard would surely not operate differently.

"Not in deeds, but in their mind," was Nae's reply. "You see, laugh as you will, there is a big difference between a man who kills you in a mocking spirit and one who does the same with pain in his heart."

Etcetera, etcetera. Can I summarize a conversation with Nae? A million different things—a million judgments, naive assertions, clarifications, threats, solutions, explanations.

From all that, I did not take away any indication regarding myself.

Yesterday morning, a brief visit to Blank. I am so disoriented that I look everywhere for information and opinions.

"All we Jews can wish for," he argued, "is the continuation of the Goga government. What would come after it would be infinitely worse."

I realize that I am becoming a little apprehensive about what I write in this journal. It's not impossible that I'll be awakened one day by a house search, and there can be no more "scandalous" evidence than a personal diary.

Saturday, 8 [January]

Yesterday evening I wasted three hours, today four, with the manuscript in front of me. I force myself to take it up again, but it doesn't work. I don't know whether it is because I am dispirited, or disgusted with literature, or quite simply lazy.

In the end I gave myself up to reading instead: Malraux's *L'espoir*. I'll work some other time. . . .

Tuesday, 11 [January]

I was determined enough to resist any "resumption" gesture on my part, but not sufficiently firm, nor sufficiently prepared, to resist a call from her. She 'phoned twice yesterday—and so I met her.

What now?

A big disaster in the theatrical world. At the S.C.I.A. an evening's receipts are two to three thousand lei. It's possible that the Regina Maria will shut by next Sunday.

And in such times I become a dramatist!

The Comoedia has announced a play by Sân-Giorgiu for one of its future premieres. Well, that's another matter!

Thursday, 13 [January]

Massoff has been dismissed from the National Theatre, at the minister's express request.[3] It's one of those wretched details that depress me more than a "general measure." It is oppression on the quiet—cowardly and petty. And I cannot help thinking that I'll be sacked from the Foundation in the same way, today, tomorrow, or the day after. . . . I await this calmly—after all, I'm not going to tie my whole life (or perhaps my death) to 5,935 lei a month.

If, amid all this filth, I didn't have to bear my old personal unhappiness, how readily—or so I think—would I tear everything up and start life again from the beginning! Where? No matter where. In the Foreign Legion, for example. But thirty is not the age for adventure seeking, especially with my terrible weariness of life—weariness because I have not lived at all up to now.

It's nearly two months since I last saw Mircea, nearly ten days since we last rang each other. Should I let things unravel by themselves? Should I wrap it all up with a final explanation? I feel such revulsion that I would prefer us both to stop speaking once and for all. I have nothing to ask him, and he certainly has nothing to say to me. On the other hand, our friendship lasted for years, and perhaps I owed it one harsh hour of parting.

I still indulge myself by listening to music in the evening. Yesterday, from Strasbourg, Mozart's *German Dances* and a Schumann concerto for four cellos, which I did not know existed.

It's a kind of narcotic, or a kind of bravado—as if I am saying that absolutely everything is not lost.

Sunday, 16 [January]

She was here yesterday evening. I kept expecting her to ring and say that she was not coming, that she couldn't come. That seemed to me simpler. But she did come—with some violets that she took from the flap

---

3. Ioan Massoff, the National Theatre's literary secretary, was Jewish.

of her cloak, and which I still have here in a glass, on my bedside table. We listened to the *Kleine nachtmusik* and smoked a cigarette, then I took her in my arms. She did not resist or waver, but awaited everything with consent. As she closed her eyes in "abandon," I looked at her before kissing her, as if I wanted to be sure it was really her.

But there is still something murky in all this, something awkward between us. I don't have the strength to refuse, point-blank, things that life has taken away from me, things that it has forbidden me to have.

I went to Mircea's today. I thought we would have it out, but as we spoke I realized that there is no point—that it may even be impossible. It's all over between us, and we are both perfectly aware of the fact. The rest—explanations, excuses, reproaches—does not lead anywhere.

I told him that I am thinking of leaving the country. He approved of the idea—as if it were obvious, as if there were nothing else to be done.

Thursday, 20 [January]

Cuvântul has come out.[4] I can't hold back a quiver of surprise, almost of emotion, when I see its calligraphic title that I used to hold before me every morning and every evening for so many years. It seems both very familiar and utterly strange. As in the old days, whenever I see someone in the street or on a streetcar carrying a copy of the paper that used to be so much my paper, I have the feeling that he is a friend, someone from the same family.

How ironic that sounds today: "from the same family"!

Yesterday evening, for the first time in four years, the windows were lighted up in the editorial offices. I passed by feeling a little sad, but not too much. A sense of irreparability attenuates a farewell. Here, as in love, it is hard if you keep feeling that all is not over, that things can be taken up and put back together again. But when the break is final, when the departure brooks no return, the forgetting is quicker and the consolation easier.

Aderca has been moved to Cernăuți as a reprisal.[5] I read a letter he sent to his wife: no laments, almost no bitterness. He lives in a room rented for a thousand lei a month, and has fifteen hundred lei for food. That's at forty-five years of age, after two wars and twenty books.

4. *Cuvântul* was banned on several occasions for its pro–Iron Guard articles.
5. Felix Aderca, a Jewish novelist, was also a civil servant whom the Goga-Cuza government was unable to dismiss because he was a decorated veteran of World War I. He was forced to move with his job to the provinces.

It's no longer possible to enter the law courts. There were terrible fights yesterday, and apparently more of the same today. I don't upset myself, I don't get worked up. I wait—without knowing exactly for what.

The day before yesterday, a long night's drinking at Mrs. T.'s. I danced all the time, either with her or with her sister; they were equally indiscreet in offering themselves. It was a "louche" atmosphere, which I did not have the energy to reject with the brusqueness it deserved.

And when I think that B. introduced me only so that I would have the opportunity to meet *"un être rare."*[6]

A dream from last night.

I am in Sinaia, in a carriage together with Marietta Sadova and Lilly Popovici. We climb a steep road, looking for a villa where none other than Jules Renard lives. We pass alongside the villa, in the front yard of which are three gentlemen: Virgil Madgearu, Mihail Popovici, and, between them, a thin man with greying fair hair. I stop the carriage and ask:

"Vous ne savez pas si M. Jules Renard habite par là?"

"C'est moi!" the unknown man replies.[7]

I go up to Renard and speak to him with great emotion (Lilly and Marietta remain in the carriage and drive on, or anyway disappear from the dream). He suggests that we go for a walk in the town. We set off together while a young woman—his daughter? his wife?—asks if he will be back soon, gives him a lot of anxious, affectionate advice not to catch cold, not to tire himself, and so on.

On the way I talk in detail about his *Journal* and quote from it. In particular I quote a phrase he uses about the theatre: *"une conversation sans lustre."*[8] The discussion lasts a long time in the dream. (I remember that it is not at all incoherent—well structured, rather.)

We come to a kind of café-restaurant. On the right, in a kind of separate room, there are a number of familiar faces—including, I think, Izi. We avoid them and sit at a table on the left, in a cubicle like those at the Corso.

That is all I remember. This morning, before waking up properly, I mentally repeated the whole dream and there were, I think, more details. But in the course of the day I forgot the dream, and it was only a short while ago, at the Philharmonic, that I remembered it again.

6. A rare creature.
7. "You don't know if M. Jules Renard lives nearby?"—"I am he."
8. "A conversation without sparkle."

Sunday, 23 [January]

Marietta's play will not be performed after all; the dress rehearsal has been banned by ministerial order. *Porunca Vremii* denounced it on the grounds that Lucia Demetrius has a Jewish mother.

I am sorry for her but not unhappy about Marietta. She'll have the chance to feel, in a way that directly affects her, the wild absurdity of her own "political ideas."

An atmosphere of panic, of disorderly retreat. Always the same questions without an answer, always the same laments. It is tiring. The only way to forget is to get drunk. But I am too tranquil, too fond of staying at home, to do that every evening.

Apparently there are dozens, indeed hundreds, of groups in the city to promote all kinds of solutions: mass conversion, emigration, an association of pro-government "Mosaic Romanians," etc., etc. They are desperate people, whose despair takes comical forms. I can't take part in this agitation, this turmoil, except by shrugging my shoulders.

Sunday evening: alone at home. I have no one to see in this big wide city, nor anything to say to anyone, nor anything to hear from anyone. I read, without too much conviction. If my radio were not broken, I'd listen to some music. It's a drug that agrees with me.

A few days ago I started work again on a French translation of *De două mii de ani.* Do I have some definite hope? No! But just as I buy a lottery ticket every month, which gives me a fraction of a thousandth of a chance of winning the "million" prize, I am preparing a text that one day, through some absurd fluke, might find a French publisher. Most important of all, it is mechanical work suitable for my free hours—so free and so disoriented, the poor things!

Tuesday, 1 February

A long lunch yesterday at Vişoianu's. Later, over coffee, Ralea.[9]

They are more disoriented than I am, a "mere individual." If that is Romanian democracy—and there is none other—then it is a dead loss. I no longer have any hope, any expectation. They've given up completely. In their view, the next elections will double the success of the Iron Guard; the National Peasants won't win more than 10 to 12 percent, with roughly the same for the Liberals.

9. Mihai Ralea: minister of labor, March 1938–July 1940.

After a five-hour session there, I left with my head in a whirl. The same grieved shrugging of shoulders, the same stupid consolations "of an external order," the same more or less confidential tidbits of news: Ostrovski spoke, Nae Ionescu squinted, Micescu got into a tangle in Geneva, Eden won't accept, etc., etc. That must be how people discussed the rise of Hitler in Germany, over black coffee after a good lunch. The last comforts on the eve of the final collapse.

I saw Belu Zilber[1] for the first time in four years (he had coffee at Vişoianu's); he is unchanged.

Sunday, a night of heavy drinking with Leni and Jenica Cruţescu. I could drink all the time; I'd do nothing else.

Wednesday, 2 [February]

Another drunken night. But it'll be the last in the series—otherwise there will be no end. It's a promise.

Wednesday, 9 [February]

The days are getting longer. It's still light at six in the evening. It frightens me to think that spring is coming, that a year has passed and I have done nothing at all. No book, no love.

Friday, 11 [February]

The Goga government fell last night! A sudden reflex of satisfaction spreads over me, an irresistible easing of nervous tension. I said to myself—and I say it all the more after a night of troubled sleep—that things are very unclear and may remain just as grave (for us at least), that the anti-Semitic repression may continue. Nevertheless, I cannot stop myself rejoicing; it is such a consolation to see a great imposture suddenly go flat.

But what gave last night its dramatic tone—its nervous joy, its excitement, its cheerful restlessness, its optimistic agitation—was the news, or rather the rumors, about Germany.

Revolt, street-fighting in Berlin, three army corps in open battle with assault troops, etc. etc. etc. Incredible, but enough to make one dizzy.

1. Herbert (Belu) Zilber: a friend of Sebastian's, Communist economist and journalist who later was imprisoned as the victim of an East European Communist show trial.

My old despondency tried to dismiss the reports, but my thirst for happiness—even momentary, even illusory—wanted to believe and began to believe.

Until two in the morning I was lost in the crowd near the Palace, latching onto now one, now another—Carandino,[2] Camil, Ghiţă Ionescu—asking questions, passing on things I heard, convinced when they came from a skeptic, incredulous when they came from someone convinced. I couldn't go home—I'd have wasted the whole night. For indeed, the atmosphere in the streets was feverish, stimulating, charged with expectation, doubts, and supposition.

Now, after some hours have passed and I have read the papers (unclear about Germany, where the situation is confused but not acute in any immediate sense), I am calmer and a little distrustful. I feel as I would after a night of boozing.

Saturday, 12 [February]

The night before last (the night of the crisis), Camil came across me in the Palace Square, where I was waiting to hear some news. He seemed taken aback by what was happening, and I liked having things to say with Camil "reduced to silence."

"You ought to see how the Jews have overrun the Corso. The whole café is full of them. They've really 'taken possession.'"

"What an anti-Semite you are, Camil! Come with me and I'll show you how wrong you are, or how much you like getting things wrong."

I took him by the arm. We went into the Corso, did a tour of the café, stopped at each table, and counted up the suspect faces. In all, there were fifteen Jews in a lively and jam-packed café full of groups heatedly arguing.

With a smile, Camil took everything back in the face of the evidence.

This morning Perpessicius—whom I met at the Foundation—told me about *Cuvântul* and how its editorial life is not much different from what it used to be. There are the same administrative squabbles, the same ironic hostility to Devechi, the same old pathetic stuff (which nevertheless constituted a family life).

But, in addition, there has been an influx of Legionary types. The relaunch dinner took place at the Legionaries' restaurant.

---

2. N. Carandino: journalist.

Monday, 21 [February]

Three days in Predeal at the Robinson villa, from Saturday morning until this evening.

I left Bucharest to escape the tiredness and exasperation and repugnance. So many wretched things, both little and big, which I felt were becoming unbearable. . . .

I return feeling restored to health and strength—or at least partly restored, despite the terrible night of insomnia and nightmares that I had on Saturday. (I find it so hard to get used to an unfamiliar house!)

The snow relaxes me, makes me younger, helps me forget. The Veştea course is the most exacting I have yet encountered in my brief skiing career. I fell innumerable times. But I think I also learned a few things. This morning I finally managed to ski from top to bottom of the highly uneven slopes, and, without falling once, to reach that little island of ice that marks the end of the course, just at the beginning of the forest.

Three days of skiing—and I return with calmer nerves, back where they belong. It's just that this Bucharest, this life I lead . . .

Monday, 28 [February]

Again a couple of days, Saturday and Sunday, in Predeal. Impressions of sun, much light, endless childhood—something resembling happiness. Nothing remains of my usual bitterness, of my stupid questions and futile regrets; nothing remains of that life made up of scraps, of broken promises, endless waiting, confused discontent, weary little hopes.

Here everything becomes simple again. Only a day at Balcic—naked, basking in the sun—has the same intensity.

Yesterday morning, with the snow bathed in sunlight, I no longer had any thoughts, any melancholy, any expectations. I was quite simply happy.

I wore only a shirt, and I would gladly have removed that too: it was a day for the chaise longue and bathing costume. I am returning with sunburnt cheeks, as in my best days of old.

As to the skiing, I am making visible progress. I descended—this time without falling once—the slopes that only last week intimidated me. I learned a kind of "christie," which I find easy enough and which gives me an unexpected feeling of *"maitrise"* on the ground. It is true that, as soon as I leave the practice area and "venture" onto an unknown track, all my experience ceases to be of any help. Yesterday afternoon I kept falling on the way from Veştea to Timiş, where I went with Devechi, Lupu, and two people from their circle. But it was a useful outing, at least as a stamina-building exercise.

On Saturday I went skiing with Virgil Madgearu. Skiing turns everyone into a child again, even former ministers.

But, of course, we must become serious again when we return home.
I have a mass of things awaiting me. I'm thinking of going back to my
"Romanian Novel" essay. Since Roman is leaving for London, and since
we still can't get into the courts, I shall try now to spend my mornings
working at the Academy.

Monday, 14 March

Emil Gulian, whom I met after a long time, is still the same disoriented
boy full of personal questioning (loves, lassitudes, scruples, expectations),
indifferent to political events, corrupted by poetry. . . . The Goga-Cuza
"period" depressed him. He tells me he felt ashamed—and I believe him.

I saw Săn-Giorgiu the other day at the Foundation. He is unrecognizable. He no longer wears a swastika. He speaks of the mistakes made by
their government.

"In short, old man, that's not the way to do things either. . . ."

He is friendly and communicative. He tells me of his theatrical successes in Germany.

"Not even Ibsen had such a triumph: not one unfavorable review!"

The skiing was a splendid distraction. The last two Sundays I haven't
been to Predeal—where I don't think there is any more snow—and I am
beginning to feel the effects. I am not at all content with the life I am
leading. I read a book by fits and starts, I write nothing, I don't work,
I waste my time at Roman's or at the Foundation, and I come away restless and a nervous wreck. I'd like to work—but I don't have the mettle
to begin. It would require an effort of organization and discipline.

Will I go to Paris for Easter? Or to Balcic? Will I ever get back to
writing *Accidentul*? Will I ever write that book about the Romanian novel?

I live by fits and starts, from day to day. I have no money, my clothes
are wearing out, and I just wait for evening to come, for morning to
come, for it to be Thursday, for it to be Sunday. What's the point of it
all? For how much longer?

Wednesday, 16 [March]

I don't know what's the matter with me. I'm tired all the time, incapable
of keeping at anything for a few hours. I spent a couple of days on my
last review for the Foundation, deleting, reading aloud, losing the thread,

overemphasizing the incidental, cutting short the main ideas. I read by fits and starts—no more than a quarter of an hour at a time. A few pages of Saint-Simon last night; today a bit of Carlo Gamba's *Botticelli*, which I never manage to finish. Even these lines are hard for me to write. The letters dance before my eyes.

I wasted the whole of today tinkering around with a little drama review for *Viața românească*. The article I promised about Camil's book gives me the frights.

All this is quite serious. I think of my novel, I think of my critical work—and I wonder how I'll ever complete them, or even start them, with these tired eyes and this broken concentration.

If I had the money, I'd see an eye specialist again.

Thursday, 17 [March]

Headline in today's *Cuvântul*:
"Pseudo-scientist Freud arrested in Vienna by National Socialists."

Friday, 25 [March]

Spring, oh unbearable spring—all week I lived in the hope of leaving for Balcic today. It's a holiday, Annunciation Day. And if I'd made a long weekend of it and come back to Bucharest on Tuesday, I could quite easily have had a five-day break, with four whole days in Balcic.

I see myself in the courtyard at Parușeff, alone on a chaise longue facing the sea. I see myself in a track suit in a deserted Balcic, idling away the time at Mamut, on the pier or in a boat. . . . Everything would have been forgotten, everything healed. I have so much to forget, so much to heal.

But out of laziness, indecision, or stupidity, I stayed to drag myself around this springtime Bucharest, where I have no one except at home, where I am neither alone nor not-alone, where the days and the hours pass in lifeless exhaustion.

Waiting for what? Wishing for what? Maybe an effort of will, maybe a cold determination to work—not for the pleasure of it, but to escape this sense of futility.

Tuesday, 29 [March]

Cella's book has appeared,[3] with the following words on the cover band: "The writers Liviu Rebreanu, Camil Petrescu, and Mihail Sebastian recommended this novel to the publisher."

Epilogue: this morning Mrs. Rebreanu rang Camil Petrescu in alarm and asked how they could permit such effrontery; the names of Rebreanu and Sebastian alongside each other.

One day I'll tell Rebreanu of this little incident—with a laugh, of course.

Saturday, 9 April

Last night I casually switched on the radio, not having gone near it since it broke down a couple of months ago. Its latest whim is that it picks up only Budapest on all wavelengths. But chance had it that last night I was able to hear a beautiful Mozart concert: the *Double Piano Concerto*, and the *Symphony in A Major*. A good hour of music—and the pleasure of again being alone. I have gone out so much recently—evening after evening!

Since I stopped being able to use the radio, I have no longer made a note of my musical itineraries. Actually, "itinerary" is too big a word—listening sessions, rather. The repertoire at the Philharmonic (where I still go regularly) is by now completely known to me. After three years that is hardly surprising. This year seems the poorest in musical terms: only the *Goldberg Variations*, played a fortnight ago by Kempff, has been a real event for me. This evening I'll hear Backhaus: the *Italian Concerto* by Bach, and two Beethoven sonatas.

Ten days or so ago at Grindea's, I listened on disc to a Stravinsky work that I did not know: the *Histoire du soldat*. Very witty, very ingenious. When it comes to the moderns, I'm afraid that I am most receptive to "ingenuity."

One evening I came across Nina on the 16 streetcar. I was just about to ask a lady in front of me if she was getting off at the next stop (so that I could pass by). She turned her head, and it was her. I can't say that I didn't feel pleased to see her again. I'd have liked to kiss her.

3. Cella Serghi: novelist.

Tuesday, 12 [April]

Dinner at Mircea's on Sunday evening. It was a long time since I had seen him. He's unchanged. I looked at him and listened with great curiosity to what he said. The gestures I had forgotten, his nervous volubility, a thousand things thrown together—always congenial, straightforward, captivating. It's hard not to be fond of him.

But I have so much to say to him about *Cuvântul*, about the Iron Guard, about himself and his unforgivable compromises. There can be no excuse for the way he caved in politically. I had decided not to mince my words with him. In any case, there's not much left to mince. Even if we meet again like this, our friendship is at an end. . . . I couldn't talk to him because of the Pencius, who came unexpectedly just as we were rising from the table. I don't know when I'll see him again.

Dinner at Ralea's yesterday. It's the second time I've seen him since he became a minister. Again we discussed his exit from the National Peasants. His explanations seemed inadequate for such a betrayal, even if it was committed out of honest conviction.

According to Ralea, the Iron Guard is still a great danger. He told me some incredible things. Three-quarters of the state apparatus has been "Legionized."

Wednesday, 13 [April]

Yesterday evening, the *St. Matthew Passion* at the Ateneu. By now I know it too well not to notice when it is badly performed. The lack of an organ began to bother me. The choruses were deafening, the soloists inadequate, the orchestra rusty, the general tone confused. It is no longer enough for me just to read the text; it has become too familiar to deliver by itself the emotion that I used to feel. I'd like to hear a proper *Matthäus-Passion*. But even so, I enjoyed again hearing the arias I have come to know. And I listened more analytically, more grammatically, more closely than before.

Saturday, 16 [April]

There are some simple things that I have always known, but that sometimes give me the arresting sense that I am discovering them for the first time.

On Tuesday, as I listened to the *St. Matthew Passion*, I couldn't get the Evangelist's words out of my mind: "Now, the first day of the feast of unleavened bread, the disciples came to Jesus, saying unto Him: 'Where wilt Thou that we prepare for Thee to eat the Passover?' And he said: 'Go into the city to such a man, and say unto him, "The Master saith: My time is at hand, I will keep the Passover at thy house."'"

It was the feast that we too have been celebrating since yesterday evening, the bread we eat, the wine we drink . . .

I suddenly remembered that Jesus was a Jew—something of which I am never sufficiently aware, and which forces me to think again about our terrible destiny.

In the same way I stopped last autumn at Chartres Cathedral to look at the *Circumcision* of Jesus. It was just like at an ordinary *bris*: an old man, holding the ritual knife in one hand and the child's "willy" in the other, looked like the "Moishe shoikhet" in Brăila.

I have been reading Nietzsche's *Daybreak* since yesterday evening. Somewhere it talks of the "Jewish ballast" in Christianity.

How terribly ironic is that ballast, but somehow also a kind of consolation for us.

Tuesday, 19 [April]

Cuvântul was closed down on Sunday.

What was the point of its reappearing? So that it would have time for two or three acts of infamy! So that it could speak of the "pseudo-scientist" Freud? So that it could claim that the Jewish attorneys mutilated each other fighting at the law courts? I'd like to speak to the professor one day about all this: not to reproach him, but to bring back to mind a *Cuvântul* that once really did fight "with its visor raised."

Restlessness, anxiousness, questions without answers. Iron Guard people arrested, a plot discovered or "staged," rumors to your heart's content—and not a single word in the papers, which leave it to you to believe whatever you like.

I want to go for ten days or so to Balcic, but I wonder whether it would not be unwise to leave town. I can't forget that my Christmas holiday was cut short by that dreadful Goga government, so unexpected, so implausible, so absurd. Another such incident cannot be excluded—and I wouldn't like to be caught a long way from home.

On Sunday—because all kinds of rumors were circulating about the arrest of Iron Guardists—I telephoned Mircea and then went to see him.

He was there, and Marietta came a little later. They were all indignant at the arrests and shutdowns, considering them mindless, arbitrary, and illogical. I should have liked to tell them that that is dictatorship (which they want too, so long as it does not strike them personally but allows them, and only them, to strike at others).

But I held my tongue. What good would it do, through irony or allusion, to begin the settling of accounts that I must one day have with them, openly and without sentimentality?

Balcic. Saturday, 30 April

I have been here for a week. I found the same room that I had last year at the Dumitrescu villa.

Why haven't I written a line since I arrived? Maybe because I have been haunted by the thought of those journal pages that I wrote here exactly a year ago, in the same room and facing the same sea with its thousand colors and sounds—but that I lost a few months later in Paris, together with the manuscript of the novel. I see the pages before me, as if it were just yesterday that I held them in my hand. . . .

How many things there have been to record! I let them all pass randomly, but now that my return is approaching I feel that I leave behind not a week of idleness but ten, fifteen.

Yesterday, naked in the sea. I went to Ecrene with Cicerone, Julietta (even today I don't know her full name), her sister, and the major. On the beach at Ecrene, barefooted, undressed, I walked through the forest (an unlikely forest, fifty meters from the sea), pulled a branch from a wild pear tree in blossom, tore off a stem of bulrush as tall as a spear, wrestled, shouted, wilted in the sun—and returned late in the day to Balcic, sunburnt, with a fever in which I could feel mixed together the sea air, the wind, the few hours of revelry on the beach, the whole day of sun and childhood.

I still don't know the name of the major's wife. For some reason they call her "Iancu"—and I like that rather odd male name said to a melancholic woman. She is not beautiful. I'd even say she's far from beautiful. But a certain meek tenderness, moving in a woman of her age (thirty-five?), gives her so much femininity. Their conjugal tragedy is simple: a husband who is both impotent and wildly jealous; a provincial life with no escape, watched over by the whole little town.

She came here one afternoon: she cried as she quietly told me everything, letting the tears run and wiping them away like a child. She stroked me, kissed me, but I declined her sallies, not sharply but firmly. Yesterday evening, as we returned from Ecrene, she told me of the sudden passion she could not help "having" for me.

No, Iancu dear, no.

Nae Ionescu was here over Easter. As my way to the center of town passes by his villa, I called on him. (I think he was actually here on my first day, last Saturday.)

Still the same perennial Nae! Suddenly, without leading up to it in any way, he told me everything he said to Nicholson—which was to get stuffed, of course. His inimitable tone of pert modesty! How childish he is, how he wants to shock people! And how much I enjoy helping him, with my air of forbidden admiration, constant amazement, and curious expectation. This childishness of his is one of the last things for which I am still fond of him.

To Nicholson (the Labour M.P. who was in Bucharest two weeks ago), he said that he would understand nothing in Romania if he judged it by the criterion of "individual liberty." It wasn't a value with which we were familiar; we'd just borrowed it from somewhere, but the natural, organic evolution of the Romanian people passed it by as something dispensable.

Very well—I'd have liked to say in reply to Nae—but when you say such things on the terrace of a magnificent villa in Balcic, or on the balcony of a sumptuous palace in Băneasa, when a Mercedes-Benz is waiting for you outside, when you get your clothes from London, your linen from Vienna, your furniture from Florence, and your toiletries from Paris, this theorizing is all terribly reactionary. Isn't it somehow an unconscious act of defense?

When I opened the window yesterday morning, the first thing I saw was a young girl leaving the villa opposite mine and running down the street in white shorts, a white sports shirt, and an orange blouse, all gleaming in the sunlight.

She may have been an ugly girl (and later, when I saw her more closely at Mamut, she proved to be not at all out of the ordinary), but at that moment she was youth, freedom, morning itself.

Une jeune fille en fleur . . . (especially as I am reading Proust, as I usually do on holiday).

I learned to my surprise that Virginica Rădulescu—the little tart I met five years or so ago at one of Carol's parties and with whom I had a bit of a fling (she was standing in for Mîntuleasa at the time)—has married an architect who is head over heels in love with her. I met them both in Balcic, and I couldn't help remembering the dreadful story of Aurică Rosenthal and Geta—a rather similar incident.

Well, who should I meet Thursday evening walking by the Fishing Lake with Virginica and the architect? *Je vous le donne en mille*[4] . . . It was Geta, of course, with her new husband. A secret solidarity of destiny, profession, and temperament.

Poor Swann. Poor Saint-Loup. There is always a new Odette, a new Rachel.

And you, who write these lines, are you sure you don't have an Odette of your own in Bucharest, one to whom you even sent a couple of love letters from here, which she may have read on her way to or from a rendezvous?

Bucharest, [Sunday], 8 May

Since I returned from Balcic a week ago, I have been leading the inexcusable life of an idler, who wears himself out by wasting his time. I haven't managed to stay at home for a single evening. I've wasted my nights either with Nelly Ehshich (after *Götterdämmerung*), or with Cicerone (after the *Rosenkavalier*), or with Cella (an evening at the movies), or with Leni and Froda at the Melody (tonight I returned at four in the morning, not even too distraught to have watched her flirting all the time with Lazaroneanu, Hefter, and a hundred other guys to whom she flashed smiles, greetings, summonses, remarks . . .). I must give her her due: all of last week she was extraordinarily affectionate, coming to me no fewer than three times in seven days.

I promise to be more hardworking and sensible. I can't bear myself when I become lazy and let myself go. Idleness is all very well at Balcic, the only place where it doesn't demoralize me.

[Wednesday], 11 May

Nae Ionescu has been arrested. I haven't been able to find out any details. Mircea doesn't call, and I can't very well keep insisting—that would seem indiscreet in present circumstances.

It seems he was arrested on Saturday morning. What will happen now, I don't know. Is he really at Miercurea-Ciuc?[5] Will he be kept there

---

4. I give you a thousand guesses.
5. Both Nae Ionescu and Mircea Eliade were interned in the Miercurea-Ciuc camp for their Iron Guard activities.

under house arrest? Will he be implicated in the trial of Codreanu? Will he lose his professorship?

I'm distressed at what is happening to him? What a strange turn of events!

Friday, 20 May

Yesterday evening at *Viața românească*, Suchianu[6] and I were talking with each other and moving toward the open window (it all lasted no more than three minutes or so). Then who should appear on the pavement below, walking slowly and in her amorous way with an elegant young man? Leni!

I don't know if I gave a start, but in a split second I sized up the situation, felt the shock, made up my mind, left Suchianu hanging in mid-conversation, and reached the street door in a few steps. Leni and her flirt were just then in front of the building, and I called out:

"Leni!"

I think she was stunned, but I don't really remember. All I could see were her big eyes and a kind of smile that said nothing.

"Leni, I'm glad to see you. I was at the Court of Appeal until seven o'clock for your case. It's been postponed until the 17th of September." ("The 17th of September," she repeated, as if making a note of it.) "I rang you at home, but there was no answer. I 'phoned *Rampa*, but I couldn't get hold of Mr. Froda to tell him. . . . Look, this is *Viața românească* here. I tell you so that you won't think I was on lookout duty."

All in a single breath. I kissed her hand and went back inside.

(I know the guy. He's the architect who gave expert testimony at the Maryse–Anghelache trial.)

I felt dizzy. Or, to be more precise, I didn't know what I felt. "Does it hurt?" I asked myself attentively, with some concern. I didn't feel that it hurt, but there was a kind of agitation, an emptiness in my heart, an oppressiveness that was hard to define—come on, I'm familiar enough with all that! I had one clear thought: how lucky I was to have been at the window just at that moment. A second later and I wouldn't have seen anything. I'd have remained in ignorance, continued to make a complete fool of myself.

(No other interpretations were possible, of course. A man with whom Leni goes for a walk at seven in the evening, on a little side street, is a

6. D. I. Suchianu: movie critic and journalist.

man with whom she has already slept, or with whom she will sleep in the shortest possible time.)

I went away flummoxed from *Viața românească*, and all the way on the No. 32 bus (I was going to Mermoz and Lilly Pancu, the young couple I'd met at Easter at Balcic) I kept repeating stupid little phrases to calm myself down: just so that the time would pass more and more quickly. For the moment I had a single wish: that it should be nine o'clock, when she'd finally be at the theatre and therefore alone. Not that I wanted to see her (from that moment I knew I'd never see her again), but it was necessary for my immediate peace of mind that she should be alone. Alone, above all else. As for the rest, we'll see . . .

At Mermoz's, where I thought I'd stop by for half an hour, a Balcic-style party was awaiting me. There was the whole of our group from late April, plus two young women—one of them Zoe Ricci, the painter I met last November at Lena Constante's.

We had some drinks. I had decided to get drunk, and never was an evening's boozing more timely. The memory of Leni faded. From time to time it still hurt, like a sore spot that suddenly throbs again for a while. Maybe it's not quite right to say that "it hurt." I just saw again the brief scene that took place at seven o'clock. It had all been so sudden; I hadn't even noticed the color of her dress.

I spent all evening close to Zoe Ricci—at first by chance, later because I found it pleasant. Soon our mutual attraction was being helped along in the usual way by the other people there, who teased us, drew attention to silences, gave an occasional prod, and turned a simple joke into the beginning of a relationship.

We went onto the balcony, which looked onto open fields. Mermoz's house was on the outskirts of Bucharest. Beyond there was grass, trees, a few solitary houses, some telephone poles. It was quite similar to the "zoned" landscape in the grounds of the Herald Hospital.

We sat chatting for a long time, Zoe in a chaise longue, I at her feet. She seems very young. Her body, in particular, is extremely youthful. She has slanting eyes, slightly overdefined cheekbones, a child's mouth. She kisses timidly, but also with a kind of desperation. Later, at her place—for we left the others without too much embarrassment and went to her third-floor studio flat on Piața Rosetti—she cried in my arms:

"How nice it is not to be alone."

That's something that Nora could have said.[7] She actually says it in a way. So here is life, a year later, repeating a situation in a novel. . . .

7. Nora is a character in the novel *Accidentul*.

I don't know what will come of the incident with Zoe. Certainly not love. *J'en sors,*[8] and I'm not aching to start again. But she'll help me *"d'en sortir."*

Anyway, whereas I might have spent a night of insomnia and suffering, I spent one of wine and love. So it's not so serious. . . . And when I think about it, the affair with Leni had to finish in any case, so this ending is perhaps not the worst that could have happened.

Baltazar has gone mad. Creeping general paralysis. They're admitting him tomorrow. What a terrible business!

Tuesday, 24 May

"You have a face that's easily forgotten," Zoe said to me the day before yesterday, when I went to see her again.

I started. Nora said the same thing: "You have a face that's hard to remember."

I don't know where this new affair will lead me. I accept it with a certain lack of responsibility. I don't know how it may end. For the moment I'm happy that she is so young, so beautiful. Naked, she is miraculously beautiful. Her breasts are small, firm, and tender—rather like a teenager's. Her face is serious, and she has a severe way of looking at you—something sad and disconsolate in her expression. But her body is lively, youthful, athletic, undulous. I felt good listening to her breathe in my arms, stroking her dark, slightly wiry hair. I especially liked it when she made simple and unrealistic plans for a summer holiday together, in a mountain village somewhere, just the two of us, working alone during the day (she painting, I writing) and making love at night.

That is happiness, my impossible happiness . . .

Monday, 30 [May]

Sleepless hours add up until I can no longer count them. I should sleep for three days on end to recover. . . . I've hardly stopped drinking recently (the whole day on Friday at Condiescu's, the whole night on Saturday at Siegfried's). Almost every day I go to bed at two or three, when I return home from Zoe's, a little drunk even if I haven't been drinking.

Yesterday, Sunday, I was at her place from five in the afternoon until after midnight, both of us naked (or almost naked), sprawled on her green

---

8. I extricate myself.

blanket (in the grass, as she says). The telephone rang, the doorbell rang, and we held our breath until the danger had passed.

Yesterday she told me "the story of her life." How different from what I had imagined! This girl was close to suicide! This girl wanted to hang herself! This girl carries inside her an unhappy and—however much she denies it—unhealed love. She is so young, so beautiful, and so eager to die. She speaks with great simplicity, but with a despondency that no longer seems to allow of any hope. Yet she is twenty-five, and one day somebody or something will release her from this torpor and carry her back toward life. Why can't I be the one?

Sunday, 5 June

Blecher has died. His funeral was on Tuesday, at Roman.

I thought not of his death, which was a merciful release in the end, but of his life, which has been shaking me to the core. His suffering was too great to allow compassion or tenderness. That young man, who lived as in another world because of his terrible pain, always remained something of a stranger. I could never completely open up and show real warmth toward him. He scared me a little, kept me at a distance, as at the gates of a prison that I could not enter or he leave. I tell myself that nearly all our conversations had something awkward, as if they were taking place in a *parloir*.[9] And each time we said goodbye, where did he return to? What was it like there?

I won't write today, and maybe never will, about what has happened between Zoe and me this last week. Our terrible nights on Wednesday and Friday!

But she is an exciting girl—much more, an exceptional person. I don't know if I love her, but I'm convinced that I could. In any case, after a fortnight I feel she weighs more in my life than Leni ever did in four years.

Leni? Who's that? She is so far away and means so little to me. I've seen her two or three times, and it was as if she had not been there. How refreshing it is to look at her with normal eyes, neither questioning nor stupefied, somewhat indifferent, somewhat bored.

9. A visiting room in an institution.

Monday, 4 July

I'm a bit crazy. I have no money and live from day to day off little loans; sometimes I can't put a hundred lei together, I can't catch a streetcar or buy stamps for a letter. There are moments when I don't know whom to ask, or above all how to ask (because I die with shame, and poverty makes me suffer more in my pride than in anything physical). But at the same time I'm planning a trip to Italy!

This morning I went by chance with Tuţubei Solacolu into Citta; I looked through some brochures there and took a few away. Since then my head has been roaring with Italian names: lakes, mountains, valleys. Misura, Siusi, Carezza, Breyes.

Isn't it madness? Of course it is. At the moment all I have are three hundred lei, left over from a five-hundred note that I borrowed last night from Carol.

But if I'm to leave on holiday on the 15th, and if I have to find the money for it, why should I pay 230 lei a day for a Romanian chalet on the Schuller, Ghilcoş, or Iacobeni instead of using it somewhere in Italy?

My madness becomes sensible as soon as I do some detailed calculations. But they do make me dizzy. . . .

I'll try to get an airplane ticket to Venice—and if one is available, I'll need fifteen thousand lei (without any extra charges), that is, two thousand lire. It's a lot of money, and hard to find, but is it impossible?

I haven't written a line here for a month. Too much has been going on, and it's been too muddled. Leni's return, her visits, her departure, her letters. Then Zoe, Zoe, Zoe, always Zoe, every day Zoe. My mind will clear only on the day when I am alone and far away. But will I be?

Bran, Sunday, 24 July

I've been here in Bran since Thursday—I myself don't know how I got here. I left Bucharest without a clear destination but with a thousand regrets. Why didn't I arrange a trip in time to Italy? Why didn't I write to Fräulein Wagner at Ghilcoş? Why not Iacobeni? Why not the chalet on the Schuller, like last year?

I'd kept the chalet in mind as a fallback solution, but I'm glad I didn't go there in the end. It would have depressed me too much to return to the place where, just a year ago, I wrote the lost novel.

Bran, at first sight, seemed rather like Breaza. How hesitant I was about staying there! I walked a dozen times around Mr. Stoian's villa, unsure whether to pay the deposit or not. If something made me decide, it was the beautifully clean and peaceful villa, with the forest a few steps away, a kind of park of its own, and a stream almost beneath the window. I hear it constantly, day and night, whispering with the sound of rustling leaves. It is restful, soothing, full of forgetting.

I gradually explored Bran in several walks yesterday, the day before, and this morning. Of course, there is not the same sense of being in wild parts amid high mountains that I had on the Schuller or even in Ghilcoş. Everything here is calmer, gentler, more subdued. But nor is there any comparison with Breaza. The landscape is infinitely more varied, more colorful, more rich in surprises. I have done four longish walks, and each time I discovered something, a new aspect, a new forest. There are places where I feel I am in France, at Cluzes. The Queen's castle, not typically Romanian at all, looks like a château in Haute-Savoie.

I'm not "overwhelmed," as I was the first year in Ghilcoş, nor do I have the sense of great solitude that the chalet on the Schuller gave me. But I am contented and have confidence in this Bran, from which I ask a little rest and some luck in my work.

I allowed myself three days of repose, sleep, and idleness. Tomorrow I start working again. Will I make any headway? Will I be diligent enough? Will I manage to pick up the broken threads? I am anxious, as usual, but also determined not to give up. This month is my last chance to finish the book, which has been dragging on for two years, with so much heart-searching, so many regrets. Everything has been at a standstill because of it. When I see it come out, what I will feel is not that I have finished a book but that I have ended an overlong relationship that was beginning to wear me down.

Tuesday, 26 [July]

Yesterday three pages, today four. Of course, I still can't consider that I am safely on my way. My main aim has been to keep to the work schedule I set myself for this week: I am at my table from nine to twelve in the morning, from three to six in the afternoon. The rest will be decided by chance and the Good Lord above. How terribly difficult it is to train myself to write! Whenever I set a blank page before me, I do so with fear and trepidation, with doubts and perhaps a little repugnance. . . . How beautiful it is outside on the lawn: green, bright, and sunny, calling you to idleness and reverie. All I have of the hardworking writer are the pangs of conscience; they take the place of real professionalism. And in order to still those pangs, so that I don't have the unbearable sense of wasting time, I go back to work in a spirit of resignation. There is no enthusiasm—not yet, at least.

Wednesday, 27 [July]

A little better than yesterday: six pages. But they are insignificant pages, neither good nor bad, which can be either kept or discarded without spoiling or solving anything.

I still don't feel at the heart of the book; I don't see my characters, feel them beside me. I grope along, hesitate, wait. . . .

Sunday, 31 [July]

It's hard going, and it has certainly been slow. I'm into my seventh day of work—and maybe it's not too bad that I've written only thirty-five pages. That makes an average of five a day, a satisfactory yield especially as I have been a little unwell and couldn't work at all for two afternoons. On the other hand, it is worrying that the "scenario" of the novel has advanced so little. I'm still only on Chapter Five, which is becoming a kind of autonomous novelette within the book as a whole. I give too much space to episodes that should not count as more than incidental. The one with the photographs takes up twelve pages! That's too much—especially in comparison with the part of the novel that has been lost and redone, where much more important events (precisely because I could reconstitute them in their entirety) have something elliptical and unintentionally concise, which makes the new pages seem digressive in contrast. I ought to be frightened when I think that I am still only halfway through the plot. At times—now, for example—I feel that everything remains to be done, and that all the work up to now counts for nothing.

Wednesday, 3 August

Two days (Monday and Tuesday) lost on the review for *Fundații* and the proofs of the study of Proust, which arrived in galleys.

Today I returned to the novel. Any interruption is dangerous, because it draws me away and makes it difficult to go back. So things went rather slowly: not even five pages—about four and three-quarters—in more than seven hours of work. But I enjoyed Paul's stop in Cologne, and I especially liked my rethinking of the Belgian visa incident (Hergenrath, 23 July), a chance happening in the first chapter which I had thought I would take up again.

Friday, 5 [August]

I thought I would finish Chapter Five today (which has taken so many unexpected turns), and I could indeed have finished it if I had resigned myself to a little effort. At the last minute, however, there were a few "scene" changes—Ann's quite unexpected departure with Paul to Sinaia—which meant an addition to the chapter. So I decided to leave it until tomorrow, when I am determined to finish it, come what may.

"Determined to finish it" is, frankly speaking, childish nonsense. I never know what will happen, and each morning I face the manuscript with the same trepidation. In the evening, when I count the five or six pages written in the course of the day (yesterday six, today only five, though I worked hard this morning and thought I would set a new record), I don't have the feeling that they were too difficult to write, but the next morning I am still afraid and hesitant. Will I never firmly establish myself at the heart of the novel? Will I never, right up to the end, have the feeling that I am in control, that it can no longer get away from me?

Saturday, 6 [August]

So you see, *qu'il ne faut jurer de rien.*[1] I didn't finish Chapter Five—in fact, I wrote only four pages, and I've no idea when I'll finish this chapter. Just now, at the end, I begin no longer to see properly what is happening. I am completely dissatisfied with my day's work, and it frightens me to think that my holiday is passing and the novel is still at a standstill.

Sunday, 7 [August]

I have been thinking of a whole host of books that I could have written, that I promise to write. This always happens when I am caught up in work: I see possible themes, I decide not to waste any more time, I make all kinds of promises to be more assiduous. Later, of course, when I return to my impossible life in Bucharest, I forget everything, let myself go, and become disheartened.

The truth is that when I have a publisher like the Foundations, where I could regularly publish one or even two books a year, it is unforgiv-

1. One should never swear anything.

able that I should put so much into all these reviews, for which I need only have an orderly schedule of reading and writing.

With a regular life of that kind, would I find it difficult to write in three to four months the first volume of my book on the Romanian novel? These last few evenings I promised in a long conversation with myself to get seriously down to work on this.

I can also envisage a few studies on "letters and journals" in French literature. The study of Proust's correspondence may have been a beginning. But the list would contain Stendhal's journal and correspondence (including *Souvenirs d'égotisme* and *Vie de Henry Brulard*), Flaubert's correspondence, Goncourt's *Journal*, Renard's *Journal*, the Rivière–Fournier letters, Proust's correspondence, and Gide's *Journal*. Even that would mean a book of four to five hundred pages, all the more tempting to write since I could publish each chapter in the *Review* as I finished it and be paid for the work twice (though, of course, such work may be unpaid).

I can also see a volume of criticism about several Romanian poets: Arghezi, Blaga, Maniu, Baltazar.

Indeed, what works of criticism could there not be? But I tie everything to the appearance of *Accidentul* as the necessary prerequisite. I absolutely must see it published; only then will I have clear ground ahead. Consequently, even if I cannot stay here in Bran for more than another fortnight or so—which, given how slowly things are going, is certainly not enough for me to finish—I am thinking of leaving Bucharest again in September for two to three weeks, perhaps to Braşov, and this time completing the manuscript at any cost.

Plans, plans . . . We'll see what will come of them.

Today I finally completed Chapter Five. Apart from the pages that were lost and then reconstituted, it has sixty pages that I have written in Bran. I didn't think it would assume such proportions. From tomorrow I'll have to go back to Nora, whom I haven't seen for such a long time. I fear that I am losing the thread and no longer know how things will develop, in unfamiliar territory. Chapter Six exists only in very broad outline. It is the one that should take me into the book's "plot," properly so called. Perhaps I should prepare myself for major obstacles and resistances.

I can't help thinking that, if I hadn't lost the manuscript, I would now have 171 pages written—that is, material that could have been safely sent to the printer's. But I should put regrets to one side and see what can be done from now on.

Monday, 8 [August]

A day lost in wavering. I am always afraid to start. I reread what I had written before, skimmed several times the chapters that concern Nora— on the pretext of getting to know her again, of regaining the tone that best suits her, but in reality because I didn't have the will to get seriously down to work. Out of superstition (Mircea once told me it was good to start working on Monday), I have nevertheless written a few lines.

Tomorrow I shall have to be more resolute. Just shut your eyes and press on: that's the only way a book can be finished.

Last night I thought it wouldn't be a bad idea to reverse the order of the fifth and fourth chapters, precisely to smooth the transition from Ann to Nora. Besides, whatever I do, the Ann chapter will interrupt the flow of the book; it will be a digression from which it will be a little difficult to return.

Tuesday, 9 [August]

There are no inspired days, but—alas!—there are bad days when everything you write, or force yourself to write, comes out dull, clottish, inert. You can't see anything ahead; it is all, if not false, then flat, otiose, unmeaning. I write a sentence, then wonder whether to leave it or cross it out. I cross it out, then afterward everything seems better than the one with which I have replaced it.

So that's how I wasted the whole of today. I wrote three to four pages against my inclination, but they are so colorless, so inexpressive, that I am embarrassed to look at them again. This chapter, the sixth, doesn't want to get started.

Am I lazy? I don't think so. Or, in any case, I am no lazier than I used to be. I sat dutifully at my desk for the regulation six hours (maybe half an hour less), but to no avail. And everything is dull and inert before me. I'll wait patiently for some light to appear—though, of course, there is only one possible way of waiting: *"la plume ferme au-dessus du papier,"*[2] as Renard said, and the poor man knew what he was talking about.

---

2. With the pen held firmly above the paper.

Tuesday, 11 [August]

All day yesterday, all morning today, I didn't even pick up my pen, didn't even dare to approach the manuscript. I have ground to a halt.

Only this afternoon did I try to get back to it. But it's seven now and growing dark, and I have to break off with not even three pages written. But now it's a question not of counting pages but of knowing whether I shall be able to write, or whether I shall be "stuck" here for a long time to come.

Work accidents that cannot be foreseen.

Sunday, 14 [August]

It's still hard going. Friday three pages or so, yesterday five, but today again only three. Now, when things are nevertheless a little clearer, it should flow more easily. But it doesn't want to. I need whole hours for the simplest movement, the slightest gesture. I long for things to ease up a little. I wish I didn't feel so many obstacles, so much resistance. Maybe it's all a bad habit of mine. Maybe it would be simpler if I let the pen rush on ahead and skip over some difficulties, which, if need be, could be looked at again later. But I cannot leave a sentence until I feel it is complete.

I have finished my third week of work, and the yield has been decreasing: thirty-five pages in the first week, twenty-five in the second, only twenty in the third. Why is this?

Tuesday, 16 [August]

The morning was looking good, but I stopped work at 11:30 to go out a bit in the sun—I haven't had a proper fill of it for ten days or so—and this afternoon I can no longer find the good disposition in which I thought I would be able to write. Of course, if I were to stick to it I'd eventually manage to do something, but I am near the end of a chapter and I don't want to spoil it—all the more so as the whole chapter is weak. Until tomorrow, then. Now I'll allow myself an hour in the chaise longue.

I have had all kinds of dreams during the time here, some of them most peculiar: Nae Ionescu, Corneliu Codreanu, Silvia Balter, Leni, Maryse . . . I say them over to myself a few times before opening my eyes; I try to remember them and promise to note them down when I am awake—but then I lose them: they become too vague, and I can no longer extract anything from them.

In today's *Timpul* the new season at the Comoedia is announced as opening with *Jocul de-a vacanţa*. Rehearsals on the 20th of August.

I don't say either yes or no. I have grown used to expecting nothing
in relation to the theatre. We shall see.

Wednesday, 17 [August]

An intricate, absurd dream, from which all I remember is that Romania
went to war to occupy "Pocuţia." I asked myself: war with whom? With
Poland? With Czechoslovakia? And where might Pocuţia be?

The streets were decked with flags. I seemed to be in Brăila, racing
uphill with Poldy on Bulevardul Cuza, toward the center of town. I no
longer remember if I was on a bicycle, but I do know that the faster I
went, the more I felt in my mouth, between my teeth, a kind of contraption that turned with a deafening sound, like a dentist's little wheel.

There were other marvels galore, which I have since forgotten.

No news anywhere about Mircea. Nor is there anyone I can ask. But as
I don't see his name under any articles in *Vremea*, I assume he is still
under arrest. Rosetti, in a letter to me from the day before yesterday,
spoke of "Mircea's deportation." Does that mean to Miercurea?

I have finished Chapter Six. It has thirty pages, though they are full of
defacements. I wouldn't be wrong to say that it is the least successful
chapter so far. It has gone badly, and apart from a few moments of walking in the street there is nothing in it that satisfies me. But maybe it will
get lost in the general effect.

From now on I don't know what to do. I have only three days left
in Bran—which gives things a provisional feel and may make it hard for
me to work. Still, tomorrow morning I shall try to be at my desk as
usual. Chapter Seven, which is also no more than a transition, shouldn't
cost me too much effort. Only when I've reached the top of the Schuller
with my characters will I be on the other side of the book.

Sunday, 21 [August]

I leave for Bucharest this evening, in the car of the lawyer Virgil Şefănescu
(last-minute relations, but very friendly . . .).

The last few days I haven't done any work at all. In the same way
that I began my month in Bran with three days of complete holiday, I
decided to end it with three days of the same.

I lay on the chaise longue in the sun, I bathed in the stream, I started an English novel (Meredith, I see, goes down very well on holiday), I played all kinds of games: chess, backgammon, billiards, table tennis, and volleyball. Like the schoolboy I am.

And now I am returning. I'd like to start my life differently from how I left it a month ago in Bucharest.

Bucharest, Monday, 22 [August]

My first day in Bucharest, an exhausting day. I was awakened early by the buses, the street shouts, the suffocating heat. Where are my good nights in Bran? Where are the mornings with the smell of the forest? Where is that calm, intense silence, broken only by the rumbling of the stream?

How much resistance I would need not to succumb to the pressure of the horrible life I rediscover here! It makes me furious to think that I could have stayed another week there, because I could have handed in the continuation of my study of Proust (which I returned to write) in a month's time. Cioculescu told me only today over the phone that he doesn't need it right away. What a stupid business!

I dropped by Marietta's to see if there was any news of Mircea. (He was not answering his telephone.) He has been at Miercurea-Ciuc since the first of August.

On this occasion I saw Marietta unrestrained: she is choking with anti-Semitism. Not even the fact that she was talking with me, nor the fact that I was in her house, could stop her from ranting and raging against potbellied Jews and their bloated, bejeweled women—though she did make exception for about a hundred thousand "decent" Jews, probably including myself since I have neither a potbelly nor a bloated wife.

Otherwise her language was just as in *Porunca Vremii*. I didn't hesitate to tell her so. And I left there feeling poisoned.

Wednesday, 24 [August]

The rehearsals start tomorrow.[3] I did a reading today with Leni and Sică, to check the text for any possible changes.

It frightens me how little Leni understands at certain points. The last scene in Act Two went completely over her head. She asked me to re-

---

3. The state's anti-Semitic measures went through phases of severity. Sebastian's play was produced during a time of lessened strictures.

move some things that had moved me a lot as I was writing them, and which—since I had loved her at that time—I had written for her.

"Do you really want to keep that?" she asked me today, about some lines that she literally had not understood. ("I haven't met him, but I have been waiting for him. I have always expected to find him, in every man I've known . . ." etc.)

I don't want to sound like an author peculiarly wedded to his text, whose "heart bleeds" for it. I think I am more skeptical, more sensitive to ridicule. I lost a novel that meant a lot to me, and I didn't die—all the less will I die for a play that they'll screw up in the theatre. But I'm amazed to see how difficult it is for her to grasp the simplest shades of meaning.

What upsets me more is that Sică has arranged things beforehand so that my play will not run for more than three weeks; the first night is scheduled for the 15th of September, and on the 7th of October Leni leaves on tour with *Ionescu R. Maria*. Does it bother me that a hit has been ruled out in advance? Will the play be successful? I don't know. Let's suppose it won't. But if there is even a small chance of a hit—even 5 percent, let us say—then I don't see why it should be denied me. The chances are even slimmer in the lottery, but that doesn't stop me playing it.

At the end of the day I tell myself that none of this matters. I shouldn't work myself up about it. I should let them do what they like, as they like, and tell myself that the play is mine but the show is theirs. Once that distinction is made, I can consider myself free and unattached.

Thursday, 25 [August]

It's not out of the question that they'll take the play off the schedule. I am grateful to Zoe, who helped me understand how unacceptable is the deal proposed by Sică. I have absolutely nothing to gain from a shoddy premiere followed by a three-week run and disappearance from the publicity boards. If this play doesn't bring me some money, it brings me nothing. I'm not such a child as to turn the theatre business into a question of "literary prestige."

Monday, 29 [August]

I got home around eight, rather fed up at having promised to go out later with Zoe. How good it would be—I thought—if I could stay home, read a little, and have an early night. I had decided to pluck up my courage and tell Zoe, when she rang a quarter of an hour later as arranged, that I would stay home and beg her to forgive me.

The telephone rang, and before I said a word she told me that she was not at home:

"I've been kidnapped. I'll explain to you."

So I am free. So I can stay quietly at home. So I can read a bit and have an early night. Exactly as I wanted.

Yes . . . but I am a jealous person. And now I feel uneasy. Now I am troubled by the thought that she has gone out with someone else. "I've been kidnapped" says a great deal. Tonight she'll return home with her kidnapper. She'll doubtless sleep with him. All that should be a matter of complete indifference to me. In the end, separation is the only possible outcome of our affair. And I can't refuse her the right to find a man to sleep with.

What's the point, I ask myself, of complicating your wretched life with such regrets, with such impossible hopes, with such insane hopes, which all eventually leave the same taste of ashes?

Tuesday, 30 [August]

I keep dreaming of Nae Ionescu. Last night I saw him after his return from Miercurea-Ciuc. We seemed to be in the schoolyard in Brăila. We were talking heatedly—he with great violence, because I was denigrating the Iron Guard. Then a lot of things happened—it was a long dream—but I don't remember any more.

The rehearsals have started. I still haven't been there—nor shall I go unless I cannot avoid it. I have no feeling of enthusiasm. I'm not at all happy with the business deal we have agreed to. I have to make an average of 24,000 lei an evening for them to keep the play on after the 7th of October. Only if I make that average will the tour be postponed. I have a sense that I am being quite simply hoodwinked. All Sică's big successes—plays that stayed up on the boards for two months—made no more than an average of 15,000 to 17,000 lei. But I can't put up a fight with these theatre people. They've licked me before we start.

I went to see Aristide Blank this morning, and I gave him ten thousand of the twenty thousand lei he lent me before I left for Bran. That leaves me with empty pockets, but I'm glad that my account with him is clear. Apart from that, I have to admit that he behaved perfectly in the circumstances. He gave me the money and took it back as discreetly as he might have offered or accepted a cigarette. If he hadn't, I would have died of shame.

I went to see Nina the other day. Only Joyce, who shouted with joy when she saw me, reminded me of the time when I felt somehow at home in that house. Nina and I were ill at ease.

Naturally I deplore all that has happened, I feel sorry for Nae and sorry for Mircea, I'd like to know they were at liberty. But I can't believe that their "action" was anything other than a miscalculation on Nae's part and childish nonsense on Mircea's. Half farce, half ambition. I don't see any more in it.

Saturday, 3 September

Autumn. It's only seven o'clock but already quite dark. For the last hour I've been reading with the light on.

Sunday, 4 [September]

In today's *Timpul* there was the first advertisement for the premiere. "Comoedia theatre. Wednesday, 14 September 1938. Opening of the winter season. *Jocul de-a vacanţa*, by Mihail Sebastian. With Leni Caler, George Vraca, Mişu Fotino, and V. Maximilian."

All day I read in Renard's *Journal* and the Goncourts' *Journal* their notes about rehearsals and premieres. I especially enjoyed what the poor Goncourt brothers had to say about the disastrous flop of their first play, *Henriette Maréchal*. It was a prophylactic reading.

Thursday, 8 [September]

This afternoon I go to a rehearsal for the first time. I promise to stay calm, to take things as they come, not to make a tragedy of anything. It would be ridiculous to blow this theatrical business out of proportion; it has a point only if I can look at it with relative indifference.

Again they tell me that at least twenty-five plays like mine are written each year in Europe—so the whole thing can have the significance of only a minor incident.

Although it was originally announced for the 14th, the premiere is now scheduled for the 16th of September. But from what Leni says, I don't think it will happen before the 20th.

Marga the day before yesterday, Carol Pascal yesterday—because they had seen *De ce nu mă săruţi?* and enjoyed it—asked me:

"Does your play also have music?"

Plopeanu's wife asked Leni the other evening:

"*Jocul de-a vacanța?* Another play with schoolgirls?"

What a difficult legacy I have: recollections of *Absențe nemotivate* and Elly Roman's music from *De ce nu mă săruți?*

My play doesn't even have any schoolgirls or any music. . . . What a letdown for the audience.

Theatrical mentality: Froda, who is no fool and actually likes the play, suggested to me a few days ago:

"How about changing the scenery in the third act? The audience gets bored with plays where there is only one stage setting."

He doesn't understand that this "one stage setting" is actually part of the play's poetry—however much of that it may contain.

Saturday, 10 [September]

To my amazement, Thursday's rehearsal was not a catastrophe. I left there feeling rather buoyed. In general, I get the feeling that things hold together; but there are still a million details that need to be adjusted and put right.

Leni's performance is moving. I say this after two days of calm reflection since the rehearsal, and at a time when I finally feel no love of any kind for her. As regards her acting, I think I am more inclined to be severe. Nevertheless (unless the surprise that things don't look catastrophic has made me err in the opposite, optimistic direction), I do believe that she was moving. It was a very simple performance, but also very nuanced, with something loyal in the quarrelsome scenes, something faintly ironic in the moments of reverie. Nearly all the time she acted within the limits of the role; only very occasionally did I feel a need to call her back "to order," "to earth."

Maximilian is Maximilian. Not for a moment was he Bogoiu. All the time outside, all the time ham-acting.

Vraca was very good at some moments—those of idleness—and very bad at others which required some frivolity, a little fantasy. If I don't manage to get him changed, the long final scene in Act One will be completely ruined—and with it the whole play.

Some of the others were amusing, others inexpressive, but none unacceptable.

To return to Leni, I must point out that she spoke most beautifully and sincerely those very passages that she had asked me to delete.

"I haven't met him, but I have been waiting for him . . . etc."

It had something muffled and melancholic, a kind of resignation that opened out—without too much fire—toward an unexpected hope.

How strange and subordinate is the profession of actor, in which you can do something very well without even understanding it. Maybe that is precisely the mark of a true actor. Maybe that is what people call "instinct."

(Yesterday I went to Leni's to read the role with her one more time.

"Why does Corina feel her pulse in Act Three," she asked me. "Is it because it beats harder since she has been in love with Ştefan?"

"No, Leni dear. It's because, being alone for the first time, she has the time, the curiosity, and the need to turn inward and observe herself, know herself. She puts her hand on her pulse as she might put her hand on her heart—a heart that she did not know she had."

"Do you think so?" Leni wonders, remaining thoughtful and a little incredulous.

Yet that moment—whose meaning clearly escapes her—she acted to perfection.)

Sandina Stan, beautiful, vulgar, good to fuck, says to me:
"I'm delighted finally to be acting in a play of ideas."
And I don't even dare laugh.

Agnia Bogoslav (who plays Agnes, and says her few words very funnily) came timidly into the box from which Sică and I were following the rehearsal.

"Excuse me," she said to Sică, "would you please urge Mr. Sebastian to write a few more lines for me. I have so few . . ."

"Okay, okay," he replied jokingly. "I'll ask him to write you a couplet."

I laughed at that girl for being so keen to have me lengthen her role—but when I thought about it, her childlike behavior seemed touching. It was an actor's childishness, made up of posturing but also of passion. The theatre is perhaps the only place where people do not flee from work but actually seek it out.

Leni had reached the moment of the lines:
Je hais le mouvement qui déplace les lignes
Et jamais je ne pleure, et jamais je ne ris.[4]
when Sică leaned toward me and asked very softly:
"Who are those lines by?"

4. I hate the motion that moves the lines/And never do I cry, never do I laugh.

Yesterday afternoon I had tea in private with Marie Ghiolu, Miss Lupa,[5] and, later on, Mrs. Cantacuzino. Loads of things to note down, but I don't have the time now.

Marie is very beautiful (maybe really beautiful for the first time since I've known her) but a little hotheaded, if not altogether hysterical.

"Don't I have beautiful legs?"

And she lifted her dress to show me her calves.

It's true that there were just the two of us.

Sunday, 11 [September]

Victor Ion Popa's play flopped disastrously at the Regina Maria last night.

The terrible thing about the theatre is that people don't realize what they are doing; the merciless lights of the premiere are needed for the truth suddenly to leap to their eyes.

I went away feeling annoyed that I had wasted the evening, and a little worried about what is in store for me. Is it possible that I too went so badly wrong in writing my play?

Mitică Theodorescu said to Froda the other day:

"How on earth can you be putting on Sebastian's play? It's inadmissible."

"It's a good play," said Froda.

"It can't be good," Mitică stubbornly retorted. "How can it be? Listen to me: it's bad, very bad."

"Well, but you don't know it; you haven't even read it."

"I don't need to read it. I tell you: it's really bad."

The smart jackal!

Monday, 12 [September]

The first posters went up on Saturday. Now they're all over town, wherever you go. I took a couple myself: one to send to Mama in Paris, the other for me to keep. I stuck it to the wall with drawing pins and stared at it in a childish way. I liked looking at it. . . . Then—with the same good humor—I did something equally stupid: I went to the photographer's to have my picture taken for the program.

But now the mood has passed. I feel bored and indifferent: I no longer look forward to the premiere, nor do I have any unease or the slightest curiosity about it.

---

5. Luli Popovici-Lupa: a friend of Nae Ionescu's.

This afternoon I went to the rehearsal—and everything seemed stupid to me. What a meal they are making of it! They put a thousand intentions and gestures into each piece of dialogue. I get the feeling that their eyes are on me, on the empty auditorium, on the prompter—calling us as witnesses to what is happening. No naturalness, no conviction, not an ounce of truth.

I won't go again tomorrow. I leave it in the lap of the gods. In fact, I am thinking of not going at all, even of heading off to Balcic for a few days to get as far as I can from this business, which is all the odder today, when war may be just around the corner. The radio is right now broadcasting Hitler's speech in Nuremberg. My own set is broken, but snatches of the broadcast drift up from the floor below, or maybe from across the way. I can't make out what he is saying, but I easily recognize Hitler's guttural voice and especially the cheering that constantly interrupts him: cheers and roars that are quite simply insane.

On such a day, am I supposed to take a mere play seriously?

Wednesday, 14 [September]

This morning's press dispatches are alarming. The Sudetenlanders issued a six-hour ultimatum, and the six hours have passed. Now war is the only possibility left. We may have it by this evening. Maybe we already have it as I am writing.

In town, people were saying that the Germans have already entered Czechoslovakia, so far without meeting any resistance. Is it possible that I could be a soldier tomorrow?

Thursday, 15 [September]

I went to yesterday's rehearsal after all, this time with Froda. The only act that went well—to everyone's surprise, of course—was the third act, which none of them wanted to believe in at the reading.

The first two acts, on the other hand, are acted stridently, superficially, always incorrectly. Fotino's entrance is unacceptable. Can't a comic scene ever be acted without laying it on thick?

Those ham-actors frighten me! When I think that they call themselves "artists," I wonder that the irony of the term does not frighten them. I felt I was in the middle of a company in disorderly retreat. Each one for himself! Let the play crash, the show perish—so long as I am a success, so long as I'm all right, so long as I am applauded.

Froda laid it on the line to Sică until he made him turn yellow. I could feel in Sică, too, the wounded pride of a ham-actor. After a moment of panic—when the whole show seemed in danger of collapse—he called someone from administration.

"Tell the papers this, I say. Premiere on Wednesday evening. And two rehearsals a day till then."

It would have been a happy solution. For a lot of things can be put right in a week of rehearsals. At the very least the lines can be learned properly—because at the moment no one, except perhaps Leni, has really got on top of them. What kind of interpretation can there be under the terror of memory exercises?

"Interpretation"—a stupid word, which means nothing at all in the theatre. No one interprets anything. Everyone comes with his own gestures, his own grunts, his own homespun coughs—and then applies them to his role. That's all.

In three acts, I don't think there was one piece of dialogue that didn't sound false. I should have gone through it piece by piece, setting the right tone and clarifying what was meant. But that's a craft that is beyond me. I ought to curse and shout, shake and threaten, risk everything, spare no one's feelings, no one's prestige. I should fight with no holds barred, determined to quarrel forever, if necessary, with each turn and all together, with Sică, with Siegfried, with the prompter and the stage hand, with absolutely everyone. Maybe that's the only way I could get the play back on its feet and defend it.

But is it worth it? Do I believe in it enough to take it that seriously?

No, I don't. It's a joke, a game. And it would be grotesque to forget that. Maybe I'll have more serious things in life to defend. I hope that, even in my career as a writer, there are more honorable battles in store. After all, between *De două mii de ani* and *Jocul de-a vacanța* there are differences that I have no right to forget. In the one, there was something very close to the bone; in the other, there is childishness, trifling stuff, a mere nothing.

So the premiere will be on Saturday. Sică immediately went back on his decision to postpone it; too many people advised him otherwise. Each of them used the same argument: don't worry, you'll see it will be a success.

That's easy for everyone to toss out, because none of them carries any responsibility for it. "It will be a success." I can just hear Bereșteanu[6] saying that—and I wonder what kind of art it is in which even Bereșteanu can have opinions and make predictions.

6. Administrator of the Comoedia Theatre.

"It will be a success." But there are two days left till the premiere—and no one is sure of his part, no one knows what to wear, no one knows when to enter, when to exit, when to speak and when to be silent . . .

Friday, 16 [September]

"Dans les choses théatrâles," Goncourt says, *"c'est abominable ces hauts et ces bas, et sans transition aucune."*[7]

Yesterday evening's rehearsal was infinitely better. It was even satisfactory. Now and then I was carried away with emotion like a child. Some of the spectators (Fifi Harand,[8] Mrs. Maximilian, Zissu) were straining to follow the performance. It amused me to hear them laugh, to see them wipe away a furtive tear. (At this afternoon's rehearsal, Beate Fredanov had a really good cry in Act Three. But it's true that that girl cries so easily. . . .)

Yesterday Timuş seemed quite won over, but I shouldn't suspect him of any friendly feeling! It's so awkward not to like it, so convenient to show one's approval. . . .

Sică was happy. Jubilant.

"That's a play, sir, that's a real play. It'll certainly travel abroad. We'll translate it into French."

I made him repeat the wonderful words of praise a few times—though, of course, they won't stop him cursing me to the skies if the play isn't a success. I can almost hear his voice: "Who the hell got me mixed up with these intellectuals?"

In general terms, then, in very general terms, I may have come away satisfied. In the details and finer shades, though, a million things remain to be done. I have to accept the situation as it is—and to look at everything with indifference. That's why I can't complain: I feel no emotion, no impatience, no nerves of any kind. Not yet, anyway.

I went out yesterday with Leni, after the evening rehearsal. I dined just with her at the Wilson, and we went home late, around three o'clock. She had acted her part so beautifully, had been so simple, so intense, and so sincerely emotional that I felt for her a rekindled tenderness, as in the early days of my love for her. We stopped in front of a poster and read our names printed alongside each other. We seemed to be alone on the deserted boulevard.

7. In theatrical matters, all these highs and lows without a transition are abominable.
8. Actress.

Saturday, 17 [September]

An hour to go till the premiere. How much I could write! But I've had an anxious day, all of it—from one to seven—coincidentally spent in court on Leni's case. A day in court usually wears me out—and it had to be today!

I regret not being able to note everything there is to be noted, at least in connection with tonight's dress rehearsal.

Now all that remains is to wait.

Sunday, 18 [September]

A big success—really big. Dozens of curtain calls, a warm, vibrant atmosphere in the audience.

I went to the cinema and watched a film in complete calm, as if nothing exceptional had been happening this evening.

Then I showed up toward the end, in time to feel the lively atmosphere of celebration and satisfaction.

This morning's reviews were full of praise. The matinee performance was sold out, and there are scarcely any seats left for this evening. Dozens of telephone calls, dozens of congratulations.

I certainly feel pleased, but I don't think it has gone to my head. I'm still fairly skeptical—and, above all, very tired. Too tired to note now what should be noted about the premiere.

Maybe tomorrow.

Monday, 19 [September]

The reviews (*Viitorul, Semnalul* . . .) continue to be good. Yesterday the box office closed after it had sold every possible extra ticket. The matinee netted thirty thousand lei, the evening performance sixty thousand.

But I still don't believe it will be a great success with the public, or that it will be kept on for what is called a series. I don't have the patience to list the reasons for this now, but I am perfectly aware of them.

Tuesday, 20 [September]

Today's reviews are overwhelming. Ionel Dumitrescu in *Curentul,* Carandino in *România,* write with an enthusiasm, friendliness, and ardor that leave me speechless. . . . No, I wasn't at all expecting such a reception. Even in *Universul* there is a review that, though perhaps not well meaning (its tone is cold and somehow sulky), is full enough of praise. So far, no one has said anything against it. In a way that makes me uneasy. *Je ne demandais pas tant.*[9] . . . *Neamul românesc, Porunca Vremii, Frontul*—which ought to attack me violently, as they have in the past—remain silent, at least for the time being. Is this because the success is too great to be contested? Or, on the contrary, is it the kind of silence that precedes and paves the way for a thundering outburst?

Yesterday evening, which is usually the quietest of the week, had receipts of 24,000 lei. Bereşteanu, who checked the figures, assures me it was 26,000. That seems to be a great deal. (On the same evening, Popa's play made a little under 5,000.) Camil couldn't believe that the figure of 24,000 was correct; it seemed to him enormous.

It may be embarrassing to inquire about each day's receipts, but when so many people live constantly obsessed with them, when everything in the theatre depends on them, you cannot help feeling curious yourself.

This morning I found Bereşteanu with the plan for the tour spread out in his office, and with a series of letters to provincial impresarios.

"You see what troubles we've got! Now we'll have to postpone the tour."

But I still ask myself whether it will be a lasting success. Act Three doesn't go smoothly—maybe in part because of the production. There is so much stress on the comic effects in the first two acts, and so much laughter, that Act Three remains suspended in a void.

I went to the Sunday evening performance and felt upset at the childish, absurd way in which people were laughing. I too laughed like a fool, caught up in the general atmosphere of jollity—it's hard to resist a packed theatre, with the boxes, balconies, and stalls all in fits. But although I too laughed, at the same time I felt dismayed. What can those people understand of the play if they rollick about as at any old farce! The proof that they don't understand anything is that Act Three leaves them baffled. They are still laughing when the curtain rises—but after the first few exchanges, and especially after the first scene, they realize that their laughter is out of place and their mirth is left hanging. Quite possibly this third act will stop the play from being taken on for a really long series.

Rosetti did not at all like either the play or the performance. He didn't tell me so straight out, but he hardly needed to. It was enough that he

---

9. I didn't ask for that much.

didn't ring me once after the premiere. When I saw him yesterday, his congratulations were so evasive, so awkward, that I almost felt I had to apologize for the play, as if it were something shameful.

Of course, Vişoianu didn't like it either. (He was in the same box with Rosetti, and he hasn't shown any sign of life since then.)

That's all to the good; it brings me back to earth. It's time I remembered all the things I have never liked in the play; time to keep telling myself that all this fuss may be agreeable but should not be taken too seriously.

What a strong impact the theatre makes! I have written five books but have never before had this sense of being in direct touch with "the public," of having reached it, engrossed it, moved it. A first night was enough for a whole current of curiosity, impatience, and friendly feeling to appear. I receive dozens of telephone calls, dozens of messages, from the most surprising and unexpected places.

Wednesday, 21 [September]

This evening's receipts: 32,000 lei! Apparently this is altogether unusual.

It was a nice packed audience, with a good ear for the play. Almost a concert audience. People laughed less wildly; they smiled more. From time to time I had the feeling that I was at a session of chamber music.

But it is time I freed myself from the theatre. It would be a good thing if I never showed myself there again. It is high time I returned to serious matters.

Saturday, 24 [September]

War may break out from one hour to the next. Czechoslovakia mobilized last night. France also seems to have mobilized, without actually using the term "general mobilization." During the night, war was imminent. There was an atmosphere of panic in town around three o'clock: or perhaps not even panic, but a kind of weary pallor of people who have given up.

Now we have a moment of syncopation. Chamberlain has returned to London with the Hitlerites' new demands. Will they be accepted? Will we have a "German peace" that suppresses freedom in Europe— who knows for how long, perhaps for a whole historical epoch? Or will they not be accepted? If so, we will have war. It's all a matter of days, maybe less, a matter of hours or minutes.

Things are slowing down at the theatre. Yesterday seventeen thousand lei!—a most worrying figure. Can the "success" have passed so rapidly? There are many possible explanations. It rained, there was bad political news, people were feeling the pressure of events, and so on.

But reasons can always be found for a lack of success, whereas no explanation is required for a really great success. And that will probably not be the case with my play.

Sunday, 25 [September]

Yesterday was a sellout. But I don't think it is going to be a "great success," or a success and nothing but. Yesterday's matinee seems to have been very poorly attended, and today's brought in only around fifteen thousand lei—half last Saturday's figure. Maybe things will pick up again this evening—though it is the first evening of Rosh Hashanah—but I fear that tomorrow, Monday, will be really bad. I no longer dare to make calculations, to engage in childish plans. . . . The hundreds of thousands of lei of which I dreamed, mainly in jest, can no longer be dreamed of even as a joke.

I passed by the theatre and watched a few scenes from Act Two. I was appalled at how badly they were acted: with no conviction or poetic fire, with jabbered lines, bits left out and others added, as if at one of the worst of the rehearsals. I fled in horror.

Tuesday, 27 [September]

A telephone call from Poldy, who is in Paris. He thinks that France will order a general mobilization tonight, and that war will break out on Saturday. He asked what he should do with Mama. He wants to send her back to Romania, but I'm terrified at the thought that, God forbid, war might erupt when she is somewhere en route—in Italy, for example. Alone, speaking only Romanian, terrified, penniless—what would she do? How would she cope?

On the other hand, she can't remain at Sceaux, because Poldy and Benu would have to enlist on the first day and she would be left alone.

Mother dear, if only this war could pass your heart by! Or at least if you could lose in it only what is lost anyway! If only I could pay everything for you all! That's the final consolation for which I ask.

Saturday, 1 October

Peace. A kind of peace. I haven't the heart to rejoice. The Munich Agreement does not send us to the front, it lets us live—but it prepares terrible times ahead. Only now will we start to see the kind of pressure that the Hitlerites exert.

It seems logical to expect a move to the right in France and a powerful anti-Semitic lurch in Romania. I can easily envision a new Goga-Cuza government, or perhaps even a gradual transition to a Legionary regime, suitably decked out.

But we shall see . . .

Yesterday I didn't even dare call in at the theatre. Thursday evening had been alarming: eleven thousand lei. I was dejected and had pangs of conscience toward the people at the theatre, as if I had pushed them into a bad business deal. Everyone said that I shouldn't panic, that the theatre was empty because people had been anticipating at any moment the outcome of the events in Munich—and, at the same time, because defense exercises had plunged the whole city into darkness and given it a sinister appearance, with streetlights off, windows blacked out, sirens wailing, bells tolling, and so on.

Yesterday I didn't go and ask at the theatre: they just said that Friday had been one of the worst days of the week.

Well, this morning, to my great astonishment, I came across Axente the typist and was told:

"You beat us yesterday at the Comoedia: we took in 24,000 at the Regina Maria, and you netted 26,000."

I couldn't believe my ears. But I plucked up courage and went to ask the theatre cashier. Yes, it was true!

Could there be a change of fortune? Could it still be something of a success?

Last night was a year since I arrived in Paris—and since my luggage and manuscript were stolen.

Wednesday, 5 [October]

Yesterday I spoke to Ocneanu about the novel.[1] I think I'll publish it with him. He's the only publisher with whom it is possible to work. I just wonder what I'll do about the contract with Delafras.

---

1. *Accidentul.*

Today I read Chapter Six, which I hadn't touched since Bran and had forgotten. It seemed much better than at the time of writing it, when I had been so dissatisfied.

I'd like the novel to appear in late November or early December. But for that I'd have to do nothing but write, day and night, from the 15th of October. No law courts, no Foundation, nothing else.

The advertisement for the play in today's *Timpul* says "last performances." I wonder why. The tour with *Ionescu G. Maria* has been postponed until the 19th of October, and *Jocul de-a vacanța* could play all the time until then—especially since, even if it hasn't gone brilliantly, it has hardly been a flop either. Monday and Tuesday were quiet (today is Yom Kippur), but Saturday and Sunday made a little over forty thousand lei—which is not all that bad.

With regard to both Zoe and Leni, complete withdrawal. It's more sensible, more simple—even if, God alone knows, it's no fun at all.

Tuesday, 11 [October]

Saturday and Sunday were rather quiet (a little over thirty thousand lei), but yesterday and Monday were really very bad. By eight o'clock they'd sold around five thousand's worth. I didn't ask what the total receipts are up to now. I went into the auditorium for a moment during Act One; there were quite a lot of people in the stalls—probably many complimentary tickets—but the balconies were empty.

How sad is a play that is nearing its end. A novel is less ostentatious, creates less of a stir, but it also drops out of circulation more slowly and insensibly, without a sudden wrench. For better or worse, the play will continue this week, because they don't have anything else to put on until the tour begins. But its "career," as they say in the theatre, has come to an end.

Last night Sică seemed a little disheartened.

"Please," I said to him, "don't start blaming me."

"I have nothing to blame you for. I'm very glad we put on your play, but I'm depressed about the audience. Again I conclude that we can't fill the seats for anything subtle. Not only was your play good, not only was it well performed, not only did the premiere make a big impact, but the whole of the first week indicated general enthusiasm, a surefire success. Tell me! What can be made of all this?"

Saturday, 15 [October]

As if Leni and Zoe were not enough to complicate my life, now there is Alice Theodorian. She 'phones me ten times a day (even at night); she always asks me to eat with her, is insistent, allusive, provocative.

It's all getting too comical. What an irony of my fate: to be Jewish and to look an *"homme à femmes"*![2]

In this respect, yesterday was completely idiotic. There was Zoe at lunchtime (Tata was in Brăila). Leni came in the evening, and later I also went to Alice Th.'s. It is too difficult to know what's what with each of them. And when I think that, in a more orderly life, I'd have been the most faithful and least frivolous man in the world. . . .

I am being torn apart in so many ridiculous affairs, none of which is going anywhere.

Monday, 17 [October]

Mama arrived yesterday morning, after spending twenty-four hours in a kind of "quarantine" at Jimbolia. Through Ralea, I had to get a telegram sent from the Ministry of the Interior before she could continue her journey home. It seems that not only Jimbolia but all the other frontier crossings are filled with Jews who have come to a dead end, unable either to return to the country they have traveled from, or to enter Romania—even though all are Romanian passport holders. No explanation or justification is given for this barbarous behavior.

"We are living in terrible times!" lamented Ralea, clearly feeling embarrassed.

But that embarrassment does not prevent him from being an accomplice—a passive accomplice whose conscience is torn, but one who finds it quite easy to bear the conflict.

I dread to think what awaits us from now on!

Sunday evening's was the last performance. They've played the dirty trick of putting *Ionescu G. Maria* back on for the last two days before the tour, yesterday and today. So now the impression is given that I've been taken down from the boards and replaced with an old play—as if it would have been such a disaster to keep me on for another couple of days! For a moment I was quite indignant. But then it passed. In the end, I don't want to make a tragedy out of anything that's happened to me at the theatre.

2. A ladies' man.

It's been an adventure—and now it's over. I didn't gain a lot from it, but nor did I lose much.

On Saturday evening, at the last performance but one, I watched the whole play for the first time since the Sunday immediately after the premiere. I've seen bits of each act at various times, depending on when I dropped by the theatre on my way back from the cinema or to see Leni. But I have only twice seen the play from beginning to end. I'm used to it by now, and it is almost impossible for me to judge it. The image of this production has almost completely covered the image I originally had of it. At first the differences between my conception and the stage performance were quite glaring. Little by little, however, the actors' gestures (even if they were wrong) and their tones of voice (even if they were false) substituted themselves for what I had imagined at the time of writing. Sometimes I'd have liked to protest, to get them back on the right track, to restore my original text, to force them to act the play I actually wrote—but it would have meant too great an effort, and I wasn't even sure it was worth it.

On Sunday evening I again watched the third act—for the last time! I was in the balcony, from where the stage appears far off and for that very reason somehow magical, and sometimes I shut my eyes to listen to the words. Maybe it was the thought that this really was the last time, that none of these words would be spoken again, that they would remain in a typewritten file or, at best, in a printed book—maybe all these thoughts, with their sense of leave-taking, made me listen with emotion for the first time. I said to myself that something was dying, departing forever, breaking loose from me. Never again will I see the audience's heads turned toward the stage, in the silence of an occupied auditorium, in the darkness broken only by the footlights, listening, taking in, echoing, answering the words written by me. Never again will I hear that laughter rise in warm animation toward the stage.

Next to me a girl was crying. She is the last girl who will cry for *Jocul de-a vacanța.*

Leni leaves tomorrow on tour. She came here today. I don't know if she is beautiful; surely not. But she has gleaming white skin, soft young flesh.

"Wait for me in your new home on the 17th of November," she said as she left.

And I do have the feeling that I will wait for her, though I realize it is not possible. The last deadline in this old love affair is approaching.

19 November. Saturday

I have been in my studio flat for two days now. I ought to keep in mind that this is one of my old dreams—and to be contented. But for the last few days I have been feeling gloomy. No hope, no expectation, no decision.

It's a large white room with a lot of light, on the eighth floor. It is right on Calea Victoriei—which I don't like in principle—but from this height it cannot be said that I live on any street in particular. The terrace is quite spacious—easily enough for three open chaises longues— and from there I have a semicircular view of half of Bucharest. It is reminiscent of the entrance to New York harbor. I float among buildings.

I don't want for the mom[3]

Sunday, 20 [November]

Last night Zoe interrupted me while I was writing. I can no longer continue the note I began yesterday. Nor do I remember exactly what I meant to write.

She was the first woman to enter this apartment. I couldn't help feeling a surge of tenderness. I undressed her and lay her on the bed, let her purr beneath the blanket like a cat in the warmth, and went down to buy some cakes at Nestor. How good it is to know that a young woman is waiting for you upstairs in your room!

But, of course, none of that has any meaning.

This morning there was a stupid matinee performance of *Jocul de-a va-canţa* at ten o'clock. (The tour did end on Thursday, and Leni came back then.) I have so little confidence in my play that I don't think it is good even for a six o'clock matinee.

I didn't go to the theatre—not as a sign of protest, but out of honest indifference.

But Mama, Benu, and Tata went instead and passed by here on their way from the theatre. Mama brought me two chrysanthemums: it is good that the first flowers to enter this flat came from her.

---

3. Sentence incomplete.

Wednesday, 30 [November]

Corneliu Codreanu was shot and buried during the night, together with Duca's assassins and Stelescu's assassins.[4] Attempting to escape. It has all been too sudden and unexpected for me to have a clear idea of what might happen next.

Once again I have to say that the situation inside the country is unexpectedly stable and may point toward a return to normality. The external situation is so adverse and confused that it stands in the way of even a timid attempt at optimism.

Friday, 2 [December]

Stupor and silence. A kind of dumbfounded silence. I get the feeling that no one has yet recovered from the consternation of the first minute.

It would be in the logic of things if all this hushed fright burst out in an anti-Semitic explosion. It's a safety valve whose use cannot be excluded, even on the part of the government. And again we may be the ones who pay.

Tuesday, 6 [December]

Cella was here and—without my realizing how we came to speak of it— she told me a lot of things about Zoe, about Zoe's "past."

In particular, she gave me numerous details about a love affair in which I did not find it hard to recognize the *grand amour* of which Zoe herself told me last summer. He is one Bisco Iscovici—and Cella, who knows him very well, helped me not only to "see" him clearly but to reconstitute the whole story of their love. Suddenly I had the feeling that Zoe, this admirable girl whom I see so often, who slept in my bed on Saturday afternoon and rolled head over heels naked on the floor, just like a child, this girl with whom I went to the cinema last night, is a stranger to me.

This feeling scares me a little. It's as if familiar things around me on which I depend had suddenly lost some of their solidity, had changed their color, their dimensions, their reality. . . .

---

4. Mihai Stelescu, a former leader of the Iron Guard, split with Codreanu and created another fascist organization, Cruciada Românismului. Condemned as a traitor by his former comrades, Stelescu was set upon in his hospital bed, shot many times, and axed to pieces.

Saturday, 10 [December]

On Tuesday, on St. Nicholas's Day, I sent Nina a flower for her birth-day, together with a few lines in which I said that I hesitated to visit them because Mircea, though back in Bucharest for some time, had not given me any sign of life.

Yesterday at the Foundation I found a letter of thanks from her, a letter of simple politeness, neither cold nor friendly but precisely indif-ferent: "The difficult trials through which we have passed, Mircea and I, have made us cut ourselves off from the world."

I understand them very well. They must consider themselves in mourning since the death of Codreanu. If they were to have me round, they might feel they were betraying a cause. Certain things are beyond repair and leave no room for memories.

Nae has signed a declaration of solidarity with the 318 "comrades from Vaslui." A facsimile of the text appeared in all the morning papers. When I saw Nae's handwriting in the picture—clear, decisive, almost print-qual-ity writing that I know so well—I had a vague sense that these matters also personally concern me a little.

Friday, 16 [December]

This morning at the Foundation, Mircea was in a group with Cioculescu, Biberi, and Benador. I went up to say hello and, to my surprise, Mircea stood up and embraced me.

A reflex gesture? Old memories stronger than recent events?

Saturday, 17 [December]

Dinu Noica sent Comarnescu a letter from Paris, in which he announced that, after the killing of Codreanu, he has decided to join the Legion. He therefore considers null and void all the contracts he has with the Royal Foundation, and is prepared to return in the shortest possible time all the sums he has received as advances.

I can clearly recognize Dinu Noica in this.

On the other hand, Mircea called on Rosetti to tell him that he remains a writer and man of science, that he wants to publish books, and that he wants—more than ever before—to occupy himself with the oriental in-stitute that is to be created within the framework of the Foundations.

That's not a bad thing either.

Yesterday the National premiered Wilde's *Bunbury*, in a translation done by myself. (No one knew this, because Sadoveanu, of course, did not want to risk putting my name on the poster. Nor am I too proud myself of an English play translated from a French translation.) All the same, it is amusing to hear on stage sentences that you have written yourself. I felt a certain author's curiosity (as if the text belonged to me), but also a complete detachment from what was happening on stage.

1939

Thursday, 5 January 1939

I had lunch at Hurtig's house,[1] where he described for me yesterday's scene at Titeanu's office.[2]

The principal secretary enters:

"Minister, the Writers' Association has applied to join the National Front[3]—but there are a few awkward names."

"Which ones?"

"Mihail Sebastian, Sergiu Dan . . . What is to be done?"

"You know the orders. We can't compromise the movement. Delete them."

So we were deleted. In today's papers our names are missing from the Writers' Association list. And to think that yesterday at the Foundation they got me to sign a membership application.

Monday, 9 [January]

I don't know why I wasted my Christmas holiday staying in Bucharest. I could have finished my novel, or gone skiing, but instead I frittered away days and nights doing nothing. So here I am at the end of the holiday, tired, listless, with no desire to work, idle, disoriented, full of regrets. Again I have no money—which reminds me that I am thirty-one, that life is passing me by, that I am wasting it, have already nearly wasted it.

Outside it is an unlikely spring day, warm and sunny, which makes me twice as sad.

1. Alexandru Hurtig: journalist.
2. Eugen Titeanu: undersecretary of state for press and information.
3. Frontul Renașterii Nationale (National Renaissance Front), the only political party allowed to function during the royal dictatorship of King Carol II (1938–1940).

Tuesday, 17 [January]

The comical, absurd, and in fact terrible situation that I have been enduring for eight months with Zoe will now have to be acted out again with Leni.

She came here yesterday, took her clothes off, and then, when I caved in, behaved with a grace and simplicity that got us through a moment that seemed to offer no way out, no salvation.

She is very beautiful, much more beautiful than I could have thought in my most credulous moments of expectation.

What a pair are these lovers of mine, Z. and L., who differ and complement each other precisely through the ways in which they agree. What a life—complicated, to be sure, but also full—I could lead between the two of them!

A complicated life! Is there a life more complicated, more stupidly, more senselessly complicated, than mine is?

I look at it with a kind of resigned stupor, which is probably the only thing that stops me from putting an end to it all.

There is no more room in my life for anything but suicide, or perhaps a departure for good into a solitary existence somewhere.

Friday, 20 [January]

Horror, disgust, something dirty, obscene, immeasurably somber.

How powerful my inertia must be to go on living after such a day!

Thursday, 26 [January]

Returned tonight from the Schuller, where I had gone skiing for five days. Too little time for an escape. But anyway, a respite. A deferment, a moment of pause. I tried not to think of anything, tried to forget. I knew it was not possible, but I tried to find at least some means of anesthetization.

And now comes the awakening?

Tuesday, 7 February

Lunch yesterday at Blank's, with Monsieur de Norpois. In fact his name is "Comte de la Rochefoucauld," but he is a typical Norpois. I was tempted to ask him if he has read Proust and if he is not struck by the similarity. It would have been an impertinence, of course, but I don't think I was in any event very tactful in my conversation with him.

I didn't realize at first that he was "Ambassador of the Order of Malta at the Court of Bucharest." As he talked all the time of his diplomatic passport, I thought he must be in the French diplomatic service—and for that reason I was amazed at his violent hostility to the Socialists (especially Blum), his ardent support for Franco, his disdain for the Spanish Republicans, and the joy with which he awaited a "Nationalist" victory. Feeling something close to indignation, I reminded him that France would now have another frontier to defend. I think I was a little aggressive, a little irritating. I should learn to listen calmly and politely, without reacting in too sharp a manner. For God's sake!—I should have learned that much at least from my knowledge of Proust. I think that La Rochefoucauld–Norpois would have "given away" much more yesterday if I had inspired his trust and if—not feeling me as an opponent—he had been at his ease. Maurice Turbé, in such a situation, would have made himself seem perfectly modest, surprised, admiring, and obedient.

But even so, the guy was entertaining. He is so much the "diplomat in retreat"! (His very position as ambassador of a fictional entity makes him overdo the mannerisms of a diplomat.)

He speaks about everything with an air of false modesty, but a sense of self-importance is exploding beneath it—as he condescends to initiate you into great secrets, unofficially and a little "incognito." *"Vous savez, mais je n'en sais rien; je suis d'une totale ignorance."*[4] And when he said *"totale ignorance"* he seemed to be inviting you to read a mass of great mysteries behind his smile.

Tittle-tattle from the Italian or Spanish court, stupid little trifles spoken with a touch of mystery and briefly underlined: *"et vous savez, ça c'est déjà de l'histoire."*[5] A kind of comical respect tinged with familiarity for the great European dynasties. *"Victor Emmanuel est un grand roi."* *"Don Juan est marié à une charmante Bourbon. Des gens très sérieux."* *"Lors de la marche sur Rome, Victor Emmanuel a agi en chef de la maison de Savoie."*[6] And, talking about Mussolini's first interview with the king, he added: *"Je le tiens d'une personne qui était présente et qui n'était pas le roi."*[7]

4. "But you know, I don't know anything about it; I am in complete ignorance."
5. "And you know, that's already history."
6. "Victor Emmanuel is a great king."—"Don Juan is married to a charming Bourbon. They're very serious people."—"During the March on Rome, Victor Emmanuel acted as head of the House of Savoy."
7. "I have it from someone who was there and who was not the king."

Aderca—whom I met last night at the Sephardi circle, where we both spoke about Baltazar at a kind of "festive" soiree—told me that he deplores the death of Codreanu, who was a great man, a real genius, a moral force without equal, whose "saintly death" is an irreparable loss.

Leni comes all the time—and I call her and receive her all the time. I don't know where this whole business will lead me—but I'm glad that I have her beside me and have not lost her. But later? What then?

Thursday, 9 [February]

Nina and Mircea came round the evening before last. It was as if nothing had happened, as if between us there were not a year to be forgotten.

There were lots of graphic details about his life in the camp at Ciuc, and especially about his companionship with Nae, whom he mentioned with such warmth that I suddenly felt a longing to see him. How I regret that I didn't manage to see him before he was rearrested!

I have been learning English for the past three weeks. I bought my first book the other day, and I shall try to go through it syllable by syllable. Lawrence's *Letters*. It's premature, of course, but I should like to have an "Albatross" volume among my books.

Otherwise, all as before: that is, absurd, humiliating, and unbearable. I don't know where I find the strength each day to drag along this wretched life of mine. Probably from laziness—my only strength.

Saturday, 11 [February]

Yesterday Camil was made director of the National Theatre. After his appointment, we dined together at the Continental.

I'm apprehensive about what he will do. I'd like him to succeed; it's one of the few great chances he's been offered.

Sunday, 12 [February]

I have decided to return to my novel. I want to complete it. It is absurd for me to leave it unfinished for so long. All my activity as a writer (but am I still a writer?) is at a standstill because of it.

Besides, I have no money and I don't know where to find any. The spring rent will soon be due. If I can send the novel off to the printer's, I'll immediately have twenty or maybe even thirty thousand lei.

By working I will also—for a time, at least—find a meaning again in this wreck of a life. At least if writing can still be that for me—a refuge!

If necessary, I'll shut myself up indoors—and if that's too difficult (Zoe, Leni, the Foundation, the telephone, etc., etc.), I'll go away from Bucharest. I must.

Today I reread the manuscript, which I quite enjoyed. The first thing to do is to knock the reconstituted part into shape. I must set aside my regrets and the feeling that the loss is essentially irreparable, that the reconstituted part is inadequate if not a complete write-off; set aside my sighs and misgivings (are these not another form of laziness?); set aside everything and get straight down to work on what has already been written. In a few days—two, three, certainly no more than four—I must be able to give a typist the six chapters I have already written. Then the rest will have to follow. I won't allow myself more than a month for everything. The aim is for the book to come out in March!

It's a solemn promise, a binding vow, a question of how serious I can be.

8 March, Wednesday

Marietta Sadova wants to take *Jocul de-a vacanţa* on tour from 8 April to 1 May.

Of course I can't refuse (there's no plausible reason or pretext I could give), but this surprising turn of events is frankly a nuisance. The money I might make from it is derisory. And what I could lose, though not grave, is certainly not pleasant. I'm not so attached to this play (especially now that its "career" is over, without glory!), but nor can I bear to see it hauled around the country with a troupe of ham-actors cobbled together from somewhere, in wretched halls either three-quarters empty or filled with free tickets issued through district prefects, residential homes, garrisons, and revenue offices.

There is something sad, disheartening, and promiscuous in such a business, and I'd have liked my name not to be associated with it in any way. I tried to persuade Marietta to choose another play—when she was here yesterday—but for the moment she is refusing. In the end, if obstacles of some other kind don't emerge, I'll probably have to resign myself.

Tuesday, 14 [March]

I had lunch today at Alice Theodorian's, after a "break" of two months; it happened in the most comical circumstances (a few aspects of which might have been worth recording at the time). I was listening to her talk today when I suddenly glimpsed the whole network of relationships in which absolutely everyone I know is caught up, as if each of their lives were but a ramification of a common social life.

I need only take a single name or character, almost at random, to see how all the others are implied in his or her personal existence. From incident to incident, ramification to ramification, I start from Alice and arrive at Blank, Leni, myself, Lilly, Zoe, Maryse, Marie Ghiolu, Lupa, Nae, Mircea, Camil—and through Camil back to Alice, where the circle closes. But I can start again in another direction, another itinerary, drawing along other people and adventures, each with a certain autonomous importance, but always enmeshed in the same "system" of social relations.

For the first time I have realized how large is the surface over which my life unfolds, monotonous and cramped though it feels to me. For the first time it occurred to me that what we put into a three-hundred-page novel is ridiculously insignificant in comparison with the huge number of things involved in the most ordinary of our gestures. It is enough to say a name—Cella Seni, for example—and dozens of people, dozens of comedies, dozens of adventures start moving in an infinite number of rotations.

If I were to write a novel containing all this material (which I seem to have seen only now for the first time, in its full extent), how many thousands of pages would I need?

Will life allow me to write it sometime, later on?

Marietta's tour is off, for the moment at least. I think she understood the danger of setting off with a troupe of obscure actors, put together from various bits and pieces. For a few days she struggled to assemble a worthy cast: Soreanu as Bogoiu, Valentineanu as Ștefan; she was even prepared to ask Elvira to play Madame Vintilă. But Soreanu is busy with *Duduca Sevastița*, and Camil doesn't want to hand over Valentineanu— so Marietta preferred to postpone the tour till October, when she hopes she will get them both.

For the time being, then, my disgruntlement of the other day no longer applies. As for the autumn, we shall see.

Monday, 20 [March]

The obliteration of Czechoslovakia has affected me as a personal drama. I was reading in the street an account of Hitler's entry into Prague—and I had tears in my eyes. It is so abject and humiliating that it offends everything I have felt able to believe about people.

It would appear that—despite the denials in yesterday's papers—Romania too received an ultimatum. For the moment it is being asked only to dismantle its industry and to revert to a strictly agrarian country supplying Germany alone, which would thus gain a monopoly on Romanian exports and imports.

If this is accepted, we shall have the Germans here by autumn at the latest. If it is not accepted, we shall have war in ten to fifteen days.

Meanwhile, Daladier and Chamberlain are making speeches in protest.

Everything seems grotesque. If you were watching from another planet, you'd feel like laughing. But like this . . .

Yes, it's possible that there will be war this spring, and possible that I'll die this spring in a trench somewhere.

Emil Gulian, with whom I spoke over the phone on Saturday, suggested that some of us get together and swear that whoever remains alive will edit the manuscripts left behind by the ones killed in battle.

I must confess that I am not particularly bothered about my manuscripts. What concerns me more are the books that I may no longer write—and especially this life, with which I have done nothing up to now.

Tuesday, 21 [March]

By tomorrow I'll probably be a soldier. It seems that the whole of the Second Corps has been mobilized. I went with Cicerone[8] to the Twenty-first Regiment (we are both part of it), and a captain who is a friend of his said that all the contingents from 1928 to 1938 have been called up. Only some of the call-up papers have been sent out, but it is almost certain that there will be no more than a twenty-four-hour delay.

This turn of events has caught me rather unawares. I have no money. How am I going to pay the rent? What will I leave at home for daily expenses? What will I take with me?

If I at least knew that they'd have enough to eat at home, I'd go off with my mind at rest. This evening I ate at home, played *belote* with

8. Cicerone Theodorescu: poet.

Tata, tried (with some success) to make them think I was cheerful and untroubled. Mama could scarcely hold back her tears. "I haven't had any joy in life," she said. Maybe she's exaggerating. But she hasn't had any great joys, and not the one she always awaits: to see us married, with grandchildren of whom she can feel proud.

As far as I am concerned, I don't want to make plans of any kind. It's best if I leave with my eyes shut.

Thursday, 23 [March]

I report to the regiment tomorrow morning. I don't want to give this excessive importance. It could be just a call-up from which I'll return in ten or twenty days—and that's it. Then I'd feel embarrassed to have blown up an unpleasant incident into a full-scale drama.

But there are other possibilities. It's all so confused that anything could happen—even war. Personally, I don't think it will come to war. France and Britain will rest content with speeches. Italy will get some kind of concessions. We'll cave in. Germany will continue its southeast-ward march. I have a feeling that *"le coup de la Tchécoslovaquie"* will be repeated in exactly the same way. Who said we are living "in the midst of adventure"? This adventure has started to become monotonous. Everything is predictable, everything looks the same.

But there is still a "margin" for accidents. There is a chance—let's say 5 percent—that the machinery will break down after all and war will be unleashed. In that case, my departure tomorrow will have been a real departure. I have to take some measures for any eventuality.

I'll stop my journal here for the time being. Perhaps the most sensible thing would be to destroy it, but I don't have the heart. I'll seal it well and give it to Benu to put in Uncle Zaharia's safe—or better, perhaps, in Roman's office. That's also where I'll get him to take my manuscripts. I see I am calm enough still to think that they are of some importance. Maybe I'll find them again one day.

Friday, 31 [March]

Although I have been free since Saturday evening, I haven't got round to noting the ins and outs of my "discharge." Two days spent in the rain, in the barracks yard, suddenly placed a value on my civilian life, and I felt that, if I ever regained it, I would know how to use it better and care for it more.

So here I am back—and nothing has changed. The same indifference, the same laziness, the same loss of sensitivity.

The Easter holidays will soon be here, and I'm afraid I'll fritter them away, without going off anywhere and without doing any work.

Monday, 3 April

Two days in Sinaia, at Roman's villa. The car journey was refreshing. It's enough for me to see fields, trees, open skies, and I forget my absurd everyday life.

I read, slept, and lazed about. I return in the mood for work.

From one of Conrad's letters to Galsworthy:

"I have begun to work a little—on my runaway novel. I call it 'runaway' because I've been after it for two years...without being able to overtake it. The end seems as far as ever! It's like a chase in a nightmare—weird and exhausting. Your news that you have finished a novel brings me a bit of comfort. So there are novels that *can* be finished—then why not mine?"

Friday, 7 [April]

Good Friday! A glorious spring day. I'd like to spend it on a chaise longue, in the sun. This morning I had half a mind to leave for Balcic. I even went to Lares[9] to ask for information. There's a flight on Sunday morning and I could be back on Wednesday, without having neglected things at the Foundation. (If Cioculescu hadn't been called up, if the *Review* hadn't been left entirely in my hands, I would certainly not have let this holiday pass without going off somewhere to work....)

I might still go away for the three days over Easter, but I'm not sure. I feel quite good alone at home. The telephone is keeping quiet and may leave me, if not to work properly, then at least to read, to write something, and to put some order into my papers.

23 April. Sunday

Today I read the first part of *De două mii de ani* (my usual habit of taking a book at random from the shelf and not putting it down)—and it

---

9. The Romanian national airline.

seemed very fine to me. Suddenly I saw myself in Paris, carrying a French translation of the book to someone or other—Benjamin Crémieux, René Lalou, Jean Paulhan, even Gide—and the idea didn't strike me as absurd. I almost know what I'd say to them: *"Lisez, monsieur, les premières 120 pages. J'ai l'impression qu'elles sont bonnes. Le livre est raté sur sa fin, mais il commence bien. Et de toute façon, je suis certain que, traduit en français, il ne passerait pas inaperçu."*[1]

In last week's *Curentul* magazine, there is a highly laudatory article about *Corespondența lui Proust* and myself, signed P.S. Who is P.S.? It seems impossible to believe, but it's Pamfil Șeicaru. I wasn't sure whether to thank him or not. In any case, yesterday I sent him a few lines in the post—more because a violent attack on him had appeared in *Azi*, precisely for his article about me. But I don't think my letter contained any platitudes, and certainly not anything overfriendly.

I am swamped with things to do. *Revista Fundațiilor* takes up a lot of my time, especially now, when I have to read and approve the page proofs. Moreover, being strapped for cash, I am translating a play by Jean Sarment for the National Theatre (*Les plus beaux yeux du monde*).

Wednesday, 3 May

Two days in Balcic. I returned yesterday morning by plane. My journey there—on Sunday morning—had also been by plane. As usual, I stayed at Dumitrescu's. I am getting to be a real old "Balcician." I even stay at the same place: no longer at Parușeff's (he has sold his house, I was very sorry to hear) but at Dumitrescu's.

I had three mornings there, all of which I spent at the sea. I return with a tanned face, as after a full holiday.

Of course, I no longer—or less and less—feel so awestruck at finding the same miraculous places in Balcic. I have grown used to them; they have lost their unfamiliar aspect. Nevertheless, there are moments when I tremble before them as before fantastic, fabulous, unimaginably distant apparitions. On Monday evening (alone with Cicerone Theodorescu) I went well beyond the Iunian villa and stood "in the moonlight," with my eyes riveted to the sea, for one long hour as full as ten. Balcic has something that intoxicates me and tears me apart. I feel like lying

---

1. "Sir, please read the first 120 pages. I have a feeling they are good. The book is botched toward the end, but it begins well. Anyway, I'm sure that a French translation of it would not pass unnoticed."

on the ground with my arms outstretched and saying: "Enough, this is as far as I go." I could remain like that for the rest of my life.

When night really set in, we went through the Tatar quarter to the outskirts, high on a hill, where we stayed a long time gazing at the moon-flooded sea, and at Balcic gleaming in the light.

Seen from there, my whole life seems misguided, idiotic, full of meaningless effort.

Monday, 8 [May]

Friday was the Day of the Book: and I had to go there in the uniform of the Front.[2]

Did I have to? I don't know. It may be that if I had taken a really hard look at things, I would have resisted. Maybe I wouldn't even have placed my position at the Foundation in jeopardy. So many plausible pretexts can be found. Was it so hard for me to be sick that morning?

I feel ashamed, and I felt even more ashamed at the time. Do I have the right to judge anyone's moral qualities when I didn't have the strength to resist that comedy? What would I do in the face of greater pressures? How would I behave in a concentration camp? How much pride would I retain in front of a firing squad?

I am paying with my personal liberty for a 5,535-lei-a-month job! Doesn't that seem rather a high price to pay?

Assuming that what I write may one day mean something to a still distant reader, will not this livery cancel out any moral significance, any moral value, in what I have thought, felt, and written?

I am a writer who wore livery. And to think that writers have died at the stake for refusing to put up with much less!

I feel disfigured and disqualified—as if I have forfeited the right to use the word "I" with that sense of self-esteem, of pride in oneself, which alone justifies the writing of it.

"I am a civilian," I wrote in *Cum am devenit huligan*—and I was proud of what seemed to me a declaration of liberty, independence, and nonconformism. . . .

"*Avez-vous remarqué,*" Princess Bibescu (Antoine's wife Elisabeth, not Martha) asked me at lunch on Saturday, "*que les fanatiques ont les yeuxs clairs? Seul un homme aux yeux clairs peut être un fanatique.*"

2. King Carol introduced the uniform of the National Renaissance Front. It was mandatory for government employees.

"Et moi, madame?"

"Je me le demande. Vous les avez presque verts, mais pas assez pour un fanatique. Enfin, votre cas n'est pas résolu."[3]

That isn't the only piece of wit that I remember from her conversation. At first sight she seemed quite stunning. "The most intelligent woman in the world" is something you might say off the top of your head. But I would retain it in this case, because no other woman I have known has ever given me such an impression of verve and nervous spontaneity. In two hours she said dozens of words of which Oriane would have been proud. (*"Moi je m'ennuie une fois tous les vingt ans. Eh bien, avec Calimachi je me suis ennuyée pour les vingt ans."*

"Les domestiques sont terrifiants. Ils sont les seuls à se rendre compte, avec une exactitude absolue, si quelqu'un est un homme de qualité ou non. Moi je voudrais fonder une société pour la protection des nouveaux riches, contre les domestiques."[4])

But she says it all good-heartedly, without ostentation, almost without being aware of it. I'd like to see her again, though it's possible that, once you get to know her, she might lose some of, I wouldn't say her spell, but her extraordinary power to surprise you with each new word.

She is ugly, dresses with an amusing lack of taste and attention, appears to have no trace of feminine coquetry, and yet is not in the least vain about what she is: a princess, an Englishwoman from a great family, a friend of all considered in Europe to be the most illustrious, most refined, most eccentric. Her best friend is Léon Blum, but another "best friend" was Antonio Primo de Rivera (about whom she spoke a lot, with warmth and passion, though this does not prevent her from remaining on the extreme left: *"Je savais qu'il allait être fusillé, et pourtant ma sympathie pour les républicains n'a pas fléchi"*[5]).

I am enough of a snob, or perhaps enough of a child, not to be pleasantly bowled over by the fact that the woman sitting opposite me at table is a close friend of royalty and Socialist leaders, with the King of Spain (who calls her *"ma petite Elisabeth"*), and with the head of the Spanish

---

3. "Have you noticed that fanatics have clear eyes? Only someone with clear eyes can be a fanatic."—"And I, madam?"—"I wonder. Your eyes are almost green, but not enough for a fanatic. Well, your case is still open."

4. "I get bored once every twenty years. But with Calimachi I was bored *for* the twenty years."

"Domestics are terrifying. They are the only ones who can tell, with complete precision, whether someone is a person of quality or not. I should like to found a society for the protection of the newly rich against domestics."

5. "I knew they were going to shoot him, yet my sympathy for the Republicans did not weaken."

Communists, who in 1931 did her the favor of allowing the Duke of Alba ("Jimmy," as she calls him) to cross the frontier without being checked. I also like her for her philo-Semitism, which relaxes me in conversation in a way that would otherwise be difficult. *"J'aime les Juifs. Je les aime passionément. Ce n'est pas parce qu'ils sont malheureux. Non. Je les aime parce qu'ils éloignent l'horizon."*[6]

I shall send her some flowers and add a few lines. I don't know if it is the done thing, but I feel bound to tell her how she filled me with wonder.

Tuesday, 16 [May]

I've been called up. This time I don't think I shall get out of it. Nor do I want to. Since it has to be done anyway, it's better to do it now than in July or in autumn maneuvers. Tomorrow morning they'll give me my "things" again, and the next day it looks as if I'll be off to Mogoşoaia, where my company—the Eleventh—has its training camp. I don't know how it will go, but I am determined to remain very calm and resigned, even good-humored.

On Friday I was in Brăila between two trains. (I have a train pass again, thanks to Rosetti. I don't know how, but the thought that I have this in my pocket gives me a peculiar sense of freedom: I can go off whenever I like. It is true that the capacity in which I have it is no longer that of a journalist but of a state employee. The distinction is without practical consequences but significant nevertheless. Since the decree issued by the Goga government, not a single Jewish journalist—do they still exist?— has been able to get back a train pass.)

Anyway, I was in Brăila—a Brăila with all the acacias in bloom, but heartrendingly sad, neglected, decrepit. Not one new building (or rather, a single horrible one, where the Diana Baths used to be): everything is as I knew it ten or twenty years ago, only older, more worn, more sunk in poverty. Even Bulevardul Cuza looked a wreck: I had preserved an impression of its majesty, but that is not what I found there.

I can't say that I am making progress with my English. I've stopped my lessons with Mangeriu. Besides, he no longer has anything to teach us.

But I continue to read. I read quite easily Arnold Bennett's *Grand*

---

6. "I like Jews, I like them passionately. Not because they have had an unhappy time of it—no. I like them because they move the horizon forward."

Babylon Hotel. Now I am reading, less easily, a novel by Joseph Conrad: *Almayer's Folly.* I have not used a dictionary for either. There are certainly dozens and hundreds of words I don't know, but I don't like reading with a dictionary (though I ought to); I prefer to be carried along by the rhythm of the sentences, whose general drift I always manage to understand. I would need something to compel me to work with a dictionary: a translation, for example, which I had to do meticulously, with a sense of responsibility. I intend to ask Rosetti if I can do a translation for *Energia.*

Thursday, 18 [May]

I collected my army things yesterday—some foul rags, which are impossible to keep indoors without all the windows open. All night I tossed and turned in bed, terrified at the thought of lice. It's impossible for me to don such repulsive things. I forced myself to put together a uniform from various clean bits: my old tunic from 1933, my puttees from the same period, my summer boots. The trousers I got from Comșa.[7]

A little while ago I had a dress rehearsal. My God! What a wretched figure I cut! I look miserable, downcast, crushed, and disfigured. I am no longer myself: I am nothing, nothing, nothing. Something that can be killed off in a scramble, without the slightest importance; something that can be dragged through the mud, dumped in stables, abandoned in a field; something without a name, without identity, without eyes of his own, without a will or a voice, without life—a Romanian soldier.

Since I heard that I'd be going to a "training camp" in Mogoșoaia, I have lived with the illusion that I need only tell Princess Bibescu that I'm nearby and she would call me into her castle and offer me a room. I saw myself installed there as on a country holiday, and I counted the evening hours that would be left for reading after I returned from the training grounds. I also wondered if I shouldn't begin work there on the Sadoveanu chapter in my "Romanian Novel."

From the regiment I called Antoine Bibescu at the Athenée Palace to tell him what was happening, but I was informed that he was away in Strehaia.

I decided to write to him there, though I didn't quite dare. But yesterday afternoon, around five o'clock, I received in the mail from Stre-

7. Ioan Comșa: friend and law firm colleague of Sebastian's.

haia a book about Proust (Arnaud Dandieu) and a few affectionate lines from Antoine. Several hours later, when I returned after midnight from Ralea's banquet (where I had gone to spend a final evening as a civilian), I found the following telegram: "WANT TO DISCUSS EXTRAORDINARY AND ADMIRABLE BOOK ABOUT PROUST—PLEASE LEAVE SATURDAY AT ONE—WILL SEND CAR TO COLLECT YOU IN STREHAIA AND YOU CAN STAY AS LONG AS YOU LIKE—BIBESCU."

It felt like a telegram from heaven. There could have been no better pretext to speak to him of the training camp in Mogoșoaia. I therefore wired him straight back: "SORRY CANNOT COME STREHAIA—AM CALLED UP AT 21 INFANTRY REGIMENT AND FROM FRIDAY WILL BE AT MOGOȘOAIA TRAINING CAMP—LETTER FOLLOWS."

The letter did follow this morning. I wrote at length about everything that has happened to me, and since Mogoșoaia is a kind of Doncières for me, I asked him—as Marcel would have asked Saint-Loup—to approach Martha Bibescu and ask her for hospitality.

At the same time I rang Dumbrăveanu's wife and told her about my military experiences. She promised to call the princess, and at four in the afternoon she rang me with the reply: "The princess is sorry, but as she has not received any officer in the castle, it would be hard for her to receive a soldier."

So that's it. Maybe she is right. Maybe my being a soldier strips me of any other quality. I am neither novelist nor critic nor playwright nor friend: I'm nothing, a soldier—and a soldier cannot be received in a castle. I force myself to understand, force myself not to feel slighted, force myself to accept that she is right, and yet I shall keep from this episode a painful sense of having been insulted.

In any case, I am just now sending Antoine Bibescu another telegram: "IF YOU RECEIVE LETTER I SENT TODAY I BEG YOU WRITE NOTHING TO PRINCESS MARTHA—HER SECRETARY TELLS ME ON PRINCESS'S BEHALF THAT I CANNOT BE RECEIVED AT MOGOȘOAIA—I KNEW IT WAS MADNESS—THOUSAND PARDONS AND IN FRIENDSHIP AS EVER."

With that, my little princely comedy has come to an end; I shall return to my fate as a commoner. Tomorrow morning I leave with my kitbag on my back.

Sunday, 21 [May]

What is terrible about my situation as a soldier is not the physical tiredness but the moral degradation. I would have to lose my pride as a human being for such a life to appear bearable. Anyone, absolutely anyone—my doorman, the humblest street sweeper or shopboy—counts for more than I do beneath these clothes, which at best arouse one's pity.

I effectively joined the army only last Friday, but it feels as if ten days have already passed since then. How terribly long is a day that starts at four in the morning, with the rising of the sun! And especially, how endless is such a day when you spend it in the training grounds, running, throwing yourself down, jumping, taking imaginary objectives by assault, then falling to the ground in moments of rest, in a kind of brute stupefaction from which you would like never to awake.

I came back home on Friday night, and when I saw again my white room, my gleaming bathroom, my clean bed, the terrace, the bookshelves, the light, I felt I was returning from an infernal molelike existence to a free, dignified, magnificent life above ground.

I tell myself that millions of people, tens and hundreds of millions, normally live in conditions that seem to me quite hellish—in filth, in promiscuity, in physical and moral squalor, exhausted, famished, and ragged—and I tell myself that it is not a bad thing to encounter, at least on army exercises, a fate which, if it doesn't make you better, at least makes you more skeptical, less sure of yourself, more modest.

I am beginning to understand why the poor cannot make revolutions. Physical degradation destroys the resources of human dignity. Revolt is then a luxury.

Thursday, 25 [May]

I haven't written anything here about my last days on call-up. I haven't been able to. When I return home at nine in the evening, I am completely wiped out. A hot bath and cold shower liven me up for a few minutes, but then I drop, unable to read a page before falling asleep.

I have two alarm clocks, set five minutes apart to eliminate the possibility of an accident. It would be a disaster if I were late one morning for roll call. Besides, I have timed with such exactitude my fitting operations and my journey to the North Station—where I meet five comrades each morning before traveling together by taxi to Mogoşoaia—that I have gradually succeeded in gaining an extra forty minutes of sleep. Now I wake up at 4:55 on the dot, not at 4:15 as in the first couple of days.

Everything becomes mechanical, every movement habitual, routinized, automatic. I found so many things unbearable in the first few days, and now I am growing indifferent to them. The physical brutalization is stronger than any moral revulsion. Little by little you lose not only the power to resist but even the taste, the fancy, the urge. . . . You let yourself be overwhelmed and dragged along. The morass of vulgarity at first disgusts you, but then you sink into it without realizing when.

This morning in the tent—where, because of the rain, the whole of our third platoon had gathered to disassemble a t.B 1932 submachine gun—didn't I too guffaw at Mălai Vasile's obscene jokes? Doesn't the stupid, never-changing dialogue between Private Spiegelmann and Private Crişan begin to amuse me too? How long would it take for me to become birds of a feather with them, to lose all pride and share everything really abject in barracks life, made up of pranks, dodges, bad jokes, and everyday misery endured without self-respect?

Yesterday I ate the food from the bucket, out of curiosity. Another day I might eat out of hunger—and then each day out of habit. Habit kills everything: disgust, dignity, the need to be alone.

I like being with people who don't laugh: one such, Săgeată Iulian, always has a rather severe look on his face, and another, Răduelscu, a sad, disarmed expression that I find heartrending.

Starting from today, I shall be free every afternoon. This is a great favor, all the more surprising in that the regimental commander, Colonel Mardare, is said to be a stern disciplinarian. I don't know to whom I owe this exceptional arrangement. He was told about me by Mişu Fotino[8] (who brought him a theatre program with my photograph and "biography": "Look who you've got here in the regiment!"), and by a Colonel Manolescu, who had himself been set up. Also, Antoine Bibescu's telegrams—one sent direct to the colonel, another to me via the regiment—must have created something of a sensation. I don't know what was in the one to the colonel, but mine sounds really over the top: "TO THE WRITER MIHAIL SEBASTIAN 21ST INF. REGT BUCHAREST—HAVE INTERCEDED WITH REGIMENTAL COMMAND TO GRANT YOU 60 HOURS LEAVE TO COME STREHAIA ON IMPORTANT MATTER—BIBESCU."

At first the telegram both amused and frightened me; it was so unmilitary, so fanciful, and so venturesome. It must have done the rounds of the battalions before it came into my hands, open and read by all and sundry. But then I pondered that—at least from what I had been given to understand by the lieutenant and my captain—things did not have for them the importance I had assumed. In their eyes, all this remains "civil-

8. Actor.

ian matters," "business between civilians." The fact that I am a writer, that Antoine Bibescu is also a writer, doesn't impress them at all; indeed, it arouses in them a slight feeling of contempt. Didn't Lieutenant Neguţi say the day before yesterday, while he was explaining the submachine gun, that what we do in the barracks is much more interesting than anything anyone might do in "civvy street"?

Another telegram today from Bibescu, delivered to my home this time: "WHY NOT COME TO CORCOVA FOR FEW DAYS? HAVE WIRED COLONEL 21ST MOGOŞOAIA—BIBESCU."

At the same time I received an envelope, also from him, containing just a telegram sent by Martha Bibescu from Mogoşoaia to Strehaia: "SEBASTIAN INTROUVABLE MOGOŞOAIA—TENDRE MARTHA."[9]

I can't say that this flood of telegrams doesn't amuse me.

I think I'll go to Strehaia on Saturday.

Monday, 29 [May]

I am back from Corcova, where I stayed from Saturday evening until this morning. I think whole pages could be written about these two days. If I were not so tired, the pleasure of being lodged in the Bibescu household (albeit for such a short time) would certainly have been more intense. Elisabeth Bibescu is, without doubt, "somebody." And her husband is interesting at least in Proustian terms and for "what goes on behind the literary and theatrical scenes in Paris."

Maybe I'll try after all to note something here about those days in Corcova. But only if the army leaves me in peace. Tomorrow morning at five I'll be in Mogoşoaia—a soldier again.

Sunday, 4 June

I cannot note here everything that happens day by day at the regiment. What makes an "army journal" almost impossible is the terrible physical tiredness. In the evening, when I get back from Mogoşoaia, I simply do not have it in me to write a few lines, nor even to pick up the receiver and telephone someone. Today is Sunday, and after a good night's sleep (nearly nine hours), I am still more dead than alive. But I will try to write the review for *Viaţa românească*.

9. "Sebastian cannot be found in Mogoşoaia. Fondly, Martha."

Sometimes in the morning, when I am running in fields with the kitbag on my back, panting, sweating, breathless, my heart ready to burst, I tell myself that death in war must be indescribably restful—a death that stops you short, a death that means you will no longer have to stir at the order: "Jump!," a death that finally allows you to sleep . . .

There must be something incurably civilian inside me, which military people find irritating by instinct. Otherwise I cannot explain Lieutenant Neguți's obvious dislike for me; it reminds me of the antipathy shown by Captain Keicik in 1932.

In principle I am supposed to have afternoons off (by written order of the colonel). But the lieutenant has done everything he can to cancel in practice this rather favorable dispensation. On Tuesday because of firing practice, on Wednesday because of night exercises, on Friday because of more night exercises, I had to stay the whole day (and night) in Mogoșoaia. It seems, however, that the major has been ordered by the colonel to make sure I am free in the afternoon—which seems to have put the wind up Neguți. Let's hope I won't have any incidents before discharge day.

I am quite good with a gun. On Tuesday morning, at Cotroceni, both my "random" fire and my "precision" fire were satisfactory. Just think, I felt a little proud!

On Wednesday morning I was on guard duty from six till one, at a bridge over Lake Mogoșoaia. (I found it rather amusing that I was acting as sentry on the lands of Martha Bibescu. Twice her husband drove over the bridge, just a meter away from me.)

I don't quite know what I was guarding there. (No one in the army quite knows what they are guarding.) Maybe I was guarding the lake and the forest from poachers. "Entering the forest, fishing and bathing strictly prohibited. *Prince G. V. Bibescu.*" What I find really amusing in that notice is the signature.

Seven hours of guard duty—that's seven hours of loneliness, without a book in your hand, without writing paper, without the right to smoke, without the possibility of sitting down. I don't know if I have ever felt the hours dissolve so slowly, pass me by and pass through me, then vanish somewhere into nothingness. I said to myself: it is the morning of 31 May 1939, six o'clock, seven o'clock, eight o'clock—this day, this hour, will never exist again.

To pass the time I tried to make a kind of recapitulation of my musical repertoire. I "mentally" searched for the phrases lodged in my memory. But at that time I was unable to recollect the short phrase in Schumann's cello concerto that had followed me for a whole year.

In fact, my memory for music is execrable. The only thing I know reasonably well is the *Kleine nachtmusik*. Sometimes I can recall a few motifs from the piano concerto I gave Leni for the New Year. Also a phrase from *The Marriage of Figaro*. That's all I remember from all my Mozart. As to Beethoven, I think I accurately know only two themes from the violin concerto, a phrase from the *Kreutzer Sonata* and one from the *Ninth Symphony* (associated with a typical gesture of Georgescu's that helps me recall it). Otherwise, only isolated fragments that come to me quite by chance, and which I never know where to place. From Bach, a single aria from the *St. Matthew Passion* and the beginning of the violin concerto in A; the rest is lost in oblivion. Strangely enough, I feel the presence of certain pieces (for example, Franck's *Sonata* or the beginning of his *Symphonic Variations*, Reger's *Variations on a Theme by Mozart*, Schumann's *Fourth Symphony*, Brahms's *Violin Concerto*, or Lalo's *Symphonie Espagnole*). It is as if I see their outline, their contours, their shape—yet it is impossible for me to recall them.

At yesterday's medical visit (an anti-tetanus jab I couldn't get out of), a second lieutenant from another company called me over and, quite irregularly, introduced himself first:

"I am a reserve officer. By profession I am a schoolteacher, in Sibiu. I have read your work for many years. I am happy to meet you; please allow me to shake your hand and congratulate you."

I listened all the while standing at attention. I was more embarrassed than happy. I have begun to distinguish almost instinctively between my civilian life and my army life—and this incident seemed to confuse the two.

A lot could be said about the men in my company. The ones I like most are simple people not on special reduced-length service: Sergeant Plăcintă Gheorghe, for example. Those who irritate me, on the other hand, are the ones known by the almost regulation term "Bucharesters": that is, smart kids, always talking and joking, with more than a little guile. (Guile is the only basis of distinction in the barracks.)

I still wonder what Antoine Bibescu wants from me. Maybe he thinks I could be a kind of agent for his plays in Romania; that I could place them and get them performed. The day before last, when I dined with him and his wife at the Capşa, he almost suggested ceding me all royalties on a play of his, *Jeux d'enfants* ("*et de vous intéresser aussi à sa car-*

rière européenne"[1]), if I would agree to translate it and place it with someone like Sică. I agreed in principle to translate it—but I firmly rejected
his monetary proposals.

Anyway, I think he is completely wrong about my potential as an
"agent." He doesn't know how lacking I am in contacts and influence,
nor, above all, how little the theatre interests me. I am all too well aware
that his friendly overtures (nearly every day I receive from him a message, a book, an invitation . . .) represent not an intellectual interest but
an interest *tout court*—though I don't yet know exactly what it is. His
offer to get my "Proust's Correspondence" published in the *Nouvelle revue
française* may therefore be no more than a tactical act of friendliness out
of which nothing is likely to come.

Nevertheless, for someone defter than I am, someone more enterprising and more adroit (for I am disastrously maladroit), relations with
the Bibescu household could well be of practical interest.

Sunday, 11 [June]

I am a civilian again. But my last day on call-up was so irksome that it
cast a pall of loathing and disgust over the whole period. I had no idea
that the "handing over of weapons" could become a tragedy. There I
was, already in civilian clothes in the regimental yard, walking with
weapon in hand from the company to the armory and back again, dozens
of times, to convince either the major in charge of the armory or the
lieutenant that the rifle barrel was not rusty and could be "taken back."
When I left there, I no longer had the strength to whistle with relief.
From the whole business I shall preserve a sense of misery and decay.
Nor can I at least say that I am glad to be back in my civilian life. I am
completely penniless, alone (I don't see or want to see anyone), with no
desire to work or do anything. Who knows, maybe a few days of Balcic
could put me back on my feet.

Tuesday, 20 [June]

On Sunday I was at Grozăvești—in Romanați—for the funeral of poor
General Condiescu.[2] It is so hard to accept the death of someone I have

1. "And for you to interest yourself in its European career."
2. General N. M. Condiescu: novelist, president of the Romanian Writers' Association.

known. And the passage from life to death always seems to me so absurd, so disarming!

I owe quite a lot to the general—including my position at the Foundation, which doesn't help me live but doesn't let me die. So many other people, rich or poor, who claim to be my friends (Roman, Blank, Ralea, Bibescu . . .) have done nothing for me, whereas "Squire" Nicu—perhaps in memory of the *Cuvântul* years, perhaps out of real literary sympathy (as he often said)—always made me feel I could rely on him. Now that he's gone, I feel great affection for that honest, sentimental man, a little muddled but kind and upright.

From Grozăvești I went with Rosetti and Camil to Cîmpulung, where we stayed the night. On Monday morning we drove up the Rîul Tîrgului valley to the foot of the Iezer. We were in the middle of the forest, alone, with the odor of fir trees around us and no sound other than the water. I wished I could stay there and never return.

Serious money problems. I don't know how I'll solve them, how I'll pay the rent, where I'll find the money to go off somewhere and write.

Wednesday, 21 [June]

A fortnight ago, Suchianu told me that Nae Ionescu had "begged" Armand Călinescu to grant him an audience,[3] and that, when he was given one, he "threw himself on his knees" and asked pardon for all he had done.

The story sounded idiotic, and I didn't even bother to remember it.

But now I have heard through Mircea that Nae was indeed in Bucharest, that he did have a very heated conversation with Armand, though Armand apparently remained quite calm and restrained, whereas Nae lost control of himself. They were due to have another talk the next day, but it was canceled on orders from above and Nae was actually sent back to Ciuc during the night. At the moment he is in Brașov, in the hospital.

I can't be sure where the truth lies. But what I gather from all this is that the poor professor—far from calmly awaiting "the unfolding of events" (which would have meant that he still believed in his destiny)—is struggling to find a way out of the impasse in which he finds himself.

How terrible is that man's fate. I can't help thinking very often about him.

3. Armand Călinescu: prime minister 1937–1939, coordinator of the repression against the Iron Guard.

Tuesday, 27 [June]

Two days in Balcic. I came back yesterday evening. For two days at least I was able to think about nothing, to forget that I am broke, to forget my rent, the landlord, and so on.

But now I am back, I wonder how I can escape this tight corner. I shudder at every sound of the lift, every footstep in the hall outside: is it not perhaps the landlord, or the doorman, or someone from the block administration, to demand the rent that fell due yesterday?

I would need to find fifty thousand lei—but from where? from where?

I am very lonely. I haven't seen Zoe for a week, and my mind is made up not to see her again. She rang this morning, but I think she will understand and give up. It's better for both of us—and in any event it's better for her.

Leni left yesterday morning, while I was away in Balcic. Anyway, we hadn't met at all over the past month. There is no longer any talk of love between us.

I'm not sad. I am lonely. I don't expect anyone, or anything. To feel I am doing something, I read Sadoveanu with the thought of writing the first chapter of my critical work for the Foundation. I don't even know whether I shall write it; or even whether I shall read all the books I have collected. Time is passing, passing—and nothing more can happen in my life.

Friday, 7 July

Plagued with money troubles. (I made some 25,000 lei last week, with God knows what fretting, what anxiety, what rushing around, but, of course, hardly anything is left of it and I haven't even paid the rent in full.)

I am exhausted, as in my worst days in the past. My eyes worry me, in particular. I can't read for more than half an hour without a tired feeling in them.

I am overwhelmed with things that I let drag on and am unable to complete; there are a thousand intricate matters at court (including an appeal deadline that out of indolence I let slip—I don't make a good lawyer!); a host of things to be written for the Foundation, for *Viața*,[4] for *Muncă și voie-bună*, for *Independența*—all postponed from day to day;

---

4. *Viața românească*, a literary magazine.

and a mass of urgent reading that frightens me. Rarely have I felt more shattered, more drained, more gloomy.

And yet, amid the giddiness of the past two weeks, I feel literary projects bursting out almost in spite of myself, ever more necessary, ever more imperious.

Since I have been reading Sadoveanu (only five volumes so far, unfortunately), my book on the Romanian novel has begun to be more than a chore. I am sure it will be a pleasure to write. But when?

Accidentul cannot go on being a problem. I must either finish it during a month's holiday or else give it up forever. It's absurd to think that this little book has kept me at a standstill for two and a half years. I had no right to invest so much time and nervous tension in a book which, without any play on words, is becoming a kind of personal "accident."

I feel this all the more sharply now that I can glimpse a major novel of many hundred pages, with many characters and a broad compass. On Sunday I kept thinking of this book as I climbed Piatra Mare (a moment of intense emotion at the Seven Steps), and now, when I am in the street or on a streetcar, I see all kinds of incidents that branch out and join together.

1) Margit/director Hellmann—departure from Oradea, car journey through Romania—nights in hotels in various provincial towns. A stay in the Pension Wagner. Rendezvous, departure for Gheorghieni.

2) An actress—the Lilly type, but with the reputation of Marioara Voiculescu. In love with a young man, a shady character. Scenes at theatrical rehearsals. Departure on tour. They are due to meet in a certain town. The boy doesn't show up. In despair she goes to Bucharest, searches for him, abandons the tour.

3) The young man in love with Margit has secluded himself in the Pension Wagner for political reasons. (You can see Georoceanu's ascent in Cristianul Mare, when the police were looking for him in Brașov.)

Saturday, 22 [July]

Scorching days, stifling nights. I won't leave Bucharest even for a day, because I want to go away for a whole month next Saturday (probably to Stîna de Vale), and until then I shall spend every free hour on a translation I am doing for Biblioteca Energia. It's a biography of Lincoln, not too big, not too hard, but it goes rather slowly. Still, I translate without difficulty, and I am almost no longer surprised at what might be some kind of record: to be a translator from English after just six months. Once again Rosetti was my savior. The ten-thousand-lei advance on the translation helped me pay off part of the rent, and the final fifteen thousand lei—for which I shall ask even if I don't finish everything by Friday—will take care of the month's holiday.

My health is worrying, unstable, full of strange turns. A sustained effort of a few hours is enough to wipe me out. Yesterday evening, when I went out at nine (in this deserted, sun-baked Bucharest), I felt at my last gasp. Fortunately I had eight hours' sleep—the first such night since I don't remember when.

I ought to ask a doctor, but I don't have the courage. Maybe in the autumn, if I somehow get to Paris.

Since I have had Mozart's *Concerto in A-flat* here with me (Leni left it when she went away), it has become daily more beautiful. The andantino is one of the purest, saddest, and most limpid pieces in the whole of music.

Yesterday afternoon Petrică from Brăila came to offer me—just imagine!—a "deal" from which I could make 30,000 to 35,000 lei. While waiting for a telephone call, I put on the Mozart concerto for him—and since we both felt moved as we listened, I suddenly glimpsed a possible scene in my future novel: a businessman, precise, exacting, and unscrupulous, but also very intelligent and sensitive, makes a strike, and as he waits (the waiting should be intense, maybe full of risks or even dangerous, but apparently calm) he plays some Bach on the gramophone.

The hero could be a kind of Mihail Mircea, with elements of Wieder and Blank—if I don't use Blank for a completely different character.

Moreover, since I was talking with Petrică yesterday about Judge Doiciu, I thought of creating room in my novel for a great legal tussle, which might even form the pivot of the action. Doiciu could then serve as my model for a certain type of judge.

But the possibility of war still impinges on all this. It may even break out in August, though by now we are too tired to await it in a state of alarm.

On Thursday evening I had a meal in a garden restaurant on Strada Călăraşi with Mircea, Nina, and Giza. It was like the best times of old.

Sunday, 23 [July]

In a deserted Bucharest, depopulated, shuttered, burnt by invisible white flames, I translate and translate.

Last night, with all the doors and windows flung wide open, there was not the faintest breath, not the most distant murmur in the whole house or perhaps the whole city.

And yet I manage to keep going. I even feel fresher than I did a while ago—maybe it's the thought of leaving at the end of the week that encourages me.

Sunday, 30 [July]. Stîna de Vale

I didn't leave Bucharest: I fled. After a day of rushing around, I packed in fifteen minutes, jumped into a taxi with my suitcases not properly closed and my overcoat and gabardine fluttering behind me, arrived at the station two minutes before the train's departure, and raced madly to my carriage (followed by the porters, who picked up everything I dropped: one my left glove, the other my right). When the train pulled out I felt completely dazed. I couldn't believe I had made it.

Last night I slept nine hours, without waking up once. When did such a miracle happen to me last? Of course, I still don't feel rested. How many nights will I need to catch up on my sleep and become normal again? For the moment I am incapable not only of writing but even of thinking about writing. In principle I shall allow myself a week of holiday. Then we'll see.

This morning I went for a trip in the mountains with Comşa. We walked for nearly five hours, up to some rocky peaks that the local papists have named Golgotha, but which must be called something else by the peasants.

My room is clean, white, and luminous, with a view over the whole glade that constitutes Stîna de Vale proper. "You have a room with a fine view," said the boy who helped me move my things from Room 47 (where I slept last night) to Room 43 (where I'll be from now on). Beate Fredanov is staying in Room 45—an honest, pleasant girl who won't get in my way, I hope. The road from Stîna de Vale station up to here is served by an indescribable "shuttle bus." There is also a forest train, which is worth every penny.

Wednesday, 2 August

I am still on holiday. After a few exploratory walks (Aria Vulturului, Muncei Custuri), and after a longer trip to Golgotha, I went on a proper excursion yesterday to the source of the Someş, or rather to Cetatea Redesii, a huge cave through which the Someş passes still warm. I left at seven in the morning (with Fredanov, Comşa, and Furnarache) and returned at eight in the evening—ten hours of walking, three of rest. It is a splendid region, where each turn of a corner opens up new countryside, different mountains, valleys, and forests.

Some color is coming back into my face, my eyes are less tired, and my brow looks less of a wreck than when I arrived.

But the deadline is approaching for me to start work—and I feel the first signs of fear.

Sunday, 6 [August]

Tomorrow morning sees the start of my work schedule. I think I am sufficiently rested. But I would like to be on my own: Fredanov and Comşa are both very pleasant, but I need to be alone. Today I read everything I have written up to now. The number of pages, and their density, mean that I can consider myself past the halfway mark.

As for the rest, we shall see.

Monday, 7 [August]

Two and a half pages written. It's true that I worked only three to four hours in all. I am too exhausted: I find it hard to pull myself together and concentrate. As always, it is difficult to get going.

Tuesday, 8 [August]

Very slow, very difficult, very unsatisfactory. Some three and a half pages in six hours of work, none of them at all interesting.

But I have to be patient.

Wednesday, 9 [August]

Yesterday evening I listened to the general staff communiqué on the radio and suddenly felt that nothing matters any more. There will be large-scale mobilizations and, judging by the tension over Danzig, there could be war.

I had a difficult evening and a troubled night—a kind of disgust or weariness at being human. This morning, however, I am again at my desk. At all costs the novel must be finished.

Friday, 11 [August]

Yesterday evening I had a real "anxiety attack," and I don't think I was the only one. The whole hotel seemed in a state of apprehension. The news is bad. There will be a coup in Danzig over the next few days, and war could break out this very month. The communiqués of the general staff, which I hear every evening on the radio, have something alarming about them.

We are a long way from all that is happening there; it is as if we were on a ship—and the panic is all the greater for it.

Late yesterday I listened to the *Ninth Symphony* and the *Third Brandenburg Concerto*, not only with emotion linked to the music, but above all with a sense of sadness at all the things we are losing in the most stupid, criminal, and demented manner.

And I continue writing. It is still heavy going. Yesterday was a long rainy day, in which I worked for more than seven hours (I didn't time myself exactly), and all I got out of it was a little over four pages. I am arduously climbing up to Gunther's chalet, where I still don't quite know what awaits me. But things will become clearer, if I have the time.

Evening

Six and a half hours of work, five pages written. I am beginning to work more normally, but I must point out again that this "normality" is a poor yield. I ought to get a move on, but I am incapable. I am arduously climbing up to the chalet. The action is brief, with no possible incidents (Nora and Paul climb up from Poiana to S.K.V.—that's all), but I feel the need to write at a slow, relaxed pace, to make the distance greater between what they leave below and what they will find above. Nothing is more difficult than to indicate the passing of time, if you do not refer to any particular incidents. For all my complaints, however, I shall be able to work and reach the end, so long as I am left in peace. Gunther—completely unknown up to now, because I haven't gone near him—is beginning to take shape, though not yet enough. He is still in shadow.

Saturday, 12 [August]

Only three pages written. (I have finally reached the chalet—or at least its threshold.) It's only 5:30 and I should certainly go on working for a couple of hours, but I am too tired. I'll go for a short walk, maybe to the Aria Vulturului, and try tomorrow to make up these hours spent "playing truant." Then I should finish this eighth chapter, which I already have clearly defined in my head. I am looking forward to it with impatience, curiosity, and a lot of sympathy for Gunther.

Sunday, 13 [August]

Five pages written—but the chapter is still not finished. Here I am stopping work at seven, though I ought to see through to the end this chapter that I can already see so clearly, and that I feel at this moment so clearly and intensely. But I am tired. I don't congratulate myself at all on the state of my health. I really must take it seriously and go to see an eye specialist. Someone in robust health would not get up from his desk—whether it took ten hours, twenty, or a hundred—until he had finished writing everything he could see with precision. As I advance, things become clearer, more precise, and more substantial. Gunther is stepping more and more into the light. But I still haven't got to him.

On my evening walk (to Muncei), I met a shepherd from Meziad and started chatting with him. I ought to find the time to record what he said to me. It was disturbing for what it revealed about "the human condition," simply but also with a certain pathos.

Maybe tomorrow I'll go on an "excursion" to Meziad—a diversion, if you like, from my work schedule, but I may come back feeling refreshed.

Tuesday, 15 [August]

I was convinced that I would finish Chapter Eight today at least—since I wasted the whole of yesterday in Meziad—but now I am wasting today as well, along with five and a half working hours. For I must abandon the two pages I wrote this morning, as well as the half-page I wrote this afternoon. I was very pleased with them, and everything seemed to be going well (I even said to myself that I'd write four or five pages to make up for yesterday's break), but then I suddenly realized that I was on a false path and had to turn back. The whole section was misdirected.

Nora should set off at night on skis, in a kind of desperate state of giddiness. Only then does Gunther's chalet become a miracle, a salvation. In the version I wrote this morning she was calm and composed as she put on her skis and thought of the next day. But at that moment there is no "next day" for Nora. Unless I grasp that, I'll botch the whole passage and risk giving an artificial tone to the encounter with Gunther.

I shouldn't forget that the whole episode with Gunther has something artificial, and that I need infinite tact if the somewhat literary, somewhat "made-up" character is not to become thoroughly phony.

But none of this will redeem my further lost day. So little time is left until the end of the month, and it scares me, yes, scares me, to think that I might leave here without having finished it.

Wednesday, 16 [August]

I have eliminated yesterday's two pages and replaced them with another two that I wrote this morning, which seem much closer to the mark. But I have been at a standstill for the last hour, unable to move forward. The resistance is stupid and incomprehensible. The whole scene seems to me clear and straightforward: it shouldn't be difficult to write. Yet difficulties appear without rhyme or reason, just where I expect them least.

I am not happy with my morning. It rained—a dull persistent rain that I gladly welcome because it keeps me indoors, gives me a taste for work and creates quiet in the hotel—and yet all these favorable conditions were not much help.

I'll go down to lunch and wait and see what I'll do this afternoon.

Evening
I have worked from three o'clock until now—that is, a quarter to eight. I have finished the chapter. I wanted to finish it at all costs. I don't know how it has worked out. I feel a little dazed. Maybe I'll see more clearly tomorrow.

Thursday, 17 [August]

It doesn't work, no, it doesn't work. I don't mean the chapter that I finished yesterday (having reread it today, I find it acceptable and anyway won't go back over it). I mean the new chapter, the ninth, which I was due to start today. It is stuck and simply won't budge, though at least the first part seems clear and—or so I thought—simple.

The weather is ideal for writing: rain, the forest hidden from sight, the whole hotel slumbering, perfect quiet. Yet here I have been, from nine in the morning until five in the evening, trying to open the same chapter, starting dozens of sentences, erasing, replacing, and going back over them, deleting them again, incapable of moving a single step forward.

I am disgusted. I don't mean to say that I am losing heart. I realize that the only thing that can still see me through to the end of this wretched book is stubbornness—I mustn't let go of that, at least.

Saturday, 19 [August]

Gunther's chalet (in which Nora finally settled yesterday) is becoming a stage set. I realized this fifteen minutes ago, and in the space of fifteen minutes I feel I have sketched a whole play in my head that I could sit down and write *immediately*. I see things so precisely that I have already distributed the roles.

Gunther is called Gunther Grodeck (I don't know if I'll keep the name in the novel, but I probably will in the play, if I write it). He can be played by Tomazoglu. He doesn't have a fair complexion, nor is he as young or does he have the same childlike beauty as Gunther—but he does have the character's intensity of feeling. Grodeck Senior can be played by Bulfinski, and Hagen by Storin. The whole drama unfolds between those three. A girl too is involved, but *she is not Nora*. The Gunther episode, insofar as it is capable of becoming a play, will deviate completely from the novel. The starting point is all they have in common.

Grodeck Senior is a big industrialist. But the fortune is his wife's, who has been dead for two years, and all or most of it will be inherited by Gunther. Gunther is still a minor: he will be twenty-one in March. He has gone to live high up in the mountains and wants to remain there. He is waiting to come of age so that he can take possession of the fortune and put a stop to his father's exploitation of the forest for lumber. I am not yet quite sure of the reasons for this decision. The basis is a terrible hostility toward his father, who may not even be his real father. Then there is the mysterious Hagen (mysterious for me too). Was he the lover of the deceased Mrs. Grodeck? Perhaps. In any case, he was the only person with whom the young woman was on good terms in the Grodeck family—she who had come from distant parts (maybe the Austrian Tyrol) to a Saxon settlement in Sibiu or Braşov.

These are the characters. I don't really know yet what will happen to them. But I can feel them with every nerve, so strongly that I think I need only set off to find my way through to the end.

I wanted to write this note now (at eleven *in the morning*), in order to get it off my chest. I felt that otherwise I would not be able to continue working on the novel.

As regards the novel, I have recovered from the depressing breakdown of the day before yesterday. I went out in the rain, furious with myself, with the book, with everything, and walked as far as Băiţa and back, along the road to the general store—a trip of some two hours. I tried to put some order into this ninth chapter and divided it into three distinct scenes, precisely to mark out the ground for the next day. Then the name Hagen came into my mind (*Götterdämmerung*), and I suddenly saw a whole new character come into being. I could feel that there would be any number of secrets in Gunther's chalet. Everything, it seems, was triggered by the name Hagen—his looks, his clothing, his behavior, even his still not completely clear life story.

Yesterday I wrote five pages. What I'll manage today, I don't know. I really ought to finish the chapter, and would if I were serious.

Sunday, 20 [August]

Last night I dreamed of myself off at war. We were attacking an enemy patrol, which fired at us from a kind of house—or shop, rather—with its doors and windows shut. We followed every movement they made, separated from them by only a few meters.

The dream ran on from yesterday's troubled evening. A long conversation with Longhin[5] (recently made president of the Court of Appeal, having been provisional secretary-general at the Justice Ministry) frightened me. It seems that last week there was a real war atmosphere in Bucharest. Germany sent a sharply worded demand for an explanation of our troop mobilization. Armand wired the King on his cruise ship. France and Britain warned that war might break out not in Danzig but through a Hungarian attack on ourselves. By Friday evening the catastrophe appeared imminent. Longhin, who was just preparing to leave for Stîna de Vale, was told by Iamandi to stay where he was. The next day, however, things calmed down and he was able to leave. But no one knows anything, and everything—*même le pire*[6]—seems possible.

Maybe it is madness on my part to remain here in the forest writing literature. But these things are too dear to me. If I die in the war, I'd like it not to be before I have finished the book. It's nothing much really, I know it's nothing very much, but when I am immersed in it I feel that these characters—Nora, Paul, Gunther, Hagen—are alive. I wouldn't want to lose them, at least not before reaching the end of their story and putting it somewhere secure (in a safe, for example).

5. Vasile V. Longhin: judge from Brăila.
6. Even the worst.

Evening

I have finished Chapter Nine. Four pages yesterday, three and a half today. I must confess that I haven't been assiduous enough, attentive enough. Yesterday I kept daydreaming about the play, drawing up the cast list, going over and over the same things. It took a great effort to break from this "reverie" and force myself to remain with the novel.

Today the play (which weighed on me yesterday like some pressing matter) has moved into the distance. Ah! if only thinking were enough to see things in literature! The misfortune is that you also have to write; that's where the agony begins.

Concerning Chapter Nine, I was happier with the first part than I am with the pages I wrote today. Gunther will certainly be an interesting character, but also, I fear, a little "artificial," a little "too obvious." I can see him—or, rather, am beginning to see him—very well. But that may not protect him from a certain degree of unreality (which wouldn't harm him and may even be necessary), as well as from a visibly literary kind of fictitiousness.

I find it amusing to think of the little details that gave birth to Gunther—and of how different he has turned out from what I envisaged. The one who first made me think of him was Margit from Ghilcoş, who told me of a winter she once spent ill, on a chaise longue, at the Wagner villa. Then there was the inscription I found high on the Schuller, in memory of a Saxon boy (Walter Maschendorfer?) who died at the age of sixteen. Then there was Blecher—though I thought of him more in order to avoid any resemblance to my hero. Gunther's name I took from one of the children who went up the mountains in July 1937. And now see how strange and unexpected is the person who emerges from all this.

It may be that Gunther interests me too much. For I risk shifting my attention from the book's main story to what should be no more than an episode. In any event, I tell myself, I must begin tomorrow to return to Paul, whom I have left rather abandoned. I am afraid of losing him now, just toward the end.

Monday, 21 [August]

I won't escape from this play until I have written it. Again today I wasted a huge amount of time thinking about it. It's possible that I could write it over the winter, to be performed in February/March. There could be a role for Mme. Bulandra. (I'll call her Aunt Augusta.) But I am afraid that, if I do write in such a part, it will detract from the role of Grodeck Senior. One of them will have to represent the "Grodeck spirit" with profundity, severity, and intolerance. And I can easily see the graceful phantom of the young Mrs. Grodeck (Gunther's deceased mother) floating over the whole play.

What I don't see yet is what will happen to the girl who goes into Gunther's chalet, at the beginning of Act One. Similarly, I don't know whether the whole drama will unfold up there in the chalet, or whether it will come down to Sibiu or Braşov (where the "Grodeck factories" are located) in the second part. If it does, the play might have four acts.

The first two acts are almost clear. The first is the "winter evening" of the novel (Chapter Nine), evidently with certain alterations due to the fact that the emphasis now falls on Gunther, not on people from outside. The second act, set a few days later, will be the arrival of Grodeck Senior; it too will become clearer as the novel progresses. After that, the direction is open. . . .

As to the novel, I am very dissatisfied with myself. Not even three pages in a whole day: that's inadmissible. I don't blame myself for the fact that these two and a half pages are completely and utterly uninteresting. The Good Lord is the one who decides that. But I cannot forgive myself for having written so little.

Time is passing, young man. You must understand that. You must understand that in Bucharest you won't have these long free days, free from dawn till dusk.

Wednesday, 23 [August]

A German-Soviet nonaggression pact!

I feel it as a stunning blow. The whole course of world politics has suddenly changed. Just try to grasp, from Stîna de Vale with newspapers three days old, what is happening in the world!

Last night and early this morning I struggled to put some order into the chaos of my papers. If the present European chess game were a stage play, one would consider that the plot had been excellently handled. The Russians are settling accounts, a year late, for what was done at Munich—and they are settling them with the other side of the coin. Everything is perfectly symmetrical. In September 1938 Britain and France came to an understanding with Hitler, over the head of Russia and against it. In August 1939 Russia comes to an understanding with Hitler, over the heads of France and Britain—and against them. In September 1938 the immediate price was Hitler's pocketing of Czechoslovakia. Now it is Danzig. Nothing is lacking for Act Two to resemble Act One, with roles reversed. But it is hard to judge things just from the point of view of dramatic construction. The Russians haven't made their move only for the sake of its technical beauty.

So then?

So then, I have no idea. Will France, Britain, and Poland maintain their opposition over Danzig? If they do, there will most likely be a war, because I can't see why Hitler should go back on his firm stand on Danzig, now that he knows he is covered on the Russian flank. Will they give up their opposition? Then Danzig will become German in two, three, or five days—and Hitler will immediately, automatically, start turning the screws on Bucharest. In that case I think the whole of southeast Europe will fall.

Where am I in all this? The hotel is in a state of disorder. Everyone is leaving, or talks of leaving. Longhin is in a panic and wants to catch the train this very day. The lady in Room 44 has received a telegram for her to hurry back to Bucharest. By tomorrow the hotel will be empty of people from the capital. I cut an absurd figure, of course, with my manuscript, but it is so hard for me to drop it and leave!

Yesterday I wrote all day (a little over six pages). I keep at my desk, but I don't rule out the possibility that I will decide to leave in five minutes' time, if the news somehow grows worse.

Just after I wrote the last note, I went downstairs to ring Rosetti and ask him for some political news. I didn't get much ("easing of tension," he says, but I've no idea what that means), but he did tell me to return to Bucharest. Comarnescu has been called up, and they have urgent need of me at the *Revistă*. I'll leave tomorrow at one and be in Bucharest by Friday morning.

I am quite simply desolated. I'm sick of this novel, which I now have to interrupt without knowing when I can return to it. I'll try to finish Chapter Ten today, so that it won't be left completely up in the air.

Evening

No, I didn't manage to finish the chapter. I didn't even write three pages (pretty awful ones at that), though I kept at work all morning and afternoon. I am too agitated, too anxious. This is not how I wanted to be leaving here. In Bucharest I'll make a balance sheet of these seventeen days of writing. I'll try not to lose hold of the novel, and do everything possible to start work again soon and see it through to a satisfactory conclusion.

In the evening, a farewell walk to Muncei. I wish I could have been alone, but even so I return from there feeling a little emotional. Tomorrow I'll spend a few hours in Cluj, then catch the evening train to Bucharest.

Saturday, 26 [August]. Bucharest

I realize that it will be hard for me to work regular hours here in Bucharest. The Foundation, Roman's office, the restaurants, the telephone are stronger than my desire to be alone.

Yesterday I had dinner at the Continental with Rosetti, Camil, and Lassaigne;[7] and today lunch (also at the Continental) with Soare, Corin, Camil, and Carol. Black coffee with Vișoianu, Țuțubei, Mrs. Ralea, and Mrs. Brătescu-Voinești. This evening I am invited—I don't know why—to Alice Theodorian's. Things can go on like this forever unless I stop in time.

I'll lose the novel if I let it slip away from me now—and I won't have any excuses. No excuse other than war . . . I still have the feeling that it won't break out, though in that case the Germans will have carried off another Munich-style victory—one that we will be the first to pay for.

How great it was at Stîna de Vale! In fact I could have remained there, because there was nothing at all at the Foundation that needed to be done urgently. But when I think of it, maybe it was rather light-minded or even irresponsible to stay hidden in a mountain gorge in these terrible days.

Wednesday, 30 [August]

On Monday evening war seemed inevitable. Yesterday peace seemed possible. This morning things are again confused. Will Hitler give way? Or is a last-minute betrayal being prepared in London? Are we heading for another Munich? Personally, when I look calmly at what is happening, I think that Hitler has pushed his blackmail to the limit and that, if Britain resists, he will back down a split second later. Rationally speaking, I have thought continually over the last few days that there will be peace (through a rebuff to Berlin). "Rational!" The word doesn't have much weight. There is a "margin" of the unknown, a limit beyond which things are more powerful than the will and initiative of human beings.

If I had a radio, I'd listen to music. A lot of Bach, a lot of Mozart—only that can save me from anguish.

---

7. Jacques Lassaigne, French art critic.

"Mon roman cesse de m'intéresser lorsque je cesse d'y travailler,"[8] Gide noted, at a time when he was working without much inclination on *L'école des femmes.* Yesterday evening I came across this phrase by chance (I was cutting the pages of Volume 15 of his *Oeuvres complètes*), and I felt it as a warning. If I don't get straight back to my manuscript, I shall lose it.

Friday, 1 September

A gloomy letter from Poldy, who has enlisted as a volunteer and probably gone off already.

Rosetti rang to tell me that Danzig was annexed this morning. War starts today. It may have begun already.

I don't know where I have found the terrible calm that I feel in this hour.

Saturday, 2 [September]

Strange days of war. The first moment was overwhelming: when the first dispatches appeared yesterday morning about the bombing of Warsaw, I felt that everything was crashing down. I quickly wrote a letter to Poldy, not even knowing whether it would reach him, but feeling a need to say something, to embrace him and offer my best wishes. But I didn't have it in me to finish the letter; I couldn't find a word that said everything. I had an intense and painful feeling of farewell—and broke into tears alone.

Lunch at the Capşa (Rosetti, Ralea, Vişoianu, Camil, Lassaigne, Comarnescu, Păstorel,[9] Steriadi,[1] Oprescu,[2] Cantacuzino[3]) seemed lugubrious. People laughed, cracked jokes—and I couldn't understand how such thoughtlessness was possible. All day and all evening (right up to three o'clock), I went about trying to find more news—but it was all vague and strangely lacking in precision, realism, and evidence. The bombing reported by both the Germans and the Poles seems to be an invention. At the present moment, though thirty-six hours of what seemed like "the beginning of war" have passed, the war may not yet have actually started. The French and British are still at the stage of diplomatic notes (though Chamberlain's speech yesterday seemed to burn all the bridges).

Everything is confused and uncertain, still not started, still not de-

8. "My novel stops interesting me when I stop working on it."
9. Păstorel Teodoreanu: poet and writer.
1. Jean Steriadi: artist.
2. George Oprescu: art critic.
3. Ioan Cantacuzino: poet.

cided. What I find completely implausible is this brightly lit Bucharest, animated and filled with people, with packed restaurants and lively streets, a Bucharest at best curious about what is happening but not panic-stricken and not aware that a tragedy has begun.

I don't know how to pass the time. If I had a radio, I'd listen to news and music.

Yesterday morning I forced myself to read some manuscripts for the Foundation, as if nothing out of the ordinary had happened. But I was suddenly seized by the thought that these might be my last hours of liberty, or even of life, and that it was absurd to waste them in this way. I went into town, feeling dazed and disoriented.

In the afternoon I began writing out again the first part of Chapter Five—but then I dropped that too. One book more or less: what can it matter now?

The whole of today I waited for something decisive to clarify the situation. But nothing is heard from anywhere. So here I'll be this evening, alone at home reading André Gide's journal and probably turning in early.

All this on the 2nd of September 1939.

Monday, 4 [September]

Yesterday morning at eleven Britain declared war on Germany. At five in the afternoon came France's declaration of war. So far, however, there does not seem to have been any military engagement. Are they still waiting for something? Is it possible (as some say) that Hitler will immediately fall and be replaced by a military government, which will then settle for peace? Could there be radical changes in Italy? Are they waiting for Italy's neutrality to be made clear? Or will Italy be forced to follow behind Germany? What will Russia do? What's happening to the Axis, about which there is suddenly silence in both Rome and Berlin?

A thousand questions that leave you gasping for breath, and that you would like to have cleared up at once. I rush around, make telephone calls, ask questions, thrash about, keep turning things over in my mind. I should get a grip on myself and wait calmly for events to unfold, without hysterics, without despair.

I'll try to stay in, to work, read and write, to reflect alone, with clearheaded resignation, on all that is happening. Above all, I must not complain. Above all, I must not go mad with anxiety.

Let's take everything with sadness, but also with self-respect.

Tuesday, 5 [September]

For the moment all is quiet on the western front. In Poland the Germans are continuing their advance; no one seems to be resisting them. The Polish communiqués strike me as downhearted. No one knows what will happen in Romania. The most terrible stories and predictions are whispered around. Yesterday there was one devilish hour at the Foundation. Lassaigne, who had just been at the French embassy, told us that we were at the point of going to war alongside France. Germany is demanding all our grain and all our oil! France and Britain want to land troops in Constanţa! But we won't accept either one or the other! That's war for you.

I don't know what to believe. I come home dazed and disoriented, filled with anxiety. What is certain is that I won't be at my desk for much longer. I'm bound to be in the army soon. Big call-ups are taking place all the time, and people say this will lead to a general mobilization in all but name. For the moment I am not in one of the categories on today's call-up list. But it can't be ruled out that the general staff will issue another communiqué, from one day to the next.

I wait. And while waiting I do all kinds of things without enthusiasm, without perseverance. I ought to make a decision: either to read a long book, or to settle down to a translation for the Foundation, or to continue work on *Accidentul*—so that I finally stick at something in an orderly way. Yesterday evening I tried to read a Dostoevsky novel, but then I gave it up to read some Thomas de Quincey in English, and ended by again writing out the beginning of Chapter One—most reluctantly, however, because the version I reconstituted two years ago seems to me extraordinarily stupid.

Camil Petrescu asked me to suggest that Rosetti arrange an interview with Ralea and Armand, about a question of "capital" importance. He intends to leave the National Theatre and take charge of the technical side of our anti-aircraft defense. He is convinced that only he can save us from disaster. He refused to divulge his plans to me—but he is determined to lay them before the prime minister, or perhaps even the King. He also told me that he has close links to the general staff of the Second Corps, and that any military operations of ours in Dobrogea will follow his instructions.

I listened to him and am unsure what attitude to take. Sometimes I'm afraid I will burst out laughing; sometimes I ask myself with sudden concern whether he has not gone off his head. And, beyond all that, there is the most amusing possibility of all: that he is right.

Wednesday, 6 [September]

The mornings are bearable, but the nights are difficult, full of apprehension, poisoned by foreboding. Yesterday I felt deep inside me that
this life is over, that I'll have to abandon everything beyond recall. I don't
know if I'll die or not, but I do know that when I go off to war it will
completely change my life, and that any return will not be a real "turning back."

I [don't] think I am reconciled to it.

I leave this evening for the recruitment center in Brăila, to put my military papers in order. Very many of those called up for service in May
have received individual orders. It's quite probable that I am among them.

Friday, [8 September]

It seems that I haven't been called up yet. I am part of that mysteriously
safe category "D.1"—which in March, too, left me as a civilian. Obviously my liberty is only provisional and revocable; obviously I can be
called up from one day to the next, and in the event of a general mobilization (which I think likely), no letter on earth could save me (and I
wouldn't want it to). But for now, the fact is that I remain at liberty.
Never has a "for now" been more precarious and more treasured.

Things have been continuing in the same way. The Germans advance
in Poland while the French and the British stay where they are. Krakow
fell the day before yesterday. Warsaw is said to have fallen this evening.

Bucharest, which went through a couple of days of panic, has calmed
down. The restaurants, cinemas, and streets are full. Who would say that
we are in a city of Europe at war?

Some people—Camil for one—think that peace is a possibility and
may even be imminent. The Germans will propose it through the Italians—and the others will have no alternative but to accept. Although I
am beginning to think anything is possible, that seems to me an absurd
solution. I can't see France and Britain losing a moral-political battle
without firing a shot; it could simply wipe them out of history.

No, no. I shouldn't start planning for peace or thinking of the books
I shall write. I shouldn't look ahead to a winter of skiing, reading, or
traveling. It will be a winter of war, a year of war, years of war, and I'll
live them to the bitter end.

On Wednesday evening I went down alone to the port in Brăila—and
saw a picture-postcard Danube beneath the moon. Even the empty white
ships in the deserted port looked as if they were made of cardboard.

There was absolutely no one in the whole port—except myself and a watchman, who kept such a worried eye on me (a spy? a saboteur?) that I was forced to return to town, though I would gladly have stayed there a while longer.

"You're getting old," said Moni Liebsiech, who had stopped me in the doorway of a shop on Strada Regală. Yes, I'm getting old. Everything tells me this in Brăila—the houses, the streets, the people, the photographs from my youth that make me feel bad when I linger over them at Aunt Caroline's.

Zoe called round this afternoon. I read her the Gunther chapter, not too seriously, more as a joke, but not totally excluding the possibility—which I mentioned to her ten days ago when I returned from Stîna—that I'd like her to play the part of the girl that I am thinking of writing.

So I read her the chapter, and not only did she understand it very well, but her vision of it was so accurate that she offered me some most valuable suggestions for the play. Until today I had not been able to envisage this girl, who enters Gunther's chalet in Act One, and I had not known what would happen to her. Zoe helped me to see her—more, she outlined her role in the play.

Gunther has to die—says Zoe—but his death will be a victory both for himself and for Nora; for him, because the Grodeck clan will have been conquered; for her, because she will have broken with her oppressive past and (by entering Gunther's chalet) moved toward a new life.

We talked for whole hours about the play—and again I felt how the need to write oppresses me, weighs me down, robs me of my peace of mind.

Saturday, 9 [September]

I think of the Jews in Poland who have fallen under Hitlerite occupation. Anyone who has a revolver or a rifle will shoot as much as he can—and keep the last bullet for himself. But what about the others?

Camil Petrescu tells me that he refuses to write the military chronicle that Vinea has asked him to do for *Facia*.

"No, old man, I've had enough of dishing out my ideas for nothing. I won't speak up unless I'm offered a place in the government."

He has no respect at all for Gamelin, and now he commiserates with the French and the British because they don't have a Camil Petrescu.

When I hear all this, I don't know how to keep a straight face—but nor can I stop myself from agreeing.

Sunday, 17 [September]

Today the Russians signed an accord with Japan. At 4 a.m. they entered Poland to occupy what had been left by the Germans.

How happy are people with an *idée fixe*! They, at least, can keep calm and still think they understand. For Communists, even for our own, things are in order and "the revolution is marching on." Whatever the Soviets do is the right thing.

For the Legionaries (a term that is being resurrected), a German victory is assured and a perfect life will arrive in its wake.

And I? I who believe in neither the one nor the other, and who try to make up my mind not with prejudices but with facts? Isn't it enough to drive you out of your mind, to make you give up in despair? Don't you have to tell yourself that from now on absolutely everything is lost?

What is there left to do in these days, which may be my last? I'd like to listen to music all the time—it's my only drug. We'll die one day like chickens, with our throats slit. I ought to await the looming disaster more sturdily, more alertly.

Wednesday, 20 [September]

Titel Comarnescu tells me of a political conversation he had recently with Mircea, who is more pro-German than ever, more anti-French and anti-Semitic.

"The Poles' resistance in Warsaw," says Mircea, "is a Jewish resistance. Only yids are capable of the blackmail of putting women and children in the front line, to take advantage of the Germans' sense of scruple. The Germans have no interest in the destruction of Romania. Only a pro-German government can save us. A George Brătianu / Nae Ionescu government is the only solution. The Soviets are no longer a danger, both because they have abandoned communism—and we shouldn't forget that communism is not identical with Marxism, nor necessarily Judaic—and because they (the Soviets) have given up on Europe and turned their eyes exclusively to Asia. What is happening on the frontier with Bukovina is a scandal, because new waves of Jews are flooding into the country. Rather than a Romania again invaded by kikes, it would be better to have a German protectorate."

Comarnescu assures me that these are Mircea's exact words. Now I understand perfectly why he is so reticent with me when it is a question of politics, and why he appears to take refuge in metaphysics to escape "the horrors of politics."

Just look at what he thinks, your ex-friend Mircea Eliade.

Thursday, 21 [September]

I was in court, waiting my turn for an adjournment, when a woman pale with fright leaned across the counsels' bench and whispered to someone: "They've shot Armand Călinescu; it was on the radio."

I took a taxi and raced home, where I found everyone downstairs at the Pascals, panic-stricken around the radio, though it was broadcasting a normal musical program. What had happened? Half an hour before, the announcer had broken in with a cry of alarm and then hastily said a few unclear words about the killing of the prime minister. After a pause, service resumed and another announcer said that "the interruption to the broadcast was because of an unfortunate incident."

I was convinced that it had all been a bad joke. Rosetti said on the phone that he thought the same, but that in any case he knew nothing about it. I went into town, and nowhere was there the slightest sign of unrest. The afternoon papers came out at four, as usual.

Back at my place in Calea Victoriei, however, I received a call from Alice Theodorian with news from Armand's sister-in-law (whom I met myself at Alice's the day before yesterday). Yes, Armand was murdered today in his car between one and one-thirty; a group of Legionaries had waited beneath a timber cart and opened fire several times when his car approached. At the same time, another group burst into the radio station and broadcast the news. Both groups were captured—but Armand is dead.

If it is true, the situation is disastrous. It is a question not only of the internal situation (which could be dealt with one way or another), but also of the Germans and the Russians, who might enter the country "to establish order" and "to protect their kith and kin."

From one hour to the next, one day to the next, we could lose everything: a roof over our heads, bread to eat, our modicum of security, even our lives.

And there is nothing, absolutely nothing, to be done about it.

It is a wonderfully sunny autumn day. I lie on the chaise longue on my terrace and look at this city, which can be seen so well from above. The streets are full of life, cars drive along in every direction, traffic policemen direct the traffic from their boxes, the shops are open for customers—the whole machinery of this great city seems to be working normally, and yet somewhere at its heart a terrible blow has been delivered, without yet being felt. It is as if we were in a city strewn with dynamite due to explode in five minutes' time—a city which, for the moment, carries on unawares, as if nothing has happened.

A short while ago I saw a group of Polish refugees coming toward my block. They were raggedly dressed, each carrying a battered backpack, but they were alive—do you know what I mean?—alive and saved. Maybe we (Benu, Mama, Tata, myself) won't even be that by this evening, tomorrow, or the day after—not even refugees who have escaped the fire with nothing but their lives.

I am probably one of those who are made to await death with resignation, to accept it. I don't see any defensive gesture I could make; no thought of escape or refuge crosses my mind.

Saturday, 23 [September]

The assassins—six or nine, I still don't know—were "executed at the scene of the crime" and left on the pavement for a day and a night, with a placard saying: "Traitors to the country!"

Yesterday morning I went there (the other side of the Elefterie Bridge). Thousands of people came by streetcar, by car, by bus, or on foot. It was like a big fair. They were laughing and joking. A company from my regiment only just managed to keep the crowd at a distance from the killers' dead bodies. (If I had been called up, I might even have been there myself, on guard!) Those who were unable to squeeze through to the front saw nothing. A lady beside me said:

"They should keep order, put us in two rows so that everyone can see."

People from nearby had brought some wooden stepladders, and those who wanted a better view paid two lei to climb up and look over the rest.

"Don't do it!" said one guy who had paid his two lei but had been disappointed. "Don't do it! All you can see are their feet." It all seemed appalling, humiliating, shameful. Apparently the same spectacle took place in Craiova, Ploieşti, and Turnu Severin. Radio London said last night that there have been "dozens of executions," but it is whispered that there have been not dozens but hundreds. Some even give a precise figure: four hundred. It seems that all the Legionaries in the camps and prisons have been executed.

I wonder what has happened to Nae. Rosetti asked and was told that he's been "missing for two days." What does "missing" mean? Escaped? Taken elsewhere and kept under guard? Shot?

I rang Mircea, also feeling anxious about his fate. He himself answered, and I told him about the proofs of an article of his for the *Revista*. But I found out what I wanted to know: he is alive.

It seems that the assassination was planned when the Germans were advancing with dizzying speed to the Polish-Romanian frontier. With the Germans already in northern Bukovina, nothing would have been easier for them than to enter the country at the moment of Armand's assassination, especially as a plot had been organized among the Bukovinan Romanians to be "liberated by their brothers." It was all supposed to be a perfect copy—in both design and execution—of the assassination of Dollfuss.[4]

What spoiled the plan was the unexpected entry of the Russians into Poland, and especially their quite unexpected arrival at the Polish-Romanian frontier, which meant that Romania had no common border with the Germans. That is the only thing which, for the moment, saves us from immediate disaster.

I am at my wit's end. There is nothing to think, nothing to foresee. Let us wait and, if possible, not lose our heads too much.

Monday, 25 [September]

I came home last night with a heavy heart, terrified at all that is happening and all that might happen. The number of dead is still not clear: tens, hundreds, or thousands.[5]

At Rîmnicu Sărat, at two o'clock in the morning, Mişu Polihroniade, Tell, and the others were shot ("machine-gunned," according to Nina) and thrown into the prison yard for all to see. In the other towns it was the same story (at least as reported by Constandache[6] and Onicescu, who had been in different places and—again according to Nina—seen things with their own eyes). At yesterday's rehearsals at the Studio, Marietta was in tears in her dressing room, saying that "all the kids at Ciuc" have been shot, as well as the ones at Vaslui. Among them were Belgea and

4. The Austrian chancellor, murdered in July 1934 by Austrian fascists in an abortive coup d'état.
5. Two hundred fifty-two Legionaries were shot in retaliation for the murder of Prime Minister Armand Călinescu.
6. V. Constandache: journalist.

Gârcineanu. It's thought certain that Nae will be shot by this evening. Rosetti, whom I saw in the evening at Camil's, confirms this. Only late at night was I rung and told that Nae is alive—ill in bed at home, but alive.

I cannot judge this drama politically. I am horrified as a human being. I know that all these people, whether collectively or separately, would have calmly witnessed Legionary terror and killed us with the utmost indifference. I also know that their blindness went beyond all limits. And yet, and yet, I feel sad, troubled, overwhelmed by a bitter taste in the mouth.

I stayed home alone, both yesterday evening and this evening, and the first thing I did back in my room was listen again to Mozart's andante, which serves me as a refuge. Then I read some of Dubnow's *History of the Jews*: the pages about Venice, Padua, Prague, Vienna, and Frankfurt in the sixteenth century. As I read, I felt that I was moving away in time. It is good to know you are from a people that has seen many things down the ages—some even more terrible than what is happening today.

Mişu Polihroniade as a martyr for a political cause? Nothing destined him for that. It's a mistake, a misunderstanding, a tragic joke. He didn't want that, didn't believe that, never imagined that. How life makes of us more than we wish or are able to be! How few things actually depend on us! What a chain of remote, unforeseen consequences is within one of our gestures, one incident, one chance event. That guy wanted a deputy's seat in parliament—at least as a junior minister. And then he ends up a revolutionary. I think that, right up to the last moment, he couldn't understand why things had taken the turn they did, where exactly they had started to go wrong.

I went to Mircea's yesterday afternoon. I had already seen Nina at the Foundation, pallid, tear-stained, wringing her hands in despair.

"They're going to kill Mircea," she said. "Don't let them kill Mircea."

I went to see them because I know that right now no one has the courage to visit them. Everything pulls us apart, of course, absolutely everything, but I told myself that it will give them a little heart to speak to someone, even if that someone is me. I found him much calmer and at ease. Rosetti will talk to Ralea and Iamandi, maybe someone even higher, to get Mircea out of harm's way. We made our laments together— but in different ways. I think I am morally more entitled to feel distressed than he is. For, in one way or another, he willed it, he assented to it.

But today his attitude is pessimistic. "Attitude" is to put it too strongly: rather, remnants of attitudes, barely controlled rages, deep aversions, a terrible hatred that would like to scream but cannot. He said that the current repression is criminal "now that the enemy is at the gates." But wasn't the assassination of Armand Călinescu also committed "with the enemy at the gates"? I put the question to him and he shrugged his shoulders.

I didn't call round to argue with him, nor to be in the right. We shall never settle accounts between us. Or maybe later, when everything has become more remote—if we are still alive then. I have the feeling that what he awaits now, as a kind of desperate revenge, is a German or Russian invasion.

"I believe in the future of the Romanian people," he said, "but the Romanian state should disappear."

I left feeling irritated. My attempt to communicate with him, to be of some use by making him feel that he was not abandoned, had been a failure.

Wednesday, 11 October

A disturbing letter from Dinu Noica. I wrote on Rosetti's behalf suggesting that he publish his thesis at the Foundations. His reply is negative. He doesn't want to have anything to do with F.R.

"We haven't seen each other for a long time, dear Mihai, and you don't know how much I enjoy the pleasure of refusal. How could I not be delighted to refuse one of the things to which I used to be most attached!"

At the same time he wrote a letter to Rosetti (which I read this morning)—a perfectly straightforward refusal, without any ostentation or bravura. It is his way of disowning everything that has happened, his way of remaining faithful to his "ideas." They are the one and the same ideas that require nothing of Mircea, for example, yet compel Dinu Noica to change his life, his gestures, his everyday behavior.

Monday, 16 [October]

Leni has slept with "Handsome Bubi," or so Zoe claims. Zoe is mad about "Handsome Bubi," or so Leni claims. I listen to them both—and laugh. It is a chain of comic situations in which I, without wanting to be, am one link. "Handsome Bubi" hears confessions from the one and the other, learning that I in turn was mad now about Leni, now about

Zoe. The whole story is like a vaudeville show, in which I don't seem to have the most flattering role. The tenor's part is already taken. But anyway, all this has been going on for several months—and it is only now that I hear about it. Calmly enough, though, to be able to smile.

A splendid autumn day, after a few weeks of cloudy weather. I'd like to lie on the chaise longue in the sun, or go for a walk somewhere on the Stîna, or be on the pier in Balcic.

The war still exists, but somewhere far away, on another continent.

Wednesday, 18 [October]

Thirty-two years. I feel old, ugly, worn out. It gives me no pleasure at all to look at myself in the mirror. Sometimes I feel disgusted at the sight of this man, pale, baggy-eyed, and balding, but still with a kind of air of haggard youth. I try not to think of my life—either that which is past, or that which lies ahead. There is a sense of futility that fills me with despair, and that I would like to avoid, to forget.

Leni was here yesterday, and I let her talk again about the affair involving Bubi, Zoe, Leni, and myself. Again I couldn't help noticing the comedy in this quadrille.

I cannot deny, however, that I still have pangs of feeling and a certain embarrassment at everything that has happened, and everything I failed to anticipate.

I want to go to Predeal next week, for ten to fifteen days, and to finish the novel in that time. Rosetti wants to publish it himself, and I can't refuse him, but I would have preferred Ocneanu, even if it would have been less secure financially. The Foundation's style of book cover, impersonal, austere, and uniform as it is, is quite suitable for a study or an essay, but I fear it would do disservice to a novel.

But it goes without saying that no consideration, however well grounded, will make me offend R. by refusing him the book once he has asked me for it.

Besides, the only important thing in all this is that the novel should appear—as soon as possible. I must get free of it—and I have the feeling that I would thereby also get free of many other old matters that are connected with it.

Thursday, 26 [October]

Maybe in the end I shall manage to leave on Sunday afternoon for Predeal for five or six days, and later for another five or six days. Will that be enough for me to finish the novel? I don't know, but it will have to be. I have so many things waiting to be done, calling out to me. I keep thinking of the play (which could not bear for long not to be written). More and more, I also think of my future novel, which is occupying more space as it grows both deeper and denser.

If I go, I shall stay at the Robinson villa, where Crăciun has the kindness to take me in for only three hundred lei a day. I have fond thoughts about that welcoming, luminous, almost elegant house, and I hope it will also be favorable to my book.

The last few days have been terrible. I was as tired as a packhorse. Each day there was business in court (not all happily resolved—the loss of Leni's case with Mr. Şerbescu was especially distressing), and each day I had to rush to the printer's in alarm that, because of me, the *Revista* might not appear on time. Everything I do—office, court, editing—I do with absurd tension and unease, in panic and disorder, with neither method nor mastery. Am I really incapable of putting a little order, I won't say into my fragmented life, but at least into my work?

When I came home yesterday, and the day before yesterday, I was not only dropping from fatigue but ashamed of the state I had reached.

I am so inconsiderate that over the last few days I have not even paused for a moment to think of Poldy, who has probably already left Sceaux for his regiment (as he anticipated in a letter I received on Saturday), or anyway for a training center in the Pyrenees.

He must come out of this war in one piece. I would like him to understand that this is his duty. I would like to tell him straight that his life (at least with regard to Mama) also has to make up for my failure of a life.

A little music—Enescu, Franck's *Sonata*, a couple of Beethoven pieces, one Mozart, one Bach, one Fauré; a Brandenburg concerto (the fifth, I think), Brahms's *Fourth Symphony*, more beautiful than ever—and a two-day excursion to Cîmpulung with Rosetti, in the miraculous weather of a glorious autumn. These have been my only relaxation, my only escape.

Predeal. Sunday, 29 [October]

The Robinson villa. I am in the room that Suchianu had two years ago. There is only one other lodger in the whole villa—an Italian diplomat, it would seem.

In this quiet I hope to be able to work. I have arrived feeling very weary, with a kind of tightness in my chest (am I a heart case? I keep wondering). But I think that I shall rest and write at the same time. What shatters me in Bucharest is the disorder, the rushing around.

This morning there was a disgusting meeting at the Writers' Association. Had it not been for Ralea's candidacy (which he anyway withdrew at the last minute—those democrats make themselves scarce at the first sign of danger), I wouldn't even have gone along. Herescu the president![7] What a farce!

Monday, 30 [October]

Midnight

I have finished Chapter Ten, the one I broke off when I left Stîna de Vale. I worked all day, from nine in the morning until now, with a break at midday and another in the evening, to eat and to walk for an hour through Predeal.

The result: ten pages. That's a record. Don't let's talk about quality. I can't tell what they are like, and I could almost say that it doesn't interest me. I want to write and to be over with it. May God take care of the rest.

Tuesday, 31 [October]

Three degrees below zero (26 F.]—snow. It also snowed yesterday morning, though by evening the weather had become autumnal again. Now it is well and truly winter. If it stays like this for a couple of days, we'll all be skiing.

Yesterday I went out *en skieur.* Why is it that all I have to do to feel more youthful is put on my skiing boots and costume?

Since yesterday we have a new lodger in the villa: a fairly young woman (thirty-two?), not beautiful but with a certain distinction. A

7. N. I. Herescu: a philologist and newly elected president of the Writers' Association.

brunette. She reads books in French (*Sparkenbroke*), and also, I think, Polish newspapers. Maybe she is a refugee.

So there are three of us at table and later in the foyer room, but we do not speak to one another. I cannot describe how comfortable this silence makes me feel.

What I like most in the villa is the brightly lit foyer, with its wall-length window, its flowered armchairs, and its scattering of delightful prints (Utrillo, Suzanne Valadon, Pissarro, van Gogh).

Evening

Only seven hours' work and only five pages written. I must understand that it won't be easy to repeat yesterday's performance. I am tired and have to call a halt. The Gunther episode is absorbing. I don't want to continue haphazardly but to have things clearly in view. I am halfway through Chapter Eleven. I hope to finish it tomorrow.

Wednesday, 1 November

I am beginning to understand what it means "to get free of a book."

These characters of mine tire me with their obsessiveness; they eat away at me and wear me out. I'd like to forget about them, to escape. I walk with them in the street, sit with them at table, doze off with them.

Sometimes I am afraid they will wriggle away from me before I finish the book, but at other times it pleases me to think that I'll get away from them, that I'll be free to forget them.

I try to remember whether other characters, in my other books, obsessed me so much. The ones in *Orașul cu salcîmi* are another matter: I never saw them for one moment. But the rest? I don't remember whether they took so much out of me in the way of nervous tension. But if they did, how could I have forgotten them so completely? How could they have become so indifferent to me?

Thursday, 2 November

Only just now, this morning, have I finished Chapter Eleven. If I had kept at it, I would have finished yesterday. But I didn't want to: I was afraid of continuing into the evening. All the time I wrote in an overwhelming state of nervous tension. To say it all—however childish—I was afraid for my heart, which I felt scampering away like Gunther's, about to burst.

When I reread the chapter this morning, I found it less exciting, less intense, and certainly less demonic than it seemed yesterday. A night's sleep clarifies a lot of things, makes them appear more subdued.

Yesterday began badly, with a splitting headache that lasted until evening and ruined my schedule. I had to go out in the morning to get some painkiller. As I walked down toward the Timiş, I passed the monument to Săulescu (only now do I realize how horrible it is, with that bird that looks like a little owl from behind), and then I came back past the railway line. The view is magnificent: the Schuller and Piatra Mare are in clouds, but the lower slopes are green and white, with snow-covered fir trees. I feel happy and alone there.

I recovered only toward evening, when I managed to do some more serious work. Five and a half pages, plus another two this morning—which concludes the chapter I began on Tuesday.

Friday, 3 [November]

The short chapter I finished this morning (which I shall call 11A for the time being) has four pages. I wrote three yesterday afternoon and one just now. I have been writing very slowly, with great difficulty and a thousand obstacles that are still not resolved. It is certainly not in its final state. Besides, I had not been planning for it; I had intended to go straight from Chapter Eleven to the *Christmas Oratorio* chapter. But I felt the need to insert a chapter which, though not constituting an episode (that is, a distinct scene in the story), would create a little time and distance from the events. Right from the beginning of the book, the action has unfolded chronologically—day by day, almost hour by hour. But here I needed a jump, a caesura. I hoped that this little unforeseen chapter would provide it. But I don't know whether I have got what I wanted. We'll see later.

At midday yesterday I went for an exciting walk to Plestera, where winter has really set in. I was alone in the snow for an hour.

This afternoon I shall "attack" the chapter dealing with the descent to Braşov and the *Christmas Oratorio*—a long chapter in which a lot of things happen, and which carries the book into its final section. I am not really worried, but I do feel a little uneasy, a little apprehensive.

Sunday, 5 [November]

The *Christmas Oratorio* chapter has eighteen pages up to now: five written on Friday afternoon, five yesterday, eight today. And, you realize, the "concert" hasn't even begun. I'm still not sure how long it will turn out to be. The "scenario" is in place, however, and I have a feeling that I won't experience the same difficulties that I had yesterday (so idiotic that the day's work felt wasted).

I'd gladly go on writing now, but it is past eight o'clock and my train leaves at ten—I haven't even packed my luggage yet. I am breaking off at a moment when I feel in full flow. I hope this good working mood will come back to me.

To be concluded—maybe in Bucharest. I could have noted a thousand things in connection with this chapter, but after eight, nine, or ten hours of work I always feel a need to take some distance. In this way I delay noting things and then never manage to write them down later.

Bucharest. Thursday, 9 [November]

Don't ask me what I have done since Monday. I haven't done anything. I have been in Bucharest. That's enough for time to slip by without my knowing when or why.

I haven't even managed to sort everything out at the *Revista*. The next issue has been completed, but I don't have everything in proof, nor do I even know how many pages are missing. I also still have to write something myself, and to put together the "review of the reviews" section.

Tomorrow I leave for Predeal—only tomorrow!—and leave things still up in the air. But that means I will have to return very soon.

What is depressing in Bucharest are the telephone calls, the going-out, the first nights, the dinner invitations. On my first day back I felt that—in comparison with my simple life in Predeal—I was entering one big madhouse.

The day before yesterday I sent a clean copy of 176 pages to the printer's. I still have sixty pages to write out again, and the last four or five chapters to compose.

Predeal. Sunday, 12 [November]

I arrived on Friday evening. It felt like returning home. The whole villa was asleep, but Room 1 was waiting with its lights on. And to make me feel even more "at home," there was a letter from Marie Ghiolu on the bedside table.

To stop writing for five days does not mean only to waste five working days. It is more serious. You lose the right tone, you move away from your characters, you can't find them again, they no longer recognize you.

Yesterday was very heavy going. I'd got it into my head that I had to wrap up the concert *at any price*, and after six hours of work (with an hour on the chaise longue, in wonderful sunny weather) I did indeed finish it, with midnight already past. But that yielded only six pages, and I don't think they are a success.

Moreover, it may have been difficult in principle to write without listening. It is true that I worked all the time with the score in my hand, but to feel it properly I would have had to know it, to hear it. My memory for music is too poor for me to have something in my head after listening to it just three times (I don't think I've heard the *Christmas Oratorio* more than three times).

Publication before Christmas now looks unlikely. I may receive the proofs of the first nine chapters this week, but will I have time to do a fair copy of the other chapters and, above all, to write the finale?

Maybe it's a mistake to speak of the "finale"? Who knows, there may still be a hundred pages to write before then. The outline of the last few chapters already exists, but I've no idea what unexpected things may turn up.

Besides, I have to be in Bucharest again on Wednesday, for the *Revista*. Will it ever be allowed me to write a book straight through from beginning to end, without interrupting it, without losing it, and without becoming disconnected from it?

Monday, 13 [November]

A wonderful spring day. Twenty-five degrees above zero [78 F.]. There is a soft, pure light—without melancholy.

This morning I went to Creasta Cocoşului. The ground was still wet from the melted snow (you'd have thought it was March!), but where the sun had been shining there was green grass and moss. I threw myself down and lay in the sun. How easy it always is to recover this bliss.

In the afternoon, another hour in the sun on the chaise longue.

I am wasting time—but I don't feel any pangs of conscience. Everything I wrote yesterday (not even five pages) was bad. Today I feel it will be even more difficult. Last week I was like a well-tuned instrument; everything I wrote had the right tone. Now I feel out of tune: everything is false, clumsy, ungenuine. Sometimes I see things, feel and hear them, but the phrase fails me. It falls like lead, colorless and unfeeling.

For a moment it occurred to me to return to Bucharest. What's the point of staying here if I don't write, when so many other things are waiting for me there? Maybe these standstills should be accepted as one accepts insomnia. Nevertheless I shall stay on—at least until tomorrow evening. The *Christmas Oratorio* chapter, for which I had such high hopes because it was so rich in detail and incident, has turned out a complete failure. But failure or not, I shall at least finish it.

I have decided to split it in two. It will consist of Chapters Thirteen and Fourteen. The thirteenth I consider already complete. (I say "consider" because in fact I am well aware that it lacks something, but yesterday evening and this morning I struggled in vain to find a better way of ending it.) Now I am starting on Chapter Fourteen. I feel no enthusiasm and have no confidence in it. I shall write it in a spirit of resignation.

Midnight

In the end, the day was not as bad as I expected. I wrote six pages and—much more important—came up with new incidents for the final chapter of the novel. So far I haven't been able to see this conclusion very well, but today I could quite precisely outline the whole "scenario" for it.

Paul will meet Ann again in this last chapter, and this meeting will mark the final break between them and the forgetting of each other.

Tuesday, 14 [November]

It's not advancing, not at all.

I wasted the whole morning on writing and crossing out, and was left with not so much as a line that could be used. I consoled myself with the thought that I might catch up in the afternoon. (That's what happened yesterday.) But now I feel there is no chance of that. I really have ground to a halt. Why should I resist? What's the point of keeping at it?

I leave for Bucharest on the five o'clock train. So much is waiting for me to do there. The novel will stay on hold for a few days. In the meantime, perhaps a way forward will open up by itself.

Sunday, 19 [November]. Bucharest

In the five days I have been in Bucharest, I have managed to do scarcely anything on the novel. Wasted days and nights. All I have done is again write out Chapters Ten to Thirteen; I'll send them to the printer's to-morrow. To make a fair copy is, for me, a strictly mechanical operation. Again I must confess my powerlessness to alter a text once I have writ-ten it; I am unable to put right even the simplest things. It is therefore pointless and imprudent for me to make a note in the margin and promise to go back over a certain passage. Pointless, because it is impossible for me to go back over it. Imprudent, because I deceive myself with the thought that I will complete the text at the copyediting or "proof cor-rection" stage, and therefore leave things poorly expressed, in a provi-sional state that I later will be forced to accept as definitive.

Maybe it would be worth trying to explain this incapacity of mine to go back over a first draft. Is it just laziness? I don't think so.

There is something irrevocable in a scene that, by writing it down, I have lived once and for all, and that I can no longer repeat at any price.

This may also explain the failure of all my attempts to reconstitute the lost chapters. What I did manage to remember and write down two years ago, after my return from Paris, remains as it was then: inadequate, desiccated, featureless, lacking in warmth and depth. I haven't been able to add anything, to rectify anything. This is where my great fear lies. I ask myself whether, in the book as a whole, the reconstituted pages will not prove too inert for the rest to come alive.

Friday, 24 [November]

The governmental crisis seems to be more than a crisis of government.[8] There is talk of a German ultimatum. Radio London claims that Ger-man troops have been massing in Slovakia, ready to attack us. I don't know what will come of it all. The specter of disasters is again becom-ing plausible.

I can't go off to Predeal. I don't dare leave. Who knows what may happen from one day to the next, from one hour to the next? I'll try to work here. Today I'll actually get down to Chapter Fourteen.

Publication before Christmas is very doubtful indeed, both because I myself have not had the tenacity to finish the book, and because the

---

8. On this date the Argetoianu government was replaced by one headed by Gh. Tătărescu.

printers, who have a backlog to clear, are taking a long time to process things. More and more I realize that it was a mistake to give a novel to the Foundation. I, who publish one novel in three or four years, am stupid enough to bury it with a publishing house that is better at factory-style production than at organizing a proper launch. The Foundation will publish twenty-six titles in December. Mine would be the twenty-seventh. Who will look after it, who will even care? So far I have received galleys only for the first three chapters—pathetically little. It depresses me to read them. Again the reconstituted chapters make me feel down at heart. They seem stupid, and I know there's nothing that can be done.

Monday, 27 [November]

Maybe it wasn't the right time to get myself a radio, just when I have to finish my novel and do nothing other than write and write. But I have been planning it for so long, and if I put it off any longer who knows when I would do it. I have had it since Saturday evening (a large Philips with 4+1 tubes) and listened to countless pieces. Bach, Mozart, and Beethoven on all the wavelengths.

Yesterday there was Schumann's piano concerto from Paris, a program of Mozart from London (a symphony, a flute concerto, and—what seemed a welcoming sign—the *Kleine nachtmusik*). From Budapest, a Bach cantata with the proportions of a small oratorio. This morning, from a German station (to which I listened with some pangs of conscience), the *Egmont Overture* and a Boccherini cello concerto. Plus dozens of shorter pieces from all over the place. And now, as I write this note, a Mozart symphony from Budapest.

But I must put a stop to this musical excess and get back to the novel—switch the radio off. . . .

Sunday, 3 December

A conversation last night with Camil Petrescu. We were both worried about the situation. We wondered whether the Soviets, after polishing off Finland, would not come to us next.

"Only Germany can defend us against the Russians," Camil said. "In the end, what we must wish is that we won't be divided, that we will remain under the same scepter. If Germany takes all of us, that's still all right. The situation of the Czechs, for example, is very good."

What he said seemed too serious for me not to note it here (word for word, I think)—though I have so many other things to do.

I'll pass over all of yesterday's funny "Camilisms"; I am used to them, and I wouldn't have opened this notebook just for them:

"Romania's one big mistake was not to have listened to Camil Petrescu, who as long ago as 1930 wrote that we need an air force."

"Even the Finns could have been saved if they had known my articles."

If he were a minister, he would bury the whole of Romania underground—and then invite the Russians to bomb us.

All this is funny, but not of much moment. I hear tens and hundreds of enormities and let them pass. ("My dear man, I am the greatest actor the world has seen since Garrick. Moissi, what does he add up to? Just an actor with a pleasant voice. But I, apart from my intense voice, have a colossal power of expression.") But the idea that this man, so thoughtless but also so intelligent, can accept in advance German domination as a possible salvation—the "German scepter," as he puts it—seems truly memorable for what it says both about Camil Petrescu and, more generally, about the atmosphere these days.

1 a.m.

At last I have finished Chapter Fifteen, which I began on Thursday evening (after I had finished Chapter Fourteen, with which I felt so profoundly dissatisfied that I was loathe to note anything about it here).

At any rate, I have put an end to my old superstition that I absolutely must leave Bucharest in order to write. On Thursday I was on the point of leaving for Predeal, when I decided to make an attempt (a stubborn one, this time) to stay where I was and strictly organize my work habits.

I "shut off" the telephone (which no longer rings at all), told my people at home to tell anyone who asked that I was away, and went neither to the Foundation nor to Roman's office—and, with these barriers, I succeeded in writing eight pages on Friday. It didn't go so well yesterday, when I managed only four pages, nor today, when I did the same. It is true, however, that I was working on an uneven chapter with which I had not even reckoned at the beginning, that I did not have a prior "scenario" for it, and that, right up to the last minute, I did not really know where it would lead me. From now on, things are more clearly defined and, I hope, more straightforward. But even so, I need to count on at least another week's work.

Thursday, 7 [December]

Wasted days. Of Chapter Sixteen—which should go very easily, because it consists of events and dialogue—I have written only three pages. Three pages in four days! I am ashamed to think of this standstill, which nothing can justify.

The proofs have been catching me up; the whole of the rest of the book has been set and is at its third proof stage, while I am stuck en route. Why? I don't know why. Everything has a clear shape, and the scenario of the four chapters still to be written is firmly fixed. The only problem now should be the purely material one of writing—and yet here I am in a depression from which I have been struggling for days to escape. There is no point in poisoning myself with coffee and cigarettes; no point in stupefying myself with music (a Mozart flute concerto and a Johann Christian Bach symphony, tonight from Hamburg); no point in inflicting sleepless nights on myself as a punishment. It simply isn't advancing; it refuses to advance.

Saturday, 9 [December]

Yesterday evening I finished Chapter Sixteen. I am very unhappy with it, taken separately, and extremely worried about its function within the book as a whole. I am more and more afraid that the whole Grodeck episode will seem like something "added on." I wonder whether its links with the main "subject" are not too vague and, above all, too arbitrary. Does not the reader's interest split at this point? Do not Nora and Paul take a back seat? Does not the whole story begin to seem too self-consciously fictional? It is true that from now on I abandon the Grodecks and return exclusively to Nora and Paul, but I wonder whether there is still enough time and space, within the setting of the book, to restore its center of gravity after it has shifted so much.

The whole afternoon and evening I struggled to write the chapter I began today—Chapter Seventeen—but so far (at midnight) I have written no more than four sentences. I am calling it a day. I am too tired and feel that, however much I forced myself, I wouldn't overcome this new obstacle that has appeared in my path.

I am certainly going through a difficult period. Bad luck has hit me precisely when I should be reaching the end. Everything is plainly visible and clearly defined, everything should be straightforward—yet my pen is stuck. If I were not ashamed in front of Rosetti and the typesetters, I'd give it up completely. This book seems fated to drive me to despair, right up to the last moment.

Monday, 11 [December]

A strange laryngitis. I have never had anything quite like it before, though I often have a tiresome bout of tonsillitis. My voice has gone and I can hardly speak. I seem to have a slight temperature.

My general condition is bad, in addition to the period of idiocy in which I have been for several days. There is no point in saying any more about the novel. It remains at a standstill.

I seem powerless to do anything at all. Yesterday I had to write something for the Foundation (commissioned by Cioculescu), and although I racked my brain for ten hours, I could not come up with anything more than a bad journalistic piece that I am ashamed to have to sign. Today the article for *M.V.B.*[9]—which never requires much application on my part, because I feel that, as it is not mine and no one will read it anyway, I can write it no matter how—also turned out shamefully uninteresting and badly written.

I lack inspiration, talent, wisdom, and vocation. I cannot see anything ahead of me and do not manage to express the simplest ideas. Something pulls me toward platitude, toward indifference.

On such days, when you are healthy, you should cut wood, go for a walk, drink, and screw.

But when you are ill, you should be thankful to lie dozing in an armchair.

Friday, 15 [December]

Call-up papers, dated today.

Saturday, 16 [December]

I still don't know what will happen at the regiment. The colonel—an old school friend of Rosetti's—said that I should report to him on Monday morning. If I am given time to finish the novel and see it come out, I shall accept the call-up with resignation and, in any event, without any drama.

9. The journal *Muncă şi voie-bună*.

What is terrible in the passage from civilian life to the barracks is that it takes place so suddenly. If I were given warning, if I knew now that I'd be called up on the 15th of January, for example, it would start to become bearable—not only because it would be a long way off (*qui doit à terme, ne doit rien*[1]), but because I would have time to prepare myself, to "soften" the blow. Moreover, I would be happy that I could have a skiing holiday—perhaps the last in my life, if there were war.

The novel has been marking time for a fortnight. I am still on Chapter Seventeen, the second to last. All three chapters that have still to be written are straightforward, clearly defined, and without difficulties. Yet it is impossible for me to write them. I don't know why. Maybe because the novel has become unimportant to me. Maybe because I have entered a dark period—one of my well-known periods of imbecility. Having abandoned everything for a few days, I got up yesterday with a grim determination to work "at any cost." But scarcely had I sat down at my desk when someone rang the doorbell. I opened the door, and it was the call-up order!

Yesterday evening, after a day full of anxiety, I nevertheless tried to write. My present inability to start and finish a sentence fills me with disgust. I write a word and cross it out, write it again and cross it out again. I don't even think it is due to exaggerated doubts with regard to style. Rather, I have the feeling it is a nervous tic. The last few pages of my manuscript have been literally butchered. Two pages of manuscript, when written out again, amount to no more than a third of a normal page.

A little while ago, out of curiosity, I looked out at the manuscript of *De două mii de ani* to see if I used to write with the same difficulty. Well, no, I didn't! In those days my manuscript was amazingly fluent: two or three words deleted or added per page; very few passages crossed out; nearly four hundred clear and legible pages composed without fretting and worrying, or at least without the visible kind that now makes my writing so hard to read. Why do I find it harder to write than I did six years ago? I ought to have more experience by now, greater skill and less fear of the written word—and yet I face obstacles that did not exist before. Is it because I used to write journalism then? Did the habit of writing an article every day—for which Albu sometimes gave me only an hour—make my pen swifter and more practiced? I don't know, I can't make it out. I look for all kinds of explanations. I ask myself whether

1. To owe in the long run is not to owe at all.

this journal itself may not hamper my writing, whether it may not in the end be impossible to write a novel together with a journal, whose critical observations and ceaseless questioning may result in paralysis. But maybe this is not true, either. I try to pin the blame wherever I can. For example, the cyclamen flower I have had here for the last two weeks is driving me up the wall, because I haven't been able to work since it came into the flat.

In the manuscript of *De două mii de ani* I came across the following sentence (one of the few I deleted in the text of the book): "I write with difficulty, with numerous obstacles, with much hesitation and a constant fear of overstepping my thoughts. For a mistake in expressing yourself is a twofold blunder: it says something other than it should, and it ties you to what you made the mistake of saying."

Sunday, 17 [December]

Six pages written. Nearly seven. It is true that I worked all day and that it is now past two in the morning. But at least I have got moving again. Tomorrow morning at nine, though, I must report to the regiment.

Will I be able to pick up the manuscript again tomorrow afternoon?

Monday, 18 [December]

The whole day wasted at the regiment. It was impossible to obtain a deferment. Only tonight, from ten until two, have I been able to return to the novel. I have written two pages, which bring Chapter Seventeen to an end. It lacks expression. But I fear it is worse than that: false, arbitrary, amorphous. I feel sorry for this book, which could have worked out differently if I had been more tenacious and events had been less antagonistic. But it is an ill-starred book—and there's nothing more I can do to help it.

Tuesday, 19 [December]

All day at the regiment. I came back at 8:30, worn out and with my left arm numb from pain. They inoculated me at the infirmary, and this has given me a fever. It is impossible for me to write any more; almost impossible for me to think about the novel, which has left me with nothing but regrets. I should give it up, postpone it, submit to the inevitable. Can't you see that something always stops this wretched book from breaking out of the circle of obstacles and misfortunes that surrounds it?

Wednesday, 20 [December]

A night of fever and insomnia. I didn't sleep for a second. I can no longer feel my left arm. I went to the regiment with a temperature of 39 degrees [102 F.]. I'm fed up with explaining, requesting, complaining. I am still sick. This inoculation seems to me one of the most barbaric things in a soldier's life.

At the barracks, or at least at the company supply room, there is a refugee-type atmosphere. As I was still a civilian, in that sordid dormitory I looked like a refugee shut up in a camp.

This evening I listened to the *Christmas Oratorio* from Braşov, which has ended just as I am writing these lines.

I could have noted a lot of things (especially in connection with the *Oratorio* chapter in my novel), but I don't feel capable of thinking, or of formulating anything.

Tomorrow morning at 6:30 I have to be at the regiment.

Saturday, 23 [December]

The army, the army—always the army. I don't have a weapon and am receiving no instruction, yet I have to be at the barracks before seven each morning and to remain there until 7 p.m., if not 8 or 9. Altogether that means some fourteen hours a day wasted in a maddeningly pointless way. All of Rosetti's efforts (not to speak of mine) to obtain eight days' leave to finish my book have come to nothing. Only today (after a day of rushing around to do all kinds of chores for the colonel) have I been given four days off for Christmas.

Tomorrow I leave, or hope to leave, for Roman's villa in Sinaia. At least I'll have a day or two of skiing. And when I return, maybe I'll pick up the threads of the novel that I have recently felt to be broken.

Thursday, 28 [December]

Monday and Tuesday in Sinaia—at Roman's villa. All of Monday with Lereanu and Comşa in the mountains, where we reached Vîrful de Dor after an exhausting hike of six hours. Thick snow and ice made it impossible to ski. But the sun was full of youth, and the wind as gentle as a spring breeze. Only on the way back could we go a few hundred meters on skis. We returned by the light of the moon—a round, yellow moon, set against white mountains and a blue sky that was as tender and delicate as an April sky at twilight.

On Tuesday we spent a few hours in Predeal, at Veştea, where the same moon, so implausible for December, again took us by surprise. I returned on skis to the railway station. The snow was bluish beneath the moon.

Tomorrow morning, back to barracks. My novel is still not finished. Yesterday I read it all the way through, in order to get inside it again. Three days of uninterrupted work should be enough for Chapters Eighteen and Nineteen, the only ones still to be written, but for which the scenario is firmly set.

On Saturday evening, as I was passing by taxi along Bulevardul Dacia, I had an extraordinarily precise feeling that there in one of the blocks, on the sixth floor, was the locked flat of someone I knew—of Nora. Had I rung the bell, I would not have been surprised to hear the doorman say that she had gone off to the mountains.

Sunday, 31 [December]

The last evening of the year.

I thought of staying by myself and working, but I am not strong enough to do that. I feel alone and left out of consideration. I have never before felt so strongly that I am becoming a bachelor. Worse than a bachelor. Zoe is in Predeal, Leni I know not where. I think of them both with a certain sadness. And yet I do not need them.

My only regret at this year's end (apart from the old incurable ones) is that I still haven't finished the book. I now feel that there is nothing more to be done, that the last part is an irreparable failure. But one way or another, I should have liked to free myself of it, not to have it trailing after me into 1940.

1940

Monday, 1 January 1940

From Zurich, a long divertimento for orchestra by Mozart. Let's take it as a good sign for the new year.

I began New Year's Eve in the most stupid way, at Carol's, in a Jewish "family" group, vulgar, noisy, without grace or charm or even the excuse of being my family. I continued with Camil, Elvira Godeanu, and Marietta Deculescu to Poldy Stern's funny little apartment, where we found a group of young girls (seventeen to eighteen years old), slovenly, a little hysterical, with a kind of exaggerated cynicism that did not dispel their terrible youth. At first I felt scared, then old, and then I got some drink inside me. I returned home at six in the morning, without the usual disgust of my wasted nights.

I worked from 7 p.m. until just now (midnight) and did not manage to write more than a page. I am still on Chapter Eighteen, having so far written only six pages of it. It is true that the regiment stops me from writing, but it is also true that when I have a day off and finally sit down at my desk, I do not have the patience to stay fixed in front of the manuscript, giving it my full attention without reverie, without distraction, and without the breaks I all too easily allow myself. Most ridiculous of all is that, with the last section now under way, three or four days of serious work should be enough for me to wrap it up.

Tomorrow morning, though, I'll be back at the regiment.

Tuesday, 2 January

I have no talent for landscape. When I speak about the weather, the light, the forest or mountains, I am unforgivably short on expressions and color. In general, my vocabulary is poor. A word keeps following me, and I cannot escape it and find other equivalents. The whole book is filled not only with words but also with phrases that are repeated dozens of times: "It seemed to him that . . . ," "He had the feeling that . . . ," "suddenly," "briefly," "he thought"—it infuriates me how often I find these in one chapter, without being able to do anything about it. And in addition there are the repeated gestures, the persistent asides. It indicates a serious lack of imagination and inventiveness, with regard not so much to the actual incidents (which can be quite bold, even far-fetched at times) as to the vocabulary and mode of expression.

Thursday, 4 January

From Paris, the Ravel quartet played by the Calvet Quartet.

I think that my exclusive preference for Mozart, Bach, Haydn, and, to some extent, Beethoven is becoming a kind of musical indulgence or even indolence. With them I am on familiar ground. I can listen to them with pleasure, without an effort of attention, almost without any active collaboration. I think I am not sufficiently curious and discerning to go beyond this. I ought to be a more disciplined, a more patient listener.

I've finished Chapter Eighteen. It has fifteen pages, butchered as usual with deletions. I am profoundly dissatisfied. I wrote without seeing it before me, without feeling personally involved. But this whole business disgusts me. It has become a torture, a duty, a chore. I'll finish Chapter Nineteen, the next one, in two, three, or four days—then I'll try to forget this whole thankless task as quickly as I can.

Although so many days have passed since my call-up, I still don't feel that I have "settled in" at the regiment. As there is no roll call and no one asks after me, I have begun to arrive at nine in the morning and not to go back at all after lunch. I don't know how long that will work. When I am there, I stay in the company bunkhouse and wait for time to pass.

I have been taking along my red Montaigne, a fairly small and supple volume that fits into my overcoat pocket. I read all morning.

In Chapter Nine, Book IIa of the *Essays*, I found a note about a lost first draft of a passage, which Montaigne never tried to reconstitute: ". . . *mais ce lopin de mes brouillars m'ayant esté désrobé avec plusieurs autres par un homme qui me servoit, je ne le priveray point du profit qu'il en espère faire: aussi me seroit-il bien malaisé de remascher deux fois une mesme viande.*"[1]

---

1. "But as this part of my notebook was stolen along with several others by a man in my service, I shall not deprive him of the profit he hopes to gain from it. Besides, it would be difficult for me to chew twice the same piece of meat."

Friday, 5 January

From Breslau (Abendroth conducting), Reger's *Variations and Fugue on a Theme by Mozart*—then a Mozart piano concerto (K. 537) which I don't think I knew before. I tried listening to it bar by bar. It all seemed to sing along—"singable" music, "like a bird." I picked out one phrase from the andante that could have been a veritable romance.

This afternoon, quite unexpectedly, Franck's *Sonata* was on shortwave from Berlin. I always listen to it not only with pleasure but with a sense that it is favorable to me, like a good omen or a promise.

Monday, 8 January

Two splendid days skiing in Sinaia—Saturday and yesterday. On Saturday I did slalom exercises on the bowling ground, and on Sunday morning I went with Comşa and Lereanu to Stîna Regală. The snow was thick, exaggeratedly so—which was a joy in itself (how nice it is to roll in it, to fall and pick yourself up again!), though it didn't allow us to do much in terms of technique. We had to work hard for a couple of hours to stamp down a track for our slalom exercises—and it was still heavy going, maybe because we were by then very tired.

From Stîna, the landscape is one of *"haute montagne."*[2] Mount Caraiman can be seen close up, Clăbucet is across the way, and at the back lie Mount Postăvar and Piatra Mare. There was a heavenly sun. I shut my eyes and stayed for minutes without thinking of anything.

The greatest delight, however, was our return to Sinaia. We had a long course: with excellent snow deep enough to glide over it, and with enough ice for our turning movements to be easy. It was the same course on which I fell so many times, especially at the bends, when I put on my skis three years ago for the first time. Now it went extremely easily. I realize that skiing is not a great feat—because it poses no problems or difficulties—but the pleasure is indescribable. I sang all the way down.

Back home I find the regiment and, above all, the novel—that still unfinished novel.

Tuesday, 9 January

I should write a note about military rapaciousness. Nothing seems too much to them; everything seems just right. When they take the trouble

2. High mountain.

to thank you for something you have done for them, they wear a kind of condescending expression that creates a further sense of obligation on your part.

I took the colonel some books from the Foundation worth several thousand lei. I thought he would be overwhelmed. But on the contrary, he was severe:

"Is that all?"

Then, almost contemptuously:

"Do you expect me to build a regimental library with that?"

And a brief last word:

"Bring me the books by Queen Maria!"

He didn't ask if I could bring them, if I could get hold of them, if they would cost money or not.

If the company is missing a bridle, we buy one ourselves. If there is need of three hundred plates and three hundred sets of cutlery, we buy them ourselves.

Today at the adjutant's office, Ghiță Ionescu—who has been called up and is working there—told me that the next call-up on 15 January will be especially for Jews. There will be fifteen hundred Jews and not one Christian.

"I don't understand why," he said. "I suppose it's okay in time of war. You can form special units of Jews and send them to be mowed down at the front. But what sense does it make now?"

I left there depressed. Everything is bearable until you start feeling acted on not as a soldier, not as a citizen, but as a Jew. Thousands, tens of thousands of Jews have been called up to lug stones and dig trenches in Bessarabia and Dobrogea. That too is a form of slavery.

Wednesday, 10 January

From Vienna, a Mozart piano quartet (K. 493).

Friday, 12 January

Yesterday evening from Breslau, a Mozart flute concerto.

The day before, on Deutschlandsender, Mozart's *Symphony for Two Orchestras* (which I first heard two or three years ago, conducted by Scherchen), and then something I didn't know existed: *Les Djins* by César Franck, a tone poem for piano and orchestra.

I listen with displeasure, even with pangs of conscience, to the German stations, even when they put on music. What is happening to the Jews now in Hitler-occupied Poland is beyond all known horrors.

I thought I would finish this evening and, if I had made a greater effort, I would certainly have succeeded. But after eight hours' work (from three in the afternoon until now, 11:30) I feel a little dizzy, though I have written only five pages or so.

I'll have to go back over the final evening in the chalet. The parting from Gunther is too brief, too lacking in emotion.

Monday, 15 January

I didn't want to finish on Saturday because it was the 13th. Yesterday, on the other hand, I was sure I would finish. But late at night, after struggling for several hours, I gave up the attempt. I still have two or three pages to write—and it's best if I wait for a favorable moment. Even so, the final chapters have been written most reluctantly, without continuity, without a close relationship between them. They feel patched together from various fragments.

This evening I'll take Chapters Fourteen to Twenty to Rosetti. I still have to add a few things to Chapters Nineteen and Twenty. Maybe I'll have more luck with the proofs. Anyway, this time I'm at the end.

Monday, 22 January

A day's skiing yesterday in Sinaia. I arrived there at ten in the morning (with Comşa and Lereanu) and immediately set off in the sledge for Stîna Regală, but it was impossible to pass beyond the point where the ways to Stîna and Altitude 1400 separate. The snow was colossal, and the sledge could not get through. We set off on skis for Altitude 1400, forgetting about Stîna.

The snow poured down like white rain: "thousands of tons" of it. So much snow that our skis barely slid forward. All the way back (the same route on which I usually descend at dizzying speed), I had to advance like a skater and make constant use of the sticks. Even at the bowling ground, where there is quite a sharp slope ("precipitous" it once seemed to me), it was possible only to slide slowly forward. The fine sticky snow was too soft. After a few hundred meters I had to stop and wipe the skis, which had a few centimeters of snow stuck to them like cork or rubber heels.

I enjoyed the stop at the 1400 refuge. I generally like these mountain refuges: girls and boys who arrive white with snow, as on a long journey; a mixture of vivacity and indifference, idleness and vigor, closeness and solitude.

It wasn't really a day of skiing. The snow didn't allow us to do much. But it was a happy day. The forest, literally overwhelmed by snow, is a landscape from a fairy tale or fable.

I don't know why I haven't written here about last Sunday's escapade at Călugăreni. I've talked about it several times, but I was too lazy to write as well. It would be worth it, though. It was funny how we scared a village in Vlaşca as we entered it in our skiing costumes.

A lot of music all week, of all kinds. As usual, Bach, Mozart, and Beethoven. One evening there was *Psyché*, a very beautiful tone poem by Franck.

Zoe, whom I hadn't seen for such a long time and with whom I thought I no longer had anything in common, came to see me on Saturday evening before leaving for Braşov. She was puzzling, affectionate, beautiful, good to hold close, warm and velvety. Were I a little less of a skeptic, I'd find nothing with which to fault her in the whole evening—an evening I hadn't looked for and hadn't expected.

Zoe is a striking girl, even in her colorful defects and her disarmingly ingenuous way of doing some despicable things (objectively "despicable," as is her acceptance of money from her lover, Tantzi Cocea).

Sunday, 28 January

Dorina Blank, still beautiful, still youthful (though with light wrinkles that she didn't have three years ago), came here yesterday after numerous insistent phone calls that I met with sincere indifference. A woman cannot say more clearly that she wants to go to bed with you.

Voichiţă Aurel, my comrade in the Twenty-first Infantry, said something yesterday about Captain Căpşuneanu, something that sums up a whole Romanian style of politics:

"He's a real mean bastard who'll beat you and swear at you. But there's one good thing about him: he can't stand yids and lets us have a go at them too."

That is precisely the consolation that the Germans offer the Czechs and the Poles, and which they are prepared to offer the Romanians.

Last night I dreamed of Stalin. He had the look of an amiable Russian peasant, and I was surprised at his great simplicity.

Yesterday from Paris there was again Ravel's quartet, which I like more and more.

This morning a Mozart sonata from Paris (which struck me as very Beethovenesque), and then a delightful Mozart trio from Berlin. Finally, from Bucharest, Beethoven's fourth symphony.

Zoe rings me every evening from Braşov. Will even this parting not be the break on which I decided?

The proofs of the final chapters have arrived. I didn't do anything special to hurry them up. It's very nearly February and the book's publication is still quite a long way off. It has become a thing of such indifference to me! And I still have to write a few pages at the end of Chapters Nineteen and Twenty—pages that I can no longer see or feel inside me.

It is snowing beautifully after several days of thaw. I promise myself a few days' skiing at the end of next week, especially if I am called up on the first, as people are saying.

Monday, 29 January

My inability to go back over a text I have written is playing another nasty trick on me. Not only am I unable to write the few pages I planned to add to the last two chapters, but I am beginning to convince myself that I do not need to write them, that they are not necessary. I am well aware that this is a clever subterfuge on my part, an obstacle course that my incurable laziness has set up for me. A check needs to be kept on such tendencies. Whenever I am tempted to do away with an incident, I should first compel myself to write it and only then eliminate it. That is the only way of being sure that you have genuinely discarded something, and not just run away from difficulties.

If I leave Chapter Nineteen as is, the departure from the chalet loses its weight. Gunther, who seems such a powerful presence in the early pages, completely eludes me toward the end.

Things are even more serious with regard to the end of Chapter Twenty, because the denouement of the whole book depends upon it. Is it a good idea for me to abandon the marriage of Paul and Nora? I would be inclined to say "yes"—not only because it is simpler that way, not only because it spares me a final hurdle, but above all because, as things have worked out, the close relationship between Nora and Paul does not imperiously require, and may not even justify, their marriage to each other. It is certainly my fault, for although the whole of the last part beginning with Chapter Fourteen was written in accordance with a fixed plan, it has departed from the underlying facts of the book. What is lacking here is the necessary intensity of emotion, the necessary power of life and suggestion, so that the final scene (which I already saw very well when I began to write the first lines of the first chapter) becomes a kind of "pleasant" denouement. On the other hand, if I give it up I fear that the whole book will remain suspended in air, with no paths leading anywhere.

Wednesday, 31 [January]

From morning to evening I spent yesterday's leave from the regiment reading through the whole book. Why should I not say that I enjoyed reading it and was caught up in the unfolding action, as if it were surprising me for the first time? It is true that I'm not sure whether it works as a novel, whether it all hangs together as a whole. Above all, I ask myself whether it will not appear to a reader as made up of three distinct parts, without a necessary connection among them. There is a Nora episode, an Ann episode, and a Gunther episode. Do they all fuse together? Is there a balance among them? I don't know. I'm too close to the book to tell.

I also wonder whether to write the final scene with the marriage proposal or to leave things hanging. Yesterday I thought about it a lot and decided that the finale really must be written—well or badly, as it please the Lord. Otherwise the book lacks a denouement, and the "accident" remains without consequence. Nevertheless I have sent the galleys back to the printer's to be made up into pages, with the idea that I may be able to have another go on the page proofs.

Friday, 9 February

I still have time to change the ending of the book. I can still revert to the initial denouement by making Paul ask for Nora's hand in marriage. But again, such an ending is beginning to seem too obvious a resolution, too neat a conclusion. On the other hand, if I leave things as they are, everything will end without sense.

In any event, I shall keep the proofs tomorrow and Sunday—the printer doesn't work then anyway. Come what may, I'll give the go-ahead for printing on Monday morning.

I have read it all through once more, yesterday and today. It's not a bad book. Up to a point, it's not even badly done.

Saturday, 10 February

Yesterday evening I didn't finish the preceding note. Ghiță Ionescu rang—and then I no longer had the time to continue.

I constantly think of the book—in the street, on the streetcar, at meals. I know now that I'll leave it as it is and give the go-ahead on Monday, because I can't delay it any longer. I can't stand the thought that this business might drag on for God knows how much longer. I am full of doubts and misgivings.

It occurred to me to seek someone's advice: Camil, Mircea, maybe Cioculescu. I'd have liked to ask one of them to read the book and tell me what he thought about the ending. But what's the point? No one will know better than I that it is an evasion. No one will know better than I what should be done.

I think that between Chapters Eighteen and Nineteen there should be a chapter of passionate love and intimacy between Nora and Paul. There should be something so intense that it restores the book's center of gravity, which broke up with the intervention of Gunther. Such a chapter would then modify the finale, because Paul's marriage to Nora would become natural, indeed obligatory. In the end, the departure from the chalet—which I have left completely unfinished—should be written properly. It would all be a matter of three or four days, not only of intensive work but above all of total and sincere absorption in the world of the book (which I have now left behind). I move around it as a "novelist," but I can't manage to identify with it. I face it as a writer, a critic, a reader, whatever you like; but I am not, as I was so often before, an astounded witness to things happening beyond me and without my consent.

Since yesterday I have been a civilian again, though I can't say I have been demobilized. I handed back my things, but the discharge papers still have not come through.

Monday, 12 February

I have delivered the final corrected proofs.
So there are novels that can be finished.[3]

A depressing visit to the regiment this morning. The discharge papers still haven't been issued. Captain Căpșuneanu had heard from the call-

---

3. In English in the original.

up office "what's what"; my corrected name does not sufficiently prove my identity for him. So who knows how much longer I shall have to wait. A yid can wait. Not even the simplest thing can be done for us. We are lepers. The orders are officially anti-Semitic, but even stronger than the orders are people's minds. Captain Căpșuneanu's hatred is a fact that nothing can escape.

A few hundred new recruits were in the barracks. Civilians without weapons were marching three abreast and receiving "individual instruction." (How indescribably sad are those no longer young enough for that game!) The majority of them—90 percent, I would say—are Jews. Collected as they are in special units, how easy it will be some day to have done with them!

I left feeling sick at heart.

I don't know how long I'll remain in civilian life. Assuming they let me go in one, two, or seven days' time, how long will I be free? It's said that we'll be called up again on the first of April, maybe even sooner.

I wonder what to do in the meantime. For better or worse, the novel is now finished. I shouldn't allow myself to be ground down between the Foundation and the courts. I must work with some degree of application. I could get down to the "Romanian Novel" project—which would give my schedule some discipline, though I'd then have to go every day to the Academy. But a book of criticism holds no attraction for me now that my days of liberty—perhaps of life itself—are numbered. What would be the point of such a book if I'm dragged off to war in the spring and everything comes to a complete end?

I'd be happier writing the play, which has been constantly in my thoughts today. I am still close to Gunther, since the novel has not yet completely detached itself from me. I even feel that I owe it to Gunther to take up again the things I did not manage to say, or even suggest, in the novel. He is so alive for me, with so many secrets to unravel. What makes me pause is my weariness with writing. I know the joy of starting, of being swept along, of feeling things come alive—but I also know the horror of seeing them grind to a halt in the mud. When I begin it seems a simple matter to wrap a play up in a few weeks, but then there is no way of escaping the torture, the bondage, the obsession.

Wednesday, 14 [February]

Last night on Deutschlandsender, Mozart's *Flute Concerto in G Major* and his *Divertimento for Two Horns and Strings*.

Zoe is back from Braşov. Beautiful, tender, sensual. But why doesn't she give up? Why is she still waiting?

Still a soldier. Rung up by the company, I raced as a civilian to the regiment, took five minutes to disguise myself in uniform, reported double-quick to the colonel, and in another five minutes got rid of my "things." By two o'clock I was outside the regimental gates, a civilian again. It is a farce that might amuse me if my place there on the "active" list did not give me a constant feeling of insecurity.

"I won't let you go until you've built a library for me," said the colonel.

Just now, from Radio Paris, the finale of a violin concerto by Max Bruch. I was surprised I knew it so well—from where, I wonder?

I am trying not to think any more about the novel. Otherwise it will never give me any peace. It looks as if it will come out on the first of March.

Wednesday, 21 [February]

I left Bucharest on Friday evening and came back last night after three days in Predeal and one in Braşov.

The days in Predeal were the most serious from a skiing point of view. I did nothing but ski from morning till evening, with passion, perseverance, and a firm resolve to learn. I feel regenerated, renewed, freer and younger.

On Saturday morning, in Veştea, I did no more than inspect the lay of the land. But a few hours later I had recovered the ease with which, two years ago, I used to speed down to the edge of the forest. After lunch I went out with an instructor and worked on nothing but sharp christies until dusk fell. I repeated the action dozens of times, resisting the temptation to take on one of the "dizzying" courses. My problem is that, at the point when I shift my weight from one ski to the other, I "lift" the freed ski into the air instead of dragging it on the ground.

On Sunday, while Comşa and Lereanu (who had arrived the day before) did exercises in plowing and controlled avoidance, I continued with my sharp christies and made visible progress. Toward evening I was managing to do some joined christies all the way from top to bottom—but I still haven't mastered the action, and I'd need a few more days of concentrated work to get it right. The three descents to the base of the ski lift were vertiginous: the speed there is truly terrifying. I cannot describe, or even mentally grasp, the sensation at that moment: it is one of extreme lucidity in a vertical fall. Everything happens in a fraction of a second. When you reach the end of the course, you are breathless and cannot remember anything.

On Monday I left the practice area and set off for Diham. It was a wonderful trip, both because of the weather (sun, sun!) and because of the route itself. The approach was the most beautiful and varied ski course I have ever done. The run down to Forban is a sheer delight. I fell three times in all, but was generally pleased with myself. By evening I was exhausted but happy, youthful, with a profound feeling of strength and vitality.

A day of love in Braşov. Zoe was nice and affectionate. Alone at Scheeser's,[4] it felt a long way from town. Sometimes I like to mimic happiness.

I saw Leni for a moment in her room at the Hotel Aro. She struck me as especially ugly.

It was a funny coincidence that all three of us—Leni, Zoe, myself— were in Braşov on the same day. As in the final chapter of *Accidentul*.

Monday, 26 [February]

The lover of Tantzi Cocea (the "Miciu" Zoe keeps telling me about) is Ciulley. So Zoe is receiving money from Ciulley! Gina Cocea[5] confided this to me when she was here the other evening with Ghiţă Ionescu.

I met Nae Ionescu on Saturday evening at the Ateneu (a very fine Walter Gieseking concert). It was a great pleasure to see him, and we agreed that I would pay him a visit one morning.

Yesterday in Buzău, for the birth of Marcu's son. An amusing provincial reception. I was interested in everything Dr. Brofman told me about his work as a specialist in abortions. I could use it one day in a novel.

Evening
The first copies have arrived from the printer's. I cut the pages of one and leafed through it. I am calm, though not actually indifferent—which would be asking too much. Anyway, it makes me feel good to see this new book on my desk.

4. A wealthy Braşovian family with an interest in the arts.
5. Wife of the novelist N. D. Cocea.

Wednesday, 28 [February]

Rosetti doesn't like the book. By yesterday evening he had read some 250 pages—but that is all he said to me. This morning (by which time he would have finished it) he didn't say anything at all to me. The silence is all the more significant in Rosetti's case, because usually he never stops sending words of praise, both in writing and by telephone.

I honestly feel bad that he agreed to publish me with his eyes shut.

Yesterday evening I was suddenly seized with real panic. Maybe *Accidentul* is just idiotic nonsense; maybe it contains outright stupidities that will discredit me forever. These were not doubts about such and such an episode (the kind of doubts I have always had). I feared that the book was a blunder from beginning to end, a trifle that said nothing and led nowhere, a pointless and mediocre failure. I went home literally terrified. I didn't have the courage even to pick up the book and open it. I had a sense of irreparability. I felt compromised and discredited. I'd have liked to sleep and sleep, to forget and to escape.

Mircea Eliade, having read the book, gave me a telephone call that seemed more kindhearted than enthusiastic. "Your best book," "a modern novel," "very interesting," "a book with a lot of character"—all said fast and furious, with a kind of forced warmth. I'm not sure it means much, or is even what he really thinks about it. His friendly volubility seemed to disguise a lot of things about which he was reticent. I'd like to tell him that I need to know his real impressions, clear, blunt, and precise, but I realize that it is very difficult to obtain such honesty from anyone. Did not I myself—after *Şarpele*, *Domnişoara Christina*, and, very recently indeed, *Ifigenia*—use a few admiring declarations to cover my real sense of dissatisfaction? (It is true, also, that what discourages me in my relations with Mircea and stops me from speaking plainly, honestly, and, if necessary, sharply is the thought that Nina would not tolerate any withdrawal of admiration.)

Of those who have read my book up to now—Benu, Comşa, Rosetti, Mircea—not one has been won over by it. Benu, though keen on the Ann episode, was silent and seemingly embarrassed about the rest. Comşa gave the impression of being altogether puzzled.

Whom shall I ask? Who will tell me something enlightening? Maybe Camil.

By myself, I can no longer see anything.

Thursday, 29 [February]

A musical evening yesterday. I read the "Berlioz" chapter in Combarieu as I listened to the *Symphonie fantastique* from Budapest (I'll hear it again this evening at the Philharmonic, conducted by Philippe Gaubert). A little later Radio Bucharest had *Le carnaval roman* on disc, as if it were a real Berlioz evening. What I find more interesting than the music is Berlioz the man, so stormy and so intelligent. In the end I must confess that I listen to his music more out of sedulity than out of any real liking—but he is extremely interesting as a person.

Also yesterday there was a Bach mass from Vienna (the *Great Mass*), divinely beautiful, sometimes more so than the oratorios. The *Benedictus*, in particular, sounded quite angelic, with the violin and tenor answering each other in the foreground, and the organ austere and powerful in the distance. It is a long time since I felt such clear emotion in music.

Mircea is right to point out that *Accidentul* sometimes resembles Norah James's *La reine équipée*.

Wednesday, 6 March

Skiing on Sunday and Monday. I caught the seven o'clock express to Predeal on Sunday morning (again with Comşa and Lereanu), and immediately set off by sledge to the "huts" and from there to the Vînatori cabin. It was sunny, but with a fierce wind. In the forest it was indescribably beautiful because of the thick powdery snow, but conditions became cruel as we came into the open. My cheeks were clenched tight from the cold; I no longer felt or saw anything. The devilish wind flung snow into our eyes—yet the sun shone as on the brightest of mornings. The ascent on Forban was terribly hard: a few times we stopped dead with the thought of turning back; but when we reached the top the wind died down and we were able to keep going to Diham. A dizzying wealth of colors: dozens of shades of mauve, of violet. I don't think the Bucegi range looks more beautiful from anywhere else.

We spent the night in the cabin and woke up the next morning in another winter: the sky completely overcast, the wind diminished, the snowfall calm and vast. Nevertheless, up on Diham the ground was favorable for skiing because of the ice and the winds of the day before. At ten we set off for Predeal, keeping to the familiar way as far as the "huts," but then we abandoned the rather monotonous highway that passes alongside Sanatorii and climbed up to Fitifoui before coming down again on the other side. (A splendid view over Predeal, as in a color sketch.)

All told, they were two happy days, restful and full of life—but I have to say that in terms of skiing, they were not at all up to scratch. There has been a big regression since last time. Is it possible for me to lose my touch so easily?

Had lunch at Rosetti's yesterday, with Derek Patmare,[6] Lassaigne, Comarnescu, and Basdevant.[7]

Patmare, a young Englishman of thirty-one, speaks excellent French, is easygoing, witty, and friendly, very Latin, very Parisian. I heard today from Camil that he is a pederast—which explains a lot of things.

Camil pointed out that the ending of *Accidentul* has something demonstrative ("go skiing and you'll be cured of your sorrows in love"). It is a fair observation. I realized from the start that the final chapter—or, to be more precise, the final sentences—trivialize the book, diminish its significance.

Thursday, 7 March

Haydn's *Symphony No. 13* (the first time I've heard it, I think) from London, a few Scarlatti sonatas from Rome, Borodin's quartet played by the Calvet Quartet from Paris, Beethoven's *Seventh Symphony* from Bucharest, a sinfonia concertante for violin and cello by Haydn, plus Schubert's *Fifth Symphony* from Vienna—all in the course of today.

Blizzard, thick snow, terrible frost. Winter's back with a vengeance. But I have a number of court deadlines to meet and I don't think I'll be able to go skiing.

Friday, 8 [March]

Mama, who read two hundred pages of *Accidentul* yesterday, said she was so upset that she couldn't sleep all night.

"How can you love and suffer that much?" she asked me. And I tried in vain to convince her that I am not Paul, that Ann does not exist, that Nora is an invention, that nothing in the book actually happened.

This morning at the Chamber of Labor I had to plead in a case involving Hachette. It had no importance, of course—but I left there feeling angry. In my own judgment, I had not remained calm, had not spoken convincingly, and my usual ironic tone had not impressed the judge.

6. English writer and journalist.
7. Jules Basdevant: French diplomat.

Monday, 11 March

Friday evening from Paris, Acts Two and Three of *Pelléas et Mélisande*. Greatly enjoyed listening to them.

Yesterday I was in Braşov. Zoe had asked me to go because she didn't want to come back to Bucharest alone.

A snow-covered Braşov, such as I don't remember ever having seen before, even in the depths of winter. I went to Poiana, where the snow was ideal for skiing. I got there too late to "work" on it, but the return to Braşov was nonetheless very pleasant. Zoe, who was doing a course for the first time, fell at each bend—which reminded me of the difficulty I had had in covering the same ground two years ago. Now it struck me as child's play.

An emotional phone call from Froda. He has read *Accidentul* from beginning to end, without putting it down once. He is astounded, doesn't know what to say, how to congratulate me, how to thank me. He hasn't read such a fine book in years—not since Maurois's *Climats* (well now!); it is a book that should be read only by initiates, only by people who have lived such things and can understand them. He followed the book in the minutest detail. He knows Ann. He knows who she is.

I can well understand F.'s excitement. It is not a literary emotion; it is something else, which I find less pleasant but also more interesting— a feeling that he too is personally implicated in the book.

"Please don't tell Leni that I've spoken to you with such feeling about it."

An unwise request, I should have said, except that all the time I had the impression that F. was not trying to gloss over the intimate aspect of the book, that he actually wanted to talk to me about it but did not dare, or did not know the right way to go about it.

Friday, 15 March

Nae Ionescu has died.

Saturday, 16 [March]

Nervous, uncontrollable sobbing as I entered Nae Ionescu's house yesterday morning, two hours after his death.

He takes with him a whole period of my life, which is now—only now—over for good.

What a strange fate he had, that extraordinary man who has died unfulfilled, beaten, and—hard though it is for me to say it—a failure.

He is so dear to me precisely because he had so little good fortune. How insolent, how insulting seems to me the success of others! Şeicaru is healthy, wealthy, and triumphant. Manoilescu will become a minister. Tătărescu is prime minister. Herescu is a tenured professor and president of the Writers' Association. Corneliu Moldovanu has the national prize for literature and appears at café events. Victor Eftimiu gives receptions.

But Nae Ionescu dies at the age of forty-nine, not taken seriously, defeated.

Tuesday, 26 March

Two days at Cîmpulung, with Rosetti and Solacolu.

Money worries again. I feel the cost of living continually rising and my budget becoming more and more unbalanced. After paying the rent I have nothing left from the twenty-thousand-lei advance on the novel. How laughable is the amount I have gotten from that book, which meant several years of work!

I feel poor, and humiliated by my poverty, though I should have grown used to it by now.

Friday, 29 March

I happened to be at Cartea Românească and couldn't help but ask Mişu how things were going. "Fairly well," he said—by which he obviously meant "pretty badly."

The truth is that the book is not selling. Did I need to learn again that I am not a successful author? If a publisher pulls out the stops on the publicity and distribution, a book of mine may sell three thousand copies; if not, it can lie around in bookshops unnoticed.

This lack of success doesn't surprise me, and doesn't upset me either. It may be that *Accidentul* could have sold more copies than any other of my books. But that would have called for publicity, for a persistent effort—and unfortunately I am not capable of either.

Otherwise people like the book. Mrs. Ralea, Mrs. Vianu, Mrs. Brătescu-Voineşti, G. M. Cantacuzino (all of whom read French books and usually steer clear of novels by Romanian authors) seem to talk about it wherever they go. On the other hand, I think that Gulian is not happy with it.

1 April, Monday

I thought again this morning about the "Grodeck mysteries," and a novel—or rather, a story—set twenty years before *Accidentul* seemed to me a possibility. I'd tell about the relationship of the young Mrs. Grodeck with Hagen, the betrothal to Grodeck Senior, the early years of marriage, the birth of Gunther, and so on. This does not mean that I would have to give up the play. For in a sense the play takes up the action of *Accidentul*, whereas this novella would precede and prepare it, explain it and make it possible.

A possible title would be "The Young Mrs. Grodeck."

Mircea has been appointed cultural attaché in London. He leaves in a few days' time. Apparently with a fantastic salary.

Giurescu[8] told Rosetti that the King, at his audience this morning, said he would appoint as general secretary of the Foundations none other than Herescu. This is a great blow for Rosetti and a great misfortune for me personally. I am dismayed twice over. That was the only thing missing for me to enter a period of gloom, of depression.

Tuesday, 2 April

Yesterday there was a Schubert rondo for violin and orchestra on a German radio station—very beautiful and, above all, surprising. In places it sounded like Mozart.

Feeling intrigued, I read the chapter on Schubert in Combarieu and realized that I have known nothing about him, not even the approximate period in which he lived. I'll pay more attention to him in the future.

Thursday, 4 April

Yesterday from Vienna, Beethoven's *Missa solemnis*, though I caught only the concluding parts (*Sanctus, Benedictus, Miserere*). Then, from Bucharest, some works by Bach, including the *Second Suite*. This morning, from Paris-Colonial, a Vivaldi concerto followed by Manuel de Falla's *Nights*

---

8. Constantin Giurescu: historian, official in the administration of King Carol.

in the Gardens of Spain, and this evening (now, as I return from the Jacques Copeau recital) a splendid trio by Ravel, also from Paris.

Wednesday, 10 April

Yesterday the Germans occupied Denmark, with no resistance, and landed at a few points in Norway, where they met a strange kind of formal resistance.

After so many months of calm, we are being reminded that there is a war on—that it may flare up anywhere and at any time, that the life we lead is no more than chance, an accident, a coincidence. This evening, or tomorrow, you can suddenly lose everything: home, family, life.

On Sunday I went to Sinaia and Predeal (with Camil, Rosetti, Lassaigne); an implausible winter's day, with snowdrifts as in January. I was sorry not to have my skis with me.

Dupront[9] told Rosetti at a lunch the day before yesterday that he intends to send me to France. Well, that's another idea!

Saturday, 13 [April]

Cioculescu's review in *Jurnalul*[1] talks mainly about the skiing: not a word about Ann, not a word about Nora, not a word about Paul. The Grodeck episode is described as a "drama with shades of Ibsen" (?). The rest of the article is made up of vague words of praise, old all-purpose epithets such as lucid, graceful, limpid, and so on. All rather disheartening, I must say.

What depresses me most is that the novel is not selling. Today I saw a report to management on recent titles: *Accidentul*, "fairly well at first, slowly at present."

It has disappeared from bookshop windows, aging and forgotten.

In Norway the German victory looks greater than one would gather from London's propaganda dispatches. After the first hours of euphoria, when we believed in a great naval battle involving the destruction of isolated German pockets in Narvik, Oslo, and Bergen, there has followed a lull of disappointment. Not one British or French soldier has set foot in Norway, not one airplane has landed, not one port has been occupied. The

---

9. Alphonse Dupront: head of the French Cultural Institute in Bucharest.
1. Daily newspaper.

Germans, on the other hand, are continuing to shore up their presence there.

Tuesday, 16 April

The British victory in Narvik at midday on Saturday (which I heard about late at night, after writing the last dejected note), and especially yesterday's announcement of the landing of British troops on the Norwegian coast, have brought a little hope, a degree of confidence.

Sometimes I see ahead a somber Hitlerite world, but at other times the ugly dream fades and I start to believe in a Europe that I myself may even live to see, a free Europe without terrors, without superstitions. Then I feel younger, more courageous, more contented to be alive. The truth is that—however unhappy I am—I wish with all my heart that I will personally live to see the collapse of Hitlerism.

Music all the time and everywhere—but so much and so varied that I no longer manage to record it all here. From Paris-Colonial, I find nearly every morning some Mozart, Haydn, and Bach. Yesterday, on Deutschlandsender, there was a Mozart piano concerto that I did not already know, and Haydn's *Symphony No. 13*, which I think I heard for the first time.

Wednesday, 24 April

After a few days of physical weakness, in which I felt sick without having the will to rest in bed, there followed days of complete idiocy. I feel downhearted, deadened, and carry with me a taste of bitterness, of demoralized laziness, of futility. No one anywhere can do anything for me, no one anywhere can come to my aid.

Sometimes I tell myself that I must get down to work again, perhaps on the play, or go to the Academy to work on the history of the novel—so that I finally do something that makes me feel my life is not totally pointless.

When I see people, it is more out of disgust with myself, out of fear of again being alone. Belu, Ghiţă Ionescu, Comşa, Lena, Leni: all of them I met by chance, without seeking them out, and in the end without really seeing them.

I am writing these lines with the radio switched on (short pieces of Gluck, Beethoven, Weber). Maybe music could still be a consolation, a drug. But now spring has come and I can no longer bear anything. The other day I listened inattentively to a Handel organ concerto, and one evening to Haydn's *Symphony No. 101*. This afternoon there were two Beethoven piano sonatas. Almost every day I have listened to something or other, but apathetically, without passion and almost without pleasure.

I wrote Poldy a long letter, sad and resigned. I feel that my fate is sealed, but why can't at least they be happy?

I think I'll go to Balcic on Friday for a few days (ten, if possible). I'd have left yesterday, but there are fresh problems at the regiment, where they are trying to extend my call-up period by another month. In principle this would start on the first of May—and thus cut my Easter holidays in two.

I am hoping that something will come of these days in Balcic. I'd like to change my pale, tired, ugly appearance of a man at the end of his tether, at whom I dare not look closely in the mirror. I'd like to regain a little self-confidence, a little courage.

Friday, 3 May

Six days in Balcic, a cloudy, chilly, damp Balcic, more like November than April. Yet I return rested, my face tanned by the wind if not by any sun.

A trip to Ecrene on Easter Monday turned into a minor shipwreck, because, though the sun had been shining when we left, we immediately had to abandon Ecrene beach, chased away by clouds that gathered in a few moments. The storm broke when we were still in the open. With the rain and hail pouring down, we moored on the other side of Hilalgi and took refuge, barefoot and soaking wet, at Pen's way, where we broke the cabin door. I laughed like a maniac, and it all seemed to me in the end a wonderful adventure.

The next few days were so cold that I kept wanting to run back to Bucharest. It is also true that Comșa and Lereanu wearied me. They were very reliable, as usual, but I found their very presence tiring. In Balcic, unless I am alone and free to walk or be idle, I do not recognize myself. Benu alone (whom I took to show him Balcic) would not have bothered me, to be sure.

Still, *tout compte fait*,[2] it was a holiday: a few excursions to Hilalgi, to the Tatar areas, and in the direction of Cavarna, some hours idled away

---

2. When all is said and done.

in cafés, some mornings of sleep—and everywhere the sea, green, bluish, mauve. It has all left me in a much better state than the dreadful one in which I arrived.

After the flight back yesterday evening I found a sunny Bucharest that also turned autumnal in a couple of hours. It has been snowing in the mountains. It is cold in the street. Nothing to do but stay indoors and work.

Things are serious in Norway. It's not yet clear to me whether the British withdrawal is a local setback or means the collapse of the whole operation.

Tonight I had a long and irritating discussion with Camil Petrescu; he saw it all coming and is now afire with jubilation. His philosophical system, which "achieves things that haven't been done for two and a half thousand years" (his very words), is finding fresh confirmation. I have the feeling that he himself is scared by so much success.

Sunday, 5 May

Yesterday was a day of panic, with the most fantastic rumors flying around. The King has met Horthy. No, it was Goering. Correction: it was Prince Paul. A German attack is imminent. Italy is preparing to enter Dalmatia, perhaps also Greece. Our own days are numbered. The Germans will occupy Hungary exactly as they occupied Denmark, and our role will be that of Norway . . .

But I calmed down toward evening (after I had seen Vişoianu and, quite by chance, Read from the British legation). Of course things are serious. Of course anything is possible. Of course destruction may one day come out of a clear sky, and there's no telling when or how. It's not just round the corner, though. It could be a matter of several days or several weeks. Dare I say "several months"?

Tuesday, 7 May

Yesterday evening, the delightful *Rondo for Violin and Strings* by Schubert (very Mozartian). Yesterday and Sunday, a host of chance discoveries: a Haydn cello concerto (once on disc from Sofia, a second time from Berlin)—a concerto which, as I get to know it, is beginning to strike me as simplistic; a Mozart symphony which I don't think I knew; Beethoven's

Second Symphony, Haydn's *Clock Symphony*, a Vivaldi concerto for cello and violin, and so on.

Great financial difficulties, which I don't know how to overcome.

Lazy, dejected, unable to concentrate. I must think that I'll be called up again soon, and that free time will then be so precious to me.

Zoe keeps coming. Yesterday evening, Saturday evening—and I don't have the heart not to receive her.

Friday, 10 May

At dawn today the Germans occupied Luxembourg, crossed the Belgian and Dutch frontiers, and bombed the Brussels airport.

It is twelve o'clock, and I have no other news at the moment. This time, perhaps, the whole of Europe will be ablaze. There is a strange silence on the Italian stations, which broadcast trivial news items unrelated to the issues of the hour. I don't think it impossible that Mussolini will also strike in the Mediterranean, now that the Allies are probably reeling from the fresh blow. I am terribly afraid of what might happen in the next five days.

Tuesday 14 May

Liège has fallen. At least that is what the German communiqué says. The French one claims there is still strong resistance, but it does not actually deny that the city has been occupied.

In Holland things are continuing in the same way. The fall of Rotterdam is imminent, even according to the French communiqué.

The German attack has been devastating. A stunned desperation can hardly be concealed in the Allied dispatches. Italy too is preparing to enter the war. In Rome the classic "student demonstrations" are paving the way for a kind of popular enthusiasm to be put together. An Italian attack could happen any hour now—in Dalmatia, in Greece, in Switzerland, no one quite knows where.

There is no telling what lies ahead here. Will the Russians attack us? Will the Germans occupy us? Will we wake up one morning with parachute troops in Bucharest? Will we put up a fight? Will we still have time to fight?

Tomorrow morning I report to barracks again. Call-up.

Wednesday, 15 May

A very serious situation on the Franco-Belgian frontier. The Germans
have crossed the Meuse at a number of points, the thrust being especially powerful at Sedan. The tone in the press and in the Allied communiqués is very dejected. Maybe it is not a full-scale rout, but I can
feel a great despondency in all the Allied reports—even the sense of a
possible disaster. Some are speaking of a French capitulation: this is certainly untrue, and unlikely, but the idea is ceasing to be completely absurd, as it was before.

Holland capitulated last night. It is appalling—after just four days of
war! The German army appears devilish in its power to overwhelm resistance.

These events have affected me deep inside. I wish I had greater
courage, I wish I could spread more courage around me. I wish my spirits were stronger, more secure, less anguished. I can see Mama terrified,
Benu without hope (without hope at twenty-four, why? oh why?), and I
so much wish I could do something for them, tell them that nothing is
lost, that everything still can be, and one day will be, made up for.

I find the problems at the regiment too frightening. In my army life
my reactions have always been too catastrophist.

Thursday, 16 May

An exhausting day at the regiment. How hard it is for me to get back
into barracks life! This is my third call-up, yet I still find exasperating—
rather than comical, as I should—all the miseries of the first day after
"reporting for duty": the registration office, the allocation, the medical
checks, the counting up, the handing over of equipment, etc., etc.

Maybe it is a sign of childishness that I find all this tragic (or anyway humiliating, crushing, disfiguring), but the fact is that I suffer in the
barracks as in a hospital, a prison, or an asylum.

Today, moreover, I was alarmed at being mistaken for a deserter.
When I was eventually allocated to a new company (the Fourth, "fortifications"), I was at a disadvantage because the commanding officer did
not know me, and I had to face both a new warrant officer and an unfamiliar "program."

Everything was cleared up very late, at 9 p.m., when I was finally
able to "report to the colonel." But I was feeling most apprehensive, because for two hours (in the waiting room) I had heard him shouting in
his office, and at one point he had beaten a soldier there amid great up-

roar. When his voice called out for me, it shook me to the core. By some miracle, however, he was calm and jokey, gave me a friendly tap on the cheek, and ordered the mistake at the registration office to be put right tomorrow. Also tomorrow I'll be transferred to another company (maybe supplies?) so that I can remain in Bucharest and—as in the last call-up—occupy myself with the library.

What gave my day at the regiment its almost suffocating "anguish" was the awareness that, in those very hours, our whole destiny was being decided in France. This morning's news seemed even worse than last night's. But when I returned this evening from the regiment, I heard some heartening words from Paris and London. The battle ("the greatest in world history," say the papers) is still going on. In France the military resistance seems to be recovering its shape, if not yet its composure. No, nothing has yet been lost.

A little music, the only thing that calms me down after such a day: Beethoven's overture to *The Ruins of Rome* (?), Beethoven's *Romance for Violin and Orchestra*, and a Mozart violin sonata.

On that note, good night!

Saturday, 18 May

Yesterday and today the situation has become ever more serious, maybe even critical. In Belgium, one town after another has been abandoned: Louvain, Brussels, Antwerp. The Germans have announced that at Sedan they broke through the French fortified lines over a distance of a hundred kilometers. The French themselves do not categorically deny this, speaking of a wide "pocket" that the Germans have made in their defensive system.

The current formulation is that the final outcome depends upon this battle. Or, in plainer language, France's immediate fate depends upon it. If it can find a way out, it will gain time. If it can't, it loses everything.

What especially depress me are the signs of panic: no one is allowed to leave Paris (which means that everyone is jostling to escape); no one can cross the border into Spain (which may mean that the frontier is besieged by refugees); General Gamelin has issued a desperate order of the day, Marshal Pétain has been urgently summoned by Reynaud. On the other side, the German communiqués have the kind of triumphant air that nothing else can match. Their losses may have been large, but their successes are mind-boggling. And this is just the ninth day of war on the new front.

I think of Poldy and wonder where he might be. Perhaps the only desirable place, after all, is in the French army. At least he would feel he is taking part in this drama, that he is present and fighting. In a Sceaux in the throes of retreat and panic, what difficult hours, what desperate days he would be living through in his loneliness.

At my parents' I cannot and do not want to talk any more about the war. We all see eye to eye, without having to speak. We know that our whole life is at stake there, at the front.

The barracks are the only place where the war is neither seen nor felt, where it almost does not exist. From the colonel to the sergeant, everyone is busy cursing, fighting, raging, thundering. What a terrible factory for the wasting of time, energy, and work! Everything there is empty and futile.

I feel oppressed, disgusted, in a constant state of tension.

Sunday, 19 May

The Germans have reached Laon. Battles are taking place ten kilometers from Rheims. Half the way to Paris has already been covered. Today's German communiqué announced the capture of more than a hundred thousand prisoners. Reynaud said yesterday on the radio that the situation is "grave, but not desperate." And from Churchill this evening, "It would be madness to say that the situation is not grave, but even greater madness to think that we are lost."

It seems hard to judge the scale of the disaster. The news from the front is vague. The only precise facts are the names of places occupied by the Germans. The rest is impossible to follow. Everything is lost in an immense and confused battle, from which you cannot isolate any French initiative or detect any sign that the army of Gamelin (replaced this evening by General Giraud) has the situation under control.

Mrs. Tătărescu—according to Rosetti—said last night in despair that the French have lost 400,000 men.

It is all like a terrible nightmare, from which you expect to wake up. Lord, have mercy!

Monday, 20 May

Weygand has replaced Gamelin as commander-in-chief. There is great German pressure to the west, around Saint-Quentin. It is still impossible to tell how the battle will end. The initiative still lies with the Germans.

Oprescu, back from London and Paris, says that people are more calm and confident than they are here.

Tuesday, 21 May

Amiens and Arras fell today. The Germans report they have reached Abbeville and the Channel. A Franco-British-Belgian army of a million men is encircled. Boulogne, Calais, and Dunkirk are in this region.

At Rethel the Germans have captured General Giraud and the whole of his general staff.

It is disaster, collapse, perhaps the end.

Hour by hour I keep thinking of Poldy. I pray to the Lord that he will have the will to live, to resist, and to wait.

Friday, 24 May

I entered the barracks on Wednesday morning and did not leave again until yesterday evening at nine. The whole regiment was confined to barracks. Why? Because the colonel is not happy with the soldiers' "behavior" in town.

What horrified me was not so much that I went a couple of days without washing, shaving, eating, or sleeping as that I was out of the picture just when so many terrible events were taking place hourly.

I managed to phone Rosetti from time to time, and he told me that the French had retaken Arras. All sorts of news was circulating in the regimental yard: Gamelin had committed suicide, Giraud had been captured while asleep, the Germans were everywhere victorious.

I dragged myself around like a soul in torment. On the first day I had nothing to eat and didn't even feel hungry. I looked longingly at the gates and walls. At night I lay on the floor in the adjutancy, completely exhausted. But after an hour or two of stupor, I woke up at 1:30 and spent the rest of the night waiting open-eyed for dawn to break.

Regimental life is a crushing experience. Only in prison can people endure so much humiliation, so much mockery, so much stupid terror (not to be seen, heard, or asked questions). All the time I feel as if I am in a concentration camp.

By some miracle I do not understand, however, as soon as I walk out through the gates and cast off my army tatters, I forget everything.

Despite the optimistic tone of the Allied stations yesterday, the situation at the front appears to be extremely grave, even catastrophic. The Germans are at Calais. The really grave outcome now on the horizon is not that they will descend upon Paris, but that from Calais (and at this rate, Dunkirk's fall is probably not far off either) they will be able to cut all links between France and Britain.

All the attempts to boost morale are in vain. France is capable of not losing its head. It is no longer a question of nervous resistance, however, but of holding a force that has shown itself to be absolutely overwhelming. I look at the map and feel scared out of my wits.

Saturday, 25 May

No, Calais has not been taken—not yet, at least. I was confused by the map in yesterday's *Universul*, which I did not look at closely enough.

For the moment, the Germans have reached Boulogne but have not occupied the whole town. Their situation on the coast—according to French commentators—is "precarious." I am a little irritated by the Allies' habit of empathizing with the Germans whenever they have a victory, by using such words as "insecure," "adventurous," or "non-strategic." After all, it is such insecure advances that have brought them right up to the Channel!

Nevertheless, in the last two to three days the onslaught has been, if not halted, then somewhat retarded. Will a front be stabilized? Will a barrier finally be raised? I don't know. I greatly fear the German pauses, from which you never know what will burst forth.

During the two days of my confinement to barracks, grave and (for the moment) confused events have been taking place inside the country: a Legionary plot, an assassination attempt organized by a terrorist group recently returned from Berlin, arrests, and even, it is said, executions. If one adds the new and extensive call-ups, and the suspension of the Sixth of June celebrations,[3] the panic of yesterday and the day before becomes understandable. Today everything seems calmer.

The Italians are still wavering. They could enter the war tomorrow—but they may decide to postpone a decision, to give up their plans and change their attitude.

3. Commemoration of King Carol's return to power.

From Paris-Mondial, the Ravel quartet played by the Calvet. In the last few days I haven't been listening to any music. I have a horror of the German stations, which I cannot bear even when they play music. And now, apart from the war, nothing preoccupies me. I am obsessed with it.

Monday, 27 May

A letter from Poldy dated 18 May, when he left Sceaux for a "health instruction center" in I am not sure which region. In a previous letter he spoke of the Midi.

I think that, having enlisted, he will feel more up to facing the war, which has so far been so demoralizing for him, as a foreigner and a civilian, in a little town such as Sceaux.

The Germans report they have entered Calais. The French deny this but confirm they have given up Boulogne. With a delay of a day or two, all the German communiqués are proving to be true.

For the moment, however, the invasion has lost its virulent momentum. The advance is more difficult, more uncertain. But I don't yet dare to begin feeling hopeful.

I visited Uncle Avram at the home. He is disfigured, shriveled, stooping, infinitely old, looking more blind than ever, half dead already. But at the same time he is obsessed with a sum of money he has in state retirement income (111,547 lei, he said with amazing precision) and concerned about what to do with some written receipts: to whom should he give them? how should he hide them?

What a terrible people! In this respect at least, I do not resemble them at all.

I do not live: I vegetate, wait, endure. I go to the barracks, return home, go to bed. I cannot read or write—nor do I have any wish to write or read.

I am in a very bad physical state. I am running a kind of flu, which aggravates my idleness and disintegration. The only thing that still keeps me alert is the war. Otherwise I'd be in a state of slumber.

This afternoon from London, some beautiful works by Purcell: a sonata for two violins, and a chacony. I read with surprise the relevant chapter in Combarieu: it is incredible that he lived nearly a century before Handel and Bach, whom he seems to me to resemble so much. (Less austere, of course, and less capacious.)

Tuesday, 28 May

The King of Belgium capitulated at dawn today. Dunkirk is left wide open; maybe it has already fallen. Leopold's betrayal is humanly incomprehensible. A harrowing speech by Reynaud.

Stupor, gloom, bitterness deep inside me.

Friday, 31 May

The Army of the North is still resisting at Dunkirk and trying to take to the ships. Calais and Lille have fallen. There is no longer any talk of a possible linkup with the armies of the South. No one expects anything other than an end to the fighting in the north, through either capitulation or retreat, in the next twelve, twenty-four, or forty-eight hours. And then? I fear that the Germans will resume their attack on Paris, and even more that there is no stable front on the Somme. What has happened on the Meuse may be repeated on the Somme (more easily, because there are no fortifications there). It is possible that the Italians will await this new offensive before entering the war—an event they keep announcing and preparing.

I can no longer be "objective." The so-called "objectivity" that I see in so many people (Camil included) seems to me a way of accepting things, of reaching an accommodation with them. Almost everywhere, not only fear of the Germans but respect and even sympathy for them are on the rise. "What devils!"

People are stunned when they should be horrified.

I thought about this yesterday evening as I listened to Ion Marin Sadoveanu giving his impressions of Vienna (from which he had returned). For him the German victory is no longer in doubt. He claims that the Germans have so far committed only 4 percent of their resources (men, raw materials, food, etc.) to the war. All that drives me out of my wits, especially when it is explained "objectively" and even with a protective-melancholic feeling for the French: "I feel sorry for them, but there's nothing I can do."

Not for a moment does it occur to these objective minds that a German triumph will bring enslavement, their own enslavement.

But the difference is that whereas it will bring them only enslavement, it will bring us death. This is a difference that completely changes one's way of looking at things.

Sunday, 2 June

Dunkirk is still resisting. The Allied radio stations claim that most of the Army of the North has been shipped across to England. In any case, the resistance is exceeding expectations, and the disaster—which seemed immense after Leopold's surrender—has been somewhat attenuated.

. Now the fighting in the north is expected to end, and the next stage will become clearer. A new German offensive? An Italian attack in the Mediterranean? A pause?

I saw Dupront yesterday, and he reckoned that if the Germans want at all costs to break through at the Somme, they will break through—though it would mean very heavy casualties. He has a feeling that Weygand will try to wear the Germans down by making them pay a high price for *"quelques percées successives."* [4]

In general, my conversation with Dupront was highly instructive. He blames the French disaster on the powers-that-be: "general staff, civil service, diplomatic corps." He believes that a victorious France will emerge structurally changed at the end of the war.

Gafencu was replaced yesterday by Gigurtu. [5] This expresses politically the terrible wave of defeatism that has been sweeping the country for the last ten days. Actually, "defeatism" is not the right word. It is a kind of admiring, stunned acceptance of the German triumphs. And beneath the startled amazement that has held sway for a number of months, ever since the beginning of the war, the old Romanian anti-Semitism (with its eternal promise of deliverance) has been expectantly bubbling up.

Blank, Zissu—both terrified and cracking up—telephone me and invite me round. I am a little sick of my millionaire friends. I don't have money to pay the rent, and they are set on having abstract conversations.

On Friday I drew the last ten thousand lei for *Accidentul.* From now on I don't know what I'll do. If war comes it will find us without money, without food, without anything. If I knew that they would have enough to eat at home, things would feel a little easier to bear.

4. A few successive breakthroughs.
5. Ion Gigurtu: foreign minister and, from July to September 1940, prime minister. A pro-Nazi politician, close to Goering, he enacted racial legislation based on the 1935 Nuremberg laws.

Wednesday, 5 June

Dunkirk was occupied yesterday, and at dawn today the Germans launched their new offensive to the south, mainly along a line from Laon to Soissons. It is clear that they are aiming for Paris, which they bombed yesterday (250 people killed).

During the days that resistance continued in the north, I lived in a state of relative calm. It is true that the Allies suffered heavy casualties. But the fact that last week Dunkirk did not seem lost and was by some miracle actually resisting, as well as the fact that in the end 350,000 soldiers were carried to safety by sea, reduced the scale of the disaster and made it to some extent bearable.

Now, however, we are in another period of high tension. The Somme offensive seems to be as violent as that on the Meuse. The French communiqué this evening was confused, and I don't have the stomach to listen to the German one. The thought that Paris might fall takes my breath away. I don't have the courage to consider it full on, or to think it through to the end.

Sunday, 9 June

The situation is very serious. *"Nous sommes dans le dernier quart d'heure,"*[6] said Weygand in this morning's order of the day. Paris is in the zone of operations, and evacuation seems to have begun. Until yesterday the front seemed to be more or less holding. But in the evening twenty new German divisions went into action. The battle is terrible along the whole length of the front, from the sea to Montmédy, with the pressure especially acute at Soissons. I don't have a map of France and cannot follow the references in the communiqué. I can feel in it the effort not to give in, not to fall prey to despair, but there is no disguising the awful danger.

Poldy is at a training center in Toulouse, but we have no direct news of him.

Monday, 10 June

Yesterday German motorized columns reached Giross and Rouen! How much further is it to Le Havre? How much more to Paris? The French

6. "We are in the last quarter of an hour."

communiqué says by way of consolation that the Germans have not managed to cross . . . the Seine.

It is excruciating news.

And, as if a final humiliation were necessary, the British are departing in haste from Narvik.

You ask yourself how much longer the French will resist. You ask
yourself with dread whether everything is not going to collapse from one
hour to the next.

Nevertheless, somewhere deep inside me, I still hope and wait . . .

Midnight
Italy has declared war on France and Britain! Hostilities begin at midnight Italian time—that is, in ten minutes from when I am writing these
lines.

Reynaud made a short speech that was deeply despondent but also
deeply resolute. I listened to it with tears in my eyes. I could have cried,
but I stopped myself. I spent the evening at the French Institute, among
French people. It was a depressing yet consoling evening. No, I don't
believe everything is lost—I don't want to believe it, I can't.

So here we are cut off from Poldy. We have to accept that we will not
receive any letters, any news.

This evening the French communiqué was very grave. The Germans
have crossed the Seine at several points.

Tuesday, 11 [June]

The battle is taking place to the north, northwest, and northeast of Paris.
The city appears to be surrounded on three sides. Will it resist? For how
long?

The government has left for the provinces. The newspapers have
ceased publication. The Paris radio stations no longer operate. I can still
listen to Lyon P.T.T., with considerable difficulty, as well as to French
voices on shortwave that are no longer the familiar ones of Paris-Mondial.

Even now, however, I can pick up Radio Paris on longwaves: a symphonic concert conducted by Engelbrecht (a Liszt Mass). So, if I can still
hear an orchestra playing there, it means we are still not speaking of a
city that is about to fall in a few hours.

Yet the communiqué I heard a short while ago leaves no room for
hope, at least as far as Paris is concerned. A few times during the day,

at home and in the street, I felt like bursting into tears. I still find it impossible to grasp all that has happened, to believe that it is all true.

Friday, 14 [June]

Has Paris fallen? According to Radio London, Bullitt cabled at 2 a.m. that the Germans had entered the city. The French legation in London knows nothing. If I understood the news program just now in English, London was still in telephonic contact with Paris at seven o'clock this morning.

In any event, when I went to bed at eleven last night, Paris-Mondial was still broadcasting news and music. The Germans were thirty-two kilometers away from Paris. At one point the French were launching a counterattack. The situation was extremely grave, but it did not look as if everything would come to an end in the space of a few hours. Two days of resistance still seemed a possibility.

Reynaud spoke on the radio last night. It was a testament, a leave-taking, a final cry of despair—the kind of declaration that is made on the brink of surrender. The shock delivered to France appears to be mortal. The messages exchanged between London, Paris, and Washington are no longer even expressions of alarm. One might say that the situation has been accepted. There is more stupor than alarm.

Saturday, 15 [June]

Paris was occupied yesterday. The communiqué states that fighting is continuing to the east and west, but it does not say where. The Maginot Line has also come under violent attack. An attempt is being made to cut off French troops in Alsace-Lorraine from those in the rest of the country.

Surrender is starting to be mentioned: I don't believe it, I don't want to believe it. But the truth is that you can't see a front being put together that will hold.

Eugen Ionescu, who is back from Paris, says some disturbing things.

Mircea Vulcănescu, on the other hand, who has returned from London, believes that the Allies will end up victorious. In his view, it is a war that will be decided not in Europe but at sea.

Maybe, maybe . . . but meanwhile our lives are lost.

Sunday, 16 [June]

At Bordeaux the Council of Ministers is in almost permanent session. Yesterday evening, this morning, this afternoon . . . It may be that they are preparing a form of surrender. All the signs are that resistance has ceased. Even more depressing than the military disasters (the Maginot Line broken, Verdun occupied . . .) is the style of the communiqués. You would say there is no longer a high command, no longer a front, no longer any attempt to resist or to check the advance. In another three days, maybe five, it will all be over.

On the Eiffel Tower, the swastika. At Versailles, German sentries. At the Arc de Triomphe, the "unknown soldier" with a German "guard of honor."

But the terrible things are not the trophies or the acts of provocation: they could even arouse and maintain a will to survive among the French population. What scares me more is the "harmony" operation that is about to follow. There will be newspapers, declarations, and political parties that present Hitler as a friend and sincere protector of France. When that time comes, all the panic and all the resentments will find release in one long pogrom.

Where can Poldy be? What will he do? What will become of him? And what of us here?

Monday, 17 [June]

France is laying down arms!

Pétain, who replaced Reynaud last night, announced at two o'clock today that he will "attempt" to put an end to hostilities. Through the intermediary of Spain, he asked the Germans to inform him of the terms of surrender. Hitler is demanding unconditional surrender.

It is just as at the death of someone very close. You don't understand, you don't believe it has happened. Your mind has seized up, your heart no longer feels anything.

A few times the tears welled up inside me. I should like to be able to cry.

1941

Wednesday, 1 January 1941

I have lost the habit of keeping a journal, and now it is hard for me to recover it. Since the fall of Paris last June, when I decided not to write any longer (I felt disgust and, above all, a terrible sense of futility), I have tried only once, last October, to start keeping entries again, but I did not have sufficient perseverance.

You must have a certain energy, a certain stubbornness, to maintain a journal—at least at the beginning, until you get used to it and find the right tone. In the end, there is something artificial in the very fact of keeping a private diary; nowhere does the act of writing seem more false. It lacks the excuse of being a means of communication, just as it lacks any immediate necessity. (I remember that in Paris with Poldy, we never spoke French when we were alone, though we would have liked to do so for the sake of practice. It seemed to us unnatural, pretentious. To speak French freely, we needed to be constrained by the presence of someone who knew no other language.) There is some of the same embarrassment in the difficulty of writing "for myself." For if writing does not help me communicate with someone (whether through a letter, an article, or a book), it begins to seem—at least initially—absurd and lacking in personal depth.

Nevertheless, I regretted so many times not having the stoutness of heart to continue my journal over the last half-year. I needed to look with my eyes open at everything that was happening during that time. Now I think of my months "under arms" and do not seem to recapture their atmosphere of terror. I tell myself that I was close to death, I remember that several times I wanted to do away with myself—but now all that has been blotted out, become immaterial and almost incomprehensible. There was the night of my call-up, the departure from barracks, the seemingly unreal journey to Oltenița, the arrival one rainy dawn at the Valea lui Soare, the four weeks there, the repetitive scenes with Niculescu and Căpșuneanu, the brief leave of absence in Bucharest in early August (with the violent feeling that "life under arms" and "the other life" were two completely separate things, as if on two different planets). Then came the sudden return to Olteniţa, and that terrible night of 11 August 1940 in the railway station, like a nightmare in which the shouting voices of Căpşuneanu and Niculescu kept interrupting each other; the two nights and three days in the regimental train, the endless hours in Bucharest station, the long climb to the Prahova Valley and on to Braşov and Sighişoara, the crossing of Transylvania, the detour toward Lugoj; then the day in Lugoj station, the never-ending torture on the platform, the arrival in Boldur, the tragicomic night "changing our effects," and the rest of that fortnight in Boldur, culminating in the return home with a detachment of Jews. But the march from Boldur to Lugoj! The arrival at the regiment! The morning's work unloading the timber wagons! All this has now lost a lot of its intensity, at once tragic and grotesque. At the time I thought I would never erase from my mind the loathing, the disgust, the weariness. I ended up in a kind of stupor, which made me receive unprotesting, as in a dream, all the blows that rained down one after another: my exclusion from the Bar, my dismissal from the Foundation,[1] my assignment to an agricultural work detachment.[2]

Maybe I should have written about all these things; maybe it would have been good to keep them in my memory. One day I shall try to reconstruct them—and it will be hard to come up with anything but faded images and withered words. Even the November earthquake is beginning to grow distant. As long as my studio flat still bore traces of the disaster—cracked walls, bare bricks, fallen plaster—I kept an image of that terrible night. But now, after the repairs and redecoration, it is as if nothing had ever happened.

It was a tragic, nightmarish year full of terrors, miseries, and unhappiness—and yet I finished it last night without despair. With horror, but without despair. I still hope, I still believe. In June, when Paris fell, everything seemed lost and gone forever. Today it seems that life will be possible in a distant future. Even that is a lot.

Happy New Year![3] Perhaps it won't be "happy": we shouldn't ask too

1. Immediately after the Iron Guard took power together with General Antonescu on 6 September 1940, Jews were excluded from employment by all government agencies.

2. The Iron Guard legislation excluded Jews from military service but organized army-supervised forced labor for them.

3. In English in the original.

much. But if our lives are spared, maybe the light will be closer, the shore within closer reach, when we come to the end of this next year.

Thursday, 2 January

This morning I met Cioran in the street. He was glowing.

"They've appointed me."

He has been appointed cultural attaché in Paris.

"You see, if they hadn't appointed me and I'd remained where I was, I would have had to do military service. I actually received my call-up papers today. But I wouldn't have gone at any price. So like this, everything has been solved. Do you see what I mean?"

Of course I do, dear Cioran. I don't want to be nasty with him. (Especially not here—what good would it do?) He is an interesting case. He's more than a case: he's an interesting person, remarkably intelligent, unprejudiced, and with a twin dose of cynicism and idleness, combined in an amusing manner.

I should have liked—and it would have been worthwhile—to record in greater detail the two conversations I had with him in December.

I have a temperature of 38 [101 F.]. A bad start to the year.

Sunday, 5 January

Still ill. The day before yesterday I had 39 degrees [102 F.] plus; yesterday and today, between 37 and 38. Nights of fever, insomnia, nightmares. The night before last I dreamed of an unreal Balcic, yellow and red. "This is like Gauguin," I remember remarking in the dream. Last night, in the grip of fever, I firmly promised myself to write the play with Gunther (who has been coming very alive again), and I sketched the scenario of another play. I was dizzy and exhausted—and I didn't manage to get out of bed, as I wanted, to jot down a few things in this connection. Today writing—literature—again seems to me a stupid gesture. A brackish taste, one of futility.

Terrible news from Bz.

Wednesday, 8 January

Still ill. I don't even know if I can think of myself as on the mend. I no longer have a fever, but I am recovering slowly and with difficulty.

Eugen Ionescu, who visits me now and then, is anxious to leave the country as soon as possible, to run away. It is the same panic as Cioran's, the same alarm, the same haste to escape the country as quickly as possible, to find a refuge. Strange that I've never thought of running away (since the fall of Paris)—except as a mere nostalgic dream, which does not bind me to do or even plan anything.

Yesterday evening and this morning I read Shaw's *Androcles and the Lion*. I laughed a lot.

Tuesday, 14 January

I had a restless evening, without knowing exactly why. I feel obscure threats—as if the door were not shut properly, as if the window shutters were transparent, as if the very walls could be seen through. From anywhere, at any moment, it is possible that some unspecified dangers will rush in—dangers I have always known to be present, but to which I have grown so used that I no longer feel them. Then suddenly everything becomes overwhelming, suffocating. You'd like to shout for help—but from whom? With what voice? With what words?

Friday, 17 January

A phrase written by Giraudoux in 1938 and read by me today: *"ce pays que rien ne menace et qui vit dans l'obsession de la guerre"*!![4]

On Wednesday, an evening of phonograph records at Lena Constante's.[5] Ravel's *Quartet*, Franck's *Sonata*, a Beethoven piano concerto, some of Bach's *Goldberg Variations*, some piano pieces by Mozart.

Somnolence, apathy, defenseless fear—that's almost everything. From time to time I make promises to read and write something—but they all soon collapse, without any enthusiasm, spirit, or conviction.

Tuesday, 21 January

Revolution? Coup d'état? On Saturday night a German major was murdered on Bulevardul Brătianu. It is not yet known whether it was an assassination or a street incident. If, as some are saying, the man who fired

---

4. "This country that nothing threatens and that lives in the obsession of war."
5. Artist, friend of Sebastian's.

was not some "Greek subject" but the former boxing champion Axiotti, there is more likely to have been some quarrel or argument at the bottom of things. Maybe an affair of the heart.

Anyway, what happened was not directly connected to the political events of yesterday morning. The morning papers published a decree that disbanded the Romanianization commissars. In the afternoon I heard that General Petrovicescu[6] has been replaced at the Interior Ministry. Toward evening a student manifesto came out calling for: 1) the removal of Rioşanu,[7] blamed for being the man behind the major's killing and an Anglo-masonic puppet; 2) the reinstatement of General Petrovicescu; and 3) a government made up entirely of Legionaries.

After ten in the evening, some five to six thousand Legionaries demonstrated on Calea Victoriei, chanting, "Down with Rioşanu! We want a Legionary government! Masons out of the government!"

At midnight the student manifesto was broadcast on the radio. This morning's papers, which appeared later than usual, published not the manifesto but the decree replacing the minister of the interior, plus (except in *Cuvântul*) a note from General Antonescu explaining that the change had been necessary to restore order and to avoid an economic slump. As I went home about one o'clock, the traffic on Calea Victoriei was interrupted between Alcalay and the Deposit Bank. It seems that police headquarters had been occupied by Legionaries and was now under army siege. When I returned at about four o'clock, the situation was the same. In the evening, Rosetti told me that the regional prefects had been changed overnight throughout the country. General Antonescu has issued an appeal to the country: "Order will be restored in twenty-four hours!"

It is nearly midnight. From time to time I hear groups of Legionaries passing beneath my window, singing in chorus on their way to the Ateneu or the Finance Ministry. Yet the city appears very quiet. On the radio, a presidential communiqué tells people not to go outdoors after ten o'clock.

This evening I finished La Fontaine's *Fables*—which I have been reading with delight for some time. The last fable, with its invitation to solitude, is a conclusion to the whole collection.

6. General Constantin Petrovicescu: was the pro–Iron Guard minister of the interior in the first government of Ion Antonescu (September 1940–January 1941). When the Iron Guard rebelled against Antonescu, Petrovicescu was dismissed.

7. Colonel Alexandru Rioşanu: head of Siguranţa (the state security police), sided with Antonescu in the conflict with the Iron Guard. Later he was governor of Bukovina.

Cette leçon sera la fin des ouvrages
Puisse-t-elle être utiles aux siècles à venir.[8]

Wednesday, 22 January

9:30 p.m.

Alone. The telephone has been cut off since midday. Powerless to know what is happening at home, at Strada Antim. I'd like to be able to say a word to Mama. I'd like to hear her speak. I try to think of the moments of fear they are experiencing there. I regret that I was not sufficiently resolute this morning—when I still had the chance—to run to their place and stay there. With us all together, the waiting might have been easier. I absolutely promise to go there tomorrow, if there is a "tomorrow," so that, whatever happens, we shall be together.

The shooting never ends. You can hear rifles, machine guns, and a few artillery blasts. In the morning the noises were a long way off, apparently on the outskirts of the city. Then they drew closer to the center. When I went out at one o'clock, the buses were no longer running. I had a few moments of hesitation: should I go to Strada Antim or not? It did not seem possible to get beyond Bulevardul Elisabeta, and so I came home and decided to stay put. I managed to call home and tell them I wasn't coming—then all the telephones went dead. The street, on the other hand, remained lively, almost normal. Around four I saw some soldiers taking up positions at Piața Amzei, and a cordon directly opposite our block on Calea Victoriei. Around five the shooting started. I couldn't follow exactly what was happening, because all the balconies had to be immediately cleared. I just saw several hundred demonstrators coming from the direction of the Palace. I went into my room, leaving the door to the terrace ajar. The gunfire did not obscure people's voices. They were shouting, singing, vociferating. Two or three voices (always the same ones) stood out from the tumult: "Don't shoot—we are your brothers!"

It all lasted an hour. Then the demonstrators went off singing—I couldn't see whether they were being driven back toward the Ateneu, or whether they were passing through the cordon and approaching the finance ministry. I went onto the terrace. Down below, next to the pharmacy, there was a lake of blood and a lighted candle on the pavement. I went down for a moment to ask the doorman exactly what had hap-

---

8. This lesson will mark the end of this work/May it be useful for the centuries to come.

pened. He said that a soldier had been killed, and that the troops—who had all the time been firing into the air—then moved back and let the Legionaries through. The street was filled with people looking dazed, disoriented, and—did it only seem so to me?—rather indifferent. I went back upstairs. It would have been absurd to try going any farther. I switched on to Radio Bucharest: the broadcast was normal until 7:45, when neither the news in German nor the interval signal followed. After a long gap of ten or fifteen minutes, a voice announced that the Legion would be victorious, that in Constanța, Tecuci, and Craiova a large part of the army had sided with the Legionary revolution, and that the Judaized ministers (Mihai Antonescu,[9] Cancicov,[1] Mareș[2]) would pay, along with the traitors (Dimitriuc[3]). So the radio is in the hands of the Legionaries. The newspapers that have appeared—even the non-Legionary ones (*Evenimentul, Seara*)—publish Legionary manifestos. There is not a word anywhere about General Antonescu. Yesterday evening, in a statement read over the radio (when it was still under his control), he said that order would be restored within twenty-four hours.

And now? Anything is possible tonight. It's only eleven o'clock—still eight hours until daylight. Will I sleep? Can I try to sleep? I am so alone, and all my thoughts are at home with Mama, Benu, and Tata. The city is pitch dark, the telephones do not answer, the radio is silent.

Thursday, 23 January

10 a.m.
The machine guns and artillery kept at it all night. I slept with sudden awakenings and short, intricate dreams. Whenever I woke up, I found the same sound of gunfire. There was complete silence in my building, as on an ordinary night. At daybreak the roaring was more powerful, more frequent. Then the noise abated. At nine o'clock I switched on the radio; the usual announcer (not yesterday's unfamiliar one) said that official broadcasts would be made each hour. So the radio station was reoccupied by the army during the night. General Antonescu has issued a new manifesto in which he declares that, given the rebel attacks on the presidency and other institutions, the state apparatus and the army have automatically swung into action. He advises everyone to defend them-

9. Mihail A. Antonescu: minister of justice in the first Antonescu government, soon to become deputy prime minister and minister of foreign affairs.
1. Mircea Cancicov: economics minister in the first Antonescu government.
2. Nicolae Mareș: minister of agriculture.
3. Victor Dimitriuc: deputy economics minister in charge of oil and mining.

selves if they are attacked at home. A communiqué from the general staff denies that there have been any defections from the army.

I go out onto the terrace. It is a hazy morning, as in autumn. The shops are open, but not many people are in the streets. Some groups stand peacefully in conversation. A special edition of some paper or other has been published. On my terrace there are debris and brick dust. A bullet must have hit my wall last night, above and to the right of the door. I can see perfectly the hole it made in the wall.

Friday, 24 January

I have been to Strada Antim, where I spent the whole of last night and this morning. Being together, we did indeed feel calmer. We hugged each other, as after a very long separation.

Yesterday at about 11 a.m. (just after I had written the previous entry), a procession started along Calea Victoriei and on toward the Şosea—long motorized German columns, with rifles and machine guns at the ready. They certainly made an impression. And it was crystal-clear that the German army was on the side of General Antonescu against the insurgent Legion. When I went out I found both this morning's *Cuvântul*, with intransigent calls for revolution, and a special edition of the same *Cuvântul* published a few hours later, containing Sima's order to cease fighting. Nevertheless, isolated shots—even some bursts of machine-gun fire—could still be heard. I went into a couple of stores to do some shopping. People were still bright and breezy in their "Bucharestian" way, more curious than terrified. Now and then pensive faces, shrugging of the shoulders: "Let's just have some peace and quiet," "So long as things calm down."

At two in the afternoon, Alice came in a car to take me to Strada Antim. She was with Comănescu (one of her Legionary types), who was haggard, taciturn, docile. Only now, as we drove through the city, could I see tangible evidence of revolution. On Calea Victoriei, below Naţional, there was an air of complete desolation. Tanks, machine guns, and army patrols on a deserted main street with shutters drawn. I heard from Alice that the Văcăreşti and Dudeşti districts had been set on fire and looted during the night. The same seems to have happened on Calea Rahovei and in many other parts.

By nightfall the shooting had completely stopped. Clear, reassuring communiqués were read over the radio. Everyone had twenty-four hours to hand in any firearms, even hunting rifles. Anyone who continued to fire weapons or to pillage would be shot on the spot. The only remaining danger came from robbers in the smaller side streets. Alice—kind, enterprising, and generous, but hotheaded and (as she so often is) childish and a little crazy—came back later to Strada Antim and kept insisting that she would drive us all home. But we remained there, barricading ourselves in as best we could. The telephone, to our great relief, started working again in the evening, and suddenly we felt less alone. But this did not stop us from jumping at the slightest sound during the night.

Both yesterday evening and this morning, the telephone never stopped ringing. People wanted to make sure we were still alive, to confirm that nothing serious had happened, that it had "blown over." Apparently there have been a lot of casualties, but you can't find out yet how many. The revolt has undoubtedly been quashed as an "armed coup." Sima has issued a new order, making outlaws of those who continue fighting. People are falling over themselves to disclaim allegiances and retract opinions. The general appears inflexible: not a word that suggests hesitation. He has announced harsh penalties for leaders and instigators. The fallen soldiers will be buried tomorrow with great solemnity, the rebels also tomorrow, but "without any honors." Things are still very confused politically. Who will be in the new government? The general has announced a reorganization of the Guard under his own direct leadership, but it is not yet known which people he will rely on to do this. The German attitude also remains to be explained: it must have stunned the life out of them in the ranks of the Guard. I am thinking of Ghiţă Racoveanu, or Haig, Cioran, Dinu Noica, Mircea Eliade (lucky as ever, if he's still in London).

It was a minor event, then, which fortunately had no consequences (up to now, at least) yet explains a lot of other things. Yesterday morning, candles were burning opposite our building at the corner by the Thoiss pharmacy, where one of the soldiers fell. Passersby stopped and asked about him. Agitated little groups looked toward our building, running their eyes up its nine floors and down again, with a strange expression of wonder and menace. When I went out, I also walked up to one group (new ones were forming all the time). In the middle of five or six passersby, I glimpsed that poor madman who once used to wander with a switch and whistle from one streetcar to the next, giving imaginary signals for it to stop or start, and who often came up to Maryse's Ford in the evening and offered to keep an eye on it (Maryse used to give him a few coppers). Well, that stuttering half-wit was telling how "a yid woman fired with a revolver last night, from the roof of that building over there—and a trooper was hit."

"A yid woman, you say?" asked an elderly gentleman, quite well dressed, quite unruffled.

"Yeah, one o' them yid bitches!"

"And didn't they do anything to her?"

"You bet they did. They arrested her, took her away."

I looked closely at the people listening. Not one of them did not believe what was being said; not one had the least doubt about the truth of this absurd story. For a moment I thought of interrupting and saying something myself: that it was all completely stupid; how could they imagine that a Jew, especially a woman, could be so mad as to fire with a revolver from the roof (!!) of a nine-story building, or that she could have aimed so precisely from that distance? Did they not know that the soldier fell yesterday in a real street battle, in which hundreds of bullets were fired? But what was the point of asking these questions? Who would have listened? Who would have tried to think rationally? Isn't it easier and quicker to believe what others tell you?—"A yid woman opened fire."

I walked on to do my shopping. When I came back, other passersby were talking about the same thing. But this time the "yid" was a man, not a woman; some said he had been captured, others that he had not; some specified that he fired from the fourth floor (where no one has lived since the earthquake), others that no one knows where he fired from. I think someone suggested making inquiries in the building, or expressed surprise that this had not already been done. Later I spent a little while at the window, watching how the news spread, how the groups became larger and more agitated. Was it far short of an attack on all the Jewish apartments in the building? Look, that's how a pogrom begins.

Tobruk has fallen. It happened the day before yesterday, but the news came from so far. It seemed so remote to us, for whom everything could be over in a flash!

Saturday, 25 January

Not much news. The Legionary papers have been closed down. (Again I think of the fate of *Cuvântul*.) A new declaration from the General [Antonescu] explains how the revolt and the repression unfolded. The street still does not seem the same as usual where the fighting took place. In the imposing square before the National Theatre, the shop fronts and the big windows of the central telephone exchange are riddled with bul-

lets. In Văcărești and Dudești,[4] apparently, everything is like after a big
earthquake or a terrible fire. The number of dead is still not known.
Hundreds or thousands of Jews—but no one can say exactly.[5] Nor is it
known how many soldiers died, or how many Legionaries. Maybe the
count has not yet been made.

Troops and tanks are still moving about the streets. The last buildings in which Legionaries took refuge are being cleared. This morning,
on Bulevardul Elisabeta, I witnessed the occupation and emptying of the
Regal cinema—until now a Legionary stronghold. The city is dead after
ten in the evening, with shows prohibited after nine; the restaurants are
closed and no one is allowed to move around. But during the day, people are lively, talkative, full of curiosity, and in the end relieved. This
also has something to do with the incredibly fine weather, as on a sunny
day in late March, except that it is mid-January. Especially in the morning, the streets are as packed as on a public holiday. People embrace each
other, noisily exchange greetings, ask each other questions. At the barber's today everyone was talking about what happened in tones of approval, surprise, excitement. Mr. Costel, the owner, said that "the army
was a match for the situation," and that "those Legionaries are a bunch
of criminals."

Yesterday Cioran said to Belu that the "Legion wipes its arse with this
country." This is more or less the same as what Mircea said at the time
of the Călinescu repression: "Romania doesn't deserve a Legionary movement," when nothing would have satisfied him but the country's complete disappearance.

Haig presented himself this morning at the office—*comme si de rien n'é-
tait*.[6] More amusing is the fact that Gyr[7] did the same thing, having made
intransigent speeches the day before yesterday in the Theatre square.
Now comes the moment for telegrams of devotion.

Sacha Roman spent all three days of the revolt in the cells at police headquarters, arrested by Legionaries. Very many Jewish prisoners were killed.
He had a miraculous escape. Pity that, being a vain and "pretentious"
man, he does not know how to keep his story simple.

4. Jewish neighborhoods in Bucharest, heavily damaged during the Iron Guard rebellion that turned into a pogrom.
5. The Iron Guards killed 121 Jews during their rebellion against General Antonescu.
6. As if nothing had happened.
7. Radu Demetrescu Gyr: poet and fanatical follower of the Iron Guard.

Sunday, 26 January

Lassaigne called round yesterday and told me some priceless details. On Thursday he was at a key point, on Balkan Federation Square, a few dozen meters from the Legion's headquarters on Strada Roma. The square was literally blocked by Legionary demonstrators. Some German motorized units arrived and were greeted enthusiastically. The Legionaries shouted, applauded, acclaimed: "Heil Hitler! Duce, Duce, Duce, Duce! Sieg Heil, Sieg Heil!" Without saying anything, the Germans took up position at the entrance to each of the streets leading into the square: Roma, Sofia, Londra, etc. The demonstrators constantly shouted their acclaim, convinced that the Germans had come to their aid. The troops kept arriving, greeted with the same enthusiastic cries. But then what a stunning blow! Once all the exits had been closed and the encirclement was complete, an officer ordered the demonstrators to leave. And everyone left. Just like that.

I had a talk with Camil about the events. It would be quite funny to note the variations in his attitude over the last few days. But that is not what I want to write about now. On Wednesday evening things were at fever pitch at Cîmpineanu 58. Camil had lost his head (he who loses it so easily). The only other person in the whole building was Marietta Rareş. The other Marietta and Haig were at the theatre, "on the barricades." Much later Marietta Sadova, looking pale, haggard, and tearful, arrived from the Presidency where she and Codreanu's wife had tried in vain to gain an audience with the General. "They've started shelling us!" shouted Marietta (how well I can hear her voice!). But she was no less certain of victory. "Everything is in our hands. General Dragalina is on his way to Bucharest. General Coroamă is on our side. Antonescu is lost." I think of the bewilderment she must have felt the next morning, when she heard how much things had changed overnight.

No definite news about the development of the political situation. Who has been arrested and who not, who sides with the regime and who is leaving—we know nothing at all.

Monday, 27 January

Yesterday afternoon I went with Lereanu and Comşa to see the "battle-fields." It is clear that there was a lot of shooting in the air. Apart from a few bullet-scarred buildings on Strada Londra, nothing indicates that there have been major battles. Neither the Legionary headquarters on Strada Roma nor even the Guards' barracks (which is said to have been shelled) are seriously damaged. The greater disaster was in Văcărești, and especially Dudești, where not one house or makeshift hut escaped plunder and burning. Try to imagine the district ablaze on Wednesday night while gangs of hooligans went round shooting all those terrified people. Here and there, a few premises with Romanian names have been left standing. But the "Romanian Shop" notice on a window or wall did not always stave off disaster. You can see quite a few devastated houses and shops with a sign that, by a sad irony, was supposed to protect them: "Christian Property," "Romanian House," "Romanian Owner," or even— somewhere in Văcărești—"Italian Property." Yesterday, Sunday, was the fourth day since the cataclysm, so a lot of the damage would have been concealed or removed. But it is still an overwhelming sight. And all this has hit the poorest of the poor, living in the most wretched conditions— small-scale craftsmen and traders, humble, careworn people barely able to scratch out a living. Here and there, beside the ruins, you see an old woman or a near-naked child crying and waiting. Waiting for what? for whom? In front of the morgue, hundreds of people wait in line; there are so many missing, so many unidentified corpses. Today's *Universul* is full of Jewish obituaries; the cemeteries are full of fresh graves. The number of dead Jews is still not known—several hundred, in any event.

Today, as yesterday, there is no official statement, no news, no indications. Is this hesitation? Reticence? Fear? A change of attitude? Compromise? An attempt to reach a deal? It's a strange silence that allows anything to be assumed.

Last night I dreamed of Nae Ionescu. He was headmaster of the school in Brăila, I one of the pupils (though at my present age). He stopped me downstairs, to the left of the staff room, and shook my hand. Then he said: Don't be surprised or angry if I sometimes don't answer your greeting as I do that of any other pupil. But the dream was longer and more complicated, with many other characters.

Evening
The dead soldiers were buried today. There were seventeen of them: two officers (a major in the geographical section, a captain in the medical corps), a platoon commander T. R. [reduced service] and fourteen sergeants, corporals, and privates. Very few, fortunately, for three days of revolt in which there was a lot of shooting on both sides. The number of casualties among the Legionaries is also probably not as high as rumor would have it. (There was talk of six thousand! Absurd!) The real figure is not known.

The new government has been formed. All its members are generals with the exception of Crainic[8] at Propaganda, an appeals judge at Justice, and a doctor at Health. The only civilian remaining from the old cabinet is Mihai Antonescu, now without portfolio. Of course, the Legionaries will interpret Rioşanu's departure as a concession to themselves. Otherwise no indication of how things will develop.

Music. I have listened to a lot of things recently, at least on the calmer days. Brahms's *Piano Concerto* (to which I must return: I had thought it was boring, but as I get to know it I feel closer to it), a trio in B minor, and a quintet. A beautiful Beethoven serenade, and this evening his *Ninth Symphony*. I enjoyed listening to Tchaikovsky's piano concerto (I didn't recognize it, but I guessed it was by a Russian from the last century— most likely Glazunov). Franck's symphonic variations. Chausson's symphony (surprised I knew it so well, and that it was so beautiful). Finally, last night, a Mozart serenade that I didn't know before. With the *Kleine nachtmusik* and the serenade for two orchestras, that makes his third serenade I know. Also a symphony I didn't know (No. 29—or 31!—the "Paris").

During the days of the revolt, I read only Shaw and Molière; Shaw's *Fanny's First Play*. Now I'm on Act Two of *Man and Superman*. Coping quite well with it from the language point of view.

Wednesday, 29 January

The official toll of civilian deaths was published today: a little over three hundred. It does not mention how many Legionaries, how many Jews. The figure seems too low. It is still being said that more than six thousand Jews died. But maybe it will never be possible to know for sure. Many Jews were killed in Băneasa forest and dumped there (most of them naked), but another batch seems to have been executed at the Străuleşti abattoir. In both cases it is likely that they were horribly mutilated before being killed. Jacques Costin's brother could hardly be recognized at the morgue by his relatives; he had four holes in the head alone. Beiler, the lawyer, was riddled with bullets, and his throat had been cut.

There were some miraculous escapes. (Aderca, almost comical in his naiveté, went knocking on the door of a den of Legionaries at Strada Burghelea 3, like a peaceable citizen in search of information! He was

---

8. Nichifor Crainic: extreme right-wing journalist, author of a xenophobic and racist National Christian fundamentalist theory.

freed that evening, beaten up but alive, whereas others were killed in the same place on the same day.) The most amazing of all the cases I have heard is that of a lawyer, Mircea Beiner, who was grabbed off the street on Tuesday morning, taken to Băneasa, shot in the back of the head, and left for dead in the snow in the middle of the night; but early next morning he was awakened by the cold. Among hundreds of corpses, only himself and three others had not been finished off. Quite incredible!

Biberi,[9] who was in Turnu Severin at the time of the revolt, says it was so calm that if you didn't have a radio, you were not even aware that anything unusual was happening in the country. The Legionaries there gave themselves up immediately, like so many sheep.

Haig was arrested yesterday. This evening, Camil tells me, their house was searched from top to bottom. But I don't think that anything will happen to either Haig or Marietta. Nothing ever does to revolutionaries of their ilk. I met Cioculescu and Streinu[1] yesterday; they were very happy with events, not at all worried about how things would turn out. I could not say the same myself: I have all manner of doubts and fears. In my view, the regime is wavering and giving ground as it concocts a formula for temporizing appeasement. The difference between Cioculescu and me is that his judgment is "detached" whereas mine is made with the knowledge that my life is at stake in what is going on around us. I am beginning to think that, at least in moments of major crisis, "detachment" is not the best vantage point from which to understand things.

Thursday, 30 January

I see devastated houses, pillaged shops on absolutely non-Jewish streets that I would not have thought the pogrom could have reached in a single night. For example, this morning I saw a wretched little workshop on Strada Traian, beside the Tabacu streetcar stop, and again I trembled at the thought of what might have happened at home on Wednesday night. Some people, like myself, spent that night apart from their family—and the next morning they found no one left, nothing left. I see and feel again all the horror of that night.

Derna fell this morning.

In Berlin this afternoon, Hitler made a long speech in which he declared that he would win the war in the course of this year.

9. Ion Biberi: writer.
1. Vladimir Streinu: literary critic.

Tuesday, 4 February

I cannot (and would not wish to) forget the horrors through which I have lived. For the last few days, all I have read are the chapters in Dubnow's *History of the Jews* about the great pogroms of the late Middle Ages. Whether the official figure is correct (three hundred Jews killed) or the much higher one that people mention in whispers (six hundred to one thousand), the fact is that we have experienced one of the worst pogroms in history. It is true that there have been moments in the past when the butchery was greater (during the First Crusade, eight hundred were killed in Speyer, eleven hundred in Mainz—and again very many in 1348, at the height of the Black Death), but the average for a single pogrom was usually much smaller—fifty, eighty, or a hundred dead is the kind of figure that appears in Jewish martyrology, and Dubnow sometimes writes at length about smaller losses that have nevertheless remained in memory.

The stunning thing about the Bucharest bloodbath is the quite bestial ferocity of it, apparent even in the dry official statement that ninety-three persons ("person" being the latest euphemism for Jew) were killed on the night of Tuesday the 21st in Jilava forest. But what people say is much more devastating. It is now considered absolutely certain that the Jews butchered at Străulești abattoir were hanged by the neck on hooks normally used for beef carcasses. A sheet of paper was stuck to each corpse: "Kosher Meat." As for those killed in Jilava forest, they were first undressed (it would have been a pity for clothes to remain there), then shot and thrown on top of one another. I haven't found anything more terrible in Dubnow.

There have been countless Adolf Hitlers throughout Jewish history. Favorable surroundings and critical moments were all they lacked for their local action to become worldwide policy, but in terms of ideology, methods, and style there is hardly any difference between them and the Führer. A certain Zimberlin in the fourteenth century, whose very similar movement in Strasbourg had its own uniforms (a strip of fur on the shoulder) and veritable assault battalions—the so-called *Armleder*. Two centuries later in Austria and Bohemia, another, more plebeian movement—called the *Rindfleisch*—was reduced to mere hooliganism. Most interesting and most significant, however, was the anti-Semitic, agrarian-based political and social movement led by Vinzenz Fettmilch in 1614 in Frankfurt.

I think there is much else besides to be learned from Dubnow.

People are never more interesting than at moments of sudden political change. Overnight they abjure, modify, attenuate, explain, fall into line, justify themselves, overlook what they do not care to see, remember when it suits them. If this is all done with a little cynicism, it is still bearable. But there is a demon of consistency that forces people to show that both yesterday, when they were for the old regime, and today, when they are against it, their attitude has remained "in principle" the same. No one beats Camil in this respect. Sometimes he is amusing: no one is more disoriented than he is, more convulsed with fear, more hysterical at moments of uncertainty, more catastrophic in his forebodings—and then, with his old triumphant smile, he explains not only that he foresaw everything but that he could have prevented it "if people had listened" to him. To the Legionaries he gave every banal assurance (that too, though, via second fiddles, secondhand women, young down-and-outs). He didn't even hesitate to write, and then spread around "confidentially," his deplorable September memorandum in which he showed that he had always been a Legionary and that, though he had been friendly with me, so too had Nae Ionescu (which was no doubt enough for it to become a precedent in case law).

But today he claims, as stoutly as ever, that he was never a Legionary and that (in his own words) he could not feel better than under the present regime, which is the regime of national values.

The most pronounced feature in that man is his blithe lack of awareness—for only that can explain how he can talk about something he did a while back without realizing how odious it was. When Poldy Stern[2] asked him to take home some personal papers and hide them, not only did he refuse, but he telephoned and reported it to Zăvoianu, the chief of police at the time, adding that he, Camil Petrescu, declined all responsibility and could not say for sure whether the papers in question were merely business contracts or dollars! What a vile act of denunciation! And Camil does not even have the awareness to understand this and to take fright!

A month ago, when Zoe left my place at night, she almost never forgot to remind me that no one should know we were seeing each other. "You see, my brothers are Legionaries, and I don't want to make things awkward for them." But today she rang me, asked me to go round, and when

2. Leopold (Poldy) Stern: lawyer and writer, friend of Sebastian's.

I hesitated on leaving to pass through her brother's room (he being there), she told me not to worry.

"Go on, darling. What does it matter?"

Indeed, it doesn't at all.

Haig is still under arrest.[3] Yesterday Margareta Papagoga—who is also acting at the National Theatre—told me some funny things about the satisfaction with which people there learned of Haig's departure, and especially of the much-hated Marietta's sudden downfall. It has been impossible to collect signatures for a petition in support of Haig. (He seems to be in a serious predicament because he allowed speeches to be made from a megaphone attached to his balcony. Frankly, I think it will be sorted out, and there is no way Haig will be made a martyr. Nor would I want him to be.)

It was a terrible thing that Naταşa Alexandra said aloud at a rehearsal in Marietta's presence: "Wherever the General is, I kiss his balls, I suck his cock, for delivering us from the Legionaries." You can't get more enthusiastic than that!

Thursday, 6 February

I keep thinking of my play about the Grodeck family. I should make up my mind to write. A few months ago the idea of writing literature would have seemed to me an aberration, and in fact even today I wouldn't dare or feel like writing anything other than plays—that is, slightly mechanical pieces that you do somehow "by rote." "Grodeck" would be especially easy to write, both because the first two acts, like the scenario, are already clearly defined, and because, by contrast, the direction, meaning, and denouement of the last act—or the last two, if there are four altogether—are still very uncertain. Thus, having set out with firm ground under my feet, I would have enough space ahead of me for surprises and enough room for maneuver.

But I should make up my mind. How much longer will my relative liberty persist? By spring, will things be as favorable for solitude, reading, and writing as they are now? Are not fresh calamities in store right now, without our yet being able to see them?

For some time now (several years) I have been thinking of a comedy that takes place in the editorial offices of a newspaper. At first I imag-

---

3. Haig Acterian was sentenced to prison for his participation in the Iron Guard rebellion. Like many other Iron Guards in the same situation, he was freed on the condition that he would volunteer for duty on the eastern front.

ined a simple one-act comedy set on a summer's day (1928–1929) at the height of the political holiday season, with no events, no news, a short print run, bored reporters not paid for weeks, expectations about a major political figure who has been at death's door for some time and whose final passing will require a special edition that is already set and waiting to roll. The obituary is written, the photograph measured to page, the biography assembled—only the dead man does not want to die. And this goes on for several days.

Suddenly there is a sensational event (I'm not yet sure whether a murder or a tempestuous romance), which makes the whole staff sit up and momentarily gives the paper all its old bustle. When the telephone rings with the news that the famous dignitary has finally passed away, the editor briefly orders it to be mentioned somewhere on the back pages—and the curtain falls.

Not much of a story, you might say. But I would be interested mainly in the milieu, the atmosphere, the character types—which I know so well from *Cuvântul.* Altogether I think something very funny could come out of it.

I don't know why I was reminded today of this old project (which up to now has remained so vague that I haven't felt moved to write any notes about it). But not only did everything suddenly become more co-herent; the material itself seemed richer than for a mere joke in one act. Why not a full-length play? Why not try to capture, in a newspaper mi-lieu, some changes in the general social situation? That, of course, would imply something quite different from a light comedy. But this inclina-tion of mine to write for the theatre is encouraged by the thought that I would not be caught in the vise of three acts. I have made up my mind to write (if at all) with the greatest freedom to cut between scenes (a lot of very brief tableaux), with much moving about on the part of the char-acters.

I am so light-minded that I forget all that has happened, all that is still happening, all that is in store, all that is awaiting us! No, I don't forget. But I too get carried away by an evening's calm.

I have resumed the English lessons that I gave up nearly two years ago. I am doing them with quite an interesting American, but I'm not yet sure how much he will help me learn. Meanwhile I continue to read (Shaw's *Man and Superman*). It is strange that I read English much more easily than I do German. My German vocabulary is certainly much richer than my English (and I can still utter a sentence fairly intelligibly in Ger-man, whereas I find it quite impossible to put three English words together), and yet I read Shaw fluently—or almost fluently—but have to struggle quite hard with Dubnow. The wild thing in German is the syntax. You can go four or five lines until you find the subject or complement relating to the definite article with which the sentence begins.

In today's papers there is a new law aimed at political repression. It surpasses everything so far devised on the matter.

Friday, 7 February

Benghazi, the capital of Cyrenaica, has fallen. A very large town for Africa: 65,000 inhabitants. After Bardia, Tobruk, and Derna, I think this will be the end of the Cyrenaica operation. It is hard to imagine that General Wavell[4] will try to go any farther. There are another thousand kilometers of desert before Tripoli. The Italian empire is coming apart at the seams. But it goes without saying that the whole of the war in Africa (however interesting and dramatic) is only a sideshow. The struggle is between the British and the Germans; that is where everything will be decided. The closer we get to spring (longer days, less and less cold, almost no more snow), the more my feelings of last year come back. Will there again be a heavy blow in March, April, May, or June? Bad health. I regret it. I ought to be stronger and more resilient for everything that may happen from now on.

Monday, 10 February

The British legation is pulling out of Romania. Today Hoare[5] delivered a letter of protest in justification for the departure. I don't yet know whether it means that diplomatic relations are being formally broken off. Yesterday evening there was a blackout everywhere in the city: no light of any kind from shop windows, offices, cars, or anywhere else; no street lamps on. From today, strict lighting restrictions will be in force. "A British air attack is expected," everyone was saying yesterday. It seems that a German attack on Bulgaria (or through Bulgaria) is imminent, if it is not by now a *fait accompli*. Yesterday evening, Churchill said in a radio speech that the Bulgarian airports have been occupied and that German troops have crossed the Danube. A Bulgarian denial this morning declares that there are no German troops there but does not men-

---

4. General Archibald Wavell: then commander of British troops in the Middle East and North Africa.
5. Reginald Hoare: British ambassador to Romania.

tion the airports. In any event, with or without Churchill's declaration, with or without the Bulgarian denial, all the signs are that in a few hours or days the long-prepared German operation will be unleashed. There will certainly be consequences for us in Romania, perhaps major changes in our lives. Everything, absolutely everything is still in the realm of the provisional.

Eugen Ionescu, who doesn't take long to get drunk, suddenly started talking to me about his mother after a few cocktails on Saturday morning. Although I heard some time ago that she had been Jewish, the issue had always been closed as far as the two of us were concerned. But as the drink went to his head, he started to "spill the beans" with a kind of sigh of relief, as if he had been gasping all this time under its weight. Yes, she had been Jewish, from Craiova; her husband left her with two little children in France; she remained a Jew until her death, when he—Eugen—baptized her with his own hand. Then, without a transition, he went on to speak about all the "Jews" who are not known to be such: Paul Sterian,[6] Radu Gyr, Ignătescu,[7] and so on. He mentioned them all with a certain spite, as if he wanted to revenge himself on them or to lose himself, unobserved, in their great number. Poor Eugen Ionescu! What fretting, what torment, what secrets for such a simple matter! I would have liked to say how fond I was growing of him—but he was too drunk for me to start being sentimental.

What an unbearable style Mitică Theodorescu has on the radio![8] With the same phrases and epithets he used to serve three regimes, he is now serving a fourth. "Serve" is perhaps not the right word. Can anyone believe that that exclusive language, without measure or nuance, which outbids itself with each new sentence, corresponds to any genuine thought, any honest sensibility? He is a monstrous character, paralytic, evil-minded, cynical, without ideas, without likings or even real hatreds, without feelings or disgust for anything, who nonetheless speaks of a "new world," a "youthful Europe," a "powerful civilization," a "vigorous regime," a revolution of the victorious races, etc., etc. I don't feel angered by his immorality, his endless versatility; it is simply his style that irritates me. His vocabulary, his syntax—everything is false, artificial, flashily inauthentic. I think the microphone also accentuates his contrived mode of speech. When I read him in *Cuvântul*, I found him merely "mannered,"

6. Paul Sterian: poet.
7. Constantin Ignătescu: writer.
8. Dem. Theodorescu: journalist.

but readable and sometimes even intelligent. When he is read aloud, however, he becomes squeaky, irritating, clownish. I have always thought that reading aloud is a tough test for a prose writer. And I wonder whether it is not absolutely necessary for critical purposes.

Tuesday, 11 February

Yesterday evening, as I listened to Beethoven's *Ninth Symphony* (from Budapest), it sometimes seemed to me of an indescribable triviality, or banality. The opening, with that grave entrance of the cello heralding the later bass aria, is still very beautiful. But some parts of the chorus are aggressively vulgar: you'd think it was a chorus in an opera, or even an operetta; Verdi, or even Kalman. Yes, Kalman. It reminded me perhaps of the choruses in *Silvia*.

Evening
There is an atmosphere of war, of general mobilization. The city seems even darker than yesterday, with only an occasional street lamp on. The shop windows are covered with thick curtains or blue paper; all the shutters are drawn. By nine o'clock there is emptiness all around. A few pedestrians run after taxis, but these just speed past. The grey vehicles used by the German army are mostly full of mud; they come from afar and are heading afar. The German soldiers, who up to now have sauntered around as in a resort, look hurried and lost in thought. In the streetcars and the streets, people talk all the time of a possible air raid by the British. Strangely enough, though, I don't see any concern—rather, a kind of lively curiosity, as if they are waiting for a show to begin.

The Lassaignes leave tomorrow morning by plane for Sofia and Istanbul, and then on to Cairo. A sad farewell. I was more emotional than I should have allowed myself to be, given that our friendship is not all that old or close. But this sense of remaining in a world that is closing up! You feel abandoned. What you see is not just someone going away, but a bridge falling down. When will the bridges be rebuilt? When will contacts be established again?

Wednesday, 12 February

The premiere of Mircea Eliade's *Iphigenia* at the National Theatre. Of course I didn't go. It would be impossible for me to show myself at any premiere, let alone at one which (because of the author, the actors, the theme, and the audience) was bound to be a kind of Legionary reunion.

I'd have felt I was at a meeting in their "den." Giza[9] told me over the phone that it was a great success, but, without meaning to, she confirmed my suspicions. "I just hope the performances won't be banned," she said. I assured her that they won't—and I am indeed convinced that nothing will happen. It is true that the text is full of allusions and ambiguities (which I already noticed when I read it last year), but it is rather difficult to ban an *Iphigenia*. The symbol does strike me as rather crude: the play might be called "Iphigenia, or the Legionary Sacrifice." Now, after five months of being at the helm and three days of revolt, after so much killing, arson, and pillage, you can't say it is not relevant.

A visit to Lovinescu. (I hadn't been to his house for some twelve years.) He is the same as ever. I found him patiently listening to a young writer read a short story, and then coughing evasively. A little anti-Semitic touch caught in passing: we were speaking of Grindea and of my surprise at seeing him succeed in London.

"Well, it's race, it's race!" he said laughing, but with obvious conviction.

My American, who is giving me English lessons, is anti-Roosevelt, anti-British, pro-German. A kind of Senator Wheeler.

Cioran, despite his participation in the revolt, has kept his post as cultural attaché in Paris, a post that Sima gave him a few days before he fell. The new regime has even given him a pay increase! He leaves in a few days. Well, that's what revolution does for you!

Friday, 14 February

A concert from Turin (Beethoven's *Violin Concerto* and Tchaikovsky's *Fourth Symphony*), conducted by Igor Markevitch. How many times have I thought of him in recent months and envied his safe refuge in Vevey! Whenever I dream of a calm and protected place, favorable to solitude, reading, and writing, Lake Geneva comes before me as the very picture of happiness. Not Geneva itself, but somewhere higher up, more modest, and less well known: Vevey, for example. And when I say Vevey, the figure of Igor Markevitch appears as I knew him on that sunny Saturday afternoon in September 1931: so young as to be almost childish; excitable and full of life, friendly almost to the point of intimacy from the very first words. Suddenly I see it all again: the lunch with Marie Ghi-

9. Stepdaughter of Mircea Eliade.

olu, Creața, their respective husbands and Igor at that restaurant (Le Globe, I think) filled with politicians, including Jouhaux[1] at the very next table. Then the long visit to the city museum (the first time I'd heard of Liotard), the long walk, the tea by the lakeside—and one of the few calm and clear evenings in that rainy September. So, Igor Markevitch is conducting in Turin. For him there is no war. Music, activity, career, successes—it all goes on. And we live clinging to memories.

Dupront is going back to France on Tuesday; he came round yesterday to say goodbye. With each new departure (Dupront after Lassaigne), the feeling grows that we remain here locked up, that the circle is constantly tightening around us, that we can no longer escape in any direction. "We should act as if the war did not exist," said Dupront. "We should not think about it—just forget it, abstract from it, prepare tomorrow's world." In a sense, he may be right. The war is an obsession, an *idée fixe*—and, in that way at least, it is paralyzing. It would be good if we could forget it. But is that possible when our whole life, our whole fate depends upon it? I fear there is something a little bookish in Dupront's attitude. Even the suggestions for action that he made to me, even his plan for "the best minds" to link up in a series of loops that form one big chain, are vague, ineffective, and unrealistic. And when I think about it, I wonder whether Dupront's talk of forgetting the war, of treating it not as the key phenomenon of the present day, is not an unconscious attempt to excuse and compensate for the French defeat. For if the war is not the decisive event, the fact that France lost it is no longer so grave.

As far as I am concerned, I feel that my whole being hangs on the war. I cannot detach myself from it, nor do I think I would want to.

Sunday, 16 February

The murderers at Jilava forest, who, according to the official report, killed ninety-three Jews in a single night, have been condemned to terms of one to twenty-five years of imprisonment with hard labor. Capital punishment exists in the laws of Romania. For whom? I wonder. How many people does someone have to murder before he is liable for the death penalty? Ninety-three is obviously not enough. In the next pogrom the murderers will know for sure that they are not risking their necks.

Last night I dreamed of Nadia, and then, without any connection, of Maurice Turbé—in two separate dreams without any digressions, both

1. Léon Jouhaux: French trade union leader.

neatly wrapped up and with a perfect sequence of events. Clear, symmetrical dreams, almost uninteresting precisely because of their clarity.

I keep thinking of my conversation with Dupront. I understand very well that, instead of remaining here or going to take up a university chair in Algiers, he is eager to be in France.

In the end, it is possible that France—though so quickly and disastrously defeated and taken out of the war—will be a determining factor in the new Europe, not politically of course, but morally and, above all, socially. (Ah! how badly I write.) More than any other country, France will tomorrow have human material ready for any revolution. There are two million prisoners in German camps, and it is possible that these two million will one day decide the shape of everything.

Tuesday, 18 February

I forgot to note in time the dream I had on Sunday night, and now it is beginning to break up. I am in a provincial town with Șerban Cioculescu, Ionel Teodoreanu, and Păstorel. Vladimir Streinu is also there, though we come only to four if we count ourselves up. We go into a hotel. There is a clean provincial room. Șerban Cioculescu writes an epigram (one of the verses ends with the rhyme "Gyr"). Păstorel writes another epigram in reply. Meanwhile the hotel proprietor comes and says that the room costs five hundred lei a night, which strikes us as rather a lot. I realize that there are only three beds in the room and go into the corridor to see if there is another room. The hotel corridors are filled with whores bustling around half naked. When I return to the room, I find the Teodoreanu brothers, Șerban and Streinu, dressed as cossacks and dancing a fiery kazachok in front of the proprietor. He seems well pleased and wants to hire them for his cabaret.

I am ill again. The "anaphylactic shock," which goes back to last September and originally seemed little more than a joke, has started to become intolerable. I have seen four doctors and find their limitations quite distressing. The same remedies, the same diet, the same language—and, in the end, the same profound ignorance.

All the Malaxa enterprises have passed by royal decree into the hands of the state: some ceded "of his own accord," others expropriated. The list of reasons given is crushing for Malaxa.

As a spectator—a very distant one at that—I cannot help feeling a certain satisfaction, as at the end of a well-acted play, especially one that concludes with a brilliant *coup de théâtre*. Malaxa's mask (a pale effigy, mysterious and unsmiling) served no purpose. Everything is sinking into one great morass. What an extraordinary novel could be written by someone with intimate knowledge of the events!

It is not yet clear what and who lies behind the Bulgarian-Turkish agreement, signed yesterday in Ankara. *Cui prodest?*[2] Is Turkey going back on its commitments to Britain? Is Bulgaria trying to stop the German action in Bulgaria? Is there a Russian hand somewhere behind the scenes? In any event, a German attack no longer appears imminent.

Wednesday, 19 February

In today's *Universul* there are two letters (one to a girl, the other to his parents) from a reserve officer and Legionary named Scîntie Ion, who committed suicide yesterday. It is worth copying down both letters.

"You know, Mioară, I took part in the so-called 'revolt.' I can give you an honest account of things. I think that I was the cause of at least half the deaths suffered by the army. So I deserve to die, and now I have done it. It's not that I wanted a Legionary regime to be established (I didn't think one would be capable of giving real leadership), but I never had any confidence in this army, whose only heroes have been created by others. I happily fired with the aim of destroying it. I wanted it to happen because I am constantly pursued by it."

The second letter:

"I have never loved you. You have been so much like strangers to me. I never thought of you as my parents, only as a world in which I woke up and to which I felt attached as to something that might offer me shelter. That's all—nothing else. Don't give anyone alms on my account. If you hear I have died, don't come and collect me. I don't want to be taken to church or buried in a cemetery, because I have never believed in those things. Let them burn me and scatter my ashes to the wind."

That is how Scîntie Ion, the son of farm laborers from Copăceni-Ilfov, writes and pays with his life. It could have come from any page in Dostoevsky.

I recently read *Jocul de-a vacanţa* again. The first two acts are excellent in terms of plot. Act Three is rather "cooked up," literary, "*languissant*,"

2. Who benefits?

too low-key, almost lame. But it still reads nicely, even if the action of the play falls off after Act Two. I hesitate to write for the theatre. I'd have to have more of a will—and especially better health—to get down to work.

Monday, 24 February

Fabi has died.

Thursday, 27 February

I mourned a lot for him and still am mourning, but I'll forget him—am already forgetting him. For a day or two I couldn't think of anything else. I had him constantly before my eyes, heard him talking, saw him. Now other thoughts are returning to preoccupy me: the war, communiqués from the front, daily events both big and small. And among them, as through a cloth that suddenly tears, or through a fog that lifts, his dear face reappears.

He was so handsome. I couldn't help marveling each time I saw him. "How come you're so handsome, Fabi? It shouldn't be allowed. It's a scandal." He laughed in a childlike way, a little embarrassed, a little ironic. He had a strangely timid gesture of confused disbelief, as if to say: "Drop it. Let's talk about something else."

The last time I saw him in good health, up and about, was at my place a couple of weeks ago. It tears me up to think that I let him go away so quickly. He had come for me to give him some books to read. Why didn't I make him stay? Why didn't we have a chat? Why did I get to know him so little? Why didn't I draw him closer to me?

The poor dear boy! It's so hard for me to understand that I have lost him forever; so hard for me to see, instead of his bright sixteen-year-old image, with silky fair hair, dark eyes, and bushy eyebrows blocking his forehead—to see instead of this a grave.

I'll wait for a fine morning to take him flowers.

Wednesday, 5 March

This morning, from Zeesen, a Schubert cello sonata (a melancholic, meditative Schubert). From London, a delightful little oboe quartet in F by Mozart. And yesterday evening, also from London, an unremarkable clarinet quintet by Brahms—dull, flat, uninspired. The other evening I chanced upon a harpsichord concerto from Vienna. As I listened, I wondered what it could be. The first phrase told me it was definitely eighteenth century. But by whom? I started a process of elimination: not Bach (too light), not Mozart (not light enough), not Handel, not Haydn. Maybe an Italian? Maybe one of the two or three lesser Bachs? This last assumption seemed the most plausible. So, Carl Philipp Emanuel or Johann Christian. And it was indeed Johann Christian Bach. Great personal satisfaction. Flattered by my skill in working it out.

German troops have been in Bulgaria for three days. Filov[3] signed the Tripartite Pact, and that same morning—a few hours before it was signed, in fact—the Germans crossed the Danube.

On Monday evening there was a surprising Russian note of protest. But whether the Soviets are opposed to it or not, Europe is closing all its gates and windows. Greece will not be able to resist much longer, with German tanks already on its coast. As for Turkey, which has done nothing up to now, I think it is too late for it to defend its positions in the Balkans. The German game is always the same and always victorious: to break up possible alliances and associations, to paralyze one zone of operations after another, and then to occupy them as those still on their feet wait their turn in a resigned stupor. Yugoslavia will fall soon. Turkey will give up a little later. It is stupid and simplistic—yet inexorable.

Thursday, 6 March

I have been to see Mircea Eliade's *Iphigenia*. (A Thursday matinee, with prices pitched at ordinary people: forty lei the most expensive seat. It has been one of the National's worst flops.) The play is much more interesting than I remember from when I read it. The performance is crude, however, and lacks style or dignity. Acting is terrible in Romania—and you never feel this more acutely than after a long time away. Hoarse voices, which scream and shout. False, declamatory gestures. I tried just keeping my mind on the text, and it did seem really beautiful. Only here and there were there annoying Legionary allusions.

This evening, from Zeesen, Beethoven's *Trio for Piano, Violin, and Cello in D, Op. 70/1*. Combarieu says of it: *"claire idylle qu'on a comparée à la modeste et jolie sonate en mi bémol."*[4]

3. Bogdan Filov: prime minister of Bulgaria.
4. "A clear, idyllic piece that has been compared to the lovely and modest sonata in E-flat."

Finished *Black Mischief*, Evelyn Waugh's whimsical novel. I read it without a dictionary, but ruthlessly skipping hundreds of unknown words. If I had more patience, and more scruples, I would make more progress in English.

Sunday, 9 March

A long, strange, complex dream, with numerous incidents and all kinds of forgotten people (I wonder where Uncle Hainerich came from, for example)—impossible to reconstruct it now. I still recall the basic schema, but terribly pared down. Prince Niculae is visiting my studio flat on Calea Victoriei. Poldy and Benu are up there with him (but they are not alone, because there is a kind of reception). I am downstairs in the street, coming from Piața Amzei. I see, or rather guess, that it is Niculae and Poldy at my window; they are probably waiting for me. I bump against a little contraption, a kind of child's scooter, that a general has left by the side of the pavement. I go into a grocer's shop (on the left pavement, near Dr. Ambrosi's) and buy some cigarettes and matches, also having a little argument with the boy who sells them to me. I come away loaded with packets and with a bottle of cooking oil. I feel embarrassed that the people up there at the window will see me in this predicament. I pass Tata and Uncle Hainerich without stopping, and finally go into my building. Collected around a table in the downstairs lobby, a group of men seem to be commenting on my entrance. I go into the elevator, where I am not alone but with Cella. The elevator travels up for an unusually long time. I am surprised we are not there yet. I tell Cella something is probably wrong with the elevator. We look through the windows and observe that, in fact, we are flying among tall, unfamiliar houses. Then we suddenly fall to the ground and die. But our death does not end the dream. We continue to take part in all that happens, even though we know we are dead. I cannot remember any more.

Marietta Rareș stopped me in the street, though I was about to pass her with a simple greeting. I listened to her complaint: Haig is still under arrest, charged with all kinds of things; the statements made by actors at the National are crushing; he is accused of communism and of revolt. Marietta Sadova has been expelled from the Conservatory, Giza has disappeared, her house is constantly searched, etc., etc. I let her speak, without interrupting and without making any reply. What more can I do than shrug my shoulders? If they had won, I know they would have been ten times fiercer. And other people's suffering would have been a matter of terrible indifference to them.

I read by chance Jules Romains's *Le Dictateur.* What childishness! What naiveté! Maybe in 1926 such things were not necessarily ridiculous. But today, after all the things we have seen . . .

Friday, 14 March

Yesterday, after several months of intermittent reading, I finished the first volume of the Pléiade edition of Balzac: *La maison du Chat-qui-pelote, Le bal de Sceaux, Mémoires de deux jeunes mariées, La bonne modeste mignon, Un début dans la vie, Albert Savarus, La vendetta, Une double famille, La paix du ménage, Madame Firmiani, Étude de femme.* It will be hard for me to keep reading everything in chronological order. I don't know when I'll be able to read Balzac again systematically. (I'd need a year or so!) But so as not to stop just like that, I have decided to read his most characteristic novels (*Eugenie Grandet, Père Goriot, Le lys dans la vallée*, etc.) and to leave the rest for another time.

According to Rosetti, Mircea has been appointed to the legation in Madrid. He won't even be coming back to Romania; he'll go straight from Lisbon to his new post.[5] This way he'll be spared having to take a stance. And later he may feel just as well in one camp as in the other.

The spring war seems to have begun. Major bombing of London and Berlin on the same night.

Roosevelt's pro-British legislation has been in force for three days. There is muted annoyance in Berlin. "The Jews are to blame," says the German correspondent of *Universul*. I wouldn't be surprised if there is a new anti-Semitic wave, as a riposte and a diversion.

Always long, complex, uncanny dreams, almost every night. But I forget them before I can write them down.

Sunday, 16 March

Yesterday was a year since Nae Ionescu's death. The requiem at Visarion Church was interesting for the people it brought together, but with sad memories of all the things it forced you to think about. Two months

---

5. Eliade was not transferred to Madrid: he remained at the Romanian legation in Lisbon.

ago, before the "revolt," Nae Ionescu's political error, his pointless ad-
venture, did not appear the great failure it does today. Old people from
Cuvântul: Onicescu, Devechi, Voglberg, Alexandru Devechi, Pretorian.
All have grown old. It felt more like their requiem.

There were also a few conspicuously Legionary figures: recently grown
beards, mysterious looks, young desperados with their hair sticking up.
Somewhere at the front was Codreanu's widow, to whom various people
pushed through and paid their respects. What is Nae Ionescu doing
among such types? What did he have in common with them?

An amicable supper yesterday at Cantacuzino's. I had a strange feeling
of being in a different city, with books, paintings, and friendly people,
instead of war, Germans, and Hitler.

Roosevelt's speech tonight was violently anti-Nazi, full of confidence, expectant of certain victory. Glued to our radios, we lived in a world which,
though so far away, we consider our own. Then we go into the street
and wake up in a city with German troops—their prisoners.

I keep thinking of my plays but cannot make up my mind to start work
on them. It is true that the one with the journalists should be left to
clarify itself, to acquire sharper contours. The material is rich enough,
but I can't yet see the structure. Sometimes I think it should be more
serious and more substantial than a mere Bucharest comedy of manners.
Is not the way Nae came to *Cuvântul* and ended up controlling it a theatrical adventure? But the "Grodeck" play is fairly well defined, and I
could—or anyway should—get down to work on it.

Tuesday, 18 March

The dismal text of the Rent Act was published in today's papers. I don't
know why, but "legal" anti-Semitic measures seem to me more depressing, more humiliating, than beatings and window-breaking. Maybe this
law will serve as a warning, will remind us of all the threats that are
ever-present. Jews forget so quickly, with such a childish lack of awareness, that someone has to remind them from time to time what their
destiny is.

I have been sad all day. My heart is heavy not simply because I shall
have to pay a rent beyond my means, or perhaps to give up my flat and
hunt high and low for somewhere else to live, but because all this stupid, senseless cruelty has no aim other than to harm and mock for the
pure pleasure of harming and mocking.

Titulescu has died in Cannes. I did not know him, never heard him speak, and had neither a personal liking nor political admiration for him. I was more inclined to think of him as a slightly hysterical meddler (some images from *Cuvântul* have stuck in my mind). Neither through Maryse and Gheorghe,[6] nor through Sacha Roman,[7] nor through Aristide (who could have familiarized me with him) did I get at all close to him. All I remember is that late-September morning in 1930 when I saw him in Geneva presiding over the General Assembly of the League of Nations, in the *Bâtiment electoral*. It was so sunny and I was so young, coming from Annecy and on my way back to Paris. Everything ahead seemed open and possible to me. *Quantum mutatus ab illo . . .*[8]

Absurd dreams every night. When I wake up, my head still cloudy, I promise to make a note of them. Then I forget. Last night I dreamed I was a soldier in some zone of operations. I was with Picu Mironescu and Major Răceanu, who at first seemed to have become a lieutenant colonel. Every dream in which I am a soldier is a nightmare. The day before yesterday I had one that ended in a funny way. I was with Poldy in a streetcar in Brăila, going to see a statue of Take Ionescu. When the streetcar stopped, we turned indignantly to the driver or conductor and asked him to explain why the statue had disappeared. The driver was Dr. Dumitrescu-Brăila. He said that the statue was in fact there and told us to get off. We found a very beautiful marble statue (black, I think) and looked at it for a long time.

The other night I dreamed again that I was in Brăila, with Nina. We were walking along Bulevardul Cuza toward the Danube. Near the Lutheran church there was a military prison in which Mircea was being held; all kinds of detainees were walking around the yard. I went into an office and telephoned a civil servant (his name was Constantinescu, but he also had another, somewhat ridiculous one, such as Policarp). As I left, they hoisted some flags, including four black flags as a sign that four men had been executed. But all the dreams are much more complex than I ever manage to note. The very act of writing them down simplifies them.

A Handel evening, quite by chance. First, from Geneva, a few choruses and a long, very beautiful concerto for string orchestra. Then immedi-

6. Gheorghe Nenişor was a relative of Titulescu's.
7. Sacha Roman: Titulescu's secretary.
8. How changed from what he once was.

ately afterward from London, some soprano arias and a trio for two violins and piano. All very beautiful, grave, and soothing.

Friday, 21 March

An evening of music such as I have not had for a long time. From Munich, played by the Mozarteum Orchestra of Salzburg, the C major piano concerto by Mozart, and at the end an andantino from the "Paris" symphony in G major. Then I switched straight to London (the Home Service) for another Mozart concert: first a piano concerto, then the minuet from the *Kleine nachtmusik* (in English: the *Little Evening Serenade*). Also from London, as I am writing this note, a concert of Spanish music: small orchestral pieces by Granados, Albéniz, Falla.

Sunday, 23 March

I'll probably be forced to leave my flat. My landlords' demands frighten me, and I dare not take on such major obligations when my whole situation (is it a "situation"?—the word seems a mockery) is up in the air.

I am well aware that to move from here would mean a terrible upheaval in my whole way of life, but I shall just have to resign myself to it. I shouldn't forget that we are at war.

"I shouldn't forget"—that's a manner of speaking. Could I possibly forget? I feel it in all my thoughts, in every step I take, in every minute of the day. Sometimes it is a sharp, physical pain, a kind of nervous choking. And so the days pass, one after another, slowly, heavily...

I saw Titu Devechi yesterday morning. He looks thinner and more tired, with more grey hairs. He has been ill. Political events don't seem to have affected him too badly: he is always skeptical, humorous, pleasant. I think the war has aged me much more. As I listened to him speak, explaining and offering solutions, I felt like laughing at the naiveté of what he said— as if he were a young boy whom you can't be bothered to contradict. All you want to say to him is: "You'll grow up, then you'll see. . . ."

But it was nice being with Devechi. Last autumn he thought a German victory absolutely certain; now he is beginning to have doubts. "If they don't win by November, they never will."

Yesterday Yugoslavia appeared to have been defeated—offered some formal concessions and marks of respect, but defeated nevertheless. They were due to sign the Tripartite Pact yesterday, or at the latest today. But now things seem to have been put off again, no more than "put off," I think. There is an attempt at last-minute resistance. Government resignations, protest meetings, memoranda, telegrams, demonstrations.

But they'll sign all the same.

It's a strange feeling to go into a large, brightly lit restaurant with lots of people and music. It seems like an unreal world, a theatre setting, lying altogether outside our lives. I went to the Cina with the Zissus. (I swear it's the last time I'll go out with them. From now on I'll avoid them as much as possible. She is the perfect example of a Jewish parvenue. How dear to me, by contrast, are becoming the careworn mothers of Văcărești and Dudești; how beloved yet again is Mama, my mother, so simple and so good.)

I left the Cina feeling dazed, having eaten all the while with pangs of conscience. I was ashamed. I felt guilty.

That Zissu is impossible to understand: a theorist of full-blown Jewish nationalism who goes out every evening to a cinema or restaurant, two months after a pogrom.

Wednesday, 26 March

Yesterday Yugoslavia signed the Tripartite Pact in Vienna. The hesitations served no purpose, and regrets will not make up for anything. The game is always played in the same way. Yesterday afternoon I listened on the radio to the ceremony at which the pact was signed. Tvetkovič gave a speech in Serbian, the only note (sentimental though it was) of "independence." It will be Turkey's turn next. But first Greece will have to be occupied by German troops (which is very likely to happen). The Turks, who now seem disposed to resist (and who, to this end, have safeguarded their rear through the nonaggression declaration with the Russians that was published yesterday), may nevertheless surrender when German troops are available to be released from the Greek front. It is the same comedy, in an endless number of identical acts.

Later, much later, a study may be written about a strange phenomenon of these times: namely, the fact that words are losing their meaning, becoming weightless and devoid of content. Their speakers do not believe them, while their hearers do not understand them. If you analyzed word by word, grammatically, syntactically, and semantically, the declarations to be found almost daily in the newspapers, and if you opposed these with the facts to which they refer, you would see that there is an absolute split between word and reality. It is not the first time that such thoughts (written here badly) have occurred to me, but the occasion today was a sentence in a speech that the General made yesterday. "Those who, in their relations with defenseless people, have revived in today's world the terror and barbaric savagery of the past will themselves be branded by contemporaries and punished by history as they deserve."

Dinner yesterday with Vişoianu, Gina Strunga, and Ghiţă Ionescu (who vanished in the Legionary period, when I think he tried to "adapt," and who has now calmly reappeared *comme si de rien n'était*). Vivi said some astounding things about Gheorghe and Maryse Nenişor, who appear to have been left as Titulescu's sole inheritors after some devilish scheming on Gheorghe's part. Poor devilish Gheorghe!

Leni was moving on Sunday evening when she celebrated at home a year since her last premiere. "I'll die if I don't get a part this autumn. I can't take it any more." She has learned to play the accordion, and when she wanted to show us what she knows, she had anxious tears as at a real premiere.

More moving, however, was Eugen Ionescu, who again came to see me yesterday morning. He was desperate, hunted, obsessed, unable to bear the thought that he may be barred from working in education. A healthy man can go mad if he suddenly learns that he has leprosy. Eugen Ionescu is learning that not even the name "Ionescu," nor an indisputably Romanian father, nor the fact that he was born a Christian—nothing at all can hide the curse of having Jewish blood in his veins. The rest of us have long since grown used to this dear old leprosy, so much so that we feel resignation and sometimes a kind of sad, disconsolate pride.

I have been reading Shelley the last few days. It is a great pleasure.

Thursday, 27 March

A bewildering coup d'état in Yugoslavia. King Peter takes power at seventeen years of age. The regent resigns his office. Prince Paul flees abroad. The head of the general staff forms a new government, which includes Macek and the three Serb ministers who did not resign in protest at the Tripartite Pact. Tvetcovič and Činčar Marcovič are under arrest. Stupor and then frenzy! Here in Bucharest you could feel in the streets a nervous excitement, as on decisive, momentous days. What must it be like in Belgrade! Overnight, in less than twelve hours, the whole situation in the Balkans has been turned upside down—perhaps not only in the Balkans. I spent the day fretting with impatience, curiosity, hope, and expectation. I am tired of excessive surprises!

Keren was occupied today by the British, after a three-week siege. No doubt the rest of Eritrea will now fall much more easily, almost automatically.

Harar, in Abyssinia, also fell today. The news arrived late, in the evening, as if to crown a day so rich in events.

Nor was that the last news of the day. At 11:30, just now, Radio Bucharest announced that Jewish real estate has been expropriated. Houses taken from Jews will be given to teachers, officers, magistrates, and so on. What worries me is not the measure in itself (because it is unimportant in the only perspective that counts: the war), but the fact that the government, in adopting such a serious anti-Semitic measure, has jumped over a whole series of anti-Semitic blows that it might have dealt out as graduated diversions. What can follow after such an expropriation? Maybe the establishment of a ghetto. And then? All that will be left is a pogrom.

As before, only more so than ever, I keep telling myself that the only thing to do is to be patient, to wait and endure. It's a question of time. If you are alive, if you stay alive, all the rest will pass.

Friday, 28 March

I am distraught by what happened last night, and anxious about what will happen now. Previously—even under the Legionaries—anti-Semitism was bestial but outside the law. That, in a way, was how it was excused. And at any moment, however formally, you could appeal to the authority of the state; a minimum of legality was preserved in official actions. Now, however, even that precarious sense of official justice has gone. All the morning papers give banner headlines to the expropriation of the Jews. The rest of the news (the war, the victories in Africa, the coup in Belgrade) is pushed to the back. What is important in Romania today, on Friday, 28 March 1941, is that the Jews have had their homes taken away from them. The rest has no significance!

This morning once again, though more acutely and painfully than ever, I felt as I spoke to my school pupils about "literature,"[9] even Romanian literature, that we are clinging pointlessly and absurdly to things which no longer have any meaning or reality for us. In the seventh grade the boys were doing test papers, and I got them to write about *sămănătorism*.[1] But as I watched them, bent (so seriously!) over their exercise books,

9. Sebastian started work in 1940 as teacher in a Jewish school established in the fall of 1940 when Jewish children were expelled from Romanian schools.
1. A Romanian literary movement of the early twentieth century.

I had a feeling of fraternal pity for their labors, for their wasted time, for the daily trials of their youth. So many of these boys' parents had been ruined overnight, thrown into the street by a mere decree—and now they were here writing about "problems of Romanian literature." How grotesque!

Camil Petrescu complains that he probably won't get even one of the houses taken from Jews.

"They never give me anything," he said, disheartened.

"Well, this time," I replied, "even if they gave you something, I'm sure you wouldn't take it!"

"Not take it? Why shouldn't I?"

He spoke so calmly that I could not fail to understand what he was saying. Not only did he see no reason not to take possession of a house that was not his and had been taken from a Jew; he actually expected to be given such a house, and would be disappointed if this did not happen.

Marietta Sadova has been interned at Tîrgu-Jiu for several days. She seems to have been agitating recently as at the height of the revolt. I don't know why, but there seems something comical in her political adventures.

In Marseilles today, ten thousand French people demonstrated for Yugoslavia. The police had a hard time dispersing them. Secretly, silently, the whole of Europe is celebrating. In Rome and Berlin there is a confused silence. The coup in Belgrade has upset the whole program of Matsuoka's visit.[2] I think the Germans will try to claim a bloody price for the unexpected blow they have received.

From Geneva this evening, Beethoven's *Missa solemnis*. An hour of calm.

Saturday, 29 March

A brief conversation with A.B. as we drove home by car. He reminded me (most delicately) that our agreement had been valid for six months and had therefore now expired. From the first of April, everything will be up in the air. Suddenly, as in a fit of choking, I feel again all the fear of a poor and wretched life.

---

2. Yasuke Matsuoka: foreign minister of Japan.

Tuesday, 1 April

There was a great sea battle in the Mediterranean, 150 miles south of Crete, during the night of Friday and Saturday. A great, very great victory for the British. The Italians have definitely lost three 10,000-ton cruisers and two destroyers, each between 15,000 and 18,000 tons [sic]. A large 35,000-ton battleship was so badly mauled that it is not known whether it managed to reach the safety of a port. Another cruiser and another destroyer are also thought to have been lost. A thousand Italian and German officers and sailors were fished out by the British and put ashore in Greece. Hundreds more Italians, perhaps thousands, remain battling the waves in the region of the action. The British lost no more than two airplanes, and all their ships have returned to Alexandria without a scratch. Admiral Cunningham issued the briefest possible order of the day: "Well done!" In Eritrea the British keep advancing toward Asmara and are already halfway from Keren. In Abyssinia they have occupied Dire Dawa and are now heading, from several directions at once, toward Addis Ababa.

While the Italians are losing on all fronts, the Germans are probably preparing an offensive behind their great cloak of silence. The mystery is the same as last spring, with some stunning blow possible at any moment. But where? Very probably, in fact certainly, in Yugoslavia. The game there is starting to become clearer. Attempts are being made to provoke a Croat diversion, which might serve—in an eventual disintegration of Yugoslavia—the same role that the Slovaks played in the destruction of Czechoslovakia. But even if it does not take that form, the Germans are bound to strike in one way or another. It is the first of April. We turn the page of the calendar with mixed feelings: on the one hand, relief that a month of this spring has passed; on the other hand, anxiety that we are still in the middle of spring and that things cannot mark time much longer.

Madeleine Andronescu paid me an unexpected visit yesterday, accompanied by Titel. What a real pleasure to discover that some people still think of you, even when nothing—not even a past friendship—obliges them to do so.

Wednesday, 2 April

Asmara surrendered yesterday, and it is unlikely that Massawa will hold out. Resistance is no longer possible in Eritrea.

Until yesterday, the Bucharest papers showed a quite undisciplined sympathy for the new regime in Yugoslavia. A photograph of King Peter was printed alongside commentaries full of praise, and the headlines announced "perfect order in Yugoslavia." Today all the papers speak of "the atrocities in Belgrade," "the inevitable disaster," "Serbian provocations." The Germans are preparing to attack in the familiar manner. First there will be a propaganda barrage about the martyred German population (as in the Sudetenland and in Poland), then—probably—a border incident, and finally an invasion. They can't even be bothered to think up something new.

I have the feeling that there are fewer German troops in Bucharest. Rapid troop movements seem to be taking place in the direction of the Yugoslav frontiers. It could be that the attack will come simultaneously from Bulgaria, Romania, and Germany.

I met Lilly Popovici this morning on Calea Victoriei. I think she was more embarrassed than pleased to see me. She claims that Marietta was arrested after being denounced by Marioara Voiculescu. I accompanied her as far as the Café Nestor. A German officer passed alongside us.

"I can't stand them," Lilly said. "I hate them. I feel ashamed when I think of the Serbs and the Greeks—ashamed of ourselves."

I listened to her without agreeing or disagreeing. I have a vague sense that when the Legion was still going strong, she must have been less intransigent. The role of a Legionary Clytemnestra—which she acted in Mircea's play—suits her very well.

Today I thought of a three-act political comedy set in Bucharest during the revolution of 1848. A lot of topical things could be said like that, under an amusing period camouflage.

Why does everyone I meet seem startled at how bad I look? "You've gotten thinner! You've aged!"—they keep telling me. And it doesn't give me any pleasure at all.

As the 23rd of April draws near, the thought that I shall have to leave my flat becomes more unbearable. I'd have to find 100,000 lei to keep it until autumn. But how could I? From where?

Thursday, 3 April

The "political comedy" of which I was thinking yesterday has become less vague. As I walked in the street this evening, I enjoyed developing a clearer idea of things. The play might be called "Freedom." It would have several acts, and would in any event be divided into a number of tableaux: one in Bucharest, in the editorial offices of a revolutionary paper; another in the French consulate; another—after the repression— on a country estate where the play's hero takes refuge. In order to write the play I would have to study newspapers from the period, a history of the movement, various documents and proclamations, and so on. I don't think of it as being too serious. A light comedy of politics and love.

The Italians have retaken Benghazi! I didn't think such a turnaround was possible. It will sober me up after the euphoria of recent events. So, the war will last a lot longer.

Friday, 4 April

Act One of *Freedom* (if I ever write it) will not take place, as I thought yesterday, in the editorial offices of a newspaper. That would have two drawbacks: 1) the problem of having an "editorial office" in 1848 Bucharest (I don't even know if there was such a thing); and 2) the weakening through repetition of the "press comedy" idea, which I have been considering for some time and do not want to abandon. It may be better to have the first act set in a public administration office; that would give me an opportunity to present the change of regime at the very moment of the seizure of power.

I wrote the above note from a kind of copyist's sense of obligation. This morning I would have written it with joy. I still liked the idea of the play, which was vividly present to me. But now it is evening and, after this long day (another and another day—all of them long), I feel tired, jaded, defeated by all that has happened, all that awaits us, all that I no longer have the nerves to endure, conceal, cover in silence. On such evenings the thought of my ever writing literature again seems absurd. I feel terribly old and worn out.

Saturday, 5 April

The British retreat from Benghazi gave me a sleepless night. I had thought that that front was sewn up. The blow seemed so serious not in itself, as a loss of territory, but for what it signified. It was possible for an offensive force to be re-created at Tripoli, for fresh troops and materiel to be brought in, for a counterattack to be prepared—and the British, with their notoriously bad intelligence, knew nothing about it. Absolutely nothing, so that they could even move all their troops to Eritrea or perhaps Greece, leaving Cyrenaica undefended. Now it is possible that the whole of Cyrenaica will again fall into the hands of the Italians, with the Germans doubling up for good measure. A fight to recapture it will have to be waged once more—who knows when?—after the complete occupation of Eritrea and Abyssinia, but it remains to be seen whether, in the meantime, the outbreak of war in Yugoslavia will leave the British with enough troops to send to Libya. I have done all this reasoning today. Yesterday, and even more the day before, I was incapable of any rational analysis. The news, coming so unexpectedly, had depressed me too much!

In Abyssinia the British occupied Aduwa today. The advance to Addis Ababa is continuing.

A summer's day, as warm as in June. I think nostalgically of Balcic. In the morning I went for a walk with Madeleine Andronescu around Lake Floreasca. She is pleasant and amusing—but I know that I'll soon tire of her. I told her frankly that I don't like to get to know people. And it's true that I don't like it. I have nothing to ask of them, nor anything to give.

Sunday, 6 April

The Germans have declared war on Yugoslavia, in exactly the same way they did before their invasion of Poland, Norway, Belgium, and the Netherlands. "German troops have received instructions to restore order in the Balkans," Hitler said. The Serbs will resist. But for how long? German troops have already attacked Yugoslavia and Greece, though it is not yet known where or with which forces. We'll have news by this evening.

Evening
Belgrade has been bombed twice, in the morning and in the afternoon. Communications are broken, the radio silent—no direct news from there. In Greece the attack is taking place through Thrace and Macedonia. At the moment it seems that it is not a lightning advance. Yesterday the Russians signed a nonaggression and friendship pact with the Serbs. Turkey is reserving its positions. I don't think they will launch anything unless they are directly attacked themselves. Addis Ababa has been captured by the British. Yesterday this would have seemed to me extremely significant, but now, with the avalanche of new developments, it arouses no feelings.

Monday, 7 April

Still no news from Belgrade. The German communiqués give no geographical precision (how far have they advanced? in which sector?), and
there are no Yugoslav communiqués at all. I fear that the Polish campaign will be repeated there. Massive bombing that disorganizes communications, cuts road and rail links, dislocates armies, and fragments
the country, before people have even realized that there is a war. So far
there is no sign of a German attack on Albania (the only action that was
to be expected all along). It is possible that the whole war in Yugoslavia
will be over in five to ten days, without a battle properly so called, and
anyway without enough time for a "front" to take shape. Maybe things
will unfold differently in Greece. Salonica will probably fall soon, but a
front might be established farther south. That is the only thing that
counts. In the end, no one is so mad as to hope that the Germans will
fail to occupy Greece. The question is: how long will it take? with how
many casualties? If the war in the southeast is still occupying the Germans in four or five months' time, forcing them to make serious efforts
and sacrifices, it will be a very bad business for them (even if they are
victorious). But if the war there finishes soon, it might represent in April
1941 what the war in Norway represented in April 1940: the prologue
to a great offensive in May–June, on the decisive western front.

I am full of fears and worries, which I am unable to conceal. I am
also irritated by other people's optimism. On Saturday I dined at Alice
Th.'s, with Braniște,[3] Hillard,[4] and Aristide. All three were certain of victory (it's true that the new German attack had not yet begun); there is
no doubt in their mind. I, on the other hand, am terrified at what might
happen. Are the terrible days and nights of last year about to begin again?

Strange Yugoslav bombing (but is it Yugoslav?) of Sofia, Timișoara,
Arad, and Budapest. No damage, no casualties. "A provocation"—shrieks
Berlin. It is being said that the Germans are determined to throw Bulgaria, Romania, and Hungary against the Serbs. Yesterday and the day
before there was constant talk of a general mobilization.

Last night at the Ateneu, a wartime *Matthäus-Passion*. Many cuts that reduced the whole work to about a third. *Ich will bei meinem Jesu wachen*
was missing, for example.

3. Tudor Teodorescu-Braniște: journalist and writer.
4. Richard (Ricci) Hillard: journalist, friend of Sebastian's.

Tuesday, 8 April

A Greek communiqué says that the Yugoslavs are retreating on the southern front and meeting up with the Greek left wing. No indication that
there is coherent Yugoslav resistance.

Anguish, despondency, unbearable loneliness. But above all else a will—
more "as a matter of principle"—to keep going.

Wednesday, 9 April

Salonica has fallen. The whole Greek army of eastern Macedonia is cut
off from the rest of the country. Either it will be annihilated or it will
surrender: there is no other way out. Belgrade is a heap of ruins. In the
south of Yugoslavia, as in the north, great destruction, large-scale retreats, thousands of prisoners. Everything is collapsing into a rout. In
Eritrea the British have occupied Massawa, but in Cyrenaica they have
lost Derna. The terrible blows they are receiving make you forget the
successes they had all through the winter. Once more Germany gives
the impression of being an invincible, demonic, overwhelming force. The
general feeling is one of bewilderment and impotence.

These are bitter days, with the old taste of ashes, and with tears that
one is too proud to allow oneself. But I can't say I feel desperate. Tired,
oppressed, defeated—but not at the end of all hope.

Thursday, 10 April

An autumn day, cold, rainy, with a chill damp typical of November. It is
warm at home, but I no longer feel "at home." In ten days I have to
hand my place over to the new tenant. Next week I'll already begin moving my things—where, I don't know. It would have been nice to have a
room at home with Mama. But their place is too small for me to have
any more than a bed. Books, desk, clothes cupboard: none of that would
fit there. I don't know whether Sacha Roman's offer (to give me a room
at his place) is all that serious. But I don't want to go on too much about
how bad I feel at leaving my studio apartment. I felt good here: I was
alone and sufficiently "left in peace." I don't know what will replace this
solitude. But I'll find shelter somewhere—for the time being. However
bad the conditions, it may not be worse than in the Valea lui Soare.

I can't say that I am very brave. Physical squalor frightens me, as does
moral squalor. I am not made to wander around. And if you can't even

glimpse some rest at the end of the wandering, what is the point of all
the worry and suffering? Today all is grey, all is desolate. I'd like to be
overcome by a long, leaden sleep.

Sunday, 13 April

The war in Serbia is confused. You can't tell whether there are any battles and, if so, where they are and between which forces. Yugoslav communiqués are nonexistent. The only information comes from Berlin,
Rome, or Budapest. Not even the British in Athens seem to know how
things stand. Zagreb fell in the first few days, and this was followed by
a declaration of independence by a so-called Croatian state. The Italians
have occupied Ljubljana, and at Lake Ohrid they have met up with German forces. There is no word of a Serbian attack on Albania. The Hungarians crossed their border with Yugoslavia on Friday, "in order to
protect the local Magyar population." Yesterday and the day before there
was talk of a similar Romanian attack on the Serbian Banat. For the moment, the Bucharest press is in the van, jubilant that "an artificial state
is tumbling down." Yet a Romanian military action against Yugoslavia
seems too difficult to be a real possibility. The Germans reported today
that they have occupied Belgrade. We do not have a map to show us the
situation on the ground. Perhaps there are still some areas of Yugoslav
resistance, but no one knows exactly where! All is lost, of course, so you
can feel only surprise that the occupation has not yet been completed.
In any event, it will all be over in a few days' time. In Greece the British
have started to link up with the Greeks, and some kind of real resistance
is under way. But I can't believe it will lead to the consolidation of a
front. All that can now be done in the Balkan war is to inflict heavier
casualties on the Germans and force them to extend their efforts. But
there is no way the business can last more than a month. I think that
by the first of June at the latest it will be completely wrapped up, and
the Germans will be free to start a fresh action somewhere. Berlin reports that German troops have surrounded Tobruk and, farther on, have
occupied Bardia. So now they are at the Egyptian frontier. The Suez
Canal will be their next objective.

   In Moscow, two events are more interesting for their hidden significance than in and of themselves: one, the official protest against Hungarian intervention in Yugoslavia, and two, the neutrality pact with the
Japanese. War is becoming possible between Germany and Russia.

I don't have the energy to tell Madeleine that she should be on her way.
I feel really bad that I let her stay with me on Thursday night. It was

another painful night (like the one in May 1938 with Z.)—except that this time a love affair is completely out of the question. If I don't want fresh complications, pointless time-wasting, and insoluble difficulties, I shall have to cut it short.

Monday, 14 April

The Germans are at Sollum, where fighting is taking place. Meanwhile, however, the British garrison in Tobruk is resisting. I don't think they can break communications between the German troops who have advanced beyond Bardia toward Sollum and the German supply bases in Derna and Benghazi. A war on Egyptian soil, for Sidi-el-Barani, Alexandria, and perhaps even Cairo, is now an immediate danger, probably so great that General Wavell will ask the Egyptians to join in the fighting.

In Greece the Anglo-Greek front is holding. But can it really be called a front? I think that if their defensive lines are still holding, this is more because the Germans are not attacking them. They want to finish off the Yugoslavs first, and so may delay until later a direct attack on the Anglo-Greek front. The situation resembles the moment last May when the Germans, launching their offensive toward Dunkirk, halted their southward push for two weeks at the Somme. For a moment I thought then that Weygand would consolidate a front. But, of course, it fell apart immediately after Dunkirk.

There are unconfirmed reports that the Serbs have occupied Durazzo[5] in Albania.

My reading has given me much food for thought about the Revolution of 1848. Despite the depressing military disasters and my own gathering troubles (my approaching move), the play remains present in my mind. I even enjoy thinking about it.

Today I finished *La femme à trente ans*, the silliest of the Balzac novels I know.

Wednesday, 16 April

I am obsessed with my approaching move. This house in which I have lived for two and a half years, and where—God knows—I have not been happy, has nevertheless become as dear to me as a living being. I look

---

5. Italian name for the town of Durrës.

at my belongings, as they are spread out here, and I feel that together they make up a live "presence." This closeness is breaking down: a relationship is ending, and with it another period of my life. Sometimes I tell myself that I have no right to get depressed over such things. We are at war, and it is no misfortune to lose one comfortable dwelling for another less comfortable, or even for one that is very uncomfortable. Indeed, I might say that retrenchment will reduce "the area to hit"; that I will be less exposed to blows, less visible, more "camouflaged." Besides, the rent will be lower. And even if I could have paid the rent here now, how would I have found the next payment in June? As life gets ever more bitter and expensive, and the money shorter and shorter, how will we manage to cope in two or three months' time? Being all together at Strada Antim, we'll spend less and hold out longer. Yes. But at other times (especially this evening), I tell myself that a lost position is a lost position; that renunciation is a slippery slope which, once you start going down it, is very hard to climb back up. Up to now I have struggled to keep my head above water, as if nothing had happened. I have struggled to keep everything as before. And this house that I am leaving is the first thing I have lost.

I am no longer following the war in the Balkans. What's the point of working myself up over each episode when the thing as a whole is already settled? Whether in one week or in two or four, the Germans will be the masters in Yugoslavia, Albania, and Greece. Until then we'll be told one evening that Durazzo has been occupied by the Serbs (as we were the day before yesterday), only to have this denied the next morning; or we will be told in the morning that all the Yugoslav armies have surrendered (as we were yesterday), only to have it denied in the evening.

In North Africa the situation is unchanged: that is, very serious.

For the last three days I have been immersed in 1848. I read the documents of the revolution collected in six large official volumes—some four thousand pages of diplomatic reports, proclamations, statements, newspaper articles, letters, and so on. They are fascinating and strikingly vivid. The degree to which the epoch resembles a theatrical comedy may be seen from the memoirs of Colonel Locusteanu. Still, the documents add a great deal to what I previously knew or suspected. The material is so rich that it is becoming dangerous. For I am afraid of being carried away and losing myself in the "local color," the atmosphere surrounding particular incidents, the anecdotal charm of history. The best method would be to get to know the epoch well, with its people, language, and events, and then to write a play completely free of "historical truth." In any case, my hero will not be a real character but a complete invention of mine, with only a vicarious role in the revolution itself.

Thursday, 17 April

How can I explain the fact that today—in the midst of war, with so much bad news and so many worries, plus the obsession of moving my home (about which I dreamed a real nightmare yesterday)—I was able to have a whole day of literary exultation, of feverish impatience and nervous curiosity? When I got up this morning I could immediately see my play (my "latest" play, because I have put my other two projects aside for the moment), but I saw it with a sudden urgency that did not allow me time even to wash properly. I sat down at my desk and straightaway sketched out the scenario for Act One—not just in summary but, on the contrary, with a mass of incident and detail. Only then did I dare enter the bathroom. I also did an outline of the second and third acts, but of course it was more summary! I had no rest all day, and in the evening I returned to the manuscript and again found this morning's extraordinary inclination to write. So I did the scenario for Act Two, also with a great wealth of detail. I think that tomorrow I'll press on with Act Three (which I also now see quite well). If I'm left in peace (by whom? by life!), I think I could write the whole play in three to four weeks.

A terrible air raid on London last night, the worst since the beginning of the war. Hundreds of houses destroyed as well as hospitals, cinemas, theatres, large stores. But still the same determination to resist. "From Greece bad news, from Libya not so good"—someone said from London a little while ago.

Friday, 18 April

Good Friday! But I don't feel I am on holiday. Nor is it a holiday for me. A dull rainy day—very fitting weather.

I continued all day my reading of the 1848 documents. The problem is that they are too vivid, too entertaining, so that I allow myself to be carried away by them. I think there is no longer any danger as far as Act One is concerned, because it is too clearly fixed, both as a historical moment (10 June 1848, the day of the attempt on Gheorghe Bibescu's life) and as a scenario. But Act Two (which will probably take place on the day of the burning of the "Organic Regulations") could involve a lot on top of yesterday's scenario; here more than anywhere else, if I am not very careful, I could be overwhelmed by the material. It must be quite clear from the start that I am not writing a historical play, nor even an evocation of history. The play must, above all else, be a play: that is, it must have a plot that develops independently of the actual events of the revolution (so independently that, in terms of dramatic action, the same play could in theory be situated in a different epoch). In the end, what I want to write is not a play of the 1848 Revolution but a play about revolution in general. If I settle on 1848, it is partly because of the charm of the period, but above all because the unexpected similarities with the January revolt give rise to a whole series of allusions. I fear that the plot will have nothing dramatic; there is nothing in the projected scenario that points toward a climax. Like *Jocul de-a vacanța*, it will be more a succession of vivid incidents than a plot properly so called. Indeed, as in *Jocul de-a vacanța*, the action will slow down after Act Two. I shall have to be very careful here. The experience of my first play should have served some purpose: a weak third act can throw everything away, however good the start; whereas a "strong" third act can raise and sustain a play, even if the first two have been dull.

I feel less giddy than I did yesterday, more skeptical even. But I like the idea of the play, and I realize there are some things in it which could work well in the theatre. I would even go further and say that it could be a big hit at the National. For precisely this reason I propose to keep calm and say no more to anyone about the play (I have talked to too many people: Leni, the Zissescus), so that when it is finished (if it ever is), I can, if necessary, remain anonymous and put it on in great secrecy, with someone else as the ostensible author. But it is true that, without a change in the general situation, the play could not be staged under my name or anyone else's.

The war in Yugoslavia is over; there are no more regular troops to fight. Again today the surrender of all Yugoslav forces was announced, but this time it is probably true. The Greek front in Albania has started to give way. Yesterday the Greeks pulled out of Climia, three days after abandoning Gorica. In Greece there are hard battles and a continual German advance, not too rapid but certain enough. Things are pretty quiet in Libya. Last night Berlin suffered the heaviest British bombing since the start of the war. But there is a big difference between the "heaviest" British bombing and the "heaviest" German bombing. None of the communiqués indicates that the bombing of Berlin was comparable to the inferno in London. Nevertheless . . .

Sunday, 20 April

G. B. Shaw, quoted by Frank Harris: "I shall never have any real influence, because I have never killed anybody, and don't want to."

How absurd was the "love affair" with Madeleine Andronescu! After Nadia, who at least had the excuse of age, came Madeleine, who had no excuse at all. With the greatest simplicity and in complete good faith, without trickery, archness, or play-acting, I tried to convince her that she was making a big mistake.

Continual retreats in Albania and Greece. Argirocastro has been evacuated in Albania, and Larissa abandoned in Greece. But the front is still holding.

Evening
Radio sets are being confiscated. Today, the first day of Easter, the operation began without any warning. It does not come as a surprise; it was even to be expected! But the blow makes me feel depressed again. I was so unaware and childishly irresponsible as to live for five days with my literary projects, to let myself be stupefied by the joy of writing, to make plans and dream of future successes—forgetting everything around me, everything that has happened and that is in store, everything that is there all the time, lying in ambush. We have ahead of us a long and terribly difficult summer. And I have been preparing to welcome it as a kind of holiday! How stupid I can be sometimes!

Wednesday, 23 April

The last day in my apartment. I must hand it over by Friday at the latest. I'll pack all my stuff tomorrow and move it on Friday morning. Then we'll have to organize ourselves as best we can in Strada Antim. I still have moments of sadness and regret—but that too will pass as I get used to things. I have got used to greater, more profound suffering.

I spent all afternoon putting my papers, manuscripts, letters, and photographs into some sort of order. It was a kind of stock-taking. And throughout I had a sense of greyness, of a life wasted in pointless fretting. This war, with its constant anxiety, has overshadowed my old sources of personal unhappiness, but they still hurt when I get close to them. Through a kind of replacement effect, the war has taken me a little outside myself and my horrible secrets. Indeed, it has given me reasons to live and wait—I who, for so many years, have had no expectations. And yet I don't want to leave here with my head bowed. I still want to hope.

I still want to say and believe that there are chances of escape, and that at least the things which can still be made good will be made good. I was saying to Zoe—who came round so that we could spend the last day in this house together, as we did the first—that I sometimes have bursts of vitality. I count on them, even if they are intermittent. I'll do what I still can to stop myself from going under. Since I must leave here, may something good come of it.

Thursday, 24 April

The last night in this house on Calea Victoriei, where I am no longer "at home." I lie down among wooden boxes, upturned furniture, and heaps of torn paper. I think I could leave Bucharest, Romania, and Europe with an overcoat and nothing else—but it is so complicated to move from Calea Victoriei to Strada Antim. I haven't had a radio for four days! It seems to make me feel more lonely, more disoriented, more lacking in support. The familiar voices from London were like friends' voices, and it is difficult now that I have lost them. Only yesterday could I listen at Alice's to a British news bulletin. The news gets worse and worse, but for me at least it is not unexpected. In Greece the armies of Thessaloniki and Epirus have surrendered. The war in Albania is over. The Greek government and king have withdrawn to Crete. Even if the armies manage an orderly retreat, resistance is not likely for some time in the Peloponnese. In ten days at the most, Hitler will be free to strike another blow. Toward France and Spain, aiming both at the French navy and at Gibraltar? Toward Turkey? Or Suez? Everyone talks of war soon against the Russians. But I don't believe it. Hitler won't do the British such a favor.

Do you see how good general politics can be? It makes you forget your own miseries, both large and small.

Tuesday, 6 May

Since I have been in Strada Antim, my only pleasure and joy has been to turn the pages of the calendar in the morning: that's another day gone.

A letter from Shaw to Frank Harris (quoted from the biography I still have not finished because of the many interruptions): "What was wrong with Frank Harris? Wasn't he a Jew, or a financial blackmailer journalist, or another Verlaine, or a German spy or something!" This in connection with the naiveté of those who expect a British victory to result in the end of anti-Semitism.

From a letter sent by D. H. Lawrence in 1913, just after he had finished writing a play: "I enjoy so much writing my plays—they come so quick and exciting from the pen that you mustn't growl at me if you think them a waste of time."

Thursday, 8 May

The war in Greece has been over for ten days or so. We are certainly on the eve of another German offensive, without knowing where it will be directed. Turkey? Gibraltar, Alexandria? Tunisia, Algeria, and Morocco? The decision will certainly come very soon. By the 15th or 20th of May at the latest, *nous aurons du nouveau.*[6] Even war with the Russians no longer seems to me completely excluded (though it is still the least likely from every point of view). This May will not pass without some major events.

I have at last finished Shaw's biography of Harris. No difficulty in reading it. Almost everything I read is English, all jumbled together: Ruskin, Shelley, even Shakespeare. I tried *The Tempest* and it went a little more easily than I had expected.

What I miss most is my place in Calea Victoriei. I long for it as for a person I have lost. I am resigned to Strada Antim, but I can't say I am getting used to it. I think of myself as being in a provisional state, not knowing when I can leave it.

I try to discourage Madeleine Andronescu, but I don't succeed. Maybe I shall have to be nastier, firmer. Maybe even brutal, if there is no other way.

Too bored to note here last week's delightful encounter with "Mrs. Mateescu." I have told it several times as if it were a scene in a comedy, always with great success. It is so funny it seems made up.

Saturday, 10 May

A year since the German invasion of Belgium and the Netherlands! On the morning of 10 May 1940, nothing tragic or definitive had yet happened; paths were open in every direction. Then followed that terrible year we commemorate today, a little surprised to be alive, to be still be-

6. We shall have something new.

lieving and hoping. Yesterday and today there were groups of people opposite the closed bakeries, waiting for bread. Shouts, scuffles, growls—
and above all a kind of stupid weariness. Old images of Brăila in 1917.

Signs of a new German-Russian accord. The Russians are probably
making big concessions, but it is not known what they are.

Sunday, 11 [May]

Cold and rainy. A wet chilly spring. But from my window on the eighth
floor, even the rain was beautiful.

This morning I called in briefly at the Simu Museum, where I hadn't
been for some fifteen years. (I find it hard to stay indoors, so I walk in
the street, pay visits, wander around.) Among hundreds of very ordinary
paintings, signed by various obscure artists, the ten or fifteen interesting
ones easily get lost. A Renoir landscape, two or three Monets, a Paul
Signac, a few by Luchian. The rest are pompous bric-a-brac, old-fashioned, academic, dusty, most often stupid. And this is called Bucharest's
main art gallery.

I am still reading documents from 1848, and sometimes I think of my
play, but from a kind of duty rather than with pleasure, as if I had signed
a contract with myself to write this play. And perhaps—who knows?—I
really will write it some day.

The fresh German offensive we await from day to day, hour to hour, has
still not started. Perhaps we are in an interlude for diplomacy (an agreement with the Russians is possible), but the pause cannot last much
longer.

With great difficulty, by getting up at daybreak and waiting in line for
two hours at the baker's, our maid succeeded in buying a single loaf of
bread today.

Tuesday, 13 May

Rudolf Hess has disappeared: he fled with an airplane on Saturday night.
The National Socialist party has stated in a communiqué that: 1) Hess
was suffering from a serious brain disorder; 2) Hitler had forbidden him
to board the plane; 3) he should be considered lost in an accident; and
4) his adjutants have been arrested. The first logical supposition is suicide. The second, assassination. But neither the one nor the other is correct. It is all more sensational and fantastic than anything we could have

imagined or believed. Hess is right now in Britain: he flew a' Messer-schmitt alone to Scotland, where he parachuted somewhere near Glasgow and immediately presented himself to the authorities. Nothing more is known at present. The comedy begins with a *coup de théâtre* whose likes have not been seen before. Neither Sardou nor Arnold nor Bach would have gone so far in the most absurd of their farces. It literally makes you dizzy. For a few moments you suspend all political judgment and contemplate the event with stupefaction.

Friday, 16 May

I have seen Nina Eliade for the second time in the four weeks she has been in Bucharest. On Monday morning she flies with Giza to Lisbon, where Mircea is waiting for her. The last year in London has changed her a little (simply dressed in the English style; speaking with some self-assurance; ironical, reserved, "*à l'aise*"). But after the first fifteen minutes she becomes the old Nina I know: an honest, rather simple girl, re-spectfully repeating things that Mircea has said. The funny thing is that, arousing curiosity by the very fact of coming from London, she has been a real personality here in Bucharest, sought after, questioned, quoted. She casually tells me what she said to Marshal Prezan, what the head of the German general staff asked her, what she chatted about with the pro-paganda minister. How remote is the poor Nina Mareş from the Imo-biliara arcade! Suddenly the ten years since then come back to mind. There is a large distance to cover between the two images (Nina then, Nina now), as with an open pair of compasses.

In London they had 120 pounds a month (roughly half a million lei at the current rate of exchange!). In Lisbon, where Mircea is a Grade 1 press secretary, he makes 12,500 escudos. I don't know what that repre-sents—a lot, in any case. (A mere functionary cannot afford a plane trip right across Europe.) But Mircea, according to Nina, is not content. He works like a slave at the legation and is upset that he cannot write. His genius is being torn into tiny pieces. He'd prefer to return to Strada Palade 43, moneyless but free. Sometimes it occurs to him to drop every-thing and withdraw to a monastery. He would like to become a monk.— I tried to calm her, to tell her not to worry. Mircea won't return to Palade 43, nor will he become a monk. Not for the moment, anyway.

Saturday, 17 May

The Hess business is still the latest sensation, with the political side of it still a mystery. The Germans' stupor has manifested itself in the most comical ways. Several official explanations have been issued and withdrawn over the past three days: 1) that Hess is insane; 2) that his flight has no importance, since he was not in possession of any of the Reich's secrets; 3) that he won't divulge anything to the British, since he may be a utopian idealist but in no case a traitor; 4) that he fled to London only to warn the British that they have lost the war and that it would be a good idea if they sued for peace.

I have never read such hilarious eyewash as in this Hess affair. Politically speaking, the very first assumption seems plausible (and is to some extent confirmed by the drivel from the DNB, the German News Agency): namely, that Hess's flight is more a symptom than an event, indicating conflict inside Germany over the accord with the Russians. Direct consequences should not be expected at once. The war goes on. The Hess case (which puts Hitler in such a tricky position from a propaganda point of view) could at most precipitate some military actions that were already in preparation. A German operation (which we have been expecting since the first of May) could be launched at any moment. The areas toward which it might be directed have become clearer: Gibraltar, Iraq, Suez. Agreement already seems to have been reached with the Russians and with France. Admiral Daran has shown himself willing to sign anything. American pressure on the Vichy government will not stop him now, at the last moment. *Les jeux sont faits....*[7]

Yesterday the British retook Sollum. If they didn't also have to face a German attack on Syria and Iraq, they would be in a position to repeat last winter's successful battle for Cyrenaica.

Aderca, whom I saw the day before yesterday, regrets the death of Codreanu. He is convinced that he, Aderca, would have got from him a better deal for Jews. He thinks that Codreanu's *Pentru legionari* [For Legionaries] is a historic book. He regrets that the Iron Guard is anti-Semitic—had it not been, he would have joined it himself. He regrets that he did not know Codreanu, who was a great figure (like Sarah Bernhardt, like Goga). He thinks that Hitler has the mind of a genius, equal to Napoleon's or indeed greater.

7. The die is cast.

Monday, 19 May

The Duke of Aosta has surrendered, at Amba Alagi. A spectacular joint communiqué. The last two points of resistance in Abyssinia are at Gonder and around the southern lakes. But the Abyssinian war as such is over. At Sollum there are attacks and counterattacks; positions occupied now by one side, now by the other.

Since yesterday we have ration books for bread, sugar, oil, and meat. It will be announced later when they take effect.

Rosetti has been replaced by Cacaprostea[8] at the Foundations publishing house.

Addition to Saturday's note on Aderca: He says that Groza[9] and Trifa[1] are Communists and are now in Moscow. That shows his level of political competence.

Tuesday, 20 May

Camil Petrescu rang and woke me early this morning to say that, by analyzing the German communiqué on Hess "according to his own method," he has established that Hess did not *flee* but was *sent*. It was not an escape but a mission, in order to propose peace, or at least to cause confusion among the British.

The war has not yet entered a new phase. We are still in a pause which, because of its length and inactivity, bears some resemblance to an armistice. There are some skirmishes at Sollum and Tobruk, and some reconnaissance flights over Germany and Britain. But for some days there have been no battles, no heavy bombing. We are passing through a phase of diplomacy. Everyone seems to be negotiating: the Germans with the French, Turks, and Russians; the Americans with the Japanese and Russians; the Russians with the Japanese; the British with everyone. So many diplomatic conversations, at what looks like a moment of tacitly agreed suspension of hostilities, are leading to some talk of the possibility of an unexpected pact. That's a joke. This war won't end with deals. *Il y va de tout.*[2]

8. A nickname for the aesthetician D. Caracostea.
9. The Iron Guard Workers Corps leader, Dumitru Groza.
1. Viorel Trifa was president of the students' faction of the Iron Guard. He was later a Christian Orthodox bishop in Detroit and was expelled from the United States following a court decision. Both Groza and Trifa were accused by the Antonescu regime of being Soviet agents.
2. Everything is at stake.

Wednesday, 21 May

Titu Devechi drove me down the Şosea to see his house. From the outside it looks like a splendid English country house, with something of a Swiss "chalet." Large rooms, huge windows. A long gymnasium, two bedrooms, a spacious living room, and a dining room suspended above it.

"All that really needs good European order," I said to him.

I don't know if he understood what I meant. In any case, he smiled.

Devechi also thinks that Hess went on a mission from Hitler. "This war can only end in a compromise peace. Neither Britain nor Germany can be annihilated, and they have no interest in annihilating each other. They'll strike a deal very soon; we'll have peace in a fortnight at the latest."

I told him how superficial such a view seemed to me. We are involved in a much more complicated catastrophe.

"Compromise peace" is a formula that is starting to do the rounds. Timuş repeated it to me this evening, in almost the same terms. But we won't have long to wait until it becomes clear that this war is not a joke (has it been so far?!). Yesterday the Germans launched an air attack in Crete, with many landings and parachute drops. We don't have enough information, but it sounds like business in the grand style.

Sunday, 25 [May]

Only today, after five days of fighting, do the Germans speak of their offensive in Crete and report that they have established themselves in the western part of the island. The British communiqués, too, more through their tone than through any real information, are preparing the ground for an announcement of defeat. Intense fighting continues—but as soon as the Germans have a firmly occupied position, with even one point on the coast where they can freely land, the conquest of Crete will be almost inevitable. There will be fighting, resistance, perhaps delays— but the game is over. So this proves that a landing is possible! In Greenland an important naval battle is going on. The British have lost a ship of the line: 49,000 tons and some 1,400 men. But both battles—in Crete and in Greenland—are still only the preliminaries. The great German drive to win the war for good will probably follow in June, July, or August.

I have read *Die vertreibung der Juden aus Spanien* [The Expulsion of the Jews from Spain] by Valeriu Marcu. I'll look for the same period in Dubnow, where it is treated at greater length. With no qualities other than simple, naive exposition, Valeriu Marcu has made a name for himself in Germany as a *"glänzender Historiker und Essayist."*[3] I tell myself that if I had had a more precise view of things in 1929 (when I left Paris) and had decided to leave for Germany, Britain, or the United States, or even France, not to do some pointless studies but to learn perfectly one of these three great languages, with the definite intention of working in it instead of being a Bucharest writer, I might by now be a creative force in Britain or America, writing not for three thousand readers but for thirty thousand.

A.B. has offered to translate my *De două mii de ani* for possible publication in America. No, no. Even if the idea were not a fantasy (an extreme one at that!), I still would not accept. I no longer have anything in common with the books I have written. To the extent that I can still make plans for the future (though I am too despondent, too weary, too embittered), I think of leaving after the war to write plays and film scripts in a big city somewhere. It's an occupation for which I think I am suited. And I don't consider it as anything other than an occupation.

In the end, we Jews are childishly, absurdly optimistic, sometimes without being aware of it. (It's the only thing that helps us to live.) In the midst of catastrophe we go on hoping. "It'll work out all right"—we always say mockingly, but in fact we do think "it'll work out all right." I do so myself, I who am the least entitled to hope. Valeriu Marcu rightly points out: *"Diese ewig Geschlagenen sind vor ihrem Schicksal die ewig Optimistischen. Sie glauben immer, es könne nicht gar zu schlimm kommen."*[4]

Cacaprostea's first measure at the Foundation has been to remove the chapters about Jewish writers from Călinescu's *Istoria*, which is already at the typesetters.[5] I haven't thought much about it, or tried to analyze the strange sense of satisfaction with which I heard the news. The honest fact is that I laughed, and that, without knowing why, I thought a favor had been done to me.

Wednesday, 28 May

The German battleship *Bismarck*, which on Saturday notched a great victory off Greenland by sinking the battleship *Hood*, has been sunk in turn

---

3. A brilliant historian and essayist.
4. "These people, forever beaten, are forever optimistic about their fate. They keep believing that things can't turn out too badly in the end."
5. This *History of Romanian Literature* was nonetheless published in full.

this morning after a dramatic four-day chase. What a lightning riposte by the British! There has been no end to the phone calls giving the news: Rosetti, Madeleine, Aristide . . . Heavy fighting in Crete, with major casualties.

Saturday, 31 May

The fighting in Crete will continue for a day or two, but the island already seems lost. The capital—Canea—fell yesterday. The British are retreating and will probably try to leave by sea.

The schools were due to remain open until 20 June, but an urgent directive from the ministry has brought this forward to 14 June, when everything (universities and schools) is supposed to shut. Today everyone has been asking with concern the reason for this decision. Again there is talk of mobilization, and rumors are spreading of a war with the Russians. I have the feeling it is another farce.

On Thursday evening there was a meeting at Vianu's[6] with Ralea, Papilian, Pippidi,[7] and Eugen Ionescu. A long discussion about Nae Ionescu, who for Ralea and Vianu was no more than a café regular, a spinner of yarns, an impostor, a "smart aleck." I enjoyed telling them that for me, Nae Ionescu was the devil.

Sunday, 1 June

So spring is over—that "Spring 1941" from which we feared so much in the way of calamities, if not the final calamity itself. *Et pourtant nous sommes encore là.*[8] We are still alive, still on our feet; nothing irreparable has happened. I wonder whether the spring really did pass easily, or whether—since we are now at the end—we have the false impression that it was bearable. (Alas, everything is bearable!) It may be that if someone had told us on 1 March that spring would see Bulgaria occupied, Yugoslavia destroyed, Cyrenaica reoccupied, Greece fallen, and Crete invaded, the perspective of so many defeats would have seemed to us disastrous. But now, when all these things have happened, they seem to have become unimportant. Again and again, the only thing that counts is that we should remain on our feet. So long as Britain does not surrender, there is room for hope.

6. Tudor Vianu: literary critic.
7. Dionisie Pippidi: historian.
8. And yet we are still here.

We are moving into summer, and evidently into a new phase of the war. Crete was an episode. Now the Germans must soon decide on a fresh action. All directions are possible: Suez, Gibraltar, Turkey, even the British Isles.

And Russia? Could there be a war between Russia and Germany? For three days everyone has thought one imminent. Since yesterday we have had a climate of mobilization in Bucharest. On Friday there was a black-out; yesterday an order was issued that air-raid shelters must be built in every yard in a maximum of two weeks. Today a number of trains have been canceled, probably because of troop movements. There is a wave of call-ups and requisitioning. At the height of the working season on the farms, horses and cattle are being taken away from people. Those who have been to Moldavia (e.g., G. M. Cantacuzino) say that there is a clear war zone in the region of the Prut. On the streetcars, in the streets and restaurants, people talk of war, war, war. From a political point of view, it seems unlikely to happen. But the actual state of things cannot be denied. Is it again a big bluff? But such a *mise en scène* would be too costly and, in the end, without any point. The same comedy could be acted with less ostentation and equally good results. In the space of a year and a half I have seen the most absurd happenings, the most incredible turnarounds. I should stop trying to judge, to understand, to predict. The facts carry more weight than anything else.

What a character from a novel is Danacu, our landlord! I thought of him in connection with the novel I was planning some time back, and there seemed to be a suitable place for him in it.

I spent a pleasant day with Zoe, whom I had not seen since I left the studio apartment.

Monday, 2 June

War, war, war: people talk of nothing else. Each person I meet has something new to tell: the Fourth and Fifth Armies have been called up; the financial administration in Moldavia has taken refuge in Oltenia; a general mobilization has been decreed for the 5th. You don't know what to believe, how to check it, whom to ask. Panic sets in, and everything escapes the control of calm judgment. I went round to see Vişoianu, who has been called up. Like me, he thinks that war with the Russians is a politically dangerous business for the Germans (even if it would be militarily straightforward). Nevertheless I think that war is possible—even imminent. Radu Popescu, whom I met at Vivi's, received his call-up papers yesterday and must report tomorrow to the Twenty-first [Regiment], which has already left for the Prut. He showed me his green-colored summons, and I shuddered at the mere sight of it. (What will happen to us Jews? What will be our military situation if there is a general mobilization?)

A meeting between Hitler and Mussolini at the Brenner Pass is another sign that we are on the threshold of a major action. This is the decisive moment. Even if it is a complete fantasy, I should note my thought that we may be about to witness a formidable *coup de théâtre*, with a sudden switch in enemies. Germany starts a de facto armistice with the British (negotiated and concluded by Hess) and immediately turns against the Russians. Absurd? Of course. But it is very strange that, since Hess's arrival in Britain, the British and the Germans have stopped bombing each other. And ten days on, the Hess affair has been completely forgotten. It is understandable that the Germans are silent. But why should the British be too, when they have an interest in the most almighty propaganda barrage? Is it conceivable that there is a tacit complicity between them? No, of course not—not if you think about it rationally. But we've seen so many things!

I visited Pippidi this afternoon with Eugen Ionescu. He read us some strikingly topical pages from Thucydides. It could have been a pamphlet against the Germans.

I finished *Père Goriot* today. It is by far the best thing of Balzac's that I have read up to now. (Countess Beauséant's ball reminded me of Mrs. Saint-Euverte's reception. Goriot's illness and death agony do not stop Baroness Nucingen from going to the ball, just as Swann's illness and the Marquess of Osmond's death agony do not stop Oriane from going to the reception.)

I continued to think of my possible future novel. The first two or three chapters are already sketched in my mind. In particular, I have drawn some connections between various "floating" characters about which I have been thinking for so long. But, of course, it is a very remote project that will not happen before my play, nor—alas!—before the war. No, I am not oblivious to everything, believe me. Literature is too weak a drug for all that is happening.

Tuesday, 3 June

Last night I dreamed I was at the regiment, still a civilian. I report to an officer (a lieutenant colonel, I think), and he takes me into Ilie's office. Feeling very scared, I stand "at attention" and salute with my hand at the side of my hat. Ilie barks at me, checks my clothing, and makes one or two adjustments. When he asks me what I want, I say that I want to enlist. He accepts and says that he is doing me a big favor; there is just one other Jew in the whole regiment. He gives an order for me to be issued my uniform and equipment. The regimental yard has the appearance of a mobilization. I am very unhappy. "What the hell got into me to come here!" I move away alone to a kind of field. When I come back, I meet Neumann (my classmate from 8th Year in Brăila), who is dressed in a lieutenant's uniform. All the Jewish officers have been called up, he tells me. I again approach the barracks (but they are not the barracks of the Twenty-first) and find the regiment in full uniform, apparently waiting for an inspection. I pass by a small platoon of male army nurses with strange equipment, some or all of whom are Jews. They prepare to swap their caps for huge red velvet berets—part of their parade uniform. Far off I can see a car belonging to the royal court. The King is coming, someone says. I am the only civilian in that whole uniformed multitude. "I hope no one sees me." I flee in terror, run, run, run—and wake up.

Lovinescu (whom I met at Alcalay this morning) tells me that the baccalaureate examinations have been suspended because of the war. It looks as if this will break out any day now, or even any hour.

Rosetti rang to say that according to the very latest information, the war will not take place. The Germans and the Russians have reached an agreement. As for yesterday's meeting at the Brenner, the topic was France and the Axis's intention to seal an official peace with it in the next few days. In return for losing nothing more than Alsace, in its colonies France will assume an obligation for armed resistance to Britain.

Evening
Again it is being said that war is imminent. A directive from the Ministry of Education, ordering all schools to close at the latest by the evening of the 7th, was published this evening. Ministers (according to Alice) are hurriedly evacuating their offices. Call-up papers are arriving in a flood. There are talks about a national government, with George Brătianu, Mihalache, Cuza, Codreanu Senior, and Gigurtu. I had supper at Alice Th.'s

with Branişte, Vivi, Hillard, and Aristide. All of them, including Branişte,
think that the war preparations are very grave.

Saturday, 7 June

Rumors of war are continuing to mount. By now the most sensible people think it inevitable. On Thursday, Bucharest Radio broadcast a new
signal—a trumpet blast—which is supposed to precede any solemn news.
On Thursday evening, Ciorănescu—a member of the Radio Broadcasting Council—told me that the radio programs have been ordered gradually to step up their propaganda for Bessarabia, until 15 to 20 June,
when war is certain to break out. Alice (who, it is true, usually has the
most fantastic information) was certain that a German ultimatum had
been presented to Russia, and that a Romanian ultimatum would follow
in the next few hours. Pan Halippa, on the General's orders, was working to map out territorial claims on the other side of the Dniester.

This morning what do we find in the papers? A dramatic official communiqué that contradicts the rumors of war spread by "thoughtless people," "alarmists," "unwitting tools of the enemy," "scandalmongers," "dens
of idle swindlers." No, no: *la guerre n'aura pas lieu!*[9]

Tuesday, 10 June

On the night of Saturday to Sunday, British and Gaullist troops entered
Syria. They seem to be advancing swiftly, without meeting any serious
resistance. Vichy has protested and is sending Dentz's troops to fight.[1]
The Germans speak indignantly of "aggression." It is possible that the
whole business will be over in a week or ten days (though speed is not
an English quality). Only later, when the Germans attack Suez through
Turkey, will Syria become a key point again. It is strange that Hitler has
not deeply committed himself in either Iraq or Syria. Because he couldn't?
Out of the question. Right now he can do anything. So why? Does this
relative indifference to the Middle East not signify that his theatre of
diplomatic and eventually military operations has really shifted? Toward
Russia, for example? There is constant talk of a German-Romanian-
Russian war, which will break out today, tomorrow, or the day after, or
at the latest in ten to fifteen days. I met Engineer Lupaş the other day
(not your ordinary man in the street), and he told me that the two armies

9. The war will not take place!
1. Henri-Ferdinand Dentz: French general.

are girded and ready on opposite banks of the Prut, just waiting for the first shot to be fired. On Sunday evening at Madeleine's, Titel Comarnescu told me—in one of his well-known fits of hysteria—that war is absolutely prepared, and absolutely inevitable. And I still don't believe it.

Wednesday, 11 June

Yesterday evening, at Alice's, the telephone suddenly rang. Someone on behalf of Colonel Lovinescu to say that a date has been fixed for the offensive against Bessarabia: 20 June.

Yesterday A.B. saw Gunther, the envoy of the United States.[2] He doesn't know either if there will be a war between Russia and Germany. He thinks there is indeed a German ultimatum, with such tough conditions that he finds it hard to believe the Soviets will accept it.

Yesterday at school we had a meeting to discuss the 8th Year. (In general, my experience as a teacher has been uninteresting. Neither my pupils nor my "colleagues" have taught me anything new.) Yesterday, however, I felt for the first time at close quarters the terrible tragicomedy of school. The elderly Latin teacher, finicky, tired, ridiculous, so worn and ineffectual as to be moving, insisted on failing an insolent pupil and making him repeat the exam. We defended the boy and tried to get him moved up to the next year while the poor teacher resisted almost in desperation, almost in tears. We felt that for him it was a question of pride, revenge, personal prestige. He didn't want to let his victim go, and clung to him with a stubborn, relentless effort. He virtually begged us to help him by not allowing the boy through; this seemed to be his way of making up for wounded pride.

"The boy will kill himself if you don't pass him."

"Well, so what? It wouldn't be any loss. None at all."

I got the feeling that that man was capable of murder.

Thursday, 12 June

More than yesterday or any other time, everyone now believes there will be war. Yesterday evening I heard several times at different places: "The ultimatum expires tonight." Some people were actually expecting an air raid last night; others expect one tonight. Those who can are leaving

---

2. Franklin Gunther Mott: head of the U.S. diplomatic mission in Bucharest.

Bucharest, especially if they have children. Gina Strunga (at whose place I had supper yesterday) is leaving for Sighișoara. Begoghina[3] is leaving tomorrow morning. Since yesterday, General Antonescu has been in Germany having meetings with Ribbentrop and Hitler. It looks as if the final decisions are being made.

"Do you still not believe it? really not?" Eugen Ionescu asked me this morning, eaten up with panic.

Jews are being arrested in the street, and it is said they will be sent to concentration camps. I don't know what the criterion is. At Strada Lipscani, I myself saw a whole column being marched along between bayonets; it was made up of all sorts of people, most of them well dressed.

On the Șosea, where I went for a walk toward evening with Comșa and Lereanu, an endless German motorized column was heading out in the direction of Ploiești. Across the road from the Minovici villa, an elegant young lady accompanied by two men in civilian clothes had stepped out of a limousine and, with her arm raised, was shouting "Heil!" to one lorry after the other. They were the first civilians I have seen saluting the Germans in such a hearty manner.

Saturday, 14 June

TASS has issued a communiqué about "rumors of a war between Germany and Russia." The news is false, provocatively put about by the British and especially by Stafford Cripps.[4] It is true that German troops are massed on the border with Russia, but this is "probably" for other purposes. It is also true that Russian troops are on maneuvers in the same region, but these are normal training maneuvers. Germany has presented no ultimatum to Russia, nor any territorial or economic demands. Relations between the two countries are excellent.—That is what is known as a *"malencontreux"*[5] communiqué. It comes at a time when, in Bucharest, the war atmosphere has reached a paroxysm, at the very moment when everyone is expecting the bugles to sound. The morning papers put the communiqué somewhere on their inside pages, among news items devoid of importance. The evening papers no longer publish it at all. So far there has been no response from Berlin, no sign of what is to come. Here, people are stupefied. Only tomorrow will heads begin to clear.

3. Riccardo Begoghina: Italian businessman.
4. British ambassador in Moscow.
5. Inopportune.

For several hours this morning, nearly all telephones in the possession of Jews were out of service. Maybe the first little diversion. Anti-Semitism covers up many disappointments.

Today is the first anniversary of the fall of Paris.

Sunday, 15 June

The same silence continues to surround the TASS communiqué. Berlin appears not to have taken note of it. In Bucharest there is "great disappointment."[6] But the evacuations go on. Everyone talks as before of the war that is about to start—on Wednesday night, apparently. Nevertheless, I have the feeling that the critical moment has passed; there is less panic, less impatience, less enthusiasm.

Haig has been sentenced to thirteen years' imprisonment.

Yesterday evening I went with the Zissus (they rang and insisted) to the Pescăruş restaurant. Unpleasant company: she, vulgar and showy; he, honest but uninteresting (how could Nae Ionescu have thought him intelligent?). It depresses me to go out to elegant places, where people seem to be living on a different planet. Elegant, indifferent, wealthy, untroubled, remote from the obsession with war, remote from the other extreme of penury. In that world I feel my poverty, failure, and disgrace as a physical humiliation.

Monday, 16 June

Eugen Ionescu burst in this morning to tell me that there is no longer any hope: war with the Russians has been finally decided. Vinea, Carandino, Ciorănescu, Nădejde—all assured him that it was imminent. Vianu has gone off to Sinaia, to settle his children there. The TASS communiqué of the day before yesterday not only denies nothing but confirms everything. Those of us who still don't believe there will be war are stupid or blind. He stayed with me all morning, tormented and convulsed. But I think he was calmer when he went back home.

This morning's papers and this afternoon's are silent. Still no hint from Berlin.

6. In English in the original.

In Marx (*The Eighteenth Brumaire of Louis Bonaparte*) there is a passage that perfectly fits the France of today: "It is not enough to say, as the French do, that their nation was taken unawares. A nation and a woman are not forgiven the unguarded hour in which the first adventurer that came along could violate them. The riddle is not solved by such turns of speech, but merely formulated differently. It remains to be explained how a nation of thirty-six millions can be surprised and delivered unresistingly into captivity by three swindlers."[7]

Evening

Starting from this evening, the city is again in complete darkness. The measure was suddenly taken during the day and announced by radio and on posters. There is a fine drizzle, and it is pitch-black. I stayed home. Outside the police are going from house to house and drawing up lists of children to be evacuated. The general feeling is one of oppressive worry.

Tuesday, 17 June

All driving permits have been canceled by decree. There will no longer be any taxis or private cars. Petrol will be rationed for cars that do have special permission to move around.

Open-air theatres and restaurants have been closed. There is no light anywhere in the city.

Longhin (whom I haven't seen since that time at Stîna de Vale) tells me that war is absolutely certain. Today the courts and appeal courts evacuated their valuables. Army Headquarters has installed itself in Snagov. The General has left for "the front." Today or tomorrow a military parade will take place in Piatra Neamţ, and then it will begin. Ovidiu Lupaş assures me that the Russians will be crushed in a couple of weeks. Horia Roman (from *Timpul*) thinks war might even break out tonight, Jebeleanu that it might be delayed until Thursday.

I am trying to "reconsider" the situation. War between Russia and Germany still seems to me unlikely—but not out of the question. The *coup de théâtre* of August 1939 may be repeated today in the opposite direction. If Hitler realizes that he won't finish the British off this year, and if he resigns himself to this fact, then what is there left for him to

---

7. "The Eighteenth Brumaire of Louis Bonaparte," in Marx/Engels, *Selected Works* (London, 1970), p. 100.

do with such a huge army? Let it be worn down through inactivity? Obviously he'd prefer to beat the British first and only then take on the Russians. But since the British have resisted more than he expected, the objectives may be posed in the reverse order. That would be logical. But I still think that we won't go to war. (It's true that my predictions are usually poor; nor did I think in September 1939 that it would come to war.)

The British are on the offensive in Libya, at Sollum and Port Capuzzo. It started before daybreak yesterday with a lightning attack, but so far the advances have been pretty mediocre. In Syria, too, the operations have lost momentum. The British seem to be going easy on the French, who are now counterattacking in their turn.

It is a year since Pétain took over the government and asked for an armistice. A day of mourning that will not be forgotten. We were brokenhearted, and since then our dear image of France has been constantly degraded and disfigured. Paris itself, having remained unscathed and unscratched, seems cold, lifeless, indifferent. In the past I had only to utter the name of a Paris street and my heart would beat faster; now everything appears frozen, motionless, dead. Still, it is possible that France will come out of this too. Was the regime of Napoleon III less abject than the Pétain regime?

Wednesday, 18 June

Rain and darkness. How strange the city looks, sunk in darkness and pierced by the brief, almost momentary glow of flashlights that people use to find their way without falling or hitting themselves.

The British offensive, repelled at Sollum, has been abandoned. Once again the depressing thought occurs that nothing can be done anywhere on earth against the German armies.

Nothing new on the internal front. War is still expected today, tomorrow, or the day after.

"It seems funny to speak of Eminescu as a philosophical poet. Actually, I am the only philosophical poet!" Who else but Camil could utter such a sentence? But since I have been seeing less of him, I again enjoy listening to him speak.

Thursday, 19 June

A very broad agreement has been concluded between the Germans and the Turks: nonaggression, friendship, inviolability. But from the text it is not clear whether "inviolability" means that German troops have no right to cross Turkey.

Carandino, on his way from *Curentul*, told me that in all likelihood the war will begin tonight.

I saw Călugăru for the first time in several months. He was unchanged: the same small, nervous, confused, hysterical, obsessed man from *Cuvântul*. He has written a play about John the Baptist, and another one about Charlie Chaplin for both the theatre and the cinema, using a new technical formula. He has also written a book of poems in Yiddish. For an hour he talked about himself and his writings, and read some aloud. He speaks terribly fast, without even looking to see whether you are listening or not. He asks no questions and waits for no answers: he just talks and talks. As far as war with the Russians is concerned, he thinks it is a complete impossibility, a propaganda invention on the part of the British. Moreover, he argues, if Hitler dared to attack the Russians he would be crushed. I left shrugging my shoulders, not saying a word. What would have been the point?

Evening

Many people claim that at 5:30 this afternoon London spoke of a German-Romanian ultimatum to Russia. But this evening at Alice's, between ten and eleven, I listened to the broadcasts from London in German, Romanian, and English, and there was no mention of such an ultimatum. All they said was that there are dozens of German divisions on the Russian frontier, and that "one way or another" the situation will have to be clarified in the next few days.

Our teacher gave an interesting interpretation of the Turkish-German agreement: namely, that Germany has been forced to give up any idea of attacking through Turkey, and to conceal this through a so-called accord.

If I were to record everything that people say, believe, guess, invent, affirm, or deny, I would have to blacken hundreds of sheets of paper. There is general bewilderment, total confusion. Days of the most terrible hysteria I have ever seen.

Pippidi told me over the phone that the war will begin tomorrow morning if it stops raining. Dr. Weber knows for sure that all the ministries have drawn up lists of functionaries to be appointed in Bessarabia. He also knows that the General is determined to enter Chişinău[8] on the 27th of June, a year to the day since the province was lost. Aristide tells me that all the factories (including his paper factory—so the information is accurate and precise) have been instructed to prepare the necessary reserves to be sent to and distributed in Bessarabia.

Saturday, 21 June

Private telephones are not working. There is a strange sense of danger, isolation, siege. You feel you can no longer communicate with anyone. The buses no longer run; they are said to have been converted into ambulances. Maybe I am mistaken, but the streets seem emptier than before. Adania[9] tells me that the National Theatre is rehearsing plays for the theatres in Chişinău and Cernăuţi.[1]

I have been reading Thucydides—splendid and soothing. How stupid is our fretting over things that have remained the same down the ages! There is hardly one page in Thucydides in which you can't find things directly applicable to events today. Sometimes it even seems like a contemporary pamphlet. I regret that I do not have a room of my own where I can collect myself. I feel a great urge to work. I would read and write as never before.

Sunday, 22 June

In two proclamations to the country and the army, General Antonescu has announced that Romania, alongside Germany, has begun the holy war to liberate Bessarabia and Bukovina and to eradicate bolshevism. This morning Hitler issued a long declaration, explaining the reasons for the war that began last night against the Soviets. Before the sun rose, German troops crossed the Russian frontier at several points and bombarded a number of towns. No precise geographical details are given. Molotov, speaking on the radio at dawn, protested against the "aggression," the "brutality," and so on. Here is the Soviet wolf forced to play the role of the innocent lamb—as if it were just another poor Belgium.

8. The Romanian name for Kishinev.
9. Alf Adania: translator of the works of Eugene O'Neill and of other American authors.
1. The Romanian name for Czernowitz.

"*Les bobards*"[2] are invented and spread with amazing speed. Just an hour after news of the war was reported in the papers, the lawyer Schwartz came to tell me that Romania had occupied Cernăuţi, occupied Chişinău, and broadcast a *Te Deum* from Cernăuţi. Three hundred Russian aircraft heading for Bucharest were all shot down. An acquaintance of his spoke on the 'phone with a nephew in Cernăuţi, who reported with tears in his eyes that the city had been liberated.

Until the last moment I did not believe that there would be war. Yesterday evening still, this morning still, I was convinced of the contrary.

Evening

The city is as deserted as on a Sunday in midsummer. You would think everyone is off on holiday. In the evening we gather early at home. With the shutters drawn and the telephone out of service, we have a growing sense of unease and anguish. What will happen to us? I hardly dare ask. You are afraid to imagine what you will be like in another day, another week, another month.

Tuesday, 24 June

The first real air-raid alert. (There were two others yesterday, but they weren't taken seriously.) Today anti-aircraft weapons and machine guns were being fired. Those who were out in the street claim to have seen two "black" (?) aircraft flying at a great height. It all lasted no more than fifteen or twenty minutes. Being at home, I did not feel any alarm. But in the street there seem to have been moments of panic. We'll get used to that, though.

In town, on the walls and shop windows, there are two propaganda posters by Anestin.[3] (He did not actually sign them, but Anestin's line is much more than a signature: it is a fingerprint.) One depicts Stalin in a white smock that carries the traces of bloody hands. The text: "The Butcher of Red Square." The second—with the text: "Who are the masters of bolshevism?"—shows a Jew in a red gown, with side curls, skull cap, and beard, holding a hammer in one hand and a sickle in the other. Concealed beneath his coat are three Soviet soldiers. I have heard that the posters were put up by police sergeants.

I still don't know if it is true that Leni and Froda are, or have been, under arrest. Worried by what I had heard, I called round to see them yesterday, but no one answered the door.

2. Tall stories.
3. Graphic artist.

Camil claims that Zambaccian,[4] who went to Malmaison[5] to intervene on behalf of Zaharia Stancu, saw Leni and Scarlat there. Yesterday I rang Mircea Vulcănescu to ask him about the arrests. Will they continue? Could I be targeted myself? Is it true (as I was told some ten days ago) that the simple fact that I am Jewish and once belonged to a press association is good enough reason? Without even saying "hello," he snapped back over the phone: "Well, what of it?" Well, obviously nothing. He gave me an appointment at the ministry, but I didn't go.

No German or Romanian communiqué about how things are going. It is said that Cernăuți and Chișinău have been occupied, that the Dniester has been reached at several points. But it is also said that the offensive on the Prut[6] is still not under way, that a strong push is expected from the direction of Poland before the advance on Bessarabia begins. Of course, no one knows anything for sure. There are rumors of air raids on Galați and Iași, Brăila and Constanța. But they are so exaggerated as to be implausible.

Thursday, 26 June

Midnight. The fourth air-raid warning of the day. The first two, almost one after the other, lasted from 5:30 a.m. until 9:00. Bombs fell in our part of town, at the junction of Strada Sfinții Apostoli with Strada Rahova. The first loud explosion was accompanied with a brief flash, as of lightning. There are dead and wounded, but it is not known how many. It was not a major attack, and I think the bombs were dropped more or less at random. Now I am too tired to note any more about this first day of alarms.

The news from the front is still imprecise. In the north, the Germans seem to have penetrated some 150 kilometers, to the vicinity of Vilna. The rest of the Russian front seems to be holding out. From the Prut, no reliable news but dozens of rumors. At first the talk was of a Soviet disaster, but now it is rather less heady. In any event, neither Chișinău nor Cernăuți has yet been occupied. It is even said that the Russians have counterattacked in the Sculeni–Fălciu region. But I refuse to believe all the things that are said or whispered. I'll wait for the official communiqués.

The day before yesterday there was more serious bombing at Con-

4. Wealthy businessman and collector of modern art.
5. Prison in Bucharest.
6. River, former border between Romania and occupied Bessarabia.

stanța and Galați. People coming from there "brag" about it, but they are stupidly garrulous and terribly hysterical. A little more calm and patience are needed.

Friday, 27 June

A relatively calm night. Scarcely had I written the last note and retired when the sirens sounded again. But we decided not to go to the shelter. In the end, I don't think we are less "protected" on the ground floor or three floors above us than we would be in the basement. I slept until morning and did not even hear the other two alerts of which people later spoke.

Among yesterday's dead was Zanea Alexandru, a pupil from my 8th Year, a tall, handsome, and sturdy boy, with a certain personal distinction in that rowdy class. I have one of his exercise books that he gave me on the last day of school.
"What shall I do with it, Mr. Zanea?"
"Please read it. I'd like to know what you think of my writing."
"Okay, I will."

Some people (Comșa, Lereanu) are completely indifferent to the course of the war. Sometimes this makes me angry: it seems callous, egoistic, unimaginative.

"The Jews will be removed from villages in Moldavia," say today's papers. The measure may be extended to other regions. The banner headline: "Yids to Labor Camps!"

Saturday, 28 June

Twenty-four hours of calm. Not one air-raid warning. I went to bed early, being very tired, and slept through till morning. The third Romanian communiqué appeared today. Again it is sober and restrained: no official news, no real indication of what is happening. The German press dispatches speak of great victories without spelling out anything. The same goes for the German communiqué. It does seem, however, that there has been a major advance in the north of Poland, and that there is fighting in the Minsk region (on the old territory of Russia). Someone told me today that Smolensk has been occupied, so that Moscow itself is now directly threatened. As I have no radio, I cannot verify anything, cannot know anything. I always wait for an official communiqué.

Meanwhile I go on reading Thucydides. Book Five, which I read yesterday, is more a history of diplomatic operations among Athens, Sparta,
and Argos than one of war operations as such. Some of the similarities,
of the analogies, are incredibly striking. What an easy game Giraudoux
invented! And in the end, how little he drew from material so rich in
suggestions!

I am worried about the anti-Semitic tension that is being fueled by the
press, radio, and street posters. Why? Why? I know perfectly well why,
but I can't break the habit of asking this silly question.

I stay at home all the time, though I find it suffocating. I dare not
go too far into town; it is best not to be seen, not to have people talk
about me. Toward evening I walk around outside the house. What I really
need is a big yard, with a little sky and a little grass to roll in.

Sunday, 29 June

Book Six of Thucydides, which I read today, recounts the war of Athens
against Syracuse, the Sicilian expedition, the diplomatic negotiations with
the colonies in Italy, and the treachery of Alcibiades. It seemed the finest
of all the books, the one most susceptible to comparisons with the present war. The analogies between the Peloponnesian War and the wars of
1914 and 1940 are so great that they sometimes seem to merge into one.
Only the element of anti-Semitic diversion was lacking in the war policy of the Greek city-states—a lack all the more glaring in that they were
waging a war for economic interests but (like today) camouflaging it beneath a war in the name of ideology and public opinion. The Jews would
have been very useful to them, if they had had any, but closer analysis
might reveal who then served that function. It amuses me to recall that
when Victor Ion Popa produced Aristophanes' *Plutos* a couple of years
ago, he put a starkly Semitic mask in among all the Greek ones. The
poor man felt that something was missing there. . . .

I intend to read Aristophanes after I have finished Thucydides. I find
the Peloponnesian War too absorbing to set it aside so quickly. With
Aristophanes, I shall remain within its framework.

There were alerts last night and this morning, each one lasting an hour
or an hour and a half. But no bombing. A few roars, but that could have
been anti-aircraft fire.

From today, Jews are forbidden to fly the Romanian tricolor or the German flag. Police lorries went around confiscating flags in various parts

of town. It seems that at Huşi, the few remaining Jews are forced to wear a distinctive yellow sign.

A constant sense of oppression and anguish. I don't see anyone, don't communicate with anyone. Only my reading helps to keep my unease in check. If my eyes were better, I'd read more.

Monday, 30 June

The pompous German communiqué reports 4,000 aircraft and 2,500 tanks destroyed, with 40,000 prisoners taken. More than the news as such, the style in which it is drafted gives you the sense of a major Soviet military disaster. On the map the catastrophe is not so evident. But in town everyone is talking of a definitive German victory.

In Iaşi, five hundred Judeo-freemasons executed.[7] The government communiqué, printed in special editions of the papers, states that they had been aiding and abetting Soviet parachutists.

Tuesday, 1 July

One more month over, one more beginning. This time we are in the midst of catastrophes. Fewer questions than on the first of June, but more terrors.

Powerless to speak or write. A kind of dull, muffled terror. You hardly dare look beyond the passing hour, beyond the day that has not yet passed. An alert from 8:30 until 10 this evening. The first since Sunday morning, but longer and apparently more serious. The roar of anti-aircraft fire, machine-gun bursts, and some strange isolated bangs, as if from a revolver.

Yesterday a streetcar driver saw me with a newspaper in my hand.

"Have they entered Moscow?"

"Not yet. But they will for sure—today or tomorrow."

"Well, let them. Then we can make mincemeat of the yids!"

A conversation between a man and a "nice" lady, overheard in the street:

"Well, what do you think they've found out? It was a Jewish girl, fourteen years old. She threw the bombs with her own hands."

---

7. Sebastian quotes from the official communiqué that followed the pogrom in Iaşi (June–July 1941). Actual numbers were closer to thirteen thousand victims in the city itself and in two death trains.

The fall of the democratic regime in Athens, after the terrible defeat in Syracuse (which Thucydides describes in all its pain and suffering), is so similar to the fall of the French Republic after the collapse of the Somme front. Alcibiades is a kind of Laval, but probably more daring and adventurous, more willing to expose himself to blows, less abject. You feel a tightening of the chest, a strange sense of humiliation as you read all about the fall of Athens.

Wednesday, 2 July

The official communiqué in all the papers today: "In recent days there have been several cases when hostile alien elements opposed to our interests have opened fire on German and Romanian soldiers. Any attempt to repeat these vile attacks will be ruthlessly crushed. For each German or Romanian warrior, fifty Judeo-Communists will be executed."

Saturday, 5 July

Days of extreme disquiet. You feel weighed down, pursued, as in a nightmare. Then, feeling so weary, you stop thinking and seem to fall back into a leaden apathy, to be aroused by another piece of news, another whisper. Maybe, alone in Calea Victoriei, I'd have felt the unease even more sharply. But here at home, where some kind of daily routine goes on (mealtimes, bedtimes, discussions, *belote*, incidents with the maid or the landlord, and so on), things become greyer and more indifferent. And yet, on top of all this gluelike apathy, there is a constant sense of danger.

In Buzău, Ploiești, and Rîmnic, all male Jews between ten and sixty years of age have been interned in camps put together somewhere or other: in schools, at the synagogue, or wherever. I don't know what is happening in other towns, and I keep wondering what will happen to us here in Bucharest.

I have stopped following the course of the war. Anyway, I do not have the means. To read the papers is like an exercise in textual decoding for which you do not have the code. And yet it is so interesting! For the first time it occurs to me that truth is definitely something that can never be camouflaged. Beneath all the fakes and lies and all the mental aberrations, however deeply hidden or wildly deformed, the truth still breaks through, still glitters, still breathes.

I can't see on the map where the fronts lie. Everything remains so confused. Who can tell what has been captured, what not captured? Beneath a daily avalanche of thundering but imprecise dispatches, the contours of the front continue to be unclear. In broad outline the situation does not seem to have essentially changed in the last week: the Germans have advanced in the center, around Minsk, but the flanks are still holding in the north and south. Nonetheless, the press and the dispatches speak of a final great catastrophe for the Russians. Here are the headlines on just one page of one of today's papers (*Universul*): "German and Romanian Forces Pursue Enemy to Dniester and Dnieper"; "Atrocities Committed by Retreating Bolsheviks"; "Nothing Can Stop German Advance in Russia"; "20,000 Soviet Soldiers Desert Encircled Army at Minsk"; "Huge Quantities of Bolshevik Weapons and Ammunition Destroyed by German Armies on Baltic Coast"; "Numerous Bolshevik Airfields Occupied by Germans in Baltic Lands"; "Soviet Attempt to Stop German Advance Fails"; "Bolshevik Transport Column Destroyed by German Air Force"; "Hungarian Troops Continuing to Advance."

Sunday, 6 July

At Lereanu's and at Dr. Silberstein's (in two completely different parts of town), policemen have called to register them on special lists of all Jewish males between the ages of eighteen and sixty. The father of a friend of Benu's—a man called Leibovici, who seems to be of no special importance at all—was picked up yesterday morning and taken away in a car. No one knows exactly who took him, or where. At Cotroceni (where I myself worked last year in the labor detachment), young Jews are continuing our work in a state of veritable reclusion. They cannot go home or receive visits; no one is allowed to take them food. I wait dazed for evening to fall, for daylight to come, for the hours and another day to pass—one more day, then another one. . . . I am not even frightened. I seem to have accepted in advance whatever may come. Were it not for the thought that Mama may suffer, anything would seem bearable.

Luckily I can still read. It's a sign that my nerves are holding out. I read in turn the many things on my desk, switching as if randomly from one to the other: Thibaudet (*La campagne avec Thucydide*), Aristophanes, Whitman's verse, and an English popular novel by Mary Borden. In reserve I have Balzac and Sainte-Beuve, which I have been reading all this year.

Monday, 7 July

The special evening editions have a communiqué on the occupation of Cernăuți.

Tuesday, 8 July

Folklore. Gypsy children sell *Romanul măcelarului roșu* [The Story of the Red Butcher] in the street, shouting at the top of their voice:
> *Pleacă trenu din Chitila*
> *Cu Stalin în Palestina.*
> *Pleacă trenu din Galați*
> *Cu jidanii spînzurați.*[8]

Rosetti, back for a few days from his holiday in Cîmpulung, thinks that the Russian defeat is a disaster and that resistance may collapse from one day to the next. Camil, on the other hand, whom I hadn't seen for at least a week, reckons that the whole situation has been turned around by a new and unforeseen factor: the Soviet soldier and his immense fighting capacity. "For the Soviet army," he says, "it is a question not of a national war but of a civil war." The whole conversation with Camil was interesting—with the inevitable "Camilisms." If he were in Hitler's place, he would know how to weaken Soviet resistance. (He would drop five thousand parachute troops on Moscow and make a rout.) If he were in Antonescu's place, he would know how to capture the Russian fortifications. (He would keep attacking them at short intervals with little squads of twenty to thirty men, thus bringing the enemy to the point of nervous exhaustion.) I think that with Camil (as with Nae Ionescu, only much more easily) I have developed a real technique for getting him to speak and listening to him. It is to listen admiringly, with occasional exclamations of surprise and false objections or doubts that he can easily dismiss.

I get the feeling that the anti-Semitic tension has fallen a little, by a fraction of a degree. I don't quite know where this feeling comes from—maybe from the fact that no new anti-Semitic measures have been officially published for two or three days.

8. The train is leaving Chitila / Taking Stalin off to Palestine. / The train is pulling out of Galați / Full of hanged Jews.

Wednesday, 9 July

Today's papers carry a decree of the Buzău mayor's office: Jews cannot move around between 8 p.m. and 7 a.m., do not have a right to enter cafés, are forbidden to visit one another, even if they are friends or relatives, and cannot call a doctor except through the local sergeant. So much for my wrong impression yesterday that the anti-Semitic tension is declining. Whenever I go into town, I come back feeling even more depressed than before. There are terrible cases (yesterday, the death of a nineteen-year-old boy), abominable news reports. You have no way of checking—but everything seems to be true, and anyway everything is possible.

I have finished *La campagne avec Thucydide*. Begun *War and Peace*. I long for a little music: Bach or Mozart would bring a moment of peace and cheer me up.

Saturday, 12 July

It has been impossible to record anything here the last four days. I do not have the words, or the feeling or attitude, to relate the simple facts that people report about Jews killed in Iaşi or transported from there to Călăraşi. A dark, somber, insane nightmare.

All that is left is for us to meet death as we would a death at war. Whether you fall or stay on your feet is a matter of pure chance. Are those who die at the front less defenseless than we are? We all fumble around in the dark, in a huge sad crowd of millions and millions of people—and death does not discriminate, does not wait for anyone. No one knows who will remain.

I saw Camil again this morning. It's strange that, out of the blue, he started to tell me once more—with unexpected violence—about last winter's incident with Poldy Stern. Why? Does he have a bad conscience about it? Is he haunted by a vile deed that he cannot cover up well enough? I suspect there is another explanation. He imagines that I could land, as Poldy has landed, in some kind of serious trouble—and he is warning me not to rely on him. "How shameless to turn to a friend, just because he is less exposed than you are." Maybe he wants to warn me against one day being so "shameless." But Camil is the last person to whom I would turn in a difficult moment.

It would appear that the Russian front is more or less where it was, and that operations have entered a phase of waiting, regroupment, preparation. For several days the communiqués have again been subdued; all they have reported has been in connection with the "encirclement" of Bialystok and Minsk. This time it seems that at least this operation is over. Today's German communiqué has the character of a balance sheet: 323,898 prisoners, 3,332 tanks, 1,809 artillery pieces, 6,233 aircraft. The absolute precision of the counting is certainly impressive. But somehow these big figures lack expressive power. When you reach those levels, you lose your feel for proportions and values.

On Wednesday, Thursday, and Friday, three evenings in a row, there were alerts of twenty to thirty minutes at more or less the same time (around eight o'clock), without any gunfire or bomb explosions, even in the distance.

I have been reading *War and Peace* with interest, more for the possible historical analogies than for the work in itself.

Monday, 14 July

Is the German "pause" over? Yesterday's German communiqué reported the occupation of Vitebsk (to the northwest of Smolensk) and advances toward Kiev. The press dispatches claim that the occupation of Kiev and Leningrad is imminent.

The Jews of Ploieşti have been forced to leave town. There have been air raids there in the last few days, and some fires at the refineries.

This evening, after a two-day pause, there was an air-raid alert, with intensive anti-aircraft fire.

Wednesday, 16 July

A complicated dream during the night. I remember only one bit of it. I was with Nae Ionescu in Brăila. We were both going to a kind of literary soiree, where he was supposed to give a lecture and I to speak about him. I think he asked me to lay on the praise.

On Monday night there was a long alert from one to three, with many incendiary bombs (nearly all of them dropped on our area). Small fires, quickly put out. Yesterday, at about 10 p.m., a brief alarm that led to nothing.

Impossible to know what is happening at the front. I have pinned a map of Europe on the wall, but I can't work out where the front line is.

Since Sunday the German communiqués have again been subdued while the press dispatches have noisily announced the imminent fall of Kiev, Leningrad, and Moscow.

Thursday, 17 July

Yesterday I read in proof (from Rosetti) the page about me in Călinescu's *Istoria literaturii.* It is probably the harshest thing ever written against me, beginning with "no artistic talent" and ending with "no aptitude as a writer." I was annoyed, but no more than that. It is vexing to have a page like that in a literary history, whose character as a work of record gives it a certain irrevocability. A thousand-page book of this kind gets written once every thirty or forty years, so I shall have to wait four decades for the record to be set straight. Nevertheless, after the initial irritation it no longer seemed so important. At most annoying. In present times I can't take seriously these literary vexations or even dramas. *Il s'agit de vivre.*[9] Death is possible any day, any hour. What happened in Iași (and I still can't make up my mind to write everything I have meanwhile heard about it) can be repeated here at any time.

So, then?

My "career" as a writer has never obsessed me; now it doesn't even interest me. Will I still be a writer after the war? Will I be able to write? Will I ever recover from all the disgust I have accumulated in these terrible, bestial years?

Apparently Chișinău has fallen at last. I am told that a German communiqué reported it this evening. There is not yet anything in the papers. This morning's communiqué mentioned the defeat of Russian counterattacks at a number of points. (But to be "defeated" they must have taken place.) The press dispatches continue speaking of the imminent fall of Leningrad.

Friday, 18 July

An official Romanian communiqué reports that Hotin, Orhei, Soroca, and Chișinău have all been occupied. The city is again decked with flags. Tomorrow there will be great celebrations. The German communiqué reports that operations are continuing to proceed in a satisfactory manner. DNB dispatches add that Smolensk has been captured. The situa-

---

9. The point is to go on living.

tion on the map is still unclear, because DNB also announced today the capture of a town, Polotsk, which is west not only of Smolensk but even of Vitebsk.

Alice Th. told me that, according to an officer friend of hers back from the front, the army has orders to shoot all Jews they find in Bukovina and Bessarabia. Ricci Hillard, who was also there, confirmed it. *Ordinea* of the evening before last printed a photograph that I regret not having cut out and kept. A long wretched line of women in tatters, with small children equally ragged. Not one male face. The text said these were Judeo-Communists, rounded up by the army in retaliation for their criminal deeds.

Saturday, 19 July

I found the following today in one of Lawrence's letters. It gives me pleasure to copy it down: "I feel I must leave this side, this phase of life, for ever. The living part is overwhelmed by the dead part, and there is no altering it. So that life which is still fertile must take its departure, like seeds from a dead plant. I want to transplant my life. I think there is hope of a future, in America. I want if possible to grow towards the future. There is no future here, only decomposition."

The headlines in today's *Universul*: "German Units Continuing Their Rapid Advance to Moscow"; "Soviet Armies in a Grave Situation"; "Smolensk-Moscow Railway Destroyed."

Sunday, 20 July

I have been reading in *War and Peace* the episode of the fall of Smolensk in August 1812—and just as I read, the same battle takes place in front of the same Smolensk, 129 years later. Tolstoy is even more absorbing, instructive, and topical than I expected. Napoleon's conversation with Bolokhov, Tsar Alexander's emissary, is amazingly similar to Coulondre's[1] last interview with Hitler in August 1939. And the atmosphere in Moscow at the start of the war (whispers, rumors, clarifications, consternation) is the atmosphere in which we have been living for the past two years. Then too, funnily enough, there were people who saw Napoleon in the

---

1. Robert Coulondre, French ambassador in Berlin.

Book of the Apocalypse and calculated that the letters of his name added up to the number 666.

Apart from the advance in the Smolensk region (where things do not seem to be rushing ahead, since the German communiqué says only that they are "*planmässig*,"[2] the rest of the front is unchanged. Fighting at Pskov, fighting at Polotsk, fighting at Novgorod-Volinsk: which means that the situation of Kiev and Leningrad has at least not worsened for the Russians since last Sunday, when they were regarded as all but fallen.

We are now entering the fifth week of war and nothing decisive has happened. The game is open, still to be played.

Lovinescu told Eugen Ionescu the other day that no one can be an Anglophile any longer. The Russians must be defeated, and the Germans must remain victorious. Otherwise we'll be ruled by "Jews and cobblers" (?).

In the street today, Georgică Fotescu called out to me that "by the first of September the Germans will polish off that big Russian pie, then propose a peace the British won't be able to refuse."

Sfîntu Ilie. What a terrible day I spent a year ago in the zone, at Valea lui Soare.

Monday, 21 July

A conversation with Titu Devechi. (He called out from his car when I was waiting for a streetcar on the boulevard, and we took a walk together for half an hour.) In his view, the situation is quite simple: Russia will fall by the first of September—perhaps even sooner. Leningrad will fall in a week at the latest, Moscow in a fortnight. In any event, the Germans will have completed the Russian campaign by the first of September, and will then propose peace to the Anglo-Americans. It's possible that the Anglo-Americans will reject it—which would be a terrible mistake on their part. Anyway, Europe can live without them, especially after the Russian windfall. Ukraine will supply grain to the whole continent. The destruction in Russia is insignificant. Large quantities were found in Bukovina: full granaries, untouched factories. I listened to it all without raising any objection. I didn't even want to give the impression that I had any doubts. Just once I asked:

2. As planned.

"But what will happen if Russia doesn't fall by winter?"
"That's absurd! Impossible!"

Tuesday, 22 July

A month since the start of war with the Russians. Impossible to predict how it will work out. Week after week I had the feeling that we were close to the "decisive" phase—and I kept having to postpone the "decision" to "next week." Are the Germans exhausted by their great offensive? Will they be forced to call a halt for the time being? Or are the Russians virtually finished? Has their resistance been using up their last reserves? I don't think that either is true. The Germans will continue to attack, and the Russians to resist. It is all a question of time: not *whether* Leningrad, Kiev, and Moscow fall, but *when* they fall. And we, however well or badly informed, cannot know anything. We have to wait and, if possible, keep calm.

Two alerts last night: at one and at three. Exhausted by insomnia, we wonder whether we will be allowed to sleep at all during the night.

They are going into Jewish homes—more or less at random—and carrying off sheets, pillows, shirts, pajamas, blankets. Without explanation, without warning.

Aderca, met yesterday evening:
   "Anyway, though it is not his aim, Hitler is doing Europe the great favor of opening the gates of the great Soviet prison, in which 200 million people were suffocating."

Today I read the section in Tolstoy about the battle of Borodino. A bit too labored. *"Grande toile d'exposition."*[3] Instructive nevertheless.

Thursday, 24 July

A long sleepless night. The first alarm was at ten (loud thundering, strange lights streaking like lightning across the sky), the second at two o'clock. I returned from the shelter absolutely all in, but I found it impossible to get to sleep. The police came and woke up the whole building; there was a constant sound of voices and boots on the stairs, doors slamming, people shouting. Apparently a maid had left an attic light on

---

3. "A great exhibition canvas."

during the air raid. All the maids were taken to the police station, and until six or seven o'clock someone or other—sergeant or gendarme—kept returning to investigate, to check, to question. We were petrified that they would take us too. A building full of Jews—*quelle aubaine!*[4] A kind of cardiac constriction kept choking me.

Moscow has been bombed for three nights in a row. Is a direct attack on the city under way? Too soon—as long as there is still heavy fighting in the Smolensk region, and even farther west, in Vitebsk and Polotsk. But all the papers have the headline: "Moscow in Flames!"

On the morning of 2/14 September 1812, a few hours before entering an evacuated Moscow, Napoleon said: *"Je dirai à la députation (de boyards) que je n'ai pas voulu et ne veux pas la guerre, que j'ai fait la guerre seulement à la politique mensongère de leur cour, que j'aime et respecte Alexandre et que j'accepterai à Moscou des conditions de paix dignes de moi et de mes peuples."*[5]

The burial of Danacu (who died in two days somewhere in the country and was brought back yesterday to Bucharest). At two in the afternoon, when the family of mourners was preparing to get into cars and drive to Bellu, the air-raid sirens sounded. We all huddled together in the shelter, they in black funeral clothes, we tenants in pajamas and white trousers. A grotesque situation.

Friday, 25 July

Yesterday evening's German communiqué: "On the whole of the eastern front, the operations of the German and allied armed forces are continuing methodically, despite important local resistance and despite the poor state of the roads."

Last night there was an alert between two and three. We went down to the shelter, dropping from sleep and convinced that the disturbance was pointless, but irritated and resigned.

Zoe has been trying to reach me by phone despite my long silence (I haven't wanted to see anyone since the 23rd of June), and she says that once she was so worried that she came to Strada Antim to see what had happened to me, but did not dare ring the bell. She was about to leave

4. What an opportunity!
5. "I shall tell the deputation (of boyars) that I did not and do not want war, that I made war only on the deceitful policy of their court, that I like and respect Alexander, and that in Moscow I shall accept peace terms worthy of myself and my peoples."

"voluntarily" for Bukovina, where the ministry had offered her triple pay on condition that she remain there for at least a year. In the end she gave up the idea for fear she would not be able to return. I asked her why she didn't go away from Bucharest for a month—and she protested that she would feel like a deserter. She is in an unusual phase of civic awareness.

Last night I dreamed Brahms's *Double Concerto for Violin, Cello, and Orchestra*. It's the first time something like that has happened to me. I don't remember anything else at all from the dream: neither who I was with, nor where, nor in what surroundings. I only know that I listened to a long piece of music, and that, after the first bars and a little hesitation, I said it was the Brahms concerto.

Saturday, 26 July

Yesterday evening's German communiqué: "All along the eastern front, operations are proceeding as planned, with sometimes fierce fighting."

I met Camil Petrescu yesterday:

"The war with the Russians is hard, very hard. It was the intuition of a genius that Hitler attacked now. In another year they would have been invincible."

(Gafencu, back from Moscow, would agree with that.) But for all their resistance, Camil continued, they will be defeated by autumn, and then we shall have a compromise peace. As Hitler will no longer be able to attack Britain this year, he will have to get through another winter. He will therefore prefer peace. As for the British, the war has tired them, and even if they don't want to accept peace, they will be forced into it by the Americans. Russia will pay for everything. The West will be left to the Anglo-Americans. France will be put together again. Poland and Yugoslavia will be reconstituted in one way or another. Germany will get the whole area of Russia, and Hitler general recognition for having saved the world from bolshevism. In the end, concessions will also be made to the Jews ("it can't go on quite like this"); they will be given a state somewhere in Russia, maybe even in Birobidzhan.[6]

Two hours later, Carandino:

"The situation is grave. The German losses are incredibly high. At present it is still not known whether the Germans will crush the Rus-

6. The "Jewish Autonomous Region" created in eastern Siberia in 1928, on Stalin's orders, as a "homeland" for Jews.

sians, or the Russians the Germans. Probably Moscow will fall—in two, three, or four weeks, but it will fall. But only then will the crucial moment arrive. If the Russian armies collapse (having been promised land by Hitler, in a repetition of Lenin's "coup"), then all will be perfect. But if they don't collapse, if an army of Russians remains somewhere far off, even beyond the Urals, they will launch a counteroffensive and nothing will stop them until they reach Finisterre. They will conquer the whole of Europe. It will be terrible: we'll be ruled by a Georgian, Tartar, or Kalmuck general, with no escape for anyone."

Berlin was bombed last night by the British. A response to the bombing of Moscow?

We had a night without an alert. I woke up at two, surprised that "they haven't come yet." Will they let us sleep tonight as well?

Sunday, 27 July

A night with no alert. Pretty sound sleep.

After Napoleon's retreat from Russia, Alexander—back in Vilna—said to his generals: *"Non seulement vous avez sauvé la Russie, mais vous avez sauvé l'Europe."*[7] To save Europe—an old stylistic figure. Yet no one tires of repeating it.

The German communiqué speaks of Russian counteroffensives repulsed to the south and southeast of Vyazma. (Vyazma is halfway between Smolensk and Moscow, so that would mean that the pocket keeps getting deeper.) In Ukraine "the Russian rearguards have been crushed, even though the weather is bad and the roads poor."

Today I saw Vişoianu. In his view, the war will last at least another year, because only after next June will the British begin to have air superiority.

Again, out of the blue, a feeling of exasperation, impotence, weariness. Until when? I keep asking. "Out of the blue" is rather a ridiculous thing to say. All I mean is that nothing new has happened, that everything is as it was yesterday, the day before yesterday, a week ago, two weeks ago—and yet I suddenly have a sharper and more oppressive sense of choking. I should like to shout, to scream.

7. "Not only have you saved Russia, you have saved Europe."

Tuesday, 29 July

The German communiqué of the day before yesterday said that "operations are continuing successfully." The one yesterday evening said that "the battle in the Smolensk region is on the point of being victoriously concluded," while in Ukraine the pursuit continues "even though the roads are washed away." There is no longer any mention of Vyazma. The general impression, both from the communiqués (uniform for the last ten days or so) and from the commentaries (a little stilted), is that the front has more or less stabilized. Lightning war has given way to positional warfare. The official German press warns its readers that time will be needed. "More time than in the old days on the western front" is how a Rador[8] dispatch put it this morning.

The optimists get on my nerves. For two or three days there has been a mindless wave of optimism. Yesterday Suchianu assured me that the war will be over in another four months at the latest.

I finished *War and Peace* yesterday. It is a great work, both as document and as novel. Anyone who wants to write the history of our times will have to wait until at least ten, twenty, or maybe thirty years after the end of the drama. How ridiculous was my attempt in *De două mii de ani* to chronicle dramas that were still only beginning! Can youth be a valid excuse? Will life allow me to have my revenge sometime later?

A Stefani[9] dispatch, printed in large letters, reports that "plague has broken out" in Russia. Material, or at least suggestions, for my newspaper comedy.

Camil Petrescu. He told me this afternoon that he feels the Jews in Bessarabia really did fire on the Romanians. What is happening to them now is no more than they deserve. They started it.

Ghiță Ionescu. It amused me some time ago when I first learned (I meant to record it here) that he was doing great business at the Economics Ministry, where he went to work a couple of years ago. By chance I heard Paltin say that he, Ionescu, had claimed and taken from him forty thousand lei for some official formality. But what I found most amusing (I heard it today) was the fact that, in his capacity as official of the Romanianization Bureau, he compiled and signed a report on the expropriation of Sacha Roman's villa in Sinaia, a villa in which—a delightful

8. The Romanian news agency.
9. The Italian news agency.

touch, this—he now lives with Gina and another couple from the same ministry. Communism, like journalism, *mène à tout. Même sans en sortir peut-être.*[1]

I am so terribly weary. For some time I have been writing even this journal mechanically, without any real inclination. And I'm afraid of losing the taste for reading.

If I could spend a few days somewhere in the forest, in the countryside or a mountain chalet, I would be able to breathe and come to myself again.

Thursday, 31 July

Vague communiqués, muddled commentaries. No definite information, only all kinds of interpretations, formulas, and euphemisms, so chaotic as to be amusing. One thing does seem fairly certain: the front has hardly changed; the central battle is still at Smolensk. But there too the situation is confused. Who holds the town? Who is attacking it? Who encircles whom? The encirclers seem in their turn to be encircled. I wait for the morning paper, then for the evening paper. These are the two events that divide up my day. I am tired of not being able to think of anything but the war. Not a moment of freedom, not a moment of rest.

Lunch with Branişte and Aristide at Alice's. I like Branişte, but how uninteresting he is! He is as honest as they come, but *quelle pauvreté dans tout ce qu'il dit.*[2] Not one idea, not one broader view. Still, life is possible with people like that.

Friday, 1 August

There was a time—not so long ago—when the first was a day to celebrate: another month has passed! But now, the more time passes, the more the circle draws in on us and the more suffocating life becomes. It is true that the way we must still travel is ever shorter, but it is all the more dangerous for that. You hardly dare look back at the thirty-one days of the July just passed—but nor do you dare look ahead to the thirty-one days of the August now beginning. Our life is a miracle that is repeated every day, every hour.

1. Can lead to anything. And perhaps never withdraw from it.
2. What poverty in everything he says.

Saturday, 2 August

All Jews aged twenty to thirty-six must report to police headquarters this evening or tomorrow morning, with three days' food and a change of clothes. That means both Benu and me. For a moment I felt dumb-founded, petrified, desperate. Then came my old sense of futility, of sub-mission in the face of adversity, of open-eyed acceptance of catastrophe. And now, this evening, after a few hours of fretting, I promise myself that I will sleep and try to forget. We'll see tomorrow.

Sunday, 3 August

A day of fasting (Tishah b'Av). A day of feverish activity and tension, yet calmer than yesterday. For the moment it does seem to be simply a call-up for labor service (if "simply" is the right word). Anyway, it is not—or is not yet (as I feared yesterday)—a repetition of the calamity in Iaşi, which also began with a "simple" summons from the police. We have been assured that we will be decently treated. And the fact is that so far no acts of brutality have been committed. I shall make various attempts to find a solution. If they don't work, I'll leave with a brave face! I am worried only about Mama and my poor state of health. I feel tired and worn out.

Monday, 4 August

Early this morning the sergeants and policemen went from house to house in various parts of town—and woke people to inform them that not only Jews aged twenty to thirty-six, but also those aged thirty-six to fifty, must report to police headquarters. The alarm I felt at first is re-turning. Are we again facing a mass roundup of Jews? Internment camps? Extermination? When I went out at ten, the city had a strange air: a strange kind of nervous animation. Agitated groups of people hurrying around. Pale faces lost in thought. Looks that wordlessly question one another, with the mute despair that has become a kind of Jewish greet-ing. I quickly did some shopping to prepare our rucksacks for this af-ternoon, for when we had decided to present ourselves. Shops were taken over by Jews buying all kinds of things for their departure. After a cou-ple of hours there were no more rucksacks on sale anywhere. The shops selling canned goods had only a few odds and ends (it was impossible to buy a tin of sardines, for example). The price of the simplest things sud-denly shot up. I went to Calea Văcăreşti to buy a couple of canvas hats for Benu and myself, and the labels with yesterday's price (160 lei) had been covered over with the new price (250 lei) in ink that was not yet dry.

From Văcărești, small groups of pale, famished, ragged Jews, carrying wretched bundles or sacks, head toward the center of town. Apparently several thousand are gathered in the square in front of police headquarters. On Calea Victoriei, sad women with worried, stupidly imploring looks turn round and round, not daring to get too close and probably waiting for news from their husbands inside. I know that look, I know that waiting. I have seen them so many times in the last two years, in the area around army barracks.

The whole day was one of torment and exhaustion, spent in an atmosphere dominated by the sense that something terrible was in store. The Iași massacre is an obsession that we cannot shake off. Toward evening, however, things seem to have grown a little calmer. The news has come that they have given up the plan of calling up people between thirty-six and fifty. It is also said that tomorrow or the day after, an official communiqué will clarify the situation and bring some order into the recruitment process. Meanwhile nobody knows what to do. To report? Not to report? To keep waiting? Everyone has a hope, a "protection," an answer for which they are waiting. And many groups have already been enlisted, allocated, and sent off.

As for ourselves, we have decided to wait. I have run all kinds of errands, as I did yesterday. (Alice, Braniște, and Vișoianu are admirable in their devotion, their friendship, their eagerness to do anything they can.) We'll see how things look tomorrow. There is extreme confusion: I don't think even the authorities know our exact situation, the purpose of all this turmoil, who ordered it, why, and for whom.... One possibility among others is that it is a form of pressure (and security), to ensure that the Jewish population comes up with the ten billion lei that have been demanded of it. I am too tired to write any more now. It's only eleven, but I am absolutely done in. Maybe tomorrow.

Tuesday, 5 August

Nothing new. We didn't report today either, and I don't yet know whether we will tomorrow. Confusion, bewilderment, constant uncertainty. People aged thirty-six to fifty were again summoned and kept this morning. There seems to be a conflict of authority between the recruitment office and the police, and this may explain the fact that no coercive measures have yet been taken. It is impossible to get certificates from the doctors who treated my food poisoning. Dr. Kahane advised me to eat contraindicated food so as to bring things to a crisis: only then will the commission believe I am really sick. And this evening I did begin methodical eating of Sibiu salami. Tomorrow I'll drink black coffee. Then we'll see. . . . I'm just afraid of causing something too serious from which it will take weeks to recover.

Madeleine Andronescu on the telephone:

"You make me ashamed, Mihail. I feel ashamed that you suffer and not I, that you are being humiliated and not I."

Vișoianu (who is no sentimentalist) said something similar in the street the day before yesterday, when a group of Jews came out and passed alongside us.

"Whenever I see a Jew, I feel an urge to go up and greet him and to say: 'Please believe me, sir, I have nothing to do with all this.'"

The tragedy is that no one has anything to do with it. Everyone disapproves and feels indignant—but at the same time everyone is a cog in the huge anti-Semitic factory that is the Romanian state, with all its offices, authorities, press, institutions, laws, and procedures. I don't know if I should laugh when Vivi or Braniște assures me that General Mazarini[3] or General Nicolescu[4] is "staggered" and "disgusted" at what is happening. But whether or not they are staggered or disgusted, they and tens of thousands like them sign, endorse, and acquiesce, not only tacitly or passively but through direct participation. As for the mass of people, they are jubilant. The bloodying and mocking of Jews have been public entertainment *par excellence*.

I have not been able to keep up with the course of the war. I don't even know how the battle of Smolensk ended (has it actually ended?), or how the battle of Kiev began. I have a feeling that the situation has not substantially changed. Anyway, for lack of information, the only thing that would really mean a lot would be the fall of one of the great target cities: Petrograd, Moscow, Kiev, or at least Odessa. For the moment the German communiqués are written in the same low-key style.

Wednesday, 6 August

Reporting to police headquarters has been called off for the time being. Those taken up to now are well and truly taken. The rest of us will re-

---

3. Nicolae Mazarini: Romanian general.
4. Constantin D. Nicolescu: general, former defense minister.

port to the recruitment office at some time and in some order. I await clarification. Meanwhile we have an unexpected breathing space. How long will it last? A few hours? A day? Several days? At least I feel calmer.

I paid Marie Ghiolu a visit. (I rang her yesterday evening and asked her to get me an appointment with the heart specialist Dr. Iliescu.) It honestly felt like entering a showy asylum, where a whole apartment is set aside for a "high-class" madwoman. Never before has the Ghiolu house struck me as so theatrical, so unoccupied, so calculated to produce an effect. Everything looks as artificial as in a shop window—above all, the glaring excess of color. In the reception room there are huge violet-blue armchairs, with little red cushions. The dining room is a pale rose, with yellow lighting, as if from an electric lamp, filtered through a rectangular window. The upstairs lounge is red. And everywhere the colors are strong and overpowering. She herself, Marie, was wearing a long dress or wrapper in the same shrieking violet as the armchairs downstairs, and a darker blue (equally strident) turban on her head. She had never seemed so mad, and this time she did not have her old childlike ingenuousness. What Marie (and therefore her husband) thinks, believes, wants, and expects is not difficult to summarize: you just have to read *Gringoire*[5] to find out. She is for Pétain and the Germans, against the British, against the Russians, and against the Jews. If the Germans do not win, there will be a total disaster that does not bear thinking about. If the Germans do win, Romania will get back Transylvania and the Hungarians will be wiped out. Anyway, a German victory is certain. Their armies are a long way past Moscow, three or four hundred kilometers past Moscow, which has been left behind surrounded. Exactly as in a lunatic asylum, where it is forbidden to contradict the patients, I kept nodding my head in agreement.

Alice tells me something I find hard to believe (especially as I have so often seen her exaggerate the simplest facts into some cock-and-bull story). It seems that Vişoianu visited her yesterday, went down on his knees, and made a declaration of love. I can't see Vivi at all in such a position—which is precisely why I find it so piquant. How Rosetti would enjoy it if I could tell him!

5. French anti-Semitic magazine.

Thursday, 7 August

A day of freedom more or less (I even went to see a film!), but a freedom that could end tonight, tomorrow morning, tomorrow evening, any
time at all. The Council of Ministers has adopted various provisions for
labor camps and concentration camps. When these are made public, we
shall know what awaits us. Anyway, I can't believe they've given up the
idea of interning us, either in camps or in labor detachments. Until then,
each peaceful hour is a peaceful hour.

A long German communiqué, with three "reports" and a "conclusion."
It is a kind of history of last month's operations. I read it carefully three
or so times, but I still can't work out the actual situation on the map. It
says that the fighting in Smolensk has ended victoriously, but I don't see
the natural sequel to such a victory, which should obviously have been
an advance on Vyazma. Nor is it altogether clear that Smolensk itself
has been occupied. The account of operations in the south is even more
confused. Is Kiev really encircled? Is it on the point of falling? The whole
communiqué seems more geared to the requirements of public opinion
than to a rigorous technical description. There is an interesting claim,
asserted twice, that "a new phase of operations has begun," and that "the
German army is preparing to take the fight it began into a new sector
of operations." In the end, the fantastic figures are more colorful than
interesting: 895,000 prisoners, 13,145 armored cars, 10,380 guns, 9,084
aircraft.

Sunday, 10 August

Comme les jours sont lents; comme la vie est lente![6]
    Sometimes, I don't know why, you suddenly feel more sharply than
before the futility, narrowness, and terrible mediocrity of this life, its
gradual disintegration as in a long, protracted death. Why? For whom?
For what? Until when? You sleep and eat, sleep and eat, sleep and eat.
You read the morning paper, read the evening paper, then again the
morning paper, again the evening paper. Everything is lost in a taste of
ashes, without memories, without real, profound hopes. I think it was
last Saturday or Sunday, in moments when everything seemed lost, that
for some reason I looked up from the street to the sky. It brought tears
to my eyes: a clear blue sky, with some weightless white clouds floating
across it; a southern sky, you might say. It could have been somewhere

6. How slow are the days; how slow is life!

else: in Annecy, Geneva, Lisbon, or Santa Barbara. I could have lowered my head and no longer found myself in Bucharest, in August 1941, but in a free city where I could move about freely, unknown and alive.

I have been reading quite a lot, rather mechanically, to dull my senses. The pleasure (the only one) of reading in English is that I see myself making more and more progress. I have on my desk the first volume of Taine's *History of English Literature*. If nothing happens to stop me, I want to make a systematic journey from the seventeenth to the nineteenth century.

Worries, regrets, melancholy thoughts. If in 1938—or, to make it simpler, in 1937 when I had the invitation to Geneva—I had left for England and remained there (which would have been possible with some effort), then how extraordinary these years of war would have been! I think I would still have been young enough to treat England as a second youth, to have lived studentlike with diligence, concentrated attention, and passion. There is a line of Dante Gabriel Rossetti's that sums up my whole life.

Look in my face; my name is Might-have-been.

A new German offensive in Ukraine seems to be making headway. I don't have enough information to follow it on the map, but there is talk of a great outflanking movement between the Dniester, the Dnieper, and the Black Sea. Nothing much on the rest of the front.

The government is relentlessly demanding ten billion lei from the Jews. What if that much can't be found? The threat is direct, with absolutely no beating about the bush. If it can't be found, we could pay with our lives.

Monday, 11 August

We have again been called up for labor service, this time through an official announcement from the recruitment office. We must all report in order of age, from eighteen to fifty years. Benu's turn comes on Wednesday, mine on Friday. This time, I don't think there is any way out. I have taken the news quite calmly—so far, at least.

After the Jews of Cernăuți, those of Iași are now obliged to wear a yellow Star of David.[7] It is said that the measure will soon be extended to Bucharest and the rest of the country.

7. The obligation to wear the yellow star was enforced only in certain areas of Moldavia and in Bessarabia, Bukovina, and Transnistria.

11 August. That terrible night of 11 August 1940 at Oltenița station! It was a nightmare—and it feels as if it is not yet over.

The German communiqués of yesterday evening and this evening do not say anything new. Advances in Ukraine, but nothing specific. Elsewhere on the front—"*planmässig.*"

A pleasant evening at Sandu Eliad's,[8] with Benu and Agnia Bogoslav,[9] on a twelfth-floor terrace. The city is a long way off, with its miseries and infamies. But when you go back down . . .

Tuesday, 12 August

So, we won't be going now either—not for the moment. "For the moment"—everything is "for the moment." At the last minute they canceled yesterday's notice to report for service. An announcement today said that "the labor call-up of Jews has been suspended for ten days," and that new instructions will be issued after the 21st of August. I don't know the exact reason for all this dillydallying; it could be just the good old administrative disorder. But it could also be that they have not yet decided what to do with us. Or it could be that they have decided to give us a few more days, until the subscriptions to the war loan have been arranged, so that the prospect of compulsory labor can be wielded as a constant threat and means of exerting pressure. Anyway, there will be a few more days, or maybe only hours, of relative quiet. *Autant de gagné.*[1]

Wednesday, 13 August

The German communiqués of yesterday evening and this evening are vague. "Operations are continuing successfully." In fact, the only sector where something is probably happening is southern Ukraine. Odessa is said to be on the point of falling. Any day, any hour—quite imminently.

But I have a feeling that the war is no longer in the phase when a swift blow could transform a situation in twenty-four hours. We'll have to wait until September to see more than we can glimpse or guess today. The Romanian press itself seems less categorical than three or four weeks ago. There has been a certain softening of tone.

---

8. Sandu Eliad: theatre producer.
9. Agnia Bogoslav: actress.
1. That much has been gained.

The lawyer Poenaru (a Brăilan with whom I was not on good terms at school) told me that Odessa has been occupied for four days but that the Germans do not want to announce it for the time being.

Thursday, 14 August

A possible topic for my doctoral thesis (if I ever submit one): anti-Semitic legislation around the world during the Hitler period.

Friday, 15 August

This evening's German communiqué: "The city of Odessa has been encircled by Romanian troops, and the city of Nikolaev by German and Hungarian rapid-deployment troops. To the east of the Bug, German troops have occupied the important mining region of Krivoi Rog. Operations are continuing successfully in other sectors as well."

It feels as if time is stuck, at a standstill, no longer moving, no longer passing. Will it be like this for ever and ever? I am dead tired. I no longer have the will to read the paper, to discuss, to ask questions, to give answers.

Sunday, 17 August

Long, hot, monotonous August days which overwhelm you with sadness, weariness, and a sense of futility. No hope, nothing to look forward to. I am physically exhausted. I feel empty, desolate, mindless, embittered. What could bring me back to life? Maybe the sea, maybe the forest, maybe a few days in the mountains. I need a wave of health to wash over me. I ought to be able to go on believing in life, in my lost youth, in my vocation to live, love, and achieve something.

Two or three weeks ago, at the height of the battle of Smolensk, there was a general sense that things were speeding up. An end to the war seemed possible in the near future. Now the war is in a less dramatic phase, and peace seems more distant, more unlikely. There is no news from the front. Everything appears to be stagnating. The German action in southern Ukraine continues according to plan—"*planmässig,*" as the German communiqué always puts it. And the conference between Churchill and Roosevelt[2] (whose note of spectacular optimism is lost on us here) is drawing up plans for 1942.

2. Churchill and Roosevelt met in Newfoundland between 8 and 11 August and adopted the Atlantic Charter, which called for national self-determination.

Monday, 18 August

Yesterday evening's German communiqué announced the occupation of Nikolaev. This evening's says that the Russian retreat from Ukraine has "speeded up" and that "major successes" have been registered in the other sectors.

A casual visit to Aderca's. He has written—and he read out to me—a long reply to Călinescu's *Istoria*. Very nice, very accurate—but how did he find the strength, the inclination, the curiosity to write it? A sign of youthful vitality. It may be that, in my profound weariness, there is something more and something worse than indifference and skepticism; perhaps there is a deficiency of life. Why do I not feel personally "aimed at" in what is said, done, or written against me? Why do I not feel a desire for revenge? Why is it that I, who used to be so jumpy and combative, am now so placid?

We had an alert last night between two and three—the first for nearly four weeks. It is said that they were bombing Buftea station. But my impression is that the Russian air raids are always aimless and ineffectual.

Thursday, 21 August

The Germans have occupied Kherson in southern Ukraine. As to the central front, they report fighting and victories to the south of Smolensk—at Gomel. The main pressure now seems to be on Leningrad to the north, where Voroshilov has issued an urgent appeal to the population.

Lunch at Alice's with Vicky Hillard, a cavalry lieutenant, who returned yesterday from the Ukrainian front. His general view of the war is not that interesting (it's anyway not very different from what you hear in Bucharest), but he gave a simple and precise account of detailed events. A lot about the massacre of Jews on both sides of the Dniester. Tens, hundreds, thousands of Jews were shot. He, a simple lieutenant, could have killed or ordered the killing of any number of Jews. The driver who took him to Iaşi had himself shot four.

Last night, an air-raid alert at one o'clock.

Friday, 22 August

Two months since the war with the Russians began. If I leave aside the new German push in the north—it is just starting, and I don't know how it will end—the war seems to be assuming a clearer shape. In any event, these two months represent two distinct periods. The first shows that a German blitzkrieg won't work; the second shows that a Russian counteroffensive cannot break through either. The halting of the German advance at Smolensk was a decisive moment: it was the first time that a German offensive had been stopped. This fact made it legitimate to ask whether the Russians, after absorbing the first tremendous shock, would not be capable of taking the initiative themselves. This was more than just a question: it was an eager expectation, mingled with fear, optimism, and surprise.

Now everything has quieted down. The Germans have repeated the "tremendous shock" in the south, around Odessa-Nikolaev-Kherson, and they are repeating it in the north around Leningrad. The Russians cannot do anything other than resist and retreat. But assuming they can do that, and assuming that nothing unexpected happens, the war may go on in the same way until the first snowfall. Then it will hibernate, or move down to warmer climes, and wait for the thaw to come.

The drive toward Leningrad looks more serious than I at first thought. Only now do I see on the map the position of Novgorod, which the Germans have reached. It won't take much more for Leningrad to be cut off from Moscow. It is true that, in the declaration he made yesterday, Voroshilov said that Leningrad had not been and never would be occupied—but Rostopchin said more or less the same about Moscow, in August 1812.

How strange—now that I think about it—seems the calm with which Hillard spoke yesterday of the murders and butchery of the Jews in Bessarabia. (Among other things, a captain in his regiment shot a young Jewish woman because she refused to sleep with him.) Only now do I remember that Hillard himself is Jewish on his father's side—and I think to myself that he witnessed all the horrors without going mad, or indeed without being shaken to the core.

Saturday, 23 August

A communiqué issued by the Ministry of the Interior: "By order of General Ion Antonescu, the Head of State, let it be known that if any act of sabotage should be committed by Communists, 20 Jewish Communists and 5 non-Jewish Communists will be shot."

A communiqué from Romanian army headquarters: "On all sides we are 15 km from Odessa. Threatened by the pistols of Jewish commissars, the Russians fight on until they are wiped out."

Yesterday evening's German communiqué presented a new balance sheet: more than 1,250,000 prisoners, 14,000 armored cars, 15,000 tanks, 11,250 aircraft.

Uncle Avram died this morning. It is a terrible thought (which I have never completely driven from my mind) that in a way I resemble him and his fate.

Monday, 25 August

Called up again for labor. This morning's papers had the announcement by the recruitment office. In the street, newspaper placards blazoned in huge letters: "Jews Aged 18 to 50—etc., etc." Benu has to report the day after tomorrow; I, on Monday. That's all I know for the moment. Will we remain in Bucharest? Or leave? For where?

This morning the Soviet and British armies entered Iran.
Nothing new on the German-Soviet front. Fighting in Odessa. The pressure in the Leningrad region seems less acute than of late.

Tuesday, 26 August

It seems that most of the young (eighteen to twenty-one) Jews who reported today at the recruitment office have been kept in Bucharest to work at the Poligon. Only one detachment of three hundred was sent to Găeşti. I anxiously wait to see what will happen to Benu tomorrow. I'll be happy enough if he is assigned to a local detachment; only the thought of his leaving Bucharest frightens me. As for myself, the fact that I still have five days to go makes me calm, even indifferent, as if the whole business did not concern me.

Heavy fighting on the Russian front, without any major changes. The resistance of Odessa has sent a new wave of anxiety flooding over last week's optimism in Bucharest. Ţuţubei Solacolu, Rosetti, and Camil—whom I saw today—complained that the progress was slow and difficult.

From Killinger's[3] speech yesterday at the German legation: "As Germans and Romanians continue fighting side by side, their friendship will become solid and ingrained."

---

3. Manfred von Killinger: German ambassador in Bucharest.

We lack information about the operations in Iran. The military aspect is not that interesting (though the country is so vast and the geographical difficulties considerable). I suspect there will not be a proper war, and that things will go quite quickly. The political aspect is much more interesting, and more unpredictable. What will the Germans do? Will they protest and leave it at that? Will they allow the British *démarche* to go unanswered? That is hard to believe. Will they attack Turkey? It's not out of the question. But then they would have to move hundreds of thousands of men to the Balkans—which would probably be no easy matter, now that the whole eastern front is open and heavy fighting is either under way or imminent.

The closer we get to autumn, the more complex and dramatic the war may become.

Wednesday, 27 August

I am beginning to feel departure nerves, afraid that all my hustle and bustle will have been in vain. Benu has to report tomorrow morning. Other young men from his contingent have been sent to Dadilov, Fierbinți, or Videle. Is it possible that he will be kept in Bucharest? The chances are very slim. I myself, who probably have some protection as a teacher, do not know whether I can escape.

Thursday, 28 August

Benu has been sent to Fierbinți. He leaves tomorrow morning.

In Iran the new government—formed yesterday—has ordered the troops to end all resistance.

The Germans have occupied Dnepropetrovsk (Ekaterinoslav) in the south, and Luga in the north. In the center, in the Smolensk sector, the Russians seem to have been counterattacking for several days. The Romanian losses in Odessa are said to be heavy.

Yesterday in Paris, a twenty-nine-year-old from Calvados by the name of Paul Colette—a volunteer in the French anti-Bolshevik expeditionary corps—opened fire with a revolver on Laval and Déat, at the end of the ceremony of the handing over of the flags.

Friday, 29 August

Benu left this afternoon for Fierbinți. All day I ran around in vain, hoping to do something so that he could remain in Bucharest. But since he has now left, may the best of luck go with him. Some day the experience will stand him in good stead.

Saturday, 30 August

Emil Gulian called round to see me. He hasn't changed: still affectionate, kindly, straightforward, sensitive. We have fifteen years of friendship between us, and I feel that nothing has budged it. And yet . . . The simple fact that he was in his lieutenant's uniform made me feel awkward. I spoke with him and at the same time said to myself: you see, he didn't feel embarrassed to come here, he wasn't afraid to be seen. We went out together, but I was obsessed by the thought that he, being in uniform, might find this disagreeable. When we reached Calea Victoriei, I said goodbye on some pretext or other. I had the feeling—perhaps mistaken, perhaps exaggerated—that I would do him a disservice by going any farther with him.

Emil works at P.O. and edits a daily information bulletin on the basis of all the reports received there. He knows an enormous number of things. The most worrying is the possibility of a Legionary government. Apparently Antonescu has for some time been negotiating with so-called "moderate Legionaries" (Codreanu Senior, Virgil Ionescu, Herseni, Vojen,[4] and so on); whereas the German press is outspoken in its support for the diehards. Anyway, it is thought that the "moderates" are themselves only (temporarily more subdued) front men for the diehards. Gulian thinks that there is a very serious danger of a Legionary comeback. He also told me some strange things about a certain tension between Romania and Hungary. The Hungarians have been violently attacking Romania in their press. The Romanian government does not respond but lets it be known that the problem of Transylvania will soon be posed. I was surprised that the affair did not strike Emil as strange, or at least naive, at the height of the war with the Russians.

This morning I met the painter Daniel in the street, and he too spoke of a possible return of the Legionaries. "Vojen is at the Propaganda Ministry every day."

4. Victor P. Vojen: extreme right-wing, pro-Nazi journalist.

At the front, the broad lines of the situation are unchanged. The Germans announced yesterday that they had occupied Kiev, and the Finns today that they had taken Vyborg. Fighting is still going on in Odessa.

Comşa gave thirty thousand lei so that he could be assigned to Bucharest. As a result, he is doing some construction work or other at Otopeni.

Sunday, 31 August

Rain, pitch-darkness, frequent flashes of lightning that illuminate the deserted streets. I think of Benu—and then of the men in the trenches. Tonight will be two years since the beginning of the war.

I don't know what the exact situation is at the front. Yesterday evening's German communiqué does not even mention ground operations. It would appear that things have again come to a halt. But even if this is true, it cannot last long. Will there be a German offensive to cross the Dnieper? Will they again try to break through toward Vyazma? Will they throw even greater forces against Leningrad? Or, finally, will they attack Turkey?

I feel the lack of a radio, especially at such moments of relative inactivity before major news events.

Yesterday there was a police raid at the bathing place on Lake Floreasca. All the Jews were rounded up and taken to police headquarters. There are all kinds of unwritten prohibitions.

I am reading *Tristram Shandy*. Rather long and padded out. Enjoyable, of course, but far from being a masterpiece. It sometimes resembles Montaigne—but what a distance!

Tedium, disgust, indifference, disintegration.

Monday, 1 September

The first of September! With what difficulty August passed! And how unreal today's date, 1 September 1941, seemed to me in the past—in the spring, for example. Today, the first of March 1942 seems to me equally remote, equally implausible. Time passes and solves nothing. Theoretically we know that we are drawing ever closer to the end of the nightmare—but for now we are in darkest night, thrashing around in the same sorry anguish.

Two years of war! But have we reached the bottom of our misfortune? Have we climbed the whole hill of disappointments? Can we consider ourselves on the other side of the slope? There was a time when Autumn 1941 seemed to me the outer limit of the war. But now another year or two seems quite plausible, even on the moderate side.

Some DNB dispatches suggest between the lines that there is indeed a Russian counterattack in the central sector of the front. Otherwise the communiqués and dispatches are so vague that you are left with the feeling that something is being confected in the shadows, something that could break out very soon.

I don't know why, but yesterday's papers again printed the official announcement that "20 Jewish and 5 non-Jewish Communists" will be shot in the event of any act of sabotage.

A cold, greyish blue autumn morning. I went for a long walk with Eugen Ionescu along the banks of the Dîmbovița; it was like being in a strange town.

Tuesday, 2 September

To-morrow, and to-morrow, and to-morrow
Creeps in this petty pace from day to day.
                                        —Shakespeare, *Macbeth*, Act V, scene v

An anthology could be made of euphemisms in the daily press. The following sentence in today's *Azi* struck me as especially tasty: "Given that German troops have already been on the other bank for several days . . . , the final operational phase of an encircling action is being carried out here, which in all probability *is approaching maturity at lightning speed.*"

Wednesday, 3 September

Autumn, rain, cold. Gloomy November weather. It is dark by seven, and then it becomes extremely difficult to move around the city. The streetcars go slowly, with people clinging to steps and buffer rails. Both yesterday and today there were police raids all over the city—which slowed traffic even more. Yesterday I jumped off a streetcar in the nick of time, just as the police were closing in on it.

I don't yet know how the comedy of going off to work will end. Complicated operations are slowly continuing at the recruitment office, with all manner of deals, agreements, and bargaining. It is a huge money market in which everyone is involved. I am waiting to see whether the school will obtain an exemption for teachers. They asked us for money—ten thousand lei per teacher—but even so, nothing is certain.

Within two days the Jewish population of Bucharest has to come up with four thousand beds, four thousand pillows, four thousand blankets, eight thousand sheets, eight thousand pillowcases, etc.[5] The Community has been asked to collect the things itself—but if it does not do this in time, the operation will be handled by the police. Teams of "intellectuals" have been hastily formed to get the business started.

It is being said (Vişoianu, Rosetti) that the German attack on Turkey is just days away, perhaps even hours. A certain pause on the Russian front. The last four or five German communiqués have again been very low-key. The bad weather is probably also complicating things. Perhaps for that very reason the war will shift to warmer climes. It wouldn't surprise me if there were a lightning attack in Turkey and the Turks' resistance were rapidly overcome. A short war, giving the Germans total victory in three to four weeks (which is not impossible), might offer them political compensation for the major delays in Russia. With an autumn success like that, it would be easier for them to go into winter from a propaganda viewpoint.

I am reading with great pleasure Shakespeare's *Sonnets*. With the idea of one day doing a verse translation, I wrote down two sonnets in Romanian this evening, for the time being in a simple literal translation.

Thursday, 4 September

Translated three more Shakespeare sonnets this evening. Of course, they are no more than rough sketches. Not even that. I would have to do a lot of work to raise them above their formless state.

In the army, when something was needed (office supplies, plates and dishes, gaps in the storehouse, etc.), the solution was quite simple: let the Jews come up with it! And that is what the Jews did. Yesterday's order, which makes us responsible for the provision of hospital beds and linen, is essentially a barracks solution.

Even more than yesterday, people are saying that the outbreak of war in Turkey is imminent. Von Papen is in Berlin.

5. The Antonescu government forced Romanian Jews to pay special taxes in household items.

The German communiqués continue to be subdued. Yet it seems (from telegrams and commentaries) that the pressure is mounting on Leningrad, while to the south the Dnieper has been crossed at one point. As to the central sector, they admit that there is a Russian counteroffensive, but also assert—in flat contradiction—that the Germans have reached Bryansk (?).

Eugen Ionescu pointed out to me in Gide's *Journal* a thoroughly anti-Semitic page that he wrote in 1914 about Jewish literature. It could very well have been published in Romania by *Porunca Vremii* or Sân-Giorgiu.

Friday, 5 September

I went to the Bar association to take my diplomas from the files. It is a year since they struck me off, and today was the first time I have been back at the courts. No emotion (I have no memories, regrets, or hopes there), but I did feel a certain disgust. There was a funny guy at the administration department who, I don't know why, spoke to me from time to time in German:

"I'm not an anti-Semite. Oh no, I've got different ideas. How much will you give? *Wie viel? Fünf hundert?*"[6]

I gave him three hundred—and he took them with an amusing air of generosity and broad-mindedness. He addressed me all the time with the familiar *tu* and kept lapsing into German, especially when it was a question of money.

A pitiful sight in the courtyard of the Great Synagogue, where they are collecting beds, mattresses, bedclothes, and pillows. Crestfallen people keep arriving with things on their backs—resigned, mournful, not rebellious, almost not surprised. No one is surprised any more at anything. The people in charge are unhappy that the work advances so slowly, without enthusiasm. Old things are brought in. They have been told that if we do not carry out the instructions by tomorrow, the army will do the requisitioning itself. And another ultimatum arrived this morning, demanding five thousand suits, hats, and boots. Finally, also this morning, the Community was informed that beginning Wednesday we will have to wear a piece of material with the "six-cornered star" stitched to the top left of our coats. I returned home feeling poisoned. More patience is needed than I have, a more stubborn will to endure anything.

6. How much? Five hundred?

I feel like dropping everything and saying: shoot, kill us, put an end to it. But of course it is not with that kind of despair, and anyway not with that kind of surrender, that the Jews have survived down the ages.

I tried staying home and reading. Perhaps it is a kind of desertion (I said to myself full of scruple), but anyway I could not be of greater use, and I don't see why I should subject myself to such torture.

I continued reading Shakespeare's sonnets.

Rosetti tells met that Pălăngeanu (General Ciupercă's chief of staff) said to some friends that he expects Odessa to fall the day after tomorrow, on Sunday. Mrs. Goga told Rosetti today that twelve thousand Romanian soldiers were killed in Bessarabia and Bukovina, and that eighteen thousand have fallen before Odessa.

Sunday, 7 September

The German communiqués maintain the same silence, which has been continuing for a week or more now. ("Vom Schweigen im Kriege" [On Silence in War] is the title of an article by Goebbels in *Das Reich* in which he speaks of a *Nachrichtenpolitik* [news policy]. I do not have a mental picture of the front, nor do I know where the present lines are. There is the battle of Leningrad in the north, and the battle of Odessa in the south. In the center there is a Russian counteroffensive, but I do not know how big or intense it is, nor what are its chances.

On Saturday I had a day in the dumps, but then I suddenly got over it. I have no right. I mustn't. In a sense, I would even say that I do not have any reasons. If I look at the map of the continents in my mind's eye, the game comes to look more straightforward. There is no need to follow it day by day, and no point in fretting about every individual episode. The final outcome is ineluctable. The day will come when it will be possible to breathe. *Il s'agit de durer. Il ne s'agit que de cela.*[7]

Yesterday I went into a grocer's shop to do some shopping for Benu— and I had a fright. I have done hardly any shopping since I moved to Strada Antim in April, and I no longer knew the prices. They have risen three, four, or five times. It is terrible. And we are still only at the beginning of September. What will it be like in the middle of winter?

---

7. You have to hang on. That's all there is to it.

I have no money left. Today I gave Mama my last thousand-lei note. And now? I don't know.

Monday, 8 September

Three air-raid warnings last night, in a clear blue moonlight that was translucent and gentle as never before. One of the most beautiful nights I can remember. Everything was transfigured, everything gentler and purer. The still, silent city became something quite different from the usual city. I spent the first two alerts (at eleven and one) in the shelter. But I did not go down for the third (it was after two o'clock, though when I opened my eyes I thought from the light that it was well into morning). I didn't have the impression that the bombing was serious. But I heard in town today that a textile factory in the Colentina district received a direct hit and was destroyed.

A Havas telegram says that Petrograd will fall in two or three weeks at the latest.

Virginio Gayda[8] says that Germany does not intend to occupy the whole of Russia, only Petrograd, Moscow, Kiev, and Kharkov, after which the war with the Soviets will be effectively over and the Axis will be able to carry the war to other fronts in the winter of 1942.

Ceacǎru:[9]
"After the war I'll take you on as chief editor of my paper."
Look at why Ceacâru thinks this war is being fought. And look at how he imagines things ending!

Tuesday, 9 September

We were supposed to start wearing the "six-cornered star" tomorrow morning. The order was given to the Community and passed on to police stations. But there was a change of mind following an audience that Filderman[1] had tonight with the Conducǎtor.[2] The change of mind does not give me any pleasure. I had grown used to the idea that I would be wearing a yellow patch with a Star of David. I imagined all the un-

---

8. Italian journalist.
9. Demetru Ceacǎru: journalist.
1. Wilhelm Filderman: lawyer, chairman of the Federation of the Union of Jewish Communities in Romania, the principal Jewish umbrella organization.
2. The Romanian equivalent of Führer, referring to Antonescu.

pleasantness, all the risks and dangers, but after a moment's alarm I not only resigned myself but began to see in that sign a kind of token of identity. Even more, I saw it as a kind of medal, an insignia certifying my lack of sympathy for the vile deeds around us, my lack of responsibility for them, my innocence.

In the courtyard of the Great Synagogue, where the commissions carry out their requisitioning, I meet all kinds of old familiar faces from my days at university and in journalism—people I have not met for many a year. I seem to have grown terribly old, if I compare myself with them. (Ludo's schoolboy face.[3] He's unchanged after so many years—I don't think I have seen him since 1932–1933—whereas I have aged so much!)

In the afternoon I went with Ceacâru to a few Jewish homes to collect beds, clothes, and linen. Painful and sad. I don't have the courage to insist and give way as soon as anyone protests. I shan't forget a doctor's "waiting room" on Strada Polizu: a wretched provincial interior, with shabby old furniture. Plush, mirrors, flowers—everything sordid and dispiriting.

"Take a seat," said the doctor's assistant, who did not know why we had come.

The doctor was some five minutes late, then suddenly appeared from an adjoining room. All the time I was tortured by the thought that he might think we were patients, and that the truth would come as a great disappointment to him.

The Germans have announced that Leningrad is now completely encircled. Today's papers again say that occupation of the city is imminent. In the central sector, it seems, the Russians are continuing to attack and to make some advances. Timoshenko's[4] plan is to attack the flank of the German armies in the north, forcing them to disengage from Leningrad. It would be an operation on a grand scale, but I don't think the Russians are capable of carrying it out at the present stage of the war.

Thursday, 11 September

There is no news from the front. Neither the official communiqués nor the press telegrams say anything. In the last few days German propaganda has focused almost entirely on Leningrad, which it considers to be completely encircled. But it also hints that the city is more likely to fall through a siege, however long, than through a direct attack.

3. I. Ludo: Jewish novelist.
4. Marshal S. K. Timoshenko of the Red Army.

Emil Gulian (whom I met today at Margareta Sterian's) told me that the German officers at his office said that the main pressure is actually on Moscow, which will fall more quickly than Leningrad and even sooner. Nothing is being printed any more about Odessa. They wait in silence, and with a certain embarrassment, for a battle to end there.

Rosetti (who returned yesterday from Cîmpulung) saw en route some long German military trains heading from Timişoara toward the Danube. He also said that Dobrogea is full of German troops. They keep trickling through Giurgiu toward Bulgaria. It would seem, though, that the Germans are going to attack Turkey (though in the last few days the question has no longer seemed immediate).

The Lereanu family. A commission from the Community went to see them yesterday, to ask them for bed linen, clothing, and money. . . . Their answer: "We won't give any. We don't belong to the Community." And as they nevertheless had some things to donate, they sent them directly to a hospital—just so that they would not be giving them as Jews. Under the Legionaries, however, I think it cost them hundreds of thousands of lei to escape from a difficult situation.

This morning a Jewish merchant from Strada Blănari (an honest man, basically), whom I had visited with Ceacâru for him to sign our contributions list, said to me: "So you see, that's how it is. Now you're a Jew! And if things are put right tomorrow, you'll forget it again." He too had heard that I had written a book ("The Year 2000"!?), that I had had a big argument, that I had become a renegade. After so many years, the wretched business is still continuing.

Gunther, the American envoy (says Rosetti), told someone yesterday that at the peace conference the Romanians would not be forgiven two things: that they crossed the Dniester, and that they behaved as they did toward the Jews.

Friday, 12 September [1941]

Today they disconnected my telephone, after leaving it on (probably by mistake) for two months. "If Mr. Sebastian is Jewish, the telephone will be cut off," someone phoning from the company told Mama today. Two hours later it was all over.

"The German army is also prepared for a winter campaign," states a Rador telegram from Berlin that appeared in today's *Universul*.

It seems that Roosevelt's speech last night was extremely forceful. We had no way of listening to it, but a lot can be gathered from the little that comes through in the DNB[5] account. In fact, the declaration that the American navy will attack German ships sailing in American "defensive waters" is a step toward war—especially as the concept of "defensive waters" is rather elastic.

I read with pleasure, almost emotion, a copy of the *Tribune de Genève*. I even closely read the cinema announcements and the small ads. Street names bearing a kind of nostalgic sadness. I found the rental advertisements especially moving. There are numerous vacant apartments: Rue Neuchâtel 4, Rue Carouge 46, Rue des Grottes 17, etc. I could live in any one of them. A holiday ad depressed me: *"Jura Vandois. Pension famille à la campagne. Alt. 600m. Situation tranq. Gd. verger. Cuisine soign.[6] Prix 5.50. Reverolles-sur-Marges (Vand.)"* What refuge there!

Today I remembered (I wonder how and why) the days I spent in Ploieşti in Autumn 1931, at the Lupeni trial.[7] The hotel room there seemed like a theatrical setting—and I saw a play rapidly taking shape around that business. Very vague as a dramatic idea, but the temptation to write is immediate.

Sunday, 14 September

The 14th of September. The day Napoleon entered Moscow. From now on, Hitler is lagging behind the 1812 schedule.

The lack of a telephone is a real nuisance: it severs the few contacts I still have with people. But I'll soon get used to that too.

Monday, 15 September

The Germans have crossed the Dnieper at Kremenchug, roughly halfway between Kiev and Dnepropetrovsk. It is a major blow that puts Kiev and Kharkov in danger. London does not hide the gravity of the situation. It also admits that the threat to Leningrad is growing.

---

5. Germany's official press agency.
6. "Country Guesthouse. Alt. 600 meters. Peaceful surroundings. Large orchard. Carefully prepared cuisine."
7. Trial of miners who participated in a 1929 strike.

Rain. I ate at Alice's and returned a short while ago—a little before midnight. The streets look sinister in the cold, the rain, and the dark. Everything smells of November.

Yesterday and today I tried to define more clearly the plan for a play that I glimpsed the other day. I got down to writing, though everything is so obscure. I hoped that with pen in hand I would be able to carry further my first vision of things. I wrote the stage settings and the first few words of Act One, but then I had to stop. It doesn't work—and there's no way it can. It's too little, and too unclear. Yet I feel that some of the knots could be untied. There isn't—or isn't yet—a subject, but there is a milieu, an atmosphere, a framework. I have started to reproach myself: I leave too many projects hanging; they grow old, lose all meaning, shrivel, and die. The war is an excuse for me to abandon too many things. I have resigned myself to treating it as a long hibernation, but around me there are people who still live, who still work and stir themselves. Why can't I too come back to life?

Wednesday, 17 September

The Dnieper seems to have been crossed not only at Kremenchug but at several points downstream from it. There is talk of a great outflanking maneuver, endangering both eastern Ukraine and the Caucasus. After three weeks of relative standstill, the war is entering another dramatic phase. But the key problem remains the same. Will the Russian army collapse or not? Can the Germans avoid a winter war? Are they in a position to settle matters now?

A day stupidly spent on Calea Văcărești, between temple and synagogue, waiting for news about the "requisitioning on the spot." This morning, unexpectedly, the schedules presented by the Community were rejected. Tomorrow we are supposed to report again to the recruitment office. Disorder, confusion, uncertainty. And yet I don't know why I am so calm. Probably I have become so numb.

On this evening three years ago the dress rehearsal of my play was performed. I remember everything very well: the darkened auditorium, the raised curtain, the incomplete stage settings, the few people in the audience, the meal late that night at Mircea's. Had I known then all that would follow in the next three years, there would still have been time for me to run away, to escape. Today I feel half dead: indifferent, insensitive, with no desires, hopes, or expectations.

Thursday, 18 September

London reports that, according to a German news item (which I haven't seen in the Bucharest papers), the isthmus linking the Crimea to the mainland has been occupied—and adds that, if this is true, the Russian armies in the Crimea will be cut off and unable to receive help. I look at the map and realize that if things are so, Kherson has virtually fallen. In fact, they have all "virtually" fallen: Odessa and Kiev and Leningrad. For the moment, though, they do not fall. How much longer can this "moment" last?

It had been announced that police raids would take place today, to catch Jews who are not performing their obligations for "labor useful to the state." But the raids seem to have been postponed. Why? how? until when?—no one knows. I have been told that I am one of the few teachers excused from labor for the time being (everything is for the time being). I don't know anything—but on this matter I am calm and more or less resigned.

I have dropped the play about the trial in Ploicşti and returned to "Freedom." I couldn't say that I am in the mood for writing, but I'd like to finish at least one of those theatrical projects of mine that have been losing all point through neglect. I think I'll add a Jewish banker (the Hillel Manoah or Davicion Bally type[8]) to the dramatis personae. I have already fitted him into the plot and can clearly visualize his entrances in all three acts. If I were persevering, I could wrap up the whole thing in a few weeks. But I am not persevering, and I have lost the habit of writing.

Friday, 19 September

I have reread yesterday's note. Kherson fell three weeks ago (at the same time as Nikolaev and Dnepropetrovsk), but I had forgotten. As to Kharkov, it is farther away. The situation in that region is certainly very difficult for the Russians. The German offensive is breaking a deadlock there, and I don't know how things will look afterward. I should give up following the different phases of the war. I should understand that these are all episodes and wait for the end (which, at such moments, again seems a long way off). From day to day the war is hard to bear. Let's see what it will be like in a month, in three months, in a year.

---

8. Sebastian's great-grandfather who supported the 1848 Revolution.

Belu[9] is very, very disheartened—he who is usually so optimistic. He thinks the British should land now in France—otherwise everything may be lost. But to believe in the possibility now of a British landing strikes me as childish.

Titel Comarnescu. I hadn't seen him since June, when I was prepared to bet anything that there wouldn't be a war with Russia. He hasn't changed: still voluble, confused, agitated. In his view, the Russians will be beaten, the British will conclude a compromise peace, and the Germans will organize Russia. He talked of the Slav danger, from which no one other than Hitler can save us. Hitler is the devil—but he is doing Europe a huge service. In any case, between the Russians and the Germans, he prefers the Germans. Not even the British have anything left but to accept a compromise.

Sunday, 21 September

Kiev has fallen. It would seem (even from the way in which the German communiqués of yesterday and the day before were drafted) that there is still street-fighting in the city. But one way or another, the city is lost. That's another chapter ended. The Germans have now drawn an arc all the way from Gomel to Kremenchug, where a great Soviet army (estimated by London at 750,000 men) is encircled. The next immediate objective will be Kharkov, which, after yesterday's announcement of the capture of Poltava, cannot hold out much longer. One gets an impression of rout and haste. Until now the Russians seemed to be in control of their movements, and to be somehow limiting their defeats. Now, however, you sense for the first time that they have lost their grip on the helm. The Germans are complementing their military offensive with a new propaganda barrage. The catastrophic headlines that have not been seen for a while are again appearing in the papers. "Collapse of Soviet Armies Inevitable"—says a banner headline in today's *Universul.*

The German losses for the period 22 June through 31 August were given in today's official communiqué: 84,354 dead, 292,690 wounded, 18,921 missing; airmen: 1,542 dead, 3,980 wounded, 1,387 missing; aircraft lost: 725.

9. Pavel Belu: journalist.

Monday, 22 September

Benu came back from Fierbinți yesterday evening for a couple of days. He is suntanned, healthy, and handsome. The open-air life, even in a labor camp (where the word "open" seems a mockery), has done him good. What a false, mindless, suffocating life we lead here! In the past, skiing, the sea, and the mountains helped me get away from it.

Three months of the German-Russian war. If the powerful offensive in the south does not settle matters, if it does not break all the Soviet resistance (and I don't think it can), the war will continue with the same alternating rhythm of blows and pauses, until the first major snowfall. In any event, after the Germans have polished off the whole Ukraine and occupied the Crimea, they will find a new field of operations in the Caucasus. And meanwhile, they might also launch the attack on Turkey that has been expected for such a long time.

A pleasant afternoon at Tudor Vianu's: with Șerban Cioculescu, Eugen Ionescu, Pippidi, Victor Iancu, Professor Rusu from Sibiu,[1] Ciorănescu.[2] We talked about literature—as if it were not September 1941.

I read with emotion a splendid play by Priestley, *Time and the Conways*. I, who for some time have been obsessed with the idea of growing old, entered their sad comedy as one of the characters.

Rosh Hashanah. I spent the morning at the temple. I heard Șafran,[3] who was nearing the end of his address. Stupid, pretentious, essayistic, journalistic, shallow, and unserious. But people were crying—and I myself had tears in my eyes.

Tuesday, 23 September

A strange dream last night. I was with Aristide Blank and (?) Octavian Goga in a small, crowded hotel, where we were looking for somewhere to sleep two or three to a room. We found a kind of lumber room, with a shower or a fountain in a corner among the junk. When I turned the tap, water gushed out to both right and left; I was surprised and distressed, not knowing how to stop it.

An autumn day, grey, cold, and gloomy. I don't know what is happening at the front, nor do I want to know. A bitter taste, as in the grim days of June 1940. But I mustn't be like this. I mustn't.

1. Liviu Rusu: aesthetician.
2. Alexandru Ciorănescu: literary historian.
3. Alexandru Șafran: wartime chief rabbi of the Jewish Communities in Romania.

Benu has left again for Fierbinţi. I seemed to find the parting more difficult than last time. And I think that a lot of bitterness lay hidden beneath his apparent good humor.

I have no money, and I don't know where to get any. The rent must be paid in three days (if the landlord wants to renew the contract), and then I don't know what I'll do. I'll have to try speaking to Zissu one day—but with what chances?

Wednesday, 24 September

"It is hard for a man to say: all the world is mistaken but himself. But, if it be so, who can help it?" (Defoe)

Today I began teaching 7th and 8th Years at the *liceu*. A wretched place, with uninteresting, impudent pupils. I'm not cut out for this job.

I heard yesterday at Vianu's, and had it confirmed today by Rosetti, that an electric power station has blown up in Iaşi. Looks like sabotage. Thousands of arrests. I am terrified to think what consequences this might have for Jews.

I don't know how things are going at the front. For the time being they are still winding up the Kiev sector; each German communiqué publishes incredible figures. Meanwhile, a blow is apparently being prepared against Turkey. The pretext has already been found. The Italian navy has a right to pass through the straits into the Black Sea, flying Bulgarian colors. Legally speaking, Turkey has no right to refuse, since Bulgaria is formally a neutral country.

I have come up with a good ending for "Freedom." But I haven't found the right tone for the first scene. I'll wait for it to become clearer, then try to write.

Thursday, 25 September

The landlord wants 93,000 lei to renew the lease. I'll accept, of course, because it is impossible to move now. The rent office probably does not even consider cases involving Jewish tenants. I have heard that new leases for Jews are only possible in the Black Sector[4] (Dudeşti–Văcăreşti). I am completely at the mercy of my landlord, who can ask any amount and

---

4. One of the color-coded districts into which the city of Bucharest formerly was divided.

force me to pay any amount. I talked with him for half an hour, trying to get a reduction. It was painfully humiliating and depressing. I left with my nerves on edge. As I returned home, I'd have liked to be able to shout out and weep.

This journal is not much use to me. I read it over sometimes and am depressed by its lack of any deep resonance. Things are noted without emotion, dully and inexpressively. Nowhere is it apparent that the man writing it goes from day to day, hour to hour, with the thought of death alongside him, inside him. I am frightened of myself. I run away from myself. I avoid myself. I prefer to turn my head, to change the subject. Never have I been so old, so flat, so listless, so unyouthful. Broken threads, pointless gestures, deleted words.

Friday, 26 September

A sleepless night, then a whole day of fretting, despondency, weariness. A sense of collapse. I feel as if I've hit rock bottom, with no way back up. I don't even feel any curiosity about what will happen. How will the war end? How will we get out of the nightmare? I don't know; I don't want to know. I must resign myself to living. But never have I felt so down on my luck.

Saturday, 27 September

"Oh, the dreaming! the dreaming! the torturing, heartscalding, never-satisfying dreaming, dreaming, dreaming, dreaming." I copy these lines from Shaw (*John Bull's Other Island*); how well they suit me! I live, as always, in a mindless series of dreams, passing from one to the other, incapable of waking up to reality. Around me are so many people—including the most simple and ordinary (Ficu Pascal, Willy Șeianu, Nene Zaharia, Nene Moritz, Manolovici, Ficu Cahane, Iosi Rosen)—who, with the same hardships and obstacles, manage to clear some space for themselves, to keep their heads above water, to earn money, to live. Only I sink to the bottom, defenseless, defeated, resigned, incapable of any gesture or effort. I feel too disgusted, too full of loathing, and in an attempt to forget things and bear up, I take open-eyed refuge for days on end in all manner of ridiculous dreams. I see myself in Geneva with a million Swiss francs (or sometimes only 300,000 or 100,000 or even 30,000); I settle into my old room in the Cornavin,[5] or into an apartment on the

5. Hotel in Geneva where Sebastian had stayed.

lake (Igiroşeanu's apartment) at Lausanne or Nyon. I see myself in London, as an editor at the BBC for forty pounds a month, or working all day at the British Museum and spending misty holidays somewhere by the sea. I see myself at the Russian front as the special correspondent of an American or London newspaper, where I am naturally an editor. I see myself in New York, and then—weary of all the noise—in a quiet provincial town, where I write smash-hit plays for Broadway without feeling curious enough to go and see them. I stay alone at home, with a powerful radio, an automatic gramophone, and hundreds of records of Bach, Mozart, and Beethoven. I have a car and travel around unknown parts of America. I see myself with Nadia in New York or California, but I have some problems because I don't get on too well with her parents. I see myself on a yacht headed for Alexandretta, Egypt, Palestine, the Pacific—a small yacht on which there are only ten or twelve of us. We are poor but hardy, and in every port of call we are met with sympathy and curiosity. In a letter to the president of the PEN Club, I point out that, as a writer in exile who is a member of the association, I have been called upon to give a lecture (for a lot of money) about our life on board, and that I shall repeat this lecture in each port of call.

I carry ten such dreams around with me. I never get to the end of one but keep switching among them and picking up where I left off. It is like a drug, a sleeping pill. Meanwhile, life is closing in and crushing me. Where will I get money? What will I give Mama for the market on Monday or Tuesday, when the last two thousand left after the rent have been used up? When I don't think of killing myself, I think of begging. (Zissu, Blank, Vişoianu—I'll have to speak to one of them.) This is all I can do at thirty-four years of age.

Oh! the dreaming, the dreaming, the dreaming.

Sunday, 28 September

Last night I dreamed I was in Uncle Zaharia's shop. I read (or write?) two letters that have come from Poldy or which I am supposed to send to him. I quarrel with Anghel. I go out and walk up the right-hand side of Calea Victoriei. An unknown woman desperately cries out that the Legionaries are in revolt and are approaching the city center. I can't believe it and am about to go calmly on my way when I realize that the whole of Calea Victoriei is indeed brimming with Legionaries. Fierce, dark figures full of menace stop and loiter in front of Jewish shops. What are they waiting for? Probably a signal to attack. I go into the barber's and see that it is empty. Next to the elevator a major is setting up a machine gun. Sandbags are brought from various places to serve as barricades. I take Mama, Tata, and Benu—and we run to hide. Where? To Alice's is my first idea, but for some reason I give it up. "The best would be home at Granny's." That is indeed where we go (the house in Brăila on Strada Unirii), and I feel calmer. No one will come here; no one will guess where we are. In the house we find Granny and what looks like Auntie Caroline. In an adjoining room Benu is in bed with Mali (a girl who lived near us in Brăila some fifteen years ago, the niece of the Lubiş family). I get into bed beside her. She is naked, unexpectedly beautiful, warm, and with firm breasts. At which point I wake up . . .

"The great battle of Kiev is over," states yesterday's German communiqué. The balance sheet: 665,000 prisoners, 884 tanks, 3,718 guns. "A victory without historical precedent has been won." Using the same tone as the official communiqué, the DNB dispatches go even further and suggest that the whole war may now reach a resolution. "A great turning point in the campaign against the Soviets." "It is possible that the war may now take a sensational turn."

Camil Petrescu claims that Odessa is resisting because of the Jews. He says there are a hundred thousand Jewish refugees from Bessarabia inside the city; they know they will be shot if they are captured by the Romanians, so they prefer to fight and resist. The Anglo-Americans— Camil continues—will undoubtedly win the war, but that too will be because of the Jews. For it is they who (especially in America) are insisting on war and making any compromise impossible.
  "Et voilà pourquoi votre fille est muette."[6]

Monday, 29 September

Also from yesterday's conversation with Camil Petrescu: The Romanian government has denounced the Vienna agreement with the Hungarians. Horthy went running to Hitler, who told him that the Romanians are right, that the problem of Transylvania will have to be reviewed, and that in any case the Romanians deserve satisfaction because they have been fighting well and making great sacrifices within the framework of the Axis. Horthy then appealed to Mussolini but received the same reply.
  Vişoianu tells me that Grigorcea, the Romanian envoy in Rome who

---

6. "So that is why your daughter is mute." The exact quotation from Molière's *Le Malade imaginaire* is: *"Voilà justement ce qui fait que votre fille est muette."*

returned a few days ago to Bucharest, describes the situation in Italy as desperate, with unimaginable poverty and extreme discouragement. The only fascist in Italy is Mussolini, surrounded by a band of profiteers. The masses hold him responsible for everything: war, hunger, poor military preparation. Grigorcea thinks that if the British air force gave Italy a good drubbing for a couple of weeks, the regime would not hang on any longer. The situation is even worse than at the time of the defeats in Albania.

I read in yesterday's papers that the daily bread ration in Italy has been set at two hundred grams—until the next harvest. It's a bit early in September to be looking forward to the next harvest.

In Prague, Baron Nemeth [actually von Neurath] has been removed (sick leave), and the Czech prime minister has been arrested and put on trial for treason. The DNB dispatch hints that the anti-German agitation in the protectorate is very serious.

I still had 130 lei in my pocket. I gave Mama 100 and now have 30. Tomorrow I'll have to find some money from somewhere. But from whom? I'm embarrassed to ask Aristide—and I haven't yet decided to speak to Zissu.

Wednesday, 1 October

Yesterday I ended up with three lei in my pocket. It's a strange feeling to be in the street without any money at all. You feel defenseless. You can't even get on a streetcar. I don't know what I'll do. Today Uncle Moritz unexpectedly gave Mama back ten thousand lei that she lent a few years ago to Poldy. This will last another ten days or so. And then?

The headline in today's *Universul*: "Germany Is Prepared for Winter Campaign." The psychological effect of the victory in Kiev has come to an end. Now there is another pause in the war with the Russians. The balance of hopes and disappointments is again slightly tilting toward London—until, that is, a new German blow causes the propaganda to take off in the other direction. Be this as it may, we are now in October.

Numerous executions in Prague: three Czech generals, several university professors, as well as engineers and architects. A Karl Čapek was on the list of those condemned to death. But I don't think this was the writer, who died—I think—in 1939.

Yom Kippur. I fasted and in the evening went to hear the shofar at the Temple. I felt a certain indifference. How much more moving it all used to be in Brăila!

Benu arrived yesterday evening and went back this evening.

Friday, 3 October

The German communiqués have returned to the old vague formulations: "operations are proceeding according to plan"; "the offensive is continuing successfully"; "our actions are developing methodically," and so on. In town, people say that the Russians have reported successes in the Leningrad region, regaining fifty kilometers of territory and freeing the rail link with Moscow. I haven't listened to London for a long time and have no direct information about this.

In Prague the prime minister and, two days later, the mayor have been executed. The death sentences continue.

Hitler spoke this afternoon. I was with Eugen[7] and Rodica in Cişmigiu around six o'clock, just when the speech was being broadcast. We went to the Buturugă (where there is a radio) and sat down at a table. I wanted to listen—but after a few seconds Eugen turned pale and stood up.

"I can't take it! I can't!"

He said this with a kind of physical desperation. Then he ran off, and of course we went after him. I felt I could have hugged him.

For some time I have been dreaming of all kinds of things, nearly all of them in Brăila, in the house at Strada Unirii 119. I don't know where they are coming from, what they mean, what they are trying to say.

I went out this morning with a complete schedule. It can't go on like this! I thought to myself yesterday. I must do something. I must find some money. I must find some work. Anything, anyhow—but I must get out of this dire poverty. So I made up my mind: 1) to see Rosetti and ask him to speak with Rebreanu about a translation, and with Byck[8] about a few hours of Romanian teaching at his school; 2) to see Ocneanu and ask him for a translation; 3) to make contact again with Roger, also for a translation; and 4) to see Zissu and ask his help for a job, or some kind of business. I went to see Rosetti, but I didn't manage to say anything.

7. Eugen Ionescu.
8. Jacques Byck: linguist, director of a wartime secondary school for Jewish children from Bucharest who had been forced out of the Romanian schools.

I called in on Ocneanu, but he was busy and I was too shy to wait. I didn't have the courage to see Roger, because I feel guilty toward him. So nothing in my schedule actually happened. A day wasted. And then, feeling ashamed of my faintheartedness, I rang Zissu.

"Come at once. I'll be waiting."

On the way, I already regretted my haste. It would have been better to postpone it, to wait for a suitable occasion. Still, I did speak to him. I don't know what I was like; I can't even remember it too clearly. He offered to give me some money. I refused. I asked him to think of a solution, and he promised to do so. I left feeling relieved, without too much hope in what might come out of it, but pleased that I had done one thing on my "schedule."

Saturday, 4 October

Hitler's speech yesterday contains one interesting point: "A new operation on a huge scale began forty-eight hours ago. It will help to destroy the enemy in the east." In which sector is this operation taking place? What are its objectives? How will it unfold? A mystery, for the time being. The German dispatches say nothing, and I haven't had an opportunity to listen to London. In any event, it must be something serious and it is probably expected to bring results soon, for Hitler would not risk anything that looked uncertain.

Rosetti (I saw him last night at Camil's) thought the speech was masterful. It struck me, rather, as insignificant, as what is called a "moderate" speech. It did not touch on any of the problems of the hour. Not a word about America, nothing about Turkey, nothing about Prague or Paris, nothing much about war policy. Unexpectedly circumspect toward Britain, so that one had a sense of vague peace overtures.

Forty-four lei for a hundred grams of butter. From one day to the next, prices increase, sometimes even double. It is not speculation; it is rout, panic, the desperation of those with money "set aside" who see it melting before their eyes, turning into pulp or ashes!

"Inflation is mass murder," said Camil, fearful that his thirty or forty thousand lei a month would lose its value.

"It doesn't affect me, Camil, old boy. I don't have any money."

"Ah!" he said, shrugging his shoulders.

Indeed, was there any more to be said?

Sunday, 5 October

The German communiqué reports "large-scale operations," thereby underlining what Hitler said the day before yesterday. Yet neither the Russian communiqués nor the British commentaries seem to register anything special at the front. We'll have to wait a few days to see what is going on.

An official Romanian communiqué reports that Soviet attacks have been repulsed in Ukraine, east of the Dnieper, in the region of the Sea of Azov, and on the Odessa front. The last part of the communiqué puts Romanian losses so far at 15,000 missing (half dead, half captured by the Russians), 20,000 dead, 78,000 wounded.

Monday, 6 October

Neither yesterday evening's German communiqué nor this evening's gives any new indication about the front. Vague phrases: "operations are continuing successfully"; "we are chalking up fresh successes." The major action announced in Hitler's speech has not yet shown itself.

A day of rushing around. I am determined to do something to get some money. This morning I drew up a long list of telephone numbers—but I rang everywhere without results. I went to Hachette's (taking my heart in my mouth), but I couldn't find Roger. I'll try again tomorrow. I spoke to Ocneanu about translations, but he didn't give me many grounds for hope. Finally, on Mrs. Zissu's suggestion, I decided to try the art trade. I'll see Oprescu tomorrow, and Devechi also tomorrow. I must try everything.

I am still reading Taine's history. It's hard going, because I keep alternating it with Sterne, Shakespeare, and Shaw. Taine strikes me as opaque and often obtuse. What he says about *Tristram Shandy* is plain stupid. I am at the chapter on Byron, from which I have retained two sentences *pro domo meo*. On the personal need to write: "To withdraw myself from myself has ever been my sole, my entire, my sincere motive in scribbling at all. . . ." And on the impossibility of reworking texts after the first draft: "I can never recast anything. I am like the tiger. If I miss the first spring, I go grumbling to my jungle again. But if I do it, it is crushing." The last point does not fit me: "Never crushing."

Tuesday, 7 October

I have heard from two different sources (Rosetti, Jianu) that, according to Radio London, the new German offensive is directed at Moscow from three directions: from Lake Ilmen, from Smolensk in the center, and from Bryansk in the south. The Russian lines are said to have been "deeply penetrated" in the center.

I have been to see Devechi. I asked him to speak to Antoine about a possible job in one of his firms. I have no illusions, but, *par acquit de conscience*,[9] I want to do everything possible to find some money. I hadn't seen Devechi since July, when he told me that the whole war in Russia would be over by the first of September. I thought he might now be forced slightly to modify his political line of argument. But I found him cool as a cucumber. No, no—nothing exceptional has happened in Russia. Hitler will win without difficulty; everything is simple and inevitable.

I also visited Oprescu, at the museum. The Șosea was empty, with many dead leaves. A pale yellow that made everything look beautiful. I could have been in a different country, a different city—maybe Lisbon or Geneva. Oprescu has arranged an appointment for me with Petrașcu for Thursday afternoon. We'll see what comes of it. It is hard for me, but I just have to shut my eyes and press on.

Wednesday, 8 October

Yesterday evening's German communiqué reports a major battle in the northern sector of the Sea of Azov. This evening's communiqué, graver in tone, speaks of an encircling operation around Vyazma, where several Russian armies are awaiting the "inevitable end." So the great blow is being delivered at what has so far been the stablest point: the center. The main objective is undoubtedly Moscow.

Thursday, 9 October

"The whole Soviet front has collapsed," declared Dr. Dietrich today to the foreign press. And he added: "The operations under way have only a secondary importance. The ground is being methodically occupied." This evening's German communiqué says that, apart from the troops sur-

9. For the sake of conscience.

rounded in Vyazma, "three army corps will soon be destroyed in the Bryansk sector." In London the Russian defeat is being described as a disaster. The greatest battle in history! The greatest victory in history! The breakthrough in the central sector is taking place at two different points, over an area—according to the British communiqué—of one hundred miles. The town of Orel has been occupied.

I walked with Branişte toward Alice's, where we had lunch together. He confided in me that a year ago he started and almost completed preparations for us to leave the country. Why didn't he succeed? Because he didn't take enough trouble, because he didn't hurry enough. I felt dazed as I listened to him. So everything could have been different—absolutely everything. We depend on chance, on coincidence, on a little luck and some persistent effort.

I visited the painter Petraşcu. He opened the door himself. An old dodderer, hardly able to stand up. He took me into his studio, where he sat down in a corner without saying a word, huddled as if from cold beside an imaginary fire. He let me look around and take notes; he didn't ask any questions or point me toward anything in particular. He introduced me to his wife, who came and went without a word.

"What's the price of those flowers over on the left?"

"We're not selling those."

"Do you have any other flowers?"

He searched in a corner and found an old painting in a frame with broken glass.

"Forty thousand," he said as he showed it to me. Then immediately, with a frightened haste:

"No, fifty. That's right, fifty thousand. What with the money changing like this, we ourselves don't know how much to ask."

But this did not stop him saying a few minutes later:

"You know, they are fixed prices."

I lingered over some canvases that I shall mention to Mrs. Zissu. But I don't think there will be much doing.

I saw Zissu this morning. He offered to lend me some money "until you find work." I didn't say either yes or no, but I stressed that I wanted to find a longer-term solution. I want to work, to do something—anything other than literature. Administrative work, brokerage, commerce—anything that brings in enough for the rent and housekeeping.

Friday, 10 October

The headlines in today's *Universul*: "The Whole Soviet Front Has Collapsed"; "The Decision Has Been Reached"; "The Destruction of Timoshenko's Armies Means the End of Russian Campaign"; "Disaster for Bolshevik Armies." More tersely, *Evenimentul* has one full-page headline: "The Russian Campaign Is Over."

The following comes from Hitler's proclamation to the army on the night of 1 to 2 October, only now published for the first time: "This is the result of twenty-five years of Jewish domination, which calls itself bolshevism but is essentially the same as the most general form of capitalism. In both cases, the people in charge of the system are the same: the Jews, only the Jews."

Zissu gave me ten thousand lei in an envelope. As I came down the stairs I immediately thought of giving it back to him. I really will have to return it—and as soon as possible. Small amounts are wretched and humiliating. When Zissu gave Nae hundreds of thousands of lei, it certainly never crossed his mind that he was performing charity. I don't want him to be able to become my benefactor at so cheap a price.

Saturday, 11 October

A slight, almost imperceptible lowering of the tone in today's papers. "The Hour of Collapse Is Near," said one headline in *Universul*. Yesterday the collapse was already an established fact. But the fact is that fighting is still taking place. This evening's German communiqué says that the destruction of Bryansk and Vyazma "is proceeding." One's impression is that there can be no question of a general collapse, only of major fighting in different sectors, and with different prospects. This evening Rosetti spoke of "bluffing"—very witty of him. Simionescu-Râmniceanu said that the new offensive was Hitler's contribution to winter relief. I think that yesterday's panic and today's ironic skepticism are both premature. We'll have to wait a few days before we can be clear about what is happening.

My career as a *marchand de tableaux*[1] has fallen through. Madame Zissu is more perceptive than I am. I had lunch at her place and felt a terrible urge to scream in her face about all that is weighing me down.

---

1. Art merchant.

I have finished reading *A Midsummer Night's Dream* with my teacher.

Leaving on my mind. I'd like to run away, to escape.

Sunday, 12 October

Fighting continues. That's all that can be said for the moment. A grave, extremely tense situation—but nothing devastating or definitive. In the south, the German communiqué reports that the battle of the Sea of Azov is finished. In the center, fighting continues in the regions of Bryansk and Vyazma. Nothing new in Odessa or Leningrad.

Visited Pippidi in the evening. Returned through total darkness. The city had never been so dark, and I didn't even have a flashlight to help me. Rain—and as hot as a summer's night.

Monday, 13 October

"The battlefields of Bryansk and Vyazma are well behind the front," states yesterday evening's German communiqué. The Russians also admit that they have lost Bryansk. The offensive against Moscow is in full swing. The German pressure is increasing from Bryansk, Orel, and Vyazma (all three of which have been passed). A "titanic," "gigantic" battle—but beyond these vague appreciations we know nothing for certain.

The Bukovina Jews have been taken from various localities (Vatra Dornei, Cîmpulung, Gura Humorului) and sent off to an unknown destination. To Transnistria, some say. God knows what awaits us too, this winter. It hasn't yet started and already seems dreadfully long.

Smoky rain, biting cold, damp November wind.

I finished *Much Ado About Nothing* last night. What childishness—in places, even stupidity! But some things, some verses, are enchanting. Everywhere in Shakespeare there are memorable things that I should like to be able to use, to quote, to keep in mind.

Tuesday, 14 October

Yesterday evening's communiqué: operations on the eastern front are continuing according to plan. This evening's communiqué: operations are following the anticipated course. But is the momentum of the battle slowing down? News placards in the street: "The Decisive Hour Is Approaching." "Peace Approaching."

I finished *Tristram Shandy* this evening, after a long time spent slowly (too slowly) reading it. Anyway, it is all too long, too uniform, too loose. After the first hundred pages there was nothing more to be learned. And there are still four hundred to go. Pleasant nevertheless. Peaceful reading for a long untroubled winter.

Thursday, 16 October

A Romanian communiqué stated that Odessa's defense lines had been broken and that three villages (probably on the outskirts) were occupied this morning. Odessa is burning. Many special editions. The flags are out.

The situation of Moscow seems to be worsening by the hour. The Germans are also attacking to the north, from Kalinin. The outer fortifications have been breached. At present the German communiqués and dispatches say nothing precise, probably because they would prefer to report a great surprise victory. The weather is extremely favorable: calm, sunny, dry. An October as in 1939. Will Japan enter the war? Will it attack the Russians? The Konoye government has resigned. Grave declarations are being made in Tokyo, as on the eve of major events.

Never have I thought so intensely about leaving. I know it's absurd, I know it's impossible, I know it's pointless, I know it's too late—but I can't help it.[2] The idea of leaving makes me dizzy. Free, free—somewhere far away. A ship with 750 Jewish migrants is leaving in a few days' time— and though I am not and cannot be one of them, it has become an obsession for me. In the last few days I have read a number of American magazines that Ocneanu gave me (*New York Times Book Review*), and I suddenly saw in detail another world, another milieu, other cities, another time.

The *Struma*:[3] to get on there I'd need a sense of adventure, and above all I'd have to be younger, healthier, less ground down by life.

Look in my face: my name is Might-have-been.

2. Last phrase in English in the original.
3. The *Struma* was due to take on board more than seven hundred emigrants bound for Palestine.

Friday, 17 October

Odessa has fallen. The streets are decked with flags. Demonstrations. The German communiqué says nothing about the offensive against Moscow, but the press dispatches say that the city is being evacuated.

The Jews of Gura Humorului have been sent to Mogilev—according to Fanny Scharch, who was in tears at the lack of news about her parents and sister. An acute sense of danger, of uncertainty about each day, each hour. You'd like to sleep, to vanish somewhere beneath the earth, to let time pass over you. All our struggling to stay alive is so futile if there is no longer any light even in the far distance.

Saturday, 18 October

Many short dreams last night.

1) I am with Alice and Aristide in a large restaurant—probably the Cina. We are planning a trip to Italy, though we don't have much money. Aristide shows me the route on a map. We are brought some cakes, I think. George Enescu comes in. Aristide introduces me, then goes with him into an adjoining room and shuts the door, because they have some kind of secrets to discuss.

2) I am with Zoe. She has decided to marry me and I don't have the courage to refuse—which gives me great pangs of conscience in the dream. The funny thing is that she made up her mind because she thought I was suffering too much, even fasting for her sake—whereas, in reality, I had been fasting for Yom Kippur. We go together to the registry officer, who is a friend of mine. I say that I want him to marry us, and he reads a passage (probably from Renard's *Journal*) about marriage. Some lists are pasted up in our courtyard at Strada Antim (lists I saw yesterday at the recruitment office, but in the dream they are lists of people's marital status). Someone congratulates Mama. I am very unhappy at the whole event. I think that we won't be able to make our trip to Italy. On the other hand, I think that my telephone will be reconnected if I marry her.

3) I am in Brăila, at the secondary school. I go into the classroom, but I have been rushing so much that all I am wearing are a shirt and underpants. Arghir is at the teacher's desk. I sit on a bench in the middle of the class. Arghir reads from the 5th Year textbook. Meanwhile a Legionary revolution has erupted. I look out the window and see a brass-band demonstration passing by. It is raining very hard. Some children on the parade can scarcely be seen beneath the driving rain and um-

brellas. I go quickly into the street (but I am no longer a school pupil), and in a kind of arcade I come across an army patrol that refuses to let me through. I am terrified, and the sounds of revolution grow on all sides.

4) I am in bed with Lereanu. We are waiting for Comşa. I undress her so that she is naked, then kiss her with a mixture of disgust and excitement. Everything is too confused—and I don't remember any more.

Sunday, 19 October

I went this morning to a Gieseking concert at the Philharmonic (the Schumann concerto, a Bach Brandenburg concerto for flute, piano, and violin, Beethoven's *Fourth Symphony*). I got the ticket at the beginning of last week, after a lot of hesitation and a sudden final decision: come what may, I'm going to go! But the pangs of conscience started at once. I was ashamed of myself. Could I possibly be so light-minded and unscrupulous as to go to a German concert in these bitter days? Hundreds of Jewish families from Bukovina are right now in forced exile! Thousands of Jews are in labor camps—including Benu! Each day, each hour, fresh horrors and humiliations press down on us—and I go to the Philharmonic! I made up my mind to return the ticket and in no event to attend the concert. But at the moments of greatest indignation, another voice began to creep through. Why should we do penance? Why should we so absurdly give up things? Why should we deny ourselves the few pleasures remaining to us? I haven't listened to any music since the spring, when they took my radio away. A concert—such a fine one at that—will allow me to forget and be happy for an hour. How many pleasures are left to me? Until yesterday evening and right up to this morning, I didn't know if I would go. I went.

It was a strange feeling as I entered the Ateneu, where I had not set foot for so long! I couldn't overcome my shyness, my shame, my fear. I'd have liked it if no one had seen me, if I had seen no one. I felt like a kind of ghost, come back to the world for a few moments. What a rustle of dresses, of white hands, furs, uniforms! So many splendid women. Nearly all the men well dressed, calm, exuding comfort and self-confidence. Sitting on my fold-down seat, I felt a wretched outcast, ugly, old, sad, and shabby. Has the war left its mark only on me? Have I alone been living through it? Do not all these people feel it, see it, know it? Half the pleasure of the concert was taken away by the obsessions I had brought along with me, and which I could not shake off for a second. I don't know if I'll repeat the experience.

Beethoven appeals to me less and less. They were operatic phrases—could have been Rossini. I think I'd enjoy listening to the sonatas more.

Regarding music, there is a curious observation in Thomas de Quincey (I began reading *Confessions of an English Opium Eater* yesterday evening) to the effect that a knowledge of instruments stops you from letting yourself go and really enjoying the music: "To the deep voluptuous enjoyment of music absolute *passiveness* in the hearer is indispensable. Gain what skill you please, nevertheless activity, vigilance, anxiety, must always accompany an elaborate effort of musical execution; and so far is that from being reconcilable with the entrancement and lull essential to the true fruition of music, . . . that even so much as an occasional touch of the foot would utterly undermine all your pleasure." If I were ever to write an essay on music (which I have been thinking of doing for some two or three years), I would try to show that musical understanding is neither "entrancement" nor "lull"; that these are indeed inferior forms of musical sensitivity.

No definite news about the course of the war. The German communiqués are still preoccupied with the twin action at Vyazma and Bryansk, where the number of prisoners is said to be in excess of 600,000. Nothing sure about the situation of Moscow; nor about the Kharkov and Rostov regions.

It is not yet clear whether the Japanese government formed yesterday is a peace cabinet or a war cabinet. My impression is that Japan will not enter the war so long as Russia has not effectively collapsed.

Monday, 20 October

Depressing news from the Union of Jewish Communities, where we went this morning to take a letter for Benu. The roads in Bessarabia and Bukovina are filled with corpses of Jews driven from their homes toward Ukraine. Old and sick people, children, women—all quite indiscriminately pushed onto the roads and driven toward Mogilev. What will they do there? How will they eat? Where will they find a roof over their heads? Death by shooting is a much gentler fate. Yesterday we heard that all Jews originating from Bessarabia and Bukovina must leave Bucharest and set off for Ukraine and Transnistria. This morning it was specified that this applied only to those who have come since January 1940. Why? No one knows. Hardly anyone asks any longer.

It is an anti-Semitic delirium that nothing can stop. There are no brakes, no rhyme or reason. It would be something if there were an anti-Semitic program; you'd know the limits to which it might go. But this is sheer uncontrolled bestiality, without shame or conscience, without goal or purpose. Anything, absolutely anything, is possible. I see the pallor of fear on Jewish faces. Their smile of atavistic optimism is frozen, their old consoling irony is extinguished. One day, far from now, the nightmare will pass—but we, you, he, I, who look into each other's eyes, will be long gone. Already (according to Gaston Antony[4]) the number of Jews murdered since June is more than a hundred thousand. How many of us are left? How long will it be before we too are murdered? My heart is weighed down with despondency. Where can I direct my gaze? What can I expect?

"Leave!" Rosetti advised me yesterday.

It was more than a piece of advice. What he outlined was a definite plan: to leave for Istanbul and to write there to Lassaigne, who would surely help me to make my way further. But everything is immeasurably difficult, beginning with the first steps of obtaining a passport, a Turkish visa, a Bulgarian visa—not to speak of money. Nor do I feel that these material obstacles are the most serious. Above all else, there is my own doubt. Can I leave on my own? Do I have the right to leave Mama alone? Can I leave Benu alone? I don't feel sufficiently robust, in every sense, to go away like that. And, with my ruined health, can I attempt such a major venture? On the other hand, is it not madness to wait—helpless and falling apart—to be killed?

Tuesday, 21 October

All Jews are obliged, under a law that appeared in this evening's papers, to deliver items of personal clothing to the state. The required quantity is laid down for each of seven categories: from those without any income to those with an annual income of 500,000 lei. It would be hard to copy the whole text, which in terms of anti-Semitism is perhaps the wildest and most unexpected thing I have read up to now. A Jewish person who earns 10,000 lei a month is obliged to donate: four shirts, ten pairs of underpants, four pairs of socks, four handkerchiefs, four towels, four flannels, three suits, two pairs of ankle boots, two hats, two overcoats, two linen blankets, two undersheets, two pillow covers, two pillowcases, two sheets. The amounts demanded of the highest income bracket are be-

4. Gaston Antony: lawyer.

yond belief: thirty-six shirts, twelve suits, twelve overcoats, and so on. It is so grotesque that I'm not sure it isn't a sick joke. I see that the law does not bear any signature, so I wonder whether it was not sent to the typesetter by some prankster. For if it is in earnest, you realize after the first moment of comical stupor that it is actually tragic. The cost of the items in question is far above the income that is taken as a criterion! If each Jew were to give all the money he earns, he still could not manage to buy all the things demanded of him. The penalty is five to ten years' imprisonment, or a fine of 100,000 to 500,000 lei.

I had a long sleepless night. Only after four in the morning did I manage to drop off at last. All the time I thought of how my departure might be organized. It is becoming the obsession of my life.

Wednesday, 22 October

A postcard received by Volcovici (a teacher at my school) from his parents and brothers: "Mogilev. My dear ones, we are healthy. We are doing a long journey on foot. At night we are in the fields. I embrace you."

Four months of war. Winter still seems a long way off. For the last few days we have had spring weather. The time of year is not hindering the German offensive. Our lack of information makes it impossible to assess the situation. Moscow will probably fall (we can't say whether in one or in six weeks), but there is no telling what might happen then. Anyway, the war is now becoming remote and immaterial to us. They'll slaughter us—and I don't think the light of victory will reach us in our graves (if we have any). At any moment we could be taken from our homes, pushed onto the roads, and killed. None of us knows if, tomorrow morning, he will turn the calendar page on today: the 22nd of October.

Evening

Rosetti tells me that the Germans have won the war, that the Russians can no longer put up any resistance, that Britain has no option other than to reach a compromise peace. I try to raise his spirits, but without success. To all my arguments that a British victory is certain (however distant), he shrugs his shoulders: no, no, there's nothing more to be done.

On another subject, he tells me that official and semiofficial circles—whose source is Antonescu—claim that Transylvania will be regained from the Hungarians in three weeks at the outside. The Marshal [Antonescu] is supposed to have written in some album: "From Odessa I leave for

Cluj." On our way home we spoke in greater detail about my possible departure, in which he insists on taking a close interest.

All day, everyone in town was speaking of nothing other than yesterday's bizarre law. It is not a sick joke, as I thought at first. It is a genuine decree, which has now been published in the *Monitor official.*

Thursday, 23 October

How glum are the streets after ten at night! Dark, cold, empty, with a chill November wind. Very rarely you hear the distant bell of a streetcar or the noise of a car; it is as if they were in another city, another time, another world.

Spent a long afternoon at a bar table with Braniște (on our way back from lunch at Alice's). My liking for him becomes ever greater. He is a decent man—which is rarer than a genius. I told him that I am thinking of leaving Romania, and he said a lot of useful things. He showed me that it will be much more difficult than I expect, and that it also has a dangerous side. The mere fact of applying for a passport is enough to make me look suspicious. I shall try nevertheless: without illusions, with something more like resignation or indifference. But I shall try.

Some people are actually preparing to buy the overcoats, suits, boots, etc. demanded by the law (Aristide, Paltin . . .). I can't even think of doing it. Where could I find that much money? Isn't prison simpler?

A fierce German attack on the Crimea, where they seem to be making important advances. In Moscow, major new attacks through breaches in the fortified lines. Timoshenko has been replaced—which may be the prelude to the city's collapse. Against your will, you think of Gamelin's replacement in the hour of irreversible disaster. But let's wait and see.

Saturday, 25 October

Nothing new on the Moscow front. But in the south (where Timoshenko has taken command), there have been serious German advances. The fall of Kharkov was announced today—a major loss for the Russians, though it had been expected for some time. The situation in the Crimea is also grave, and in Rostov almost desperate.

I saw Vişoianu today. He talked in a friendly way about my planned departure. He doesn't think it impossible and will try to help me get a

Turkish visa. I am less eager than I have been recently, but I'll press on with it. Who knows?

Sunday, 26 October

The Sunday papers publish Marshal Antonescu's letter in reply to Filderman's appeal concerning the Jews deported to the Bug ghettos. That measure—the letter states—is no more than just punishment for the crimes and atrocities committed by Jews in Bessarabia and Bukovina, in Odessa and Ukraine. "Their hatred is your hatred."

Fear, bewilderment, terrible waiting. The published text is so sharp that it makes possible any act of violence against us. Tomorrow morning we could be taken from our homes and thrown into ghettos—without this seeming excessive to anyone. I find it hard to believe that the publication of such a text can be a chance event without political intentions behind it. I find it hard to believe, or at least to write, that certain things will not follow from it.

I am petrified with fear and anxiety. I feel sorry for old people and children, and sorry for Mama. I don't know what to say to her, how to comfort her. I force myself to smile but am unable to.

I saw Zissu this afternoon. He was pale and withdrawn. The news he told me was even worse than I imagined: namely, that by the first of November our whole legal position here will change. He's not yet sure what this will involve: withdrawal of citizenship? the herding of the whole Jewish population into a single district? its removal from the city?

The Zissu family (sisters, brothers, Zimmer Senior) are thinking of escape: I think they have even started to make preparations. There was a kind of family adviser there. As they are hugely rich, I think they will succeed. I left them alone because I could feel I was disturbing them. It occurred to me how naive are my plans for going away, if this is a difficult problem even for them with all their money. Hundreds of thousands of lei are being paid for a Turkish visa—and I expect to get one for my pretty face? Anyway, now that the danger is so grave and so close, I realize that I would not have the heart to abandon my loved ones.

Late in the evening, after writing the above lines, there came the delight of Benu's return from Fierbinţi for twenty-four hours.

Tuesday, 28 October

All of today's papers comment on the Marshal's letter and violently address "the Jewish problem," calling for radical solutions to be introduced. It is not hard to see a guiding hand in this. In Berlin the German press has given a lot of space to the document, and preparations are being made at the propaganda level for new anti-Semitic blows. We cannot make the slightest gesture in our defense. We wait.

Vicky (Roman's second secretary) tells me that an officer friend of hers, recently returned from Transnistria, is horrified by what he saw there.

"They had orders to shoot all Jews, but he felt so sorry for them, he was so horrified at the butchery, that—when he had to execute a hundred Jews—he ordered the soldiers to shoot them at once, without tormenting them. Those were his very words."

Wednesday, 29 October

Details of how the Jews were driven out of Gura Humorului. (Fanny told us them on the basis of news from her parents and sister, who have reached Mogilev alive.) On Friday, 10 October, people went to bed in peace. Nothing unusual had happened that day or in the past few days. After midnight they were awakened by the beating of drums in the streets. People went outside, not knowing what was afoot. Jews were told that they must be at the railway station by 3 a.m. at the latest—which meant that they had two hours to put some bundles together, lock up, and leave. At the station they handed over their house keys and their residency papers, and were given in exchange a personal identification number. Then they were put on a train. They did some of the journey by train, the rest on foot, and crossed the Dniester on boats. They kept selling the clothes on their backs in order to have money for food. A loaf of bread was not easy to buy at eight hundred lei. Now they are in Mogilev: some have found room in a house; others haven't and are in the fields. They wait there to be sent on farther, to an as yet unknown destination.

"Let's try not to think of the Jews in Ukraine," Lena Constante said yesterday. "There's nothing we can do for them. Let's try to forget. Let's try to live."

Maybe she is right. But it is a nightmare from which I cannot detach myself. And the nightmare is also ours, even if it is not yet dragging us under, even if it still allows us to keep our heads above the surface, before we sink for good. Today's papers comment again on Antonescu's letter, even more violently than yesterday's. The echoes persist in Germany, Bohemia, and Italy. It is a European event. Organized anti-Semitism is going through one of its darkest phases. Everything is too calculated for effect, too obviously stage-managed, not to have a political significance. What will follow? Our straightforward extermination?

I listened at Lena's to Franck's *Symphonic Variations*. A moment of forgetting—before I returned to the same terrible nightmare. Sometimes I tell myself that everything is untrue: suffocating, painful, overwhelming—but not actually true. Perhaps I could make an effort and wake up. Perhaps I could open my eyes and suddenly realize that everything has vanished into thin air. Never has life seemed to me so unreal.

Thursday, 30 October

Yesterday the finance minister called to his office ten leading Jews, including the chief rabbi and Filderman. He received them standing up, without saying good day or offering his hand or asking them to take a seat. He shouted at them and did not allow them to say a word in reply. With Filderman, in particular, he was extremely harsh, again telling him that the Jewish population must make a loan of ten billion lei, and giving him one month to deliver.

I spent the evening at Alice's, with Vişoianu, Branişte, and Aristide. Always the same discussions, which obsess, tire, and exasperate us. We live with two or three *idées fixes*. None of us knows more than the others; no one can think or say anything new. Nor is there room for anything new. The war will last another two years, says Aristide. Two and a half, adds Vivi. Maybe only one year, say I. Maybe not even that, says Branişte. Tomorrow we'll set different time schedules, arguing stupidly for things about which we are ignorant. But our life is caught up in these things, and we feel each day that we are losing it.

"I am being objective," I said yesterday to Camil, who was again having an attack of anti-Semitism.

"A stupid person is objective."

I feel that this whole war does not concern me, precisely because my chances of surviving it are minute. I speak as if I am beyond life—as if it were a question not of a war in 1941 but of a long-forgotten war that is part of history.

There is no detailed news from the front. The situation of Moscow continues to be very grave; no sign that it might resist much longer. Also very grave is the situation of Rostov. As for the Crimea, the Germans report that they have broken through the Perekop Isthmus and are easily advancing into the peninsula.

Saturday, 1 November

Two hours of music. I had asked Lena to invite me round, just me, so that we could listen to some records. She let me choose the program alone: four preludes for piano by Debussy, the Ravel *Quartet*, a Bach piano concerto in D minor, the Debussy *Quartet*. We didn't talk either about the war or about the deportation of Jews.

November! Time passes without any resolution, without any alleviation. We keep thrashing about in the same fog, in the same night.

Monday, 3 November

A summons to the recruitment office. I didn't tell Mama that I had received it. There will be time enough tomorrow. I have vague hopes of escaping—who knows? Usually in such matters I am both unlucky and incapable. Anyway, I wait with resignation.

Simferopol has fallen. The German advance is making rapid headway toward Sebastopol. The whole Crimea is going. The resistance was serious at Perekop, but now the gates are wide open. Fighting continues in Leningrad and Moscow.

Tuesday, 4 November

Last night's dreams. I am with Izi at a Legionary demonstration, on the Șosea. We are marching in the front row. A girl in the row behind looks at us with surprise and says: Legionary yids! We start walking faster and distance ourselves from the column while she turns round to another column to denounce us. We reach the left-hand pavement, at the beginning of Calea Victoriei, but the girl catches up to us and asks to see our papers. We run as fast as we can. Izi says: "Not so fast; I can't take it." We are being followed and don't know where to hide ourselves. On the right-hand pavement, more or less across from Strada Grigore Alexandrescu, someone who used to be employed at the Foundation (probably Costea) suddenly appears coming in my direction. He is wearing the uniform of a ministry doorman. He points a way through the gardens of a public institution. We take it and arrive at some steps, on which a num-

ber of passersby have taken refuge. The dream continues, but I don't remember any more.

Another dream. I am at a trial for the murder of five Legionaries
(among them Mişu Polihroniade). At first I am a witness, then a defen-
dant. The presiding judge is Istrate Micescu, though I am well aware
that he is the killer (he admitted it some time ago in an interview). Filderman gives his testimony (sharply interrupted by Micescu), then Zissu,
in a calmer atmosphere. The proceedings are adjourned so that a symphonic piece may be played in honor of the murder victims. A religious
ceremony takes place at what seems like the same time. Micescu orders
us defendants (among whom I am now definitely one) to be taken away.
I am kept in a hall outside, where I meet Dinu and (I think) Wendy.
Both of them, or perhaps only he, make great sport of the statement I
made.

Evening

A day spent rushing around: to the school, to the recruitment office, to
Alice's, to Timuş's,[5] to the Union . . . I haven't done anything for the time
being. I haven't reported for duty, and I don't know if I will do so tomorrow. Timuş was very nice: he offered not only to requisition me at
the Alhambra but even to give me some work there. Nothing definite,
of course. We shall see.

For the last two or three days a major new German offensive has been
directed at Moscow. The situation there seems to be worsening all the
time. Still, it is one relatively fixed point in the course of the war. Yesterday was one month since Hitler's last speech, which seemed to announce more decisive blows. I think we can soon expect a fresh German
initiative, which might give a push to the somewhat slackened pace of
events. And the time passes so slowly.

Thursday, 6 November

A day of endless errands. Impossible to get a postponement for a week,
or even for less. Colonel Negulescu has been told that I must report to
the recruitment office, where I shall be assigned to a detachment at Romanian Railways. At school, however, they say that I shall receive exemption from labor in the next two to three days. But this is uncertain,
even unlikely, and meanwhile I could be stopped in the street (there are

5. Vasile Timuş: theatre administrator.

police checks every day). Then how would I justify myself? I greatly fear
that I shall eventually be forced to leave—which would further complicate my already sufficiently complicated life.

Rumors of a change of government. Rumors of Legionary disturbances.
There is something murky in the air. Braniște claims that a national government is being cooked up. Everyone (Alice, Camil, Rosetti) is talking
of a governmental crisis. I don't quite understand what this means—if
indeed there is a crisis.

It would seem that the offensive against Moscow has been slowed, if not
actually halted. London, which oscillates between gloom and satisfaction,
is going through a new period of optimism. The German communiqué
focuses on the southern front, saying nothing about the center and the
north. But if the war continues at its present rhythm, there will probably soon be a new German blow.

Friday, 7 November

In the end, I hope I have obtained a few days' respite. I had registered
on the teachers' list at the recruitment office, in the belief that this would
reduce my risk of being called up. In reality (and no one could say why),
teachers are being called up, whereas lawyers (even if disbarred) are not
being called up. Colonel Negulescu successfully applied for me to be re-
classified as a lawyer, and this has (for the time being) led to cancella-
tion of my call-up. Meanwhile, until my turn comes as a lawyer, I shall
try to arrange something for myself in a theatre.

I am reading *Hamlet* in English with difficulty. The vocabulary and syntax are incomparably more difficult than anything I have read before.
Even with a parallel French text, it is tough going.

I have no news about the course of the war. Tomorrow the victorious
Romanian troops will have their triumph in Bucharest. Already this
evening the city was decked with flags and, for the first time in a long
while, properly lighted up. It sounds as if the next couple of days will
be hard for Jews. A public ordinance, printed in today's papers, forbids
ritual methods of slaughtering poultry, as well as the selling of it (dead
or alive) in Jewish districts.

Saturday, 9 November

Recent German communiqués no longer mention the Leningrad or the Moscow front, and speak only of operations in the Crimea. It would seem that the war has come to a standstill in the other sectors. According to Ţuţubei (whom I saw this evening at Camil's, together with Rosetti), Hitler said yesterday in a speech not yet published in the papers that he will not sacrifice any more soldiers for Leningrad. That is another sign that the offensive has been halted. Moreover, winter is fast approaching. Today was quite cold, murky and overcast, with bluish-grey skies. We expected it to snow at any moment. It is a time when Anglophilia is on the rise again. This evening, Camil, Rosetti, and Ţuţubei were of one mind that the Germans are coming off losers. All that is necessary is another German attack or another success in the next few days, and all three will agree that the British are lost. It is a psychological pendulum, operating with clockwork regularity.

The Jews of Dorohoi and Botoşani have received deportation orders. The pharmacist Aric, who has a seventy-year-old mother and a ninety-year-old grandmother there, is rushing around in a furious attempt to escape. Nevertheless, both George Brătianu (according to Rosetti) and Doctor Lupu (according to Branişte) have received assurances from the Marshal that nothing bad will happen to native-born Jews. Nothing new there at least. But I can't believe that moderation is still possible on the road that leads to pogroms.

Last night and this morning I read with great pleasure Molière's *Amphitryon*. So much more direct, more palatable, more simple than Giraudoux! Surprising things in it about double personalities. A kind of Pirandellism *sans le savoir*.[6] I'd have enjoyed writing some notes along these lines.

Monday, 10 November

The papers publish the speech Hitler gave last Saturday. Violently anti-Semitic. Is there a need for diversion? Anyway, it is not an optimistic speech. It seems to come at a difficult moment, and the violence of the phrases is not enough to mask the concerns. There is an interesting statement that they are on the defensive in the Leningrad area. "If anyone

---

6. Unwitting.

asked why we are not advancing at present, I would answer: because it is raining, or because it is snowing, or because the railways are not yet ready."

Similarly interesting is a sentence about Italy: "His (the Duce's) country is poor, overpopulated, still badly off; it doesn't know where the next day's bread will come from."

Wednesday, 12 November

The city hall has forbidden Jews to have dealings in the market outside certain hours (ten to twelve), and has laid down penalties for traders who sell to them in breach of this order. Each day you wonder what they will think up next; it must certainly take a lot of imagination. In fact, since they expropriated Jewish housing and started the deportation and killings, all the rest has become grotesque, puerile, mindless. It is no longer even depressing. In anti-Semitism there is sometimes a demonic element, but now, when there is not a bloodbath, we have to wade through the muck of petty meanness.

Titu Devechi says that neither any information I might have, nor any use of my imagination, could help me form even the most approximate idea of what the carnage was like in Bukovina and Bessarabia. As to the war, he surprised me by saying that he no longer believed in a German victory. In his view, the Germans are on the way down; they will try to secure peace at any price, and it is possible that the British (fearing the Russians) will grant it.

Bad weather, the onset of winter, the halting of the offensive against Moscow and Leningrad, the Italian losses, Goebbels's article, Hitler's speech—all together have led to an ever more widespread conviction that the denouement is approaching. Anglophile optimism is going through a period of special intensity. I don't allow myself to be carried away. I am well aware that another bout of depression will follow soon, according to that automatic swing of the pendulum to which I have grown accustomed. The end is still a long way off. A long way.[7]

It snowed this morning, but it was not a wintry snow. November: gloomy, wet, and mucky.

7. In English in the original.

Thursday, 13 November

Snow, blizzard, a wintry day.

At Dorohoi, dozens of families wait in wagons at the station to leave. Exactly the same system is in operation in Gura Humorului: drums beating in the middle of the night, people herded toward the station, houses locked and sealed. Here in Bucharest their relatives are at their wit's end as they run around seeking compassion—but from whom? At the president's office, at the Interior Ministry, at army headquarters, they are received with a shrug of the shoulders: "We know nothing about it."

Benu, in Fierbinţi, lives in a cold house without a stove, without wood. On top of everything, he is tormented by his old attacks of sciatica. Of course he doesn't write to us about all that, but I have spoken to someone who has come from there. From Poldy there has been no news for such a long time. It is with aching hearts that we live and wait. And we even find the strength to laugh, to read, to talk!

I have returned to Balzac: *Une fille d'Eve*, an excellent little novel set in the Paris of politics, literature, and theatre, in 1832.

Friday, 14 November

A heavy November day. Thick snowfall.

Nothing new at the front. On the Atlantic, on the other hand, the British have lost the *Ark Royal* to a submarine torpedo. In Washington the neutrality law has been repealed after a long hard battle in Congress.

"The Jews Are to Blame" is the title of Goebbels's latest article in *Das Reich*.

A few hours of music at Lena's. A lot of Bach, a lot of Vivaldi, the *Goldberg Variations*, the first Brandenburg concerto, a concerto for four pianos and orchestra, a concerto for string instruments.

Monday, 17 November

A bad day with the blues. I have no money and don't know where to turn. There are only four days left until I have to deliver the shorts, underwear, socks, and so on. We should buy the missing things, but with what? Sometimes a feeling of powerlessness leaves me paralyzed. I no longer see anything ahead; all paths are closed, everything is pointless—and suicide seems the only escape.

Kerch in the Crimea has fallen. Sebastopol is still holding out. Nothing new on the other fronts. Winter seems to have snowed in the war.

Pippidi's room (I called by to take him some books) is the kind of island in which I wouldn't have minded living myself. A desk, a library, solitude, light, quietness. He is working on a study about the date of Tiberius's enthronement.

Tuesday, 18 November

I met Corin Grossu.[8] He is recently back from Odessa, which he entered on the very day after it was captured. Intelligent, measured, and well informed, he told me a number of interesting things. (How hysterical by comparison appears Camil, who shouts and thunders and blindly rushes into the most stupid enormities!) Grossu does not think the end of the war is in sight; rather, everything will sooner or later come crashing down in a catastrophe whose nature is hard to predict. He too is sure that the Germans cannot win, but nor does he believe in a swift British victory.

Lunch with Ghiță Ionescu at Gina's. I had the feeling that he is making more than a career for himself—a fortune. He told me that he was at the Melody one evening, and that everyone there was "a grafter from the Economics Ministry." Does he say that to show off?

Oprescu saw G. Nothing doing. Vague expressions of pity, sighs and regrets—but that was all. Anyway, I have rather gone off the idea of leaving.

Thursday, 20 November

The British have launched an offensive in Libya! It began on the night of the 18th, and Churchill announced it today as a major event in the general course of the war. It seems to be on a large scale and to have got off to a successful start, though it is too early to tell what will happen.

8. Corin Grossu: writer.

On the Russian front, the Germans are again attacking Moscow after relative quiet for the last two to three weeks. Will they capture it? Anyway, they will certainly do everything possible, make every necessary effort. At Tula and Kalinin they seem to have broken through the Russian lines. The relief from winter (we are back in November) has given them a fresh opportunity for action. Powerful attacks have also been unleashed at Sebastopol and Rostov.

A dispatch from Berlin that appeared in today's *Universul*: "As regards the cold, the thermometer records a slight drop in temperatures, established over several months."

I am broke and feel more helpless than ever. What can I do? To whom can I turn?

Saturday, 22 November

Too little news about the British offensive in Libya. Things seem to be going well, if not with lightning speed.

In Russia the Germans report that they have taken Rostov. Major battles in Moscow, launched from the directions of Kalinin and Tula.

Vivi thinks that my planned departure is not unrealistic, after all. He has also spoken to Mrs. G. He too is thinking of leaving. But I don't dare take these ideas any further.

Last night I finished a splendid novel by Balzac—*Béatrix*—one of his finest.

Benu has at last returned again from Fierbinți.

Sunday, 23 November

In Libya the British have occupied Port Capuzzo. There is not much information about how the offensive has been going. Major German attacks on Moscow, especially from the north, where they have occupied Kalinin.

I am penniless, completely penniless—and I don't know what to do. I thought of speaking today with Aristide, but I couldn't pluck up the courage. Besides, it is a long time since I saw him alone. He seems to be somehow avoiding this.

Monday, 24 November

A night full of intricate, confused dreams. I remembered them quite well when I woke up in the morning, but then I almost entirely lost the thread. All I can still reconstruct is the first part of one dream. I am in Paris. The city is full of red and black loaves of bread, which no one is allowed to touch. The red is bright and powerful, the black burnt like charcoal.

I am told that the British have reported taking Bardia.

The Council of Ministers decided yesterday that Jews should pay certain taxes instead of performing work for the state. Those who don't pay will be sent off to work, while those who don't pay and are too ill to work will be expelled.

Tuesday, 25 November

A lot of music yesterday evening at Gina's and Ghiţă's. A Beethoven quartet (played by the Calvets), the third Brandenburg concerto, the Vivaldi-Bach *Concerto for Four Pianos and Orchestra*, a Bach chorale and fugue on the organ, the *Death of Isolde*, Ravel's *La valse*, two Chopin nocturnes. I returned home after one in the morning—the first time for so many months. It was snowing gently; the whole city white and calm.

At Ghiţă's yesterday, Ceauşescu—the general secretary at the Economics Ministry—listened avidly to the French-language bulletin from London at 11:15, happy that fifteen thousand Germans and Italians had been taken prisoner in Libya. He too is expecting a British victory. But in the interim he sees nothing odd in holding public office under the present regime. Incompatibility is not a problem that occurs to people here on the Danube.

A number of funny things in the Gina-Ghiţă family. Gina is as ever *la folle du logis*.[9] But Ghiţă is indescribable. We drank a good (and "not too expensive") wine, as we all agreed. "Ghiţă brought it from the Romanianization Board," Gina said. Just like that.

I heard people shouting in the street at one in the morning: *Unity! Unity!* A new decree on the Romanianization of Jews.

---

9. All imagination.

Yesterday I read *Le colonel Chabert* and found it surprising. A little Daumier engraving: powerful, cold, and precise. I finished the third volume of the Pléiade Balzac.

The *Struma* was due to leave Constanţa today. But last night the people were turned away from the station at the last moment. The *Struma* won't be sailing [for Palestine]. The government's permission has been withdrawn. I feel a little as if my own escape attempt has failed.

A confused situation in Libya. A grave situation in Moscow.

Friday, 28 November

I saw Balcic for a moment last night in a dream—but a wonderful Balcic full of light and color. I was on the crest of the plateau, and suddenly the green gulf (it was April or May) and the deep blue sea opened before me. It was stunningly beautiful—but I immediately woke up and everything vanished.

The headlines in the afternoon papers: "Moscow's Fate Is Sealed!"; "Moscow's Fate Is Finally Sealed!"

Sunday, 30 November

The Germans have evacuated Rostov, a week after their reported occupation of it. A powerful Russian offensive from the Sea of Azov. I cannot work out the scale of the operation. The German advance at Moscow appears to have been slowed or checked—though the situation remains no less serious. In Libya everything is confused. A junction has been partly accomplished at Tobruk. The British have superiority, but it is not completely clear-cut. In Washington, negotiations with the Japanese are on the point of collapsing. Will war break out in the Pacific?

In the past two days I have seen nearly all the few people I am in the habit of seeing: Aristide, Alice, Branişte, Belu, Eugen, Camil, Rosetti, Gulian, Lena, Harry. I spoke with all of them about the war—and the whole thing seemed more distressing, more absurd, more futile than ever. Camil thinks the Germans are unbeatable. Branişte thinks they are lost. Aristide is disgusted at the British lack of seriousness in Libya. Belu is excited about the Russian offensive. But in essence, all say the same things over and over again. Days, weeks, months pass—and all we do is talk, talk, talk. It is driving me up the wall. I can't stand this stupid game of working ourselves up over all manner of ridiculous opinions, which never change anything.

A colorful visit to the Bibescus. Antoine is the same as ever. His wife is suffering from a serious case of general amnesia, but she remains incredibly intelligent. We chatted for a long time in Antoine's room (at the Athénée Palace) until he arrived. There was an amusing episode with Speranța (I regret not recording it here, but I don't feel up to writing a longer note).

Recently I have been thinking of the major novel that I once planned. The initial episode at least (the theatrical tour in the provinces) is clear in my mind; I could start to write it now. Then there are numerous ramifications which it would be interesting to follow through. It could all grow into something even larger than I bargained for. There is enough material not for one but for five books. From 1927 to the present, a long series of situations framed by the history proper of these fourteen years. But will I write it? Will I ever write again? I am vegetating, dragging myself from one day to the next, becoming old and worn out, losing myself. Is there still anything to be done with me? Do I still have any demands? Any expectations? Can I still get anything out of life? Can life still get anything out of me? Physical decrepitude and moral disgust—that's about all there is. Otherwise, poverty, penury, lack of a solution, a sense of being abandoned and helpless.

Monday, 1 December

Skis have been confiscated from Jews. An order has been passed obliging us to hand them over at once to the Community.

Things are developing slowly but satisfactorily in Libya. Resistance in Moscow. A Russian offensive on the Sea of Azov. That is more or less a summary of the war today. But people are more restless, more impressionable, more hasty, more enthusiastic than the facts themselves. Everyone you meet tells you that in Libya the British are already south of Benghazi, that Rommel's headquarters have been surrounded, that von Kleist's army in southern Russia has been destroyed, that Taganrog has been recaptured, that the Germans are running to Mariupol and starting to withdraw from the Crimea. You wonder where all these stupidities and exaggerations are dreamed up. It's a kind of need to feel intoxicated at any price—even at the price of lies.

I have finished (after an interruption of several weeks) the *Confessions of an English Opium Eater.* It is less interesting than Quincey's fame would lead you to expect, but it is nonetheless worth reading. The right tone for confessions—direct, virile, precise.

Wednesday, 3 December

German successes both in Libya and in Russia. At Tobruk they have broken into the corridor that the British established last week between the fort and the armies outside. The situation again seems grave. As to Rostov, the Russian success seems to be more a local incident than part of a large-scale action.

Last night—after so many years!—I leafed through Spengler's *Années décisives*, which I read for the first time in 1935, I think. There are stunning predictions, some of them miraculous, but also an unexpected page (suddenly of burning topicality) about the impossibility of a war against Russia. "The population of this vast plain, the largest in the world, cannot be attacked from outside. The spatial expanse is a political and military strength that no one has ever been able to overcome. Napoleon himself had to learn this through experience. Even if the enemy were to occupy the vastest regions, it would still be of no avail. [. . .] The whole region to the west of Moscow—Byelorussia, the Ukraine, the whole region between Riga and Odessa that was once the most flourishing in the Empire—is today no more than a huge 'buffer' against Europe that could be abandoned without a collapse of the system. This being so, however, the idea of an offensive by the West makes no sense. It would run up against a void." Written in 1929, published in 1932.

Friday, 5 December

A dream the night before last. I am in a huge hall, seated at an endless rectangular table with a large number of guests. It appears to be a banquet. A door opens right behind me, and Hitler walks in. He approaches the table and asks: "Who is Radu Apotecker?" Radu Apotecker is seated to the left across the table from me. He stands up. Hitler comes beside him, grabs his tie, and violently shakes him. A beautiful young brunette slaps Hitler a couple of times—but at the same moment realizes the enormity of her gesture and bursts into tears. She is lost! we all feel it, as if a shudder has passed through us. I don't know how that incident ends (as if there is a break in the dream), but Hitler walks along the table behind me and stops at the end on the right. He orders the first six diners to get to their feet. Among these six are myself and Benu. He asks us all for our names. The first four are Romanians. Then comes our turn. We are petrified with fear, but just then Mihai Antonescu comes up and whispers to me: "I've got to leave, but I'll be back. Don't be afraid: nothing is going to happen."

I don't know what I'll do in the end because of my lack of money. I have borrowed two thousand lei from Lereanu, and one thousand from Comşa. I was supposed to pay my teacher yesterday, but I postponed it until tomorrow. Even assuming I find the several thousand I need at once, what will I do then? There are terrible nightmares from which you awake with a start, ready to scream with fear—but you do awake from them. When will I awake from this nightmare?

The street lamps are out—a general blackout. There seems to have been a British ultimatum. But even if it comes to a formal declaration of war, would this have more than a purely demonstrative significance? My only fear is that there might then be another anti-Semitic outburst and a general worsening of the climate.

A pause in Libya. In southern Russia there is fighting to the west of Taganrog (which has not been recaptured, though). A grave situation in Moscow.

Everything passes slowly and with exasperating difficulty, endless and seemingly hopeless. To escape from here seems more and more an impossible adventure.

Sunday, 7 December

The British ultimatum has finally been made known. From midnight tonight we are at war with Britain. I am writing these lines a quarter of an hour after midnight. I am very worried about the consequences inside the country. After a few days of relative calm, I fear there will be another outbreak of anti-Semitism.

Monday, 8 December

Japan has entered the war. Landings in Malaysia and Borneo. Invasion of Thailand. Aerial attacks on Singapore, Hong Kong, the Philippines, Honolulu. Once again I was mistaken in thinking that it would not come to war. I knew that the regime in Tokyo could not accept the American conditions, but I was convinced that the negotiations would drag on indefinitely. The war is spreading to the whole planet. The old reasoning that held until yesterday has become redundant. Everything is more serious, more complex, and more obscure.

It would appear that Moscow's position is less acute. In fact the whole Russian front has more or less frozen up. This evening's German communiqué opens on an unexpected note: "The continuation of operations and the form of battle in the east hinge upon the arrival of the Russian winter. Over great stretches of the eastern front, only local operations are now being reported."

Tuesday, 9 December

It will take some time before we know what is happening in the Pacific. It may be a new type of war there—quite unlike anything we have seen since August 1939. The first two days have been full of Japanese blows, with no response from the Americans or the British. The "blitz" technique perfectly accomplished. The Americans are stunned to have lost two armored battleships, and apparently an aircraft carrier, without having the chance to fire one shot. "A disaster"—my teacher says. Maybe he exaggerates, but anyway it is most disturbing to see America taken by surprise like any old Belgium or Yugoslavia.

Wednesday, 10 December

A catastrophic day in the Pacific. In the space of twenty minutes the British lost their only two battleships in Singapore: the *Repulse* and the *Prince of Wales*. There have been numerous Japanese actions all over the area, and no Allied response. I can't follow the situation because I don't know the map, but it leaves you feeling thunderstruck. It is a moment equal to the French collapse; the other fronts now move to the back of the stage. Even the war in Russia has become less important. The Russians have retaken Tikhvin in the north. The Germans are talking of a winter lull as if it were an established fact. It is the Japanese who have sensationally captured the notice boards.

Thursday, 11 December

Germany and Italy have declared war on the United States! Hitler spoke this afternoon, but I don't yet know what he said. The sensation of the

first Japanese successes, the Anglo-Saxon consternation, the general stupefaction—all this adds an aspect of pomp and theatricality, as well as
one of tragic catastrophe, to the events. It will take several days for our
heads to clear.

Apparently the Japanese have also lost a top-class ship, and here and
there the British and Americans do seem to be putting together a defense. We have had a number of shocks throughout the day. *Universul*
reported that a third British battleship, the *King George*, had been sunk.
But this was not confirmed, and the lunchtime papers did not mention
it. Then the sinking of a 32,000-ton American aircraft carrier was announced—but later, when I read the dispatch more carefully, I realized
that this was the same as the one sunk yesterday.

I have reread *The Way of All Flesh*, this time in English. My poor memory disturbs me. True, it is ten to twelve years since I first read it, but
I was still upset that I remembered absolutely nothing: not one name,
not one character, not one episode. I had not even retained a general
vague outline of the plot. Yet it is one of the books that meant something to me. I have written about it and referred to it many times! I
thought of Butler as a writer familiar to me!

Friday, 12 December

A day without catastrophe. Is the Japanese "blitz" subsiding so quickly?

This war has in a way covered over my great misfortunes and disgrace. I cling to it, live in it, lose myself in it—and thus forget my horrible old sufferings. I comfort myself with the thought that I am waiting
for something—I who have nothing to expect.

Saturday, 13 December

Romania has declared war on the United States. The legation is leaving.
A final gate has shut.

Nothing new in the Pacific. In Russia there have been Soviet advances that may be local adjustments of the front or actions with a wider
significance. In Libya the Germans are retreating west of Tobruk, leaving garrisons to maintain resistance at Bardia and Sollum.

A dream last night. Jean Hurtig has been condemned to death, but for
him to be executed someone must start a petition and pay a tax of, I
think, forty lei. I don't know why I am the one who drafts this petition

and takes it to the offices of *Adevărul*. Then I am gripped by fear and go to Hurtig's mother—Madame Sărăţeanu—to warn her of what has happened.

Monday, 15 December

Nothing new at the fronts. Sometimes I get the feeling that the war will never, never end. I am tormented by the thought that one day soon— tomorrow, the day after, five days from now—there will be fresh anti-Semitic attacks. It has been too quiet recently for something not to be in preparation. I am vegetating, falling apart, losing myself.

Apparently the *Struma* has set sail and already arrived in Istanbul. Those people still have a life.

Wednesday, 17 December

The Union of Communities has been dissolved and replaced with a "Central Office."[1] A new census will begin of all inhabitants "of Jewish blood." I think that Zissu is involved in all these developments.

"Go over to Catholicism! Convert as quickly as you can! The Pope will defend you! He's the only one who can still save you." For several days I have been hearing this same refrain. This morning Comşa, this evening Aristide and Alice, asked me in all seriousness why I am still waiting. I don't need arguments to answer them, nor do I search for any. Even if it were not so grotesque, even if it were not so stupid and pointless, I would still need no arguments. Somewhere on an island with sun and shade, in the midst of peace, security, and happiness, I would in the end be indifferent to whether I was or was not Jewish. But here and now I cannot be anything else. Nor do I think I want to be.

Today, more acutely than before, I had the feeling that it is not true, that everything is terribly unreal, that I am thrashing about as in a nightmare, that I am sinking beneath it—and that I must wake up. So long as I don't go mad! At times I feel so tired that I am afraid I will crack up and lose control of myself.

---

1. The creation of the "Jewish Central Office" was decreed by Ion Antonescu. Filderman's Federation of the Union of Romanian Jewish Communities was dissolved.

Thursday, 18 December

I am worried by Poldy's silence and the uncertain news about him. Has he been in a camp? Is he leaving for Toulouse? May God give him the courage to be patient and hang on! Duduia Mică and her husband have been baptized. This evening, Muni Goldschläger [reading uncertain] spoke to me of baptism as a possible solution. He claims that Christian Jews were not deported in Bukovina.

The new Jewish leaders: Streitman[2] and Vilman![3] They were installed today by Lecca.[4]

Saturday, 20 December

Hong Kong has fallen. The Germans are continuing to advance on the Russian front, but without any great speed. In Libya the advancing British forces have reached Derna. But nothing has changed. Everything is still the same.

Sunday, 21 December

The letter I shall send tomorrow to Zissu:
  "Dear Mr. Zissu,
  "I beg your pardon for these lines, but, believe me, it is much harder for me to write them than it will be for you to read them. You can tear them up and forget about them: I shall never forget them. I need money. I have not had any real 'money' for a long time, but now everything has become literally unbearable. Tomorrow I have to pay the rent. More-over, Christmas will find me with nothing. I tell myself that there must be someone in this big city who can make me a loan. *Loan* is not a eu-phemism. I mean a sum that I shall one day pay back.
  "Either we shall see the end of this nightmare of war, and then a person like myself, with a name, an arm, and a head on his shoulders, will easily earn what is refused him today, and will pay the sum back; or else we shall never see the end of this war, and then the money—whether lent or not—will in any case be lost together with life itself.

---

2. H. St. Streitman: journalist, first president of the Jewish Central Office.
   3. A. Vilman: journalist, member of the leadership council of the Jewish Central Office.
   4. Radu Lecca, commissar for Jewish affairs in the Antonescu government. His chief duty was to supervise the Jewish Central Office, but he oversaw many government operations related to the deportation and forced labor of Jews.

"This simple calculation makes me speak with a certain bluntness. I ask you to help me through this hard moment. If you do not have the money or are unable to give it, perhaps you could find someone in the circles close to you.

"But if not, tear this up and forget it."

Derna has fallen.

Tonight, six months of war in Russia.

Monday, 22 December

Brauchitsch[5] has been removed. Hitler has taken personal command of German land forces through a proclamation that is also a call to fight on, drafted in an unexpectedly alarmist style. The simple fact of the change in command is a recognition of failure on the Russian front. The proclamation itself heightens the seriousness of the event. All day, everyone you meet speaks of nothing else. Vişoianu, Camil, Rosetti. George Brătianu told Rosetti today that the situation is extremely serious, and that the switch from Br. marks a historic moment.

Six months of war in Russia. The papers have not published their usual monthly balance sheet. An awkward silence, which cannot be coincidental.

A sentence in a letter from Mircea Eliade to Rosetti: "This year there have been two extraordinary things for me: the amazing weakness of the Soviet air force, and my reading of Camoëns."

Tuesday, 23 December

The eve of Christmas, with its holiday bustle, its haste, abundance, and wealth—all quite remote from me. Lighted shop windows, crowded shops, purchases, white packets, presents . . . I cannot buy anything. Until this morning I did not have a penny, and I kept wondering where I would find two thousand to three thousand lei to give Mama for the house-keeping over these four days of holiday. Around two o'clock an envelope arrived from Zissu with—I think—ten thousand lei. I didn't even have the courage to read what he had written to me, or to count the money. I feel ashamed, terribly ashamed; I wish I could return the money to him tomorrow. I have never felt so bad toward anyone as I do toward this

5. Walter von Brauchitsch: German field marshal.

man who is so wealthy and so sordid. The 23rd of December—the due date for the rent. I met the landlady in the courtyard, but I didn't say anything to her. Maybe she will wait—but I am in any case in her hands, and she could kick me out whenever she wanted.

For the whole of today, as of yesterday, we kept discussing the Brauchitsch affair with very great interest. In a childlike way we glimpse great changes in various situations. It was the same at the time of the Hess business. And it will pass over in the same way.

I am old, sad, dried up, apathetic, lost. In a sense, the war is a drug.

Thursday, 25 December

The first day of Christmas, spent stupidly *en famille* (Zaharia, Debora, Marcu and his wife, Aunt Lucia, and others), playing *belote* and eating. Not a moment of solitude, not a moment of rest.

An implausibly beautiful, springlike day, with a pure sunny sky and a light wind more like a breeze. Oh to be somewhere in the mountains, with a young woman you love!

Ideas of things I might write. The play ("Freedom"), about which I thought again today after it had been out of my mind for several weeks. The novel. An essay on music. But I won't write anything—and so I'll lose beyond retrieval things that I could say only through long and careful work. I cannot count on moments of inspiration or prolificness. My writing never "bursts forth." Eight hours of work a day might lead me to surprise even myself. But without discipline, without continuity of work, without material freedom, without a lot of application—*je ne vaux rien.*[6]

I regret not having copied Zissu's letter before I tore it up. It was disgusting and attracted pity. And in the envelope were 8,500 lei, not 10,000. I'll be really glad if I can give it back to him by the 10th of January.

Without a paper or a radio, no news about the course of the war. I thought a lot about how it might work out, and my conclusions were not too rosy. I am too tired to formulate them now. Maybe tomorrow.

6. I am worth nothing.

Saturday, 27 December

Hong Kong has fallen. Benghazi has fallen. In Russia the front remains unchanged. The Germans are fighting defensively. The Russians attack and, here and there, move slowly forward.

Froda, back from six months in a camp at Tîrgu Jiu, says a number of things: some tragic, others grotesque, others downright comical. He looks quite pale, and says that now that he is out of there he will start another life. He realizes that so far his life has been artificial, ungenuine, false, and inadequate. I know about such decisions to begin everything again from scratch. After a couple of weeks, the routine sets in again as one forgets and abandons the effort.

Sunday, 28 December

Lunch at Alice's, as on every Sunday, with Aristide and Branişte. The same information, the same interpretations, the same predicted dates, the same discussions—*à n'en plus finir.*[7] The war will end in the autumn of 1942. But it's not out of the question that it will end sooner—next March, for example. But if you stop and think about it, it may go on until 1943, and even 1944 is a possibility. The Germans no longer have enough oil. The Germans no longer have food. Italy cannot hold out any longer. There are partisan attacks in Serbia. It's a hard winter in Russia. The same things over and over again, which we say dozens of times almost mechanically, and which never change anything. It is exactly as in an asylum, with lunatics both docile and manic, full of tics and *idées fixes.*

Tuesday, 30 December

I dreamed of Paris again last night. A long dream, in which the joy at being in Paris was strangely mixed with anxiety that it was under German occupation. All the time I felt threatened, pursued.

Roger from Hachette has asked me to translate a few children's books for his publishing house.
"C'est pour vous rendre service, car autrement, vous savez, des traducteurs j'en ai des tas et des tas."[8]

---

7. With never an end to it.
8. "It's to do you a favor, because otherwise, you know, I've got heaps and heaps of translators."

He offers me 80 bani[9] per line—which, he says, works out at roughly 25 lei a page, or 2,500 lei a hundred pages.

"Ce sont des livres pour enfants, car les livres sérieux je les donne aux traducteurs plus connus. J'ai par exemple un Pierre Bénoit que traduit M. Iacobescu."

"Qui est-ce Monsieur Iacobescu?"

"Comment qui est-ce? C'est un écrivain. Il est très connu. Il a beaucoup traduit."[1]

I shrug my shoulders. Roger probably thinks I am envious of Iacobescu's reputation (who could he be?) and am pretending not to know him. But he continues quite deliberately:

"C'est du travail à faire, je vous assure. Évidemment pas trop bien payé, mais si vous travaillez quelques heures par jour, vous pouvez finir un livre en deux semaines. Je vais vous donner un livre pour commencer et vous allez nous présenter un échantillon de quelques pages, que nous soumettrons à M. Ciorănescu. Vous savez, moi je m'y connais pas, mais M. Ciorănescu est notre critique et s'il est d'avis que ça marche, alors l'affaire est faite."[2]

I heard him through and kept nodding, without indignation, without irony, without even despondency. But I'd like to box his ears one day.

Mama has given me a tie for the New Year. I feel moved, but I can't disguise a certain annoyance. That's seven hundred lei we will be short tomorrow. In town there are sounds of happy people hurrying around, full of plans for their New Year's Eve party. We have two thousand lei in the house, out of the last ten thousand I managed to borrow. And then?

I have read *The Vatican Cellars*, after fourteen or fifteen years. My bad memory is almost abnormal. All I remembered from the whole book was that a character throws a stranger from a moving train. That was all. The rest had completely vanished. I had not even held in my memory the striking fact that Lafcadio was born in Bucharest and was a Romanian citizen. The book is interesting in many ways. I very well understand

---

9. One ban is worth a hundredth of a lei.

1. "They are children's books, because I give serious books to better-known translators. I have a Pierre Bénoit, for example, which is being translated by Mr. Iacobescu."—"Who is Mr. Iacobescu?"—"What do you mean who is he? He's a writer, very well known. He's translated a lot of things."

2. "It's work that needs doing, I assure you. Not too well paid, of course, but if you work a few hours a day, you can finish a book inside two weeks. I'll give you one to start with. You should send us a sample of a few pages, which we'll pass on to Mr. Ciorănescu. You see, I don't know about these things, but Mr. Ciorănescu makes the judgments, and if he thinks it's all right, then we've got a deal."

that *sotie*[3] is not an invented term but corresponds to something real. I can also see readily identifiable traces of Dostoevsky, especially of *The Devils*. All in all, the farce is still alive, even virulent, thirty years after the novel first appeared.

[Wednesday], 31 December 1941

The Russians have landed in eastern Crimea, recapturing Kerch and Feodosiya.

The last day of the year. I don't want to, or need to, look back and take stock. I carry inside myself the 364 terrible days of the dreadful year we are closing tonight. But we are alive. We can still wait for something. There is still time; we still have some time left.

---

3. A type of satirical costume drama of the fifteenth and sixteenth centuries, its mad characters alluded to aspects of the age.

1942

1 January 1942, Thursday

Days pass slowly, but years quickly. Now it's 1942! How distant it seems to me, how problematic and unreal! "The war will end in '42," people said at the beginning, a year or two ago—and I was terrified that it might last so long. "The war will end in 1942" was for me like "the war will never end." 1942 was the opaque future, the remote unknown, the inscrutability of chance. And now here we are in 1942—with all our old questions and terrors.

2 January 1942, Friday

A sentence from Hitler's New Year message: "His [the Soviet enemy's] attempt to overturn fate in the winter of 1941–1942, to move against us once again, must fail and will fail."

To overturn fate! Three months ago there could be no talk of anything like that. Today the problem is posed. It has become possible, humanly possible. It is credible, or at least conceivable, and anyway not absurd or excluded in principle, that the Russians will "overturn fate." It is possible that the front will move off in another direction, possible that there will be a fundamental change in the situation. Since the fall of Rostov, the war has taken on a new aspect. Perhaps more than this: it is a new war, a *different* war. Personally, I am inclined to look at things calmly and soberly, without illusions. I tell myself that the German army is still a formidable machine; that the winter is an enormous trial for the Germans, but does not spell the end. Moreover, the Russian offensive does not seem to be of the scale and violence of the shock delivered by the Germans; I can well imagine a German recovery in the spring, and even six months of major German successes from April to October. Only then, on the threshold of next winter, will the crisis become acute again. But if this has been my view until recently, if I have never allowed myself to be carried away by sensational expectations, I have to admit that now there are also elements that justify such expectations. Rostov marked the final point of the German offensive and the obligatory shift from war of movement to war of position. The removal of Brauchitsch showed that this shift corresponds to a deeper crisis of command, conception, and general policy in the conduct of the war. The Russians, by taking the offensive all along the front, have demonstrated that they will not agree to a winter armistice. Finally, the blows at Kerch and Feodosiya show that their army has a certain capacity to deliver sudden shocks in a totally unexpected operation. These, unquestionably, are new factors. Will they lead to an "overturning of fate"? I don't know—and I personally tend to think not. But the question is posed.

Saturday, 3 January

In the Philippines the Japanese have taken Manila. In Libya the English have taken Bardia.

Nicuşor Constantinescu[1] (whom I saw yesterday evening at Leni's) has suggested that I write a play. He is prepared to sign it, to offer to have it performed by a theatre. The author's share would be paid to me, and after the war the truth would be told. It is a moving gesture; I wonder whether I would be capable of it myself in such a situation. It is perhaps the greatest sacrifice a writer can agree to make. I tell myself that what literature means for N.C. is quite different from what it means for me; that he thinks of writing as something to be done for the fun of it; that nothing really engages him; that in the end he does not consider himself bound by any kind of artistic responsibility. I tell myself all this— and his proposal still seems of an unequaled devotion, disinterest, generosity. I want to use the opportunity he has offered me. It is a way of earning a few tens of thousands of lei, maybe even more. It could save me for a while, in terms of rent, debt repayment, housekeeping money, and so on. All day I have thought of nothing else. I must write a play fast. *Fast!* Will I be up to it? Not one of my older play projects can be used. "Freedom" is politically impossible: it could be performed only after the war. "Gunther" is also impossible, because it would give me away: it would be easy to see that the subject has been taken from *Accidentul*. That leaves *Ultima oră* and "News in Brief," neither of which is well enough defined. Besides, *Ultima oră* might also create difficulties of

---

1. Nicuşor Constantinescu: theatre director, playwright.

a political order. And I fear that "News in Brief" is too serious for Nicuşor to put his name to it—implausibly serious, in fact. What is needed is a light comedy, not so much written as put together. It's a question of dexterity, of professional skill. Will I succeed? Will I be up to it? Will I be lucky enough to come up with something? Will I be able to work so fast?

The last few days I have been reading Pascal's *Les Provinciales*. I gave them up today for Pagnol. I'll read a few plays to get a feel for the theatre again. I am determined to have no scruples about this. But will that be enough?

Wednesday, 7 January

Fresh Russian landings in the Crimea, this time on the western coast. The Russians have retaken Yevpatoriya (which, to my surprise, I found on the map to the north of Simferopol), and also, apparently, the small locality of Erilgoch, eighty kilometers south of Perekop. But this evening's German communiqué reports that the forces that landed at both Yevpatoriya and Feodosiya have been wiped out. In any event, what I am used to calling the psychological pendulum of the war has clearly swung toward London. I even feel there is again a quite exaggerated optimistic fever in the air. We shall see more of these, many more.

Oţetca (whom I saw at Rosetti's) spoke with emotion, stupefaction, and occasional fury about what happened in June in Iaşi.[2] Sometimes he covered his face with a gesture of impotence, fear, and loathing. His way of speaking moved me, but when I came away I couldn't help thinking that he is still director of the Theatre in Iaşi. No two things are incompatible in this country.

I never stop thinking and searching for the play I want to write. Until yesterday evening I had nothing in my mind's eye. Only vague ideas, insufficiently connected to one another. A stage setting, a scene, a situation—nothing coherent. Then I read two plays (Savoir, Duvernois[3]) that stimulated my theatrical fantasy, without offering anything solid. I found a clearer lead in an old issue of *Gringoire*, which had a summary of a play, *Jupiter*, performed by someone just starting up in Paris. "I too could write a play like that," I told myself. So yesterday afternoon, while I was

---

2. Andrei Oţetea, a historian, was referring to the Iaşi pogrom.
3. The French playwrights Alfred Savoir and Henri Duvernois.

watching a film, I suddenly felt that I'd "found" it. I had an idea, a title ("Alexander the Great"), and two characters. I left the cinema in a kind of optimistic excitement (as I always do when I "see" a plan for a book or play). On the way home the idea took on shape and substance—but at a certain point I realized that it was altogether too sketchy, too thin and shaky to fill up three acts. I don't feel capable now of writing an intimately poetic play for the stage. I couldn't even do another *Jocul de-a vacanţa*. No, I need something more solid, more earthy, more full of content. I need a firm structure with many characters and incidents, a proper plot, a wealth of detail that makes full use both of Nicuşor's name and of the National Theatre's troupe. *Ultima oră* could be, or could have been, such a play.

I don't know when (or indeed if) I had precisely these reflections. I don't know how I came to link "Alexander the Great" and *Ultima oră*. I think it was all a question of a minute or even of seconds. Suddenly the two projects merged into one. *Ultima oră* became Act One, and "Alexander the Great" Act Two, of the same play. I don't yet have Act Three— but there are so many comic elements in the first two acts that I think everything will sort itself out.

Et maintenant il s'agit de travailler.[4] Will I be able to? Will it come easily enough? Scruples, as I said before, are not a problem. I could just do with some luck.

Thursday, 8 January

I have paid the rent. Ten thousand lei from Papa's end-of-year bonus. Five thousand borrowed from Manolovici. Five thousand from Uncle Moritz—though I later promised to give that back by tomorrow evening. So by tomorrow I have to find five thousand lei to repay Moritz and one thousand to two thousand for the house.

The Wurm "coup,"[5] which was supposed to happen today, has been postponed. I had so much faith in it that I made all kinds of calculations about how I would divide up the money. But I shouldn't count on either "coups" or miracles. I must write the play. I must finish it at the latest by the first of February, so that it can be put on by the first of March. But until then I simply must get a loan of thirty to forty thou-

---

4. Now it is a question of working.
5. The Wurm Brothers company was in dispute with the Finance Ministry. A resolution would bring Sebastian a sizable fee.

sand lei from somewhere, to pay my most pressing debts and to have money for everyday expenses.

Last night I finished the plot of Act Two (finding new, unexpected incidents). The play's outline is now almost complete, and I must get down to some serious work. I deeply regret that my holidays are over and that I have to turn up at school tomorrow.

Friday, 9 January

I borrowed seven thousand lei from Marcu. I used five thousand to repay yesterday's debt to Uncle Moritz—which left two thousand for housekeeping. Now I'll have to find some money so that I can repay Marcel in a week's time. That is how the days pass.

My play is making great and rapid progress. Today I wrote six long pages. The first three scenes of Act One are almost ready. New things pop up with each piece of dialogue, as I am easily carried away by the tennislike rallies. I enjoy writing more than I expected. I feel I have found the right tone for the play (though it is true that I shall later have to execute delicate, perhaps difficult, changes of tone). For the moment, what I wrote today seems to me excellent. When I reread it tomorrow morning, a calmer, more accurate eye will doubtless spot things with which I am less pleased. I rang Nicuşor, feeling stupidly afraid that he might have reconsidered. Now that his plan is becoming a real possibility (a week ago I couldn't see myself writing a play), I begin to have bouts of fear, impatience, and doubt. I'll have lunch with him tomorrow and try to define our plan of operations.

Saturday, 10 January

Lunch at Nicuşor's. I spoke excitedly about the play, which I said I'll be able to finish in two to three weeks. We discussed the possibilities for putting it on stage. The National might not be available for Nicuşor either, as his marriage leaves him open to any anti-Semitic attack. Things would be simpler at the Comoedia. On the other hand, he is also writing a play—or wants to write one (together with Froda)—and he will naturally want it to be performed. Two plays bearing the same writer's name would be hard to put on in the same season. But it is too early to be thinking about all this. First I have to finish the play. All day I have held on to yesterday's good impressions, especially as I wrote another two pages this morning at the same speed. But now, this evening, it is all beginning to seem infinitely stupid. What was yesterday lively, coherent, and full of verve is now only puerile, cheap, and obvious. Maybe I'm just feeling tired. It's too early to lose heart.

Sunday, 11 January

For a few days, nothing new at the fronts. I can't keep up with the war in the Pacific: I don't have a good map, nor any precise knowledge about the possibilities and the significance of the situation there. Any tiny event on the Russian or North African front can be fitted into a familiar framework. In the Pacific, things seem too remote and indistinct.

An evening meal with Rosetti and Camil at G. M. Cantacuzino's; he told me some things about Transnistria and Odessa, where he fought in the army. He thinks that the Russian offensive has no prospects; that there can certainly be no talk of a German catastrophe, only of a certain lack of success. He explains the Russian advances by the fact that the Germans withdrew major forces from the front to send elsewhere (e.g., Turkey), or simply for a period of leave. They'll resume the offensive next spring, when they will reach the Volga and finish the Russians off. *On n'est pas prince impunément.*[6]

Cantacuzino's view should be contrasted with that of Radu Olteanu,[7] whom I also saw yesterday. He does not think that the Germans will be able to take the offensive next spring or summer; nor that they will ever be in a position to capture Moscow. He does not exclude the possibility that they will collapse even before April.

I have written little today—hardly anything. For an hour I struggled with the temptation to make a major change in the plot by introducing a new main character (a passing presence in Act One, who could become the play's central protagonist). But I resisted. I am afraid of complicating things and losing too much time. This play must be written fast, very fast, if I want it to appear this season and bring me in some money. I have school tomorrow, but for the rest of the week I'll try to find some excuse to "play truant." If I let the play drag on, it could escape me altogether.

---

6. You can't be a prince without paying for it.
7. A legal expert and translator.

Wednesday, 14 January

Sollum has fallen. Rommel has retreated from Ajdabiya to El Agheila, where he is resisting. On the Russian front, the Soviet advances are not for the moment substantial, though a larger operation is shaping up in the center. Twice in the last few days the German communiqué has mentioned Kharkov—where there is fighting to the east of the city. In the Crimea the situation is confused. It is not clear whether the Russians are still at Yevpatoriya; it seems they may also have landed at other points along the coast.

In today's papers there are hints of a German attack on Turkey and the Bosphorus. One gets the impression that a blow is being prepared and will soon come. Any day there could again be major events.

On Monday I wrote nothing. Yesterday, Scenes 5 and 6. Today, Scene 7. It's going rather slowly. Besides, I work too little. I only have three to four hours in the evening free for work. If I had ten whole days, I might be able to finish. But school, money worries, and various errands keep slowing me down. I should write this play quickly, with my eyes closed, so that scruples and pangs of conscience do not have time to invade me. Sometimes I am seized by a terrible disgust for what I am writing—but I soon manage to repress it. *C'est une vile besogne, mais il faut le faire.*[8]

Thursday, 15 January

A day spent rushing around at the Finance Ministry and Revenue for the (semibotched) Wurm business. I don't think it will work out—and my dreams of money are fading. Again I wonder what will become of me! Where can I borrow some money? To whom should I turn?

I haven't been able to write at all. All day out and about—this evening, cold at home. The heating is out of order. All I did was copy out Scene 7, which I wrote yesterday. I'll take tomorrow off with "flu" and try to get down to work. A short visit to Leni set me thinking. Froda is writing a play with Nicuşor, and they intend to have it performed at the National. I can't believe, and can't expect, that Nicuşor will give up his own play if there is a choice between that and mine. Meanwhile, though, I have to write. Who knows, maybe I'll still get a few tens of thousands of lei in return for the manuscript.

8. It's vile work, but it has to be done.

Saturday, 17 January

Small debts to pay off (Marcu, Manolovici, Zaharia) and food expenses to meet for some time. It was a pleasure giving Zissu back his money. I'd like one day to write a novel or play that centered on money.

Yesterday and today I have written six scenes (twelve pages), but there is nothing of real substance in them. I am not pleased with the conversation between Ştefănescu and Andronic, which I thought would have more to it. I am thinking of redoing it if I have time. It is all going too slowly: not because I have artistic scruples, but because I don't occupy myself enough with the play to the exclusion of everything else. At least if I could finish Act One more quickly.

Sunday, 18 January

Khalfaya has fallen—the last place held by the Axis in Cyrenaica. It remains to be seen how the struggle for Tripolitania will develop.

Today I have written only three pages—the (very short) fourteenth and fifteenth scenes. My young heroine Magda has entered the picture. Here I feel the need for a change of tone. Up to now I have written somewhat mechanically, in the style of a "situation comedy," and I think I have some talent for that. The entrances and exits, the unfolding of events, seem to happen without the author. Once a certain situation is posed, a play is constructed automatically. Theatre writes itself. Unfortunately my workload starts to get very heavy in a week's time—and I fear I won't have enough time for my play. I don't see how it will be ready by the first of February.

Tuesday, 20 January

"New statement about the Jews," shout the newspaper sellers in the street. All Jews, "without exception," are obliged to work for five days on snow-clearing. "Any irregularity that is shown to have occurred will lead to expulsion of the Jews from the country." "Jews who are found without proof of five days of snow work will constitute the first battalions of Jewish workers to leave in spring for Transnistria."

The Germans report that they have retaken Feodosiya.

I wrote nothing yesterday and today. I fear that I have ground to a complete halt. I shouldn't allow myself such dangerous standstills. It is true that I lack spare time, but this play must be finished quickly—or it won't be written at all.

Wednesday, 21 January

Fairy-tale snow—such as I don't remember ever having seen in Bucharest. Maybe in childhood, in Brăila. When I went out this morning, the whole of Strada Antim was a river of snow. I reached with difficulty Piața Senatului, where a long line of streetcars were at great pains to advance along their route. Cars, trucks, and carts struggled in vain to start moving again. Snow, I thought to myself, is an elemental force of nature. All civilization and modern technology are powerless against major snowfall. If it were to keep snowing like this for three months, everything would be swallowed up.

An idea for a short story occurred to me as I was going to school.[9] It would be called "Snow." Like "Deschiderea stagiunii" [Opening of the Season]—my only previous short story—it would tell of a moment of rebirth for a man whose life has been a failure, then of his loss of momentum and his final abandonment of the effort. The hero would be a teacher. He gets up in the morning in a desolate conjugal setting. His journey to school, through a magnificent wintry landscape (my picture of the city today), awakens in him the desire to start a new life. In the classroom, which he enters full of enthusiasm, an oaf of a boy plays a stupid trick—and the rainbow disintegrates. The man suddenly turns back into a dry pedant, and everything is as it was before.

The Russians have retaken Mozhaisk, the Germans' most advanced point before Moscow. *Mais ça ne change pas beaucoup.*[1]

I left a letter for Zissu at his office: "Dear Mr. Zissu, Please accept ten of the twenty thousand lei I owe you. I shall try to settle the rest very soon. Once again I thank you for the favor and assure you that I will remember it."

The play is being neglected. I have to focus on the course at Onescu that begins on Friday. I can't forgive my stupidity in agreeing to do it. I am determined to start working hard again on the play very soon.

21 January. A year since the start of the Revolt.[2]

---

9. Sebastian was teaching at the Onescu school, established in 1941 for Jewish students who were expelled from Romanian schools.

1. But that doesn't change much.

2. The Iron Guard rebellion against General Antonescu.

Friday, 23 January

Both the *liceu* and the college are closed for five days. The students, pupils, and younger teachers (I'll be in a later group) are off clearing snow. We get used to the most grotesque situations: when they are not tragic, when they are not deadly, we look on the funny side of them.

Otherwise it is a welcome holiday for me. I'll be able to work on the play again. Today I wrote the scene with Magda, which has been the first serious difficulty up to now. I think I dealt with it reasonably well. The rest of Act One seems simple.

The night of 23 to 24 January a year ago! Machine guns, eerie silence in the streets, my terrible loneliness, the telephone calling in the void. Yesterday evening a baby of two or three months was left in swaddling clothes at our door. I was afraid of complications with the police: statements, questioning, investigations. There was no trouble in the end. But I had a half-hour of tragicomedy.

Sunday, 25 January

In Libya the British have retreated from Ajdabiya. I was reminded, against my will, of the Italian-German recovery last spring. Is it possible that the British will for a second time lose their grip on the situation?

In Russia a Soviet offensive in the north has broken right through to Kholm. The Germans say it is a gamble, the British a major victory. We'll have to wait for things to become clearer.

I had hoped to finish Act One today, but I was not diligent enough and wasted the whole evening playing *belote*. I'll try again tomorrow. In any case, it has all been going too slowly for what I originally intended.

Monday, 26 January

I have finished Act One. By six in the evening I hadn't managed to write a single line, but from six until now (eleven-thirty) I wrote quickly, almost without rereading. I am not sure how it has worked out. I fear that the whole act is too long, and that the plot and construction are rather labored. I may read it to someone as a check. To Benu, perhaps.

Wednesday, 28 January

I read Act One to Benu last night. A satisfying impression. Roughly an hour of continuous reading. It all seems fluent, natural, well put together. At some points we burst out laughing. If there had been more of us, I think all the "effects" would have worked. I had lunch today with Nicuşor, to find out if I can rely on him. I don't think I can. I'll have to find another solution. The play he is writing with Froda is nearly finished; it will probably be ready before mine. He wants to put it on at the Studio, during the current season. I can't ask him to wait for my sake. I'll have to find someone else to put his name to it if I want to push it through quickly (and I do want to, for the simple reason that I can't make long-term plans; this play is a joke and a business proposition that have to be wrapped up quickly). But it is too early to be thinking about all this. First I have to finish it; I'll look for solutions later on.

I have started to write Act Two. In fact I haven't yet got to the heart of it, because I have done only the radio lecture that opens the act. I hope I'll be able to do more work on it tomorrow. I have no right to squander these few days off.

Steps are being taken to mobilize Jews for the snow. Today there were raids in the streets and in people's houses. I hesitate to present myself. I delay it as long as I can. First I'd like to finish the play—but am I not asking too much?

Rommel is attacking in Libya (with a halt today). It is not impossible that he will get back into Benghazi. On the Russian front the Germans are counterattacking in places—especially, it seems, in the center. Nothing is clear for the moment. In the Pacific the pace of things has slowed somewhat.

Thursday, 29 January

Until eight in the evening I was unable to write a line. The heating was frozen up, and you can't sit in the house even with an overcoat. I had to go to a cinema to warm up. But then I worked from eight until now, two in the morning. Only five pages: Scene 1 and half of Scene 2. But I have the other half in a rough copy that needs only to be written out.

I spoke with Rosetti, and later with Cicerone, about the possibility of staging a play that I might write. I was fairly vague, so as not to give myself away. Rosetti is doubtful, and Cicerone refuses to consider the question. I can very well understand him.

Nothing new at the fronts.

Saturday, 31 January

"Nothing new at the fronts"—I wrote on Thursday evening, but at that moment Rommel had already been back in Benghazi for twelve hours. Without a radio, the only news I get is late and incomplete.

Act Two is still pretty heavy going. I also have a bit of flu. Our heating comes on and off, as the fancy takes it. The cold is demoralizing me.

Sunday, 1 February

So, two months of winter have passed. Even with the heavy snow that still covers the city, there are already glimpses of spring somewhere over the horizon. It is hard to believe that anything essential can change in the war during the five or six weeks of winter that remain. As the season favorable to the Axis approaches, I grow more fearful of the coming dangers.

I am at Scene 5 (Magda and Andronic), the most difficult one in Act Two and perhaps in the whole play. I have written half of it (satisfactorily, I think), and I'll try to finish it tomorrow. The rest of the act looks more straightforward, because I shall now be returning to the situation comedy. For Act Three I have come up with some solutions that are not yet fully clear but will, I think, work well.

Tuesday, 3 February

Yesterday I wrote only a couple of snatches of dialogue. But today (just now, at one in the morning) I have finished Scene 5. Both yesterday and today have been days of discouragement. A certain disgust with writing. How I can work now at literature! I am too tired to record everything that is on my mind. Maybe tomorrow. And if I forget it, so much the better.

Thursday, 5 February

Rommel has retaken Derna. The British offensive in Libya is falling apart. No sign of a counterattack. Will Tobruk hold out at least? Will defensive lines be reformed at the Egyptian frontier? It is all deeply disturbing. The British stupidity enrages and depresses you. The whole face of the war has changed as a result of the grotesque happenings in Africa—especially as the Russian front is unaltered while Singapore is under siege and perhaps about to fall.

I was summoned to the police on Tuesday afternoon, so that they could warn me to dismiss the maid. "Jews do not have a right to hire servants." Two painful hours of fear, ridiculous and out of all proportion. My Romanian-Jewish inhibitions have a paralyzing effect.

Nicuşor Constantinescu, whom I saw yesterday, insists that I finish the play and give it to him. As I understood it, he doubts whether his own play will be accepted at the National—and if it isn't, he will put it on at a private theatre and give mine to the National. I don't know what will come of all these plans and expectations. The first thing to do is finish it—then we shall see. I have decided to read him next Thursday or Friday what I have written. I'll force myself to finish by then at least Act Two. Everything would go faster and more easily if I weren't tied up at the school and college (an unforgivable stupidity), and if I didn't also have to do the five days of snow work.

Sunday, 8 February

I started the college course this morning. The class was a failure. I thought I was a good speaker, and maybe I am—but I need a direct link with the class to be able to speak. Yesterday everything was amorphous, opaque, inert.

Nothing new at the fronts. The Japanese are a mile from Singapore! In Africa it is not yet known whether there is a British front and, if so, where it exists. In Russia there have been local actions of no importance.

The play is going slowly, unforgivably slowly. I haven't even finished the scene with the director. I feel all the worse about it because I have arranged a reading with Nicuşor. I'd have liked to have Act Two finished.

Monday, 9 February

Yesterday evening I finished the scene with the director. That leaves three more, including the only important scene, the one with Bucşan. I hope it won't cause me too much difficulty—though you never know where difficulties will arise. Then there will remain Act Three, which still has no real shape.

Yesterday at Nicuşor's I read what I have written of the play, with an audience of Leni, Froda, and Nelu. Disappointing. Not a success with anyone. No smiles. A brick wall of attentive but bored well-wishers. Act One, which I considered a "hit," raised a vague appreciation from Nicuşor—"interesting"—a smile from Nelu, and not even that from Leni. Froda, who was bored, praised me for reading well. Act Two went down even worse. At the end, everyone told me that it was too literary and too long; that it needed to be cut and changed—in short, a failure. To-morrow I'll try to give it more thought. I'm too tired now. (How exhausting it is to read or "act" a play!) Maybe this reading was, after all, necessary for me. Maybe it will help me see things more accurately.

The Japanese landed last night on the actual island of Singapore. It can't hold out much longer.

Tuesday, 10 February

I have thought a lot about the play and the lessons to be drawn from yesterday's reading. Whether people agree or not, I'll leave Act One un-changed. I at least—and why shouldn't I say it to myself?—consider it a perfect act of comedy and, technically speaking, a real "hit." As for Act Two, the conclusions are simple.

1) Magda is too screwy and too arbitrary a character. She must be given a civil status, a reality. Otherwise—especially given the realism of the play as a whole—she will appear much too artificial.

2) Her exultation needs to come down a shade.

3) The scene between Magda and Andronic is too long and cum-bersome. It will have to be simplified.

In general, yesterday's disappointment has put me out of sorts, but it has also concentrated my mind. I am less excited, but at a higher level. I think that Nicuşor's plan is unworkable. Act One has frightened them; they think the whole press will be up in arms. There may be something in that. Anyway, the name that is put to the play will have to be com-pletely untouchable. Someone new to the scene, whose personal efface-ment will take some of the sting out of any attacks. Georgică Fotescu would be a good choice. But whatever happens, I shall have to give up the idea of staging it during the present season. It would be quite good if I could present it to the National in March–April–May, so that I could pick up an advance and have it performed next autumn or winter.

Yesterday I had a bite to eat with Șerban Cioculescu. He doesn't know what he should want. A German victory? That would mean a protectorate. A British-Russian victory? That would mean sanctions. I could do nothing to ease his conscience.

Tomorrow morning Benu and I begin five days of snow work.

Thursday, 12 February

The Japanese have occupied Singapore. Impossible to calculate the consequences. The whole face of the war has changed. The moment is as grave as that of the fall of France in 1940. It hurts us less (then it was a personal, physical pain, a cardiac pain, a blow straight to the heart), but it is just as grave. Perhaps it does not spell the end. Perhaps the British will not succumb and the war will not be over. We now have a new war ahead of us, which could last for five, ten, or fifteen years. What will become of us? What will happen to our lives?

The other day I read Fox's speech in 1800—the Fox who, alone in the House of Commons, argued that it was impossible to defeat Napoleon and that a compromise peace was the only option. He was wrong, of course, but it took fourteen years for this to become apparent. Will we have to wait so long? Will we be able to? Will we be allowed to?

At the last moment, an order issued by someone or other has excused academics from snow work. So I have remained at home.

Sunday, 15 February

On Friday evening the *Gneisenau*, *Scharnhorst*, and *Prinz Eugen* happily passed from Brest through the Straits of Dover, right under the noses of the British. "The most mortifying blow to the prestige of the Royal Navy since the seventeenth century," commented the *Times*.

The British are having a run of ill luck; they have seldom looked so uncomfortable. Nor is it just a matter of their feeling "uncomfortable"; some serious questions are inevitably raised about the whole future of the war. Beyond all this bitterness, our old hope flutters stubbornly on—but it is tinged with a certain melancholy.

For three days I haven't gone anywhere near the manuscript of my play. I am completely exhausted. *Je m'épuise à ne rien faire.*[3] I lose myself in all kinds of wretched little things, at school, at the college.

How old I am! What a grub's life I lead! How gloomy and stale! I find it hard to take my physical decline. I am disgusted when I look in the mirror.

Sunday, 22 February

A mindless, tiring week. I did nothing, wrote and read nothing, yet had the constant feeling that I was overwhelmed with things to do, exhausted by work. The college course—though not serious—takes up too much of my time and attention. Moreover, I received a number of invitations, which I accepted out of inertia and later endured with repugnance. Thursday at Gruber's,[4] Friday at Leni's, yesterday at our place: three "society" evenings. And on top of those, lunch yesterday at Zissu's. I'll probably never get out of his clutches, unless I tell him plainly one day that he disgusts me.

The war is at a standstill. Nothing new at the fronts—or anyway, nothing important. The Japanese keep scoring successes. Nothing in Libya or in Russia. Today it will be eight months since the start of the Russian-German war, but the situation remains undecided. The front has scarcely changed. The Russians report advances, the Germans report encirclements, but neither appears to be serious. We shall have to wait for spring and summer. I wait with anxious unease.

Nicuşor has offered to work with me on my play. He suggests various solutions for Act Two and Act Three. He assures me that we will have a hit on our hands, and has even offered an advance of fifty thousand lei. I don't think I'll accept. I am sorry to say that I still have some literary prejudices, and an absurd, ridiculous "artistic conscience."

Thursday, 26 February

Yesterday evening a Rador dispatch reported that the *Struma* had sunk with all on board in the Black Sea. This morning brought a correction, in the sense that most of the passengers—perhaps all of them—have been

---

3. I exhaust myself doing nothing.
4. Solomon (Charles) Gruber: lawyer and personal secretary to Wilhelm Filderman.

saved and are now ashore.[5] But before I heard what had really happened, I went through several hours of depression. It seemed that the whole of our fate was in that shipwreck.

The other day, George Brătianu told Rosetti that unless Germany defeated the Russians by summer, and unless it organized the economy of the occupied territory, it would collapse by next winter—because it wouldn't be able to take another winter. Such views and forecasts lack foundation. This war keeps creating new conditions that no one can foresee even one day ahead, let alone three months.

Stefan Zweig has committed suicide. He shouldn't have done it; he didn't have the right. I reread the following sentence from an interview he gave in 1940: "I would be suspicious against any European author who would now be capable to concentrate on his own, his private work." All the less do we have the right to make individual gestures—even if we consider them liberatory. That's how it seems to me, though who knows?

For a month now at the Baraşeum,[6] Jewish actors have been performing a revue with great public success. All the seats are sold ten days ahead. I went yesterday with Benu (at the insistence of Sandu Eliad, Ronea, and Bereşteanu), and I was amazed at the text and the audience. Is it possible that Jews who have experienced all these appalling tragedies still write, act, listen, and applaud such miseries? They asked me to write a play too (and of course I would for money—because I have to find the rent in March), but I don't feel capable of writing in response to such exacting demands.

In the last few days I have been thinking that there is a solution for "Alexander the Great" that would address both my own doubts and Nicuşor's suggestions. I write the play as I want to write it, then I give it to Nicuşor and give him complete freedom to change and perform it as he wishes. We split the author's share fifty-fifty. This strikes me as an acceptable solution, especially if he keeps to the fifty-thousand-lei advance. We'll sort things out again after the war.

I finished Act Two this evening—satisfactorily, I think. But I really must change, in fact completely rewrite, the scene between Magda and Andronic, which I realize is a nonstarter. With some changes, Act Two

5. In fact only one passenger survived. A heated parliamentary debate in Great Britain followed this tragedy.

6. Baraşeum was a Jewish theatre founded in 1940, after Jews had been excluded from Romanian theatres. It functioned during the duration of the war.

will unfold at the same dramatic, nervous pace as Act One. The real difficulties begin with the final act, which threatens to lose the rhythm of the play. We shall see.

The Germans have contradicted the Russian report of a major victory in the north, where it is said that the German 16th Army has been encircled and almost completely destroyed.

Sunday, 1 March

March! Perhaps it will not yet bring major changes in the shape of the war, for spring comes with difficulty after such a hard winter. The dangerous season will begin in April to May. For the moment the Russian attacks seem to have become intense again. Yesterday evening's German communiqué noted heavy fighting all along the front: in the Crimea, "Russian attacks supported by tanks and aircraft"; in the Donets, "an attack with sizable forces." Still, I don't think that major turnarounds can be expected from now on.

N. Davidescu (!!!), back from Germany, met Rosetti and said that the Germans are losing the war, that only the British can emerge victorious, that the situation in Germany is desperate, and so on. Davidescu the Anglophile!

The five days of snow work have been increased to ten. Intellectuals may be exempted for a thousand lei a day. Where can I get twenty thousand lei for Benu and myself? I can't even think of it. We'll go out in the snow, and that's that!

Monday, 2 March

So, the six to seven hundred people on the *Struma* did go down with the ship. It seems that only one passenger—or, according to another report, four passengers—escaped. There has been no official statement. We didn't really know any of those who set sail. Two or three vague, distant acquaintances. Not one I can recall and hold in my mind's eye. (Possibly Schreiber, my former pupil in the 7th Year.) But the death of them all pains me.

We had decided to report tomorrow morning for snow work. We have been put off until the day after tomorrow.

Spring is in the air. It is still cold and overcast—but clearer and less misty. I have a sense of coming back to life, and at the same time a vague but profound sense of danger and fear.

Tuesday, 3 March

"In the Crimea, on the Donets front, and to the south of Lake Ilmen, heavy defensive fighting continues"—said yesterday evening's German communiqué. This evening's communiqué repeats the same formula: heavy defensive fighting. Is something serious happening on the Soviet front? It would seem so from the tone of the German dispatches and communiqués. But the Russians are maintaining an impenetrable silence.

We leave for the snow work tomorrow morning at six. We have prepared our things. I feel rather weary (I've been in bad physical shape for some time), but I hope I'll bear up to everything. I'm more worried about Benu, with his sciatica.

Wednesday, 4 March

The first day of snow work. Dropping from tiredness. We left home at five-thirty this morning and returned at eight in the evening. The work itself is a joke (it is at a marshaling yard outside Grivița station). What wears you out is the standing around, the journey there, the waiting, the formalities. On the way home we couldn't even cling to the outside of the packed streetcars as they went by. Never has Strada Antim seemed so far away.

Thursday, 5 March

Very tired, but not like yesterday. Things are starting to get more organized—which greatly reduces the time spent on various formalities (roll call, certificates, rubber stamps, etc.). We left at six-thirty this morning and were back home by six. If we were fitter, we might not be so tired. I have lost the habit of physical effort. The work detachment itself is a farce, perfectly resembling the Poligon detachment in October 1940, except that the work is even more absurdly pointless than it was there. We shift snow from one place to another—a completely senseless operation. If I hadn't seen so many others in the last few years, I would have died with laughter.

Friday, 6 March

As I handed over my shovel this evening, it occurred to me that millions of people around the world had been doing the same things that I had. I go home to sleep, eat, and forget. But what about those in the prison camps, in the internment camps? Where do they go? There is an inexplicable good humor in my work detachment. Each of us lives in the midst of danger and is aware of it. Each knows that tomorrow may bring greater miseries than the ones endured up to now. Each has left at home worries, bitterness, fears, and terrors. And yet, all are bound together by a kind of ironic youthfulness and martyrlike courage, which may be the expression of great vitality. I must say, we are an astonishing people.

Batavia has fallen. Not much of Java is left. The Japanese are still victorious more or less everywhere. On the Russian front the Soviet attacks seem to have weakened in the south. No major change anywhere.

Sunday, 8 March

Aunt Caroline has died: the last connection to our old Brăila, the last link to a whole past that is now lost forever. I am old. Tata left for there tonight.

There is a snowstorm. Winter has returned. Today in the open (even though we returned at two, as it was Sunday), I felt more exhausted and frozen than ever. The first five days of work are over. That leaves another five, which seems an enormous length of time. The farce of the work detachment no longer has anything new to say to me.

Monday, 9 March

In the morning I worked at Grivița station, clearing fresh snow from the platforms. In the afternoon we went back to "Sector 6," where it is less exposed and we can do what we like. The main operation was to move snow from one line to another. Spring returned around noon, when the sun came out. With a little imagination you could think you were at a hut somewhere in the mountains.

Rangoon has fallen. Java is now totally lost, and it seems that the Dutch there have capitulated. Nothing new on the Russian front.

Tuesday, 10 March

I worked on the "snow train"—an operation that looked terribly difficult when we saw others doing it in the first few days. In fact it is not
only simpler but even more stimulating than I expected. We played around
filling some wagons, treating it all as fun and games. I also think I am
getting fitter as a result. Last week I would not have been able to do as
much as I did today. Imperceptibly I am becoming a railway worker—
worse, a platform sweeper and track clearer. I am hardly even sensitive
any more to the grotesque side of the situation. Only once, when I saw
the Constanţa train passing a few hundred meters away, did I catch myself thinking that two years back I could have been one of its passengers, one of those looking from a carriage window at men on the line
with pick and shovel, at men without a name or an identity.

How terrible it is that, after these ten days that will pass—that have
already nearly passed—the old miseries and fears await us. In the evening,
as I came home on the streetcar, I saw it announced in the paper that
Jews will have to pay the special reunification tax at four times the regular rate.

Friday, 13 March

The tenth day of snow work. It was more of a struggle than the others.
On Wednesday and Thursday we had sunshine, but today was cold and
overcast, with bluish-grey skies. I can still feel the cold in my bones. I
am very very tired. But I have in my pocket a "Romanian Railways cer-
tificate" with ten blue stamps and one pink, which shows that I "worked
on snow-clearing at Bucharest-Griviţa Station from 4 to 13 March 1942."

Monday, 16 March

In three days I have seen all the regulars: Rosetti, Camil, Aristide, the
Roman office, the school, Zissu, Leni, Nicuşor, and so on. Nothing has
changed; everything is the same as ever. I am the only one who is changed
in any way: changed by sun and open air. Tanned and a little thinner, I
have something of how I used to look after a ten-day holiday in Balcic
or Predeal. I really do feel physically restored. But the tan will go, and
I'll soon return to my grubbish form. One might almost say it was better in the snow!

All kinds of troubles and woes. I find it hard to wade through them;
I feel listless and disgusted, with no wish to carry on.

In Russia the German communiqués keep reporting "heavy defensive fighting" and "massive Soviet attacks." The Ides of March find the winter counteroffensive in full swing—but the German front is holding almost intact. I don't think anything essential can happen in this regard. We must wait until late spring or early summer (May–June, because April may still be too soon). Will a new German offensive be launched then? In his speech yesterday, Hitler said that he would finally crush the Russians "in the coming months."

Friday, 20 March

Beate Fredanov suggested that I write a play about the *Struma*—a suggestion that has set me thinking, especially as it links up with my old idea of a play about some shipwrecked people trying to start a new life on an island somewhere.

Nothing new at the fronts. "Heavy defensive fighting" is what the German communiqué invariably says.

Vişoianu, whom I saw today, thinks that yesterday's speech about Transylvania is a local initiative and does not reflect German pressure on the Hungarians. He also told me some funny things about what Mircea Eliade is up to in Lisbon.

Sunday, 22 March

Nine months of war in Russia. Nothing new at the fronts. In today's *Universul*, a German dispatch speaks of the future "summer campaign"— the first time, I think, that this term has been used. Until now the formulation has been "spring campaign."

A pleasant afternoon with Branişte at a tavern. We talked at length about the Alice-Alcibiade comedy. He knows a host of things and recounts them intelligently. Beneath his naive appearance, *il sait toujours à quoi s'en tenir.*[7]

Tuesday, 24 March

Yesterday and today have been disturbed days because of the rent. Will we be able to stay where we are? Will we have to move? Kazazian wants

7. He always knows what is to be believed.

150,000—and I don't even know if she'll give us an agreement for a year. It's hard to imagine anyone more sordid, more vile and grasping. Nor am I sure there will ever be a day of judgment, either in heaven or on earth.

Rosetti told me a funny story about Russo,[8] who for some time has been trying to get space for a grave at Bellu, with a particular position, size, vicinity, and price. The episode could be used for Danacu (Dăracu) in a novel.

I have read two plays by Galsworthy, *Escape* and *The Roof*, both written in the same manner. It could, as a type of scenario, provide me with a model for my play with the shipwrecked people.

The Russian attacks have entered a "period of stagnation," according to DNB. "Weak attacks on Kerch."

Sunday, 29 March

A week of anxiety, depression, and humiliation—in connection with the house, the landlord, and the rent. I'll have to accept the exorbitant demands without even asking myself where I'll find the money. I feel helpless in all these drawn-out discussions and negotiations; I don't know how to defend myself. When I should be forceful and unyielding, I am bitter and sarcastic. Bitter and sarcastic with Mrs. Kazazian! I am ashamed of how unfit for life I am. I give away anything to avoid conflict. I allow people to cheat and prey on me, just to be left in peace. Lack of vitality? Disgust with human beings? Or just apathy and impotence? I feel sad at heart when I think of all these troubles.

For some time I have also had a fresh sense of dread and anguish. I am afraid of any stranger who appears before us.

Nothing new at the fronts. A British landing at Saint-Nazaire, which sounds more like a raid than an offensive action. It is a period of waiting. You wonder when and how the transition will take place from Russian offensive to German offensive. For the moment the communiqués invariably report Soviet attacks, some weaker, some stronger, all of which are furiously beaten off.

8. Demostene Russo: historian.

Monday, 30 March

Winter again. It snowed all night long. White streets, a morning snow-storm. The German communiqué says that frost has returned to the Russian front. "Heavy defensive fighting," according to the usual formula.

In the fortnight since I returned from snow work, I have made constant efforts to overhaul Act Two of my play. I don't think I have succeeded. Again I have to admit that what I don't manage at the first draft I will never succeed in doing. I have written, recopied, cut, redone, and altered Scene 5, the one with Magda and Andronic. I have turned it this way and that, and still it is bad. I have now decided to leave it as it is and move on to Act Three. Later, when I have acquired some distance from it, I'll make another attempt at revision. I am beginning Act Three without relish and without confidence. This play ought to be fun—and it isn't. I feel it becoming too unwieldy.

Wednesday, 1 April

April, but not yet spring. The snow of yesterday and the day before has not all melted. Clouds and snow.

Nothing new at the fronts. "Powerful attacks, heavy fighting"—you wonder when we will see the offensive phase that the Germans keep announcing. Perhaps April will not change much either, especially if the weather stays bad.

The first night of Seder. I'd have liked us to have a proper *Seder nacht.*[9] I sometimes think that our links with Judaism can be restored.

Friday, 3 April

A spring day—a little too cold, but white, blue, transparent. Toward evening I went for a walk by the lakes with Lereanu and Comşa.

A brief note from the English teacher, who is deserting us without explanation. Zissu and Aristide, to whom I imprudently recommended him, will certainly have paid him better. I didn't think he was capable of such inelegance. This way of proceeding makes me angry, and I am upset at

9. A Jewish ritual meal conducted on the first and second nights of Passover.

having lost him as a teacher. I made a lot of progress with him, and I'm sure that I'll lose a lot without him.

Will April pass without any developments in the war? I cannot believe it. April '40 was used for the Norwegian campaign. April '41 for Serbia and Greece. Why shouldn't April '42 be used in Turkey? Or (absurd as it strikes me) in Sweden?

Saturday, 4 April

It appears that the deportation of Jews from Dorohoi has started again. Gaston Antony tells me that a statute concerning the Jews is in preparation and will soon be published. Baptized Jews, he says, will have a better position in law and will, in any event, be protected from deportation. Gaston tells me that he alone in his family has not been baptized. It is an absurd, grotesque comedy. I spent this evening at the Baraşeum, where a play was in rehearsal. The auditorium was filled with Jews—but in the whole theatre (according to Bogoslav) only two or three practice the faith: the rest are Catholics, Orthodox, or Protestants.

With fifteen hundred lei I won at poker the last few evenings, I bought one of Mozart's Milan quartets and Bach's third Brandenburg concerto—to give myself a little happiness on this spring morning, so sunny and so bursting with youth. Life is somewhere alongside me, outside me.

Sunday, 5 April

So far I haven't written a line of Act Three. But I have come up with some incidents that might prove useful. I need an act with riches of its own, and if possible with new characters. This evening I thought that if I set this act too in the editorial office, the difficulties would be considerably reduced. I would have the people from Act One, and especially an already-created atmosphere. The brisk pace of the early part would suddenly be regained. On the other hand, I cannot draw Bucşan in full unless he is in his own setting. In the office where he is economic dictator, he will be more powerful and more overwhelming than elsewhere. (This is true especially of the scene with Minister Brănscu, if I decide to employ him in the end.) But this raises the problem of how I would then introduce Andronic and Magda, who would fit much more credibly into the editorial office. Each of the two settings (newspaper or Bucşan's office) has advantages and disadvantages, situational plausibility but also situational implausibility. One solution might be for Act Three to have two tableaux, the first in Bucşan's office, the second at the news-paper—but in that case other difficulties and discrepancies would arise.

Well, we shall see. For the moment I am happy that the play—which once completely sickened me—is beginning to interest me again. Not too much—but maybe enough for me to finish it.

Wednesday, 8 April

Nothing new in the course of the war. A period of waiting and prepar-ing. No one can say what will happen. We just realize that there are stormy times ahead; probably huge efforts, terrible blows, great battles. Only in the autumn will we, perhaps, be able to grasp their significance and outcome. Until then we will need strong nerves, staying power—and good luck. Once this general assessment has been made, all the rest—discussions, prognoses, information, opinions—becomes pointless.

I borrowed the Lekeu sonata from Lena for a few days—and I listen to it all the time. It reminds me of Franck at many points. Very beautiful, I must say.

I haven't written anything for Act Three; I just haven't had the resolve. There is a lot of material, not yet well organized. I promise myself that as soon as I finish Act Three, I shall get down to "Freedom." I also keep thinking of the shipwreck play, which is becoming clearer in my mind. Meanwhile the material for the novel is growing and falling into shape. Never have I had so many literary projects on which I could set to work. In a well-ordered life with relatively calm conditions, I think I could write from morning till evening every day for months. But who knows what will come of all this?

Sunday, 12 April

Nothing new at the fronts. The German communiqués of the past few days have mentioned a new Russian attack at Kerch, and local German attacks in the center. Situation unchanged. In today's papers, a kind of DNB weather bulletin shows that winter has ended but that spring is not favorable to an offensive either, because of rain, melting snow, fog, and mud. Does this mean that the offensive will be postponed until June?

The trial at Riom has been called off.[1]

---

1. The Riom trial was staged by the Vichy regime against Léon Blum and other French politicians accused of being responsible for the 1940 defeat.

Despite everything, there are certain things that France cannot commit, even if it wants to, even if it tries. A country that produces Jules Renard cannot fall too low in the moral order. Or can it? Maybe I am mistaken. Maybe things cannot be understood from afar. Poldy would know what to say. Nevertheless, it seems to me that France feels rather awkward when it comes to base deeds; they are not its style. *N'est pas infâme qui veut.*[2]

I was with Leni in a streetcar yesterday evening when a woman accompanied by a major (doubtless her husband) looked with recognition at Leni and discreetly pointed her out to him. She was visibly surprised and happy at the encounter. At the market the woman stood up to get off the streetcar but then suddenly turned and offered Leni her hand—with a shy and affectionate gesture, like a schoolgirl. The major also greeted her with an air of enchantment. Both would have liked to speak, to say something—but the gesture said everything for them. So, that too is possible.

A lot more could be written about Leni, if she were still of interest to me. She readily tells me of the affairs she had three or four years ago—affairs for which I would have felt like killing her if I'd known at the time, but which now leave me cold. How grotesque, too, was that absurd affair of mine!

Wednesday, 15 April

Yesterday evening, for the first time in six or seven years, I reread to my great surprise *Oraşul cu salcîmi*. As it happened, I had with me some of my pupils' exercise books from 5th Year, with summaries of their month's reading. Among these was an intelligent summary of *Oraşul cu salcîmi*, full of ingenious observations on its possible relations with other of my books. I read this with amusement, then took the book down from a shelf with the intention of leafing through it. But I couldn't put it down. It used to disgust me: I refused to speak about it, it irritated me just to read the title, and I considered the whole thing a foolish error. Well, now I think I was unjust. Reading it now, with the characters, scenes, and incidents almost entirely forgotten, I find the book captivating. How youthful it is! Beyond all the elements of naiveté, it has a certain freshness, a certain poetry, that move me. Or am I so old that the book's

2. Infamy is not open to anyone who wants it.

youth gains an exaggerated value, beyond literature? I don't know. The fact is that I spent three enjoyable hours reading it.

Thursday, 16 April

The marriage of Baby, Alice's daughter. Wedding at the Biserica Amzei Church, buffet lunch at the Delea Veche, then a visit to Alcibiade, who is ill. I looked carefully and with amusement at all the people in the Delea Veche, and I ran over the story of each one separately, of all together, and of the house itself—all mingled in a terrible, grotesque, absurd comedy. What extraordinary material for a novel!

I have suddenly found another subject for a play. It came into my head this morning (don't ask me how), and I kept tossing it around all day—in the street, on the streetcar and bus—until I returned home in the evening and wrote *d'un trait*[3] the whole scenario for Act One. I was in such a state of excitement that I didn't have the patience to write down the scenario for the other two acts. I went out, rang Leni, and went to her place with the intention of telling her about my find. The evening before, I had said to myself that a play was needed for Leni, Stroe, Ronea, and Marian. Well, I wanted to tell them, I have the play! Even funnier, during the eight to ten minutes I was on a No. 40 bus going toward Bulevardul Mărășești, I mentally outlined the scenario for Act Two and Act Three, and came up with a number of unexpected incidents. So when I reached Leni's, I gave her a complete exposition. Great enthusiasm. Both Leni and Froda said it was a great coup! That's all very well, but I still have to write it. Right now I am holding four plays, not one of them (not even "Alexander the Great") written. I can be a writer for the theatre, even an inventive one, but I need to have greater tenacity, greater professionalism. We shall see.

Friday, 1 May

A splendid spring night—blue, silver, transparent, airy, slightly unreal. How fantastic Balcic must be in this light! If the war did not extract us from life, if we did not have this constant sense of reclusion, perhaps such a spring—or at least such a night—would not be wasted even on a person like myself, who for a long time has felt himself to be lost.

April has passed without changes. What will May bring us?

---

3. At one go.

Saturday, 23 May

If I were not so tired—exhausted by several bad nights and several days of hectic effort—I would try to write here this evening. I feel as if I am choking with bitterness, tedium, rebelliousness, and disgust. If I were to write, I might possibly cleanse myself. To keep a journal is a matter of routine. (It's not the first time I've realized this.) If you don't write anything for ten days, it is very difficult to begin again on the eleventh. But I do want to return to this notebook, to record some things that have happened or that I have thought in the last few weeks. Maybe tomorrow.

Wednesday, 27 May

I have definitely lost the habit of keeping a journal. Over the last few days I have kept promising to write—and kept abandoning the idea. I still don't feel capable this evening of formulating a proper sentence—but as I anyway have a pen in my hand (I have spent the last two hours completing part of the census return), I shall jot down a few things at least.

Last week I translated five Shakespeare sonnets. I was delighted that I found this technically quite easy. I felt a kind of passion for all the sonnets, which struck me as splendid in the original and highly open to poetry in translation. It was as simple as a crossword puzzle—and as intoxicating as a wave of youthful lyricism. I walked in the street reciting verses, seeking rhymes, counting syllables. (How many people must have seen me talking to myself in the street or on a streetcar!) But now I have stopped, now I have calmed down. For several days I have been on Sonnet LXXI ("No longer mourn for me when I am dead"), and I cannot get started again. I don't find rhymes, I cannot match the verse—and what I do find is impossibly flat. I'd be sorry to have to abandon it. I'd be all the sorrier because this game has become a new drug for me, which takes me a little away from life's troubles.

I have to pay five thousand (but I may get off with one thousand) for five days of snow work, even though I worked ten. At first I was furious. Rosetti and Solacolu couldn't believe it when I happened to tell them. They said it was a farce. And a farce it is—though a serious one. Now I am resigned to it.

Nina has been in Bucharest for two or three weeks. Obviously she didn't try to get hold of me, nor I of her. In fact I don't know what I could say to her. It seems that Mircea will be appointed to Rome; his political views (he's more of a Legionary than ever) make him useless in Lisbon. I have been told (by Rosetti) that he gets 400,000 a month. Maybe that's an exaggeration, but even 200,000 wouldn't be bad. I must admit that, when I heard this, I felt a moment's indignation, disgust, and cheerless envy. While he is off living a magnate's life, in paradises of life, peace, luxury, comfort, and dream, while he lives the "new order" to the full, I am stuck here with a wretched prisoner's existence.

When the war is over—assuming that I survive and we meet again—I will be able to balance his years of prosperity only with my grim years of humiliation and failure.

Nothing can ever excuse failure. Successes, even when resulting from moral infamy, remain successes.

Wednesday, 3 June

Today, after such a long interval, I have reread the first two acts of "Alexander the Great." They (even the second one) seemed excellent. Now that I have finished with school and exams, I'd like to get down to work—but before anything else I really must write Act Three. It is ridiculous to be stuck en route with a play two-thirds written, the more so when I think of the straightforwardness of the subject and the richness of the situation. Only when I finish this will I be able to think of the play with Leni. What is bad is that I have still not settled on the scenario for Act Three. Until this evening I didn't even know whether it would take place at the newspaper or in Bucşan's office. Now I think I have decided—for good?—in favor of the editorial office. Tomorrow I'll try to get started.

I haven't translated any more sonnets. I am waiting for another wave of lyricism before I begin again. With Benu, Comşa, and Lereanu, on the other hand, we have finished reading *Cymbeline* and moved on to *Henry the Fourth, Part One*. It is going fairly easily. Recently my reading has been quite varied. I have revisited, after ten or eleven years, Moore's *Confessions of a Young Man*—this time in the original. Less moving than the first time.

It is now June, but the gates of victory are still closed. I couldn't say that we know more today than we knew or suspected in March. After Kerch and Kharkov, the situation is still roughly the same. Only if Rommel's offensive was successful (which does not seem to be happening) and if the offensive against the Soviets could develop also through Iran, only then would we find ourselves in a truly novel phase of the war. As it is, the development of the situation is still more or less predictable, by analogy with what happened last year.

Sunday, 14 June

I feel down at heart. Rumors, prognostications, interpretations. Everyone is saying that new anti-Semitic laws will be introduced any day now. A nine-o'clock curfew. Yellow insignia. A ghetto here in Bucharest. A ghetto at the Berşad (?)[4] barracks in Transnistria. You don't want to believe it, you refuse to listen, but you are left with doubts deep inside you. The air-raid alert on Thursday to Friday night, and the rumors of bombing, frighten me less in themselves than because of the overheated, hysterical climate they might produce—as they did last year. I shudder when I remember.

I keep thinking of Poldy. There the terror is mounting. How is he? How is he managing? He is so alone!

The absurd unreality of our life. We still read books. We still have the strength to laugh. We hold celebrations. We go to the theatre. On Wednesday evening I went to the Baraşeum. And at eleven in the morning. . . .

Sometimes it seems that our plight no longer has anything to do with the war. The war is somewhere on a different level, in a different order of events. You discuss it, you follow it on the map, you comment on it— but whatever happens there, everything remains grave and threatening for us.

But we are alive. And we must not lose the will to live.

Wednesday, 17 June

Two years since the French armistice. And we are still breathing! It is true that we carry with us the weariness of these terrible two years—but we are alive. Until when? There is an appearance of calm, but so many horrors lurk beneath it. Rumors of another anti-Semitic outbreak mingle with reassuring denials, both equally vague and irresponsible. I don't

---

4. Not clear in the original text. Sebastian was questioning if the ghetto was indeed in Berşad.

know where they come from, what worth and significance they have. And times passes slowly, so slowly. I count the days, the hours.

Tired. In a bad physical condition. My eyes do not help me read. Headaches. Otherwise I would work—reluctantly perhaps, but I would still work.

Monday, 22 June

The 22nd of June. A year since the start of the war in Russia. When you look back, you realize that nothing could have been foreseen. This should cure us of our absurd game of predictions. And yet there does seem to be a certain rhythm to the war, with its almost regular sequences of fever and calm, of ebb and flow. If this keeps up, the second year of war might resemble the first. Personally, I don't believe that something decisive is bound to happen in the short term. Autumn will not necessarily bring the denouement any more than it did last year.

For the time being (apart from the offensive against Sebastopol), the Russian front is in abeyance. But the battle in Africa, after two weeks of wavering, has suddenly been propelled forward. Yesterday the British abandoned Tobruk. I wonder whether Rommel is not aiming at much more than that. It may be that preparations are being made to turn the Middle East into a huge wing of the war in Russia.

Eugen Ionescu left Romania yesterday. A miraculous event.

Tuesday, 23 June

Tiring discussions, commentaries, suppositions, interpretations! You try to understand what will happen from now on. What may be the consequences of the fall of Tobruk? When will Sebastopol fall? Why is the German offensive being delayed? Is an Anglo-American landing possible? Will the war not shift for the time being toward Suez? What will Turkey do? So many questions that you raise and set aside. There are arguments for each hypothesis. I'd like to be able to drop the war for a while. I'd like to escape this obsession with it. I am tired. I'm afraid of neurasthenia. I wish I could have a little freedom, a little oblivion.

Sunday, 28 June

We still don't know if the British disaster in Libya has bottomed out. The fighting is now in Egypt, beyond Sidi el-Barrani, at Mersa Matruh.

If Rommel calls a halt, the whole operation will remain in the usual framework of the African war. But if he occupies Alexandria and gets as far as Cairo, the whole face of the war will be fundamentally altered. Sebastopol still has not fallen.

Monday, 29 June

I have tried for hours and days on end to write Act Three of "Alexander the Great," but to no avail. On the one hand, the final act has brought the play to a standstill; on the other hand, I myself am in a period of total lack of inspiration. I am apathetic, lethargic, lacking in energy and spontaneity, opaque, inert, dislocated. Everything I put on paper is dull, wooden, pointless. Evidently the scenario for Act Three is not a happy one. I even have doubts about where it is set. (I originally placed it in the editorial office but then began it in Bucşan's office, without knowing whether I would eventually return to the newspaper.) However good or bad, though, I'd like to finish the act, at least so that I can put it to one side. But I don't manage to do this.

The truth is that I don't manage anything: not even to read a book in a disciplined way from beginning to end. I feel bitter, drowsy, disjointed, disgusted with myself. I am waiting for a little grace to appear from somewhere.

Mersa Matruh has fallen. The road to Alexandria lies open. The whole British system in the Middle East seems to have crumbled.

Wednesday, 1 July

July–August. The difficult months of the war. Sixty days in the middle of hell. In Africa, Rommel is 190 kilometers from Alexandria. It seems that the British, who so far have beat a hasty retreat, are today trying to fight back. Will they be able to?

Sebastopol has fallen.

Saturday, 4 July

The struggle for Alexandria goes on. I have been expecting its fall to be announced at any moment. But at present the front is still holding at El Alamein. Yesterday's German communiqué reported that Rommel has taken the position and advanced beyond it, but today's communiqué speaks of "strong fortifications" and "major strengthening" at the same point. Is it possible for the British to recover? What happens there is crucial.

The whole aspect of the war could change in a flash. I can't even be sure that, as I write these lines, the die has not already been cast.

An almost overwhelming vision of a new play suddenly thrust itself forward amid a series of unfocused thoughts. It was feverishly intense, so simple and powerful that it has left me feeling a little dizzy. I wish I could write it down at once, automatically, with my eyes shut. But God knows what will come of this, as of so many other ideas.

Monday, 6 July

Yesterday I wrote the scenario for the play I visualized so giddily on Saturday evening. To be frank, my excitement yesterday at noon seemed naive after a night's sleep. The spell had passed. I felt that it was all no longer so mysterious, and I was a little embarrassed by myself. But as I wrote the scenario I became animated again—not only because I succeeded in putting Saturday's intense yet confused thoughts on paper, but also because I made them clearer, more extensive, more sharply defined. So here I am holding another scenario—the third, not counting "Alexander the Great."

Will I write them? When?

Again I must deplore the slowness with which I write. I don't think anyone has less vivacity, less freedom of movement, less spontaneous ease than I have. Certain things I lack completely. Sometimes, when I see ideas in a kind of dazzling light, I have the impression that everything could be done miraculously in a few hours, as if by a process of unconscious dictation. But when I pick up my pen, everything becomes opaque again—and then the absurd, flat, dull work of writing begins, which takes days, weeks, months, sometimes years.

As far as "Alexander the Great" is concerned, the end now seems closer. Act Three, which I began reluctantly and have been writing without confidence, seems to be taking shape in an interesting way. Today I worked quite well. I still have to write two scenes in all—the last two—but the fate of the whole act depends upon them, because if they are not a success, everything I have done up to now will fail and the whole act will have to be written differently. It seems a question more of skill and tact than of dramatic material. The situation of my heroes is at the moment a little artificial, but a pirouette could save everything.

In Egypt the main fighting is at El Alamein—seemingly at a lower intensity than before. The British resistance appears to be growing firmer. In fact the German communiqués and dispatches all discreetly pass over the African front (which was such a grave issue last week) and stridently emphasize the Russian front, where the start of a major offensive has been officially announced. Fighting is taking place between Kursk and Kharkov, up to the region of the Don.

Thursday, 9 July

A long intricate dream last night, from which I remember only the setting and the broad framework. I was one of a three-man delegation to congratulate Mrs. Antonescu on the marriage of (I think) her son. We were received in a vast rectangular hall, with many flowers. After a while the hall was filled with guests, most of them in evening dress. In an adjoining hall, larger and more sumptuous than the first, an entertainer and then a girl sang some English songs. I remember that Leibovici Camil was one of the guests, among a group of (I think) girls known to me from Brăila, and that they made a sign for me to come closer. Meanwhile, however, without a change in the setting, we were no longer at Mrs. A.'s, but at Princess Bibescu's, waiting for Valentin B. to return from an air raid or a competition, with a decoration or a trophy. And I did indeed see Valentin Bibescu, in evening dress with a male entourage, stride across the hall and on past me.

Yesterday evening at Capşa, where I had gone to collect Rosetti, as arranged. At the next table were Ion Barbu and Onicescu, with the evening papers spread open in front of them. Barbu, following a map of the African front, was very disappointed by Rommel's halt. Onicescu tried to cheer him up:

"Any piston, however powerful, draws back after it has delivered a blow. That's what is happening at El Alamein."

Barbu did not seem altogether recovered.

"And then," Onicescu continued, "can't you see what has happened in the north? They've destroyed an American convoy of fifty ships."

"That's more like it!" Barbu shouted, and his whole face lighted up.

I found both of them most amusing. They were like two Jews engaged in café politics—with the same fears and enthusiasms—but on the opposite side of the barricades.

In Russia, Voronezh has fallen and the Don has been crossed at several points. The German offensive seems colossal. Camil Petrescu assures me that they'll be at the Volga in a week. I bet that it would be the first of August. In Africa, things remain halted at El Alamein.

Saturday, 11 July

Last night I read *The Two Gentlemen of Verona*. After *Measure for Measure*, *Love's Labor's Lost*, and *Twelfth Night*, I have few of that kind of comedy left to read. Meanwhile I continue the royal plays with Benu, Lereanu, and Comşa: we have finished *Henry the Fourth* and read the first three acts of *Henry the Fifth*. The more I get into Shakespeare, the more enchanted I become. I have given some pleasant thought to the idea of writing a book about him. Maybe I'll start right now to sort my reading notes into a series of files. Before writing such a book (but when? when?), it would be enjoyable—and also, I think, useful—to give some lectures on Shakespeare.

Sleepless nights, as I have never had before. Sometimes I haven't slept a wink until six, and felt exhausted when I got up in the morning. It is not only because of the dog days but above all because of all the exasperation that has accumulated for so long inside me—and is now taking its revenge. But I must get a grip on myself. I still need my nerves.

In Russia the Germans are advancing toward and beyond the Don. The Russians are in retreat there but are counterattacking in other sectors. The war is in one of its most intense phases. The center of hell. Still waiting at El Alamein.

Saturday, 18 July

I have finished "Alexander the Great"—at last!—or, to be more precise, I have finished Act Three. The play still needs some touching up, but that should be easy to do when I copy it out. This does not mean that I am satisfied with the work I have done. In fact, if I think of my original intentions (a light play, written quickly for immediate performance to earn some money), I have failed. It has turned out quite differently: not good enough to count in my writer's corpus; not common enough to be a big hit; not innocuous enough to pass as such into one of today's repertoires. But I shouldn't grouse—not today, at least. For better or worse, I have finished it and therefore become available for something else. I'll have a go at the play for Leni. A possible title would be *Insula*.

Sunday, 19 July

I don't know exactly what is happening at the fronts. The German communiqués are vague, even if the press dispatches are enthusiastic. The propaganda speaks of disasters and final decisions, but things do not seem as grave as all that. Fighting continues at Voronezh, where the Russians are resisting and counterattacking. To the south, the Germans have occupied Voroshilovgrad and now have Rostov under attack. Another offensive is aimed at Stalingrad. Just from reading the papers, I have the impression that, however boisterous the style, the situation is not really so acute.

Yesterday I opened Montaigne by chance (I needed to trace some Latin verse), and I couldn't put it down. What delights! Not for a very long time—perhaps never—has he seemed so lively, so enchanting, so direct and familiar. Yesterday I read "De l'inutile et de l'honnête," and today I began "De l'éxperience." Everything, almost every line, seemed subversive and liable to censorship in today's world.

Not a thought for the play I finished yesterday. No affection for it. I feel it as something alien, yet I shall have to concern myself a little with it.

Monday, 20 July

An air raid at ten this evening. Why? you ask yourself. From where? The Russians are at the Don, the British have their work cut out in Egypt—so who is still so keen to fly over these parts? The sirens caught me at Piaţa Naţiunii, where it was impossible to find shelter nearby. I lay at full length in the grass, with everyone else who had got off the buses and streetcars. For the first time I witnessed operations in the open air. The firing was quite powerful. Tracer bullets, searchlights, exploding shells—the whole thing, beneath a moon slightly blurred by smoky white clouds—resembled a huge fireworks display. I didn't see a single airplane. The alert lasted an hour—after which I went straight home and read the last two acts of *The Tempest*.

I have learned with surprise, and with pleasure (from a commentary by Duval), that Shakespeare read Montaigne and was passionately fond of his *Essays*. I seem to like him all the more now, because I am reading both of them at once.

Thursday, 23 July

A letter from Antoine Bibescu, in reply to the letter I sent him a week ago to ask if he would receive me for a while at Corcova. *"Vous êtes at-*

tendu avec joie et impatience."[5] It remains to be seen whether I can obtain the necessary permission; Rosetti has already offered to try. I think a few days in Corcova would do me a lot of good. I don't feel well physically (the accumulation of sleepless nights, tiredness, a cold—all kinds of things), and my nerves are completely gone. I live with too many obsessions and *idées fixes.*

Since yesterday evening I have a little quartet by Mozart for strings and oboe. It's not one of his key works—a playful sketch, rather. But it is nice enough, and I think I could go on listening to it indefinitely. It's like sonorous froth—a little insubstantial, but delicate and full of grace.

I heard a while ago—but omitted to mention it in this journal (is it becoming so unimportant to me?)—that Mircea Eliade is in Bucharest. He did not try to get hold of me, of course, or show any sign of life. Once that would have seemed odious to me—even impossible, absurd. Now it seems natural. Like that, things are simpler and clearer. I really no longer have anything at all to say to him or ask him.

The fall of Rostov seems imminent. The Germans report they have reached the outskirts of the city.

Thursday, 30 July

In Russia the situation on the southern front after the fall of Rostov seems to have become more and more serious. The Germans have crossed the lower Don at several points and are rapidly advancing over the wide plain now open to them. Even if they do not immediately attack the Caucasus (which cannot yet be known), they will try to seal it off by drawing a line from the Azov to the Caspian.

Mac Constantinescu,[6] whom I met yesterday, told me that all of them (Vulcănescu and so on) gathered at Mircea Eliade's and also "called me to mind." The expression amused and irritated me at the same time. "What, were you having a seance?"—I regret not having asked him.

On Sunday I read aloud for Benu the last two acts of my play. A wretched impression. It all seemed to be absurd, bungled, without any charm. How often I wanted to break it off halfway through! But three days have passed since then—and I think I am now seeing things more sensibly. To be

---

5. "You are awaited with joy and impatience."
6. Graphic artist.

sure, the play is no great shakes. It could not even be put on stage in its present form, though I don't think it would require too many changes. I'll leave it for the time being, shut it up in a drawer, and get down to something else (if my health allows it, because I again have problems with my eyes and with sleeping). But later, in a few months' time, I'll try to look over it again.

I have read a Dreiser novel with great interest: *The Financier*. It is powerful, solid, and large. But he lacks a little poetry, the mysterious magnetism of a Balzac, to be a really first-rate writer. Anyway, it is enough to put me off any novel I have written or may ever want to write. Meanwhile I am getting on with my Shakespeare and Montaigne. Finished *Richard II*, begun *The Comedy of Errors*. Also read the last two acts of *Hamlet*, which I had left unfinished.

Saturday, 1 August

July passed terribly slowly—hour by hour, minute by minute. I draw time after me, I drag myself along behind it. I live with my eyes on clock and calendar: another day, and another, and another. It is exhausting. "For now hath time made me his numbering clock," says Richard II in prison. Our prison is more oppressive. I wish I could forget a little, be a little indifferent. I'd like to have a week of clear and simple living, without any obsessions.

The first of August last year! What a terrible day it was! In comparison, we are now—or ought to be—grateful.

Wednesday, 5 August

Summer. Lazy, inert, long, heavy days. I lead a grub's life. My only way of being awake is insomnia. But when I am lucky enough to sleep, I fall into a kind of general lethargy. I no longer ask myself anything. I couldn't stand it. Will I ever wake up? Will I ever come back to life? Will I ever again be a living person?

Saturday, 8 August

Again there is great concern about what is in store for us in Romania. Are new blows being prepared against the Jews? Today's papers—as if responding to a signal—are full of official statements concerning Jews (work, requisitioning, criminal offenses, threats, etc.). According to the

Interior Ministry, "the authorities have established that most violations of the law . . . and most acts of sabotage . . . are committed by Jews." On the other hand, *Bukarester Tageblatt* has a long article showing that between this autumn and the autumn of 1943 Romania plans to become *"judenfrei,"* through our deportation to the Bug. There is an oppressive climate, charged with forebodings, fears, and terrors that you don't even dare think through to the end.

And Poldy? What is happening with him? Suddenly there is talk of mass deportations of Jews from France to Poland. The nightmare is ever darker, ever more demented. Will we ever wake up from it?

Again I have not slept the last few nights. Disgusting insomnia, with dogs howling and barking in the yard next door, with flies buzzing around the room, with bedbugs crawling all over the bed, the walls, and me. A great revulsion. But I must rise above it if I want to go on living.

Sunday, 9 August

Big roundups in town. This morning, apparently, the whole city was studded with checkpoints and patrols. I don't think Jews were the only ones targeted.

Today I looked at the map for the first time in two or three weeks in order to locate all the places mentioned in the German communiqué: Armavir, Krasnodar, the River Laba, the Sal and Don regions, Kalach. There has been an important advance from the south, but the situation still seems confused and undecided, at least in that sector. As to the rest of the front, there is no change. The German communiqué indicates a powerful Soviet offensive at Rzhev—but nothing major can reasonably be expected.

I have reread *A High Wind in Jamaica,* which I first read ten or twelve years ago in French. Some difficulties with the vocabulary (because of the nautical terms), but what a beautiful, unusual book! The same strange mixture of innocence and cruelty that stunned me, I think, the first time.

Slowly, all too slowly, I have begun to write the first act of *Insula.* I'm on the third scene. I can't even say I have got to the real subject of the play. All I have done so far is a kind of preliminary setting of the scene. In fact I fear that the whole scenario for Act One is the outline of a sketch.

Sunday, 16 August

No big changes at the front. The German advance in the Caucasus is continuing, but now it has reached the mountains and slowed down. Piatigorsk, which fell a few days ago, is almost in the center of the peninsula. This looks impressive on the map, but the Germans probably won't try to cross the mountains—not yet at least. For the moment they are moving across the peninsula to the Caspian, with some two or three hundred kilometers still to go. The offensive at the bend in the Don and toward Stalingrad is being maintained. The Russians are resisting, but the attack is expected to become more intense here. In the center and toward the north, the Germans are on the defensive. In general, nothing decisive. The situation is roughly the same as it was.

What people say about the war is not interesting. Predictions, wishful thinking, fears—all are equally arbitrary. On Friday evening I dined with Vişoianu and the lawyer Gad, and on Monday I had lunch with Devechi. Although each had a different orientation (Devechi, *malgré tout*,[7] can't help remaining Germanophile, even if he denies it), each repeated the same formulas, the same arguments, the same pieces of information. It is uninteresting one might even say mindless. And it is so tiring. But you never have enough of discussing the same things over and over again. The war is following us like our own shadow.

I haven't written another line of the play all week. What did grip me, quite out of the blue, was a taste for my old plan for a novel. Suddenly things have become real, with living people and an attractive story. There are a number of series of events that I would like to bring together in the same framework, but until now I have not clearly seen how to do this. All at once everything seems to be taking shape and expanding. It will not be one epic episode but a fresco, or better a "saga," of a whole era from 1926 to the present day, which takes in not only my new heroes (whom I can already see very well) but also many characters who were not fully drawn in *De două mii de ani* and will now acquire reality. This time I shall probably work differently from my usual way. My books have all been written without drawing from a file, without a guiding plan, often even without a vague preliminary notion of the paths to be taken and the goal to be reached. But if I really am going to write a large-scale work, I shall have to organize my material. A kind of pleasure at

7. Despite everything.

inventing things that I felt jostling inside me forced me to pick up my pen, not to "formulate" anything but to jot things down in haste. So at present I have filled nearly six sheets of paper with a rough summary of the material for the first five chapters. Together with what still remains to outline, this will mean a novel of three hundred pages. But in no case will I leave things at that, because the characters in this first episode interest me more for what they will become later (ten or fifteen years later) than for what they already are. This novel too, however, like all my other projects (three plays, a translation of the *Sonnets*, a book about Shakespeare), depends on so many things! First of all, there is the question of my health and physical resilience. Am I not too run-down to carry the load of all my work projects? Maybe not. Maybe some things are still capable of repair—though not, alas! the essential ones.

Tuesday, 18 August

The German advance in the Caucasus is becoming slower and slower. Yesterday evening's communiqué speaks of stubborn resistance, difficult terrain, and tropical heat. The truth is that the acute phase of the struggle for the peninsula has passed, thereby diminishing the enthusiasm or the depression of observers on either side. The psychological balance is again shifting toward Britain. The game is still the same. But I don't think it will be long before the Germans start another major offensive in one of the sectors (maybe Stalingrad or even Moscow)—and then the corresponding depressions and enthusiasms will again be *de rigueur.* Perhaps only later, in the autumn, will it be possible to make all the important (if not final) calculations.

"The Jews hand in their bicycles!"—the main text on this afternoon's newspaper boards. I burst out laughing without meaning to. The joke about the Jews and the cyclists automatically came to mind.

Starting from tomorrow, Jews will pay twenty lei for a loaf of bread instead of the fifteen lei for Christians.

Wednesday, 19 August

A British landing in Dieppe! The first moment of emotion (full of all manner of fabulous hopes, dormant inside us beneath all the disappointments)—but then, very soon, a return to reality. It is not an invasion, not even an offensive, only a local incursion—more energetic than the one at Saint-Nazaire, but with no greater significance. It is, as they say, a "combined raid," involving tanks, aircraft, and artillery. Some of the landing forces have by now reembarked; the rest are continuing to fight.

A loaf of bread costs not twenty but thirty lei for Jews. For us that means one thousand lei more a month—quite a lot in our poor household calculations. But for the really impoverished Jews, it is a calamity. Nevertheless, so long as we are still at home, everything is bearable.

I am continuing with Shakespeare, though not at the same rhythm. I have read *Richard III* and *Romeo and Juliet*.

Thursday, 20 August

The German report on the Dieppe operation indicates that everything was over by four o'clock yesterday afternoon, that the landing forces amounted to a division and were repelled with heavy losses on the British side. All the Axis press considers this proof that a landing to open a "second front" is impossible. I don't know the opposite point of view or the account given by London, but in any case I don't understand very well the purpose of the operation. Whatever the explanation, one is left with some suspicion that it was not really serious.

Sunday, 23 August

Nothing new at the fronts.

The week ending today brought three anti-Semitic measures: expensive bread, confiscated bicycles, and—the day before yesterday—a ban on having servants after the first of October. It is disturbing that a kind of sequence is being established, in which new oppressive measures become automatic. You wonder what will come next.

I shall force myself to leave for Strehaia tomorrow evening. I think it has finally become possible, after endless interventions and obstacles.

Tuesday, 25 August

I am leaving for Corcova. A grotesque farce should be written about the adventures I had before I finally obtained the necessary papers. Once upon a time, that much effort would have sufficed to organize a journey around the world.

I met Paul Sterian[8] in the street—a Paul Sterian grown fat, almost porcine. He was so confused and embarrassed at meeting me, so eager to rush off and escape, that I did not want to rush off now myself without noting the incident.

Sunday, 6 September

I returned this morning from Corcova, rested and recovered, calm, suntanned, with that holiday look of which I used to be so proud. Ten days of the free life, in the sunshine and open air, can still make a new man of me. I am not yet so worn out as to be unable to respond to such a call from life. I thought I was on my last legs. But not so. I am still alive. I still have healthy reflexes. Life can be brought back out of all my decay, apathy, and collapse.

But in Bucharest I find the same woes and troubles—with some new ones added. I am well aware that I won't be able to stay in my present "form." *Tâchons de vivre pourtant.*[9]

Monday, 7 September

I must try to stop myself from being overwhelmed by troubles old and new. I must pull myself together. If I could draw up and stick to a regular program of work (reading and writing), perhaps I would avoid letting myself go again. It makes no sense, and is of no use to anyone, simply to relapse into our common exasperation. I am in hell—but in this hell I must discover an area of solitude, to the extent that this is possible. It tears me apart just to pass by Sfîntu Ion Nou, where Jews picked up from their homes are kept while awaiting deportation. It breaks my heart to see them, and I feel ashamed to turn my head. There are atrocities that cannot be observed with one's eyes open. They are too unbearable, like great physical suffering. Words are no longer any help at all.

Poldy is somewhere in the countryside, in the Garonne. This gives me a certain feeling of relief. We know almost nothing about how he is, but he does seem to be safer than before.

I haven't found half an hour to note anything down about Corcova.

---

8. The novelist Paul Sterian was a high-ranking official in the Antonescu administration.
9. But let's try to go on living.

Tuesday, 8 September

It would have been amusing to keep a journal in Corcova, but I can no longer reconstruct it now from memory. I don't regret this. It was a holiday—and it's just as well that I didn't interrupt it even for a daily journal entry. Here I am in a round of events that do not allow me to go back, even in my thoughts, to Corcova.

This morning the people at Sfîntu Ion Nou were loaded into trucks and driven off somewhere. I am told that there were scenes of terror and despair. Some were left there for the moment, until a final decision is made about them. One of these is Sandu Eliad.

Zissu is interned at Tîrgu Jiu.[1] This morning I went to visit his wife. The sympathy I have for him in principle (as the Central Office victim) was not enough to cover entirely the sense of a bad comedy which that woman always arouses in me.

Radu Cioculescu, back from Russia, thinks the war will last another two years because the Germans are in excellent morale, are well prepared for the winter, and have all their fighting spirit intact.

The fighting at Stalingrad is continuing. "The City's Fate Is Sealed," "Stalingrad Living Its Last Moments"—the same headlines in the papers for nearly a fortnight. Yesterday evening, however, the German communiqué mentioned Russian counterattacks (beaten off, naturally) to the northwest.

Thursday, 10 September

The train with the deported Jews left yesterday afternoon after halting a few hours at Chitila. A truck loaded with food and clothing set off too late, first for Chitila, then for Ploiești—after which it turned around and came back. A dazed stupor. There is no room for feelings, gestures, or words.

By chance I was with Aristide at the Bellu cemetery. He was taking flowers for Mafalda (it is twenty-two months today since the earthquake). But I thought of the millions of dead who have no name or grave. I thought especially of those long convoys of Jews, neither alive nor dead, who have been hurled into a satanic agony. A big earthquake would come

1. Concentration camp used for the internment of those thought to be hostile to the Antonescu regime.

as a godsend. Mafalda had the good fortune to die in a few seconds. It was a moment of terror—not days, weeks, months, and years.

Jews will have no bread every fifth day. Their sugar ration has been cut from two hundred grams to one hundred, while for Christians it remains at six hundred grams.

Friday, 11 September

I told Camil about the train carrying the deportees. For a moment, he too seemed to shudder. But no . . .

"It's nothing," he said. "I think that the Russians committed the same atrocities when they built the Volga Canal—and my conscience is at rest."

Saturday, 12 September

It seems that Stalingrad is not expected to fall to a direct assault. Fighting is going on for each kilometer. One can see that the offensive has slowed, and that there is an awkward note in the propaganda. But I think to myself that Stalingrad will not finally decide anything, any more than did the other cities (Kiev, Smolensk, Kharkov, Sebastopol) on which all eyes were turned for a while. While the situation in Stalingrad remains grave, we have the feeling that it is a crux of the war. But when it is resolved—either through the city's escape (which is hard to believe) or through its fall (much more likely)—we will realize that it was all just another episode in an ongoing war.

Monday, 14 September

I have reread *Ultima oră* with unexpected pleasure. In the end, it is an excellent comedy. I know its defects and what needs to be redone, but I realize that in three days I can make of it more than something merely presentable. It does not even have to be "redone"; only some technical adjustments are necessary. I'd like it to be put on stage (because my money problems again threaten to become serious), but the difficulties are considerable, and anyway I don't feel I have the strength to see it all through.

Yesterday evening's German communiqué states that assault troops have entered Stalingrad from the south.

Last night, two air-raid alerts. Bombs fell and there was a lot of anti-aircraft fire. But I've no idea exactly what happened.

Wednesday, 16 September

The German communiqués of yesterday evening and today speak of "ground gained" in Stalingrad, but without giving any details. On the other hand, the press dispatches, the supplements to the communiqués, and the newspaper commentaries indicate that the city is on the point of falling; the central station has been captured, the city center is in the attackers' hands, and fighting continues in the streets and houses. It would all seem to be a question of hours.

After two days in which the most fantastic rumors have spread in the street, on streetcars, and so on about Sunday's bombing (fifty dead, eighty dead . . .), an official communiqué states that the total number of victims was fourteen. All the bombs fell in the suburbs or even farther out.

Last night, in various districts, Jewish families were picked up and taken away. I don't know how many or why. But from now on, none of us can be sure when we go to bed at home that we will still be there the next morning.

Thursday, 17 September

The number of families taken away last night was 105 or 107 (I don't remember exactly): parents, children, brothers, sisters. The reason was irregularities in the performance of compulsory labor.

Solacolu tells me that Stalingrad fell yesterday but that Berlin has delayed announcing this for reasons of propaganda. They are preparing a high-flown communiqué that will have the maximum surprise effect.

Tuesday, 22 September

The families picked up on Thursday night were deported this morning. Until the last moment it was thought that the measures would not be carried out; we still can't believe in such a calamity. But last night another batch of Jews (I don't know who or how many) were picked up from their homes. Gradually, methodically, the deportation plan is being put into operation.

The fighting continues in Stalingrad. After Rador's definite assurance on Thursday that the city had fallen, after it became common knowledge on Friday that the resistance was over (Alice had information from army headquarters), and after a communiqué announcing final victory was expected on Saturday evening—the fighting is still going on. Yesterday and today the German communiqué has reported Soviet counterattacks to the north of the city. The whole battle is a dramatic event.

Yesterday was Yom Kippur. A day of fasting—and of trying to believe and hope.

Friday, 25 September

A sentence from this morning's Rador dispatch from Berlin: "The German command ... has been deliberately avoiding a full-scale assault ... and preferred to advance methodically, even if this means the German people and the whole world still have to wait for the great news of success in Stalingrad." I get the feeling that, however euphemistic this sentence may be (in not directly saying that the capture of the city is no longer absolutely imminent), it does express a reality. I think the Germans are really not throwing everything into their effort. Not only the battle of Stalingrad but the whole of this summer's campaign has been conducted economically, as in a war marked by hesitancy rather than decisiveness. It may be that the Germans could have done more and done it sooner if they had been prepared to pay the full price to achieve it. I expected that their war effort would by this summer have reached a biological outer limit (which is precisely why I thought an exhaustion crisis likely this winter)—but I wonder whether I was not mistaken. I wonder, that is, whether the relatively small number of their achievements is not due precisely to the fact that they have been sparing in their use of reserves. But who really knows? No, absolutely nobody knows. This is why I am so irritated by the futile game of commentary and prediction. "*Nous avons encore pour deux ans,*"[2] Jacques Truelle said to me when I had supper with him and the Bibescus at the Athénée. "It will all be over by December or January," said Branişte, back on a short leave from Tiraspol. Both of them had their arguments. We all have our arguments.

It would be amusing to note here many things about the Bibescus (whose circle I have reentered since Strehaia). Telegrams, letters, invitations, con-

2. "We have another two years to go."

versations, echoes crossing one another in the Corcova–Bucharest–Posada triangle: it is exactly as if I were a key figure in their life. But I know the habits of the clan (Proust helps me in this), the code to their slang, the inanity of a pompously declared liking for something that one day suddenly disappears without trace and makes way for some new craze. At the present moment, Antoine Bibescu and Elisabeth seem prepared for any sacrifice, any token of devotion. But this is the same A.B. whom I did not manage to see in Geneva for as much as five minutes; the same A.B. who, a couple of years ago, left me without saying a word one Sunday morning in the lobby at the Athénée Palace, even though he had invited me to lunch! There is a touch of madness in them, the same touch that makes them colorful and captivating. I am enough of an impressionable commoner for such a comedy to amuse me, though I am not really in the mood for it at the moment.

A very nice letter from Martha Bibescu about Antoine: sober, severe, lucid—the first letter from her that has not been showy. But what I am to do with this world of luxury, I who have to pay the rent tomorrow, I who don't know where to find the 100,000 lei for another three months' rental agreement?

At Tiraspol, according to Braniște, one of the most widely read books is *Accidentul*. The reason for this is quite simply that it can be bought there, and people read what they find. Cărăbaș[3] took thirty copies of *Accidentul* to put on sale there, and some of the officers read the book and liked it. Braniște let out to them that the author was Jewish.
   "Well, fancy that! You can't even tell!"

I paid a couple of visits to Mircea Ştefănescu, who has agreed in principle to adopt my *Ultima oră*. I left him the manuscript, and he'll give me his final answer once he has read his way through it. For me it's just a question of money. Poverty is closing in on me, as in the worst moments before.

Yesterday I was in a group with Leni at the Jewish theatre, to see Stroe's revue. Everything there—stage, actors, theatre, audience—seemed completely crazy. Death is breathing down our necks and we have a Jewish theatre, with girls in low-cut dresses, jazz, verse songs, gags, and knockabout sketches. Where is reality? The specter of the trains heading for Transnistria haunts me all the time.

3. Ion Cărăbaș: bookseller.

Saturday, 26 September

Yesterday I was in town with Antoine Bibescu. He wanted at all costs to go to the theatre—not one but two. He said he couldn't stand seeing the same show from beginning to end, so he got tickets for the National (where they are playing *Noaptea furtunosă* and *Conu Leonida*[4]) as well as for the Cocea sisters' theatre, which is doing a play by Denys Amiel. This alone struck me as pretty eccentric. I also found it personally quite embarrassing to make a sudden appearance at two theatres on the same evening, after two years in which I have not set foot in a Romanian theatre. "Make an appearance" is the right expression: both entrances seemed highly successful, and I don't think a single person there did not turn his eyes toward us. Antoine, dressed in a white drill suit, shuffled around in a pair of slippers. When we set off, I tried to persuade him to dress properly—but I failed.

"Pourquoi voulez-vous que je change de costume? Il fait chaud—et je m'habille comme ça. Quant à mes pantoufles, c'est si commode. En Roumanie les gens ne savent pas s'habiller."[5]

At the National we saw *Conu Leonida*, after which we crossed the road, where Act One had already begun. The packed auditorium watched this gentleman's entrance in a beach suit as he calmly walked to the front and propped himself up a meter from the stage. I followed him, amused and embarrassed in equal measure, fully savoring the fun of the situation but also worried about the consequences. I had told him before not to speak aloud during the performance, so at least from that point of view things went almost normally—except that occasionally, when he didn't understand a line, he turned to me and said:

"Qu'est-ce qu'il dit? Qui est-ce? Comment s'appelle la femme en vert, etc.?"[6]

We left after Act One and spent the rest of the evening much more agreeably, walking along Calea Victoriei and then sitting very comfortably on a stone wall in front of the lattice work on Piața Ateneului. "He's crazy! He's off his rocker!" people said (or felt they had to say) to me as they passed by. In fact, though a little battiness is part of this strange man's character, he is not strictly speaking mad. Romania and Bucharest represent for him a kind of barbarian province, a weird and colorful

---

4. *O noaptea furtunosă* [A Stormy Night] and *Conu Leonida față cu Reacțiunea* [Squire Leonida Facing Reaction], two plays by Ion Luca Caragiale.

5. "Why do you want me to change what I'm wearing? It's hot—and this is how I dress. As for my slippers, they are so comfortable. People in Romania don't know how to dress."

6. "What's he saying? Who is that? What's the name of that woman in green, etc.?"

colony from which he feels (and is) so far removed that he does not make the least effort to please the natives. He lives among them as among ne-groes, yellow men, or redskins, sometimes showing an interest in local customs but without feeling obliged to respect them. He told me that Asquith had been terribly bitter when he learned that Elisabeth was going to marry a Romanian. *"Pour lui, c'était comme si elle avait épousé un chinois."*[7]

I think that Antoine Bibescu feels the same about the whole of Romanian society. He is like an Englishman suddenly landed among colored people.

Yesterday evening I had an experience that was perhaps more revealing about the Romanian theatre than any other one might have been. *Conu Leonida* and Amiel seen in the space of twenty-five minutes. The performance of *Conu Leonida* was lively, genuine, and good fun—Amiel was, in Romanian, false, trivial, and absurd: Dina, Tantzi, and Critico engaged in psychology! *C'était à hurler!*[8] Romanian theatre is lost as soon as it rises above the ordinary. Perhaps that is true of everything here, not just the theatre.

Thursday, 1 October

"Si Stalingrad tient jusqu'au premier octobre, les Allemands sont perdus,"[9] Antoine Bibescu said to me a month ago in Corcova. And here we are at the first of October. Stalingrad is still holding out—but the Germans are not lost. All the predictions we make, all the dates we set, all our calculations are arbitrary. The war is a mystery that may not become clear until the last moment. And no one knows when that last moment will be: in five weeks, five months, or five years.

"The Jews will be exterminated," Hitler said in his speech yesterday. He hardly said anything else. On the course of the war, on short-term perspectives, on the length of the struggle, on the key issues—nothing. The war is again at a standstill. With the exception of Stalingrad—where the fighting has been extremely intense the last two or three days—all the fronts are relatively quiet. It is as if this war were the normal state of things, which did not necessarily have to reach a resolution and might

7. "For him, it was as if she had been marrying a Chinese."
8. You felt like screaming!
9. "If Stalingrad holds out until the first of October, the Germans are lost."

drag on indefinitely without any change. This may explain the sense of weariness that has gripped us the last few days.

This morning saw the departure of our maid Octavia, an eighteen-year-old peasant girl who felt so good in our home. She cried like a child. Our life will be even more difficult. All kinds of daily troubles—small ones, to be sure, but insoluble—will now appear: sweeping the floor, washing the dishes, laundry, shopping. Poor Mama is too ill and tired, and we are too awkward. We'll sweep, make the beds, and wash the dishes, but who will do the laundry? Still, you have only to think of deportation and all this becomes bearable. It's not tragic; it's only grotesque.

Today it occurred to me that a play could be written on the basis of Balzac's *Béatrix*. Two splendid female roles, and great scenic development.

Thursday, 8 October

Nothing new at the fronts, or anyway nothing really important. The fighting goes on at Stalingrad. It is hard to follow events just by reading the papers. There is talk of Soviet attempts to relieve the city, but I can't locate them on the map. As things stand now, you would say that neither side expects anything other than the onset of winter.

The first days at school have tired me beyond all measure. After four hours of teaching I feel exhausted. What bad health!

Friday, 9 October

Strada Sfîntu Ion Nou again has the tragic air of early September. Two schools are full of families picked up last night for deportation to Transnistria. In the windows you see pale countenances, dazed looks, but also sometimes a smiling young face or a laughing child, and you don't know which is more painful: the despair of some or the indifference of others to their fate. Long lines of people wait in the street and on the pavement to see once more their relatives inside. It is a harrowing sight. And you cannot shake off the thought that the same fate may be reserved for us all.

I kept thinking that I would manage to get enough money for a few months of peace. But now my hopes have gone. Having dreamed of half a million, I have now returned to my petty calculations. I still have seven thousand to eight thousand lei at home—but then what will I do?

Lack of friendship on the part of Mircea Ștefănescu, who has still not found the time to read my play. It would be absurd to think that he will help me put it on. That's another door closed.

Saturday, 10 October

Yesterday evening's German communiqué does not mention the Stalingrad front. Clearly, all the dispatches and commentaries are trying to shift attention to other sectors: Terek, Ilmen, Leningrad. Does this mean they have given up the idea of capturing the city? Or, because it will take more time, are they going to keep quiet about it until they are finally able to announce victory? In any event, the hour of victory has unquestionably been overtaken by the change of season. Autumn is well and truly here. We have had the first day of rain and cold.

Aristide showed me some lines attacking me in a book of Efimiu's that came out a few days ago.[1] I am a "russet contributor to an Orthodox newspaper," an "unbaptized Jew in the service of the Orthodox Nae Ionescu," and so on. One day Eftimiu will be a champion of extreme democracy and I still a hooligan. As I grow older, I realize that misunderstandings are irrevocable. *Cuvântul* is a part of my life that remains perpetually open. Nothing, neither my writing nor my life, will ever close it.

Monday, 12 October

The other day I finished Act One of *Insula*. Today I began Act Two. I work without conviction, because I know it is pointless. Leni will act in a play by Froda and Nicușor—and *Insula*, a circumstantial piece that could be acted only by Leni, only today and only at the Barașeum, will have no use or purpose. If I do nevertheless write it, it will be so that I do not drop yet another project halfway through. All my abandoned literary projects depress me. But if I am frank about it, is *Insula* a literary project? It seems to me more like a pretext for a show. There was also the hope of earning some money from it, at a time when I need money so much and don't know where to turn.

The war continues as a state of mind. It is a great calamity that we always have on our backs. From a military point of view, however, this is

---

1. See Victor Eftimiu, *Frăția de arme* (Bucharest, 1942), p. 340. The phrases cited by Sebastian are in fact condensations of passages from the book.

a moment of general standstill. For three days the communiqués have been completely trivial.

Wednesday, 14 October

Yesterday evening, everyone awaiting deportation at Sfîntu Ion Nou was set free. People returned from the dead. I have heard that there were wild scenes at the moment of their release; people were howling and fainting. Someone shouted: "Long live Greater Romania!" "Long live the Marshal!" What these releases mean, I don't know. Second thoughts? A mere postponement? Will they give up the deportations for good? An article in Sunday's *Bukarester Tageblatt* repeated the assurance that by autumn 1943 there will no longer be any Jews in Romania.

The military pause continues. Nothing new at the fronts. Stalingrad has completely dropped out of the news.

Antoine Bibescu, in a letter I received yesterday, asked me whether I needed ten thousand lei and said that he could send it to me. I wrote back at once, saying that I didn't need anything.

Thursday, 15 October

In today's *Universul*, the Berlin correspondent spoke of adjustments at the front in view of the approaching winter; the offensive will be resumed next spring, when the Bolsheviks will be annihilated. But if the German army is already entering its winter break, the hibernation will begin nearly two months earlier than in 1941.

For the first time something was published today about the deportation of Jews ("expatriation of certain elements"—as the official statement puts it). The Council of Ministers has decided that, from now on, the "expatriation" operations will be carried out by a special body, and that all such measures have been suspended until this comes into being. Can we feel reassured? If so, for how long?

Saturday, 17 October

The Germans have been on the offensive at Stalingrad for the past two days. It seems to be a final effort to capture the city. Titel Mănciulescu (whom I met just now on a streetcar) said that it will all be over in two or three days.

I have taken back my play manuscript from Mircea Ştefănescu, who hasn't read it. I preferred to put an end to an embarrassing situation.

I keep trying to write Act Two of *Insula*. After a few days of complete inertia, I seem finally to have got things moving. But what's the point? I don't think I'll do a play suitable for Leni and the Baraşeum.

Thursday, 22 October

Act Two of *Insula* is making progress, and I may finish the first tableau by Sunday. It is even possible that this first tableau will acquire the dimensions of an act—which would, to some extent, force me to rearrange the play. I am happy enough with what I have written recently (in particular, today, because I am simply too exhausted to write anything on days when I am at school). Maybe the tone is at times too serious for Leni and for what a Baraşeum audience can take. But the way I have started it means that it will not be cut to their size but will be a play pure and simple. Quite likely it will remain in my drawer, and in the end that would not displease me. But I do need money so badly: if it were not for this, I wouldn't even think of putting it on. A stage performance, a published book, an article—any sign of myself in public is an act of presence and acceptance. Well, I don't consider myself present—and I don't accept.

"Fighting continues in Stalingrad" was the laconic report in yesterday evening's German communiqué. Again the rhythm of the offensive has slackened. Again the imminence of the city's fall has been toned down.

Saturday, 24 October

"An enemy counterattack has been repelled in Stalingrad," said yesterday evening's German communiqué. In Egypt, according to what Rosetti said yesterday, the British have taken the offensive.

I feel that Act Two of *Insula* is coming along much better than I expected. The attic tableau is acquiring the dimensions and dramatic coherence of a full act.

It occurs to me that if Act One is speeded up at performance, it could be presented as a prologue, followed by three acts.

Sunday, 25 October

The headline in today's *Universul*: "The Fate of Stalingrad Sealed."

Tuesday, 27 October

Yesterday morning I finished Act Two of *Insula*. I read it in the evening to Leni, Scarlat, and Jenica—an illuminating experience. For I became aware that it is well constructed theatrically and, despite the comic rhythm, finely written. I think I may like it more than *Jocul de-a vacanţa*. There are *longueurs* in Act Two—even a certain monotony and times when it drags—but in general I feel that I have a rich situation, three well-planted characters, and a few roads open to Act Three (if there is not to be a fourth act). Their reaction was, of course, less favorable. They liked Act One a lot—which was to be expected, because it is a sketch. Act Two, where the tone becomes rather more serious and the situations acquire a certain psychological depth, pleased them at first but then started to weary them. There can be no question of a performance in the near future. Scarlat does not want one, and Leni doesn't dare to want one. He is keeping room for his play and Nicuşor's, whereas she, the poor girl, has lost her bearings. Instinctively she feels that *Insula* is a lively play and that her role has a certain warmth and intensity. But it all strikes her as too refined, too subtle, too "intellectual."

"Why can't you write more ordinarily?" she said to me with sincere regret.

I can't explain to her—nor would she believe—that *Insula* is a simple play without intellectual pretensions, a real comedy with just a little poetry here and there. But poetry, even in minimal doses, scares her in the theatre.

There is no news about the British offensive in Africa. All we know is that it is in full swing. The German commentaries suggest that it is of enormous proportions. We shall see.

Frances D.[2] would have been another one of my women if I had permitted myself such a thing. She is frankly ugly but young, clever, humorous, and—last but not least—from Yorkshire. What would I not have done for Yorkshire!

---

2. Frances Dickinson was an employee of the British Council.

Friday, 30 October

My love games are one of the most stupid tortures. They are humiliating, dangerous, futile, and meaningless—and yet I cannot give them up once and for all. I know they lead nowhere, can lead nowhere, and that they are doomed to end in the most grotesque way, but each time I embark on the same ridiculous farce, with some weird combination of imposture and good faith, as if I were trying it all out for the first time. It is hard to be a has-been, and seriously to accept that fact. What is unforgivable in my case is that I drag into such false situations people who have done nothing wrong except to know me: Cella, Leni, Zoe. This afternoon was so painful that I feel disgusted with myself. *Et maintenant, il faut s'en tirer.*[3]

Monday, 2 November

Here we are in November, and nothing has changed in the course of the war. October passed almost without military events. Stalingrad is still holding out, and the other fronts are not moving. Some people, of course, go on living: money, work, love—everything is for them more or less normal, at most hindered, and in any event fitted into their lives. For me, the war has suspended everything. I wait as I would for a train, meanwhile tossing around between torpor and exasperation. I have never known how to wait quietly for something. When I was an attorney, an afternoon of waiting in the courtrooms used to seem a terrible ordeal. Now my whole life is one long wait.

No news of the British offensive in Africa. Great caution in both sides' propaganda. The fighting continues, but so far remains stationary. If the British liquidate this front (as they might logically do after all their experiences), anything is possible. It could even bring the end rushing on. But if they do not succeed (which is what we tend to think, after all they have done so far), nothing more can be expected for another year.

L. is a delightful girl. Even if age has not left her features unmarked, her body still has a delightful youth, warmth, and firmness. She also has the most charming mixture of tact and impudence. Anyone who resigns himself to having her as a capricious and welcome gift, without making any demands, is a lucky man. The error begins with the first grain of jealousy, which in her case is so out of place. When she sleeps with another man, and then again with you, she doesn't deceive either you or

---

3. And now I have to extricate myself from it.

him. She just likes to fuck—and puts into it all her candor and grace. But I am forbidden such pleasurable compounds of sensuality and indifference.

Thursday, 5 November

A British advance—even victory, it seems—in Egypt. They report 9,000 enemy prisoners, 600 aircraft, and some 250 tanks destroyed or captured. The German and Italian communiqués both admit retreating to a second line, but do not treat this as important. In general, yesterday's and today's papers have put out propaganda preparing for the announcement of a retreat. We cannot believe anything yet. Over the past two years in Africa, we have seen the most dramatic turnarounds from one day to the next.

The Ministry of Propaganda has ordered the removal of books by Jewish writers from libraries and bookshops. Today, at Hachette, I saw two printed boards with huge letters: Jewish Writers. There too, of course, I was presented as a troublemaker or criminal, with my parents' names, my date of birth, and a list of my books. Only my distinguishing features were not mentioned. At first I laughed (especially as the whole board was full of mistakes), but then I thought that this kind of poster does us no good. I fear that it will attract attention to us, and who knows what that might lead to. For two years I have not been to the theatre or gone to restaurants; I avoid walking around the city center; I don't see anyone or try to get in touch with anyone; I keep to myself as much as possible and let others forget about me—and now here is my name in all the bookshops!

Sunday, 8 November

The Americans and British have landed at several points in Morocco and Algeria. It seems to be a major operation, preceded by a declaration in French from Roosevelt. There is fighting in Rabat, Oran, and Algiers. Pétain's troops are resisting. I don't yet know what attitude the Germans will take. Rommel's situation will become terrible if he must also face an attack from Tunisia. For the moment he has retreated to somewhere between Fouka and Mersa Matruh, roughly 120 kilometers from his original position. The retreat seems to be continuing, and the number of prisoners to be growing. The British are calling it a disaster. The DNB Agency speaks of "war of movement" and a skillful retreat.

Monday, 9 November

We still don't know the details of what is happening in Africa. Certainly the pace of events has speeded up—events that may be absolutely decisive or may be no more than important. We shall be able to see more clearly in a few days' time. For the moment we are at fever pitch, still dizzy from the first shock of it all.

Algiers already surrendered yesterday evening. It is more than a surrender; it is an accord worked out a long time ago between the Anglo-Americans and the insurgent French forces. The insurrection and landing have been running in parallel, both in Morocco and in Algeria. No news about Tunisia. In Egypt, Rommel is continuing to retreat. He seems to have abandoned Mersa Matruh and crossed the Libyan frontier, leaving behind a number of encircled infantry divisions. Is it a rout? Does he have a plan? Can he still have a plan? The answer depends on what Hitler decides about the whole matter; for it is no longer a local battle but affects the main lines of the war as a whole. I await that decision with some anxiety! Will he march into the unoccupied part of France? (I am thinking of Poldy.) Will he force Pétain into some kind of military collaboration? Or will he do nothing for the time being (which is hard to believe)? Yesterday he gave a traditional speech at a Nazi party festival in Munich; but it was overtaken by events and therefore appeared inconclusive, except perhaps in its confusion. Only one section was clear: that which again threatened the extermination of the Jews.

Tuesday, 10 November

Darlan is "in American hands,"[4] though I don't know whether as prisoner or ally. In any event, Pétain has taken over supreme command of the French army. In Oran and Casablanca there were brief cease-fires for a few hours, then renewed fighting, but it does not seem possible that the resistance will last long. The occupation of Algeria is proceeding apace. Nor is there much resistance in Morocco. Roosevelt has asked the Bey of Tunisia to allow Allied troops to cross Tripolitania, evidently so that they can fall on Rommel's army from the rear. According to the Italian communiqué, he is continuing to retreat. But where is he now? Where will he stop? Berlin has given no sign of a response to the major events, but I think that something is brewing beneath the silence.

We must try to control our emotion, to look at things coolly and

4. In English in the original.

clearly. Frenzy is exhausting; certain joys wear you out. Of course it is hard not to rejoice, but now is the time to keep calm. Yesterday evening I read over last June's pages from this journal, when Rommel was "at the gates of Palestine." I remember the Axis frenzy of excitement at that time. Everything—even the most fantastic plans—seemed simple, straightforward, original. The Germans saw themselves grabbing the whole of the Middle East, on three continents, in one enormous pincer movement. And today the reality has turned right around. Triumph and collapse at a distance of four months from each other.

Where will today's triumph lead the Allies? What will happen over the next four months? I ask these questions on the evening of a day full of such great hopes.

I keep thinking of the threats that Hitler made yesterday. He wants to exterminate us—and that is perhaps the only thing he is certainly capable of doing. The thought suddenly crossed my mind that one night—a night like this—we might all be butchered in our homes. And meanwhile the air would be buzzing with the news of victory.

Wednesday, 11 November

This morning (the anniversary of the armistice in 1918), German troops marched into Lyons, Vichy, and other parts of unoccupied France. In terms of the war, I don't think this will change anything. But my mind is on Poldy, and it is hard for me to think of anything else.

Thursday, 12 November

The thought of Poldy dominates everything. What is he doing? Through what dangers is he living? How much longer will he be able to stay where he is? In what conditions? Hundreds of questions that haunt me day and night, especially as the situation in France is so confused. No one knows what the new regime will be like. Will there still be a government? Or is it an occupation pure and simple? Will there still be any distinction between the two zones? I am afraid of the German fury. There, as here, they could find in a massacre of the Jews a kind of psychological safety valve for everything they have had to swallow during the last four days. Here too, all kinds of dark rumors about us are being whispered around: that Killinger has demanded a resumption of the deportations, that the Germans want two trainloads of Jews to be deported every day to Russia, and so on. Enthusiasm, amazement, and anxiety are mixed in equal doses, perhaps dominated, however, by the "electrifying news"[5] from which we have not yet awoken.

In Algeria and Morocco the fighting has come to a complete end. In Libya, Rommel is still in retreat. The Germans and Italians seem to have sent a not very sizable force of aircraft to Tunisia. The Americans, approaching from Philippeville, are a hundred kilometers or so from the Tunisian frontier. The spectacle is dramatic and on a grand scale. *Tout n'est pas encore couru*.[6] There is more to be seen yet.

Friday, 13 November

The British are at Bardia and Tobruk. Rommel is still retreating. Will he try to make a stand before Benghazi? Or will he prefer to use El Agheila again?

Camil Petrescu is down in the dumps. He replied with a wan smile to the news that Rosetti gave him yesterday evening. And he somehow came up with a phrase straight out of a Camil anthology: "I too will bet on a British victory, when it is absolutely certain."

Monday, 16 November

A conversation with Paul Sterian. (Aristide, whose library is being taken away and put up for sale, had asked me to try to get the order rescinded.) Sterian received me at his office in the ministry, with two civil servants in attendance. When I entered, he wasn't quite sure what to do: to stand up or to remain seated. He found a middle way: he stayed in his chair, but sketched out a vague half-movement of rising.

"What is it you want, Mr. Sebastian?"

The "Mr." was a warning to me and a demonstration to his assistants. He repeated it two or three times in the course of the interview, which could not have lasted more than five minutes. I explained to him very briefly (because I swear I felt myself choking at the farce of it) what was at issue.

"Yes, why shouldn't the library be sold? What? He's expecting a British victory?"

The question was a kind of denunciation—for the witnesses present

5. In English in the original.
6. All is not yet over.

in the room. He said it to me with a mocking smile, which testified to his confidence in a German victory.

I left feeling sad and humiliated, furious at myself for having gone, depressed at the whole encounter after eight years with a Paul Sterian grown rich and prosperous, powerful and full of himself. How distant our lives seemed from each other as I entered his sumptuous office for a moment, I a kind of humble petitioner, poor, weary, and helpless, my clothes worn thin. To compare us at all is somehow distressing, though there is also a funny side to it. I am now trying to view the whole thing as an episode out of Balzac.

Wednesday, 18 November

I gave the opening lecture in my Shakespeare course, for which nine students have enrolled. Another ten or eleven people, friends of mine, came along as an amicable gesture. The situation could be embarrassing—but it seems to me that I came out of it unworthily. I shall give up the course and hand the money back; it was a failure, though I don't think I made a fool of myself. I spoke for an hour, with warmth and pleasure, as I do when I find the right tone. But I hadn't come there to score a success. I thought I would find a solution to my money shortage. I was mistaken. That's all.

Yesterday evening and today I read *Julius Caesar*. I am returning to Shakespeare and plan to finish my reading of him.

In Africa the pace of events seems to have slackened, though there is still activity everywhere. But since we have grown used to major blows every day, to lightning changes, our suddenly aroused thirst for the sensational is somehow disappointed. Rommel is continuing to retreat. The British are at Derna and will probably reach Benghazi in a few more days. It remains to be seen whether the battlefront will not be, as it was last year, at El Agheila. In Tunisia the British report advances but do not give any geographical details. The Germans and Italians are at Bizerta and Tunis, probably to cover the back of Rommel's army. A battle is likely somewhere, either in Tunisia or in Tripolitania. In Russia it is winter: torpor and confusion. No large-scale events.

Thursday, 19 November

This evening I read *Insula*. (I have been so busy the last two to three weeks with the translation of *Bichou* and the preparation of my course that I have put *Insula* to one side, though anyway there is no more I can do on it for the moment.) Everything looks clearer after three weeks. Act One is excellent. Act Two is botched: not bad, botched. It will have to be rewritten, with the same material. The biggest problem is that Act One is pure comedy whereas Act Two verges on drama. The change in tone is too marked, almost as if they were not two acts of the same play. The initial situation is too comical to allow such a serious tone later on. If I continue writing the play (and I don't feel I can continue without an assurance that it will be performed), I shall have to shed all the ballast from Act Two.

Sunday, 22 November

Since Friday morning, Benghazi has been back in British hands. Clashes between patrols are taking place at Ajdabiya. We shall see whether Rommel, who has quickly retreated all the way from El Alamein, will make a stand at El Agheila. In Tunisia the fighting has the character of skirmishes; a battle is expected for Tunis and Bizerta. In Russia the German communiqué reports Soviet attacks in the Caucasus, at the bend in the Don, and at Stalingrad.

Monday, 23 November

As yesterday and the day before, this evening's German communiqué speaks of "heavy defensive fighting" to the south of Stalingrad and at the bend in the Don, as well as of (repelled) Soviet tank attacks at Lake Ilmen. I don't know what the Soviet communiqué says, and there is no way of telling how large the battle has been. In Africa I am told that the British First Army has occupied Gabès—which would open the gates to Tripolitania from the rear, before the battle for Bizerta takes place. But who really knows?

Monday, 30 November

I have been ill since last Tuesday, when I came home at lunch with a temperature of 39 degrees [102 F.]. A few days of fever (38 to 39) have exhausted me. Today I no longer have any, but I am so weak I can hardly stand.

There were major events all last week, but I couldn't record them here or follow them personally. The occupation of Toulon by the Germans and the scuttling of the French navy mark a serious turn. In Russia the Soviet offensive is continuing south of Stalingrad, at the bend in the Don, and at Kalinin.

Wednesday, 2 December

Nothing new at the fronts. Waiting. In Tunisia the British and Americans are approaching Tunis and Bizerta, where they will meet German-Italian resistance of unpredictable strength. In Russia, Timoshenko's offensive appears to be fading without major operational results. This would repeat what happened last September at Rzhev and last May at Kharkov. But no one can know whether major events are in store in December, similar to the ones we saw in November.

I went out this morning for a short walk, after eight days at home. I feel extremely weak and tired.

I read with pleasure (but also with some sense of monotony) Jane Austen's *Emma*. Graceful, simple, full of humor, but rather slow and too detailed—like a Dutch painting.

Depression, gloom, disgust, revulsion. I haven't properly regained my health, and now Mama has fallen ill. The lack of a maid is more oppressive than ever. Autumnal weather, dark and damp. I have no money. Just a thousand lei left—and then? How will I pay the rent at Christmas? How will I meet the household expenses until then? No prospects, no expectations, no hopes. I'd like to sleep, to die, to forget.

Sunday, 6 December

Days of lethargy and disintegration. It's not even despair. Everything is bitter. Profound disgust with yourself, with other people, with "events," with life. You don't even have the energy to commit suicide, but if you had a loaded revolver in your hand, you might pull the trigger. What do I need to come back to life? Money? A woman? Work? A book? A house? I don't know. Everything is joyless, tasteless, colorless, meaningless. The only thing I could do now would be to play cards, for hours or days on end—until my mind is completely numb.

Wednesday, 9 December

I don't think I have ever felt so acutely, and at the same time both a sense that my life is over and a desperate wish to come back to life. I did have, and still do have, some dispositions to happiness: a certain élan, an indefinable lyricism, a great belief in light, serenity, and life, a certain warmth, an endless capacity to love—but all have been ruined and lost. There is a curse that pursues me from afar. The war is a catastrophe that sometimes overwhelms (and makes me forget) my old unhappiness, but at other times deepens and accentuates it, keeps it alive like still bleeding wounds. I feel annoyed with myself for writing so badly (maybe I shouldn't write at all when I can't keep myself under control), but I feel a need to speak, to shout, to release—if only by screaming—something of my horrible nightmare.

Thursday, 10 December

In Clermont-Ferrand the Jews were arrested yesterday and sent to labor camps. According to the dispatch, this measure will be extended to other *départements*. What will Poldy do? This is always my only thought.

Yesterday and the day before, I went out in the evening to get some air. Clear starry nights, not too cold. But, I don't know why, the darkened city seems to me gloomier than ever. I feel the prison, the walls, the barbed wire—and ourselves struggling amid them. Here, or in France, the circle keeps tightening around us. Is there an escape? I am beginning to think not. There are only brief postponements: a day, a week, a month—another day, another week, another month—but our fate will be the same.

A calm appraisal of the war (one conducted without either excitement or depression) forces me to see it as a long, hard, and slow business. Peace cannot be reasonably expected in the near future. The end may be certain, but it is a long way off. The war has reached a phase in which the Germans cannot do much more than they have done up to now—but the Allies still cannot bring their resources to bear. The Germans have great staying power, and the British and Americans are not strong enough to deliver knockout blows. We are entering a long process of attrition, which will last until there is a decisive change in the balance of forces. Meanwhile the Russians continue to attack, but (though the situation is still confused) they do not seem capable of fundamentally altering the front. In all likelihood, the winter will be extremely difficult for the armies in the east, but not completely intolerable. So then spring will come, and the cycle will start again. Until when? God knows.

But there is still room for miracles.

Sunday, 20 December

I really am living from day to day. I have a thousand lei in my pocket—and I don't know where I'll find another thousand the day after tomorrow. I haven't smoked for ten days. And I have meanwhile drawn little sums from school: 2,000, 3,000, 4,000 lei, in back pay from previous months. It looks as if tomorrow they'll give me my January pay (about 6,000, I think). After that, I don't know at all. I won't pay the rent on the 26th, but it will have to be paid one day or another, in a week or two. With what? From where? I have asked Sică for some work. For the moment I am translating *Topaze*. I'd happily do work on the side, without feeling gloomy or resentful about it, if it would bring in what's needed at home. (By chance I found out that Sică has been getting the author's royalties for *Bichou*; some 10,000 lei an evening. I got 22,000 total, and I'd start the same work any time at the same rate. Maybe some people would do it for even less.) Without feeling desperate, I think to myself that this is what is called a failure: I, at thirty-five years of age, with no job, no money, no real friendship, no escape. Everything I have done has failed miserably. My clothes are tattered; my boots look worse and worse. I have grown lean. I am tired, finished, useless. How far is there to go before I put out my hand and beg?

The war goes on: nothing dramatic, no major changes. For the past eight days Montgomery has been back on the offensive at El Agheila; Rommel hastily retreated, but it is not very clear to where. Will he stop before Tripoli? Will he defend Tripoli? Will he retreat to Tunisia? In Russia the Soviet offensive is continuing in more or less the same zone, without major advances but also without slowing down. Each day the German communiqué reports that attacks have been "driven off," "destroyed," or "crushed." The daily repetition of these three expressions greatly weakens their meaning. The Germans have gradually created a kind of slang, a kind of communiqué code, which we manage to understand but which draws a curtain of mist over the reality of the war.

Tuesday, 22 December

The Soviet offensive persists all along the front (Terek, the Volga-Don region, Kalinin-Toropets, Velikiye Luki, Lake Ilmen). On Sunday, moreover, a new offensive was started at a point that the newspaper reports imprecisely call "the middle Don." The official German communiqué issued yesterday evening contains an unusual passage: "On the middle Don, the enemy has been attacking for several days with a very powerful concentration of armor, and has managed to penetrate the local defensive front. This breakthrough cost huge Bolshevik casualties. To avert a threat to their flank, the German combat divisions took up prepared positions to their rear and thereby foiled an extension of the initial enemy success. The fighting is continuing with undiminished intensity."

One day, soon after peace comes, I may write a chronicle of the war years: "Events, Texts, People"—in the genre of *Cum am devenit huligan*. A kind of personal memorial to this terrible journey. But will we reach the end of it?

For money I'd be prepared to do anything in the theatre (of course, without signing it or taking literary responsibility). Translations, adaptations, falsifications, vile tricks. I'd happily cobble together any kind of play (farce, melodrama). A few days ago I greatly enjoyed reading Soare's and Vlădoianu's rubbish (*Pămînt* [Earth]), with its sublime, methodical, formulaic triviality. If I wrote like that, I would have the dual satisfaction of earning money and poking fun at myself. I suddenly thought that an adaptation of one of Ionel Teodoreanu's novels (*Lorelei*, for instance) could be a real hit on the stage. In fact, its success would be guaranteed. False nobility, false intellectuality, falsely blasé attitudes. With Vraca as Catul Bogdan and Mimi Botta as Lorelei, it would easily run for 150 shows. This afternoon I actually went to Madeleine's to suggest that we work on it together, with the idea that she would sign it alone and present it to a theatre. But while she was busy making some tea, I happened to leaf through Teodoreanu's latest (or next-to-latest) novel and found a passage of such abject anti-Semitism that disgust proved stronger than my theoretical cynicism. I no longer said anything to Madeleine—and I dropped the project. After all, some things are just too dirty to touch even in the theatre.

Wednesday, 23 December

"The defensive battle on the middle Don is continuing with undiminished ferocity," said yesterday evening's German communiqué. There are no details that would allow you to locate the action on the map.

No news of Emil Gulian.[7] I rang Ortansa and found her at her wit's end. "Just so long as he's alive," she said. His last letter is dated the 15th of November. On the 18th there was the attack between the Volga and the Don—and since then, not a sign. It would be too terrible to lose him. Why he of all people? Mircea Eliade wanted this war. He waited for it, wished for it, believed in it, still believes in it—but he is in Lisbon. And Emil Gulian dead? At a front where he didn't know what he was doing?

Friday, 25 December

The first day of Christmas. At home all day. No one rings me and I don't try to contact anyone. My solitude is ever greater.

Of the 3,500 lei I still had yesterday, 2,000 have gone on a Bach concerto. Recklessness? No. I too felt the need to buy something in a town that yesterday seemed invaded with happy people doing their last-minute shopping—a sight that has always humiliated me, because I have always been, and above all felt, so poor. The concerto (in D minor for piano and orchestra) is of a wonderful gravity and, at the same time, a wonderful brilliance. I listened to it twice yesterday and three times today. The andante begins and ends with a phrase of Wagnerian intensity.

It is almost certain that Emil is a prisoner. An orderly on leave from the front told Vivi that his officer—who escaped by a miracle—saw Gulian at the moment of his capture. Colonel Stancov, phoning from Rostov, confirmed the news. Now begins the uncertainty. Will he remain alive? Will he return?

Why do I not write? Why do I not work? A half-written play (*Insula*) is waiting to be completed. Two complete scenarios for a play are on file. I have a novel planned to the last detail. I won't even speak of Shakespeare's sonnets, to which I have not returned for so long, or of the "chronicle" that occurred to me a short while ago but is so tempting. I put everything off—until when? And meanwhile, time passes to no avail.

---

7. Sebastian's friend Emil Gulian died on the eastern front.

I know only too well why I can't write. Bad health. Frayed nerves. Lack
of a comfortable house. Inability to remain alone with myself, in hours
filled with meditation. Worries about money—and about so much else
besides. Yet Jane Austen wrote on her knees in her father's dining room,
surrounded by a family who did not know what she was doing. Maybe.
I am not Jane Austen.

Tuesday, 29 December

I don't think that Darlan's[8] assassination (on Christmas Eve, in circumstances not yet made public) will have any influence on the course of the
war, even in the limited sector of Tunisia. There are probably moves toward a deal between De Gaulle and Giraud,[9] which will solve the problem of North Africa at a political level. The war in Tunisia is still at the
stage of waiting and preparing. In Tripolitania, Montgomery has occupied Sirta. Will he meet resistance at Misurata?

The fighting continues in Russia, especially in the southern sector,
but we are not able to follow it. The communiqués are vague and totally lack geographical precision. The tone of the propaganda deliberately matches the confusion. The Russians are always attacking, but always
advancing slowly. The whole operation is of a scale and complexity that
we can grasp in theory, but its evolution on the ground escapes us. My
own view is that the Germans will eventually reestablish a front line and
will not give up Millerovo or Kamenskaya or, above all, Rostov. They
will hold them, as they have held Rzhev and Velikiye Luki for the past
year. At some point, however, the collapse will become due. But when?
Next summer? Next autumn?

8. François Darlan: French admiral, high-ranking official of the Vichy regime.
9. General Henri Giraud assumed governing powers in North Africa after Darlan's assassination.

1943

1 January 1943, Friday

I am beginning to get used to the years of war. We seem to struggle through the same journey from first of January to first of January, in a nightmare that is itself beginning to have a certain monotony. The seasons always bring the same phases. Winters of German semislumber, when you feel the armies are tired: low reserves, no stamina left. Then spring comes and you live in expectation of a new offensive—in April? in May? in June? And when the fighting suddenly becomes fierce with the arrival of summer, the offensive and the propaganda reach dizzying new heights, and you live a few days of fear, doubt, and mortification. Could it just possibly be that . . . ? Later, in September or October, you realize that nothing decisive has happened. The pace of events slackens again in the weeks before the first snow, and the cycle begins all over again. How much longer will this continue? Will 1943 bring us peace? I don't think so. Not unless a miracle happens. I tend to think, rather, that 1943 will repeat without major differences the trajectory of 1942, certainly accentuating the German decline and the Allied rise, but not by so much as to bring the denouement rapidly closer. Perhaps in 1944. Anyway, I find it easier to say 1944, precisely because it is still far away.

What is becoming of me, of us, in all this madness? I don't know. For the moment we are still alive. We have got this far, and it's possible that we will get further. Nothing depends on me, on us. Everything takes place over our heads. All we can do is wait. But God knows, it is not easy.

Saturday, 2 January

Place names that used to be totally unknown to us now concentrate for a moment all our attention, as if everything were being decided there: Velikiye Luki, Elista, and so on. What they mean in themselves, what they represent in the general course of the war, we do not know and hardly even ask ourselves. But for one day, one hour, or one minute, our whole being is there.

Hitler's order of the day is grim but not desperate. His speech in May was much graver.

"Look, this war will go on till 1947 or 1948," Sică said yesterday. It was the first time I had heard those numbers (my thoughts have never gone beyond '44), but now I am beginning to get used to them. Yes, in the end, why not?

In translating *Topaze*, I see close at hand what is called a great play, a surefire success, a faultless construction. *Topaze* is a machine that will always work and bring people to the theatre anytime and anywhere. It is rich in material and full of drama, its characters are precisely drawn, and, above all, it has a satirical vigor that hits right on target. No wavering, nothing fuzzy or vague. In my own plays there is an inclination to "delicacy," which means that they have no chance at all of being a great success. As long as I play the key of "subtlety," I'll never win a large audience. Pagnol has shown me that you don't have to be crude, but you must without fail be vigorously dramatic. Can I stop being what I am? Can I deliberately achieve what I lack? The material for "Alexander the Great" was excellent, but after Act One (so rich, so lively, so energetic) I became "subtle" again. I keep committing the sins of a litterateur. I wish I could treat theatre as an industry and write a play with a perfect mechanism.

Monday, 4 January

Beginning today, Jews will get not fifty but one hundred grams less bread than Christians. Four of ten daily rations have been withdrawn from us.

Rebreanu is preparing *Shylock* for the National. Camil Petrescu, who reported the incident to me this evening, asked him whether the passage in which Shylock rebels against anti-Semitic hatred (Are we too not human? "If you prick us, do we not bleed?") would not be difficult to act in today's conditions.

"No, it won't," Rebreanu replied, "because we'll give it an anti-Semitic interpretation."

"And he wrote *Iţic Ştrul dezertor*," Camil added.[1]

---

1. This World War I novel, *Itzhik Strul, Deserter*, described the persecution of Jewish soldiers in the Romanian army.

Tuesday, 5 January

I have reread *Hedda Gabler*. (I think it's fifteen to seventeen years since I last read a play by Ibsen. I had a strange passion for him in my youth: I knew almost by heart *Rosmersholm, Brand, The Wild Duck*, and so many others, which I probably didn't understand but read five, six, ten times.) In the first two acts I find Hedda irritating. My sympathy goes out more to the simple characters in the play: to Thea, to the old aunt, even to the mediocre Tesman. Hedda is just mean, tense, and egoistic. But Acts Three and Four give her an intensity and depth that go beyond the others' likable honesty. While reading the play I thought of my own novel, whose first chapter features a tour in the provinces with *Hedda Gabler*. In this respect my reading was unexpectedly useful, because it suggested a lot of ideas to me. My poor heroine is a very good interpreter of Hedda, but she does not understand the work and is terribly afraid of the character she plays.

Can I start work on the novel before I finish off my outstanding theatrical projects? Is it not more sensible first to get *Insula* out of the way and then to write "Freedom"? I think it is—and again I make promises to myself in this spirit. This evening I seem to have come up with some solutions for the second act of *Insula*, and to have found a taste again for working on the manuscript.

Dr. Kahane went to Alice Theodorian's the other day to pass on some terrible information. "Madam, I must speak to you about a very grave matter. I have heard that Sebastian is an agent of the secret police. It has been drawn to my attention that he has a great deal of money (where from, no one knows), that he lives in extraordinary luxury and makes incredible purchases." His very words!

Thursday, 7 January

This evening the subject for a play occurred to me out of the blue. Another subject. How many does that make? Not counting "Alexander the Great" (but counting *Insula*), it makes four—or rather, five, because I have asked Cella Serghi to work with me on a drama of the Manolescu–Marioara Voiculescu type, and have even drafted a scenario for it. The comedy that popped up yesterday seems to me a charming idea: ingenious, lively, witty. I have written the whole scenario, in considerable detail, for Act One. The other two acts are less clear, but it has started so well that there are great possibilities for the plot to develop. I am now at a crossroads: either I move toward a sentimental comedy; or, with a little courage and lack of scruple, I can head straight for a situation comedy, if not an outright farce (which I unfortunately don't think I am capable of writing). I'm not quite sure what to do, but in any case I don't want to leave it as a mere project. I want to sell this scenario. (Quickly, before I get too fond of it; quickly, while it is still something alien.) I want it to earn me quickly several tens of thousands of lei, so that for a while I can get out of my great financial difficulties. (Today I have two hundred lei left in my pocket, and I drew my January salary from the school before Christmas.) If Nicuşor gives me fifty thousand, I'll propose that we immediately write it together. If not he, then Sică.

Tuesday, 12 January

The night of Thursday to Friday was the kind of feverish night that usually follows my first vision of a book or play. I tossed and turned almost until morning, besieged by ideas, solutions, questions—and it seemed that I was finding an answer to everything, with magical ease. The play grew, filled out, became urgent, demanded to be written at once. The next day, Friday, was equally agitated. First I rang Nicuşor, to tell him without delay of my proposal. The plan was simple: to make the scenario tend toward farce; to eliminate elements of poetry, delicacy, subtlety, etc.; to draw everything in a burlesque direction. The man's role would suit Beligan,[2] and I would write the woman's with Nora Piacentini in mind. I would ask Nicuşor for fifty thousand and we'd get straight down to work, so that the play would be finished in three to four weeks and rehearsals could begin at once (there being a slot at the Sărindar after *La petite chocolatière*). I couldn't get through to Nicuşor, and it was impossible to get hold of Nora's or Şeptilici's[3] number. I went to look for them in town, but then the front cover of the recently published *Cortina* caught my eye in a kiosk opposite the post office: Tudor Muşatescu, it seems, is under contract to write a comedy in seventeen days for the Sărindar Theatre, in collaboration with V. Timuş, with Nora Piacentini in the leading role. What a blow! But the blow was even greater when I learned from the text of the report that the first act of Muşatescu's play would take place "in a corner of North Station." The coincidence infuriates me, or actually depresses me. My first act is set on the platform of a small provincial station, on the Sinaia to Bucharest

2. Radu Beligan: actor.
3. Mircea Şeptilici: actor.

line. All the rest is quite different, of course, but nevertheless... I felt with irritation that it really is necessary to do things quickly and energetically, while there is still time (if there is still time).

I rang Sică (why?), tried Nicușor again, and went to the Sărindar in the evening to see the actors in performance, hoping that I would be able to check my first sketch of the roles. But I did more—what a stupid mistake! Not only did I tell Şeptilici that I had a scenario for Nora (which was already premature, because it committed me to the plot line), but I said I was determined to write it with him, Şeptilici. I am so angry with myself for this lack of tact.What a babbler I am! How little self-control I have! With a couple of words I shut off all my possibilities. Since then I have tried every way of wriggling out of it, but it's no use. I get pointlessly entangled in all sorts of lies from which I cannot escape. I and my scenario are the prisoners of a gaffe. For a moment I thought I might yet save the scenario by showing him "Alexander the Great" or even *Insula* in its place. But no! That's impossible. I'll have to give it to him tomorrow evening. I say "give" because I feel that the simple act of communicating will alienate it from me. The same would have been true if I had communicated it to Nicușor, but at least I would have had a chance of earning some money. I am beyond forgiveness.

Wednesday, 14 January

Both Piacentini and Şeptilici thought my scenario "fantastic" when I read it to them last night. Both see it being a great success. Both prefer the farce option (they even want music, if that's what there has to be). What will remain then of my play? Nothing. But at least if I can write it quickly, and have it put on quickly, and score a great success that brings in a lot of money fast, I won't feel too bad about it. I am so cornered by poverty that I'll write anything for the theatre if it makes me some money. But I won't even have that compensation. They are off on tour until the 15th of February, so we can begin writing only when they return. This means that the play could not be performed earlier than June or July, perhaps even next autumn. I am losing interest in the whole thing. I consider the scenario lost and have put it into a drawer along with so many other useless papers.

I have now copied out Act One of *Insula* and will try to press on with the rest. The first half of Act Two is very good, while the second half is easy to rework. If the tone is somewhat lightened and the pace quickened (through the introduction of a new character), it will be excellent.

Act Three seems straightforward. But Act Four (because I am tending to go for four acts) remains unclear for the moment. I must force myself to work. I am lagging too far behind my projects, which are more plentiful than my poor output. I also think that a serious schedule will serve as a kind of penance for my curious blunder with Piacentini and Şeptilici.

But meanwhile, where can I lay hands on some money? Gradually I have been drawing more from school, my only resource: three thousand lei on Monday, seven thousand today. This will be enough for the present week—and then? A translation for Sică would be a salvation right now, but can I ask him so soon? I am also thinking of dashing off a farce for Birlic (I have stitched together a kind of scenario from here and there, but it's not usable). In the best of cases, however, even that could not be staged before summer. I just don't know how I am going to make ends meet.

I have not followed the war this last week. I read the communiqués at random. They say nothing, but at least it is a nothing that has some special meaning. The Soviet offensive is being maintained. The Germans appear to be retreating from the Caucasus but holding firm in the Millerovo region. Amusing euphemisms sometimes allow you a glimpse of the situation. For instance, behind the description of the Kalmuck steppes and the Caucasus as "elastic zones," one senses that Georgievsk, Piatigorsk, and other towns have been abandoned. But the general view of the war remains, I think, unchanged. With greater or lesser difficulty, with higher or lower casualties, the armies will remain locked together until the spring. This winter will not "overturn fate" either.

The streets are again filled with Jews clearing the snow. Classes 7 and 8 have broken off lessons. Everyone over the age of sixteen, except those with special papers, has been called up. But will these papers protect us for much longer? I hardly dare to think so.

Once again, a childish awe at the colossal power of the snow. It fell for twenty-four hours—from Saturday night to Sunday night—and the whole city was clogged with thousands of tons of the stuff.

I have again been reading a lot of Balzac. I regret not having the patience to make notes. Sometimes I am irritated by his style—a certain melodramatic sentimentality, a certain grandiloquence—but in the end the vigor of the creation carries you away. It is an extraordinary provincial gallery, with characters profoundly drawn as if by a more fiery and lucid Daumier. (What a lot I could say about *Pierrette*, which I read yesterday and today!)

Monday, 18 January

The day before yesterday, at a private gathering at the French Institute, I listened to the whole of *Pelléas et Mélisande* on twenty crystal-clear disks. It was twelve years since I had heard *Pelléas*, and I seemed to enjoy it more in this rediscovery. At the opera the whole stage apparatus had weighed the text down, covered the music, and accentuated everything incidental. What a strange piece it is! A long recitative lasting four hours, with diffuse tuneless music, like a dull, filtered sound-light. I think I shall go there tomorrow afternoon, when they are playing it again.

The offensive on the Russian front seems to be growing sharper at each of its central points. Recent German communiqués, while reporting that attacks have been repelled with heavy Russian losses, indicate less vaguely than before the seriousness of the situation. "Attacks launched with numerically superior forces." At Stalingrad, "our troops have for several weeks been waging a heroic defensive struggle." "The enemy is attacking on all sides." "Powerful enemy attacks." "Fierce fighting." "Hard defensive battles." "Massive new enemy attacks." Today, on top of all this, there was an ingeniously euphemistic new formulation: "mobile defense." For the last two to three days a new offensive seems to have come from Voronezh, and the elastic zone has now expanded as far as Millerovo. Rostov is under attack from nearly every direction—but is it conceivable that it will fall?

Using a reworked scenario, I have written another scene in Act Two of *Insula*, but I can't tell whether it is good or bad. I could simply eliminate it and make things even more straightforward. In principle the idea of someone drunk on aspirin seemed very funny. But as I wrote the scene, everything seemed to become false and far-fetched. As soon as I lose the right tone and a sense of "truth," I no longer have any talent.

Tuesday, 19 January

In Russia, as in Tripolitania (where Montgomery resumed his offensive two days ago), we are witnessing "mobile defense." The mobility has reached as far as Schlüsselburg in the north and Kamensk in the south, and in Tripolitania it probably extends beyond Misurata. I do not have any definite geographical details. Yesterday evening's German communiqué is revealing in both style and tone, but it does not signal any actual facts: "In the south of the eastern front, the fierce winter battle that has lasted for two months is continuing with undiminished strength. . . . German forces in the Stalingrad region, who are fighting in the most difficult conditions, show firm perseverance and combat spirit in resisting powerful new attacks."

Wednesday, 20 January

I am writing Scene 6 in Act Two, with a character who did not enter into my original calculations and came to me only the evening before last. So far it seems to me successful. I'll see more clearly later on. I think the rest of Act Two will be straightforward. I should be able to finish it in three to four hours of work, especially as I'll be using some material from the first draft.

"The Stalingrad island is under attack on all sides," says the Berlin correspondent of *Universul* in today's edition.

Friday, 22 January

Two years since the Legionary revolt. The anniversary has passed almost unnoticed.

Gheorghe Nenişor is back after three years in France. He looks surprisingly youthful. The Titulescu inheritance has made him a very rich man; this is not obviously visible, but you can see it nevertheless. Wealth seems to change people physically, giving them a kind of heaviness, quietness, or physiological assurance.

I might translate another play for Birlic. It would come just in time, because otherwise I don't know what I'll do for money.

Saturday, 23 January

From yesterday evening's German communiqué: "In the southern sector, the enemy is attempting to break through the whole front . . . [but is being driven] back at many points. In the eastern Caucasus, German troops have methodically retreated in the face of the enemy, as part of mobile battle tactics. The German force in Stalingrad is hemmed in by the enemy . . . fierce resistance . . . powerful enemy pressure [with] much larger forces . . . breakthrough from the west . . . a few kilometers into our positions. . . . At the great bend in the Don and in the Don Sector, the fighting is heavy and fluctuating . . ."

In Africa, Tripoli has fallen.

Sunday, 24 January

Finally completed Act Two of *Insula*. I may add a few things to the final scene when I copy it out, but the act generally strikes me as very good. Of course, it does not have the rapid pace of the first act (which maintains a racing allegro), but nor does it have the slowness of the first version. I would pass straight on to Act Three, but I have to deal with the translation for Birlic.

Thursday, 28 January

The translation for B. has taken up all my time. I haven't had a breathing space even to note anything here. It is a silly farce, which I am translating mechanically and without any pleasure—*What a Dirty Thing*. I'll try to force myself to finish it by Saturday and then return to *Insula*, as if with washed hands to something finally clean. I think with a little melancholy—not a lot—that I am capable of writing plays infinitely better than Jean de Letraz. But what's the point? I am translating him, not the other way round.

"The major winter battle on the eastern front is continuing with undiminished strength and spreading to new areas." So begins yesterday evening's German communiqué. But it is a sentence that we find virtually unchanged in all the communiqués of the last ten days. The tone of the whole press (dispatches, commentaries, official communiqués, articles) is fundamentally altered. As if from a sudden turn of a starting handle, the optimistic style has given way to a style of grave concern. Before everything was "*tant mieux*"; now it is "*tant pis.*"[4] The explanation, I tell myself, cannot lie only in the gravity of the situation (unless there really is a catastrophe—which in my view is not the case). Rather, I think that the main lines of the propaganda are being revised. Military setbacks usually lead to a political crisis—and we may be on the eve of one now. Such a crisis cannot be overcome through the trivialization of problems but rather through their dramatization. Hence the excess of pathos, after

4. All the better—all the worse.

the previous excess of nonchalance. In any event, even for someone fore-warned as I think I am, the real difficulty is to uncover the meaning of things amid this terrible chaos.

Monday, 1 February

The battle of Stalingrad is over. General Paulus, appointed marshal yesterday, has ended all resistance today. A stunning chapter of the war is drawing to a close. No one in September would have ventured to consider today's epilogue as a faint possibility, let alone to predict it.

For two or three days the German communiqué has regained some of its old optimistic style. It signals resistance, counterattacks, new initiatives, and successes, but one does not gather from it that the fighting is less intense. All the offensive thrusts are continuing.

On Saturday evening at Camil's, I met a Legionary (the lover of Marietta Anca). It amused me to hear him talk about the war. I realized that, seen from the other side, things can even today have a different aspect. It is not the facts that count but the eyes that behold them (at least until things have gone so far that there is no longer room for different interpretations). In his opinion, nothing new has happened. The Russians will be annihilated in April ("the Führer said this to Antonescu"), or in July, or at worst in the autumn. The Germans are stronger than ever; their reserves untouched. They are developing formidable new weapons. Stalingrad will be recaptured very soon, perhaps in the next few days. . . .

There is in me something of the petty bourgeois, something of the low-grade functionary used to living on a pittance and childishly treating money with a ridiculous fear. I saw Gheorghe Nenişor in his room at the Athénée. A packet of Maryland cigarettes cost him 760 lei, a bottle of whisky 6,000. He seemed to be talking from another planet. One day, in my novel, I must write a lot about poverty and about money.

Today I read Act Two of *Insula* after a week's break, and checked my first impressions. I think it really is good. But now I must keep working at it.

With the thirty thousand lei I got from Birlic, I could breathe easily for three weeks, maybe even four. But if it proves true that I have to pay military taxes (nearly forty thousand lei for Benu and myself), what will I do then?

Thursday, 4 February

In Germany there are three days of national mourning and recovery for the divisions lost at Stalingrad. The whole press has a solemn, majestic tone, as in a funeral hymn. A kind of tragic grandeur, probably by directive, conceals the questions and doubts concerning political and military affairs.

Friday, 5 February

A possible title for an essay: "On the Physical Reality of Lying." It would be shown that lying, however arbitrary, grows, branches out, becomes organized and systematic, acquires definite contours and points of support; and that once a certain level is reached, it substitutes itself for facts, becomes a fact itself, and begins to exert inescapable pressure, not only on the world of others but also on the one who originated the lie.

Saturday, 6 February

Starting on Wednesday, evening performances will begin at seven and end by ten at the latest. Shops will close at five, theatres at ten, and streetcars will no longer run after eleven. Soon we shall probably have a general curfew, as one of a series of sweeping measures of civil defense. Everyone is obsessed with the thought of heavy bombing. The raids on Turin, Milan, and Genoa have brought the specter of air war closer to us. The Casablanca Conference, the Adane negotiations, the events on the Russian front, the approach of spring: all together create a sense that Bucharest is becoming a vulnerable target in a wider field of operations. This is leading to a certain nervousness and a few early signs of panic. There is talk of large-scale evacuation of the city, in which case Jews would be isolated in ghettos. After a lull in anti-Semitism, there is again worry, fear, and insecurity.

Tuesday, 9 February

The war on the Russian front is growing ever more intense and spreading to new sectors. The German communiqué rarely gives more than vague geographical details, but these are enough to indicate a shift toward the Oskol, Shakhty, the mouth of the Don, Zheisk. We can't know exactly what is happening—both because there is a lack of news and because the front keeps moving. In the Caucasus the retreat continues on two separate fronts: one toward Rostov, the other toward Taman, the last two bridgeheads. Rostov is under attack on all sides. In any event, the game now seems over in the Caucasus. The situation is perhaps more acute in the north, in the region of Kharkov and Kursk, where the Soviet offensive is reaching places that were part of a stable front in Autumn 1941. Is the pace of events speeding up? Are we already on the slope leading to the end? Or could there still be halts, recoveries, turnarounds? Have the scales tipped for the last time, or will there still be movements this way and that? I don't know. But the questions are becoming possible.

Saturday, 13 February

"Ursa Major" is a possible title for my latest scenario—if I give up the idea of a farce and go for a delicate comedy. "Ursa Major" because the provincial math teacher has a passionate interest in astronomy. He has a telescope at home. The book that is waiting for him at the station is a treatise by James Jeans. The woman in evening dress, who will spend the night in his house, will be fascinated by his talk of the sky and the stars. And Act Three, in which the cynical lover appears, will see him fall from sky to earth. The play thus has a nicely rounded structure. But I can't yet know whether I shall have a free hand with my scenario. First, when Șeptilici returns, I have to get out of our agreement to work on it together.

Meanwhile I am writing Act Three of *Insula*. It is going much too slowly. I work too little and am too disjointed. I think that if I could again have a month of calm and solitude somewhere in the mountains, I would enjoy working and make rapid headway. For all my theatrical projects, I would need a few months of steady hard work. Then I could get down to more serious things.

The snow tax for Benu and myself is fourteen thousand lei. I have to pay another forty thousand in military taxes by 23 February, and in March the rent will be a terrible problem. Where will it all come from? How will I find it? I dare not think.

Monday, 15 February

The Russians have retaken Rostov and Voroshilovgrad, a day or two after Krasnodar, Shakhty, and Novocherkassk. The Caucasus front has been wound up. The battle is now advancing ever westward, along the Sea of

Azov to Taganrog, and up toward Kharkov. All the territory gained by the Germans in their summer offensive has been won back. The zone of operations is extending to places that have long seemed "out of the question."[5] It is hard to look further ahead and make any predictions; the pace of events is too fast for our brains to keep up.

Tuesday, 16 February

I called on Longhin. He is stunned by events, neurasthenized, thrown into panic. He thinks that there can be no stopping, even at the Dnieper, and that the situation is serious for Jews. He has been told—from the best of sources!—that the Germans are demanding the organization of a pogrom, and that a new series of anti-Semitic measures will anyway soon be passed.

"Be careful," he said to me. "In case of danger, come and hide at my place."

He set me thinking. He is given to panic, I know, and today he was incredibly on edge. But I remember that both in August 1939, at Stîna de Vale, and in June 1940, in Bucharest, he was pretty well informed.

Thursday, 18 February

Act Three (of *Insula*) is proving harder than I expected. I wrote the first three scenes easily and quite fast, but now I have been stuck for several days. The difficulty arises from a change in the scenario. My plan last week envisaged two tableaux for this act, but I have given up that idea. I want to concentrate everything in one tableau, so that the play does not lose its lively rhythm. This removes some of the old material planned for this act (which will be replaced with new incidents), but the original structure has been lost in the process, so that I am now in a kind of "scenario breakdown." I know the characters and the settings and the action, but I don't know how things will hang together on stage. It is much easier to write in tableaux, but I don't want to use that easiness here.

Berlin denies the fall of Kharkov, which the Russians seem to have announced back on Tuesday. Yesterday evening's German communiqué, however, reports fighting both in and around the city.

---

5. In English in the original.

I had a conversation with Ovidiu Lupaş (apparently in response to the one with Longhin). The Germans are enormously strong, he argued, and the Russian advance inconsequential. Hitler did make a mistake about the size of Soviet forces (he thought in November he was facing 25 divisions, when there were actually 520), but that can be corrected. The thaw will tie down the Soviet offensive, which is anyway due to lose momentum. Meanwhile the Germans are achieving a great concentration of forces which, if not in 1943 then certainly in 1944, will wind things up in Russia. At the same time they will take action in the west. The events in Tunisia are much more important than those in Russia. Rommel will crush the British and Americans—especially once German armies occupy Spain, Portugal, and Gibraltar, as they will easily do in the summer with hardly any resistance. Submarine warfare will completely paralyze the Allies.

Yesterday Maria Magda said to Camil: "In my view, the war will end in a compromise peace." It might have been a witty remark if the girl were not a delightful little goose.

Friday, 19 February

The fall of Kharkov was announced in yesterday evening's German communiqué. The dispatches and commentaries have been more optimistic of late. "Defensive successes," "major Soviet losses," "the approaching thaw" are the general themes. Amid all this good cheer, however, Goebbels's speech last night sounds unexpectedly dramatic. Stalingrad represents a fateful moment: the Russian offensive is becoming catastrophic, and the whole situation critical. The Jews are once more threatened with extermination.

Monday, 22 February

Yesterday I outlined a scenario for Act Three of *Insula*, but then almost immediately I realized that my original plan was preferable. It is true that if Act Three is written in two tableaux, I risk a slowing of the pace, but in return the story will have more space, more perspective, more richness. This will make the transition to Act Four more natural. Strangely enough, in writing Act Three as a single tableau (with less material and a faster pace), I am actually involving myself in a digression. The basic line of the play would be more unified in the two-tableau solution. I regret that the thing is dragging on so much.

I have read with delight Jane Austen's *Pride and Prejudice*. It has the same luminous irony as *Emma*, the same gentle poetry, but it is even more sensitive, because the whole story is more rounded, better constructed.

The German communiqués of the last two days indicate that as the thaw sets in, the Soviet offensive is slowing down.

Wednesday, 24 February

A dream last night. I am at a political meeting, in a hall which, though not large, is crowded with people. Goebbels is speaking, together with a tall, dark-haired man—probably Gunther. Someone (he looks like Coşoiu, a pupil of mine from 5th Year) shouts: "Hechter! Hechter!" I make desperate signs for him to be quiet. Goebbels comes up to me but is then again speaking at the rostrum. He seems to propose the formation of an action committee. Then Perpessicius appears from a neighboring room and says: "I'll sign if you like, but I won't work." Goebbels consults his assistant in the first row and calls on everyone in turn: "And you are Aryan, and you, and you . . ." He stops in front of Camil Petrescu, hesitates, and smiles awkwardly: "Ah, I'm not sure about you. Maybe you're not." Camil is mortified. That is all I can remember. In fact, it was more complicated and richer in incident—and it was not even as coherent as my account suggests, though I think my broad outline is accurate enough.

I have dropped *Insula* for the time being. It wasn't working—so it's best to leave it in peace. I'll try again in eight to ten days, when I have some distance from it again. A play is always amazingly simple at first; the difficulties and resistance come later. In order to overcome them you have to do stubborn (almost physical) work that has nothing to do with inspiration. The worst is that, though I realize the qualities of *Insula* as a piece for the stage, it does not interest me directly, personally. I find it more pleasant to think of "Ursa Major," though with that too, an early period of captivation will certainly be followed by similar frustrations.

The press, the communiqués, and dispatches still indicate a gradual slowing of the Russian offensive. The optimistic tone is being systematically consolidated in readiness for the thaw.

Saturday, 27 February

German resistance in the Donbas is becoming sharper. They seem to have recaptured Kramatorsk a few days ago and to be counterattacking, with Stalino firmly in their hands. The Soviet advance has halted at the Sea of Azov, where Taganrog is still in German hands. But the Russians are still keenly on the offensive in the center and the north, in the regions of Kursk-Orel, Ilmen, and Ladoga. The situation in Tunisia is confused. The Eighth Army is advancing from Tripolitania, but the First Army is losing ground near the border with Algeria.

An envelope from Aristide has calmed my money worries a little. I'll try not to open it until the rent is due, and meanwhile search elsewhere for money to pay the household expenses and (most serious) the military taxes.

Monday, 1 March

Yesterday evening's German communiqué reports the recapture of two towns in the Donbas: Kramatorsk and Lozovaya. German resistance in this sector seems to be more and more active. On the rest of the front, the Russian offensive is continuing unremarkably, but with no loss of intensity.

March! You can feel that spring is coming—and with it so many unresolved questions, so many worries.

Thursday, 4 March

In the south, after Kramatorsk and Lozovaya, the Germans have recaptured Slavyansk and are maintaining their counterattack in the Donbas. In the north, however, they are evacuating Damyansk and (surprisingly) Rzhev. The Russian offensive remains intense at Orel.

Vague unease. Fears, forebodings, doubts. The evening papers published a new anti-Semitic law, with provisions for internment and deportation. Disturbing mainly as a symptom.

I am patching up for Sică the third act of a Viennese play that he is not even sure he will put on. Will I do a good job? Will I get some money out of it?

Tuesday, 9 March

The Germans are attacking and gaining ground in the Donbas, to the south and west of Kharkov, but are defending and giving ground at Orel to the north. The names of small localities find a place on the asset sheet on both fronts. But one has the impression that the overall battle has lost much of its intensity. The dramatic climax was the fall of Kharkov. Since then the war seems to have entered one of its phases of transition and waiting.

If the terms are right (that is, royalties of 10 percent), I might translate *Pride and Prejudice*. In principle it does not seem out of the question. In three days I have written a whole new third act for Sică's play—quite skillfully, I think. Why shouldn't I be able to work as easily for myself? I suppose it's because I get overscrupulous about things and feel paralyzed by my responsibility. But when I am able to shut my eyes, I "let go" and it doesn't work out badly.

Friday, 12 March

The Germans are taking back Kharkov. Yesterday evening's communiqué reported that their troops have reentered the city and are engaged in street-fighting. In the center, on the other hand, "disengagement" operations are under way. Vyazma was evacuated last night.

Monday, 15 March

The street-fighting in Kharkov has ceased. Yesterday evening's German communiqué announced that the whole city has been recaptured. On the other sectors of the front, it mentions only "reduced-scale operations." Has the Soviet winter offensive come to an end? I don't know. But there is certainly something to be learned from the latest twist: that nothing in this war is final; that any event, however important, is sooner or later lost in the general movement of the war; that a situation never changes instantaneously. The war is a slow accumulation of facts, some minor, some more sensational, which all merge into the general drama. Sometimes, when "a heavy blow is struck," we feel dazed for a moment and get the impression (whether confused or excited) that everything may end suddenly, as if by a miracle, in one great triumph or disaster. But then the dust settles and everything looks less important. We return to the long slow succession of days, until the next "major blow" again takes our breath away for a moment.

Meanwhile, our life passes by.

Saturday, 20 March

In the south on the Russian front, the initiative seems to have completely passed to the Germans. Yesterday evening's communiqué announced the recapture of Belgorod. The German advance is continuing in the Donbas, even spreading in the area of Kursk. The official attitude is quite reserved, but there has been a clear change in the situation.

I have enjoyed reading another of Jane Austen's novels, *Persuasion*, though it is less vigorous than the first two.

I have wasted a great deal of time on that act for Sică. I keep patching and patching—and never manage to finish. Together with Dickinson,[6] I today began translating *Jocul de-a vacanța* into English.

Monday, 22 March

Yesterday I had lunch at Mogoșoaia with Rosetti, Camil, an Italian prince, a French monk, and a Swiss diplomat. Martha Bibescu was simpler and less showy than before. She has an extraordinary way of leading a conversation, of trying out one, two, or three subjects until she finds the right one, of varying attitudes and bringing people together. In this sense she is a great actress. I myself was dull and silent. My French sometimes goes through a difficult period, and this was one of them. I didn't have the confidence to start a sentence unless I could already see how it would end. Poor Camil cut a sorry figure as a Balkan writer, speaking in dreadful French about his own work. I'd have liked to help him out, but his deafness amongst this group of complete strangers destroyed all the bridges between us. In the end, the nicest thing about it was the drive there and back, on a bright spring day with the fields colored in numerous shades of blue, violet, and mauve.

I have read "Esther's Letter" in the English Bible, and today Racine's *Esther.* (This too is a way of celebrating Purim!) Three centuries, a few millennia—and our story is still the same. What a fantastic mystery.

Wednesday, 24 March

In Tunisia the Anglo-American offensive began on Sunday and is in full swing. So far—at least according to the Axis press—nothing is known

6. British Council employee.

about the course of events. In Russia the German counterattack in the south seems to have stalled. The German communiqué of the day before yesterday reported a stabilization of the front. But fighting is continuing at Kursk, where the Germans are gaining ground in the battle for the city. As to Orel, yesterday evening's communiqué presents the Russian offensive as completely smashed.

The visit to Mogoşoaia transported me into the entire atmosphere of an episode in my future novel. The project has suddenly come alive again. I looked through the material in my files with great interest. It is a book that I feel obliged to write.

Saturday, 27 March

In Tunisia, after some early successes, the British have clearly been shaken by Rommel's counterattack. But the offensive is continuing, at present through fierce air and artillery clashes. In Russia the communiqué does not mention anything new across the whole front. The thaw is general. Will it lead to a kind of cease-fire until the ground dries? Or will there be new developments between now and May? In any event, the war is no longer in a dramatic phase.

This evening I have reread *Insula*. It was instructive. Act Two doesn't work even in the new version; I haven't dumped enough ballast. But I do think I am seeing things clearly. I need to make some huge cuts. Some twelve pages will go by the board—pages of reverie and lyricism. A month ago, when I was too close to the text, I couldn't have borne the thought of eliminating them, but now I can do it without feeling bad. The play will be brisker, more coherent, more simple and concise. I may be wrong, but I have a sense that this time *je suis dans le vrai*.[7] I also have a clearer picture of Act Three. I shall divide it into two tableaux, as I originally planned. I'd like to write it quickly, not only to wrap up *Insula* but above all so that I can get started on "Ursa Major," which has recently taken clearer shape and become just too tempting.

Monday, 29 March

Chesterton about Thomas Hardy: "I will not pretend to sympathize with his philosophy as a truth, but I think it is quite possible to sympathize

---

7. I am on the right track.

with it as an error; or, in other words, to understand how the error arose." This is a possible motto for a portrait of a friend in the opposite camp. But is such friendship still possible?

Tuesday, 30 March

In Tunisia, Rommel has again turned to a war of movement. The British have crossed the Mareth line and occupied Gabès. I don't have a map to follow the situation, nor do I have enough information. I can't work out the possibilities and perspectives, but if the British and Americans are bent on a serious fight, you wonder what is left for Rommel to do. Resist? Counterattack? Take to ships?

Saturday, 3 April

Nothing new at the fronts. The communiqués say nothing. Standstill in Tunisia, thaw in Russia. And it is already April.

I visited Ortansa Gulian yesterday evening. No news of Emil. Is he a prisoner? Or dead? The poor people are consulting fortune-tellers, who read things in cards or coffee grounds, and arranging for masses to be said. I stayed until Anca (Emil's daughter) said her evening prayers for "Daddy." It was harrowing.

Saturday, 10 April

Terribly tired. Almost sick with tiredness. I fear that last year's insomnia is returning. Some nights I sleep only two or three hours. I am also working too much at school: twenty-three hours of classes (sometimes eight a day) is too much for my level of stamina. I get home dizzy, hoarse, incapable of two consecutive thoughts. I await the Easter holidays as a period of convalescence. I'd have liked to go to Corcova, but Antoine—to whom I sent a letter—doesn't seem in any rush to receive me.

Camil is performing *Mioara* at the "Studio." I had no choice and went along yesterday to a rehearsal, or rather to the preview. People getting worked up, plotting against one another, trading insults and praise. I feel completely indifferent to it all. In a way, maybe I should feel scared. Am I so old, so lethargic, so disgusted that this game—in which I too used to take part—no longer means anything at all to me?

By a stroke of good fortune I have been able to reread my journal for January–June 1941, which for a moment I thought I had lost. The big surprise was that it seemed so uninteresting: too dry (despite the dramatic nature of the events), too cold, too impersonal.

In Tunisia the Anglo-American offensive resumed a few days ago and is expanding in every sector. Rommel is retreating in the south and is also yielding ground in the center. The resistance seems stronger in the north. Yesterday evening's German communiqué, as well as today's, say that the enemy forces are several times larger. From now on it looks as if it is just a question of time. Three weeks? A month? Two months? In Russia there is nothing new.

Wednesday, 14 April

In Tunisia, Rommel's retreat has become headlong in the past few days. Kairouan, Sfax, and Sousse have fallen in turn. Resistance is taking place only in the north, in a kind of semicircle containing Tunis and Bizerta. The campaign has entered a new phase, in which there is no longer room for strategic retreat. That formula, possible up to now, has been overtaken by events. From now on the alternative is quite simple: either resistance or surrender. We can't be sure how things will work out in the immediate future; for that we would need to know what forces have been committed.

In Paris, the seventy-four-year-old General Mordacq has thrown himself into the Seine. No identifying papers were found on the corpse. The dispatch gives no more information, but what a tragedy must lie behind it!

Thursday, 15 April

An unusually forceful statement was issued this morning about Marshal Antonescu's visit to the Führer. "The common struggle against bolshevism and the Anglo-American plutocrats." "The mobilization of all forces ... The Romanian people will wage this war until the final victory ... This historic contribution will be the foundation and guarantee for the future of the Romanian Nation." Is something being prepared? What? War in the Balkans? An attack on Turkey or from Turkey? There is a silence that betokens major new events. With the exception of the Tunisian front, the war is passing through one of those quiet periods from which it may suddenly burst out again, in one of a number of unexpected directions.

Thursday, 22 April

I leave for Corcova this evening. I don't know how this rather improvised *"séjour"* will work out, but a few days' holiday will do me a power of good. I'm in bad shape, tired and miserable, and I have great hopes for this week of rest.

Sunday, 2 May

I returned last night from Corcova, where I spent nine blissful days. I am suntanned, calm, and relaxed. I know I'll soon lose this sporting "form"—Bucharest and the war grind it all out of me—but the fact that these few days in the open air were enough to restore me suggests once again that my health has not been deeply undermined. A sick person would not respond so readily to the first call of life. My reflexes are still healthy. In Corcova I gave a lot of thought to all manner of personal and other problems (literature, the war, etc.), but I won't record it all here. For that I would need a few hours of solitude—which is what I lack so much in Bucharest. (I keep thinking of my studio flat, where I could be alone when I needed to be.) I amused myself in Corcova by keeping a diary in English: thirteen pages, with an entry for each day, more for the fun of writing in English than for the actual record.

Any journey is a stimulus for me. In the carriage between Corcova and Strehaia, I saw a lot of new things for my future novel. The "Princess Stana" chapter, in particular, has grown richer in incident. I'll put some notes about this into the file with material for the novel.

Antoine forced me to talk about one of my scenarios, and so I gave him a brief outline of "Ursa Major." I grew excited as I talked, and again it seemed to me that the scenario offered good chances of success. He was even more excited. *"Écrivez tout de suite. Il le faut. Tout de suite. Pas un moment à perdre."*[8] I have come back with the idea of working as much as possible in the theatre. I'll finish *Insula*, get down to "Ursa Major," dramatize *Comăneștenii*. With so many projects, I may succeed in having a play put on this autumn and earning a few hundred thousand lei to pay the rent and the household expenses. Come the end of the war, I'd like to have in my suitcase two or three plays that might go down well in New York or London. I don't say I'll succeed. But I have to try, es-

8. "Write it straightaway. You must. Straightaway. There's not a moment to lose."

pecially as I don't know many other games and would find it hard to get used to any.

What Corcova mainly meant for me was nine days out of the war—as if I had slept for nine whole days. Then I woke up and found things as I had left them: nothing new on any front.

Friday, 7 May

I am quickly returning to my daily routine, which tires me and grinds me down. I have lost my "holiday form." On Monday and Tuesday absolutely everyone was amazed when they saw me. I was "unrecognizable." Now, alas! I am more and more easily recognizable. I tell myself that the life I lead must be seriously wrong if in five days it can bring me to this state: rings around my eyes, pale cheeks, frequent headaches, insomnia. My health is too unreliable a machine for such a way of living.

In Tunisia, after three weeks of inconclusive fighting, the Americans have broken through the German positions in the north and center. Mateur was abandoned a couple of days ago. The advance is approaching Bizerta and Tunis, which are likely to be cut off soon.

On the River Kuban, "renewed Russian attacks." The German communiqué reverts to the formula: "heavy defensive fighting." What is happening in Tunisia and on the Kuban does not, however, wipe out the general impression of sluggish expectancy. It may be that the last five or six weeks have been the dullest period of the war so far—as if the war were set to go on forever.

Meanwhile, an article by Goebbels has reopened the anti-Semitic offensive, which had somehow become less topical.

Saturday, 8 May

Tunis and Bizerta have fallen, exactly six months after the Anglo-American landing in Africa. The campaign was unexpectedly long, but the denouement is unexpectedly short. Even after yesterday's rather solemn German communiqué, which reported a deep penetration of their defensive system, I still thought that Tunis, and especially Bizerta, would be capable of holding out for another couple of weeks. In no way did an immediate collapse seem possible after such a long resistance.

Camil Petrescu is affected by the *Mioara* affair as by a disease. He speaks of nothing else, is aware of nothing else. He reads the latest review for or against, organizes publicity, negotiates with those hostile to it. When I returned from Corcova and found him in his room buried beneath newspapers and magazines, I honestly had the impression that I was visiting a madman.

This evening, after he had spoken for a whole hour about *Mioara* and *Mioara*, I asked him what had been happening in the war and was amused to realize that he had no idea. News no longer gets through to him.

"Bizerta and Tunis have fallen!"

"What's that you say?"

He put his hands to his head in a gesture of uncontrolled horror, then stood up, walked a few paces and stopped:

"What will become of us?"

Poor Camil! He feels a diffuse fear—a real fear, but he's not quite sure of what. If he could stop everything as it is, so that the war continued and he kept his apartment and job, some money and personal security, he would be a happy man.

I am afraid of a possible anti-Semitic campaign and wonder whether Goebbels's article was not a signal.

We Romanian Jews, I heard, have been told to come up with four billion lei. How can that much be found? If it can't, what might happen next?

Lunch at Mogoșoaia with Antoine, Elisabeth, and the Basdevants (the first time I have met them for some three years). It's impossible to establish a relationship with Martha Bibescu. I don't really want it, but since we talk to each other I'd like to be able to get some communication going. I am terribly awkward and uninteresting in such surroundings.

Monday, 10 May

Three years ago! I'll never forget it.

In Tunisia things have been suddenly wound up. The fall of Bizerta and Tunis has broken the whole front. I'm still not quite sure how it happened.

I have translated A[ntoine] B[ibescu]'s *Quatuor* in two days, yesterday and today, dictating to a typist. It is very witty, but slight and unpolished.

Thursday, 13 May

The Africa campaign is over. The last German-Italian resistance in Tunisia ended yesterday. Capitulation. One chapter of the war comes to an end, after so many dramatic moments. In three years, how many times has one side or the other been inches away from victory or defeat?

What will happen next? This is the only question preoccupying us. Will the Allies attempt a landing? Is it not too difficult, too risky? Are they well enough prepared? And if they don't organize a landing now, will it not be too late next year? Will a year without major hostilities not give Germany the breathing space to escape its present crisis? It is only the middle of May. Ahead of us are four or five months in which anything is possible.

Yesterday evening I met the Havas Agency correspondent, Ypert, for dinner at the Bibescus. He is a right-wing Frenchman, anti-Gaullist (without saying so), and strongly anti-Semitic.

"Prince, aimez-vous les juifs?" he asked Antoine.

"Pas de gaffe!" A. broke in. *"Notre ami est juif."*[9]

A brief moment of stupefaction. For my part, I'd have preferred it if the guy had been allowed to speak.

Two hundred and fifty young Jews belonging to what are called "mobile detachments" were taken yesterday from their place of work. Within a few hours they had been formed into columns and sent off for labor in Transnistria.

Tuesday, 18 May

A long visit to Marie Ghiolu, who talked to me about Creața and how she died. She had many absorbing things to add to their story, which is already pretty strange. I'd like to note them down. Maybe tomorrow.

Two terrible dreams last night. In one I was with Hitler, who spoke Romanian and threatened me with dreadful things. In the other I was in Paris, the same German-occupied Paris of which I have dreamed a number of times. I felt horror, a choking sense of unease. Then I woke up terrified.

I regret that I can no longer remember the details.

---

9. "Prince, do you like the Jews?"—"Mind your manners! Our friend is a Jew."

Thursday, 20 May

Marie Ghiolu talked about Creața as if she were still alive. She tries to meet her, waits for her, would not be surprised if she were to come.

I have been thinking about the young Mrs. Grodeck. Unexpectedly, after such a long time, I found the whole story of the Grodecks still intact in my mind. Is it possible that I will one day write the play with Gunther? There was a time when the need to write it calmed me, gave me peace. Then I lost contact; I forgot it.

But the afternoon at Marie's has brought things back from oblivion. I think I could write it—in fact, I want to. This evening I reread some passages in *Accidentul* with Gunther, and they all seemed full of dramatic intensity.

How strange, how implausible is the story of Maria and Creața, living the same loves in turn, as Marie took relationships further than Creața could because of her physical disability (*"Elle pouvait à peine écarter les jambes"*[1]—Marie told me, to show that Creața probably never slept with Allan). But this story of theirs depended on the incredible physical similarity between them.

Zissu came yesterday morning to offer me seventy thousand lei, and to say how unhappy he had been a year and a half ago when he had been unable to meet my request for help.

I refused to take the money and told him that I didn't need anything. The man acts cheap theatre, and he does it badly. He claims to have ruined himself of his own free will, so as not to grow rich from oil under the Germans.

Thursday, 27 May

Had lunch at Alice's. Aristide is looking for some refuge in the countryside. Several people (Alice, Braniște . . .) have told him that we are approaching a crisis that could shatter the previous calm overnight. Nothing precise, but fears are secretly smoldering.

I don't know what to think, but the old anxiety suddenly gripped me.

The war is again in suspense. Nothing has happened since the winding up of the Tunisian front. We are at a crossroads—rather like the situa-

---

1. "She could hardly open her legs."

tion in Spring 1941, only in reverse. Then we were anxiously awaiting a German push in an unknown direction; now we await an Allied initiative. The Axis frankly admits that it is biding its time, and does not suggest that it might take any action. The Russians or the British will be left to take the offensive themselves.

The basic elements of the war have completely changed, but the danger weighing on us is no smaller—on the contrary, perhaps.

In one day, one hour, one second, it could be all over for us.

I have lived the last few days in a kind of mindless euphoria, making grotesque plans on the basis of nothing more than an opinion, a word, a smile. Simply because Marie Ghiolu told me on the phone that she had discussed my Shakespeare translations with the Swiss ambassador, I childishly constructed all kinds of plans (including a job at the Swiss legation!). But when I saw Marie today, she didn't remember any of it.

No one can do anything for me, nor can I do anything for anyone. Relationships with other people, unless based on definite interests, are merely incoherent gestures. We each live in our solitude, as in a glass cubicle. We can exchange smiles and greetings—that's all.

I turn for help to all my friends and acquaintances (the Bibescus, Nenișor, Alice, Marie Ghiolu, Sică, Leni and Froda, Devechi, Zissu), and in none of them do I find more than shadowy figures of varying indifference or amicability. And in this daily comedy, I am not a more interesting character than they.

Sunday, 30 May

I read *La Rabouilleuse* with passionate interest (which brings me to the end of the third volume of the Pléiade Balzac). Strange that it isn't considered one of his masterpieces. For everything in it is masterly: the construction, the range of methods, the characters, the atmosphere.

I wonder whether Dostoevsky's *The Devils* does not owe something to it. The group of *"chevaliers de la désoeuvrance"*[2]—veritable "devils," with Maxence Gilet at their head—resemble Stavrogin's people well enough to have been a starting point for them.

If I ever write anything about "Balzac's technique," I shall refer to *La Rabouilleuse* in particular, where the alternation of slow exposition and sudden quickening of the pace is so manifest.

2. Knights of idleness.

At a late hour I heard that Filderman[3] was deported this evening to Mogilev.

Wednesday, 2 June

What will June bring? Will the phase of preparation and transition in the war last much longer? We are going into summer and approaching what have each year seemed to me the "decisive months."

I met Dinu Noica yesterday. He is going to Berlin to give a lecture on "The Tension Within Romanian Culture." It seemed to me so grotesque that I couldn't stop myself from laughing.

Friday, 4 June

A brief call on Pippidi, whom I hadn't seen for several months. His little studio flat, so quiet and with so many books, is for me an image of peace.

I anxiously walk the streets looking in vain for ridiculous solutions (I have no money and don't know where to find any), when a life of study would calm me down and give me everything I want.

Spent the evening with Țuțea.[4] (I want to ask him something to do with "business.") He is an enjoyable character. The same volubility, the same amusingly arbitrary and unexpected formulations. He feels that his side has lost, so he takes refuge in metaphysics. "Europe is a pigsty. I feel disgusted with Europeans."

I have begun translating *Pride and Prejudice*. I am determined to work on it seriously and regularly.

Thursday, 10 June

Although I have worked between five and eight hours a day on the Jane Austen translation, it has gone incredibly slowly—not so much because of the difficulties of style (which are also unexpected) as because of the actual writing. With a typist I think I could triple my output. As it is, I

3. Wilhelm Filderman continued to be the de facto leader of the Romanian Jewish Community. He was deported to Transnistria because he constantly petitioned Antonescu, asking the Marshal not to deport his fellow Jews and opposed various anti-Semitic decrees and decisions.

4. Petre Țuțea: philosopher, ardent follower of the Iron Guard.

cannot do more than eight to twelve pages—which is much too little. I'd like to be able to deliver the manuscript at the end of the month, so that I have some money to pay the rent.

I don't know what I'm going to do. Again I have no money. Where can I find a hundred thousand lei to get me over this latest hurdle? Shall I ask Nenişor? Yes, I'll ask him, but without expecting anything.

Rosetti tells me I could sell my edition of Gide for a hundred thousand lei. If I find a buyer, I'll sell.

At the fronts the wait continues. You feel that major events will break out in a few days, or even a few hours.

Monday, 14 June

Pantelleria was occupied on Friday, Lampedusa on Saturday. The Sicilian Channel is completely free. One has a feeling that the coming operations will also take place there, in the central Mediterranean. But, of course, other possibilities remain open—including, we shouldn't forget, the possibility that nothing will happen. There could also be a kind of premeditated armistice, in which both sides mount a constant watch for an attack that threatens at any moment.

Wednesday, 16 June

Yesterday and today were the first hot days of summer. It is stifling indoors and exhausting in the street. I would like to be somewhere naked at the seaside or in the mountains, on sand or grass. Here I lead the life of a grub.

I keep on mechanically translating Jane Austen, but without a lot of headway. When you are doing something clear and definite, your limitations weigh heavily and depress you. You can do only so much.

How much easier, and more intoxicating, it is to think and dream!

I have no difficulty with Jane Austen's vocabulary. I open the dictionary once in twenty pages. But there are big problems with the syntax. Some sentences are so old-fashioned (how Jewish![5]) that I have to rebuild them from scratch. I won't finish it before the 10th or 15th of July. So long as all this work is not in vain!

5. In English in the original.

I have drawn twenty thousand from school for my July and August salary. A few days' respite are enough for me to lose my anxiety about this. And yet, what am I going to do?

The war is at a standstill.

Monday, 21 June

Tonight marks two years of war in Russia.

We have counted the days, the weeks, the months—now we are starting to count the years.

It is surprising that we are still alive—but I am too tired even to feel surprise.

Thursday, 1 July

June passed without any major developments in the war. After a landing seemed about to happen any day (I bet on the 20th and lost), it is starting to become not problematic but in any event less urgent. "Before the autumn leaves fall," Churchill said yesterday. That could mean either tomorrow or the 15th of September.

The fact is that once the Germans stop attacking in the east, one of the aims of a landing has been achieved. The problem of relieving the Russians of excessive German pressure is no longer acutely posed.

Undoubtedly the war now looks completely different; the initiative has passed to the Allies, at least in the present phase. Waiting and nervous tension have passed over to the Axis camp. The bombing in Germany and Italy is wreaking ever greater destruction. British losses in the sea war have declined considerably. But this does not mean that a new German push (whether in the air, underwater, or on land) can be ruled out. Maybe the balance has not stopped tipping; maybe the scales of victory have not fallen for the last time.

Some five days ago I stopped work on Jane to do a quick translation of Scribe's *Paharul de apă* [The Water Glass] for Sică. If this brings me in thirty thousand lei (not cashed yet), it will slightly relieve my serious money problems. I still haven't paid the rent. I have borrowed twenty thousand from Zaharia for daily expenses. On Saturday all we had left in the whole house was sixty lei.

Antoine was driving me mad with two or three letters and wires a day (asking me to go to Corcova), and in the end I was forced to write back that I can't go anywhere for the moment because of major financial problems that have to be resolved. He answered me today: *"Les em-bêtements d'argent n'ont rien de déshonorant."*[6] A consolation, at last!

I am back with Jane, but it is going terribly slowly. I have translated only a little more than half—which means that I couldn't finish it before the 20th or 25th of July. It also tires me too much (eyes and head), and I don't even know whether I'll get any money for all this work, and if so, how much.

I have read Monzie's[7] journal for the years 1938–1940 (*Ci-devant*)—at first with disgust, then with interest in spite of everything. I now understand better the collapse of France. With every day that passed, it was sliding politically and morally into a stupid and comfortable death agony, without realizing the huge historical stakes.

Monzie's ridiculously smug sense that he "was right," amid the most grotesque blindness, knows no bounds.

As I read him I also realized once more that political attitudes make up a complex system from which there is no escape. *Tout se tient.*[8] In 1938 Monzie is pro-Munich. So by 1940 he is inevitably an anti-Semite.

Some ten days ago I read Balzac's *La muse du département*. It is a second-rate novel, but it sometimes displays ingenious technique and is a pleasure to read, especially for its behind-the-scenes picture of Parisian literary life.

How much I would once have enjoyed writing a book about Balzac!

Yesterday evening I dined alone with Mouton[9] at the Institute. Long discussions in connection with his book about Proust, which he has given me in manuscript.

In the afternoon I listened to the third act of *Pelléas*.

Wednesday, 7 July

For two days a great tank battle has been raging in the Kursk sector, on a wide front between Orel and Belgorod. I know only the reports based on German sources, and I cannot gauge either the scale or the significance of the battle. The official communiqué claims that when the Rus-

6. "Money troubles are no disgrace."
7. Anatole de Monzie: French politician, a Vichy supporter, and a former social-ist.
8. Everything hangs together.
9. Jean Mouton: director of the French Institute in Bucharest.

sians responded to a local offensive with powerful counterattacks, the German commander threw large reserves into the struggle. We have to wait for more details.

Is this the beginning of a wider German offensive? That's hard to believe, with the specter of a landing at their rear. Or is it just a limited action, designed to reduce the "Kursk salient" or to probe the Russian forces? Maybe. But even if the original purpose of the operation was limited, no one can say for sure that things will not develop further.

In any event, it is this summer's first real episode of war.

Sunday, 11 July

The Allies have landed in Sicily. They launched the attack yesterday at dawn. No geographical detail is yet available, but there seems to be major fighting in the southwest portion of the island. The battle of Orel-Belgorod remains violent and unclear. Some German progress.

Tuesday, 13 July

According to yesterday evening's Italian communiqué, the British and Americans have established Sicilian bridgeheads at Licata, Gela, Pachino, Syracuse, and Augusta, all on the southern or eastern coast.

Thursday, 15 July

From Licata to Augusta, the whole southeast corner of Sicily is in the hands of the British and Americans. A battle for Catania is taking place.

In Russia the offensive seems to have come to a halt, without any notable progress. The communiqué has returned to the vague tone it had before the attack was launched.

Lunch with Mouton—likable, timid, friendly. What I like about him is a kind of expression of humanity, a kind of capacity for emotion, which I can sense beneath his unexpected awkwardness.

I'm nearing the end of Jane. Another three or four days.

Saturday, 17 July

The Russians report that a few days ago they launched a major offensive to the north of Orel. The German commentaries admit this but try to play it down, suggesting that it is merely an attempted diversion to relieve the front at Belgorod. Nevertheless, yesterday evening's communiqué notes that at Belgorod (where the Germans are attacking) "combat activity has diminished," whereas at Orel there are "hard defensive struggles" and "hard and fluctuating struggles." It is the vocabulary of last winter.

Je fais semblant de vivre—mais je ne vis pas. Je traine.[1]

Mechanical gestures, monotonous habits, some simulated liveliness. Otherwise, a big void that is my life.

I am waiting for the war to end—and then? For what will I then wait?

I have seen a lot of people in the last few days. Maybe no one sees that among all these living people (with their tastes, interests, loves, and relationships), I am an absent person.

On Thursday at Mouton's, then at Marie Ghiolu's and in the evening at Mogoşoaia, then at Gruber's and this afternoon at Tina's—I have seen all kinds of people. Each had something, each is set on something, each pursues something. I walk among them as a shadow. I speak, see, listen, answer, wonder, agree—and beyond all this surface agitation, I always remain alone with my irrevocable fate.

Tuesday, 20 July

In Sicily the invasion is spreading quite rapidly. Agrigento was already taken on Saturday. The deep push to the center of the island has reached Caltagirone, and now Caltanissetta. Infiltration along the coasts is thus paired with breakthroughs in the center. Catania still seems to be resisting, though yesterday evening's Italian communiqué does not mention anywhere by name.

Rome was bombed yesterday for the first time. The pressure on Italy, both military and psychological, is being continually stepped up.

In Russia the communiqués speak of formidable operations on a thousand-kilometer front. In fact, the only really sensitive spot is still Orel, where the recent German communiqués invariably signal "heavy defensive fighting."

Yesterday morning I finished translating *Pride and Prejudice*. I have already delivered the manuscript, though there is still need of serious re-

---

1. "I pretend to be living—but I am not alive. I drag myself along."

vision, especially in the passages I dictated. I'll get an advance of fifty thousand lei, in two installments.

Now, in a great hurry, I have to touch up a melodrama for Sică. I fear this will delay my departure for Corcova by a few days, but it will ease my money problems.

Saturday, 24 July

Marsala, Trapani, and Palermo have fallen. The whole Sicilian front has been broken, with resistance continuing only in the northwest corner. Catania is still being firmly defended. Probably Messina will try to hold out as long as possible.

But Sicily seems an affair of minor importance now that the war in Russia is coming to a head. The Russian offensive is spreading to hitherto quiet regions: Izyum, Kuban, Lake Ladoga. The situation remains extremely tense at Orel.

The German communiqués give fantastic figures for the Russian losses—hundreds of tanks and aircraft destroyed every day—but no geographical precision. Instead they talk again of "war of movement," "mobile fighting," and "elastic defense"—formulas familiar from last winter.

Once again, events are proving mightier than our reasoning. I didn't believe in a Soviet summer offensive, and certainly not in one of such proportions.

Nevertheless, I don't at all feel that the final scene is upon us. Maybe one reason for this is that we are not as anxious as in the past (rightly or wrongly—who knows?).

Monday, 26 July

Mussolini has resigned. Badoglio is the new head of government. It is the hour of Pétain.

Thursday, 29 July

I am off to Corcova in an hour's time.

I wish I had had an hour's peace in the last few days to note here something of the turbulent emotion, restlessness, and nervous agitation through which I have passed.

The end of fascism is a dizzying turn of events, a bewildering moment in the great drama of the last ten years. It is as if the curtain had briefly fallen after an unexpected (though theoretically predictable) twist of the plot.

I haven't had time to write, and I won't do it now.

I have worked flat out the last few days to finish Sică's melodrama—which I eventually did last night at half past three. With the money I have collected (Ocneanu, Birlic, Nenişor), I have been able to solve all my immediate problems. So I am leaving for Corcova with my mind reasonably at rest over money. In September it will start all over again. I'm used to that.

The day before yesterday I was still not sure that it would be wise to leave town. I had a feeling that the fascist collapse might speed up the whole war (which will indeed happen) to such an extent that everything could change in five or six days. Now, however, I think there is still time to spend two, three, or four weeks in the country.

I shall see how things shape up, both internationally and in Corcova.

Monday, 6 September

I returned from Corcova on Friday night, 3 September, after thirty-seven days there. I exceeded all my deadlines: I hoped to spend two or three weeks there and didn't think it possible that I would stay for five. Their hospitality is both more attentive and more discreet than anything I have ever known before. It is an art, a profession, a vocation.

I didn't even keep the "English diary" of April. I don't know why, but I felt very tired nearly all the time. Probably my old physical exhaustion was deeply rooted and was taking its revenge.

On the other hand, I did write the first two acts of "Ursa Major"—Act One quite easily, Act Two with much greater difficulty, as I kept stopping and fell prey to doubts.

I followed the war better (at least five or six broadcasts a day) and with a shorter delay than I am used to here, but with less anxiety. When I left Bucharest I had the impression that everything was speeding up. It is true that there was no shortage of developments, but amid the avalanche of events and place names a certain slowing could be detected in broad outline. Our question is always: when? Well, it won't be today, and it won't be tomorrow. Maybe in three months or six, maybe in a year.

I still haven't seen everyone. I'm not yet back in circulation in Bucharest. After I've "got back in touch" with everyone, I'll try to calm down and work. I should at least finish "Ursa Major" before too long.

Wednesday, 8 September

Italy has surrendered!

I was at the Athénée Palace. I heard the news at seven o'clock from Antoine Bibescu, who had happened to pick it up on the radio.

In the lobby I watched the news travel like an electric current from person to person. Antoine had no patience. He wanted to shout it out loud. Then an Italian officer suddenly walked into the main lobby.

"*Siete italiano?*" Antoine called out to him.

I gulped as the man approached our table.

"*Si, io sono italiano.*"

"*Monsieur, vous n'êtes plus en guerre. Votre pays a fait la paix.*"[2]

Saturday, 11 September

In Italy the situation following surrender is confused. The Germans occupy towns and regions in the north and are the masters of Rome, with the Vatican under their protection. How? When? No one quite knows.

Meanwhile the British and Americans have slowly occupied Taranto and landed near Naples. Italian forces have disintegrated and abandoned everything to the Germans or the British, whichever arrive first.

Where is the king? Where is Badoglio? Where is Mussolini? General bewilderment and breakdown.

On the Russian front the Germans have lost Mariapol after Taganrog, and almost entirely withdrawn from the Donbas. The war of elastic retreat continues right across the front, from Bryansk to the Sea of Azov.

Monday, 13 September

SS parachute troops have kidnapped Mussolini and "freed" him. It was a spectacular *coup de théâtre*, but it hasn't changed anything essential.

Fighting is continuing in southern Italy. Badoglio's capitulation took the Italian armies out of play (they were effectively paralyzed anyway), but the conquest of Italy is an objective that the Allies will only now begin to achieve, probably slowly and with difficulty.

---

2. "Are you Italian?"—"Yes, I am Italian."—"Sir, you are no longer at war. Your country has made peace."

Thursday, 16 September

Heavy fighting at Salerno, where American troops met stiff resistance when they came ashore. Yesterday and the day before, the DNB press was jubilant. Big headlines announced "a new Dunkirk," "a new Waterloo." What a great catastrophe! What a great disaster!

Today the tone is more subdued, the attitude more prudent. Montgomery is advancing from the south. If he meets up with the Americans, the situation will be consolidated.

In Russia a DNB dispatch yesterday reported the evacuation of Bryansk. The news has not appeared in the official communiqués. The offensive continues in every area affected. Kiev is becoming a possible objective.

Yesterday I read Balzac's *La vieille fille*; splendidly incisive. As a provincial portrait it perhaps stands alongside *Pierrette*, though it caricatures the oppressiveness of life in a way that somewhat detracts from the tragedy of the story.

Friday, 17 September

I have been home for a fortnight and still have not managed to return to a normal life, to organize a work schedule of writing and reading. I live haphazardly, go out too much, pay visits to people, accept invitations, walk in the street, allow all kinds of trifles to pull me here and there.

I haven't found an hour of solitude to collect myself and work out a clear picture.

What I lack most is a place of my own. Two and a half years have passed since I left Calea Victoriei, but I still keep thinking about it.

On the evening before I left Corcova, I went for a last walk alone in the vineyards and forest that was perhaps the most troubling hour I spent there. I felt the shiver of autumn coming from afar through the grass and trees, approaching and traversing me. It was a painful and nameless melancholy, which I had never felt anywhere before, because I had never looked autumn in the face as I did there.

Saturday, 18 September

Yesterday evening's German communiqué speaks of "a broad correction of the front" in Russia, in the south and center, and reports the evacuation of Bryansk and Novorossiisk.

In Italy the Allies have gone on the attack again at Salerno, which seemed for a moment to be slipping out of their grasp.

The war is everywhere in a phase of large-scale movement. It is a question not only of the front lines but above all of profound dislocations that are probably occurring (even if we do not see them) in the whole structure of the conflict. Somewhere beyond the speeches and the dispatches, great events needed in the coming period are struggling to be born; they may take a while longer to appear, but they may also burst forth from one day to the next.

In this time of unease, with its barely disguised anxieties, our own fate hangs by an invisible thread on some incident that we cannot foresee.

Thursday, 23 September

Poltava has fallen, and Melitopol is about to fall as well. Everywhere the Germans are hastening to the Dnieper. All the DNB dispatches call it a methodical retreat (and it is true that the Russians never mention a large number of prisoners), but the official communiqués, including the one this evening, keep referring to "powerful Soviet attacks," "growing intensity," and "heavy fighting." We still don't know the general significance of the operations, but the war has rarely—perhaps never—been through such a dramatic phase.

The day before yesterday, Camil and Rosetti saw gloomy prospects ahead—bombing, destruction, collapse—if the war gets closer and actually comes to Romania.

My own great worry relates to the domestic situation. If the Germans are capable, this autumn or winter, of mounting a desperate action that places their own frontiers in question, they won't hesitate to lay Romania waste. The closer the front comes, the more likely they are to brush Antonescu aside and take over the country themselves "to cover their backs," perhaps making use of a Legionary government hastily assembled for the purpose. The blow in Denmark can be repeated at any time. And the experience with Badoglio will not make them likely to exercise caution.

Who knows if the blow is not already being prepared somewhere in the shadows?

The fact is that I know nothing. But sometimes I suddenly feel a kind of anxiety—an anxiety that has never really left me throughout the war. From time to time, however, it nods off and leaves me in peace, so that I can forget it for a while.

Sunday, 26 September

Yesterday the Germans pulled out of Smolensk, after holding it for two years. If you think back to the dramatic battle of September 1941, you get a sense of the ground that has been covered since then.

The Bibescus have returned to Corcova, after three weeks at the Athénée Palace during which I spent a lot of time with them (lunches, dinners, correspondence, explanations). They were extremely nice to me at Corcova, but in the end they become tiring. I had some tense moments with them, once even a quarrel that seemed to me irrevocable. I realize that he is, if not mad, then at least "loony," and that nothing lasting can be built with such a person.

But he is still one of the most interesting people I have known.

I begin teaching tomorrow. At the same time I'd like to start a regular work schedule again.

Saturday, 2 October

Too much time-wasting, too much disorder in my life. I fall into the habit of doing meaningless things. I let myself be dragged along by petty obligations, which I accept out of carelessness, politeness, or indifference.

If I had a place of my own, I would probably lead a more orderly existence. But in any event I shouldn't make my fragmented life worse by being reckless or thoughtless.

For some three days I have been translating a play by Achard (*Je ne vous aime pas*). I don't know what Birlic will do with it, but he has paid me, and this will give me some material security for another three weeks or so.

The war goes on: quite slow in the case of Italy (Naples was occupied by the Allies yesterday); more lively, and sometimes more intense, in the case of Russia, so that you have to wonder whether major events are not in store for the autumn.

What is called "the Battle of the Dnieper" is in full swing. If the Germans can halt the Russian advance here and organize a relatively firm defensive line, then their deep retreat—though still representing a battle lost—will not be a disaster and the war will enter a new period of waiting. But if the Dnieper does not become the front line, if the Russians (who already have a few bridgeheads on the right bank) manage to press even farther, then everything is possible.

Rains could slow the advance and mire the whole war for a few weeks, but there is no sign of any. It is a warm, clear, sometimes torrid autumn, with afternoons as in July, even if the mornings and nights are cooler.

I am still worried about our fate. I keep fearing that the Germans will do something on their own authority to restore the faltering political morale throughout the southeast. A sudden pogrom is still a possibility.

Monday, 4 October

Yesterday evening I read *The Merchant of Venice*, and today *As You Like It*. I have returned to Shakespeare after a break of nearly a year. It has been enthralling: there is nothing lighter, more graceful, more enchanting. Even in *The Merchant of Venice*, the figure of Shylock is overshadowed by the glorious game with the handkerchief. And *As You Like It* takes you right into fairyland. There is something dancelike in a Shakespeare comedy. Floating movements detached from reality—as in a ballet.

The Jews in Denmark are being annihilated. A DNB dispatch leaves no doubt about their fate.

And once again I shudder.

"For sufferance is the badge of all our tribe," says Shylock.

Tuesday, 5 October

It seems that the German front is holding on the Dnieper, and that the Russian offensive is losing momentum. The DNB press speaks of the "Melitopol dam," "the natural barrier of the great river," "solid defense" from new positions.

The major battles have been scaled down to "local fighting." If the Soviet summer offensive really is over, then the pause on the eastern front will take the war out of its dramatic phase and—for one, two, or three months or more—remove that decisive aspect it has seemed to have since the 25th of July.

Should we be preparing for another hibernation?

I have to translate *Melo* for the Baraşeum. It will give me no pleasure at all. Anonymity enables me to translate anything without scruples for Sică. I'd like to have nothing to do with the Baraşeum and not to sign anything—even a translation—for the duration of the war.

Monday, 11 October

Saturday was Yom Kippur.

I do not try to put any order into my "Judaism." I fasted, and I went to the synagogue in the evening to hear the sound of the shofar. Reading over someone's shoulder, I tried to intone the "Avinu-malkenu."[3]

Why? Do I believe? Do I want to believe?

No, not even that. But it is as if, in all these unthinking gestures, there is a need for warmth and peace.

On Thursday evening I listened to Camil's play at Rebreanu's.

I hesitated a lot before going—and later I was furious with myself for having gone. I shouldn't have done it.

It's better to wait until the war is over before meeting Rebreanu. Now I have nothing to say to him—especially in his home.

It is a weakness, an act of carelessness on my part, which already holds out the prospect of forgetting everything, of compromising on everything.

Will I go back to those people? Will the war have come and gone without breaking anything, without inserting anything irrevocable or irreducible between my life "before" and my life "tomorrow"?

So why? What is the point?

In Russia the new Russian offensive has resumed right across the front after a pause of three to four days. Moreover, a new area of operations has opened northeast of Vitebsk, where Nevel has already fallen.

The DNB propaganda, which had focused on solid defense and the halting of the Soviet offensive, is going through some difficult moments.

Autumn is more and more in the air, however. (Yesterday was very cold, and this morning could have been November.) Maybe a pause will nevertheless develop sooner or later.

But things are dragging on too much for the state of our nerves.

Tuesday, 12 October

Cold, windy, autumnal.

A warm, cozy house in which I can read and write beside a woman I love—an unrealizable dream after which I have always hankered, especially on days like today.

---

3. "Our Father, Our King"—the first words of the Hebrew litany for the days of repentance.

A long meal just with Branişte, from lunchtime until seven somewhere on the Şosea. He drinks slowly and methodically, like a man on a long journey. Conversation about war and peace, but still basically café chatter.

Friday, 15 October

The Russians have retaken Zaporozhye. How will the southern front now hold? Hasn't Melitopol been left somewhat in the air? We shall see in the next few days.

It is by no means certain that the Dnieper will form a solid line of resistance. The Russians claim that the so-called "Battle of the Dnieper" is over and that "the river has been crossed at all points." The German attitude on this matter is vague, euphemistic, and insecure.

Tuesday, 19 October

The situation on the German front at the Dnieper seems more and more serious. A breakthrough at Kremenchug is on the point of cutting the whole bend of the river, in a great encircling movement similar to last year's at Stalingrad. The whole of the southern front is tottering. The offensive is almost equally powerful at other points, especially at Kiev and Gomel. For several days the DNB communiqués and commentaries have afforded some glimpse of the seriousness of the situation.

There is great concern in town. The dragon's breath can almost be felt, though it is still far away.

Basdevant (whom I visited yesterday with Antoine) thinks the Russians will be here this winter!!

This morning I finished translating *Melo*. Bernstein's technique infuriates me. It is so self-confident that it can simulate anything: even emotion, even depth, even gravity.

But there is something profoundly trivial, I would even say obscene, in this falsely noble play.

What a professional, though! What theatrical virtuosity! What a rogue! As I translated him, I saw more closely how the machinery works, but even I was tricked here and there by the dramatic pretense!

I have been reading *Coriolanus* with some irritation. (I think I'll finish Act Five tonight.) I can well understand now why it aroused such fury in Paris in 1934.

Friday, 22 October

Major battles in Russia. The breakthrough at Kremenchug is growing deeper. Another breakthrough has been announced at Chernigov.

It is not to be expected that the whole operation will suddenly reach a climax. The "new phase" (which, this time, really is new) could last two or three months before all its consequences appear. Last year the breakthrough on the Don began in December, but Stalingrad fell only in February.

The turnaround could be more dramatic at the level of politics and diplomacy. Anything can happen—at any time.

Onicescu (so Devechi tells me) has made up his mind to commit suicide if Germany loses the war. He cannot resign himself to living in a Europe occupied by the descendants of Australian convicts and American emigrants, come back to destroy Western culture. He cannot accept the annihilation of culture.

I asked Devechi to tell him on my behalf (I'd gladly tell him myself if I met him) that if culture is the issue at stake, he missed the right moment to commit suicide. It would have been much more appropriate on 31 January 1933 or 8 September 1940.[4]

Balmuş (a professor of Greek at Iaşi) told me once again—as Oţetea did last year—how the Jews were butchered there on 29 June 1941. "It was," he said, "the most bestial day in human history."

Saturday, 23 October

"Greater optimism in Berlin," reported the *Universul* correspondent today.

All the commentaries are again much chirpier. "Soviet attacks driven off." "Great defensive success." "In the last twenty-four hours the enemy has not advanced one kilometer."

The German communiqué is more hesitant, more circumspect. It signals "heavy attacks," "an attempted breakthrough," "heavy fighting," "temporary breakthroughs"—all repelled, crushed, or annihilated.

As I have no information other than what I read in the papers, I can only conclude that there has been a temporary weakening of the offensive, but that its scale and directions, if not its intensity, remain the same

---

4. Hitler took power on 31 January 1933, and Antonescu on 6, not 8, September 1940.

as before. "Relative stabilization" is one commentator's cautious expression.

I finished *Titus Andronicus* yesterday evening. In Shakespeare, if not in the whole of world literature, dreadful acts keep piling up in the most absurd way. At times it is almost coarse and puerile, when it can no longer be tragic: hands and limbs cut off, heads severed, people falling dead in almost every scene. A Chamber of Horrors museum, with everything jumbled together. Beneath or above all this bloody machinery, however, the thrill of poetry can sometimes transfigure everything it touches. Now I am reading *Antony and Cleopatra* (with language difficulties that surprise me, because the last three plays have gone easily enough).

Monday, 25 October

The situation again seems tense at the fronts in Russia. Melitopol fell yesterday, after days on end of bitter street-fighting. You look at the map—and you no longer see what might happen in the Sea of Azov sector.

On the other hand, the breakthrough at Kremenchug has penetrated almost as far as Krivoi Rog. Finally, yesterday evening's German communiqué has reported that Dnepropetrovsk is under attack on all sides.

An Indian summer, implausibly warm and clear, has made it possible for the whole operation to continue. A great encirclement, a major new retreat, or an energetic attempt to defend by counterattack: I try to visualize these three scenarios by looking at the map. The last of them is improbable, while the first two open the way to all manner of possibilities, including the most extreme.

Tuesday, 26 October

Dnepropetrovsk seems to have already fallen yesterday, as the German communiqué reported this evening.

Yesterday and today I have read *Le cabinet des antiques*, a lively short novel, fast-moving, ironical, and robust. It is Balzac at his best: concise in exposition, firm in design. The first part of the story still has a certain slowness—but the ending (with the delightful travesty of the Duchess of Maufrigneuse) feels like an excellent third act in a perfectly constructed comedy. The portrait of judicial life in the provinces is as accurate and as funny as that of ecclesiastical life in *Le Curé de Tours*.

Friday, 29 October

The breakthrough to the west of Melitopol is driving deeper. The Crimea is in danger of being cut off at the Perekop Isthmus. This is precisely why the Germans are trying to repel the attack on Krivoi Rog. If the front crumbles here too, the whole of the "Nogaic steppe" will be encircled.

The situation remains very grave, but I still cannot believe it will lead to a rapid ending.

Monday, 1 November

A cold November, but clear and sunny. Odd, unusual weather that defies the forecasters and the war. The fighting in Russia is continuing "with undiminished force," as the communiqué invariably puts it.

The breach in the Nogaic steppe is moving ever deeper toward Perekop. At Krivoi Rog, however, the Germans report powerful counterattacks.

I am still on Shakespeare. Finished *Antony and Cleopatra*. Yesterday and today I read *Othello*. This evening, the first act of *Lear*.

Theatrically speaking, *Antony and Cleopatra* is disjointed, fragmented, lacking in dramatic coherence. Some beautiful scenes and passages, especially in Act Five.

But *Othello* struck me as a work of unexpected beauty (perhaps heightened by the pleasure of being able to read it almost without a dictionary).

Lear begins in a grand manner.

I shall again be paid quite well for teaching at Onescu—and it is an opportunity to organize my material for a book on Shakespeare that I may write sometime. (Sometime!! When? In another life?)

Wednesday, 3 November

Since yesterday the Russians report having occupied and moved beyond Perekop. The German communiqué reports this evening "heavy fighting" at "the northern gateway to the Caucasus," having yesterday reported a landing in the region of Kerch.

Will the results of the Moscow Conference give the war a different direction? Should we expect another blow to be struck this autumn?

Saturday, 6 November

This evening's German communiqué reports the evacuation of Kiev "to avoid a breakthrough that was threatening to occur." The Russians have retaken the city two years after losing it. The Kerch landing seems to have established a "bridgehead." Now that the Crimea is under attack from both Perekop and Kerch, how will the Germans be able to hold on there? For how long?

The Nogaic steppe seems to be completely clear of Germans. The immediate point of attack for the Soviets is now Kherson.

The Russian offensive is continuing right across the front, with changes in intensity and violence at one point or another.

None of the propaganda formulas holds any more. No explanation stands up. The distances grow shorter each day; the obstacles fall one after the other.

Marietta Sadova never stops play-acting, as I saw when I visited her yesterday. (I need some books in connection with Shakespeare, and I thought I could get some from her—but I gave up.) I found her with the same gestures, the tears and faintness and changes in her voice, which have always made her a sublime Marietta. It's unbearable, but also funny.

I spent a couple of hours in a tavern yesterday with Cicerone Theodorescu, who was pleasant and honest as always.

We read and work, see people, listen to music, make plans, but beyond all that there is the shadow of the disasters that might yet come.

Wednesday, 10 November

I began my course on Shakespeare today at the college. An uninspired lecture—though I had good material.

In the last few days I have read *Lear* and *Macbeth*.

The war is continuing in all the areas of offensive action. The critical points are now west of Kiev and west of Nevel.

Hitler's speech of the day before yesterday *"fait bonne mine à mauvais jeu."*[5] I think it restored morale a little, even among people here, for a few days or hours at least. Even the most recent military communiqués have been less somber.

I am worried that my money is again running out.

5. "Puts on a brave face in adversity."

Sunday, 14 November

The Russians have taken Zhitomir. Their breakthrough is becoming so deep that it threatens to drive a complete wedge between the northern and southern fronts.

On the map it strikes you how short is the distance between Zhitomir and Cernăuți, between Kherson and the Dniester.

Igiroşeanu—I met him at lunch at the Bibescus', who are back in Bucharest—is terrified by the approach of the Russians; he said that the Germans have not lost the war and will not lose it. They are in a period of crisis, but they will pull through it. With the new weapons they are developing (an invisible airplane, a self-propelled projectile, etc.), they will destroy London in the spring and force Britain out of the war; they will also annihilate the Russians. All this he said with a mournful air (*"vous savez, moi j'ai toujours été pour les Anglais"*[6]), but also with a show of knowledge and "objectivity."

I spent the evening with Titel Comarnescu, first at the Gieseking concert, then at the Bavaria. He is completely distraught: the Russians will be here in two months, he says, and we will all perish wholesale, Jews and Romanians alike.

Wednesday, 17 November

Yesterday was wonderful: warm, sunny, with a soft April light in which everything stood out. It was incredible. Today is also fine but more "normal," less springlike.

Yesterday afternoon I went to Dragoş Protopescu's opening lecture—furious with myself for going, but having no other choice. (I want him at all costs to authorize me to read some works about Shakespeare in the faculty library.)

It was a "Nae Ionescu" type of lecture without Nae's magnetism; a funny, couldn't-care-less lecture in the Bucharest style. How easy that is!

What I want to note here is something quite different. He spoke of the "English genius" and said things that seemed wildly courageous in today's conditions: on "the British moral genius," on the Englishman as "the highest form of human evolution," on "the stupid prejudice about British perfidy or hypocrisy," when in reality the British spirit is an alloy

6. "You know, I have always been for the British."

of realistic common sense. He even spoke of Britain's military genius. And he went so far as to describe Churchill as a model of political courage. It was "subversive" from the first word to the last.

I thought there was a basic lack of seriousness in the fact that such a lecture is possible today, in November 1943, when Romania is in the middle of a war alongside Germany. It might have been a grave incident, but it wasn't. It had no significance, no consequence. A Legionary praises the spirit of England to an audience of students—who are themselves Legionaries, actually or potentially—but this means nothing to them. They feel no need to reexamine or abandon anything, or to stand up to anything that is said.

Yesterday evening I went with the Bibescus to *The Marriage of Figaro*. It was miserably performed, but I still listened to it with boundless pleasure. What riches, what youthfulness, what wonderful facility. Dozens of musical themes and ideas liberally tossed off, each of which could have been the starting point for a concerto, symphony, or quartet.

The front-page headline in this morning's *Universul*: "The German Military Command Again Controls the Initiative in the East."

Saturday, 20 November

The Germans have retaken Zhitomir. The Russians have been in Korosten for a couple of days, but it is too advanced after the fall of Zhitomir.

Friday, 26 November

I have been ill for several days, without knowing what is wrong. I am not ill in the true sense: I don't have a fever or any aches and pains, but I feel completely drained of energy. Yesterday evening I wanted to write a few lines here, but I couldn't hold the pen in my hand. I am just about all right in the morning (now, for example, as I prepare to leave for school at nine o'clock, I still have the strength to scribble these few words), but by evening I am dropping from fatigue. It is a real "crisis," all the more unwelcome as it finds me penniless. I haven't been so hard up since June, and I don't know what to do about it.

In Russia (judging by the German communiqué) the fighting remains intense but stationary.

However strange it may be, with its various bulges that do not look tenable, the southern front continues to hold. Things have been at a visible standstill for the last ten to fifteen days.

The German riposte at Zhitomir seems to have larger objectives. The papers are starting to talk of Kiev—an operation that would be similar to the retaking of Kharkov this spring.

Anyway, the war goes on. Nothing new has happened that might speed things up. On the contrary, a general slowing of the momentum is returning us to our old moral inertia.

To-morrow and to-morrow and to-morrow.[7]

Sunday, 28 November

Gomel was captured by the Russians on Thursday.

In the Zhitomir sector, the German communiqué has not mentioned for a couple of days the great counterattack that was supposed to retake Kiev.

Berlin has been heavily bombed in a series of air raids.

But the war is still the same: long, drab, oppressive. And our question is still the same: When will it end?

Sunday, 5 December

An exhausting week, with all manner of lunches and dinners. But with the Bibescus gone this morning, I can return to my customary life outside the social round.

Nothing new at the fronts. The Germans have retaken Korosten, the Russians continue their attacks almost everywhere; in Italy, Montgomery has reopened the offensive. But despite all these developments, we are in a period of relative quiet, perhaps because of the weather (implausibly clear and sunny), perhaps also for certain political reasons that we cannot know.

The British-American-Russian-Chinese-Turkish conferences, in Egypt and Iran, may lead to something.

---

7. In English in the original.

Monday, 6 December

Today I passed the final proofs of *Pride and Prejudice*. I'd be surprised if it had a big success in Romanian. It is too delicate, refined, subtle; no crudeness, no stabs of pathos, no wrenching. I am not at all happy with my translation, which lacks fluency. But will it bring me in some money?

I have recently listened a number of times to Mozart's concerto in E-flat major, which I gave as a present to Leni some four or five years ago. I asked her to let me have it for a few days, and I have been listening to it with real enchantment. I force myself to follow it phrase by phrase, sound by sound. I try to identify and hold on to each instrument. It is an infinite joy in the fast movements—but what sadness, what melancholy, what heartbreak in the andantino!

Wednesday, 8 December

A grave letter from Poldy, who is very ill and needs to have two operations. He was in a concentration camp for three months in 1941 and came out with his health ruined.

"*J'ai eu faim, horriblement faim,*"[8] he tells me. And I knew nothing of it. I still know nothing. Suddenly the war has again become the appalling nightmare that I have recently been so thoughtless as to forget.

Saturday, 11 December

The headline in an evening paper: "Twelve Thousand Arrests in France."[9]

My thoughts went straight to Poldy. I talk, laugh, walk in the street, read, and write—but I never stop thinking of him.

This journal is becoming absurd—a bad habit, nothing more.

The war pierces me through, pierces my whole life, everything I love, believe, and try to hope. And of this whole grinding torment, what should I record here?

8. "I was hungry, terribly hungry."
9. The reference is to the roundup of Jews in France.

Tuesday, 14 December

Yesterday evening I unexpectedly found myself reading "Ursa Major" for Nora Piacentini and Șeptilici. (I went to see them at the theatre, and they took me to their place upstairs.)

They were immediately very enthusiastic about it and decided to put it on straightaway, even though they had already started rehearsals of Michel Duran's *Barbara*.

Today things happened with a speed that has swept away all my doubts and hesitations. From eleven this morning until four this afternoon, Mircea and I dictated simultaneously to three typists. At 4:30 the manuscript was delivered to the theatre. A quarter of an hour later, Soare (already introduced to the plot) presented the play on behalf of a teacher who wants to remain anonymous—and signed it Victor Mincu. The title: *Steaua fără nume* [The Star Without a Name]. (Personally, I regret the loss of "Ursa Major"—but in their view it sounded too literary.)

I waited for Nora and Mircea in a café, and at 6:45 they arrived aglow from the "rapturous excitement" it had aroused at the reading before the board.

Everyone is intrigued and happy about it. The first rehearsal will take place tomorrow. Soare told me over the phone:

"It's a masterpiece."

That's all very well, but Act Three hasn't been written. When will I do it? It is urgent—but I don't have an hour to spare between school and college. Nevertheless I must try at all costs to finish it off, working day and night.

If this venture makes me some money, the rest is unimportant.

Tuesday, 21 December

Today I finished Act Three of "Ursa Major." I wrote it quickly, from Friday night until midday today, hurriedly, a little mechanically, almost without pausing to read back over it. Last night, "doped" on black coffee, I worked until four in the morning. It's not my favorite way of working. I can't produce anything good "under the whip." I need more freedom to move, more time for reflection. I think there are some excellent things in the act, but I know that I haven't given my all. Maybe I'll come back to it later. The ending does not satisfy me.

But I don't take this whole business too seriously. For a few moments—a few hours, perhaps—I was in a state of some tension. The casting annoyed me. I was depressed that Maria Mohor had the female lead (for whom I felt a kind of tenderness). The various echoes it has produced both amuse and irritate me. Victor Ion Papa calls it the best Romanian comedy, and Soare a masterpiece; Marcel Anghelescu is angry that he is not in Act Two and so does not want to appear in Act Three either; Nora wants an ending for herself, etc., etc.[1] It's time I said to all this nonsense: *merde*![2] Badly acted or well acted, praised or abused—the only thing I ask of this play is that it should bring me in 500,000 lei.

I think and hope that I'm serious enough for all the rest to be completely and utterly indifferent.

Wednesday, 29 December

A dream on Monday night.

I'm at the University. I meet Onicescu in a corridor. He is leaving for Berlin—and tells me to leave with him. A moment later I am in a small room, at Nae Ionescu's seminar. Here he comes. He asks me the time and notes my answer on a piece of paper. Then he asks the same question to the other students in turn, noting each reply under a special heading. The times given are not the same. Then Nae asks each of us to determine the right time—and gets us to sign our names. He turns to me and tells me that I speak with a Jewish accent. But immediately after that, he puts his hand on mine and adds that he is leaving on Saturday evening for Berlin.

Thursday, 30 December

"The town of Korosten has been abandoned after heavy fighting"—says this evening's German communiqué.

Recently I haven't noted anything in connection with the war. But some ten days ago, after a period when things had remained fairly stationary, the Russian offensive resumed with maximum intensity, at least in the Vitebsk and Zhitomir sectors.

Since the Cairo and Tehran conferences, things seem to have again entered an acute phase. Berlin has suffered a series of devastating air raids. In the North Atlantic a German ship of the line, the *Scharnhorst*, was sunk three days ago. Everywhere, in both the Allied and the German camps, it is thought that a landing in the west is now imminent.

1. The premiere of *Ursa Mare*, renamed *Steaua fără nume*, took place on 1 March 1944.
2. Shit!

Just by reading the papers—because I have no opportunity and make no effort to listen to the radio—I gain the impression of a final stiffening of positions.

I can't believe, however, that an offensive will begin in the west in the middle of winter. The Allies are exerting great psychological pressure on Germany, which is probably needed to prepare the blow at a later date.

Friday, 31 December

Certain gestures and habits, by force of repetition, have become almost like superstitions: a letter to Poldy, a book for Aristide, some records for Leni. I went to Socec to buy a calendar refill. This evening I shall go for a meal at Alice's. I have hastily reread this notebook.

The 31st of December. Like a year ago, or two years, or three years. When did this year pass? It seemed so heavy, so foggy, so uncertain. And yet it went. It has passed and we are still alive.

But the war is still here beside us, with us, in us. Closer to the end, but for that very reason more dramatic.

Any personal balance sheet gets lost in the shadow of war. Its terrible presence is the first reality. Then somewhere far away, forgotten by us, are we ourselves, with our faded, diminished, lethargic life, as we wait to emerge from sleep and start living again.

1944

Saturday, 8 April 1944

Four days after the bombing, the city is still in the grip of madness. The alarm of the first moments (no one quite knew what was happening, no one could believe it . . .) has turned into panic. Everyone is fleeing, or wants to flee. The streets are full of trucks and carts carrying all kinds of jumble, as if everyone were moving house in one vast tragicomedy.

Today a few streetcars started to run here and there, but most of the lines are still blocked. Half the city is without electricity. There is no water supply. The radiators do not work. Flocks of women and children come with buckets from various wells and fountains, where long queues have formed.

In an hour (and I don't think the actual bombing lasted more than an hour), a city with a million inhabitants was paralyzed in its most vital functions.

The number of dead is not known. The most contradictory figures are bandied about. A few hundred? A few thousand? The day before yesterday Rosetti said 4,200—but that isn't certain either.

Yesterday afternoon I went to the Grivița district. From the railway station to Bulevardul Basarab, not a single house was untouched. It is a harrowing sight. Dead bodies were still being dug up, and groans could still be heard beneath the ruins. On one street corner a group of three women, pulling their hair and tearing their clothes, let out piercing wails over a carbonized corpse that had just been taken from the debris. It had rained a little in the morning, and a smell of mud, soot, and burnt wood floated over the whole neighborhood.

It was an appalling, nightmarish vision. Being unable to pass beyond Basarab, I returned home with a feeling of revulsion, horror, and impotence.

Five years ago, when I was doing military service at Mogoşoaia, I passed every morning and evening through that station district. I avidly read the morning paper on the way out, and the evening paper on the way back, anxiously following the press dispatches. I knew that war was pressing down upon us. I knew that our fate was at stake in those dispatches, as we set off for the training fields, and the fate too of the shopkeepers noisily opening their shutters, and of all the people hurrying on foot to the market, the station, or the railway yards. But no one imagined the grim scene that would appear on a chilly spring day five years later, when the smoke of fire and massacre would hang over ruined houses.

And none of us could do anything about it, either then or now.

It is strange that while the bombing was going on, I did not at all feel that it was serious. At first I thought it was an exercise (there had been one three hours earlier). And when the thundering sounds began, I thought it was the ack-ack. There were a couple of more powerful convulsions, but they did not seem to come from bombs.

When I went into the yard, I saw many sheets of colored paper floating about (propaganda material, probably), and I thought that that was all the aircraft had dropped. The first rumors from town (a bomb on Brezoianu, another on Strada Carol) sounded like concoctions.

When I went toward the center, a strange nervous agitation animated the streets—more like curiosity than terror. Only later did we realize the scale of the destruction.

Leni's house is completely wrecked. I went there the day before yesterday to help her rummage for anything that could be saved from the rubble.[1]

Mary, the young manicurist who used to come every Friday morning, was killed. She was so young, so sweet, so honest—a shopgirl, but as graceful as a child, as sensible as a young lady at a boarding school.

When, among the thousands of anonymous dead, you come across a face you know, a smile you have seen before, death becomes terribly concrete.

Aristide, Rosetti, Camil, and Vişoianu have fled the city, each to where he was able. No one is left except us, for whom any thought of leaving is ruled out.

The consternation caused by Tuesday's bombing will gradually pass, but anxiety about a future one will remain. When will it come? What will it be like? In which district? Will we escape? Who will escape?

---

1. The Allies heavily bombed Bucharest and the Ploieşti oil fields.

Nor is it just a question of physical survival. There is also the misery that follows, and all the dangers involved in a general atmosphere of despair, fury, and hatred.

For the moment there are no signs of an anti-Semitic crisis. But one is possible at any time.

Sunday, 16 April

The second bombing came yesterday morning, between twelve and one. It struck me as much worse than the previous one. Fortunately I was at home and could calm Mama a little; she had a fit of weeping. At least once, the noise of the explosion was so loud that I felt everything was happening in our neighborhood. The aircraft always seemed to be passing over our heads. We waited tensely: now . . . now . . . now . . .

The city center looks appalling. Bulevardul Elisabeta from Brezoianu to Rosetti, and Calea Victoriei from the post office to Regală, are blocked. Most of the bombs fell here and in nearby streets. What were they aiming at? I don't know. Maybe the telephone exchange. But in that case the bombing was very inaccurate. The block containing Cartea Românească was destroyed; the University and the School of Architecture set on fire; many other buildings hit. Yesterday evening the flames could be seen from a long way off. I don't know if there were casualties and, if so, how many.

I keep thinking of Poldy. When we hear from him, everything will be easier to bear. But until then, all kinds of thoughts will beset me.

Spring! Full of anxieties, full of uncertainties. Somewhere, far away, muted hopes.

I am too alone. Old, sad, and alone.

But I forbid myself to sink into a crisis of personal despair. I have no right. *Il faut tenir le coup.*[2]

I am reading Balzac, the only thing of which I feel capable at present. I couldn't work. I have reread with disgust one of my plays ("Alexander the Great"). I didn't realize it was quite that bad. Inexorable.

I have reread with great interest *Illusions perdues (Les deux poètes, Un grand homme de province à Paris, Les Souffrances de l'inventeur)*. Yesterday and today, *Ferragus*. I have now begun *La Duchesse de Langeais*.

---

2. You have to hold out.

Tuesday, 18 April

This morning's air-raid warning caught me at the *liceu*. As soon as the "pre-alarm" sounded, I went into the street and started running home. The main square had a cinematic aspect: a scene of crowd panic, with hundreds of people running aimlessly like drunken ants.

I stopped for a moment at the corner of Strada 11 Junie, just as the siren was sounding. I went into a trench but soon came out again. What was the point? I kept heading for home, to be with Mama as quickly as possible. The streets had emptied, but there were still a few people passing by. No one forced us to move on. The terrible silence of a deserted city.

On Sunday morning they were over Braşov and Turnu Severin. And today?

No news from Poldy. I wait anxiously.

Still reading Balzac. Yesterday I finished *La Duchesse de Langeais*. (It's not the masterpiece that Antoine Bibescu suggested.) I know immeasurably better things in Balzac, even among the minor works. *La vieille fille*, for instance—not to speak of *Pierrette*.)

I read today *La fille aux yeux d'or.*

Yesterday I happened to open a volume of Baudelaire. I was struck by the affinity between his Paris and a certain image of Paris in Balzac: a dirty, fetid, gloomy city, a (scarcely theatrical) mixture of splendor and misery, a Paris I used to consider distinctively Baudelairean and that I am now getting to know better and better in Balzac.

As soon as I hear good news from Poldy, I'll try to work. A play ("Freedom") or even the novel.

Saturday, 22 April

Yesterday morning, at the fateful hour of twelve, there was another air raid—the third. I still don't know which part of town was hit. There's nothing in the center. It must have been in the outskirts—Pipera, Ford, Malaxa. Anyway, this time we don't hear any echoes of a great disaster.

This morning at eleven a rumor started, from somewhere, that there was an alert. The shops closed and people rushed home.

In the evening there has been the growing impression of a deserted city. A vague anxiety is floating in the air. You feel as if you are suffocating.

Balzac, still Balzac. I have read *Birotteau* and *La Maison Nucingen*, and begun *Splendeurs et misères des courtisanes*, where the rediscovery of Vautrin heightens the curious interest.

Tuesday, 25 April

The bombing yesterday morning was the longest and probably the worst up to now. There was no trace of it in the center, at least, where every-thing—water, electricity, streetcars—seemed to be working normally. But they say the railway line was blown up at the Chitila marshaling yard, and that the Filantropa district was badly hit. Several young Jews from a civil defense detachment died in a trench shelter. Things also seem to have been very serious at Ploieşti.

I had lunch with Ginel Bălan,[3] who told me of a "historic" conversation he had a year ago with Mircea Vulcănescu. The finance minister sug-gested to Bălan that he should assume the financial management of Transnistria, a kind of vice governorship. When Bălan rejected the offer, Vulcănescu took him aside and tried to change his mind: "This is a unique opportunity for our imperial ambitions. Transnistria means the first ex-perience of colonization in Romanian history. By planting forests in the whole of Transnistria, we'll be able to stop the icy north wind ever blow-ing on us again."

Sunday, 30 April

It has been raining for three days or so. It's a kind of anti-aircraft de-fense: we feel more sheltered beneath it. Anyway, there haven't been any more alerts.

No recent news from Poldy. A letter reached us today—but dated the 8th of March.

Finished volume five of the Pléiade Balzac. Begun volume six.

Nothing new at the fronts.

Thursday, 4 May

Last night there was bombing between one and two—the first night raid.
    I didn't go into town at all today, and I don't know what happened.

3. Eugen Bălan: journalist.

The bombing seems to have been more or less random, without precise targets. (Strada Izvor, Bulevardul Mărăşeşti, Strada Mecet—why those?) Renée Presianu was killed along with her entire family. The poor girl!

I suddenly feel in greater danger than ever. Organized bombing with reasonably precise targets is something against which you feel you can protect yourself. But no precautions are of any use against blind chance.

Sunday, 7 May

The whole city smells of lilies and smoke. Spring burst out magnificently after a week of rain, but thick clouds of smoke hang above the city from the bombing of last night and this morning. In sixty hours there have been five alerts and two bombing raids. We are having one disaster after another. On Friday, one alert in the morning and another in the evening. The same on Saturday. This evening we are waiting to see what will happen.

Last night, stray bombs also fell on our part of town—Sfîntii Apostoli, Bateriilor—but the real destruction was a long way off, around the station, around Buzeşti, around Bonaparte and Ştefan cel Mare. Apparently, whole streets are ablaze there.

Water, electricity, and telephones are out of order in at least half the city. (We still have water and electricity.) The streetcar service has again been suspended. I went into town for a while, but the main streets were deserted.

I would like to know that there is some purpose behind all this, that it is leading somewhere, that the suffering is not completely pointless.

Monday, 8 May

Bombing last night for the third time in twenty-four hours—brief but powerful. For a few hours it seemed that the bomb we heard falling was for us: a long high-pitched whistling, as of a rocket at a fireworks display, heralded the strike. We closed our eyes—and waited.

Today it seemed like Sunday in town: closed shops, empty streets, people waiting around the shelters.

It is one in the morning. Maybe they won't come tonight. I'd like to sleep. I'm beginning to feel exasperated, to think of leaving Bucharest. The shelter does not inspire any confidence; people died last night in almost every part of town.

Wednesday, 10 May

Thousands of people started leaving town at daybreak today. For two
days the rumor had been spreading by word of mouth that, according
to Radio London, Bucharest would be destroyed on the 10th of May. It
was an idiotic idea, which people believed with superstitious terror.

But it has been peaceful—at least so far, as I write these lines after
midnight.

Thursday, 11 May

Scarcely had I written the previous lines when the air-raid warning started.
We heard no explosions from anywhere, but we were kept in the shelter until the "all clear" sounded at two. I cannot take this sinister game
as calmly as I did at first. I have nervous shudders that I scarcely manage to control.

Am I too about to fall into panic? I have no right. I must hold on—
at least for Mama, if for no one else.

Vague thoughts about leaving town (everyone is leaving . . .) have troubled me for the last couple of days.

Today I saw Romulus Dianu[4] (how naive I am!) and asked him to put
in a word for me at the Ministry of the Interior. His refusal was cold,
evasive, and formal. The guy is extremely reserved, with something lizard-
like in his sleek gestures.

But this has cured me of such attempts. We'll stay where we are—
and may God watch over us.

Nora and Mircea have left. I rang them a few times today, but there was
no answer. I feel more alone than ever—a poor bachelor who clings to
his friends and tends to make a habit of them.

This afternoon I walked through town feeling weighed down by loneliness. There is no one with whom I can talk, no cinema that I can enter.
(Most of them are shut, and the rest show only the worst old leftovers,
as in a provincial town.)

I am still reading Balzac. He can be depressing at times, with his meticulous ferocity and a relentless sense of doom. *Cousine Bette* and *Cousin
Pons*—gloomy masterpieces in which "the triumph of evil" is implacably

---

4. A writer whom Sebastian had known since they had worked together on the literary journal edited by Camil Petrescu.

organized. I read them in a childlike manner, with compassion and rebellion in my heart. There is also a desperate platitude about the milieu
in which they are set; abject little furies (Bette, Mme. Matiffat, La Cibot,
Fraisier); no one has the Mephistophelean grandeur of Vautrin.

I still have some writer's tics. The idea of one day writing a book about
Balzac has remained from my previous existence. But what is the point
of such a project amid today's collapse? When, how, and with what shall
I be able to rebuild a life for myself?

Sebastopol has fallen—a couple of days ago. The war in the east will
move on from the standstill of the last month or more. Apart from the
bombing, everything has been frozen at the fronts.

Monday, 15 May

Five days without an air-raid alert, eight days without any bombing. We
don't know how long this will last, but it has given us a respite to do
something about our shattered nerves.

If it were not ridiculous to make any political judgment about the bombing, I would say that the pause is likely to continue for the time being—
so long as the Anglo-American offensive in Italy (which began three days
ago) is at its height. They have to concentrate their aircraft there at least
until they break the German lines—and it would be illogical to shift them
to other targets.

It would be "illogical." Yet nothing is logical in this war, at least for
us who lack hard information and have to judge on the basis of fragmented signs and appearances.

Did I not explain to Alice Theodorian, on the evening of 3 May, that
the British and Americans wouldn't start bombing Romania again until
the Russians launched a new offensive in Bessarabia and Moldavia? My
reasoning was perfectly logical. Yet two hours later we were all in the
cellars and the first British night bombs were pattering over most of the
city.

Tuesday, 23 May

Some rather old but reassuring letters from Poldy (late March/early
April).

I had been growing desperate, tormented by the most terrible
thoughts.

How he has suffered in his loneliness!

Still quiet. Ploieşti has been bombed (on Wednesday afternoon, I think), but nothing here in Bucharest.

The hysteria of "heightened alert," of warnings and pre-warnings, has calmed down. The city seems to be growing more lively again.

But how long will the pause last?

The offensive in Italy is continuing. All quiet on the other fronts. In fact the aerial pressure in the west seems to be slackening. The invasion fever has noticeably declined.

Finished Volume VI of the Pléiade Balzac. Begun Volume VII.

Wednesday, 31 May

An alert this morning. Air raids on Ploieşti and Braşov.

The fighting in Italy remains intense—but this does not stop the British and Americans from pummeling us too. Well, anyway, we have had three weeks' grace.

In my view, as soon as something new happens at the fronts (the fall of Rome, an invasion, a Russian offensive), we'll see another round of bombings here, perhaps worse than the last. I am thinking of leaving then—but will it be possible?

I am translating *Vient de paraître* for Sică. He has a season at the Studio and wants to open it in a few days' time with *Steaua fără nume*. But I don't think he'll actually manage it by then.

The war is here, even if it sometimes leaves us in peace for a few days.

Monday, 5 June

Rome has been occupied by the Allies.

The news thrills us less today, nine months after the Italian armistice, but it is still a splendid twist of fate!

We are too tired to rejoice. We need an end to the war, not intermediate victories.

I had a conversation with Şeicaru[5] on Friday evening at *Curentul*. He is a swine of a man. I feel disgusted that I talked to him at all.

All quiet on our air front. Four weeks without a raid on Bucharest. How much longer will it last?

5. Pamfil Şeicaru: owner and director of *Curentul*, a daily newspaper.

I translated Bourdet's *Vient de paraître* for Sică in four days.

I might leave tomorrow with Aristide for three or four days in Butimanu.

Tuesday, 6 June

The Allies are landing in France, on the Normandy coast. The invasion has begun. Eisenhower has made a declaration to the peoples of Europe. Churchill says that four thousand large ships and eleven thousand aircraft are taking part in the operation.

Saturday, 10 June

I returned yesterday from Butimanu, where I spent three days with Alice and Aristide. Nothing pleasant, apart from a visit for lunch to the home of Mrs. Culag at Bujoreanca (a splendid mansion, with a veranda straight out of Sadoveanu). The idyll of country life has too many drawbacks, what with the fleas, the dust, and so on. But the fields are beautiful everywhere. I could lie in the grass and never leave. I long for the mountains. I long for the sea. I long even for Corcova.

All the time I was in the country I was restless and impatient to know how the invasion was going. We had newspapers, but they were not enough.

Now that I am back and up with the news, I realize that since the first breathtaking moments, the rest has been proceeding at a slower pace. The crucial fact is that the landing has taken place, that the Allied divisions have a foothold on the continent. So the "Atlantic wall" was not an impassable barrier, nor did the "secret weapons" sort everything out.

Sunday, 11 June

An alert yesterday, another one this morning. Distant thunder. The dull sound of aircraft passing overhead without dropping any bombs. Yesterday, it seems, there were machine-gun attacks on cars, carts, and people on foot in the vicinity of Bucharest.

It's strange that they have time for raids on Romania when they are so busy in Italy and France.

Tuesday, 20 June

In Normandy, after marking time for a while, the Allies have cut across the Cotentin and are approaching Cherbourg.

The offensive is continuing in Italy, with Perugia on the point of falling.

In Finland the Soviet offensive launched a week ago directly threatens Vyborg.

And yet the whole DNB press has been jubilant for the past three days. Triumphant shouts, sensational banner headlines, as in the headiest moments of German victory. What's going on? The secret weapon has been unveiled! A pilotless aircraft! A mysterious rocket. *Wunderwaffe.* Hell's hound! London ablaze! Millions in England flee in panic! London destroyed! London evacuated!

I had lunch with Camil at the Continental. At the next table were Onicescu, Crainic, Dragoș Protopopescu, Ivașcu—all four beaming with joy.

"At last!" Onicescu exclaimed.

"But it's not enough," Crainic added. "Washington must be hit—Washington!"

A boy passed by with the afternoon papers. Onicescu opened one and read it aloud as the others expressed their amazement and enthusiasm.

In the end, people always see what their point of view allows them to see.

The facts are the same for Onicescu and for myself. We read the same papers and know the same things, but everything is fundamentally different for him and for me, as if we lived on two different planets.

Good Lord, can human intelligence really be such a ridiculous instrument? Is Onicescu an imbecile? In the two years since I saw him last, waiting at a table at the Capșa for Rommel to enter Alexandria, the war has changed in the most radical way. Yet the facts pass him by and leave him with exactly the same smile, the same unshaken assurance. A fixed idea signals a closed universe.

Tuesday, 27 June

The Allies took Cherbourg yesterday. The DNB press spells out how Montgomery's plans have failed. He had wanted at all costs to capture the port in two days—and it took him twenty. Moreover the town is completely destroyed and does not represent any real gain.

In Finland, after the fall of Vyborg, the Russians are advancing in two directions.

In Russia, on the central front, a major Soviet offensive was launched on the symbolically important 22nd of June. Vitebsk has already fallen.

It is a sharp moment for the whole evolution of the war. July and August may bring things to a head, but in any event we have a sense that there is no longer room for pauses.

Things are quiet here for the moment. There were air-raid alerts on Friday and Saturday morning (bombers over Ploieşti), but nothing fell on the capital.

I have finished Volume VII of the Pléiade Balzac—*Les chouans*—a laborious but interesting read. (The action takes place in Normandy, more or less in the zone of the landings.) Now I have started Volume VIII. I am reading *Les paysans*, especially for the light it throws on the origins of Balzac's political attitudes. He is a reactionary without being hypocritical about it. But the novelist is stronger than, and cancels out, the doctrinaire. I'd like to write about this—and much else besides.

Zissu's wife is a strange woman. She came here in a cab to collect me, and I couldn't get away from her. Yesterday, another walk on the Şosea.

She lets her imagination run wild, eagerly trying to be interesting. She puts on the most absurd acts, for no other reason than to arouse other people's curiosity. On Saturday she told me that Nae Ionescu once asked for her hand in marriage. And yesterday—I shudder to think of it!—she confessed that she had last year, and still has, a strong *"béguin"*[6] for me. If I had wanted and understood, if I now wanted and understood . . .

I did all I could to wriggle out of it. She is crazy and lies deliberately, setting up emotional scenes and then acting them out. A real case, that's for sure.

Wednesday, 28 June

There was an air raid this morning. I don't yet know what it was like elsewhere, but it was pretty serious in our part of the city. A bomb in Strada Apolodor, one in Bateriilor, one in Iuliu Roşca. The arsenal is on fire. Thick smoke drifts over the houses. There is a clinking of broken glass all over the neighborhood, and glass fragments and dust lie in the streets. In the shelter I felt at least once that danger was close, when the blast from an explosion hit the walls. A cloud of dust and smoke fol-

6. Amorous crush.

lowed, even though it had been quite a long way off. How strange the "all clear" then sounds! All clear for whom? For us who emerge safe and in one piece? Or for the others?

A day like any other continues amid the corpses and fires.

Monday, 3 July

Air raids last night and this morning. It seems that Malaxa and Distribuție were the hardest hit. Nothing in the city center, which looks its normal self. But all day thick clouds of smoke have been floating across.

Tuesday, 4 July

It was a quiet night, but the sirens sounded again in the morning. Distant rumbling and the noise of engines.

In Russia there has been a major breakthrough in the center and a rush of unclear movements. Vitebsk, Orsha, Mogilev, and Bobruisk have fallen one after the other. Yesterday Minsk. Today Polotsk.

In Normandy things have not moved much since the fall of Cherbourg.

Saturday, 8 July

I have finished *Les paysans* with some difficulty. The book's construction is obscure and unwieldy. A surfeit of characters clog up the action, without themselves being clearly individualized. You lose them along the way, unable to remember them. The preparation is meticulous, to the point of appearing forced, for a plot that is eventually resolved with fewer and much simpler elements. But it is an unfinished work—and I don't know what Balzac would have done in the end with all this material.

We have had four days of quiet. No alerts. The rainy weather gives us a little security.

I have translated a short play by Guitry for Birlic. The money from it will keep me afloat—we'll see how it goes later.

Fighting continues at the fronts, but with no great change.

Doubts sometimes creep in about whether it will all be over this year. Could it last another winter?

No, no. It's too early to draw conclusions. We are in the middle of the summer campaign; all outcomes are possible.

I am always alone: not desperate but not happy; rather lethargic and somnolent.

Monday, 24 July

An air raid last night at one. Again we were out of the habit. It lasted a short time but seemed to be intense.

Nothing looked different in town this morning. The bombs probably fell on the suburbs.

On Friday an attempt was made on Hitler's life at the German high command; it doesn't seem to have changed anything.

Somewhere in the background, the process of disintegration spreads like a cancer.

In Poland the Russians have occupied Lwow and Lublin.

Friday, 28 July

We're having another run of bad luck: an alert this morning; air raid last night; alerts both morning and evening the day before yesterday.

Last night's bombing was terrible. We felt all the while that waves of aircraft were heading for our neighborhood. The shaking was the kind of thing you feel in an earthquake. The walls rocked. A cloud of dust blew open the cellar door and brought with it a smell of burning.

When I left the shelter, huge flames could be seen near the Central Post Office and the Metropolitan Church. I walked through the streets with Benu, Mircea, and Nora. It seemed as if a fire in Şelari would engulf the whole city. White and yellow flames were bursting forth on all sides. Up the Dîmboviţa toward Calea Rahovei, a number of smaller fires marked out a large circle.

I haven't been into town today, but apparently all the fires have burnt themselves out and the disaster is not as we imagined it last night.

What is the point of these air raids? Are they the prelude to a Russian offensive? Are they an attempt to shift Romania from its alliance with the Germans, now that the front in Poland has collapsed and the internal German front is tottering?

You try to find a justification, a political rationale! Otherwise the bombing would be too much of a random affair.

Bialystok has fallen in Poland, as have Dvinock in Lithuania and Narva in Estonia.

At least in the center, the German resistance seems to have been pulverized. Warsaw is the main immediate objective.

Meanwhile, farther to the south, the fall of Stanislav[7] and the fighting around Kolomyya mean that the offensive may move down toward the Moldavian front.

In any event, it is hard to believe that the Romanian front, overtaken as it has been by events, will continue to remain stable.

Monday, 31 July

Another air raid this morning. It wasn't very long or particularly heavy, but the engines in the sky had a sinister sound. For a few moments I thought that Friday night's ferocious attack was going to be repeated.

If, as people have been saying for a few days, Turkey breaks off diplomatic relations with Germany (expected for the 2nd of August), the availability of closer bases could easily make the bombing catastrophic for us. The war seems to be approaching the end. It may all be over in ten weeks. The question is how we can survive these final weeks in one piece.

I spent the whole of yesterday at a farm not far from Bucharest, in an enchanting house like a stage set for *Jocul de-a vacanța*.

Thursday, 3 August

Turkey has broken off relations with Germany.

The president of Finland has resigned and been replaced by Mannerheim. This is interpreted as a prelude to fresh peace negotiations.

In France an American push toward Rennes threatens to isolate the whole of the Breton peninsula, in a repetition of the Cotentin operation.

In the east the Russians are simultaneously attacking Warsaw, Riga, and Memel. In Italy, Florence is still holding out, but not for much longer.

As the situation grows more acute, we become more and more impatient. Yesterday and today we were constantly overexcited, as if news of something definitive might arrive at any moment.

7. Former name of Ivano-Frankivsk.

Monday, 7 August

It is hard to follow what is happening in France. The German front, broken in both the west and the south, is crumbling away. In Brittany the "Atlantic wall" lies flat and useless. The Americans are inside Brest, Saint Nazaire, and Lauriau, while the respective German garrisons still hold the fortifications that were supposed to defend them from the sea. Armored thrusts crisscross the whole of the German rear, suddenly springing up where no one expects them. The operation is identical to the German advance in May 1940—only so far on a lesser scale. Paris is not excluded as an Allied objective: if things continue at this pace, anything is possible.

Tuesday, 8 August

I have written the scenario for a play. Act One: a perfect outline, scene by scene, with great wealth of material. Act Two: less detailed. Act Three: completely general, except for the denouement. For a moment this afternoon, working my thoughts out on paper as they jostled for my attention, I was in the grip of a kind of fever (my old fever that makes me a little dizzy when I "see" a book or a play). I felt impatient: I'd have liked to get straight down to work; I wanted to tell someone the great news.

I went out and walked as far as the Alhambra, where Nora and Mircea are doing rehearsals. (It was as if I needed to be in an atmosphere where everything was bubbling behind the scenes.) But I felt out of place and returned home.

Now I have calmed down. I have put the scenario aside and will leave it for a while. I have other work that needs to be done (redoing Antoine's play, rewriting Act Three for *Potopul*[8]). In a week's time I'll look again at the pages I wrote so hastily today and see what can be done.

If I write this play, I shall owe it to the idea of a stage set. That is all I saw at first: no characters, no conflict, no ideas—only the set of a house that is under construction in Act One, furnished in Act Two, and flattened by an earthquake in Act Three. All three phases of the set are dominated by a single sight in the distance, which serves to link and unify them.

Today all the living material of the play has grown up around this bare schema. A funny starting point.

---

8. *Potopul* [The Flood], a play by H. Berger.

Thursday, 10 August

Air raids last night and this morning. I don't think Bucharest was the main target, but at least once last night the gunfire was deafening. I swallowed. And poor Mama, who suffers like a frightened child!

Friday, 11 August

It seems that American armor has pushed as far as Chartres!

I see again that Sunday in October 1937, with Poldy and Benu at Chartres, when we were so excited by the beauty of the cathedral. Paris is not far.

Sunday, 13 August

Nothing new on the western front. The Russian offensive has come to a halt, more or less at the 1939 frontiers. Riga, Memel, Warsaw, and Krakow are still to be reached. Is this a Soviet pause to regroup? Or a German attempt to use massive reserves to stop the advance to the frontiers of the Reich? A new assault may begin at any time, but for the moment the fighting (though still intense) is not of the same proportions as before.

In France, on the other hand, the battle is confused but is expanding in scale. We know nothing definite about Chartres, nor how far the thrust from Le Mans to Paris has actually reached. Bypassing Alençon, it is aiming to strike the rear of the German front line in Caën—a sector that has been wobbly ever since the landings. If the operation succeeds, the invasion will become truly "invasive."

It is a hot, enervating summer's day. I am apathetic and cannot pull myself together enough to work. I have been redoing one of Antoine's plays, but I am stuck on Act Four and find it impossible to move ahead. I also have to finish Act Three of *Potopul* for Beate[9] and Finți.[1] All this has to be done double-quick, and I'm incapable of putting two words together.

Tuesday, 15 August

A Franco-Anglo-American landing in the south of France!

9. Beate Fredanov: actress.
1. Al. Finți: theatre producer.

Thursday, 17 August

Alerts this morning and evening. They surprised us because we had been expecting a period of aerial calm following the landing in southern France. They've got so much to do there—and they still find time for us.

The landing force is advancing smoothly and rapidly across the south of France: Cannes, Nice, Saint Maxime, Saint Tropez.

In the north the Allies have taken Orléans, Chartres, and Dreux. Paris is on the horizon!

Yesterday evening the Comoedia had *Steaua fără nume* "in a new production," as the poster put it.

I didn't go—nor do I feel at all curious about it.

Saturday, 19 August

I am writing these lines during a morning alert. Our run of bad luck continues. We also had an alert yesterday morning. From the street you could see swarms of aircraft passing in the distance, with their metallic glitter in the bright sunlight. Sometimes, when they show up against a whitish cloud, they become dull and hazy. Yesterday and today they have been to Ploieşti. Today they seem to be heading for Braşov. For the time being.

The advance on Paris continues, with the Americans already at Rambouillet. But the front is too fluid for the shape of the battle to be visible.

I saw *Steaua fără nume* yesterday evening.

What a splendid auditorium the Comoedia has! At the Alhambra everything gets lost, as in a huge barn. But here the whole hall is like a wonderful sound box.

A surprise: Tantzi Cocea.[2] She has quite a few false touches, but (though everything is rather "dreamed up") also a mixture of frivolity and emotion which is quite similar to my Mona's.

2. Actress.

Monday, 21 August

The Soviet offensive in Moldavia and Bessarabia has been under way for two days. Apparently Iaşi has fallen.

The war is coming toward us. It is not the war that has weighed us down for five years like a moral drama; now it is physical war. Great turnarounds can occur at any hour or minute. Again our lives are on the line.

Everything is possible—and nothing is easy. Military resistance (however quickly things are over) means destruction, perhaps forced evacuation, perhaps starvation. Capitulation means (who knows!) a repressive German response, in the style of northern Italy.

In both cases, moreover, a pogrom once more becomes possible at any time. Our relative quiet is now a thing of the past. We are moving toward the center of the fire.

In keeping with their familiar practice, the Russians are attacking in the south now that their offensive has slowed somewhat in the center and north. They will push here as strongly and as fast as they can. The Balkans are ripe for things to be wound up; all the pieces are in place. Turkey is ready. Bulgaria (after the amazing *coup de théâtre* of Bagrianov's speech[3]) is prepared for any change in the game. Together with Tito, and possibly also an Anglo-American landing (which is hardly necessary as things stand), the Russians can push the whole German front toward the Carpathians, Hungary, and Austria.

It cannot be expected that the Germans will rapidly pull back of their own accord. They will try to resist. I don't know how much longer they can keep it up, but it may be enough for them to exterminate us.

In France the Anglo-American assault is continuing in the south and the north. Everything is unclear in the south: there is no front as such; Anglo-American thrusts have made deep inroads, but it is not said exactly where. The Maquis is a real force, with Annecy and Grenoble apparently in French hands.

In Normandy the battle has shifted right over to the Seine in the east. Paris may fall within the next few hours.

---

3. Ivan Bagrianov: newly appointed Bulgarian prime minister. He moved Bulgaria from a pro-Nazi foreign policy to neutrality.

Tuesday, 22 August

Toulouse has been captured by French forces of the Maquis. Poldy may by now be a free man. But I still fear for him. I'm not sure how firmly the city can be held until Allied regular troops arrive.

Tuesday, 29 August

How shall I begin? Where shall I begin?

The Russians are in Bucharest.

Paris is free.

Our house in Strada Antim has been destroyed by bombs.

I am as tired as a dog. It is my lot not to be able fully to rejoice at the overwhelming events.

I am writing these lines in a house where some of us have managed to take shelter with whatever belongings we could save from Strada Antim. We have set up here as best we can— for how long, I don't know. The owners of the house could return at any moment and make us leave.

It would have been impossible to keep a regular journal of the events. It was all quite extraordinary—and then horrifying. Last Wednesday evening we started down an unlikely slope to we knew not where—either to salvation or to disaster.

That night from Wednesday to Thursday—which we spent with Pătrășcanu,[4] Belu,[5] and so many others in the house (the "historic house") on Strada Armenească, immediately after the coup d'état[6]—was a night of frenzy. All over the city, people shouted with delight. Antonescu had been overthrown in five minutes, the new government formed, and the armistice accepted. We hadn't had time to drink a glass of champagne to Paris (now back in French hands) when the true avalanche of events reached us.

All night I wrote for the edition of *România Liberă* that was due out at dawn. I was glad that events were making me a journalist on the very night of the victory.

4. Lucrețiu Pătrășcanu: Communist leader and minister of justice in the first post-Antonescu government. He was executed in 1954 after a post-Stalinist show trial.

5. Herbert ("Belu") Zilber: Communist publicist and friend of Sebastian's. He was condemned to prison during the Pătrășcanu trial.

6. The house in question was a headquarters of the conspiracy, involving Communists, National Peasants, Liberals, and forces close to King Michael, to overthrow the Antonescu regime and align Romania with the Allies. The formal proclamation of this "coup d'état" was made on 23 August.

In the morning I went to bed dead-tired and hoping to catch up on some sleep. But then the sirens began to wail: the Germans had launched a bombing attack on the city. We then had an unfamiliar kind of air raid, uninterrupted, with no alert or pre-alert, which kept us in our shelters for sixty hours until Saturday evening. And at the last hour, toward Saturday evening, our house was hit. We found ourselves victims just as we were about to cross the finish line. But we are alive.

How afraid we were on Thursday, Friday, and Saturday that the Germans might return to Bucharest, if only for an hour! A single hour would have been all they needed to exterminate us. Each one of us. No one would have escaped.

There are thousands of things to be said. Maybe tomorrow, or the day after tomorrow. Right now I don't feel capable. I want to sleep. From Wednesday until Saturday evening I didn't sleep a wink. From Wednesday until Monday I didn't take my shoes off once. From Wednesday until yesterday evening I didn't lie once on a bed. I only writhed about on the floor, wherever I could.

Wednesday, 30 August

I can't write today either. I am too tired, disfigured with tiredness. My poor stamina is not up to such trials. I'd have to sleep several days on end—to have a schoolboy's holiday—to recover from it all.

Everywhere there is a terrible (morally terrible) jostling, as people hurry to occupy positions, to assert claims, to establish rights.

I can't do it. It doesn't interest me. I don't want to know. The best thing is to wait. You can't speak now, only shout. It is true that for years I awaited the moment when I would finally be able to utter a cry of revenge—after so much nausea, so much disgust.

One day I'll write a book. That is still the best thing for me to do. I'm not a person for meetings and committees. Everyone is summoning me to one—at school, at college, at the writers' gatherings. What should I do there? What I have to say I'll say when the time comes. Certainly not today, when nothing can be heard above the shouting.

Thursday, 31 August

A parade of Soviet heavy tanks on Bulevardul Carol, beneath the windows of the house where we have taken refuge. It is an imposing sight.

Those tired, dusty, rather badly dressed men are conquering the world. *Ils ne payent pas d'apparence*[7]—but they are conquering the world.

Afterward a long column of trucks full of Romanian soldiers: former prisoners-of-war in Russia, now armed and equipped and fighting in the Red Army. They are young and happy, with excellent equipment. You can see they are not coming from battle. They are a parade unit, probably kept in waiting for the entry into Bucharest.

People in the street are still bewildered. Great explosions of enthusiasm, but also a certain reserve. Many passersby look askance at "the applauding yids."

Romania will regain its senses when the problem of responsibility is posed in earnest. Otherwise it would all be too cheap.

I myself am still unable to take a direct role in what is happening. To be a disaster victim is much graver than I used to think when I passed burnt-out houses and hurriedly glanced at them in sympathy.

A house is a factory. You find everything in its place, as you would a screw or a part of a machine. When this organization collapses, you are surrounded by chaos.

I don't know how, when, and where I'll be able to rebuild any kind of normal life, one that allows me to concern myself with other matters. For the time being, everything is in abeyance.

I am happy that my experience at *România Liberă* ended quickly, before I signed up for anything. I'd have found it impossible to work in that regime of secret committees. Indoctrinated stupidity is harder to take than the ordinary kind. Pătrășcanu attracted me for his human side. When we reached agreement about the paper four weeks ago, at Ulea's farm,[8] I can't say I didn't feel some regret that I would be returning to journalism. But I welcomed it insofar as it gave me an immediate way of saying aloud all the things I had kept silent about, gritting my teeth, for five long years.

In three days, after Graur and his crew pushed their way in,[9] I realized that I would be joining an editorial committee terrorized by conformism. No, no, it's better for me to write plays.

Then my house was bombed. I rang up to say what had happened, and haven't set foot there since. Later I informed them through Belu that I was pulling out for good.

7. They're not much to look at.
8. General Octavian Ulea: cousin of Pătrășcanu's, head of protocol at the Royal Palace, active participant in the 23 August coup.
9. Alexandru Graur: Jewish linguist.

Friday, 1 September

Bewilderment, fear, doubt. Russian soldiers who rape women (Dina Cocea told me yesterday). Soldiers who stop cars in the street, order the driver and passengers out, then get behind the wheel and disappear. Looted shops. This afternoon three of them burst into Zaharia's, rummaged through the strongbox, and made off with some watches. (Watches are the toys they like most.)

I can't treat all these incidents and accidents as too tragic. They strike me as normal—even just. It is not right that Romania should get off too lightly. In the end, this opulent, carefree, frivolous Bucharest is a provocation for an army coming from a country laid waste.

Toward evening an order printed in Russian and Romanian, on sheets of paper the size of a cinema program, imposed a nine o'clock curfew and instructed everyone to hand in their radios.

They seem like standard texts drawn up before the 23rd of August, which have not been revoked as a result of the new situation. Probably everything will be explained soon enough.

In the end, the Russians are within their rights. The locals are disgusting—Jews and Romanians alike. The press is nauseating: Mircea Damian, Cristobald, and so on.[1]

This morning I made the stupid mistake of going to Dorian's,[2] where I had been invited to a "writers' conference." I helplessly witnessed the constitution of "the Union of Jewish Writers," with Benador,[3] Călugăru,[4] and Dorian at its head. Unknown figures, nonentities—a mixture of desperate failure, thundering mediocrity, old ambitions and troubles, all drawing fresh life from impudence and ostentation.

I won't forgive my cowardice at not having shouted out all they deserved to hear. But that's the last time I let myself be caught in such snares.

Saturday, 2 September

Without a home, I feel things as provisional. It is as if I were in a strange city, on a platform between two trains.

---

1. Constantin Cristobald.
2. Emil Dorian.
3. Ury Benador.
4. Ion Călugăru.

I have no books and no working hours. I don't know where to find people who might interest me—and they certainly don't know how to find me.

I am exhausted and unoccupied.

I went to the cinema this afternoon. A Soviet film had been billed at the Scala, but there were no tickets for the four o'clock show. So I went to the Aro to see *Intermezzo* again after all these years, with Leslie Howard and Ingrid Bergman.

What a pleasure it was to hear and understand English; to see a film so technically subtle and accomplished. All the German and Italian wares were good for nothing. How human is Leslie Howard, how decent in his humanity!

On the way out I passed the Scala again and this time found rear balcony seats for Benu and myself at six o'clock.

The newsreel was fascinating. It showed a parade of German prisoners in Moscow. Huge columns of tired, dirty, shabby animals, with nothing recognizable from the sportily provocative elegance of the Hitlerite troops who paraded in Bucharest. Troglodyte faces, as if taken from anti-Semitic or anti-Bolshevik propaganda photos in *Das Reich*. How easy it is to turn a human face into an animal's! Those clean-shaven, well-dressed, bathed, groomed, and polished young men, who used to reside at the Ambassador Hotel, did perhaps sincerely believe that the Jews lying in mudheaps and pools of blood in Poland and Transnistria were a lower species of dog that anyone could shoot with impunity.

How stunned, how humble were the German generals in today's film, as they marched between bayonets at the head of the column!

In that one vengeful image you can see the reality of victory.

The main feature was a film with a war theme: naive, rather crude and childish. *Mais le coeur y est.*[5]

This morning I saw a small Soviet tank chasing a private car with intent.

The street incidents continue. Passersby are jostled until they hand over their watch. The watch seems to be the Russian soldier's *idée fixe*.

Yesterday's order appeared in all today's papers: a nine o'clock curfew; radios to be handed in. It's not a very clear sign of freedom—and people will find it hard to understand. But if it proves a lesson for Romanians, who spent four years pillaging the Jews, then it won't do any harm.

5. But it had heart.

Tuesday, 5 September

Still the same wearying impression that things are provisional. I am out and about all day—even I don't know why. I desperately rush around looking for somewhere to live, hesitating between all kinds of "solutions" that would not actually solve anything. Should I repair the apartment in Strada Antim? Should I wait for the Basdevants to leave, and take over theirs?

The complications will grow with each day that passes. For the moment I have some money, but its value is falling all the time. Inflation and devaluation will be catastrophic. With the ruble at one hundred lei, and with thousands of soldiers who buy anything (when they don't pillage) and pay any price, money no longer means anything.

If I had a house like everyone else, I would find the spectacle interesting. After all, hunger might not kill me. But with my present sense of living in the street, everything is becoming too uncertain.

Camil Petrescu, pale and scared, has naively fastened onto Belu and myself. I feel sorry for him. He is cracking up with fear. He would like to make some demonstration, justify and protect himself. Others, no less "fascist" than he, have the nerve to make a profession of democratism and intransigence. But poor Camil tries to exculpate himself. That is what he has always done—under Carol II, under the Legionaries, and under Antonescu.

I met Cocea by chance.

"You brought the Germans here," he shouted at me, "you *Cuvântul* people."

"No, it was you who worked with the Hitlerites," I replied in the same coin.

It had an impact. He was fuming, in quite a state. I may have made myself an enemy.

But I've had enough of that, for God's sake! Will I be "one of the *Cuvântul* people" till the end of my life?

I'd like to write my book about the war—fast, so as to get it off my chest and calm down.

Thursday, 7 September

It amuses me that one of the phrases I composed for the manifesto of the National-Democratic Bloc—"History makes no gifts"—is making a career for itself. When I wrote those four words I didn't know that I was giving birth to a historical judgment. The phrase has been taken up by Radio London. *Universul* has written a whole commentary under the same title. And yesterday I read in *Semnalul*: "History, a great Romanian statesman said recently, makes no gifts."

Friday, 8 September

Yesterday at the cinema, a film about the war in Ukraine. The horror exceeds everything. Words and gestures are no longer of any avail.

These Russian soldiers who walk the streets of Bucharest, with their childlike smile and their friendly churlishness, are real angels. How do they find the strength not to set everything on fire, not to kill and plunder, not to reduce to ashes this city that houses the mothers, wives, sisters, and lovers of those who killed, burned, and laid waste their country?

Only the total extermination of Germany could, in the ideal scales of justice, make up for all or at least part of what happened.

I had lunch with Carandino at the Capșa, where he had asked me to come and talk about "business."

He suggested I become editor of a paper he is planning to bring out with Zaharia Stancu, under their management. I told him that I don't do journalism. But why didn't I say how impudent the proposal seemed to me? What the hell! Is that my "value" as a writer? Maybe Carandino thinks it natural for him and Stancu to put me on their payroll? It's very disturbing.

I met Ion Barbu in the street. It was the first time we had greeted each other for six or seven years. For six or seven years he simply did not recognize me. But today he hurried over to me, opened his arms wide, and effusively held out his hand.

"You were right!" he shouted to Carandino and myself.

(That's all: "You were right!"—as if it were a game of chess or checkers in which he had made the wrong move.)

But he added with melancholy, with regret:

"The mistakes they made were too great. Hitler proved a dilettante. They shouldn't have left him in charge. If they hadn't removed Brauchtisch . . ."

Tuesday, 12 September

A letter from Titel Comarnescu:

"To Mr. Mihail Sebastian, writer and editor at the *Revista Fundațiilor Regale*,

"Dr. Octavian Neamțu and colleagues at the *R.F.R.* invite you to resume your post as editor at this review. Would you please come to the Foundations on Wednesday at 4 p.m. (Bd. Lascăr Catargi), where you will make contact with the management committee."

I haven't replied—but I don't think I'll accept. I have been in doubt all day. (*Mauvais signe!*)[6] I asked Belu, Aristide, and Zissu what they thought. (*Autre mauvais signe.*) If your mind is made up, you don't ask anyone else. Is it possible that I have the slightest hesitation? Isn't the disgust in me strong enough to stifle any remaining doubt?

I feel incapable of writing there again. It's dead, and that's how it should remain.

When I met Şerban Cioculescu by chance, he took from his pocket a memorandum signed by thirty members of the SSR, the Writers' Association; it calls for the holding of a general meeting to elect a new committee (democratic, of course) and to reintegrate Jewish writers.

I read the piece of paper and handed it back without a word. It doesn't interest me. Sincerely, without posturing or an ounce of exaggeration, it doesn't interest me. It was hard to explain this to Cioculescu, nor did I try. But as he insisted that I must come to the general meeting, I told him that I wouldn't be coming. Is it possible that he, who is neither a fool nor a complete lackey, cannot see how grotesque the whole situation is?

The new president of the SSR will be Victor Eftimiu. His name is everywhere: at the theatre, at the Writers' Association, at the association of property owners who have suffered war damage (where Paltin says that he gave a thundering speech on Sunday about the revolutionary spirit).

A salty detail. Cioculescu suggested to Eftimiu, the likely president, that the new committee of the SSR should include "from the Jewish writers, F. Aderca." To which Eftimiu replied: "But why? They should be pleased we're having them back."

A taste for pamphleteering alternates in me with a kind of helpless disgust. Sometimes I shudder with an urgent need to speak out against all the shameless posturing, against the whole farce being acted out around us. But then I remember that it doesn't concern me. What am I supposed to do in this great Balkan swamp?

Yesterday at Beate's I met two Soviet writers: Boris Epstein, a thirty-year-old captain and *Pravda* drama critic, and Yura (I don't remember

6. A bad sign!

his surname), a twenty-two-year-old sublieutenant and poet. Both are editors at a front-line paper. They moved on this morning.

Boris spoke German badly, Yura French badly. Both had an expression of humanity (a little melancholic in Boris, more youthful in Yura), which was impressive after the faces of Soviet soldiers in the street, *bons enfants*[7] but wild.

I saw Braniște on Sunday. He was reserved, discreet, buttoned up. No mention of our old vows to work together. Not a word about his plans for the future.

He is scared of the Russians, worried about the Communists. He strikes me as irredeemably the chief editor at *Adevărul* and *Dimineața*.

It is strange that I haven't noted anything for so long about the course of the war. I have no radio, I read the papers without attention, and above all I don't have a map. (All our maps were destroyed at Strada Antim.)

The war has interested me less since I felt the outcome was settled. The peace preoccupies me more. I think that Germany will be finished in six or seven weeks. I can't see it lasting beyond November.

But some think that the game is not yet over. Enescu[8] surprised me today when he said that all we risk by uncovering the *Steaua fără nume* mystery is execution if the Germans return to Bucharest.

"Do you think that's possible?" I laughed.

"I don't myself. But there is a lot of talk of a new German offensive, from Timișoara."

Nearly the whole of France has been liberated, half of Belgium, plus Luxembourg and the Netherlands. The Siegfried Line has been breached at numerous points. Aachen is within range of Allied machine guns. Can anyone really still imagine a "German offensive"?

Anything can be imagined in this big wide world.

We are always on the move. Today we left our temporary accommodation on Bulevardul Carol for another temporary accommodation in Strada Dmitrie Racoviță. I don't know when this "waiting room" life will be over and we will again have somewhere to call home.

I am still, above all, a war victim.

---

7. Good kids.
8. Ștefan Enescu: he signed as author Sebastian's play *Steaua fără nume* under the name of Ștefan Mincu so that it could be performed.

Saturday, 16 September

I am not willing to be disappointed. I don't accept that I have any such right. The Germans and Hitlerism have croaked. That's enough.

I always knew deep down that I'd happily have died to bring Germany's collapse a fraction of an inch closer. Germany has collapsed—and I am alive. What more can I ask? So many have died without seeing the beast perish with their own eyes! We who remain alive have had that immense good fortune.

And now? I don't know.

And now, life begins. A kind of life, which has to be lived. The only thing for which I longed was freedom. Not a new definition of freedom—but freedom. After so many years of terror, we don't need to have it explained to us what freedom is. We know what it is—and it cannot be replaced by any formula.

There are certainly miserable tricks, farces, impostures. There is Victor Eftimiu, with his impudence, his bad taste, his eternal vulgarity. There is young Macovescu,[9] who had a comfortable life under the Germans and is now a fierce Jacobin. There is Graur, obtuse, dismal, triumphant. There are thousands of incidents and happenings that offend you. There is a frightening spirit of conformism, new in its orientation but old in its psychological structure.

But over and above everything, there is the one redeeming truth: the Germans are done for.

Sunday, 17 September

I had lunch at Byck's with Belu, Rosetti, and Vişoianu. We waited for Vişoianu with lively interest, as he had just been to Moscow for three days as a member of the Armistice Commission.[1] Very interesting things, told by an intelligent, free-minded man without prejudices. I am too tired this evening, but I'll try to note something tomorrow.

9. George Macovescu: a middle-rank official in the Antonescu regime, later deputy minister of foreign affairs under Ceauşescu.
1. C. Vişoianu was a member of the Romanian delegation that negotiated the terms of the armistice with the Soviet Union.

Monday, 18 September

A lot of sadness in Russia—Vişoianu says. He didn't see anyone smiling in the street. But, as he himself added, there is a certain sadness in the big Slav cities. Moscow is sad, as Warsaw was too in peacetime.

The war in Russia really is total. You see very few men. Women have replaced them everywhere. Ugly, badly dressed women, naively eager to flirt (lipstick, clumsy and pretentious hairdos). Life is terribly hard (four or five people live in one room), and terribly expensive (130 rubles for a bar of soap). A mixture of arrogance and inferiority complex. They are aware of their great victories but at the same time fear they are not being shown sufficient respect. This upsets them.

The Romanian delegations were first summoned by Molotov at eleven in the evening. Then they were told to report an hour earlier: at ten o'clock. When they entered the Kremlin at ten sharp, a mighty can-nonade began. They asked what it was and were told they were salvos for the capture of Bucharest.

Then the door opened and they went into Molotov's office.

The discussions did not change a comma in the prepared text of the armistice agreement. The objections fell one after the other—there was no point. From time to time Molotov asked: What were you looking for in Stalingrad?

I didn't know that Vişoianu played such a major role in organizing the plot. On the night he left for Cairo, the King gave him his word that he would carry out the coup d'état as soon as he heard from Cairo that the time had arrived.

The amazing thing is that such an operation, prepared over a long period of time with emissaries and written correspondence, could take place right under the noses of Antonescu's people and Killinger.

Probably there was a kind of paralysis of will, a disappearance of self-protective reflexes, which usually sets in when a regime is on its last legs.

Wednesday, 20 September

Another long conversation with Vivi [Vişoianu], this time alone. He tells me that he doesn't dare express all the bitterness with which he has re-turned from Moscow.

He believes in freedom—but there is no freedom there. People are terribly afraid to speak their mind, to say clearly either yes or no. There can be no doubt that Romania must go along with the Soviets, but it is not easy to get through to them. People there hide away and cannot be found. The material and intellectual level is low. Great ignorance, and great poverty.

I tend to agree with Vişoianu—but then stop myself.

He is a Westerner, a man for whom comfort, well-being, good manners, and politeness are ingrained habits, necessities of life. But the regime in Russia is for workers and peasants, for people who are only now learning to write, to wash, to eat properly—tens of millions who are rising with difficulty toward an elementary level of civilization. It is a world without refinement. All the things that have been dear to me—discretion, moral elegance, irony, respect for ideas, an aesthetic sense of life— are impossible in such a world, which has to solve the immediate problems of hunger and cold.

We may be deceiving ourselves when we think that the broad masses share our same thirst for freedom. We need Montaigne's freedom: an intellectual freedom that defends its solitude. Peasants and workers—the "crowd"—have simpler and more powerful demands.

Yesterday evening there was a Soviet music-hall show (*estradă*, the Russians call it) at the Alhambra. It was a wretched front-line troupe, with a ham-handed pianist, two Circassian fairground dancers, a couple of athletic dancers, an awkward young actor (who recited Pushkin, immediately followed by some anecdotal verse), and finally a comic actress who spoke in monologues. Nor should I forget a tenor in a brand-new tuxedo, which he had probably bought off the rack in Bucharest and wore with a touching lack of grace.

It was all quite wretched, but not without a certain warmth. I still can't help feeling that there is something miraculous in the presence of these troops, so candid in their wildness. There is also something dreamlike in it. Around me were soldiers and officers with all kinds of faces (a Mongol, a Tatar, a Jewish major with a wonderfully kind expression, a nearsighted young soldier looking somehow melancholy behind his glasses). I laughed with them. I applauded with them.

Tuesday, 26 September

Still the same disjointed life. The lack of a stable home disorganizes me. I have no practical ability; I am *par excellence* the type of person who "can't sort things out for himself." I am, in the worst sense of the word, a "poet." I don't know how to talk with the landlord, or quarrel with a neighbor who is bothering me, or arrange something at the local police station. All I want is to be left in peace. I miss opportunities, I give in, I swallow things, just to be left in peace. It is absurd and very harmful. At thirty-seven years of age, I am as helpless as a child.

Monday, 2 October

I am somehow installed in the Mehedinţ household. All sorts of problems, but at least I have a room from which no one threatens to evict me (for the time being).

The house at Strada Antim is being repaired. I don't know when it will be ready, nor do I know if and when we'll be able to return there. Meanwhile I want to calm down and wait, with less nervous fretting.

I am terribly tired. I don't know why. Obviously my health has been deeply affected. I sleep badly, have dizzy spells, and look wretched. I ought to take more care of myself, but I have never known how to do that.

Nothing new at the fronts, nothing new in internal politics. The German resistance is desperate but still firm. And here the old reactionary Romanian state is putting up a dull, stubborn resistance.

It's not serious, of course. They will all go to the devil: both the Germans at the front and the Legionaries inside the country.

Meanwhile I feel a little disgust for the eternal Romania in which nothing ever changes.

Camil Petrescu read me a couple of articles in which he has taken sides with "the Left," one violently attacking the Germans, the other attacking Gide. Like hell! Didn't he have any time to write before the 23rd of August?

I advised him to take it easy. For five years Camil has been exculpating himself and joining something new.

Yesterday evening, as they returned from three shows at the theatre, Nora and Mircea were attacked by a Russian soldier. With his revolver at Nora's head, he took from them a hundred thousand lei—and a watch.

He had to run into them, of all people. There are thousands of people who might have deserved something like that (Ghiolu, Kazazian . . .). Why Nora and Mircea?

Friday, 13 October

Always tired, without any normal explanation. Am I really ill?

I live in a constant state of nervous tension, unable to regain my equilibrium. The house is largely to blame. But it is mostly my own fault, because I let myself go too easily, too quickly.

Life keeps passing me by. Some people, in these new conditions, at least try to find a position for themselves (Gruber, Comşa). But for me, nothing whatever has changed. I have some money left over from *Steaua fără nume*, and I'll probably get another two or three thousand lei from the Baraşeum. Without that, I'd be really up against it. I have no position—nor do I see any prospects. Money as such (whether it's 100, 300, or 500,000 lei) doesn't mean anything at all. We are in the grip of inflation and keep falling down and down. What counts, then, is not money but the capacity to work, to keep your head above water, to be part of some institution.

But I am always alone.

The government went into crisis a few days ago, though there have not been any resignations. The stubbornness or inertia of the old state (if not its manifestly reactionary ambition) will have to be abandoned. The Liberals and the National Peasants are caught between total disappearance and relegation to the background of political life. The Left is throwing itself into the attack. For the moment there is no question of a Communist revolution. But if democracy is to become a reality in Romania, deeply radical changes will have to be urgently introduced.

A funny incident. In a pastry shop I met a Greek doctor (I don't remember his name) whose acquaintance I made in Paris in 1930. Since then we have greeted each other whenever we meet.

"I'm glad you've developed," he said to me.

"How have I developed?"

"I heard you're no longer on the Right."

"Me? On the Right? When have I ever been on the Right?"

"Well, that's how I thought of you in Paris. Weren't you with *Action Française*?"[2]

I wasn't sure whether to laugh, to protest, or to hold my peace. What could I say? How on earth did I come to be thought of as "*Action Française*"? From where, for God's sake?

How difficult it is to communicate with people. All kinds of images and ideas are spread about you. You don't know where they come from, how they were born, what they are based on. You don't even know what they are. Meanwhile your real life is like an island.

---

2. French anti-Semitic movement led by Charles Maurras.

Sunday, 19 November

Why haven't I written here for so long? I don't know. I can give several explanations, but none of them is sufficient.

I still live with a sense that everything is provisional. Since the 26th of August I have remained a war victim. I still have no home; I am still "installed" somewhere. In theory I am looking for somewhere. In practice I stay at the Mehedinț home as if I were at a hotel where I have put up for the night.

I work—but with the same sense that what I do is suspended in the air—and I postpone things to which I really should turn my mind.

I have made a play from *Nuits sans lune*. I have translated *Anna Christie*. Now I am translating *The Taming of the Shrew*. I keep telling myself that I must finish it quickly—as if only then will I begin my main activity.

I haven't lost the wish to write my war book. I promise to do it as soon as I am rid of my theatrical chores. Meanwhile I translate, translate, and translate.

Let's be fair. The theatre does give me some money, for the time being. Otherwise how could I pay the rent or the daily household expenses?

I have no "position." I have refused in turn: 1) to rejoin the Foundation, 2) to resume my post at the college, 3) to become the confiscation administrator of a German company, 4) to work as an editor for the Radio, and 5) to join Braniște's *Jurnalul*.

It's hard to live on refusals.

What will I do in January or February, when my income from the theatre dries up?

It was a dramatic decision on my part not to go to work at Braniște's *Jurnalul*. It cost me a sleepless night and a couple of days of worry.

I am fond of the man. I wrote him a long letter in which I tried to explain why I was neither able nor willing to work on the paper. Then I had a long chat with him, in which I was on the point of crumbling. *Mais j'ai tenu bon.*[3]

Even at the risk of upsetting Vișoianu, even at the risk of somehow quarreling with Braniște, I no longer want to do journalism.

Vișoianu, Pătrășcanu, Belu, Rosetti tell me that I will almost certainly be appointed a "press adviser."[4] I don't know; I have my doubts. Nor do I

3. But I stood firm.
4. Sebastian was appointed press adviser to the Foreign Ministry a couple of months before his death.

even realize what such a function would actually mean. "Press adviser" in Romania means a kind of pencil pusher. And I don't know how much chance there is of my doing it abroad (which has always been my dream); and it is unlikely to happen for a long long time.

What if I were to drop everything (press, literature, theatre) and concentrate on advocacy? That idea comes back to me whenever my disgust with work as a "publicist," in any form, starts to suffocate me. This morning I spent ten minutes or so at Siegfried's exhibition. Lemnaru, Comarnescu, Muşatescu, and Argintescu were there! They spoke about all kinds of things behind the scenes at the editorial office. Grotesque Balkan affairs. A world that doesn't even amuse me. No, no, I need something completely and utterly different.

Sunday, 26 November

It was a big mistake to take on the translation of *The Taming of the Shrew*. A big mistake. Something like that should be done over six months, and I have to have it ready in a few more weeks. I have been working at it for a month now, and am still only halfway through. Whatever happens, I must do the rest more quickly.

Besides, I am unable to work with Leni and Froda. I swear this will be my last theatrical experience with them. My very last. Everything irritates me. Scarlat's superior airs as a "man of the theatre." The "objectivity" with which Leni agrees with him on every matter. The fact that Jenica (who is playing a commonsense character, a "voice from the crowd") always votes with them. They seem to be saying: you see, there are three of us and only one of you; if we all three say the same, why do you remain so stubborn?

And then there is Şahighian, stupid, obtuse, and superior. Were it not for Leni, I'd long since have flung the translation into their faces and run off.

Things are now becoming complicated because of money.

I made the childish (and I admit, inexcusable) mistake of not specifying terms from the start. There is no way I would have agreed to work without a 6 percent royalty. But this seemed such a normal expectation that I was sure there would be no difficulty. Yesterday I talked to Froda. At the last moment—again my absurd helplessness in money matters— I was so cowardly that I said not 6 percent but 5 percent. He took fright; he literally took fright. A second earlier, in my presence, he had laid into some program agents and imposed on them very tight financial conditions. And now, when I asked him for money, he took fright.

Leni called me this morning so that we could talk it over between the two of us. The theatre is going through difficulties, production is expensive, the budget is large; she appeals to me, etc., etc. I resisted. The only thing I would now gladly do is drop the whole business. I'd have worked a month for nothing—that's all. At least I'd become a free man; I'd be able to breathe, to rest, to tie up the whole situation. But the ridiculous thing is that I would then look like a *lâcheur*.[5] They argue that I did not specify terms at the outset—a kind of moral blackmail they can use against me. But I am determined not to give in. Either 5 percent or nothing. Yes, I'd prefer to give them the translation for nothing. All I'd ask then would be that my name does not appear anywhere.

That's a sucker's solution, of course. A naive form of revenge. But at least I'd be calm and at peace with myself.

Sunday, 3 December

A short epilogue to the *Taming of the Shrew* affair. I translate, translate, and translate, and for the last three days, without saying a word to me, they have been rehearsing something else at the theatre.

I heard about it quite by chance, on the phone from Mme. Zissu. The whole town knew—only I didn't. There's no longer any question of Shakespeare. Not only did they not take the trouble to inform me, but on Friday evening, with the new premiere already arranged, Leni did not say a word about it when she rang and asked me to speed up the translation. She can lie awfully well.

I am so disgusted that I don't even feel bad about it.

I have wasted six weeks of work, and I feel as if I have been on compulsory labor service.

The only odd thing is that they didn't tell me, so that I could have stopped working on it. I feel cuckolded—and no doubt that is how everyone sees me and laughs at me in the theatre.

Thursday, 7 December

I spent the afternoon with Captain Larry Bachman, from the U.S. Army. He flies to Italy tomorrow morning, and from there on to China. He has been fighting until this year in the Pacific.

---

5. An unreliable type.

He is a Jew with passion. He is furious that during his two weeks here he has been hanging around with a group of Romanians and that no one told him they were Legionaries. (A lawyer named Stănescu, the lover of Doina Missir.)

He is a Hollywood scriptwriter, mad about the theatre, but so far none of his plays has been performed. He has been working for years at Metro-Goldwyn. With much friendly curiosity, he asked hundreds of questions about me and my plays. He knew about the *Steaua fără nume* business. He went to the Baraşeum yesterday. He'd like us to write a play together, and regretted (as I did too) that we hadn't met on his first day in Bucharest; then we might have had time to do something.

He is young, full of vitality, honest and straightforward, concerned about us as Jews, concerned about the reality of democracy. A person. A new figure. Someone.

Wednesday, 13 December

I have heard from Marietta Rareş that Nina Eliade is dead. A telegram from Lisbon brought the news ten days ago.

A wave of memories rises up from the past: her little room upstairs at Pasajul Imobiliara; the typewriter on which she copied almost simultaneously *Maitreyi*[6] and *Femei*; the evening visits to Mircea's attic on Strada Melodiei; their unexpected love; Mircea's flight to Poiana; Nina's despair and my helpless attempts to console her; Mircea's return, their engagement, and two years later their civil wedding, in secret, at the town hall on Calea Rahovei; their apartment on Bulevardul Dinicu Golescu, then on Palade; our walks in the mountains, the summers in Breaza, the games in Floria's yard at Strada Nerva Traian; our years of fraternal friendship—and then the years of confusion and growing apart, until it all broke down in hostility and oblivion.

It's all dead, all vanished, all lost forever.

Friday, 15 December

A cable arrived today at Strada Antim, sent the day before yesterday from Vatican City and bearing the marks of the Russian censorship.

"*Etat. Mihai Sebastian Strada Antim 45 Buc.*

"*Cité Vatican, 25, 44, 13, 1020*

6. A novel by Mircea Eliade.

"Maison éditrice La Caravella—Rome propose publier traduction roman Accidentul *versant droits auteur dix mille lires italiennes. Stop. Si acceptez, somme sera déposée légation jusque possibilité transfert. Stop. Prière télégraphier immédiatement réponse Légation Roumanie Vatican.* Grigorcea."[7]

I don't know what La Caravella means, nor how much ten thousand lire are worth, nor what I shall answer, nor whether the book will actually appear. But the telegram gave me very great pleasure.

Is it possible that my writing will one day break out of this blind alley? Suddenly I seem to be less alone, less poor, less useless.

Sunday, 17 December

The last performance of *Potopul.*

How mysterious is success in the theatre. I was in the auditorium and looked carefully around me. Badly acted, badly produced, with inexpressive sets and mediocre actors (Finți false, Măruță declamatory, Vurtejeanu humorless, Athanasescu plain stupid). It all seemed worthless and inauthentic—yet it went down well. The audience listened, believed, applauded. That is what's called a hit.

It has had a run of eighty-five performances. No doubt others have done better in central Bucharest. For me it has been an excellent little business, bringing me in nearly 400,000 lei. I have never received so much before from anything in the theatre, earned with so little effort.

But can I do a job like that? It's so cheap and easy as to be dishonest. The character I added, Miss King, was made of next to nothing. A constantly repeated line ("I'm an honorable person") was the only device, simple yet infallible. People laughed whenever the line occurred, as if someone had pressed a button. It's an insultingly simple, a crudely simple, effect.

Monday, 18 December

A conversation with Vișoianu, at the ministry.[8] This is the third time I have met him since he became a minister. He received me warmly, simply, and honestly—but he can't do anything for me. He cannot and does

7. "La Caravella publishing house—Rome offers to publish translation of novel *Accidentul*, paying royalties of ten thousand Italian lire. Stop. If you accept, sum will be deposited at Legation until possible to transfer. Stop. Please cable immediately reply to Romanian Legation Vatican. *Grigorcea.*"

8. Vișoianu was now foreign minister in the Sănătescu government.

not want to. He won't give me the "press adviser" job he promised. There seems to be some legal obstacle to it. But in fact the opposition comes from Piki Pogoneanu,[9] and Vivi doesn't have the courage or the interest to override it. All he offered me was a position paid "on a daily basis." I turned it down, of course.

For him I still remain a yid. Room may be found for me somewhere in the shadows, but it would be an impertinence to try to bring me more to the front.

I spent an irritating afternoon at the Baraşeum, where there are panic rehearsals of *Nopţi fără lună*.[1] The premiere is the day after tomorrow, but nothing is ready.

Probably that's how things are always put on in the theatre. In worry, disorder, haste, and fear. No one sees anything any longer. Is that bad or good? Disastrous or admirable? No one can answer. No one knows.

I myself am quite calm. All I did in the end was the work of a translator. But if it had really been my play, I too would probably be caught up in this mad panic.

Friday, 22 December

I may be going on Sunday to Diham, with Herta, Andrei,[2] and Herant.[3] (At the last moment I learn that our numbers have grown: Leni and Harry.)

I have tried to put together a skier's wardrobe from my remnants of the past. A bit torn, a bit stained—but not too bad. I was delighted to find my skis and sticks again at Alice's, hidden in her loft some three years ago when we were ordered to hand our skis in to the police.

The 23rd of August is not, after all, the fiction it sometimes seems, if it has at least given me back the freedom to go to the mountains.

I'd like to be happy there—and I hope I will be.

In the evening, a reception at the Foreign Ministry. Vivi insisted that I go, and I went. It was agreeable as fashionable society, but disgusting as a political spectacle. These are the same people who, five months ago, were clinking glasses with Killinger!

I fear that a kind of bankruptcy is being arranged at the Baraşeum.

9. Victor Rădulescu Pogoneanu: director of cryptography in the Romanian Foreign Ministry.
1. Sebastian's dramatization of *The Moon Is Down* by John Steinbeck.
2. The name used by Lucreţiu Pătrăşcanu in the wartime Communist underground.
3. Herant Torossian: lawyer.

Nopți fără lună might be a success (at least as great as *Potopul*), but it's also possible that I won't see a penny myself. Marcovici complains that he is ruined, that he doesn't have the money for posters and publicity, and meanwhile he pockets all the box office receipts.

Sunday, 31 December

I returned half an hour ago from the mountains. I was one day in Predeal and six at Cabana Vînători, on Mount Diham. We didn't have snow for skiing, but it was still a nice holiday.

I was moved by the Bucegi mountains, which I hadn't seen for so long. A clear white light gave depth to the wintry landscape, covered with snow only in the last couple of days.

I can't say or write anything; words do not help me. A few times I stood still and watched the view, with the idea of fixing the contours in my mind. But everything was more varied, more complex, and more mysterious than I can ever remember.

I must be getting very old. I didn't find my old exuberance in the mountains. I was melancholic, rather, almost despondent. I feel an old weariness, and everywhere I go I carry my incurable loneliness around with me.

The last day of the year. I am ashamed to be sad. After all, it is the year that gave me back my freedom. Beyond all the bitterness and suffering, beyond all the disappointments, this one basic fact remains.

I think of Poldy and feel bad that he is so far away. I can't wait to see him again. Everything else melts into regrets and hopes.

On 29 May 1945, Mihail Sebastian was hit and killed by a truck in downtown Bucharest.

INDEX

28 ~~DK~~ DAYS